A THEOLOGICAL INTRODUCTION TO
THE THIRTY-NINE ARTICLES

A THEOLOGICAL
INTRODUCTION TO THE
THIRTY-NINE
ARTICLES
OF THE CHURCH OF ENGLAND

BY

E. J. BICKNELL, D.D.
LATE PROFESSOR OF NEW TESTAMENT EXEGESIS
IN THE UNIVERSITY OF LONDON

Third Edition revised by

H. J. CARPENTER, M.A.
WARDEN OF KEBLE COLLEGE, OXFORD
CANON THEOLOGIAN OF LEICESTER
EXAMINING CHAPLAIN TO THE BISHOP OF OXFORD

LONGMANS, GREEN AND CO
LONDON ✦ NEW YORK ✦ TORONTO

LONGMANS, GREEN AND CO LTD
6 & 7 CLIFFORD STREET LONDON W 1
BOSTON HOUSE STRAND STREET CAPE TOWN
531 LITTLE COLLINS STREET MELBOURNE

LONGMANS, GREEN & CO INC
55 FIFTH AVENUE NEW YORK 3

LONGMANS, GREEN AND CO
20 CRANFIELD ROAD TORONTO 16

ORIENT LONGMANS LTD
CALCUTTA BOMBAY MADRAS
DELHI VIJAYAWADA DACCA

First published February 1919
Second Edition July 1925
New Impressions (with additional references) February 1929,
January 1932, October 1933, and February 1935
New Impression October 1936
New Impression November 1939 (with additional references)
New Impressions March 1942, June 1944, January 1946,
March 1947 (with additional references), April 1948, April 1950, January 1953
Third Edition January 1955

Printed in Great Britain by Robert MacLehose and Co. Ltd
at the University Press, Glasgow

PREFACE TO THE THIRD EDITION

SINCE it was first published in 1919 Dr. Bicknell's book has been widely used as a guide to the study of the doctrine of the Church of England. Its qualities are too well known to need description here. Frequent new impressions have now made it necessary to reset the type, and the opportunity has been taken to carry out a revision of the work.

The first aim of the revision has been to construct a new list of books for further reading. The references to theological literature have been found a useful and important feature of the book. If it is to continue to fulfil its author's purpose of acting as a stimulus to wider study its book list must now take account of theological works published in the last thirty years. The new general list has been placed in a form which it is hoped will be found convenient at the end of the volume, and not interspersed, as were the original lists, at the end of sections or paragraphs. On points of detail a number of references will be found in footnotes to the passages concerned. Since the purpose of the general list is to refer the student to books likely to be of most use in the next stage of study it is deliberately selective in character. Room has been made for the newer works in a list of limited scale by the omission of some, but by no means all, of the older authorities. With rare exceptions only books in English (including some translations of foreign works) have been mentioned. A † in the text directs the reader to a section in the list. It is perhaps a sign of the times that more works by non-anglican writers are included than appeared in the original lists. Current doctrinal thinking in the Church of England can hardly be understood and studied without some attention to works coming from outside its borders.

The text itself has been revised on conservative lines. The clear arrangement of the book could not be improved and remains unaltered, but at some points Dr. Bicknell's expositions and discussions have called for reconsideration. In the period since the end of the First Great War new currents of theological thinking have begun to flow strongly and new emphases have appeared at vital points in the system of Christian doctrine. In illustration of this point it is sufficient to mention the revival of interest in the classical theologies of the Reformation period, the powerful neo-Calvinist Movement in dogmatic theology represented by K. Barth and his circle, the new phase of biblical study which is associated with the title 'Biblical Theology', and the increasing interest in problems concerning reunion. Dr Bicknell would certainly not have proceeded on the assumption that the latest work in theology must supersede all that

v

has gone before. His mind was too catholic and independent to be swayed uncritically by the most recent fashion in theological thought. If, however, he had lived to revise his book at the present time he would certainly have taken some account of the new trends. In attempting to revise his work I have not engaged in inconclusive speculation about what he would have said. A few paragraphs and sections have been entirely re-written, some paragraphs or notes have been added, and in a number of places the phrasing has been modified. It has usually been a question of restating or further emphasizing a point already contained in the original exposition. On some topics the progress of historical research (as in the history of the Creeds) or the march of contemporary events (as in the section on Church and State) have made revision or additions necessary. The general aim has been to make the book more useful to those who are embarking on theological study in the middle of the twentieth century, without obscuring those qualities of accuracy, clarity, fair balance, and loyalty to the Church of England which have recommended the book to so many for over thirty years.

My thanks are due to the Rev. H. E. J. Cowdrey, Tutor of S. Stephen's House, Oxford, for compiling the index and for assistance in the final reading of the proofs.

H. J. CARPENTER

KEBLE COLLEGE, OXFORD

PREFACE TO THE FIRST EDITION

A NEW book upon the Thirty-nine Articles by an author entirely un-known requires an apology. I can only plead that it is an attempt to meet a need openly expressed on all sides by those engaged in the teaching of theology, for a book on new and broad lines. My excuse for undertaking the task is that no one is likely to do so who has not been engaged in lecturing on the Articles, and the number of such is small. The book is intended in the first instance for students, but it is hoped that large portions of it may be found useful by ordinary men and women who are prepared to make an effort to understand Christian doctrine. It makes no claim to originality of thought, but contains a large amount of material collected from various sources into a single volume for the first time.

Proposals have recently been made that the teaching of doctrine in our Theological Colleges should no longer be centred in the Articles. They would then be treated presumably only as a historical document, illustrative of the course of the Reformation in England. However desirable such a reform may be in itself, there are grave difficulties in the way. Not only are all candidates for ordination required to give a general assent to the Articles, but the course at Theological Colleges is of necessity guided by Bishops' exam-inations. At present these proposals would hardly win acceptance in all dioceses. Moreover, though certain Articles deal with questions that in their old form have no interest for the modern mind, the majority deal with those fundamental problems of theology that are debated anew in every age. Since in certain instances such Articles represent the typical attitude of the Church of England towards such problems, their statements have more than a bare historical interest. These considerations have shaped the arrangement of the book. Like the Articles themselves, it is a compromise. The general scheme of treatment is based on the Articles, but the Articles themselves are grouped quite freely according to subject matter. The reader is asked to study the analysis in order to grasp the principles of this grouping. I would suggest that by this arrangement a minimum of attention need be devoted to obsolete or unimportant details.

Any teacher of theology to-day is faced with a multitude of per-plexities due to the increase of modern knowledge. In treating of any subject, it is difficult to know where to make a beginning. All state-ments of doctrine involve a host of assumptions, philosophical and critical. In a book of this kind these assumptions cannot always be indicated, still less defended. If, for instance, I do not mention 'pluralism', it is not because the theory is unimportant or unknown, but because I have deliberately rejected it alike on philosophical and Christian grounds. Again, on critical grounds, I accept the authenticity of all the Pauline Epistles, including the Pastorals. Those who disagree with me on this point will need to modify, let us say, the conclusions that are drawn from the Pastoral Epistles in regard to the early ministry of the Church. The old method of 'proof-texts' is gone for ever. It is no longer enough to quote a sentence of Scripture in order to prove the truth of a dogmatic statement. We have rightly come to see that not only is the context all important, but that we must look behind the letter of the text to the mind of the author. We must strive to reconstruct his mental outlook and to test his sources of information. The existence of the Synoptic problem makes it hazardous to lay undue stress on the precise form in which our Lord's words are recorded in any particular Gospel. The evidence of S. John's Gospel is more complex. Personally I have come to believe that on the historical side it gives a more accurate chronological account of certain details of our Lord's life than the Synoptists. Even in the discourses, however much they may be coloured by the lifelong meditation of the Evangelist, I would maintain that we have far more of our Lord's words in their original form than many critics have supposed. At least I would plead that they represent an essential element in His teaching that cannot be minimized or ignored without a serious loss of proportion in our estimate of His teaching and claims. A long list of such presuppositions might be compiled. It is sufficient to ask those who dissent from my conclusions to believe, of their charity, that if philosophical or literary problems are rarely discussed, it is not that they have been rarely considered.

Perhaps the hardest task of a tutor at a theological college is to stir up in a large proportion of his pupils the will to think for themselves. Partly this reluctance to think is due to the English temperament, partly to faulty education received before arrival at the theological college, partly also to the fear of approaching examinations. It cannot be denied that our too short system of theological training encourages intellectual sloth. The ordinary student is almost invited to regard what will help him to pass examinations as more important than the study of the Christian faith for its own sake. It is not the fault of the colleges: it is the fault of the system. I have tried as far as possible to write this book in such a way as to stimulate further study and to discourage cramming. If at times I have been provocative, it is because in too many cases thought needs to be provoked. I hope it may be found useful to lecturers as the basis of a wider discussion.

The book consists in the main of lectures delivered at Bishop's Hostel, Lincoln, rewritten and expanded. I am conscious throughout of the great debt that I owe to the doctrine lectures given to students at Wells by Dr. Goudge. If certain phrases and expressions from these lectures have become so part of my own thought and expression that

I have failed to acknowledge them, I hope that this general acknow-ledgement may be accepted. Of living writers I am most conscious of the influence of the Bishop of Oxford and Dr. Du Bose. My debt to the books of the late Dr. Moberly will be apparent. I must thank many kind friends for sympathy and help, especially the Rev. J. C. Du Buisson, Warden of S. Deiniol's Library, Hawarden, and the Rev. G. H. Dix, who have given most valuable assistance in revising the proofs, and to the former of whom I have owed many valuable suggestions from the moment that I first contemplated the book. For the opinions expressed I am alone responsible. For any small in-accuracies of reference or fact which have escaped my notice, my only excuse can be the stress of parish work and separation from my books during the revision of the proofs. Finally, I would gladly take for my model the tone and temper of a former lecturer on the Articles and 'claim a right to retract any opinion which improvement in reasoning and knowledge may at any time show me is groundless'.[1]

E. J. BICKNELL

S. MARY'S CLERGY HOUSE, WIMBLEDON, S.W.

[1] Hey's *Lectures on the Articles* quoted by Lightfoot, *Commentary on Galatians* [1], p. ix.

ANALYSIS

INTRODUCTION

THE PLACE OF THE THIRTY-NINE ARTICLES IN CHRISTIAN THEOLOGY

THE BEING OF GOD

ARTICLE I

xi

ABBREVIATIONS

The following abbreviations are employed throughout the book:

C.H.S.	-	Church Historical Society.
D.C.G.	-	Dictionary of Christ and the Gospels.
E.R.E.	-	Encyclopaedia of Religion and Ethics.
H.D.B.	-	Hastings' Dictionary of the Bible.
J.Th.S.	-	Journal of Theological Studies.
C.Q.R.	-	Church Quarterly Review.

N.B.—The references to Scripture should in all cases be looked up in the Revised Version. Where R.V. occurs, special attention is drawn to the difference between the Revised and Authorized translations.

INTRODUCTION

§ 1. *The relation of Theology to Religion.*—Theology arises from man's effort to understand his own life. Whether we study the individual or the race, we discover everywhere that 'Man lives first and thinks afterwards'.[1] If we select any department of human experience we can find more or less sharply defined, three stages. In the earliest stage men act with little or no reflection. They are impelled by a blind instinct or custom. They have little desire to explain why or how they act. There are as yet no laws or rules formulated to direct action. In the second stage men begin to reflect on what they have been doing. Man is by nature a rational being, disposed to ask 'Why?' So by reflection and self-questioning men gradually draw out into the light the principles by which they have long been acting. They frame general statements and rules. They attain to science. Science is 'systematized or ordered knowledge'.[2] In the third stage the science thus gained is found most valuable for guiding and correcting future practice. Not only are more certain results obtained by its aid, but the principles that have been discovered can be applied to fresh material. So the field of action is extended, and wider experience is gained, which in turn the mind is called on to analyse and explain. Thenceforward science and action go hand in hand. Science directs practice and practice affords new material for science.

We may apply these thoughts to religion. In whatever way it may be, religion arose. That is, men came to worship a God or gods. They experienced feelings of religious awe and reverence. They desired to please their God by doing His will and to turn away His wrath when He was angry. By sacrifice and prayer they sought to attain His help and to hold communion with Him. In the earliest stage such religion was based primarily upon instinct and custom. But because men were rational beings, they were bound to ask questions about their religion. They wished to make clear to themselves the grounds of their worship and obedience. The service of any God must in the last resort imply certain beliefs about Him, His character and His relation to His worshippers. These beliefs men drew out and stated and formed into a system. So we reach the second stage—the

---

[1] Cp. Illingworth, *Personality, Human and Divine*, c. i. 'Man lives first and thinks afterwards. . . . He makes history by his actions, before he can reflect upon it and write it . . . thought is always in arrear of life: for life is in perpetual progress.'

[2] We must not limit the term 'science' to physical science. The great advance made in all branches of physical science during the last few years, and its visible results, as shown in everyday life, have encouraged a popular use of the word 'science' as limited to them. Strictly speaking there is a 'science' of painting or music just as much as of chemistry.

formation of a primitive theology. Theology is the science of religion. In the third stage theology begins to react upon religion. The Hebrew prophets, for example, perceived and enunciated certain fundamental truths about the activity and purpose of Jehovah. Hence they demanded that conduct and worship that were inconsistent with such truths should be reformed. As the religion of Israel deepened out of further historical experience its beliefs became more clearly formulated, and this in turn helped to shape the religious practice and observance of post-prophetic Judaism. So in the final stage, theology and religion coexist side by side, theology explaining the principles of religion and setting them forth in an orderly system, and religion striving to realize those principles in a living experience.†

§ 2. *The place of Theology in the Christian Religion.*—The Christian religion is primarily a way of life. In its earliest stages it was known quite simply as 'the Way' (cp. Acts 9^2, $19^{9 \text{ and } 23}$ and also 16^{17}, 18^{26} and 24^{14}). But it was never an easy or an obvious way; it was in glaring contrast to the prevalent way of life in the world around it. From the first it always involved certain beliefs about the nature and character of God, the life and claims of Jesus Christ, His Death and Resurrection, the Church and the Sacraments. The Christian lived as he did because he based his life on certain convictions. The Church gradually made clear to itself what these were. Within the New Testament we see a theology growing up. The doctrines of the Christian faith are stated and drawn out, and practical consequences are deduced from them. The purpose of Christian theology is to set forth clearly the truth about God and God's dealings with mankind, as it has been made known. Christian 'Doctrine' is simply Christian teaching. 'Dogmas' are simply fundamental points of doctrine, the primary assumptions that are implicit in all Christian life and experience. No logical proof of them can be offered. Just as, *e.g.* all geometry rests upon certain assumptions about the nature of space, and if these are not granted, geometry is impossible, so Christian life and experience, if it is accepted as true, and not a mere delusion or fancy, involves certain presuppositions. If these are denied, then all that we can say is that without them the Christian experience could not exist. We may not find universal agreement as to what these 'dogmas' are, but all Christians would agree that there must be some, *e.g.* the existence and the Fatherhood of God. Christian theology is the attempt to state them in a connected and orderly system.

Theology begins like any other science. It strives to collect and verify the facts, to sift and compare them, to classify them and discover their mutual relations. Then it tries to find language that will express the facts as clearly as possible, and to set them out as parts of one coherent system. All knowledge must be based upon experience. The facts upon which Christian theology is based are found in the revelation of God to Israel, the whole life and witness of the Jewish

Church, then in the life and teaching of Jesus Christ and the whole witness and experience of the Christian Church throughout all ages. Christian theology grows naturally within the Christian religion and has a necessary place in it. But while religion is possible without any formal knowledge of theology, the pursuit of theological enquiry has no meaning apart from the practice of religion. The professional theologian can properly exercise his powers of discrimination, explanation and construction only as a living member of Christ's Body. A full understanding of the great doctrines of the Christian faith can only be based upon some first-hand experience of the Christian life.

We should probably do well to draw a further distinction between theology and religious philosophy. The intellect has a two-fold work. First, to draw out and state those fundamental truths that underlie the Christian revelation, *i.e.* to construct a theology in the strict sense of the word. Secondly, to bring these truths into connexion with the rest of our ideas derived from other sources, *i.e.* to construct a religious philosophy. As rational beings we are bound to wish not only to understand our religion, but to bring our knowledge of it into relation with the rest of our knowledge, to clothe the Christian revelation in the current terms of science and philosophy. This is a right and necessary desire, but it brings its own dangers. Science and philosophy change. Hence the religious philosophy of yesterday, expressed in the scientific and philosophical categories of yesterday, grows obsolete. It demands revision and correction so that it may be brought into harmony with the knowledge of today. The work of the intellect must be done over again. Too often men have identified religious philosophy with theology proper. Because the former has needed restatement they have supposed that the latter needed restatement too. Or it has been supposed that the truth of Christianity itself was bound up with the satisfactoriness of a particular religious philosophy. We need to point out that Christianity is not committed to any one philosophy. Christianity does stand or fall with the truth of certain doctrines, but these are independent of any local or particular science or philosophy. They spring out of the Christian revelation itself. Much unsettlement would have been avoided if men had made the distinction between 'theology' proper, *i.e.* the statement of fundamental Christian doctrines, and 'religious philosophy', *i.e.* the attempt to fit these doctrines into a general scheme of thought.

§ 3. *Theology as a practical necessity.*—On practical grounds theology is indispensable: (*a*) Some desire to understand his own activity and environment is inherent in man's nature, and religion cannot without grave loss be left outside the scope of this desire. If, while men come to understand more of the meaning of the rest of life, its religious side is left unexamined by the mind and no effort is made to reflect upon it, it will grow weak. In the competition of many interests it will be crowded out. Being intellectually unorganized, it will lack strength to hold its ground in man's attention. The deepest type of Christian conviction requires and includes some measure of intellectual assent. In an age of increasing knowledge and intellectual ferment such conviction is not likely to be maintained unless a man can give some considered account of the grounds and content of his faith. Moreover, that faith itself, if not embodied in some form of intelligible and coherent statement, may lose its integrity and ultimately its identity. The mind which has not been strengthened by definite Christian teaching according to its capacity will be most exposed to the danger of being 'carried about with every wind of doctrine'. To put the point more religiously, the use of the mind to grasp, so far as may be, the meaning of God's revelation of Himself is part of the total devotion of his powers which is demanded of the Christian. A partial unreflective devotion will stand strain less easily.

(b) Further, the need of some theology is obvious as soon as we consider the social nature of man. Religion is essentially social. The child that is born into the world inherits the religion as he inherits the knowledge and the experience of the society into which he is born. In any society that has risen above the mental level of savages, if there is to be any continuity of religious custom and belief, some intellectual expression of religion is necessary. The moment that any teaching about religion begins, the rudiments of theology are to be found. We cannot teach what we do not in part understand. A religion that possessed no theology, even in the form of myths, would be either purely individualistic or a mere barren ritual coupled with a blind obedience to rules that were out of all relation to the higher elements of life. Christian theology has a necessary place in the furniture of the Christian home. Christian dogma begins at the mother's knee.

(c) From another point of view we must face the fact that Christian morality is the product of certain definite beliefs accepted and acted upon. The Christian type of character is no casual growth. It has been wrought out of a reluctant human nature by centuries of effort.[1] Christian doctrines influence conduct through the medium of the emotions. Where these doctrines are discarded, Christian feeling and standards may last for a while, but in the end they disappear. This has already occurred in certain circles. A generation ago the opponents of Christian doctrine professed themselves anxious to preserve Christian morality as the one thing needful. Their descendants to-day criticize with equal freedom Christian dogma and Christian ethics.[2]†

---

[1] 'Men are living on a moral sense transmitted and inherited while they are restive under the discipline and claims of the systems which generated that moral sense. They are living on the fruits of a tree of which they are anxious to cut away the roots. . . . A popular audience will always cheer a reference to "true religion stripped of the bonds of theology", i.e. the results of the Christian conscience without the faith that formed it.'—Creighton, Life and Letters, vol. ii. p. 191, cp. pp. 245–247.

[2] 'Christian ethics are bound up inseparably with Christian mysteries. Clear away these and, in default of some substituted construction of the over-natural world, what

§ 4. But the fact remains that there exists a not entirely unreasonable prejudice against all dogmatic theology. This is due to many causes.

(*a*) Partly it arises from the intellectual indolence of the English race. The Englishman hates the trouble of exact thinking. Truth for truth's sake has at all times few attractions for him. He is bored by philosophy. In the case of religion his mental sloth is reinforced by a new motive. A vague religion is a comfortable religion. It makes fewer demands upon his conscience and will. By keeping his Christianity hazy he hopes to escape the moral and spiritual obligations that a definite belief must carry with it. So he has a natural dislike of Christian doctrine.

(*b*) But he has more worthy reasons than that. The responsibility for the dislike of dogma must largely rest with the theologians themselves. They have confused religious philosophy with theology. Many have claimed to have a much more complete and definite knowledge of God and the world than they really possess. They have yielded to the temptation to stretch God's revelation so as to cover whole tracts of knowledge that it was never intended to cover, as, for instance, when the Bible was made a text-book of science. Again, they have failed to respect the limits of human knowledge. Not only is all our knowledge of real things imperfect, and therefore our knowledge of God, the highest reality, must be the most imperfect of all, but also human words and ideas were formed primarily to deal with objects of this material world. We are compelled to use them in speaking of spiritual things, since we possess no others. But all doctrinal statements must partake of the nature of metaphor. They are true as far as they go, but they cannot represent the whole truth. A metaphor must never be pressed beyond the limits of the truth that it was formed to express. Some theologians have argued from doctrinal statements as if they were a final and adequate expression of divine truth. They have ventured to lay down as a necessary part of the Christian faith the precarious deductions of human logic. The result has been that assertions that rested on purely human authority have been disproved, and Christian theology as a whole has had to share the discredit. Men have failed to distinguish between the primary doctrines of the Christian faith and the fallible speculations of certain individuals or schools of thought.[1]

---

remains is an ethics without foundation, without end, without character; neither Christian nor anything else; and that love which is the substance of the inward immanent life of the Christian soul, as opposed to the life of outward conduct, gives place to a vague amiability whose roots are nowhere and its branches anywhere.'— Tyrrell, *Through Scylla and Charybdis*, p. 190.

[1] Tyrrell, *External Religion*, pp. 125–126. He speaks of men 'who carry cut and dried answers to all difficulties, wrapped up in pellets to shoot out on occasion; to whom everything is clear and common-sense and obvious; who can define a mystery but have never felt one. That the human words and ideas in which eternal truths are clad cannot, even through divine skill, convey to us more than a shadow of the realities

(c) Again, a protest against theology is often made in the name of religion. 'A living faith' is contrasted with 'dead formulas'. In part this opposition arises from the mortality of human language. Words and phrases grow old and lose their edge. Ideas and expressions change and decay. Every advance in knowledge carries with it a new vocabulary and a new stock of ideas. It revolutionizes the point of view. Each generation acquires its peculiar temper of mind. Evolution, for instance, has changed our whole mental outlook. Accordingly, language that expressed the deepest aspirations and the highest ideas of one generation becomes to the next a string of catchwords from which the life has departed. The phrases of one age are always in danger of becoming formal and unreal to the next. They are felt no longer to protect but rather to stifle religion. Further, at certain periods theology has been allowed to usurp the place of religion. A mere intellectual assent to certain theological statements has been substituted for moral effort as the test of true Christian faith. Orthodoxy, not holiness, has been regarded as the distinguishing mark of the Christian. The gulf between theology and religion has been allowed to widen. We can hardly wonder that in the ardour of a spiritual revival men have been impatient of the pious phrases of their forefathers, or have hastily cast aside doctrines that seemed to have the faintest possible connexion with practical Christianity. The only preventive of this disaster is to insist that theology shall always be in the closest contact with life. The New Testament invariably keeps its theological teaching closely related to the practical duties of worship and conduct. Frequently its most profound statements of doctrine emerge in passages primarily concerned with Christian morals or the Christian character.

To sum up. Those who wish to be both Christians and thinking persons must have a theology. If the individual is left to himself he will probably have a bad theology, a child of his limitations and caprices. To establish the best possible theology will involve the study of the history of Christian Doctrine, the record of the process of thought by which the Church has attempted to make plain to herself the meaning of her own faith and life. But the Church can never cease to reflect on her doctrines. Standing on the foundation of the Scriptures and guided by her own theological tradition, the Church will in every age discover the necessity for renewed theological thought, in order both to maintain her own life and to propagate her faith in the contemporary world.†

they stand for; that they cannot, like numbers, be added, subtracted and multiplied together so as to deduce new conclusions with arithmetical simplicity and accuracy, never occurs to them. . . .'

THE THIRTY-NINE ARTICLES

THEIR HISTORY AND PLACE IN THEOLOGY

§ 1. Our present 39 Articles are only one out of a large crop of formularies produced in Europe by the general unrest of the Reformation.
Even as regards the Church of England, they are only the last of a
series of doctrinal statements put forth as occasion demanded. The
Reformation was not a single act but a long process, not always in a
uniform direction: it was not concluded until far into the seventeenth
century. The history of our Articles can only be understood if it is
studied in the light of the history of the Reformation in England.
Changes in the formularies of the Church in the main run parallel
with changes in its worship and order. Either side illustrates the other.
In this present chapter the outstanding incidents of the Reformation
are alluded to but not explained. They are intended to serve as land-
marks by which to estimate the tendency of the various theological
statements put forth from time to time. The surest way to understand
the account of the Articles given here is to read it side by side with a
history of the Reformation.

The actual movement for reform in England may be said to start
with the repudiation of Papal authority in 1534. The breach with
Rome was complete. In itself a quarrel with the Pope was nothing
new. In the past it had not involved any change of religion. But the
English desire for independence, the disgust at the greed and exactions of the Popes, the character of Henry himself, and the doctrinal
unsettlement both at home and abroad formed a new combination
of circumstances about whose issue few could venture to predict.
Lutheran ideas had reached England as early as 1521, when a bonfire
of Lutheran books was made in front of S. Paul's. Since 1526 the influence of Zwingli had spread through Tyndale's English version of
the Scriptures. Anabaptists were propagating tenets subversive of all
order in Church and State alike. Abroad, Luther and Zwingli, with a
large part of Europe behind them, had broken with the historic faith
and discipline of the Catholic Church. Amid the general confusion
the Church of England was compelled to raise its voice. The authority
of the Pope had been repudiated. In all ranks of life some centre of
unity was needed. Within the Church itself there were two main
parties, the party of the Old Learning, who desired little more than
independence of the Pope, headed by Gardiner, Bishop of Win-
chester, and the party of the New Learning, who aimed at considerable reforms both of doctrine and discipline, headed by Archbishop

7

Cranmer. The Lutherans in Germany had already set the example of putting forward a public statement of their position. Their object in this was partly, no doubt, to repudiate 'Romish errors', but also to make clear their divergence from the Zwinglians and Swiss reformers. Accordingly, in 1529 the Schwabach Articles were drawn up: the acceptance of these was to be the indispensable condition of membership in a reforming league. On these were based the first great Lutheran confession, the Confession of Augsburg, drawn up in 1530 by Melanchthon and approved by Luther. Originally it was simply 'Mr Philip's' (i.e. Melanchthon's) 'Apology', but it became the official statement of Lutheranism, and as such was signed by the Elector of Saxony and others and presented to the Emperor. It contained 21 articles on matters of faith and 7 on matters of discipline.[1] In the same year, 1530, Zwingli himself presented a Confession of his own to the Diet of Augsburg. After his death in 1531, the Zwinglian party put forth their views in the Confession of Basel, 1534, and the First Helvetic Confession, 1536. These last had no influence on our Articles. They are interesting only as signs of the times and as examples of the type of formulary that was happily avoided in England.

§ 2. (a) The first attempt of the English Church to state its position was the *Ten Articles of* 1536. Their object is made clear in the title: 'To establish Christian quietness and unity among us and to avoid contentious opinions.' They 'bore the character of a compromise between the Old and the New Learning. The Catholic nation was satisfied that the Catholic faith still remained'.[2] The reforming party 'was conciliated by a secret infusion of Lutheranism'. They succeeded in quenching the suspicion that the kingdom had been brought into schism, and helped to reconcile men's minds to the impending dissolution of the monasteries. Politically they served to show foreign powers that England was still a Catholic country. The King had a large share in their composition. But their final form was due to Convocation, with whose authority they were issued. They fell into two parts.[3] The first five deal with questions of doctrine. The chief points to be noticed are:

(i) The rule of faith is based not only on 'the whole body and canon of the Bible' but also on the three Creeds. The authority of the Four Great Councils is recognized and all opinions condemned by them are declared erroneous.

(ii) Three Sacraments only are expounded, Baptism, the Eucharist and Penance. This last is said to be 'institute of Christ in the New Testament as a thing ... necessary for man's salvation'. The other four of the 'Seven Sacraments' are neither affirmed nor rejected.

(iii) The Real Presence is strongly asserted, but the manner of the Presence is left open. There is no mention of Transubstantiation.

[1] A survey of it may be found in Hardwick, *A History of the Articles of Religion*, pp. 17 ff.
[2] Dixon, *History of the Church of England*, vol. i. p. 415.
[3] The text of the Ten Articles is printed in Hardwick, Appendix I.

(iv) The definition of justification was borrowed from words of the Lutheran, Melanchthon, but the characteristic Lutheran formulas were avoided. It is to be attained by 'inward contrition, perfect faith and charity, certain hope and confidence'.

The second five concern 'the laudable ceremonies used in the Church'.

(i) Images are retained to be 'the kindlers and stirrers of men's minds', but idolatry is to be avoided.

(ii) Saints are to be honoured and invoked as intercessors to pray with us and for us, 'so that it be done without any vain superstition as to think that any saint is more merciful or will hear us sooner than Christ . . . or doth serve for one thing more than another or is patron of the same.'

(iii) Certain mediaeval rites and ceremonies are to be kept as 'good and laudable', but have not 'power to remit sin', but only to stir and lift up our minds unto God.

(iv) Prayers for the dead are encouraged, and the book of Maccabees is quoted to support them. Our ignorance of the details of the next life is asserted. Abuses connected with Purgatory, and especially the Pope's pardons, are denounced.

We can see how such a formula met the needs of the moment. No final settlement was as yet possible. The Ten Articles remained the authoritative expression of the mind of the Church of England down to 1543.

But meanwhile, in 1537, there appeared *The Institution of a Christian Man*, commonly called *the Bishops' Book*. This was a popular and practical handbook of instruction in faith and morals, based on the Ten Articles and incorporating parts of them. It was drawn up by a committee under Cranmer. It contained explanations of the Common Creed, the Seven Sacraments, the Ten Commandments, the Lord's Prayer, the Ave Maria, Justification and Purgatory. The articles on the last two were taken bodily from the Ten Articles. All Seven Sacraments appear, but the three, Baptism, the Eucharist and Penance, are placed on a higher level than the rest. Its lapses from accurate theology, due to haste in composition, offended the refined taste of the King. Hence it never gained his authority, though printed at the King's Press. It rested only on the authority of those who signed it, including all the Bishops.

(*b*) In 1543 there was published *The Necessary Doctrine and Erudition for any Christian Man*, commonly known as *the King's Book*. It was substantially a revised edition of the Bishops' Book, being based upon the King's own criticisms of the former work. The language was more precise and theological. It was issued on the authority of Convocation, Parliament and the King, who himself wrote the preface. As compared with the Ten Articles, it shows a reaction. This may be explained by the political circumstances of the time. In 1538 the conference between Anglican and Lutheran divines had broken down. The influence of Cranmer had for the moment declined. The character of this new formulary is in keeping with the anti-Protestant legislation of the close of Henry's reign, especially the Statute of the Six Articles. Transubstantiation is taught, though the actual use of the word is avoided. The silence of its articles suggests that all 'Seven

Sacraments' are on a level. Clerical celibacy is maintained, and a loftier view is taken of Orders. Taken as a whole it marked the triumph of the Old Learning. Probably this was designed to be the last and final statement of England's theological position. Such it remained till the death of Henry in 1547.

§ 3. After the accession of Edward VI rapid changes were made in the services of the Church, but no definitely doctrinal statement was issued till 1553. However, as early as 1549 a letter from Bishop Hooper states that Cranmer 'has some Articles of Religion to which all preachers and lecturers in divinity are required to subscribe'.[1] This was probably an early draft of the later Articles, framed as a test of orthodoxy. These Articles were submitted to the Bishops, and, after revision, submitted to the Council in 1552. At this time they were 45 in number. After they had passed the scrutiny of the Council, the King and the Royal Chaplains they were returned to Cranmer and reduced to 42—the famous *42 Articles*. An English edition appeared in May, 1553. The official edition signed by the King followed a week later, and in June a royal mandate commanded subscription from all clergy, schoolmasters and members of a university on taking their degree, in the province of Canterbury. In two later editions, published shortly afterwards, a catechism was added. The exact authority on which they were published is uncertain. It is clear that the catechism issued with them had no authority from Convocation. The titles of all the editions, but not the royal mandate, claim for the Articles the authority of Convocation. Is this true? The records of Convocation perished in the great fire of London. In any case, they were badly kept, 'but one degree above blanks,' and their evidence would have been of little value. Convocation had appointed a commission in 1551 to reform the Canons of the Church. That commission probably produced the Articles and claimed the authority of Convocation for them. In any case the question is primarily interesting as a historical problem.[2] Even if the Church was committed to them, it was only for a few weeks. Edward VI died in the following July. On the accession of Queen Mary they were dropped. As they had never been enjoined by Act of Parliament, there was no need to repeal them.

The 42 Articles are not, as it were, the natural descendants of the previous official formularies, but represent a different line of development that can be traced back as far as 1538. At that time Henry VIII, for political reasons, desired an alliance with the Protestant Princes of Germany. Accordingly, a small body of Lutheran divines was invited over to England to confer with a committee of English Churchmen, headed by Cranmer, with a view to drawing up a joint confession of faith. By the deliberate use of ambiguous language

---

[1] Quoted by Hardwick, p. 72.
[2] For a statement of the evidence on both sides, see Gibson, pp. 15-20.

agreement was reached on certain points of doctrine. But on questions of discipline the conference broke down and the Lutherans returned home. Among Cranmer's papers has been found a draft of 13 Articles of doctrine agreed upon by this committee. These are known as the *13 Articles*. They were never published, and hence possessed no authority. But they were used by Cranmer as the basis of certain of the 42 Articles. Being themselves based upon the Confession of Augsburg, they form the link between the Confession of Augsburg and our own 42 Articles. At first sight the similarities suggest direct borrowing, but it has been proved that all the borrowed portions came through the medium of these 13 Articles.

In reading the 42 Articles it may easily be seen that they are a double-edged weapon, designed to smite two opposite enemies. On the one hand they attack mediaeval teaching and abuses, on the other hand they attack Anabaptist tenets. First they deal with the doctrine of 'School-authors'. This needs some explanation. The doctrines attacked were not necessarily official Roman teaching as revised by the Council of Trent, but popular mediaeval teaching. The Reformation compelled even the Church of Rome to re-state her teaching. The Pope called together a 'General Council' at Trent. In actual fact the Council proved to consist only of Bishops in allegiance to Rome. The Reformers refused to acknowledge it.[1] It held its first meeting in December, 1545, and continued to sit, though with long breaks, until 1563. It was from its own point of view a reforming Council, and did much to purge away mediaeval abuses. In some cases its decrees are prior in time to the Articles of our own Church, in other cases they are later. It is most important to know which is the earlier. Very often the teaching condemned in our Articles cannot be the formal statements of the Council of Trent, because such did not yet exist, but is simply current mediaeval teaching. Upon this the Council of Trent is in many cases as severe as our own Articles. The Reformers kept a keen eye on all the doings of the Council. When the 42 Articles appeared the Council of Trent had only begun its work. Secondly, they oppose even more keenly the teaching of the Anabaptists. These were the extreme Protestants, in no way a single organized sect, but rather an undefined class embracing men of every variety of opinion. The name Anabaptist was given to them from their denial of infant baptism and their custom of re-baptizing converts. There is hardly any error of doctrine or morality that was not proclaimed by some of them. They were a very real danger to all order in Church and State alike. No party had a good word for them. The Reformers feared the discredit that they brought upon the whole reforming movement.

The chief instances in which Roman errors were attacked in the 42 Articles may be summed up thus:

1. The claims of the Pope are denied (Art. 36).

[1] See below on Art. 21.

2. The Church of Rome is declared to have erred in the past and therefore to be liable to err again. So, too, 'General Councils' so called have not always shown themselves infallible (Arts. 20 and 22).

3. The use of the vulgar tongue in Church and the marriage of the clergy are defended (Arts. 25 and 31).

4. Errors about merit, works of supererogation, purgatory and pardons, grace *ex opere operato*, transubstantiation and the 'sacrifices of Masses' are denounced (Arts. 12, 13, 23, 29 and 30).

5. The sufficiency of Scripture is maintained (Art. 5).

The Anabaptists are only mentioned by name twice, but the errors maintained by them and attacked in these Articles include the following:

1. They had revived all the ancient heresies about the Holy Trinity and the Person of Christ. Against these the Catholic position is asserted (Arts. 1–4 and 7).

2. Many of them were Pelagians (Arts. 8–10).

3. Others claimed that being regenerate they were unable to commit sin (Arts. 14–15).

4. Some depreciated all Scripture and placed themselves above even the moral law. Others assigned equal importance to all the Old Testament (Arts. 5–6 and 19).

5. Some denied any need of ordination for ministers, and claimed that the efficacy of all ministrations depended on the personal holiness of the minister (Arts. 24, 27).

6. Infant Baptism was denied (Art. 28).

7. All Church discipline was repudiated (Art. 20 and 32).

8. Many held strange views about the Descent into Hell (Art. 3), the nature of the Resurrection and the future life (Arts. 39–40), the ultimate salvation of all men (Art. 42) and Millenarianism (Art. 41).

9. The authority of the State was impugned and communism demanded (Arts. 36–38).

Taken as a whole, the 42 Articles 'showed a surprisingly comprehensive and moderate spirit. The broad soft touch of Cranmer lay upon them, when they came from the furnace.'[1] Their tone is conciliatory. They aim rather at concord than at accurate definition. Cranmer had a great desire to form a united Protestant Church as against Rome. Such Articles might well be a basis of union. They exclude extremists of all kinds. Again, these Articles make no pretension to set forth a complete system of belief. There is, for instance, no Article on the Holy Spirit. Unlike many continental formularies they do not attempt to embrace all theology, but are content to meet the needs of a particular crisis. They do, indeed, bear unmistakeable evidence of Lutheran influence and language. Certain Articles embody whole paragraphs and phrases of the Confession of Augsburg, taken from the 13 Articles. But on the doctrine of justification by faith they avoid

---

[1] Dixon, vol. iii. p. 520.

Lutheran extravagances. Further, at this time there was violent controversy among the Reformers on the subject of the Sacraments. The Lutherans held that they conferred grace. The Swiss reformers regarded them rather as signs or seals of grace independently received, since only the elect could receive grace. The delay in the publication of these Articles was, according to one account, due to the violent controversy on this point. Cranmer and Ridley on the one side maintained the Lutheran view, Hooper the Swiss view. In the end Cranmer won the day. Both sides agreed to discard the language of the Schoolmen, that the Sacraments 'contain grace', since this failed to emphasize the need of a right disposition in the recipient. But though the actual term 'confer grace' does not occur, the truth that it contained was clearly stated. In Art. 26 Sacraments are said to be 'effectual signs of grace'.[1] In Art. 28 'Baptism . . . is a sign and seal of our new birth, whereby as by an instrument they that receive Baptism rightly, are grafted into the Church'. Only on one point these Articles do fall short of their general spirit of comprehensiveness. In their teaching on the Holy Communion, not only transubstantiation but any doctrine of the Real Presence is denied. This was held by Lutherans no less than Romanists. The explanation of this fall below the Lutheran standard is that Cranmer's views on the Eucharist had been steadily falling. Owing to the influence of the Swiss, and particularly one John à Lasco, he had abandoned any belief in the Real Presence, and adopted the Calvinist view that the presence of Christ is to be found only in the individual soul of the faithful recipient. Any other view was excluded by the language of Art. 26 (with this we must compare the Prayer Book of 1552, into which, before publication, was intruded the famous 'Black Rubric'). So, too, in Art. 26, all use of the phrase *ex opere operato* is condemned, and the title sacrament is practically refused to any rites except Baptism and Holy Communion. On all these points considerable changes were made in 1563. We may also notice that the objectionable title 'Supreme Head of the Church' is employed in Art. 36. In the reign of Edward VI this was inevitable.

§ 4. Some mention must be made here of a work probably by the same persons as the 42 Articles. We have seen that Convocation sanctioned the appointment of a committee to revise the Canons. Their labours resulted in a document entitled *The Reformatio Legum Ecclesiasticarum*. This work was completed in 1553, but never obtained the sanction of Parliament. Its chief importance is to be found in the light that it sheds on the meaning and purpose of the 42 Articles. Which of the two in its treatment of any subject is the earlier, we cannot now ascertain.

§ 4. When Elizabeth came to the throne in 1558, she had a hard

---

[1] The phrase 'signs of grace' comes from the Confession of Augsburg, and was deliberately strengthened by the addition of 'effectual'.

C

task before her. Her aim must be to secure religious unity at home in the face of many active and powerful enemies abroad. She began not with questions of doctrine, but of worship and discipline. She recovered from Parliament the restoration of the Royal Supremacy: enforced by Act of Parliament the new Prayer-book: filled up the vacant sees: took strong measures to enforce a modicum of decency in worship. It was not till 1563 that Convocation began to undertake the revision of the 42 Articles. Till then the Prayer-book was the standard of doctrine. However, in the interval, Archbishop Parker put forth on his own authority the *Eleven Articles*. These were to be read in church by all ministers at their first entry into their cures and twice a year afterwards. Though sanctioned by the Archbishop of York and all the Bishops, they were a temporary expedient, lacking official authority.

(a) In January, 1563, Convocation met to draw up a new formulary. The Archbishop had been using the interval in preparing with Bishop Guest of Rochester a revised edition of the 42 Articles. These were to form the basis of the new formulary. A revival of Lutheran influence can be found in this revision. The Archbishop had drawn upon the Confession of Würtemburg, a Lutheran formulary presented to the Council of Trent in 1552 by the ambassadors of Würtemburg as an official statement of Lutheran views. Thus a Lutheran confession influenced the English Articles for a second time. The influence of the Confession of Augsburg was indirect, through the 13 Articles. Here the borrowing from the Confession of Würtemburg was direct.

When first presented to Convocation the new Articles still numbered 42. Four of the old had been removed and four new ones added. Three were struck out by Convocation, reducing them to the familiar 39. These were passed by Convocation and were then sent on to the Queen. The Queen herself made two important alterations in the draft sent up by Convocation: (i) She struck out our present Art. 29 in order to avoid giving offence to the Romanist party, whom she wished to retain within the Church; (ii) She added the opening clause to Art. 20, drawn from the Confession of Würtemburg. This asserted the authority of the Church to decree rites and ceremonies, as against the Puritans, who denied the Church's authority to enforce any rite or ceremony that was not explicitly commanded in Scripture. At the time these two changes rested solely on the Queen's authority: they had no authority either from Convocation or Parliament.

The 38 Articles remained in this condition till the final revision of the Articles in 1571. As the result of the Pope's bull any hope of reconciliation with Rome was destroyed. In obedience to his injunction the Papists had separated themselves from the English Church. Hence there was no longer any need to respect their feelings. Accordingly, Art. 29 was restored. At the same time a number of small changes were made, of which the chief was the completion of the list of the Apocrypha in Art. 6. In their revised form the Articles were passed by Convocation, and so the opening clause of Art. 20 gained synodical authority.

(b) We may now consider the main changes that are to be found if we compare our present 39 Articles with the 42 Articles of 1553.

1. Certain new articles were added and old articles expanded, apparently for the sake of greater completeness. Thus the statement in Art. 2 of the 'Eternal Generation' and 'Consubstantiality' of the Son and the whole of Art. 5, 'on the Holy Ghost' were added, both practically verbatim from the Confession of Würtemburg. In Art. 6 canonical books are stated to be those 'of whose authority there has never been any doubt in the church'. So, too, Art. 11, on Justification, was enlarged and made more definite. Art. 10 was enlarged to fit on better to Art. 9, and a new Art., No. 12, on 'Good Works', was added. All these changes were based on the Confession of Würtemburg.

2. Certain articles and statements were omitted, either because the errors attacked in them had now ceased to be formidable, or because it was seen that a greater latitude of opinion might be allowed. Thus four whole articles on Anabaptist errors, such as 'Millenarianism', 'the resurrection being past', 'universalism', 'unconscious existence after death', were removed. The article on 'Blasphemy against the Holy Spirit', the interpretation of S. Peter's word about 'the descent into Hell', the condemnation of the phrase *ex opere operato*, were likewise withdrawn. So, too, the reference by name to the Anabaptists as reviving Pelagianism.

3. A great advance was made in sacramental teaching, parallel to that made in the Prayer-book of 1559 as compared with that of 1552. The language of Art. 28 is at least consistent with a belief in the Real Presence, though the relation of the gift bestowed in the Holy Communion to the visible elements is left undiscussed. The language on Infant Baptism in Art. 27 is strengthened. Also the five 'commonly called Sacraments' reappear in Art. 25, though not placed on a level with the two 'Sacraments of the Gospel'. The withdrawal of any condemnation of the phrase *ex opere operato* in Art. 25 emphasized the objective value of sacramental grace.

4. Art. 37 on the Royal Supremacy was largely rewritten. The title 'supreme Head of the church' was dropped. The character of the supremacy claimed for the Crown is explained.

5. On the other hand the independence of the Church of England as against Rome was asserted and strengthened in certain quite definite ways. The Council of Trent had as early as 1546 issued a somewhat ambiguous decree placing Scripture and tradition side by side as the sources of truth and discipline, including within the canon a large number of apocryphal books. These last it put on a level with the rest as a source of doctrine. In Art. 6 the Church of England de-

liberately dissented from this view, distinguishing between the Old
Testament and the Apocrypha, and placing them on different levels.
A list of canonical books was given, and the list of apocryphal books
completed in 1571. Again, in 1547 the Council of Trent laid down that
all Seven Sacraments were instituted by Christ. In the revised form of
Art. 25 this is practically denied. So, too, in Art. 24, the Church of
England was no longer content to commend the use of the vulgar
tongue in public worship. It condemned the use of any other as unscriptural and unprimitive. A new Article (Art. 30) was added to
condemn Communion in one kind. Art. 32 on the Celibacy of the
Clergy was re-written and strengthened. Art. 36 was re-written to
defend Anglican ordinations against Romanist objections. A new
clause to Art. 34 was added to assert the rights of 'particular or
national' churches. On all these points the revision showed itself
anti-Roman.

6. In the opposite direction the revision can hardly have been entirely acceptable to the Puritan party. They must have disliked the
changes in Sacramental teaching and still more the Queen's addition
to Art. 20. Many of them did not love Art. 34. The authorship of the
saying that 'the Church of England has a Popish Liturgy and a Calvinistic set of Articles' is ascribed to Pitt. It has been widely repeated
by those who know little of the Articles and neglect the Prayer-book.
No doubt the general tone of the Articles is not quite that of the
Prayer-book. They reflect the troubled atmosphere of the times in
which they were composed. The Prayer-book, being based largely on
earlier models, breathes more of the spirit of serene and undisturbed
devotion. Its tone is more positive. Further, while the Church of
England deliberately aimed at excluding Pelagians, it did not aim at
excluding Calvinists. Hence there is much in the Articles which,
though it need not be taken in a Calvinistic sense, may be taken in
that sense. There was much, too, that was good in Calvinism: if the
Articles would never have existed in their present form without the
influence of Calvin, that does not mean that they are Calvinistic in
the sense that they accept all his teaching. There are several statements in them that Calvinists have always found it hard to accept.
Art. 16 says that a man who has received the Holy Ghost and fallen
into sin, '*may* rise again.' The Calvinist would say 'must rise again'.
Art. 2 lays down that 'Christ died for all actual sins of men': Calvinists would say 'Christ died only for the elect'. In Art. 17 the clause
'although the decrees of predestination are unknown to us' was
dropped and the phrase 'in Christ' added, both changes tending to
soften the language. Further, the same article speaks of God's promises as 'generally' (*i.e.* for all men) 'set forth in Holy Scripture'. So,
too, in Art. 9, Man is only 'very far gone from original righteousness',
not entirely corrupt, as Calvin taught. But the clearest evidence that
the Articles are not Calvinistic is the repeated attempts made by the

Puritans to alter or supplement them. In 1572 the Puritans addressed certain admonitions to Parliament complaining of the inadequacy of the Articles and their dangerous speaking about falling from grace. Further, in 1595, as a result of controversy at Cambridge, a committee, meeting under Archbishop Whitgift at Lambeth, compiled the 'Lambeth Articles', setting out the full Calvinistic system in all its stringency. Fortunately the Queen at once intervened and repressed any attempt to force these on the Church. They never possessed any authority but that of their authors. At the Hampton Court Conference in 1604 the Puritan party again tried to amend the Articles. The Royal declaration prefixed to the Articles, and dating from 1628, is a relic of the controversy that raged during the reign of Charles I, largely round the interpretation of the Articles. When in 1643 the Puritans were triumphant, the Westminster Assembly appointed a committee to amend the Articles. Art. 16 fared badly at their hands. Again, at the Restoration, similar objections were raised by the Puritans, but without success. This bare statement of fact is the best answer to any assertion that our Articles are Calvinistic.

(c) Such, then, is the history of our present 39 Articles. They express the mind of the Church of England on the questions under dispute during the Reformation. They do not claim to be a final and complete system of theology. As Bishop Pearson wrote:[1] the book 'is not, nor is pretended to be, a complete body of divinity, or a comprehension and explication of all Christian doctrines necessary to be taught: but an enumeration of some truths, which upon and since the Reformation have been denied by some persons: who upon denial are thought unfit to have any cure of souls in this Church or realm; because they might by their opinions either infect their flock with error or else disturb the Church with schism or the realm with sedition.' On this point they present a strong contrast with many continental formularies which are 'controversial, diffuse, and longsome'.[2] Our English Articles avoid the sweeping anathemas of the Council of Trent or the 'endless arguings and chidings' of contemporary confessions. They move on a higher level. If we compare them with other performances of the age, we must see in them an example of the special Providence that has watched over the Church of England. Dr Moberly has put very clearly the grounds on which we may be grateful for their tone of moderation and comprehensiveness.[3] 'It might so easily have happened that statements drawn up amid the stress and strain of the vehement passions which were raging in the struggle of the Reformation, would have been just in the form which we, in the sober thought of the nineteenth century, could not have endorsed. But this is just what has not happened. Condemnation of Roman theory or practice, failing to make any necessary distinction

---

[1] Quoted by Hardwick, p. 158.   [2] Dixon, vol. v. p. 396.
[3] Moberly, *Problems and Principles*, pp. 386–387.

or allowances, might so easily have had just the irremediable traces of exaggeration upon them. Approximations to Calvinism or Lutheranism might so easily have gone just beyond the line of what was in the long run rationally defensible. It may even be admitted that, *prima facie*, there is a certain aspect of ambiguity in some of these directions. And yet, on examination, after all, in one article after another, the almost expected overstatement has not been made. You may say that the 17th Article comes very near to Calvinism, or the 11th to the characteristic formula of Lutheran solifidianism. But, on the other hand, as the mind begins to recognize that the lengthy and apparently Calvinistic phraseology of the Article about Predestination just stops short of all that is really offensive in connexion with that theory, remaining after all within those aspects of it which are edifying and true; and again, that the apparent embrace of the cardinal Lutheran principles of justification by faith only is not in the paradoxical terms in which Luther loved to overstate it; there begins to be a certain definite and growing sense that, though the articles may carry us into forgotten controversies, and make some statements which have but little relevance to our modern difficulties, at all events there was, amongst those who drew them, too much of genuine conservatism, of reverence for what was good in old ways, of self-restraint and moderating wisdom, to allow of their committing themselves or us to the extremer and more unguarded statements even of those with whom they greatly sympathized.'

§ 5. *Creeds and Articles.*—The significance of our Articles may best be learnt by a comparison between them and Creeds. Both alike are theological statements of belief. Both alike have been employed as tests. Both are attempts to preserve the truth in all its fulness. But while Creeds are a necessity, 'in a world where all expression of spirit is through body,' Articles are a consequence 'not of the Church's existence but of the Church's failure'. 'The Church, without a Creed, would not in human life on earth, however ideally perfect, have been a Church at all. But if the Church on earth had been ideally perfect, or anything even remotely like it, there would never have been any 39 Articles. The one is a necessary feature of spiritual reality. The other is an unfortunate consequence of spiritual failure.'[1]

(i) Creeds are in origin far more than controversial statements. No doubt particular clauses in them have been added or altered at particular times to rule out certain errors, as when 'of one substance with the Father' was added to refute Arianism. But in their essential nature Creeds grew up out of the positive statement of belief required of every Christian at his baptism. The threefold division recalls the baptismal formula. They rose spontaneously out of the life of the Church to meet such a need as this. Though they conform to a common type their origin is veiled in obscurity. Their growth in the

---

[1] *op. cit.* pp. 378–379.

main has been hidden and spontaneous. Even their developments were largely unconscious. On the other hand, Articles were composed at a definite time for the express purpose of meeting a particular crisis. Their authors are known.

(ii) Creeds have behind them the authority of the universal and undivided Church. Articles have behind them at most the authority of particular or national Churches. In most cases they assume the truth of the Creeds and start from that. Further, creeds are based upon a wide and universal experience. The formularies of the Reformation—though this applies very much less to our own Articles than to others—are the product of a group of men, or in some cases a single individual mind. Hence, Creeds have a permanent value, Articles only a temporary value. We do not condemn, say, the Churches of the East, because they do not possess the 39 Articles. We should condemn a Church that rejected the Apostles' or Nicene Creed. We may reasonably doubt if the Churches of the mission-field need become acquainted with the 39 Articles. But they certainly are bound to receive the Creeds. It is possible even to look forward to a day when the Church of England may exchange or discard our present Articles, though that day is not yet in sight. That would not involve any breach of continuity or catholicity. But to reject the Creeds would be to part company with the life of the Universal Church.

(iii) The Creeds consist in the main of short and simple statements without explanation or argument. They assert simple facts of history and theology. Their field is very narrow. Their theology rarely goes beyond explaining the significance of the historic facts that they record. The whole Creed is grouped round the historical Person of Jesus Christ. The Articles, on the other hand, cover a wider field. They deal not only with the nature and being of God and His great acts of redemption, but with man's inner religious life. Questions about the meaning of sin, the relation of faith to works, grace, free-will and the like are all discussed. The Creeds are positive, Articles are often negative and controversial. The Articles also touch upon an entirely new department, the relation of the Christian to the State. This can be explained by the condition of society in the sixteenth century.

(iv) Lastly, as has already been pointed out, Articles are primarily 'tests for teachers'. They set a limit to official teaching. Creeds are for teachers and learners alike. Belief in the Apostles' Creed is demanded of every candidate for Baptism. A Creed rightly finds a place in public worship. In the service for the visitation of the sick and the dying the Christian is called upon to repeat his baptismal creed as a last act of faith. The Creeds belong to the laymen not less than the clergy. But a loyal churchman may go through his whole life without necessarily coming into contact with the 39 Articles.

To sum up, though both Creeds and Articles have arisen out of the necessity imposed upon the Church to interpret to itself the meaning of its own life: though both have been shaped by that discussion, which alone can sift out error and bring to light the truth: yet in origin, value and aim they differ. Creeds belong to the life of the Church and Articles to its life in a sinful world.

§ 6. *A history of Subscription to the Articles.*—Up to 1571 subscription was required only of members of Convocation. The Queen had not allowed the Articles to be submitted to Parliament. But the open breach with Rome in 1570 and the Pope's excommunication of the Queen obliged her to turn to Parliament in order to strengthen her hands. In 1571 an Act was passed requiring that everyone under the degree of a Bishop who had been ordained by any form other than that set forth by Parliament in the reign of Edward VI, or the form in use under Elizabeth, should subscribe 'to all Articles of Religion, which only concern the confession of the true Christian faith and the doctrine of the Sacraments.' This was aimed at men ordained under Mary. Further, in future no one was to be admitted to a benefice 'except he . . . shall first have subscribed the said Articles'. The Act was ingeniously drawn up in the interests of the Puritans. By the insertion of the word 'only' subscription was made to include no more than the doctrinal Articles: the Articles on discipline were evaded. However, in 1571, after the final revision by Convocation, Convocation on its own authority required subscription to *all* the Articles in their final form. This was enforced by the Court of High Commission, though at times with less strictness. In 1583 Archbishop Whitgift provided a form of subscription included in the *Three Articles*. All the clergy were to subscribe to these. The first asserted the Royal Supremacy. The second contains an assertion of the Scripturalness of the whole Prayer-book and a promise to use the said book and no other in public worship. The third runs 'That I allow the Book of Articles of Religion agreed upon by the Archbishops and Bishops of both provinces and the whole Clergy in Convocation holden at London in the year of our Lord God 1562 and set forth by Her Majesty's authority and do believe all the Articles therein contained to be agreeable to the Word of God.' In this way subscription was once more strictly enforced. In 1604 the Three Articles received the authority of Convocation, being embodied after small alteration in the Canons of 1604 and ratified by the King. The actual form ran: 'I . . . do willingly and *ex animo* subscribe to these three articles above mentioned and to all things that are contained in them.' This form remained in force in spite of various attempts to relax the stringency of it. In practice the form usually employed ran: 'I . . . do willingly and from my heart subscribe to the 39 Articles of Religion of the United Church of England and Ireland, and to the three Articles in the 30th Canon, and to all things therein contained.' In 1865, as the result of a Royal Commission, Convocation obtained leave from the Crown to revise the Canons. A new and simpler declaration of Assent was drawn up by the Convocations of Canterbury and York and confirmed by royal letters patent. To-day the candidate for ordination is required to subscribe to the following: 'I . . . do solemnly make the following declaration, I assent to the 39 Articles of Religion and the Book of Common Prayer and of ordering of Bishops Priests and Deacons. I believe the doctrine of the Church of England therein set forth to be agreeable to the Word of God and in public prayer and administration of the Sacraments I will use the form in the said book prescribed and none other, except so far as shall be ordered by lawful authority.' Two points need to be noted.

(i) The Church has demanded subscription to the Articles from the clergy and the clergy only. The fifth Canon of 1604 at most demands from the laity that they shall not attack them. If other bodies such as the Universities have in earlier days required subscription from their members, they were responsible for the requirement, and not the Church.

(ii) The change of language in the form of subscription was deliberate. We are asked to affirm to-day, not that the Articles are all agreeable to the Word of God, but that the doctrine of the Church of England as set forth in the Articles is agreeable to the Word of God. That is, we are not called to assent to every phrase or detail of the Articles but only to their general sense. This alteration was made of set purpose to afford relief to scrupulous consciences.†

THE BEING OF GOD

ARTICLE I

<table>
<tr><td>Of Faith in the Holy Trinity</td><td>De fide in sacro-sanctam Trinitatem</td></tr>
<tr><td>There is but one living and true God, everlasting, without body, parts, or passions, of infinite power, wisdom, and goodness, the Maker and Preserver of all things, both visible and invisible. And in unity of this Godhead there be three Persons, of one substance, power, and eternity, the Father, the Son, and the Holy Ghost.</td><td>Unus est vivus et verus Deus, aeternus, incorporeus, impartibilis, impassibilis, immensae potentiae, sapientiae ac bonitatis, creator et conservator omnium, tum visibilium, tum invisibilium. Et in unitate hujus divinae naturae tres sunt personae, ejusdem essentiae, potentiae, ac aeternitatis, Pater, Filius, et Spiritus Sanctus.</td></tr>
</table>

One of the original Articles of 1553. Its language is very close to that of the Confession of Augsburg.

It was called forth by the teaching of the Anabaptists, who were reviving all the ancient heresies. It deals with:

1. The Unity of God.
2. The attributes of God.
3. God's relation to the universe.
4. The manner of God's existence—the doctrine of the Trinity.

§ 1. *There is but one living and true God.*—The Articles, like the Bible itself, assume and do not attempt to prove the existence of God. By God we mean the one self-existent Being, the Author and Sustainer of all that is, upon whom all things depend and in whom they find their goal. All thinkers agree that God is one. The ancient Greek philosophers attained to this truth primarily by the road of reason. Every attempt to understand the world assumes that the world is intelligible, and therefore one. All philosophy presupposes that behind phenomena is a single ultimate reality. A world that is capable of being explained must be a single and coherent system. It must be one in origin and in purpose. Philosophy and science rest ultimately upon the same assumption. They presuppose the ultimate unity of all existence. This 'Absolute' or ultimate reality whose existence behind the world of change and appearance philosophy and science are compelled implicitly to assume, need not be a very interesting God. He need not be, as far as their requirements go, a God who loves men and can be loved by them. We could not sing hymns to the 'Absolute'. But He must be one. The very idea of God excludes the possibility of more than one God. All the so-called arguments for the existence of God are arguments for the existence of one God. Thus the unity of God is a truth of reason, though reason by itself can tell us little or nothing about His character. (See note on p. 52.)†

The nation of Israel attained to the truth of the unity of God, not by speculation and abstract thought, but through historical revelation and prophetic insight. We can trace out in the history of Israel a growth in the knowledge of the one true God. At first Jehovah was a tribal God, the God of the Jewish nation. To use technical language the Jews were 'monolatrous' rather than 'monotheists'. They worshipped one God, but were not concerned to deny the existence of others. Even the First Commandment allows the possibility of the existence of other Gods. Slowly, through the religious insight and experience of the prophets, the spiritual leaders of the nation, at least, came to grasp the truth that Jehovah was the one and only God of the whole world.[1] Through the exile Israel was purged of idolatry. By suffering and persecution the conviction of the Unity of God was branded for ever upon the consciousness of the nation. The Creed of the Jewish Church was the words of Deut 6[4], 'Hear, O Israel, the LORD our God is one LORD.' As such it was solemnly reaffirmed by our Lord Himself (Mk 12[29], etc.). This truth had been attained, not by any process of reason, but by a special revelation of God Himself. The Jew could go on to say what the Greek could not, 'Thou shalt love the Lord thy God.' The God who revealed Himself to Israel was above all a God of grace and righteousness, a Redeemer, who manifested His love and care for His people in a practical way through the events of history. In this aspect, too, God must be one. There is but One God, not because it happens to be so, but because it cannot be otherwise. Philosophy and religion alike make the same demand. To have more than one God is, as the early Christians maintained, to have no true God at all. To be a polytheist is to be an atheist.†

So the way was prepared for a further revelation of the nature of God. The truth of the Unity of God 'had to be completely established first as a broad element of thought, indispensable, unalterable, before there could really begin the disclosure to man of the reality of eternal relations within the one indivisible Being of God. And when the disclosure came, it came, not as modifying—far less denying—but as further interpreting and illumining that unity which it absolutely presupposed.'[2] When it is rightly presented, the doctrine of the Trinity does not destroy but safeguards the Unity of God. The highest type of unity is not a mere barren numerical unity, but one that embraces within itself a wealth of diversity.

[1] This truth is implied as early as Amos. It is Jehovah who directs and overrules the movements of all the nations.
[2] Moberly, *Atonement and Personality*, p. 85.

Opposed to this truth of the unity of God stands polytheism. In the Bible this is always represented as intimately connected with spiritual blindness and moral evil. Whether, as a matter of simple history, all forms of polytheism are in origin corruptions of a single older and purer belief in One God, is a question for the science of Comparative Religion to decide. At present very different answers are given. But the standpoint of Scripture is amply justified. From the point of view of Jewish and Christian revelation polytheism is a degraded and degrading form of religion. The Jews were always being tempted to lapse into idolatry because the faith and worship of Jehovah made too great demands upon them. The contest between Baal and Jehovah was not only a contest between two forms of religion, but between two standards of morality. Jehovah demanded personal righteousness in His worshippers. 'Be ye holy: for I am holy.' Baal did not. The prophets are always protesting against those who degraded Jehovah by putting Him on a moral level with the gods of the heathen. Throughout Old Testament history polytheism stood for a religion that corrupted the very springs of the spiritual life. It met men's desire for worship without demanding moral effort or reformation in the worshipper. Religion was regarded not as doing the will of God, but as bribing or cajoling God to do man's will. A firm belief in one Almighty God was shown to be the only basis of a moral and righteous life.

So, too, S. Paul's denunciation of heathenism in Rom 1[18] ff. was amply justified. He 'looks at things with the insight of a religious teacher: he describes facts which he sees around him, and he connects these facts with permanent tendencies of human nature and with principles which are apparent in the Providential government of the world.'[1] The Gods of pagan mythology were attractive to the multitude largely because they were on a moral level with themselves. Religion had become the enemy of morality. How far the particular individuals of any one generation were personally responsible for this may be questioned. But the multitude 'loved to have it so', and made little or no effort to follow up the truth which was offered to them in reason and conscience. 'It was in the strict sense due to supernatural influence that the religion of the Jew and of the Christian was kept clear of these corrupt and corrupting features. The state of the Pagan world betokened the absence, the suspension, or withholding, of such supernatural influence; and there was reason enough for the belief that it was judicially inflicted.'[2]

The words '*living and true*' are in Scripture applied to God in opposition to the false gods of heathenism. God is living ('*vivus*', *not* '*vivens*'): not merely alive, but the source of all life (Ps 42[2], Jn 5[26], etc.). He is opposed to dead idols (Jer 10[10], Acts 14[15], 1 Thess 1[9], etc.). So, too, God is *true* ('*verus*'): not only faithful to His word

---

[1] Sanday and Headlam, *Romans*, p. 49.   [2] *Op. cit.* p. 49.

(*verax*), but genuine (ἀληθινός). He is contrasted with the sham gods of heathenism as alone fulfilling the true conception of God (Is 44⁸ ff.); 'The only true God' (Jn 17³). The two ideas of living and true are combined (1 Thess 1⁹, 1 Jn 5²⁰).

Polytheism may appear at first sight to have lost its dangers. But its spirit is always threatening to corrupt the purity of Christian faith. Human nature desires a satisfaction for its instinct of worship. Fallen human nature desires to satisfy its instinct with the least possible moral effort. Hence men are always tempted to seek a refuge from the intense holiness of God in some object of worship that will be more indulgent towards sin and sloth. Accordingly we find in the Roman and Greek Churches a Saint-worship that in popular practice tends towards polytheism. Elsewhere we find what Dr. Hort called 'Jesus-worship',[1] *i.e.* a perverted and sentimental devotion to our Lord, not as the revelation of the Father and one with Him, but as a tender and not too exacting Saviour who will be a refuge from the Father's holiness and justice. In each case the One God is set on one side as too strict in His moral demands. A less exacting object of worship is invented or procured. The pleasures of religion are retained at the cost of its truth and purity. For practical purposes the result is polytheism. Its fruits to-day are the same as they were in the days of the prophets or of S. Paul, a relaxing of the moral life and the lowering of the moral standard. To-day as of old the Unity of God is the one safeguard of moral and spiritual progress.

§ 2. (*a*) How can we conceive of God? In Scripture, from first to last, God is represented as a 'Personal' God. He is said to possess will (Mt 7²¹, Jn 6³⁹, Eph 1¹¹, 1 Jn 5¹⁴, etc.): to know, to have a mind and purpose (2 Sam 14¹⁴, Jer 32³⁵, Mt 6⁸ and ³², Jn 10¹⁵, Acts 4²⁸, Rom 11³⁴, etc.): to love (Hos 11¹, Is 43⁴, Jn 15⁹, 1 Jn 4⁸ and ¹⁰, etc.). So, too, God is said to be jealous (Exod 20⁵, Deut 32¹⁶, etc.), and grieved (Gen 6⁶, Is 63¹⁰, etc.), to be pitiful and show mercy (Is 60¹⁰, Jas 5¹¹, etc.), to feel anger (Jn 3³⁶, Rev 14¹⁰, etc.). Further, in the teaching of Christ a wide range of images borrowed from human relationships is employed to depict the character of God. Not only is He above all 'the Father', but His acts are compared to those of a king, an unjust judge, an owner of sheep, a woman keeping house, etc. In all such images the life and character of God are represented in terms of human life. It could not be otherwise. Human personality is the highest form of existence within our own experience, and we are obliged to think of God in terms of the highest that we know. However far God's life may excel our own, it cannot fall below it. The God who created human personality cannot Himself be less than personal. We do not claim that in describing God in terms of human personality we are giving a complete or adequate description of Him. All that we say is that this is the least inadequate language that we

[1] Hort, *Life and Letters*, vol. ii. pp. 49–51.

can use. The criticism has often been made that man in speaking of God as personal is really making God in his own image.[1] It is suggested that it would be more reverent to think of God only as the 'great unknowable'. Since all definition implies negation, we should only speak of Him in negative terms, as not like anything within our finite experience.[2] Such agnosticism is not quite so reverent as it appears at first sight. It involves the assumption not only that man is unable to know God, but that God is unable to reveal Himself to man. If religion is to exist as a living force, and if God wishes men to have fellowship with Himself, men must make some effort, however inadequate, to picture to themselves the God whom they are bidden to serve and worship. We cannot love or pray to an 'unknowable'. The criticism forces us to remember that our idea of God, even at its highest, is incomplete and inadequate. We are necessarily limited by the capacities of our finite human personalities. As man's knowledge of his own personality has deepened, so his conception of God has deepened too and become less partial and inadequate. Further, to a Christian the Incarnation has proved that human personality is in its measure a mirror of the Divine Personality. In Jesus Christ God gave us the fullest revelation of Himself that we at present can receive, through the medium of a perfect human life and character. Jesus Christ has demonstrated what we may call the 'humanity' of God. However much more there may be in the nature and being of God that cannot be expressed in terms of human life and personality or embodied in a perfect human character, and that transcends human experience altogether, still all the elements of man's life and personality are to be found at their highest and best within the divine life and personality. If man is made 'in the image of God', the original cannot be wholly unlike the image. So, then, we speak of God as 'personal' because that is the loftiest conception of Him that we are able to form. We believe that, though it is inadequate, yet it is not in its measure untrue. Further, our human personalities are all of them imperfect and fragmentary. They hint at capacities that are only partly realized in our present life. No man taken by himself discloses even the full capacity of human nature as we know it here. We do not know what a perfect and complete human personality may mean.

---

[1] The German philosopher Fichte sums up the argument thus:—'You insist that God has personality and consciousness. What do you call personality and consciousness? No doubt that which you find in yourselves. But the least attention will satisfy you that you cannot think this without limitation and finitude. Therefore you make the divine Being a limited being like yourselves by ascribing to Him that attribute, and you have not thought God as you wished but only multiplied yourself in thought' (Quoted by Bruce, *Apologetics*, p. 81).

[2] In substance this objection is as old as Xenophanes, who argued: 'If the lions could have pictured a god, they would have pictured him in fashion like a lion; the horses like a horse: the oxen like an ox.' Supposing that lions can reflect, and that 'lion-hood' is the highest kind of existence known to them, the lions who conceive of God as an unlimited lion, would seem to be more intelligent than their human critics.

'We are not so much complete persons as on the road to personality.' When we think of the Personality of God we think of Him as possessing in all their completeness all those attributes which we perceive ourselves to possess tentatively and incompletely. He alone realizes the full meaning of personality.†

(b) The perversion of the truth of the personality of God is known as 'anthropomorphism'. We fall into this error when we ascribe to God the limitations and imperfections of our own finite human personalities. Anthropomorphism degrades the idea of God by ascribing to Him human infirmities.[1] It arises from the forgetfulness that our highest conceptions of Him are inadequate. We are tempted to argue from them as if they were unreservedly true. It is largely against this danger that the next words of this Article are directed. '*God is everlasting, without body, parts or passions, of infinite power, wisdom and goodness.*'

We may take these in order. By speaking of God as '*everlasting*' (*aeternus*) and '*without body*', we mean that God is raised above the limitations of both time and space. We ourselves live in time and space. We cannot get outside them. All our experience is necessarily presented under the forms of time and space. When we say that God is above them, we do not attempt to picture God's consciousness or to describe what they mean to Him: all that we affirm is that they impose no limitations upon His knowledge and activity as they do upon ours. If we consider our own mental pictures of either time or space, we can easily see that they are really self-contradictory. However far distant we travel in imagination to the beginning of time or space, there is always more time and more space beyond them. The beginning of either is to us unthinkable. This in itself suggests that our knowledge about them is only relative and imperfect. To take the thought of time first: God is eternal. We do not pretend to say what time means to God. We can only picture to ourselves eternity as an endless succession of moments. By our imaginations 'eternal' can only be viewed as 'everlasting'. But the eternal God is not limited by time as we are. There was no moment of time when He first came into being. Again, with us time is associated with change and decay. But God never grows old or weary (Is 40[28]). Time does not hamper His knowledge or His power as it does our own. In some sense the future is as present to Him as the past. He lives 'in an eternal present'. It is as being eternal that He is 'the only wise God' (Rom 16[27]); 'one day is to the Lord as a thousand years, and a thousand years as one day' (2 Pet 3[8]).

So, too, with space. God is without body, for He is Spirit (Jn 4[24], R.V. marg.). Not only does He not possess bodily needs and appetites; He does not need to be fed or to be awakened (cp. the protests of Ps 50[12–13]), as the primitive mind supposed; but His activity is not

---

[1] Cp. Browning's *Caliban on Setebos*.

limited by any considerations of space. We can only imagine God as 'ubiquitous' or 'omnipresent', *i.e.* as present in all places at the same time. But God's presence is not in space at all : it is not on a level with that of even the most subtle of material substances. God does not occupy space like a created object. He can act always and everywhere. Nothing is hidden from His sight or His control. 'Can any hide himself in secret places that I shall not see him, saith the Lord. Do not I fill heaven and earth?' (Jer 23²⁴, cp. Ps 139). In early parts of the Bible we find traces of a primitive anthropomorphism that puts God away in some distant place or confines Him to one place at a time. Thus He needs to come and see for Himself the tower of Babel (Gen 11⁵) and the real truth about Sodom (Gen 18²¹). Again, His power was regarded as limited to the territory of Israel (1 Sam 26¹⁹). But such ideas were transcended as the Jewish religion progressed. In Ezek 1⁴ ff., for instance, the elaborate symbolism is an attempt to picture God's omnipresence in Babylon no less than at Jerusalem.

Any view of God that regards Him as limited by time or space detracts from His claim to our unconditional trust and obedience. We are not likely to regard God's dominion as confined to any one country. But we are tempted to limit His dominion to certain spheres of our own life. This is a practical denial of His unlimited supremacy.

God is without parts (Latin *impartibilis* = unable to be divided).— If God does not occupy space He is indivisible, since division implies space. But the word means more than this. We think of God as possessing certain faculties. In ourselves these may be divided one against another. We may be distracted by competing interests or desires. Our reason may be opposed to our inclination. Or again, we are forced to acquire our knowledge piecemeal. Our consciousness cannot retain all that we know. We are subject to lapses of memory. But God's being is not thus divisible. All that He is, He is essentially and not accidentally. What we from our human standpoint regard as separate attributes, His mercy, wrath, love, remembrance, etc., are really aspects of one consistent and unchanging Being. There can be in Him no conflict of purpose or desire. His knowledge can never fall short of full attainment. He can never forget. He can deal with all things at once. We do not need to attract His attention. His interest is not divided. 'Before they call, I will answer' (Is 65²⁴. Contrast the taunts of Elijah in 1 Kings 18²⁶⁻²⁷).

God is without passions (Latin *impassibilis*, a word which originally meant 'incapable of suffering').—This is closely connected with the foregoing statement and is intended to rule out anthropomorphic ideas about the changeableness of God. The Bible does not hesitate to speak of God's wrath, jealousy, sorrow and love. But these are not passing emotions, passions that for a time overcome God and turn Him aside from His purpose. They are rather aspects of God's one and unchanging character. God's purpose and character are ever one and the same. But as God deals with the manifold material of our inconsistent and variable lives, His attitude in relation to us appears to change. God's wrath is not a transitory feeling: it is rather one aspect of His love as it deals with human sin. God's action seems to us to change, as it meets the varying needs of His government. God is now merciful, now punishes, now restores (e.g. Is 60[10] and Mt 18[27 and 34]). But the change is never arbitrary. Behind it all lies the one immutable purpose and character of God, giving consistency and unity to all that He does. 'God's immutability is not due to carelessness or indifference. It is rather a mark of intense moral activity. It may be defined as that moral changelessness by which all the powers of God's nature are brought under the dominion of a single consistent purpose.'[1] This moral constancy of God is the ground of faith and hope in Him. 'I the Lord change not: therefore ye, O Sons of Jacob, are not consumed' (Mal 3[6]). 'God is not a man that he should lie' or 'repent' (Num 23[19]). We cannot help using human language in speaking of God's actions. There is a certain necessary 'anthropomorphism'. The only danger is that we may argue from our imperfect human conceptions as if they were complete and adequate (cp. Is 55[8–9]). For instance, certain theories about the atonement have been constructed out of very crude and literal ideas of the wrath of God. God's mercy does not incline Him to forgive and His justice to punish: His justice is the ground of forgiveness (1 Jn 1[9]). God not only loves but is love (1 Jn 4[8]). He is 'the Father of lights, with whom can be no variation, neither shadow that is cast by turning' (Jas 1[17]). There is no contradiction within the Divine Being. Each of the divine qualities involves all the rest (1 Jn 1[5]).

We can hardly deny that since God is love, He is in some sense capable of suffering. The life and Passion of Christ are the manifestation in space and time of 'an element which is essential and eternal in the life of God'.[2] This idea of the sympathy of God with human sorrow and suffering underlies much of, e.g. Hosea, the later chapters of Isaiah, 'In all their affliction he was afflicted'[3] (Is 63[9], cp. Judges 10[16]), and the teaching of our Lord. God rejoices over the return of sinners (e.g. Lk 15[7, 20]). He can sympathize with human sorrows and sufferings. But such suffering is one aspect of His perfection.†

(c) God is of infinite power.—'With God all things are possible' (Mt 19[26]). God's omnipotence is the perfection of His will. He is almighty, i.e. all-sovereign: unfettered by any limitations in His actions, unbounded in His resources. All the power that exists in the universe, of body, mind or will, is in origin His. He is pleased to lend it to beings whose wills are free. As such, they may pervert or misuse it. But its source is all the time in Him and its exercise is never with-

---

[1] W. A. Brown, Christian Theology in Outline, p. 118.
[2] Cp. D. White, Forgiveness and Suffering, pp. 82–91.
[3] But the actual rendering of the verse is doubtful.

drawn from His control. 'Precisely in this way above all others, that He is omnipotent over a free world, does God reveal the greatness of His power most clearly.'[1] Thus God is not hindered in His activity by any foreign or independent power in the world. Nor yet is God limited by creation in the sense that He has exhausted His resources in it. He has inexhaustible power and wisdom in reserve. On all such points God's infinite power is contrasted with man's finite power.

But God's infinite power does not mean that God can do anything whatever. He cannot lie or contradict Himself (2 Tim 2[13]). He cannot do wrong or undo the past or make men holy apart from their own efforts. For all these things are contrary to His own laws. These laws are not imposed upon Him by any external necessity, but are the free expression of His own character and purpose. As Hooker writes: 'The Being of God is a kind of law to His working.' 'God is a law both to Himself and to all other things besides.' 'Nor is the freedom of the will of God any whit abated, let or hindered by means of this, because the imposition of this law upon Himself is His own free and voluntary act.'[2]

He is of infinite wisdom.—'Omniscience is the perfection of God's mind as omnipotence is the perfection of God's will.' He is 'the only wise God' (Rom 16[27]). Not only has God an immediate and perfect knowledge of the smallest detail of every event that happens upon this earth (Mt 10[29-30], etc.), but He knows all the manifold intricacies of His universe. Every piece of truth gained, of whatever kind, is so far an entering into the mind of God. Science has been defined as 'thinking God's thoughts after Him'. Further, God knows all the possibilities that lie before the world. Nothing that happens can ever take Him unawares (Heb 4[13]). In what way God views the future we cannot say. All that we can affirm is that no contingency is unforeseen by Him or outside His control.

He is of infinite goodness.—The Latin *bonitatis* shows that goodness here means 'kindness' rather than holiness. It refers to God's infinite blessings to mankind, 'the riches of his goodness' (Rom 2[4], cp. Tit 3[4]) as shown in creation, preservation and redemption.

§ 3. 'God is *the maker and preserver of all things visible and invisible.*'—These words sum up the Christian view of God's relation to the world. (*a*) When we say God 'created' the world, *i.e.* made it out of nothing, we are of necessity using metaphorical language. There is nothing in our own experience to correspond to such a process. We can only modify or rearrange within certain limits what already exists. We are driven to say that God 'created the world out of nothing' in order to express the truth that there was nothing already existing in its own right, independently of God, out of which He made it (cp. Heb 11[3], Rom 4[17]). This rules out two other views of creation.

(i) Plato taught that God made the world out of an independently

---

[1] Martensen, *Dogmatics*, p. 81.   [2] *Eccl. Pol.* I. c. ii. § 2 and § 3.

existing matter. This has never been completely subdued to the divine will. Accordingly all material things, our own bodies included, possess an inherent taint of evil, a certain rebelliousness against the good.

This theory has the advantage of explaining the universal existence of evil. But it contradicts the very idea of God, and leaves us in 'dualism'. No such dualism—the assumption of two ultimate realities —can satisfy the needs of our mind. Our intellect demands a single ultimate and all inclusive reality. Christianity holds that the world as made by God is 'very good' (Gen 1³¹). Everything in it has a purpose. The evil in the world is due to the misuse or perversion from its true purpose, by beings possessed of free will, of what is intrinsically good.

(ii) Others again holding the view that matter is intrinsically evil, and being oppressed by the pain and wickedness of the world, taught that the world was not made by God Himself but by some inferior Being—a Demiurge or Creator. Thus they imagined a series of Emanations from God. 'Imagine a long chain of divine creatures, each weaker than its parent, and we come at last to one who, while powerful enough to create, is silly enough not to see that creation is wrong.'¹ Such a view at bottom is not far removed from that of certain modern pessimists.

Against all such views Christianity maintains that God Himself made the world, and that nothing exists in the universe, whether matter or spirit, that is independent of God or beyond His control and His care.

(b) Further, God has not only created but preserves the world from moment to moment. He is the sustaining force behind all life and all existence. Accordingly we need to hold fast to two counter-truths. The first is the 'transcendence' of God. God is above the world. He is the Master whose will all created things serve (Ps 29¹⁰), the Potter in whose hands men are as clay (Is 64⁸, 45⁹). He does not depend upon the world for His existence or His consciousness (Ps 90²). Creation was an act of His own free love. The second and complementary truth is God's 'immanence'. God dwells in his own world as the sustainer of all life. We find the signs of His presence in the beauty, order and movement of nature, and we can discern something of His providential ordering of history. 'In Him we live and move and have our being' (Acts 17²⁸). Every part of His creation is present to Him at every moment, and every part is in its measure a revelation of His presence. In the apprehension of truth and the voice of conscience we are in the highest degree aware of His operation through the natural powers of our own minds and wills.†

Each of these truths has been exaggerated to the practical exclusion of the other. Thus we get:

(i) Deism.²—This view of the world exaggerated the idea of God's

¹ Bigg, Origins of Christianity, p. 135, on the Gnostics.
² We must distinguish between 'Deism' and 'Theism'. Deism is the view here described. Theism is simply belief in a God.

transcendence. The Deists practically taught that God made the world, started it and left it to run by itself like a machine. God was regarded as living afar off, apart from the life of the world, with little or no interest in its concerns. The world pursued its course in accordance with certain fixed laws. God was an absentee God, at most returning occasionally to visit the world, when His visits were marked by strange and violent catastrophes. God's active sovereignty was practically denied. His presence was recognized only in the abnormal. This view of God's relation to the world is impossible for the mind of to-day. Modern science is always bringing before us the complex and unceasing energy of God in the world of nature and in the processes of evolution. The world is seen to be not a piece of mechanism but a living organism. God is recognized as present no less in the orderly progress of life than in startling and unusual events.

(ii) *Pantheism.*—This isolates and exaggerates the truth of the Divine Immanence. It views all that exists as equally the manifestation of the one divine life. God is conceived as having no existence above and apart from His own self-realization in the world. He has no conscious life except where the one great universal world-life rises to self-consciousness in creation. At death the individual life falls back into that universal life from whence it came.

> 'The one remains, the many change and pass; . . .
> Life, like a dome of many-coloured glass
> Stains the white radiance of Eternity,
> Until Death tramples it to fragments.'

Accordingly all things must be as they are. 'Whatever is, is right.' This universe is only an eternal process which must go on along its course. Man may be conscious of his own life, but he cannot alter or amend it. The universal life realizes itself equally in all that exists, pleasure and pain, false and true, good and bad.

Pantheism has a great fascination for many minds. It appeals to man's love of consistency. The man whose interest in science or philosophy usurps a disproportionate place in his life, is readily attracted by a view of the world that gives him the unity for which he seeks. Pantheism appeals to man's intellectual and contemplative faculties at the cost of his moral and social faculties. It is found in the religions of the East and in some modern philosophy. In a slightly different form it underlies certain forms of 'scientific monism', in which the idea of one universal matter underlying all existence is substituted for the idea of one universal life or spirit. But pantheism fails to give an account of the whole of experience. It cannot explain certain facts of life. Man's indignation at wrong-doing; his conviction of the eternal difference between right and wrong; his sense of responsibility; the efforts and struggles of the moral life; all these contradict pantheism. If all things are equally a manifestation of the divine life, then the ultimate value of all moral distinctions must be denied. But our sense of right and wrong is a fact that demands explanation. Pantheism does not explain it so much as explain it away. Unless we are prepared to throw overboard the whole of the moral life of mankind as an illusion, we cannot accept pantheism. The God of pantheism is no God at all. 'The immanence of God becomes . . . a polite expression for the beauty and fruitfulness of nature, human and otherwise.'†

§ 4. *And in unity of this Godhead there be three persons, of one substance, power and eternity, the Father, the Son, and the Holy Ghost.*— (a) This formal statement of the doctrine of the Trinity did not come ready-made into the world. It is the result of the Church's efforts to express in the simplest possible terms the new truths about God that she had come to know through the life and teaching of Jesus Christ. The doctrine was not the result of abstract speculation. The Person and claims of Christ raised new problems about the nature of God and demanded new explanations. There were certain very definite concrete facts of history and experience, of which Christians were compelled to give some account.

(i) The first disciples of Jesus Christ were Jews. As such they worshipped and served the One God. Their knowledge of God was confirmed and deepened by intimacy with their Master. He Himself reaffirmed the Unity of God. He employed the Jewish Scriptures. He joined in the worship of the Synagogue and Temple. He prayed and taught others to pray to the Father, identifying Him with the God of the Old Covenant.

(ii) Through their prolonged intercourse with Him the disciples became convinced that our Lord too was divine. He spoke of Himself as 'Son of Man',[1] and Himself interpreted the meaning of that title in the light of Dan 7^{13} (*e.g.* Mk 14^{62}). They were compelled to ask 'what manner of man is this?' (Mt 8^{27}, etc.). By His question He encouraged them to think out for themselves who He was. He commended S. Peter who could find no word short of 'Messiah' able to contain all that He had shown Himself to be. He claimed a unique intimacy with the the Father (Mt 11^{25-27}). In His own name He revised and deepened the law of Moses (Mt 5^2, etc.). He taught His disciples to repose in Him an unlimited confidence that no mere man had the right to demand of his fellow-men (Mt 7^{24}, etc.). He died for

---

[1] The title seems to come from Dan 7^{13}. There it denotes not an individual but a figure in human form, which is interpreted as 'the saints of the most high', v. 27. That is, it stands for Israel, in contrast with the beasts, which stand for heathen nations. But very soon 'One like unto a son of man' came to be interpreted as an individual, the Messiah. In the Book of Enoch this interpretation is made explicit. 'The Son of Man' is a superhuman being, who executes God's judgment. How far it was a recognized Messianic title in our Lord's day, is disputed. He would hardly have assumed it if it was popularly regarded as synonymous with Messiah. For discussion of this title, see A. E. J. Rawlinson, *The New Testament Doctrine of the Christ*, pp. 242 ff. ; C. H. Dodd, *The Interpretation of the Fourth Gospel*, pp. 241 ff. ; A. M. Farrer, *A Study in S. Mark*, pp. 247 ff.

His claim to be the Christ and the Son of God (Mk 14⁶¹). The whole impression made upon them by His life and works was crowned and brought to consciousness by His Resurrection (*e.g.* Rom 1⁴). He was indeed the Son of God. No language short of this could express the place that He had come to take in their knowledge of God.†

(iii) He had spoken to the disciples of the Holy Spirit, the Advocate, as divine yet distinct from Himself¹ (Jn 14¹⁶ and 15²⁶). They were to expect the Spirit's coming when He was gone (Acts 1⁴⁻⁵). In that coming He Himself would come too (Jn 14¹⁸). At Pentecost they had a personal experience of the Holy Spirit. A new and lasting power entered into their lives. They knew that He too could be no less than God. Further, in the Baptismal formula the teaching of Christ is summed up.² Converts are to be baptized 'into the name of the Father, and of the Son, and of the Holy Ghost' (Mt 28¹⁹). The name is one. It belongs equally to the three Persons, who are associated on an equality and distinguished from one another by the use of the definite article.

(iv) We turn to the witness of the early Church as presented in Scripture. In the Acts of the Apostles, the Epistles and the Apocalypse we find evidence of a new life and experience shared by men and women of very diverse types and races. They worshipped the Father. But they placed Jesus the Messiah side by side with Him and applied to Him the divine name Κύριος,³ familiar to Jews as the translation of Jehovah in the Septuagint, and to Gentiles as a title of heathen gods. The disciples' experience of the power of Christ was not ended by the Ascension. He was still a living Saviour. The life that flowed from Him was divine.⁴ In the hour of death S. Stephen prayed to Him (Acts 7⁵⁹). The cures wrought in His name were proclaimed to be His work as really as those wrought during His earthly ministry (Acts 3¹⁶, 9³⁴). 'Jesus is Lord' was the earliest profession of faith (1 Cor 12³). He was worshipped (1 Tim 3¹⁶). The Church was His body, filled with His life (1 Cor 12¹², Eph 4¹², etc.). He was daily expected to return as judge in glory (Acts 3²¹, 1 Thess 4¹⁶, etc.). So, too, the Holy Spirit revealed His own divine power in many ways. Not only did He bestow supernatural gifts, such as prophecy and speaking with tongues, but He shed abroad in men's hearts new peace and light and strength (Rom 8¹⁵⁻¹⁶). Christians witnessed by their changed lives to His indwelling presence (Gal 5²²⁻²⁴, Rom 8², 15¹³, Eph 3¹⁶, etc.).

A practical belief in the Father, the Son and the Spirit underlies such passages as these:

¹ It is not easy to distinguish in the fourth Gospel between our Lord's actual words and the Evangelist's own meditation upon them, but on such a point we can hardly suppose that the teaching of Christ was misapprehended.

² The genuineness of this will be discussed later.

³ Either 1 Thessalonians or Galatians is the earliest extant epistle of S. Paul. See the opening words of each, 1 Thess 1¹ and Gal 1³.

⁴ We need to remember that the 'Christ' of the Epistles is earlier than the 'Jesus' of the Gospels. The Gospels were written by and for men who believed in the glorified Christ.

'If any man hath not the Spirit of God, he is none of his. And if Christ is in you, the body is dead because of sin; but the spirit is life because of righteousness. But if the Spirit of him that raised up Jesus from the dead dwelleth in you, he that raised up Christ Jesus shall quicken also your mortal bodies through his Spirit that dwelleth in you' (Rom 8⁹⁻¹¹).

'Peter, an apostle of Jesus Christ, to the elect . . . according to the foreknowledge of God the Father, in sanctification of the Spirit, unto obedience and sprinkling of the blood of Jesus Christ' (1 Pet 1²).

'Hereby we know that we abide in him, because he has given us of his Spirit. And we have beheld and bear witness that the Father hath sent the Son to be the Saviour of the world. Whosoever shall confess that Jesus is the Son of God, God abideth in him and he in God' (1 Jn 4¹³⁻¹⁴).

A long list of similar passages might be given.[1] They all spring out of a fresh and vivid spiritual experience. In every case the writer is not consciously repeating the teaching of Christ. He is giving first-hand evidence out of his own life. Nor again are such statements consciously theological. Christians knew that since Jesus Christ had come into their lives they had passed from darkness into light. Their hearts were aglow with a new-found joy and peace. S. Paul, for instance, expected his converts to understand the meaning of his phrases from their own spiritual experiences. He is confident that a share in this new life is open to all who will believe in Christ. In speaking almost casually of 'the grace of the Lord Jesus Christ and the love of God and the communion of the Holy Ghost' (2 Cor 13¹⁴)[2] he simply sums up the working faith of the Christian community.

(b) (i) In the first reception of the good news Christians were hardly aware that there was an intellectual problem to be solved. They were not conscious that their faith was inconsistent with monotheism. S. Paul can still write: 'To us there is one God, the Father, of whom are all things', though he proceeds to add immediately 'and one Lord, Jesus Christ, through whom are all things' (1 Cor 8⁶, cp. 1 Tim 2⁵, Acts 14¹⁵ and 17²⁴). ὁ θεός is in the New Testament applied to the Father alone, but, on the most natural interpretation, θεός is applied to our Lord in Rom 9⁵ and Tit 2¹³.[3] Divine names, titles and

---

[1] *E.g.* Rom 5¹⁻⁵, 8¹⁴⁻¹⁷, 15¹⁶⁻¹⁹ and ³⁰, 1 Cor 2⁶⁻¹⁶, 12³⁻⁷, 2 Cor 1²¹⁻²², Phil 3³, Eph 4⁵⁻⁷, 1 Thess 1²⁻⁷, Tit 3⁴⁻⁶, Heb 9¹⁴, 10 ²⁹⁻³¹, 1 Jn 5⁵⁻¹².

[2] These words were written not more than thirty years after our Lord's Ascension. It is obvious that S. Paul is not employing new or unfamiliar language. He expects the Corinthians at once to grasp his meaning. 'S. Paul and the Church of his day thought of the supreme source of spiritual blessing as not single but threefold—threefold in essence and not merely in manner of speech' (Sanday, *H.D.B.* vol. ii. p. 213). The form of speech suggests at once teaching on the lines of the baptismal formula of Mt 28¹⁹. See Plummer on 2 Cor 13¹⁴.

[3] So, too, the most probable reading in Jn 1¹⁸ is μονογενὴς θεός (instead of υἱός). Cp. 'My Lord and my God' in Jn 20²⁸, which forms the climax of the Gospel.

functions that in the Old Testament belong to God, are freely ascribed to Him (Heb 1[10-12], Rev 1[17], etc.). So, too, language is employed about the Holy Spirit that implies His divinity. We may sum up their attitude thus, 'In the first flush of their new hope Christians rather felt than reasoned out the conviction that their master was divine. It was a certainty of heart and mind—but the mind could hardly subject the conception to the processes of reason—the soul leapt to the great conclusion, even though the mind might lag behind. They did not stay to reason: they knew.'[1]

But even from the first it was necessary in preaching the Gospel to express in words something of what the Saviour had proved Himself to be to His disciples. In the opening chapters of the Acts we find a very rudimentary theology. Jesus is the Messiah. At least in the earlier books of the New Testament, 'Christ' is no proper name, but a title of almost incomparable dignity and honour (Acts 2[36], etc.). He had fulfilled all Old Testament prophecy (Acts 3[18], etc.). He was the suffering servant of Jehovah (Acts 3[13], [26], etc.). Through His death redemption had been won (cp. 1 Pet 1[21]). A crucified Messiah was a scandal to the Jews, and already through controversy Christians were forced to explain the meaning of His death. He was the Son of God, whose sonship had been vindicated by the Resurrection (Acts 9[20], 13[33], etc.). The Resurrection made clear before men that the Death was not defeat but triumph.

Elsewhere we find a further exercise of reflection. S. Paul bids his converts at Philippi meditate upon the divine self-sacrifice involved in the Incarnation. 'Have this mind in you which was also in Messiah Jesus, who existing ($\dot{v}\pi\dot{\alpha}\rho\chi\omega\nu$) in the form of God ($\mu o\rho\phi\hat{\eta}$ implying more than outward resemblance, essential being) counted it not a prize (a thing to be clutched hold of) to be on an equality with God ($\tau\dot{o}$ $\epsilon\hat{i}\nu\alpha\iota$ $\dot{\iota}\sigma\alpha$), but emptied himself (i.e. of His divine glory), taking the form of a servant ($\mu o\rho\phi\acute{\eta}\nu$, again. His humanity and divinity were both equally real. He shared truly both the nature of God and ourselves), being made ($\gamma\epsilon\nu\acute{o}\mu\epsilon\nu os$ in contrast to $\dot{v}\pi\dot{\alpha}\rho\chi\omega\nu$ and $\tau\dot{o}$ $\epsilon\hat{i}\nu\alpha\iota$) in the likeness of men' (Phil 2[5-7]). This is not primarily a lesson in doctrine but in humility: its theology is all the more valuable because it is incidental. The illustration is meaningless unless S. Paul and his converts shared a common belief that Jesus of Nazareth had in some sense existed as God, before He came down to earth. This same belief is implied no less clearly in 2 Cor 8[9].

Again at Colossae S. Paul had to deal with false teaching about angels. This he meets by asserting the 'cosmic significance' of Jesus Christ, i.e. His supremacy in the universe. 'He is the image of the invisible God,' 'the first-born (i.e. the heir) of all creation' (or possibly 'begotten before all creation'). 'In him all things were created,' including the angels themselves. He is the agent and goal of creation.

[1] Bethune Baker, *Christian Doctrines; how they arose*, p. 16.

'All things have been created through him and unto him.' He is the power behind the world. 'In him all things hold together' (Col 1¹⁵⁻¹⁷). In this passage S. Paul does not call Him the Logos, but he assigns to Him the functions of the Logos. He holds the central place in the history and meaning of the universe.

Similarly, the author of the Epistle to the Hebrews insists upon the unique relation of Christ to God, in contrast with that of the angels. 'God hath at the end of these days spoken unto us in his Son (ἐν υἱῷ, literally in 'one who is Son', as opposed to the prophets who are servants), whom he appointed heir of all things, through whom also he made the worlds: who being the effulgence of his glory and the very image of his substance and upholding all things by the word of his power, when he had made purification of sins, sat down on the right hand of the majesty on high' (Heb 1¹⁻⁴).

In Jn 1¹⁻¹⁴ (cp. Rev 19¹³) we find the explicit use of a technical theological term. The historical figure of Jesus of Nazareth is identified with the 'Logos' or 'Word' or 'Reason' of God. 'The Word became flesh and dwelt among us.' The contrast between Jesus Christ and all men who had gone before is between those who bore witness to the Light and the Light Himself. Jesus Christ is asserted to be the eternal author of all the life and truth and goodness of the created world. But the term Logos can only be understood by a reference to contemporary thought.[1]

Passages such as these contain a large amount of theological reflection. Their aim is primarily practical, but they mark the lines along which theology was bound to develop, if it was to be faithful to the revelation given to Christians in Christ.†

(ii) In the writings of the sub-apostolic times we find a like belief in God as revealed in the Father, the Son and the Holy Ghost. The Church's faith is shown more decisively in her hymns, doxologies and worship, or in her Baptisms and Eucharists than in formal theological statement. The heathen Pliny, for instance, speaks of Christians singing hymns to Christ 'as to a God'.[2] In the letters of S. Ignatius and S. Clement[3] of Rome passages are to be found similar to those already quoted from the New Testament. But this condition of devotion uninterrogated by reason could not be final. Human nature, and not least Greek human nature, was as inquisitive and argumentative then as it is to-day. Even in the pages of the New Testament we

---

[1] See below, p. 40.

[2] Pliny, *Ep.* 10, § 96, *Carmen Christo quasi deo dicere*.

[3] *E.g.* Clement, *ad Cor.* c. 46, 'Have we not one God and one Christ and one Spirit of grace, that was poured upon us.' c. 58, 'As God liveth and the Lord Jesus Christ liveth and the Holy Spirit, who are both the faith and hope of the elect.' Ignatius, *ad Eph.* c. 9, 'As being stones prepared beforehand unto a building of God the Father, being carried up to the heights through the engine of Jesus Christ, which is the Cross, using the rope of the Holy Spirit.' *Ad Magn.* c. 13, 'that ye may be prospered . . . in the Son and the Father and the Spirit.' So also *ad Rom.* c. 6, he speaks of 'the passion of my God.'

find traces of false teaching that raised deep theological problems. Questions were asked and could not be checked. 'Why is it right to worship Jesus as Lord and yet refuse to burn incense to the Emperor?' 'If Jesus Christ is God's Son, is he truly God? If so, are there two Gods or one?' Even a child could ask such questions. It was not unreasonable for men who might be called upon to die for their faith at any moment, to wish to be able to give some account of it. Further, not only were such questions as these asked, but explanations were given by individual teachers that the Church felt to be false or inadequate. The Church did not wish to speculate, but in the presence of teaching that denied or explained away the truth that she was commissioned to teach and by whose fulness she lived, she could no longer be silent. Not only the enquiries of religious men but the assertions of 'heretics' compelled the Church to think out her belief and find words in which to express it. Her aim was, in the first instance, practical and religious, not theological. She wished to safeguard her own worship and vitality. So she was always saying 'no' to various explanations which, though plausible and attractive, gained their simplicity at the cost of ignoring or explaining away some of the facts. The human mind naturally dislikes mystery[1] and is attracted to what is simple. But the Church, out of loyalty to the whole truth, had the courage to set aside all such inadequate explanations. Her aim throughout was that the Christian faith in all its mysterious fulness might be handed on undiminished to future generations.

(c) Christianity was born into a world that was full of religion. (i) There was, of course, Judaism, not only the Judaism of Palestine but the more liberal Judaism of the dispersion, which had gathered around itself in all lands a circle of 'God-fearing' Gentiles, attracted by its strict monotheism and its lofty moral teaching. In this way Jewish ideas of God were spread abroad far more widely than we might have supposed. Outside Jewish influences in the heathen world we may draw a sharp distinction between the religion of the philosophers and the religion of the plain man. Philosophers had attained to the idea of the unity of God, though their God was often regarded as a being unknown and unknowable, far removed from the world of common things. Popular religion interposed between the God of the philosophers and the needs of the ordinary man an indefinite number of divine beings of uncertain status, gods, demi-gods, heroes, spirits and the like, to whom worship was offered and who were supposed to have great influence on worldly affairs. These were real objects of pagan devotion. Further, Greek thought had become largely orientalized. Ideas such as that of the impossibility of a good God having

---

[1] Cp. Hooker, v. 'The strength of our faith is tried by those things wherein our wits and capacities are not strong. Howbeit because this divine mystery is more true than plain, divers having framed the same to their own conceits and fancies, are found in their expositions thereof more plain than true.'

contact with an evil matter, dominated the theological speculation of the more thoughtful pagans. Yet again the mystery-religions of the East had won their way to popular favour. They offered the hope of immortality and salvation from death to the initiated. This salvation was too often conceived in physical rather than moral terms. Such religions encouraged vague religious emotions divorced from practical holiness. There was no orthodox pagan creed. The various cults lived, on the whole, in friendly terms with one another. The result was a medley of vague and shifting popular theology, with a background of serious and more or less consistent philosophical theory. There were plenty of ideas about God in the air, even if those ideas were not always defined.†

Accordingly the Christian Church had the greatest difficulty in framing a vocabulary in which to express her meaning. She was driven to borrow words and phrases from Jewish and heathen thought, to separate them from vague or popular or pagan senses, and to stamp upon them a new and technical limitation which they were very far from possessing in popular usage. Then she had to bring her teachers to a common agreement to employ them only in this limited sense, at least in all formal definitions of the faith. 'If the church was compelled to devote an infinitely minute and subtle attention to the adaptation and definition of words it was because it had new and high and infinitely important things to express, and had to create, although out of existing materials, a language in which truly and adequately to express them.'[1] This was the source of infinite danger. Christianity had opened a new world of ideas and truths. But the familiarity and associations of the old language tended to disguise the novelty of the ideas and truths that it was being used to convey. Men were tempted to endeavour to make Christ and Christianity fit in with their own current conceptions of religion, not to expand and reform those conceptions in the light of a fuller disclosure of truth. Human nature is always conservative, and in all doctrinal controversy there was the disposition to water down the Christian faith so as to accommodate the facts to the words and not to expand the words so as to embrace the facts. This building up of a Christian terminology by conflict with false teaching was a slow process. We must be prepared to find in earlier writers tentative expressions that a later age would condemn as ambiguous or even heretical. Terms that came in time to be employed only in a limited and technical sense, were at first used with a certain ambiguity. As we follow out the course of controversy through which the formulas of the Church took shape, we shall find abundant illustrations of these difficulties and dangers.

(ii) We can now turn to contemporary Jewish ideas about God. Few to-day would undertake to prove the doctrine of the Trinity from

[1] Du Bose, *Ecumenical Councils*, p. 95. The whole passage pp. 94–95 should be read.

the Old Testament. Since, however, the Jews received a special revelation of God we are not surprised to find that Jewish faith could
not rest content in a bare Unitarianism. We find in the Old Testament
and in later Jewish theology several lines of thought which pointed
towards the recognition of distinctions within the Divine Being.
(a) In opposition to surrounding polytheism, the Jews laid stress on
the Unity and transcendence of God. Hence the need was felt of some
link between God and the created world. The idea of God's 'word',
as the creative or self-revealing utterance of God, started from such
passages as 'By the word of the Lord were the Heavens made'
(Ps 33[6]) and 'God sent his word and healed them' (Ps 107[20], cp.
147[15]). Again, the special revelation given to the prophets is called
God's 'word'. 'The word of the Lord came' (Joel 1[1], etc.). 'The word
which Isaiah saw' (Is 2[1]). God's word came to be regarded as a manifestation of God, yet distinct from Him. It is His effective utterance
by which He creates the world, directs history, and reveals Himself;
it is the active expression of His mind and will in and to His creation.
A kindred idea is found in the mention of 'the Angel of Jehovah' and
the 'Angel of the Covenant', who appear to be both identified with
and distinguished from Jehovah (e.g. Gen 16 compared with 16[13],
Hos 12[4-5], Jos 5[14-15] compared with 6[2], Mal 3[1]).[1] So, too, God's
'Name', i.e. God's self-revelation, is almost personified (e.g. Ex 23[21],
Is 30[27]). God's 'Presence' (Deut 4[37], cp. Is 63[9]) and God's 'Glory'
(Ex 33[18] compared with v. [20], 1 K 8[11], cp. Jas 2[1], where Jesus Christ is
called 'the Glory') are all in some way viewed as manifestations of
God, yet distinct from Him. In such ways as these Hebrew thinkers
strove to combine the transcendence of God with His activity in the
created world. They represented His self-revelation as mediated by
an Agent, who was viewed as more or less personal and yet divine.

In the Wisdom Literature the 'Word', though still in evidence
(Wisdom 9[1-2], 18[15] ff.) tends to give place to the conception of the
divine 'wisdom'. In Prov 8[22] wisdom is pictured as dwelling with
God from eternity (cp. Wisdom 8[3-5], 9[9] ff., and Ecclus 24[1] ff. where
wisdom is identified with the Law). The idea is of God's thought or
plan. As the plan of a work of art exists in the artist's mind before he
realizes it in his work, so the rational principle of the world existed in
the thought of God before it proceeded forth to be actualized in
creation. Similarly, in Alexandrian Judaism the 'Word' acquires
something of the meaning of the Greek term logos, which connotes
not only 'significant utterance' but also 'reason', 'principle',
'thought'. In Philo, the Jewish philosopher of Alexandria, in the first
century A.D., the Logos is the Divine Reason issuing forth from God
for purposes of creation. The Logos is not strictly personal, but on
the way to becoming so. Through the Logos God comes into con-

---

[1] Up to the time of S. Augustine the Fathers universally identified the Angel of the
Lord with the Second Person of the Trinity.

tact with the world: its presence is to be seen in the order and system of creation and in the moral and religious life of mankind.[1]

At this point Jewish and Gentile thought meet. Alexandrian Judaism was strongly influenced by Greek philosophy. The idea of the Logos or reason of God permeating all things and constituting the rational unity of all life, was common to much of the higher thought of the day. In the Stoic philosophy, which came to be the religion of most educated men, the life and unity of the world was derived from the $\sigma\pi\epsilon\rho\mu\alpha\tau\iota\kappa\grave{o}\varsigma$ $\lambda\acute{o}\gamma\sigma\varsigma$, the 'generative reason', whence all things came and in virtue of which they lived. Stoicism was pantheistic. God and man were akin because they both shared the divine Reason and in so far as men conformed their conduct to the divine Reason they shared the life of God Himself. The Stoics in reality had no personal God. If they tolerated the belief in the many gods of the traditional faith, they viewed them as like themselves, manifestations of the 'generative reason'.

(β) We find also in the Old Testament the idea of the 'Spirit of God'. The Hebrew word like the Greek $\pi\nu\epsilon\hat{\upsilon}\mu\alpha$ embraces many shades of meaning, 'breath,' 'wind,' 'life,' 'spirit.' Its exact shade of meaning in any particular instance is not always easy to discover. As in man 'breath' is the proof of life, so the 'breath' or the 'spirit' came to stand for the 'life'. By a natural analogy any unusual exhibition of power from the strength of Samson (Judg 14[19]) or the skill of Bezaleel (Ex 36[1]) to the insight of the prophets came to be attributed to the presence of the Spirit of God. It is an almost physical conception. 'The Spirit of God is the vital energy of the divine nature, corresponding to the higher vitality of man.' 'The breath of God vitalizes what the Word creates'[2] (e.g. Gen 1). To a limited extent personal qualities and acts are attributed to the Spirit, since the Spirit is God (Is 63[9-10], 48[16]). 'It is the living energy of a Personal God.' In Wisdom 1[5] it is identified with the divine Wisdom. We cannot say more than that the conception of the Spirit of God paved the way for the thought of personal distinctions within the Being of God.[3]†

(d) In stating her faith the Church tried as far as possible to employ the language of Scripture. The language and thought of the New Testament is dominated throughout by the historical facts of the human life of Jesus Christ. He lived above all as the 'Son' of God. He spoke of the 'Father' who sent Him, and revealed the Father through a perfect life of sonship. He also spoke of the 'Spirit' of God whom He would send. Thus the terms 'Father, Son and Holy Spirit'

---

[1] In Philo the Logos is styled 'the image of God', 'the elder son of God' (the universe being God's younger son), 'the high-priest of the universe,' etc. Philo would have agreed with the prologue to S. John's Gospel, as far as the statement 'the Word was made flesh'.

[2] Swete, H.D.B. vol. ii. p. 403.

[3] It is usually agreed that apart from the historical facts of the Incarnation, we could not distinguish between the activity of the Word and the Spirit.

refer primarily to the manifestation of God through the life of Jesus
Christ.[1] So, too, the Church came to speak of the Son as 'begotten' of
the Father, and the Holy Spirit as 'proceeding from' the Father, because that is the language of Scripture, shaped by the outward events
and consequences of the Incarnation. To use a technical phrase, all
such expressions refer in the first instance to the 'Economic Trinity',
i.e. the Trinity as revealed by God's threefold dealing with men. God
had made Himself known through the life of Christ and the coming
of the Spirit as Creator, Redeemer and Sanctifier.

But even within the New Testament Christians had begun to think
out the relation of Jesus of Nazareth to all history and all existence.
To call Him the 'Christ' was to find a place for Him within the eternal
purposes of God. To some extent, at least, Jewish thought had come
to regard the Messiah as existing from all eternity with God, waiting
to be revealed in His own time.[2] But for the Gentile world the title
Christ had no interest. Its value needed to be translated into other
terms. As the missions of the Church extended, one wider and more
universal designation had to be found to express all that Jesus Christ
was felt to be not only for the Jews but for the whole world. Accordingly by S. John He is identified with the Logos, the Word or Reason
of God. He had revealed to those who knew Him the meaning of all
life and all existence. And this identification had been anticipated by
S. Paul. In a passage such as Col 1^{15-16}, though he does not use the
term Logos, he attributes to Christ just that central position in the
divine economy that Jewish and Gentile thought assigned to the
Logos. By this identification the supreme claims of Christ were made
intelligible to the educated world. But even so the Christian Church
never allowed herself to lose sight of the living Personality of the
Saviour. The centre of her devotion and her penitence was always
the historic figure of Christ crucified.

So, even within the New Testament the Church was advancing in
her belief from the 'Economic' to the 'Essential' Trinity. That is, she
was coming to see that the threefold revelation of God as Father,
Son and Holy Spirit rested upon and pointed back to a threefold distinction within the very being of God. About the 'Essential' Trinity,
the relations of the Three Persons as they are to one another in the
eternal life of God, Scripture says very little. Human language and
thought can deal only in a limited way with such a subject. The terms
Father and Son, for instance, which were borrowed from temporal
and human relationships, must clearly be used with caution. We need
great care in applying any words spoken by our Lord in His earthly
life, through human lips, to the Essential Trinity. The Essential

---

[1] This explains the mention of only two Persons in almost all apostolic salutations.
They are not maimed Trinitarian formulas. Rather the writers have in mind not the
doctrine of the Trinity as such, but the revelation of God as Incarnate. See Moberly,
Atonement and Personality, pp. 188–193.

[2] Cp. 1 Enoch 48^{2-7} and 62^{5-9}.

Trinity, however, is clearly implied in Jn 1[1]. (Cp. also Jn 17[5].) It is also hinted at in Mt 11[27] and Lk 10[22], where the Son's knowledge of the Father depends on a previously existing Sonship, not the Sonship on the knowledge.

As we shall see, the very ambiguity of these terms 'Son', 'Word', 'Spirit', was the cause of much confusion of thought. The Church in using them gave them a special sense. But Jewish and Gentile Christians were in danger of continuing to use them in their old sense and carrying with them ideas of God which fell short of Christian truth.

(e) We may now turn to the attempts made to explain the fact of Christ, which the Church rejected as inadequate or untrue.

(i) First in time comes the tendency known as 'Ebionism'.[1] The term is vague and covers many shades of belief. Ebionites were those who endeavoured to interpret Jesus Christ in the light of previous Jewish ideas about God and redemption. The Jewish mind was dominated by two great conceptions, first the transcendence of God, secondly the final and unchangeable character of the Law, given by God Himself, through obedience to which salvation could be obtained. Starting from the former conception the Ebionites regarded the idea of a real Incarnation as blasphemous. It was unthinkable that the high and holy God could degrade Himself by appearing in human form on earth. Further, to suppose that Jesus Christ was God endangered the unity of God. No, Jesus of Nazareth must be a man pre-eminent for holiness, who was chosen to be Messiah because of his faithful observance of the Law and was raised from the dead.[2] Again, if salvation could be gained by the observance of the Law, there was no need of a Saviour. Jesus Christ could be at most a new prophet or law-giver, a second Moses, sent not to supersede but to fulfil and elucidate the Law. Christians were to obtain salvation by a right observance of the Law as interpreted by Him. For this purpose a uniquely inspired prophet was all that was required. Enough has been said to show that Ebionism was an attempt to explain the facts in the light of a priori Jewish ideas. Ebionites refused to enlarge their ideas of God and redemption in the light of a fuller revelation. They desired to reduce Christ and the Christian revelation to terms acceptable to the Jewish mind, and to interpret Christianity by Judaism, not Judaism by Christianity. This tendency underlay the controversy about the keeping of the Law and the admission of Gentiles. The infant Church at Jerusalem began as a sect within Judaism. The full import of the claims and work of Christ was realized only by degrees.

[1] The name is probably derived from a word meaning 'poor'. The Ebionites identified themselves with the 'poor' and meek who were persecuted by the wicked rich. Others less probably, derive the name from one Ebion, the reputed founder of the heresy. Others suppose it to have originated as a title of contempt bestowed on the first Jewish Christians.

[2] As we might expect, some, but not all, Ebionites denied the Virgin-birth.

Through controversy the distinction between Judaism and Christianity was made apparent,[1] and it became clear that Jesus Christ was too great to be confined within Jewish categories.†

(ii) *Docetism.*—If Ebionism stands for the attempt to find a place for Jesus Christ within Judaism, Docetism stands for the attempt to find a place for Him within the circle of current Gentile ideas about God, the world and redemption. Its root is to be found in the dualism that characterized so much of the Greek and Oriental thought of the day. In the attempt to explain the pain and suffering of the world, men had come to find the origin of evil in matter, which was imperfectly subdued to the will of God. Hence, all that was material possessed an inherent taint of evil. Now, if God is good and matter evil, a real Incarnation is unthinkable. The good God could never pollute Himself by entering into union with matter. Men needed rather a Saviour who would free them from bondage to matter. So the physical side of our Lord's life, His birth, His eating and drinking, His passion, death and Resurrection must all be only an 'appearance' ($\delta o\kappa\epsilon\hat{\iota}\nu$—hence 'Docetism'). His Body itself must be only a phantom, like the bodies of angels when they appeared to men (*e.g.* Tobit 12[19]). Again, the Greek mind always tended to identify salvation with enlightenment. If men only need one who will enlighten them by revealing the truth about God and themselves, a Docetic Christ would answer all requirements. Docetism can supply a picture of God and redemption. If Christianity is only a religion of ideas, an apparent Incarnation would serve to disclose them to men, as well as a real Incarnation. Docetism was a tendency rather than a system. Docetists varied in the extent to which they allowed their ideas to dominate their teaching. Within the New Testament we find evidence for the existence of Docetism. 1 Jn 1[1-4], 4[1-3] and 2 Jn 7 are aimed at those who denied that Jesus Christ had 'come in the flesh'. The letters of Ignatius are full of denunciations of this heresy.[2] The Church felt that it undermined the historical character of her Saviour.

Both Ebionism and Docetism spring from ideas about the nature of God. Hence their place is in any discussion about the doctrine of the Trinity rather than that of the Person of Christ. If they were accepted, the need of any restatement of the doctrine of God disappeared. The question before the Church was this, Are we to take existing ideas about God and God's relation to the world and make the new facts square with them as best they may? Or are we to accept

---

[1] Attempts have been made to represent Ebionism as the original Christianity unspoilt by the teaching of S. Paul. It is rather a degenerate form of primitive Christianity. The Ebionites refused to advance to the full Catholic view of our Lord's Person and so they tended to sink below the primitive conception of Christ. We must not suppose, however, that all Jewish Christians were unorthodox. Many went no further than to combine Christianity with the keeping of the Jewish Law. Such a compromise could not last, though Jewish Christians of this kind are mentioned as late as the fourth century. Others combined Ebionite with Gnostic and Docetic teaching.

[2] See *e.g. ad Smyrn.* c. ii-iii, *ad Trall.* c. ix-x., with Lightfoot's notes.

and face the new facts and, if necessary, enlarge our ideas about God in the light of this wider knowledge?[1]†

(iii) The tendencies of thought disclosed in Ebionism and Docetism underlay all the many false explanations, in conflict with which the doctrine of the Trinity was developed. In opposition to Gnosticism which interposed a large number of Emanations between God and the world, Christians were compelled to insist on the unity or 'Monarchia' of God, the Creator and sustainer of all things. The question then arose: What position is to be given to Jesus Christ? Under the influence of a conception of the Unity of God that was borrowed from Judaism or Gentile philosophy attempts were made to safeguard the unity of God either by denying the full divinity of Christ or by identifying Him with the Father. So we find two types of answer (a) 'Dynamic' Monarchianism, (b) 'Modal' Monarchianism. (a) Dynamic or Ebionite Monarchianism gave practically the answer of the Ebionites. Jesus Christ was a mere man ($\psi\iota\lambda\grave{o}\varsigma\ \mathring{a}\nu\theta\rho\omega\pi\sigma\varsigma$). From His birth or baptism a divine Logos, *i.e.* influence or power, resided in Him. As a reward of His moral excellence and unity of will with God, He was raised to divine honour. This was taught at Rome by two teachers of the name of Theodotus, by Artemon and above all by Paul of Samosata. Such views had few attractions for Christians. They destroyed any real Incarnation and were hardly consistent with the power of Christ in their own lives.

(b) 'Modal' Monarchianism (sometimes known as Sabellianism[2]) made a different approach. It originated in Asia Minor and appeared in Rome at the end of the second century. Taking as its fundamental principles the unity of God and the deity of Christ, it refused to allow any personal distinction between the Father and the Son. God is one and Christ is God. God when He so willed became the incarnate Son and suffered and died. Christ is the Father incarnate. The doctrine in this form appealed to deep Christian instincts and was welcomed by many simple Christians. In opposition to some contemporary tendencies to think of Christ as a second and subordinate God, Modalism asserted His unqualified deity. Its emphasis on the

---

[1] We may pass over the strange speculations, many of them akin to Ebionism or Docetism or both, which are grouped under the name of Gnosticism. They were for the most part Oriental speculations, antecedent in time to Christianity, which did not profess to start from the Christian revelation so much as to find room for it within their own schemes of the world. For an account of Gnosticism see Tixeront, *History of Dogmas*, I, c. iv, and K. E. Kirk, *The Vision of God* (full edition), Lect. iv.

[2] Sabellius was one of the Modalist teachers in Rome about A.D. 220 and was the only one to be excommunicated by the Roman Bishop. Contemporary evidence suggests that, like the other Modalists of that time, he taught the personal identity of the Father and the Son. Perhaps it was because he had been excommunicated at Rome that in the fourth century more elaborate forms of Trinitarian doctrine, which it was desired to brand as heresies denying the distinction of the Persons, were attached to his name. There is no evidence that Sabellius himself made a special use of the term *prosopon*.

unity of God was fully justified by Scripture and by the constant
teaching of the Church in conflict with paganism. The doctrine in
fact represented certain profound Christian convictions and a refusal
to think about them.[1] It was rightly felt to be inconsistent with the
evidence of the Gospels, for it left no room for the mutual love of
Christ and the Father as exhibited in His earthly life, nor for that
dependence of the Son upon the Father which is the constant theme
of S. John's Gospel.[2] Moreover, Modalism suggested that the Incarnation was a passing mode of the divine life. The one solitary God
whose being was without personal distinctions had no permanent
principle of self-communication in Himself. The Incarnation as Son
was a phase, and could hardly on the Modalist view be a permanent
phase, of the Father's existence. Modalism was the statement of a
problem rather than a theologically tolerable doctrine.[3]†

(iv) But the most powerful heresy in conflict with which the doctrine of the Trinity received its final expression was Arianism. Arius
started from a philosophical idea of God that ruled out in advance
the possibility of a real incarnation. In common with Judaism and
current Greek philosophy he regarded the unity of God in such a way
as to exclude all contact between God and the world and all distinctions within the divine unity.[4] Accordingly, he endeavoured to find a
place for Christ outside the being of God, yet above creation. God,
he taught, was alone eternal. He could not communicate His own
being or substance to any created thing. When He willed to make the
world, He begat (*i.e.* created) by an act of will an independent substance (οὐσία or ὑπόστασις) to be His agent in creation, who is called
in Scripture the 'Son' or the 'Word'. As the very name 'Son' suggests,
God had not always been a Father, but became such by creating the
Son. The Son is not of the same substance as the Father, else there
would be two Gods. He is only 'the first of created beings'. As such
He can only know the Father relatively, not absolutely. Still, He is
not a creature like other creatures. As a rational being He possessed
free will. By the grace of God and His own moral effort He so used it
as to become divine. We can speak of Him as 'God only begotten'.
At the Incarnation He took a human body but not a human soul.
The Holy Spirit bears the same relation to the Son as the Son does to

[1] The evidence of Tertullian, *Adv. Praxean*, and Hippolytus, *Refutatio* (Bks. 9 and 10
on Callistus) shows that Modalism under the pressure of controversy developed a
slightly more elaborate theory, viz., that in the historical Christ the deity is the Father
and the humanity is the Son.
[2] It was this Gospel which supplied some of the Modalist proof-texts, 'I and my
Father are one', 'he that hath seen me hath seen the Father'. See Tertullian *op. cit.*
[3] In the West Modalists were often known as 'Patripassians' because they 'made the
Father suffer'.
[4] Arius belonged to the school of Lucian of Antioch, which may have been affected
by the 'dynamic Monarchianism' of Paul of Samosata, who in turn was influenced by
the Jewish idea of a 'baldly transcendent God'. But the main root of Arianism seems to
have been in the 'subordinationist' tendencies of Origen's theology.

the Father. Arius' method throughout is based on the teaching of pagan philosophy. His object was to present Christianity in such a way as to make it acceptable to men who retained pagan ideas about God and life. The Arian Christ was a heathen demi-god bridging the gulf between the unknowable God of heathen philosophy and the world.

Arianism never really commended itself to the conscience of the Church. If Arian views won a temporary acceptance, it was because they were not understood. Arianism was essentially a novel exposition unknown to Scripture and tradition. It might be buttressed up by texts of Scripture isolated from their context, but its true origin lay outside Christianity altogether. It was an attempt to find a place for Christ in pagan philosophy. Arianism contradicts the elementary facts of Christian life and experience.

The Church has always worshipped Christ. If He is not truly God, that is idolatry. The distinction between God and the loftiest of created beings is infinite. Arianism is really polytheism. To yield to the Arian Christ that faith and worship that are due to God alone is blasphemy. Further, if Christ is not divine, to offer Him worship is not to honour Him but to act contrary to His own teaching. He always rejected unreal devotion. Again, as S. Athanasius saw, Arianism destroys the basis of redemption. The Arian Christ can be no true mediator between God and man, because He Himself is neither. Since He is unable to know the Father Himself, He cannot reveal Him to others. As a creature, He cannot be a source of divine light or life.[1] God remains unknown and man unredeemed. The opposition to Arianism was not due to love of argument nor even to a desire for theological accuracy. Its opponents saw that Arius sacrificed the revelation of the self-imparting love of God that met the needs of the human soul, to an un-Christian notion of God carried over from heathenism. The chief value of Arianism was that it compelled the Church to become conscious of her real belief and so to frame the doctrine of the Trinity as to find a place for Jesus Christ within the eternal being of God.[2]†

(f) We can now turn to the language in which the Church came to express the doctrine of the Trinity.

(i) The earliest technical term to appear is 'Trinity'. Theophilus of Antioch (180) used τριάς in speaking of God, His Word and His

---

[1] Contrast the saying of Athanasius, 'He was God and then was made man that we might be made God' (*Or. c. Ar.* i. § 39). His idea always is that to partake of the Son is to partake of God Himself. Athanasius' God, unlike Arius', did not hold Himself aloof from a perishing world. For his own view of salvation see his earlier tract 'On the Incarnation of the Word of God'.

[2] Arianism reappeared in the eighteenth century. Then, as in former days, it could not maintain itself. Arians were compelled by the irresistible logic of facts either to advance to a full belief in our Lord's Divinity or to descend to a purely human Christ. The point at issue between the Arian and Catholic view of Christ is well expressed in the famous question put to the Arian Dr Clarke 'Could God the Father annihilate God the Son?'

Wisdom. The Latin *Trinitas* is found a few years later in Tertullian and was commonly employed afterwards. Tertullian also was the first to use the terms *Una substantia* and *Tres Personae*. He employed the term 'substance' in a sense based on its philosophical use.[1] It meant for him a distinct existence, a real entity. It was that which underlies things and makes them what they are. It goes deeper than 'natura' which denotes only the sum-total of a thing's properties. Thus *Una Substantia* asserts in uncompromising fashion the unity of God. The term *'persona'* was borrowed primarily from its grammatical use. He employed it in the sense in which we speak of first, second and third persons in the conjugation of a verb. This use was based on texts where he regarded the Persons of the Trinity as holding converse with one another or speaking in reference to one another. While he freely used the singular *persona*, he preferred the vaguer *'tres'* where possible but in opposing Modalism was driven to say Tres Personae.[2] These terms commended themselves to the Western Church. During the Arian controversy the West was strongly Nicene, largely because it had already been provided with language in which to express the relations of the 'One' and the 'Three'.[3]

In the East agreement was less quickly reached. Only at the close of the Arian controversy was the use and meaning of μία οὐσία for the One, and τρεῖς ὑποστάσεις for the 'Three' fixed by general consent. When the Church rejected Arianism at the Council of Nicaea, in order to rule out all Arian attempts whatever to find a place for Christ outside the essential being of God, the word ὁμοούσιος was introduced into the Creed. The Son was said to be ὁμοούσιος τῷ πατρί and ἐκ τῆς οὐσίας τοῦ πατρός. The opposition to ὁμοούσιος was due partly to reluctance to go outside the words of Scripture, partly to the fact that the word had already been used in a bad sense by heretics.[4]

---

[1] See Bethune Baker, *The Meaning of Homoousios* (Cambridge Texts and Studies), p. 15 ff.

[2] He speaks of our Lord as one 'persona', combining in Himself two 'substantiae', *i.e.* Godhood and manhood (*Adv. Praxeam*, c. 29). He writes, *e.g.* 'The mystery of the providential order which arranges the Unity in a Trinity, setting in their order three—Father, Son, and Holy Spirit—three, however, not in condition but in relation, and not in substance but in mode of existence, and not in power, but in special characteristics' (c. 2). But in c. 26 he is compelled to write, 'Ter ad singula nomina in personas singulas tinguimur.'

[3] See *Adv. Praxeam*, cc. 11–12. Some have argued that this use of these terms is primarily legal. *Substantia* in Roman law meant a property which could be shared by several parties. *Persona* meant a 'party' whose existence was recognized at law. The legal sense of these terms may have assisted their use but was hardly primary. Tertullian does indeed, speak of the Father as the 'whole substance' and the Son as 'the portion' (*portio*) of the whole. This is the result of his materialism. He is laying stress on the distinction between the Persons and the full Godhead of the Son. In his writings first appear the physical illustrations of the Trinity. The Father is to the Son and the Spirit like the sun to its rays that issue from it and the light that falls upon us. Or again, the three are like the spring, the pool, and the river that issues from it.

[4] Its opponents at Nicaea failed to see that a philosophical question can only be met by a philosophical answer. 'Consubstantial is but the assertion of the real deity of

But in time even the most conservative theologians came to see that error could be ruled out in no other way. The Arians evaded the meaning of all phrases from Scripture. At the same time it was made clear that the Council added no new fact to the Creed: this new term did but compress the true meaning of Scripture into a single decisive word. In the long controversy that followed Nicaea, the two terms οὐσία and ὑπόστασις came to be adopted in a technical sense by the Church to formulate her teaching.

In current language οὐσία meant one of two things. Either it meant a common essence of being, shared by a class of things: a universal, by ceasing to share in which they would cease to be the thing at all. In this sense the οὐσία of God is Godhead. Or it meant a particular or individual existence, 'a being', as in the phrase 'a human being'. Thus its use was not free from ambiguity.[1]

ὑπόστασις was a less common word and originally was a synonym for οὐσία, the underlying essence of a class of things. As such, it was the exact equivalent of the Latin *substantia*, but it could also mean the abiding reality of a thing that persisted in spite of the variety of actions that the thing might perform or the various experiences it might undergo. Thus in the case of a person it fairly corresponded to the individuality that lasts through and holds together all our experiences. It was used in the earlier sense by Arius, Athanasius in his earlier writings, and even by one of the anathemas appended to the Creed of Nicaea. But it was the second sense that came to prevail in the formulas of the Church.

This ambiguity of language led to confusion. Those who used ὑπόστασις as a synonym for οὐσία and spoke of μία ὑπόστασις seemed Sabellians to those who distinguished between the two terms. Conversely, those who distinguished between them and spoke of τρεῖς ὑποστάσεις seemed tritheists or Arians to those who regarded the two terms as synonymous. But at the Council of Alexandria (362) under the leadership of Athanasius a reconciliation between the two usages was initiated. The orthodoxy of τρεῖς ὑποστάσεις was recognized, but the older use of ὑπόστασις (= οὐσία) was also approved. Gradually, owing largely to the influence of the Cappadocian Fathers, Basil, and the two Gregories, the usage of the Church settled down to the formula, μία οὐσία, τρεῖς ὑποστάσεις. The West retained *Una substantia, Tres Personae*.[2]

So it comes that in English we speak about 'Three Persons in One Substance', a literal translation of the Latin. The English terms are

Christ in terms of the philosophy by which it had been denied' (Mackintosh, *Person of Christ*, p. 188).

[1] Origen clearly used it in both senses. He spoke of the Son as κατ᾽ οὐσίαν θεός (perhaps he even used the word ὁμοούσιος). But elsewhere he speaks of Him as ἕτερος κατ᾽ οὐσίαν τοῦ πατρός, using οὐσία almost in the sense of 'individuality'. It was partly this second meaning of οὐσία that laid ὁμοούσιος open to the charge of 'Sabellianism'.

[2] Certain Western writers did attempt to speak of *Una Essentia, Tres Substantiae*, but the attempt entirely failed.

not altogether happy. They convey false associations that are absent from the Greek. In Greek both οὐσία and ὑπόστασις define as little as possible where the minimum of definition is desirable. The Latin *personae*, especially in its legal usage, and still more the English 'Persons', convey an idea of separateness that is happily absent from ὑποστάσεις. Owing to the fact that human persons walk about in bodies divided by space, it is hard to free our imagination from the idea of separation in connexion with 'Person'. So, too, 'substance'[1] to our ears suggests the occupation of space. The terms need explanation. The Church uses them in her own sense, and before they can reasonably be criticized it is necessary to find out what that sense is.†

(ii) In thinking of the Trinity we must bear in mind three great considerations.

(α) All theologians confess that the best language that can be found is inadequate. The Church only uses these words, because she cannot escape. 'When it is asked what are the three, human speech labours indeed under great poverty of expression. However, we speak of Three Persons not that that might be spoken, but lest nothing should be said.'[2] The Fathers are full of similar confessions of the inadequacy of human language. The Church does not claim to be able to define or explain all that Godhead means. All that is taught is that whatever Godhead means, all three Persons equally possess it. For instance, in the Athanasian creed this truth is illustrated by applying various epithets to all three Persons and insisting that they belong to all three alike.

(β) There is what is called the 'Monarchia' of the Father. The Father is not more divine than the Son, but He is the Father. The Father depends on Himself alone for His Godhead. He is ὁ θεός. The Son eternally derives His Godhead from the Father (cp. θεὸς ἐκ θεοῦ). He is the Word or self-expression of the Father, and therefore eternally dependent upon Him. So, too, the Spirit proceeds from the Father through the Son. Thus the distinction between the Three Persons rests upon the different manner in which they possess the one Godhead. From the time of Tertullian various illustrations have been drawn to explain the Trinity. It was left to S. Augustine to introduce psychological analogies and find images for the complexity of the Being of God in the complexity of the life of our own being, *e.g.* memory, reason and will, or 'I exist, I am conscious that I exist, I love the existence and the consciousness.' Such illustrations must not be pressed, but they serve to show that the unity even of the human personality is not a bare unity but one embracing distinctions.

(γ) There is the doctrine of the περιχώρησις or 'coinherence' of the

---

[1] Because 'substance' is a familiar English word, the man in the street thinks he knows what it means when it is used in theology. It is perhaps a pity that some long and obviously technical term is not used.

[2] S. Augustine, *De Trin.* v. 9.

Three Persons. This corrects the excessive idea of separation involved by the term 'Person'. The Three so indwell in one another (cp. Jn 14$^{10-11}$, 17^{21}, 1 Cor 2^{11}) that where One is, All are, where One works, All work, where One wills, All will. They are distinct but not separate. A right observance of this truth saves us from falling into Tritheism.

(g) The doctrine of the Trinity is based on fact and experience, not on speculation. But we shall expect that if it is based on a real self-revelation of God, it will recommend itself to our minds. We cannot say that reason could discover it or even prove it. But the Christian doctrine of the Unity in Trinity is really far more illuminating to our thought than a barren Unitarianism.

(i) It is almost impossible to conceive of God as personal at all if He is a bare Unity. In ourselves personality involves thought, will and love. Thought implies an object. A mind without an object of thought would be a mere blank. It is hard to see how the Unitarian God could possess consciousness apart from the world. The difficulty is no new one. Aristotle, for instance, raises the question 'what does God contemplate?' and concludes that in His eternal life God is His own object of contemplation (νοεῖ ἑαυτόν). Does not this involve something like distinctions within the Being of God? The highest type of knowledge is the knowledge of a Person.

(ii) When we turn to will the force of the argument is increased. Will necessitates an object on which it can act. At its highest will is realized in its influence on another will. How then could God realize His will apart from some eternal object on which to realize it?

(iii) When we come to love, the idea of a unipersonal God is seen to be even less tenable. If 'God is love', not simply 'God is able to love', then from all eternity God must have had an object of love. Love in any true sense of the word can only exist where there is an object able to receive and return the love. The doctrine of the Trinity renders conceivable the existence of what corresponds in human experience to knowledge, will and love within the eternal Being of God. Otherwise it is hard to see how we can avoid the conclusion that God is dependent upon the created world for the realization of His Personality.

Once again the doctrine of the Trinity makes the thought of creation easier. God from all eternity possessed within Himself a real activity. The Word from all eternity responds to the Father's love. As the indwelling source of the order and unity of the world (Col 1$^{16-17}$) He leads the world to respond to the Father also. 'The world', it has been said, 'is the poem of the Word to the glory of the Father.' Unless we recognize real distinctions within the divine life, it is almost impossible to avoid falling into either Deism or Pantheism. The Doctrine of the Trinity combines and harmonizes the truth that is expressed one-sidedly in each of these two theories. 'It can explain how God became a Creator in time because it knows how creation had its analogies in the uncreated nature; it was God's nature eternally to produce, to communicate itself, to live. It can explain how God can be eternally alive and yet in complete independence of the world which He created, because God's unique eternal being is no solitary and monotonous existence; it includes in itself the fulness of fellowship, the society of Father, Son and Spirit.'[1]

Lastly, we must always remember that the Being of God is a mystery. We are bidden to 'worship', not to understand 'the Unity in Trinity and Trinity in Unity'. Whenever the mind comes into contact with reality it is baffled by a sense of mystery. Much more must it be so when it comes into contact with God, the ultimate reality.[2] We are learning ever more the mysterious depths of our own personalities. Far more wonderful must be the Tri-personality of God.†

Note on Natural and Revealed Knowledge of God.—During the present century a revival of classical Reformation theology, associated particularly with the name of Karl Barth, has brought into prominence the question of the nature of revelation. Is anything which the Christian can recognize as knowledge of God derivable from any source but the specific action of God in Christ and the preparatory divine action in the history of Israel which preceded it? Or can the existence of God, and perhaps something of His attributes and mode of operation in the world, be discerned by rational reflection upon what is given in the natural order, apart from the Biblical revelation? The Barthian school would argue (1) that apart from the free grace of revelation fallen man cannot either reach or anticipate a true knowledge of God, (2) that the conclusions of rational or natural theology are either based on invalid reasoning or else are irrelevant to Christian faith, (3) that to admit a natural knowledge of God as a foundation or supplement to revealed knowledge deposes Christ from His supreme place as Redeemer and Revealing Word of God to sinful and self-reliant man. On the other side it is argued (1) that man's intellect, admittedly able to reach truth in some spheres, cannot be denied *a priori* the possibility of discovering some knowledge of the Creator through His creation, (2) that only the attempt to construct rational theology can show what valid results it can

---

[1] Gore, *Bampton Lect*. V. end.

[2] ' What is real is always mysterious, just because what is real is always imperfectly known. What is clear and simple is not reality, but the conceptions of our minds. Take, for example, a straight line as Euclid defines it. The straight line is simply a mental conception—there are no straight lines in nature—and therefore it presents no difficulty. Define it as Euclid does and you can know about it all that there is to be known. Now contrast with that straight line the very smallest beetle. The beetle is a humble portion of reality; the beetle is really there; and therefore you can spend a lifetime in the scientific study of the beetle and know him but imperfectly at the end of it. Take another example. How comparatively easy it is to understand the characters in fiction and how difficult it is to understand the people whom we meet every day. . . . That is because the characters in fiction are creations of the mind, while our relatives are real'—(Goudge, *Cathedral Sermons*, pp. 72–73).

reach, and that any such results cannot be ignored by the Christian theologian, (3) that the Biblical revelation did in fact pre-suppose some knowledge of God, could not have been communicated unless such knowledge had been present, and cannot be expounded theologically without the use of some of the 'rational' principles (*e.g.* that of analogy) which form part of the method of natural theology.

Three brief comments only can be made on this controversy here. First, the discussion has drawn fresh attention to the supernatural character of revelation in all its aspects. Thus it has challenged views which too easily minimize the distinction between truths of natural reason and truths of revelation ('All knowledge of God is in some sense revealed, and revealed truth is rational'). The 'particularity' of the Gospel, *e.g.* the Incarnation of God at a particular time and place, in a particular historical person, takes it out of the realm of rational speculation. It must be the object of *faith*, and this corresponds to its character as given by the divine action. Secondly, natural theology has in some of its exponents in the past claimed a power of demonstrative *proof* and an extent in the range of its conclusions which the arguments employed did not warrant. The present intellectual and moral confusion of man both emphasizes the need for 'revelation', and also puts special difficulties in the way of the construction of a natural theology. Thirdly, the conviction that the natural reason is one source (though limited) of our knowledge of God is deeply rooted in our tradition and will not easily be abandoned by Anglican theologians generally. The Bible itself (*e.g.* Rom 1[20], Acts 14[17]) suggests that the creation bears intelligible witness to its Creator apart from historical revelation. Much that is characteristic of our tradition is summarized in the following words of a modern Anglican theologian. 'Faith and reason, theology and divine revelation are organically continuous with each other. Just as natural religion requires faith in reason as a God-given guide and instrument, if it is to have the courage and confidence to affirm its conclusions, so faith in revealed religion requires the aid and co-operation of reason if it is to understand and communicate itself.' (J. V. Langmead Casserley, *The Retreat from Christianity*, p. 43.)†

THE INCARNATION AND ATONEMENT

ARTICLE II

*Of the Word, or Son of God,
Which was made very Man*

The Son, which is the Word of the Father, begotten from everlasting of the Father, the very and eternal God, of one substance with the Father, took Man's nature in the womb of the blessed Virgin, of her substance: so that two whole and perfect natures, that is to say, the Godhead and Manhood were joined together in one Person, never to be divided, whereof is one Christ, very God, and very Man; who truly suffered, was crucified, dead and buried, to reconcile His Father to us, and to be a sacrifice, not only for original guilt, but also for all actual sins of men.

*De Verbo, sive Filio Dei, qui
verus homo factus est*

Filius, qui est verbum Patris, ab aeterno a Patre genitus, verus et aeternus Deus, ac Patri consubstantialis, in utero beatae virginis, ex illius substantia naturam humanam assumpsit: ita ut duae naturae, divina et humana, integre atque perfecte in unitate personae fuerint inseparabiliter conjunctae, ex quibus est unus Christus, verus Deus et verus homo, qui vere passus est, crucifixus, mortuus et sepultus, ut Patrem nobis reconciliaret, essetque hostia, non tantum pro culpa originis, verum etiam pro omnibus actualibus hominum peccatis.

This Article dates from 1553 and is based on the Lutheran Confession of Augsburg, through the medium of the 13 Articles. In 1563 the words 'begotten . . . Father' were added from the Confession of Würtemburg. Its object was to oppose the revival of ancient heresies on the Person of Christ by Anabaptists.

§ 1. *The Son took man's nature in the womb of the blessed Virgin.*— The Church's teaching on the Incarnation, as on the Trinity, was gradually formulated by struggle with error. Once again her aim has always been to be faithful to all the facts, not in any way to speculate for the sake of speculation, but to guard the truth in all its fulness. From time to time explanations were put forward, most attractive from their simplicity and their harmony with popular ideas, but the Church was compelled to say 'no', because their attractiveness was gained at the cost of ignoring or explaining away certain of the facts. So the Church was driven to think out and state, in the best language that she could find, all that she understood by the Incarnation.

(*a*) When we turn to Scripture and study the Person of our Lord we are confronted with three main facts.

(i) Our Lord lived as true man. His contemporaries, friends and enemies alike, had no doubt of His humanity. He grew, not only in body, but in mind and soul (Lk 2⁴⁰ ᵃⁿᵈ ⁵², Heb 5⁷⁻⁹). He displayed human needs, hunger, thirst, weariness and the like (Mt 4², Mk 4³⁸, Jn 4⁶⁻⁷, etc.), and human emotions, anger, wonder, sorrow, sympathy, etc. (Mk 3⁵, 6⁶, 14³³⁻³⁴, Lk 7⁹, Jn 11³³⁻³⁴, etc.). He prayed and exhibited a true human faith in the Father (Mk 1³⁵, 14³³, Lk 9²⁸, Jn 11⁴¹⁻⁴², 17, Heb 5⁷, etc.). He was tempted and experienced the trials of uncertainty (Mk 14³³, etc., Mt 4¹, etc., Lk 12⁵⁰, Heb 2¹⁸, etc.). He won a real conquest over temptations. He displayed a true human obedience to the will of God as made known in the Law. He attended the public worship of the Synagogue and Temple and submitted to the Baptism of John (Mt 3¹⁵, Mk 1²¹, Lk 2⁴²⁻⁴⁹, etc.). He could be disappointed and disobeyed (Mk 1⁴⁵, 4⁴⁰, etc.). He asked questions for the sake of information and confessed to ignorance on one point at least (Mk 9²¹, cp. 11¹³, Jn 11³⁴, Mk 13³², etc.). In short, though our Lord lived a perfect human life, perfect at each stage of its growth, still it was a human life: there was real development, real dependence upon His fellow-men, above all, real submission and self-surrender to the Father.

(ii) On the other hand, as we have seen, the impression made by our Lord on those who knew Him was of one who was more than man. He made a divine claim, and His claim was proved true by the Resurrection.

(iii) Yet, most certainly He was one Person. His life was in all ways a unity, far more so, indeed, than our own lives, which are broken and distracted by conflicting aims and desires, and by the struggle between a higher and lower self.†

(b) When the question of the true divinity of our Lord had been settled, controversy shifted to His Person. The point at issue was no longer whether He was 'of one substance with the Father'—all parties were agreed on that—but the relation between His divinity and His humanity. How could Jesus Christ be both the Eternal Son and Word of the Father, and also truly man?

(i) Apollinarius, Bishop of Laodicea, had been a vigorous opponent of the Arians. Possibly it was in opposition to their Christological teaching that he was led to construct his theory of the relation between the divine and human natures in Christ, which came into prominence between A.D. 370 and 380. More probably he wished to correct some current theories of the Incarnation which appeared to him either to reduce our Lord to a highly-inspired man or to introduce a dangerous duality into the Incarnate life. He held that, if the Lord's humanity were complete, we should have to suppose that He possessed two wills, one divine and infallible, the other human and essentially 'free' to sin. There could be no union between two such wills without the violation of the nature of one of them, and since the rational will is the directing principle in a person, the possession of two wills would destroy the unity of the Incarnate. Christ therefore had no human mind (νοῦς), to be the seat of rational deliberation and choice; His mind and will were those of the divine Word, who took to Himself in the Incarnation only a human body and an animal soul or animating principle. The divine Word Himself was the sole mind and will of the Incarnate Christ. Only so, Apollinarius believed, could the unity of His Person and the redemptive sinlessness of His will be understood. Christ was οὔτε ἄνθρωπος ὅλος οὔτε θεὸς ἀλλὰ θεοῦ καὶ ἀνθρώπου μίξις. The Church saw that this theory contradicted many of the facts of our Lord's earthly life.[1] It left no room for growth in mind or soul or for the building up of a human character. It abolished the possibility not only of sin but of temptation. Further, such a view lowers human nature by regarding it as unable to become the means of God's self-revelation. Not only does it regard the higher part of human nature as intrinsically sinful, but it leaves it unredeemed, and it is just this higher part which is most truly human, as being that which differentiates man from the animals. All that Christ assumed was the animal side of man. If, as was constantly urged against Apollinarius, 'what was not assumed was not redeemed', man's will, the ultimate seat of his sinfulness, was left unredeemed by Christ. To our modern minds the theory of Apollinarius is wholly repugnant. We know that all human consciousness, such as acts of thought, will and desire, are conditioned by functions of the body. What purpose could a body serve when there were no real processes of human thought or will to be realized through it?†

(ii) As a reaction from Apollinarianism there arose the explanation of the facts known as Nestorianism. Nestorius was Bishop of Constantinople. Whether he himself was at any time, or at all times, a 'Nestorian' is a question for ecclesiastical history. It is enough to state here that he was condemned for the views that bear his name, and that, undoubtedly, there were those who held them. The School of Antioch had come to represent theology of a marked type. This school represented what we should call to-day historical theology. Its first aim was to discover the literal and grammatical meaning of Scripture; to ask, What did the authors mean to say? In dealing with the earthly life of our Lord it started, like the Synoptic Gospels, with the human and natural elements of that life, and then went on to see the divine and supernatural shining through them. The most famous representative of this school was Theodore, Bishop of Mopsuestia. Approaching the problem of the Person of Christ from the human side, he laid stress, in opposition to Apollinarianism, on the complete humanity of our Lord. He taught that each of the two natures of Christ was personal. An impersonal nature was an absurdity. How

---

[1] The 'heresy of the Apollinarians' was condemned at the Council of Constantinople in 381. Apollinarius and one of his followers had been previously condemned at Rome in 377.

then did God indwell in Christ? The answer given was, through
moral union, through unity of will. He postulated a divine agent and
a human agent, united completely and yet freely. Each remained
distinct and unconfused. 'We say that the person (πρόσωπον) of the
Man was perfect, and perfect also the person of the Godhead.'[1]
Thus, God dwelt in Jesus of Nazareth as in a temple, or as in saints
or prophets. Theodore speaks of it as madness to compare the indwelling of God in Christ with His indwelling in the Saints. But it was
different—infinitely different—in degree only: it was the same in
kind. So he prefers to speak of the conjunction (συνάφεια) of the two
natures in Christ, not of their union. This conjunction is compared
to the union between man and wife, who are made one flesh. So the
human life of Jesus Christ was the life of a man selected by God's
fore-knowledge, to be taken from the mother's womb into the most
intimate and indissoluble union with the divine Word. He was
ἄνθρωπος θεοφόρος. All through His life He revealed a complete
moral sympathy with the divine will, so that men could see God perfectly in Him. Through the co-operation of the divine Word with the
unfaltering loyalty of His human will He advanced to the most perfect holiness, which was consummated at the Ascension. Theodore
claimed thus to preserve the unity of Christ's Person and yet leave
room for free moral development. Nestorius did little more than
repeat his teaching. As so often happens, the controversy centred
round a catchword, in this case the use of θεοτόκος[2] to denote the
mother of Jesus Christ. Nestorius denied her the title on the ground
that it suggested the divine nature of her Son was derived from her.
His opponents defended its use as witnessing to the truth that He,
whom she bore, was none other than the eternal Son of God.

Nestorius' solution has its merits. It preserves the reality of Christ's
human example and sympathy. But for all his protests, it reduces our
Lord to a superlatively inspired man, the chief of the saints. He is
man side by side with God, not God in and through man. There is
not the oneness of a single personal life, but the concord of two
persons. Nestorianism is fatally inconsistent both with facts of the
Gospel and of Christian experience. The Christ of Nestorius could
have no right to make the unbounded personal claims for Himself
that our Lord made. In the saints there is no confusion of personality
between themselves and God. They are always conscious that their
message is other and greater than themselves. They point men away
from themselves to God. Jesus Christ drew men to Himself. The
Nestorian Christ cannot rightly be worshipped: at most we can
assign to him that reverence that we pay to holy men. Further, Nes-

---

[1] It is however by no means simple to determine what Theodore, and later Nestorius,
meant by the term here translated 'person'.

[2] 'Mother of God' is not quite a fair translation of this Greek word. It means rather
'she who gave birth to Him who was God.' The emphasis in the Greek word is on the
deity of the child rather than on the motherhood of Mary.

torianism undermines the whole basis of redemption; it rests content with a conception of salvation that has fallen below the level of the New Testament. Christ becomes at most an example and a teacher. But He can bestow on us no power to realize in ourselves His example. By His unique closeness of union with the divine Word He can save only Himself. He cannot impart to us a share in that union. It is just because Christ is more than a single human individual that His perfect humanity can be the source of new life to us. His death is not an act outside us, like, say, the death of Socrates or any other good man, only because it is not simply one of our fellow-men who died. What we need, and what Christ has proved Himself to be, is a redeemer, one who restores and quickens the soul from within, and one who can save from sin. Nestorius was rightly condemned at the Council of Ephesus in 431.[1]†

(iii) At the opposite pole of thought is Monophysitism or Eutychianism. The school of Alexandria had come to represent a theology in many ways opposed to that of Antioch. Their method was that of 'dogmatic' as contrasted with 'historical' theology. Like the Gospel of S. John, they started from the divine side, our Lord's pre-existence as the Word of God, and went on to regard His human life as a self-manifestation of God in time. Cyril, Bishop of Alexandria, had been the great opponent of Nestorius. In his anxiety to safeguard the unity of Christ's Person he used the phrase, μία φύσις τοῦ θεοῦ λόγου σεσαρκωμένη.[2] By this he meant that the Word of God in all the fulness of His divine nature had become personally Incarnate. There was only one centre of personality in Christ, namely, the personality of the Word, which gave personality to the human nature. The human nature had not a separate personality of its own. Cyril expressed this unity of the two natures in a single person by phrases such as ἕνωσις κατ' οὐσίαν καὶ καθ' ὑπόστασιν or ἐκ δύο φύσεων εἷς. Such language was easily misunderstood. After Cyril's death, Eutyches, an abbot at Constantinople, and a follower of Cyril, taught that our Lord was of two natures before the union between them, but after the union only of one nature. This could only be taken to mean that at the Incarnation the human nature was absorbed in the divine and did not exist in the Incarnate in its proper characteristics. The later developments of Monophysitism[3] showed to what lengths

---

[1] The interpretation of the Christological teaching of Theodore and Nestorius remains a disputed question. Some modern estimates would be more favourable than that given in the text above. Undoubtedly Theodore and Nestorius believed themselves to be maintaining the unity of Christ's person as well as the fulness of His two natures.

[2] Cyril believed the phrase to come from a writing of Athanasius. Unhappily, the writing is really a work of Apollinarius passing itself off under the name of Athanasius.

[3] Those later known as Monophysites were united in rejecting the formula of Chalcedon ('two natures'). Some of them merely maintained Cyril's terminology ('one nature') and were as orthodox in the substance of their teaching as he was; others developed views of our Lord's humanity which denied it all forms of corruptibility and passibility. (See Tixeront, vol. iii, c. iv.)

this theory might go in the direction of 'docetism'. Our Lord's humanity is reduced to a mere outward appearance, the veil of His divine glory. All the facts of our Lord's earthly life that make Apollinarianism impossible, make Eutychianism impossible.

(c) The teaching of Eutyches won a temporary triumph at the Robber Council of Ephesus (449), but the decision was finally reversed at the Council of Chalcedon (451). There a dogmatic epistle from Leo, Bishop of Rome, known as the 'tome of Leo', was read and recognized as the expression of orthodoxy. Eutyches was in it directly refuted, Nestorius indirectly. Leo was a Western, with all the Western impatience of philosophical subtleties and disputes about the precise difference between 'nature' and 'person'. He dealt with the whole question from a practical point of view. All that he was concerned to secure was a full recognition both of the true divinity and true humanity of our Lord. As a pastor, he was quite clear that what men needed was a mediator between God and man, who Himself remained both. The influence of Leo was ultimately decisive, and the witness of the Council of Chalcedon to the Church's faith was set forth in the following definition:

'Therefore, following the holy fathers, we all, with one consent, teach men to confess one and the same Son, our Lord Jesus Christ, the same perfect in Godhead and the same perfect in manhood, truly God and the same truly man, of a rational soul and body, of one substance with the Father according to His Godhead and of one substance with us according to His Manhood, in all things like to us except sin, begotten from the Father before the ages according to His Godhead and in the last days born of Mary the virgin, the *theotokos* for us and our salvation, according to His manhood, one and the same Christ, Son, Lord, only-begotten, being made known in two natures, without confusion, without conversion, without division, never to be separated (ἀσυγχύτως, ἀτρέπτως, ἀδιαιρέτως, ἀχωρίστως), the distinction of natures having been in no way abolished through the union, but rather the property of each nature being preserved and meeting in one person and one hypostasis (πρόσωπον καὶ ὑπόστασιν).'

The language of our Article is in large part identical with this, and is so framed as to exclude all the ancient heresies. *The Son . . . of one substance with the Father* excludes Arianism. *Man's nature . . . two whole and perfect natures* excludes Apollinarianism. *In one person, never to be divided* excludes Nestorianism. *Two whole and perfect natures, that is to say the Godhead and the Manhood . . . very God and very Man* excludes Monophysitism.[1]†

The question still remains, What is the value of the formal theological definitions of these Councils to-day? The language used by the

---

[1] The decisions of the four great Councils may be summed up in the four adverbs, ἀληθῶς, τελέως, ἀδιαιρέτως, ἀσυγχύτως. Our Lord was 'truly' God as against Arius, 'completely' man as against Apollinarius, 'indivisibly' One Person as against Nestorius, both God and man 'without confusion' as against Eutyches (Hooker, v. 54, § 10).

Church in her attempt to state the doctrine of the Trinity, 'One substance, Three Persons,' and still more, the language used at Chalcedon about our Lord's Incarnation, 'Two natures and One Person,' is often attacked as useless or worse than useless to-day—a mere encumbrance, due to the Hellenization of Christianity.

In reply, let us begin by reminding ourselves that the primary object of such language was not to speculate, but to rule out speculations that were seen to be destructive of the purity and completeness of the faith. The formulas have a lasting value. The ancient heresies all represent certain permanent tendencies of the human mind. In every age men, when faced with the mystery of the Incarnation, have inclined towards a line of solution that leads ultimately to Nestorianism or Monophysitism. We naturally pay greater attention to those facts that interest us and are disposed to ignore others that make a less forcible appeal. Here, as elsewhere, our personal leanings need to be corrected by the more complete experience of the Church.

The average healthy Englishman has an Antiochene mind. What attracts him is our Lord's character. He admires His life of doing good, His courage in facing death for the sake of duty, His self-sacrifice and the like. He regards our Lord as an inspiring example, a leader in the life of faith, but little more. Accordingly, the English mind is easily satisfied with the conception of our Lord as a good man, with whom God dwelt. The need of something deeper, of inward renewal and salvation, is hardly realized. So, teaching that is practically Nestorian is quite common among us.

On the other hand, a view of our Lord that is practically Apollinarian or Monophysite tends to prevail wherever devotion to our Lord as the divine Saviour is not balanced by a study of the Gospels. It is the typical danger of a theology based upon worship divorced from the moral life. If Nestorianism appeals to the masculine independence of the respectable Englishman, Monophysitism appeals to the emotions of the devout worshipper. It is to be found in our hymns and, *e.g.* in the cult of the Sacred Heart. In England to-day we are living in a reaction from teaching about our Lord that was practically Monophysite. Protestant piety no less than Catholic devotion had come to lay such exclusive stress on our Lord's divine work as practically to ignore His humanity. Now, the reality of His humanity, His human growth and sympathies, have been, as it were, rediscovered. His human life has been made to live before our eyes. In the joy of realizing afresh our Lord's humanity, men have been tempted to lose hold of His divinity. But we must not live in reactions. The Church's duty is to hold together both sides of the truth, as essential for the completeness of the Christian life. The formula of Chalcedon at least rules out one-sided presentations of the truth that would impoverish the Christian life. 'Of one substance with us according to His manhood' secures for us all that Nestorianism can offer. 'Of one substance with the Father according to His Godhead' secures all that Mono-physitism can offer. The primary object of the Council's decision was pastoral, to warn men off paths that must lead astray and to send them back to study the Gospels for themselves with the right pre-suppositions.

Still the fact remains that in modern theology the formula of Chalcedon is often criticized and set on one side as valueless or even a hindrance to Christian faith. Before we examine its permanent value let us remember that it is the facts that are of supreme import-ance; not the formula that expresses them. If to-day, in the light of modern knowledge, we can express all the facts more adequately in some new formula, we are at liberty to do so. If, for instance, in view of modern psychology, we come to hold that 'person' and 'nature' are indistinguishable, that is not being disloyal to the Catholic faith. The objection to nearly all, if not all, modern attempts hitherto made to restate the truth about the Person of Christ, is not that they are modern, but they ignore or explain away some of the facts. Often, indeed, they are only the old heresies in a new guise, and to-day as of old the Christian consciousness feels their inadequacy. In attempting to restate the truth, part of it is allowed to escape.

The complaint is made that 'the formula merely stated the facts which constituted the problem; it did not attempt a solution. It was therefore unscientific; and as theology is the science of religion, it represented the breakdown of theology.'[1] We may fairly reply that if the first part of this assertion is true, it is really the highest praise. The function of a council is not to strike out a new line in theology. Its primary duty is to witness to the faith once for all delivered, and to decide whether a particular teaching is in accordance with it or not. If the Council 'stated the facts which constituted the problem' so as to rule out once for all attempted solutions that did not cover all the facts, it performed precisely the service that a Council exists to per-form. It is the place of theologians, not councils, to frame a theology. All that the Council could declare is that hitherto their efforts had not proved successful. In the interests of the Gospel the Church was obliged, not indeed to explain the problem of the unity of God and man in Christ, but to insist positively that there was the problem to be solved.

Again, the formula of Chalcedon was of necessity expressed in terms of the philosophy of the day. There was at that time a single dominant philosophy. This philosophy viewed the world and experi-ence 'statically'. It thought out questions in terms of 'nature' and 'being'. It asked what a thing was in its essential nature. Our minds to-day view the world 'dynamically'. We think in terms of 'life' and

---

[1] *Foundations*, p. 231. Cp. p. 230. 'Their formula had the right devotional value; it excluded what was known to be fatal to the faith; but it explained nothing.' (W. Temple). But see his later work, *Christus Veritas*, cc. vii and viii.

'movement'. We ask not simply what a thing is in itself, but what it does and how it acts. Hence modern theologians often complain that the formula of Chalcedon throws no light on the problems that the Incarnation raises for our minds to-day.[1] It leaves us with a divine nature and a human nature side by side, without any attempt to show how they were united in a single life. To us the 'divine nature' is not something stationary, but the sum total of divine energies and activities that constitute the divine life. God is God not simply by what He is but by what He does. So, too, we think of human nature not as something that exists ready-made, but as something that is progressively realized through acts of choice, in a human life. So we ask, If Jesus Christ is God, how could His divine powers and activities leave room for a truly human life, for that mental growth and development, and for that building up of a human character of which Scripture speaks? Or again, How if He was divine could He possess a true human consciousness? For us the problem is in large part a moral problem, a problem of will. To speak of a 'divine nature' and a 'human nature' as if they were fixed quantities ignores the whole question of the will. Such terms are, indeed, not necessarily moral at all.

We cannot deny that these objections are well-founded: but what do they show? Simply that Greek theology inevitably approached the whole question from a different standpoint from our own. Our own approach tends to be dominated by psychology. Psychology discusses and explains the manner in which I come to feel and know. It investigates my states of consciousness and the processes by which I attain knowledge and perform acts of choice. But psychology has its limitations, though it sometimes forgets them. It cannot explain ultimate realities. It can describe what I do and how I do it, but it is unable to tell me what I am. That is a question not for psychology but for metaphysics. If my feelings and thoughts are not a mere series of passing illusions, they imply behind them an 'I', which, indeed, has no consciousness apart from them, but is yet not identical with all or any of them. The words 'life' and 'movement' imply that there is an abiding something that lives and moves. Accordingly, we must assert that the questions that have been raised about the life and person of Jesus Christ are not simply psychological but also metaphysical. There is, for instance, such a question as that of His pre-existence. It is unreasonable to blame the formula of Chalcedon because it gives to these metaphysical questions a metaphysical answer. In effect it says, 'If we assume the life and redeeming power of Jesus Christ as

---

[1] This is the main point of the criticisms of Dr Harnack which are repeated by Dr Temple in *Foundations*, *e.g.* 'The spiritual cannot be expressed in terms of substance at all.' 'The "substance" of the Greek Fathers, whether divine or human, has the material, not the spiritual characteristics.' 'Substance theology inevitably ignores the will and with it the moral problem,' etc. (pp. 231 –233).For criticism of this position see *C.Q.R.* Oct. 1915, p. 1.

true, if we grant that He has made men one with God, what do these experiences presuppose as a necessary condition of their truth? They presuppose that He was in the full sense God and in the full sense man. If you deny either that He was perfect God or that He was perfect man, then Christianity falls to the ground.' The vocabulary of metaphysics must be static: to condemn it for being static is to condemn metaphysics for being itself.[1] But it is not necessarily either unspiritual or materialistic. Greek philosophy was not so incompetent as is sometimes assumed. οὐσία is not unspiritual at all. The formula does not attempt to define either the 'divine nature' or the 'human nature'. It only asserts that, whatever they are, Jesus Christ possessed them. Nor does it attempt to explain how it was psychologically possible for our Lord to unite the two in the living out of His earthly life. It leaves the field open for modern philosophers to do this if they can.

What we may fairly criticize is not so much the decisions of Chalcedon in themselves, as the *Tome of Leo* and other theological writings that prepared the way for those decisions. These do attempt to deal with our Lord's life and person psychologically.[2] We must admit that the predominant theology of the Church did not do full justice to the complete humanity of our Lord or to the facts of the Gospel narrative that attest His complete humanity. As we have seen, a vital part of the humanness of human nature is that it comes to completion through growth. On its moral and spiritual side this growth is conditioned by acts of will and choice.[3] In our study of our Lord's human life we must leave room for real mental and moral effort, for spiritual progress and development of character. He was able to sympathize from within with the doubts and difficulties of our finite minds and with our moral struggles. This is where Alexandrian theology tended to fail.[4] Even in the writings of S. Leo, our Lord's conduct and His conquests over temptation are in danger of being viewed solely as an exercise of divine power. The full humanity of our Lord's bodily needs and actions only receives unreserved recognition. The activity of His human reason and will, of just that part of our human nature which is distinctively human, and by which we transcend

---

[1] The metaphysician, as it were, takes a section of experience, abstracting life and movement. In abstracting these he necessarily abstracts the activity of the will. His language, therefore, is bound to appear non-ethical and static.

[2] Cp. Weston, *The One Christ*, pp. 70 ff.

[3] It is customary to speak of our Lord's human nature as 'impersonal'. The phrase is unsatisfactory, but it was intended to guard the truth that the humanity which our Lord assumed had no independent personality. The Word did not unite Himself to an individual man but gave personality to the human nature that He assumed. Hence our Lord's manhood as assumed by Him and as progressively realized in His human life was most truly personal. For a valuable note on *hypostasis*, 'person' and 'personality', see *Essays on the Trinity and the Incarnation*, p. 392.

[4] Cp. Westcott's criticism of Cyril. 'Under his treatment the divine history seems to be dissolved into a docetic drama' (*S. John*, p. xcv).

animal life, is practically ignored.[1] Hence, our Lord's moral life tends
to become a mere appearance. But human goodness, as we know it,
can only be attained by real effort of will. If our Lord's human life
was exempt from this moral struggle, if His obedience to the Father's
will was achieved by the automatic employment of divine power, then
so far our Lord's life was not human at all. But the Gospels lend no
support to any such suggestion.

Again, Greek theology treats of the actual living out of our Lord's
life in a way that breaks up its unity. It is one thing to insist that He
was and is both God and Man. We must equally insist that He is 'one
Christ'. Our mind revolts against any attempt to parcel out His
activities among His two natures,[2] to say that He did this as God, that
as Man. Such an attempt leaves us with no continuous human life at
all.[3] The Gospels give us no hint of any such double consciousness.
In all His conduct our Lord was fundamentally one. The view
criticized ignores the mutual kinship between the divine and the
human. Man was created in the image of God. Thus God could express Himself in and through a human life without any contradiction
of the divine nature. Our Lord's divinity and humanity were not, as
it were, placed side by side. He was not only God and Man, but God
in Man and Man in God. Probably when we think of God our
imagination dwells too much on what we may call His physical
attributes, omnipotence, omniscience and the like, and we tend to
make them independent of the love and righteousness which constitute His inmost being. Greek theology was greatly hampered by
the dogma that God cannot in any way suffer. Cyril and Nestorius
were at one in their desire to insist that in the Incarnation our Lord's
Godhead was exempt from all suffering. No doubt there is a true and
important sense in which God is 'without passions'. But we may

---

[1] For the manner in which theologians explained away clear statements, *e.g.* of our
Lord's ignorance, as man, see Gore, *Dissertations*, p. 130 ff.

[2] Thus Leo can write: 'To hunger, to thirst, to be weary, and to sleep is evidently
human. But to satisfy five thousand men with five loaves and to give to the Samaritan
woman living water, . . . to walk on the surface of the sea with feet not sinking, and to
allay the swelling waves by rebuking the tempest, this, without doubt, is divine.'
'It belongs not to the same nature to say "I and the Father are one", and to say "the
Father is greater than I".' Leo is attempting to safeguard the reality of the divine and
human natures, each with its distinct operation, but the result is strangely different
from the impression made on us by Scripture. We notice how all the human acts quoted
belong only to the body. There is no adequate recognition of the activity of the reason
and will. (For a more favourable view of Leo's meaning as interpreted by another of his
treatises, see R. V. Sellers, *Two Ancient Christologies*, p. 249.)

[3] A certain attempt at unity was made by the theological device known as the
communicatio idiomatum, by which, owing to the union of the two natures in a single
Person, it was held possible to transfer names and titles appropriate to one nature to
the other in virtue of this unity of Person, to say, *e.g.* 'God died for men' instead of
'He who was God died for men'. So long as it is simply a question of titles such a
practice is harmless, but it has proved theologically dangerous. It has come to suggest
that the divine and human natures were fused into something neither divine nor
human, but a strange compound of the two, that the Godhead was converted into
flesh, as the Athanasian Creed expresses it.

question whether the unqualified denial that God can suffer is not a pagan rather than a Christian dogma: a legacy from heathen philosophy taken over by theologians without due scrutiny, and needing to be corrected by the bold anthropomorphisms of Scripture. We must distinguish between physical and moral suffering. If God is love, love must be capable of moral suffering. So we can hold that our Lord, in all the humiliation of His Cross and Passion, was active in His divine no less than His human nature. We can see God there as truly as in His acts of power. For where were love and righteousness more perfectly and more victoriously love and righteousness than in the Crucified? If God is love and holiness, then on the Cross we see God most truly, though He be self-restrained under the limitations and infirmities of manhood. Let us remember that God's omnipotence in all its forms is not the omnipotence of bare power, but the omnipotence of love. It is to be seen in the fulness of self-sacrifice as truly as in the unspeakable majesty of a theophany.

So, too, Man is most truly man in so far as He lives in that union with God for which He was created. The truest human life is the work both of God and Man. The more intimate the union, the more perfect the human life. The divine does not annihilate or supplant or curtail the human: rather it raises it to its highest perfection. In our Lord we see this perfection of human life. That life was the work of God in Man and Man in God. God could be most really God under the conditions of and within the sphere of the human. Man could be most completely man in perfect union with the divine. We cannot, therefore, draw hard and fast distinctions within the unity of our Lord's earthly life. 'In all things He acts personally; and so far as it is revealed to us, His greatest works during His earthly life are wrought by the help of the Father through the energy of a humanity enabled to do all things in fellowship with God.'[1] To sum up, the Fathers' psychology was crude and unsatisfying, even though their metaphysics were sound.[2]

The objection, however, still remains, that even though some static and metaphysical language has a right and necessary place in any formal statement of the Church's belief, still the phrases, both of the Creed of Nicaea and of the formula of Chalcedon, are Greek metaphysics. It was, indeed, inevitable that the Greek Fathers should employ the categories of their own day, but why should we be bound to them? Let us frankly admit that we are not tied down to any particular metaphysical system. But it is very doubtful whether, even if we put aside all historical associations, a change is either possible or

[1] Westcott, *Hebrews*, p. 66.
[2] We may compare the criticism of Dr Moberly (*Atonement and Personality*, pp. 96–97).
'The phrase "God and man" is, of course, perfectly true. But it is easy to lay undue emphasis on the "and". . . . In His human life on earth, as Incarnate, He is not sometimes, but consistently, always, in every act and in every detail, human. The Incarnate

desirable. After all, there are certain fundamental ideas that are common to all thought. 'The ideas of substance or thing, of personality, of nature, are permanent ideas, we cannot get rid of them; no better words could be suggested to express the same facts.'[1] The ideas of the Fathers need not be the less permanent because they are Greek. They are not limited to any particular type of metaphysics. Indeed, they are largely ideas that common sense demands. Some such ideas as 'divine nature' and 'human nature' are implied in the very notion of an Incarnation.

Further, we are coming increasingly to see how, not only in broad outline but in detail, the divine providence had been preparing the world for the coming of Christ. This preparation was religious, social and intellectual, the work of the Jew, the Roman, and the Greek. We cannot but suppose that the forms of thought as 'Christ' or 'Son of Man' under which Christ revealed Himself to His contemporaries were part of the divine scheme. He took them and filled them with a new and richer content. We may equally believe that the thought-forms of Greek philosophy were no less providentially designed that through them the Church might express to the world the wealth of her new life, filling them with a new and richer content. We cannot, therefore, lightly let them go.[2]

Lastly, the dogmatic language of the Church is confessedly inadequate. We know little about our own life, still less about the life of God. Even psychology cannot help us here. If we throw over the language of Chalcedon, we must find some substitute. Where is it to be found? To which school of modern philosophy are we to turn? For they are many. To choose any one would be to identify Christianity deliberately with one particular philosophy—the very charge that their critics bring against the Greek Fathers. The men who agree in their contempt for Greek theology as a rule agree in little else. The Church has to deal with practical needs. If the formula of Chalcedon has the right value for Christian devotion and leaves full scope for all modern investigations the Church may well claim to hold fast to it

---

never leaves His Incarnation. God, as man, is always, in all things, God as man. . . . Whatever the reverence of their motive may be, men do harm to consistency and to truth, by keeping open, as it were, a sort of non-human sphere or aspect of the Incarnation. This opening we should unreservedly desire to close. There are not two existences either of, or within, the Incarnate, side by side with one another. If it is all Divine, it is all human too. We are to study the Divine in and through the human. By looking for the Divine side by side with the human, instead of discerning the Divine within the human, we miss the significance of them both.'

[1] Gore, *Bampton Lectures on the Incarnation*, p. 105. Cp. *The Reconstruction of Belief*, pp. 848 ff.

[2] We must not be too much influenced by the fact that the Church's formularies need to be explained to men to-day. The technical terms of all science can only be understood by those who are ready to take some pains to learn the science. A theology that could be completely understood by the man in the street in five minutes would be very shallow.

until there is at least some possibility of a re-statement that would win general acceptance.

(*d*) How then can we best conceive of the Incarnation? Perhaps our best starting-point will be some such thought as that expressed in S. Paul's phrase, 'He emptied Himself.' We must beware of language that might suggest that our Lord was God before and after, but ceased to be God during His Incarnate life on earth. He laid aside not His Godhead but His glory. He willed to live a real human life, to know our condition no longer simply by divine intuition from without, but from within by passing through a real human experience. By an act of His divine omnipotence He willed to restrain His divine attributes so as to render this possible.[1] The subject of the whole human experience was the divine Word Himself. In pondering over the mystery of the Incarnation we shall get more assistance by thinking along the lines of love and sympathy than along the lines of abstract logic. The essence of sympathy is putting oneself in another's place : in the case of one less educated or less developed this must involve a deliberate holding back of our wider knowledge.[2] Perhaps some such example as this, inadequate as it is, is the nearest that we can get to a real understanding of His self-humiliation. We can dimly conceive that by a single supra-temporal act of choice the Eternal Word willed so to restrain His divine attributes as to render a true human life and experience possible. If we believe that God is love, there is nothing in such a conception that violates the central being of God. Many of the objections that are brought against such an idea are at bottom objections against the possibility of a real Incarnation at all. If we are ready to grant the possibility of an Incarnation, we must also grant that there will inevitably be much in it that we cannot fully understand. The whole question of the relation of time to eternity is involved.[3] We cannot conceive what time means to God or reconcile historical sequence with His eternal consciousness.[4]

---

[1] Our Lord did not part with such essentially divine attributes as, *e.g.* omnipotence or omniscience; rather, it was His own omnipotent power that restrained His omnipotence, His own almighty wisdom that devised the means for sharing our human ignorance.

[2] Cp. Gore, *Dissertations*, p. 219; Ottley, *Doctrine of the Incarnation*, ii. pp. 291–2.

[3] *E.g.* How could our Lord be at one and the same time living on earth and performing His cosmic functions? Was He, as Proclus, preaching against Nestorius, said, 'In His Father's bosom and in the womb of the Virgin; in His mother's arm and on the wings of the wind; worshipped by the angels in Heaven and supping with publicans on earth?'

[4] Cp. the following statement: 'It is not meant that the Logos was withdrawn from God and occupied by the Incarnation. We err if we think of the Logos as only capable of one activity at a time. The Logos is capable of all the activity of God. God was the same elsewhere as if there had been no incarnation, and the Logos was meanwhile as truly as ever the medium of God's relation with the universe. . . . The Incarnation is not a division of God. The truth is rather this: that the God of infinitely varied activity added to His other self-expressions the act of becoming man—an additional form of activity in which He could engage without withdrawing Himself from any other' (Clarke, *An Outline of Christian Theology*, pp. 294–295).

Nor can we possibly understand what change the Incarnation made in the life of the Trinity. All we are told is that the 'coming of the Son' corresponded to a sending by the Father, and that He was made man through the power of the Spirit. In the act of divine self-sacrifice the Father and the Spirit had their part no less than the Son.[1]†

(e) Special difficulties arise when we consider (i) Our Lord's human knowledge; (ii) His temptation.

(i) We can only conceive of God's omniscience as a perfect knowledge raised above all the limitations that beset our own, as an infinite and immediate intuition into the inmost being of all that is. But a real human experience includes the possession of human knowledge, attained by human means and able to be contained by the finite capacity of the human mind. It would seem, then, that our Lord, in willing to become man, willed such a restraining of the divine knowledge as would render possible a true human experience. Though our imaginations find it easier to picture a restraint of divine power, so as to allow of need and suffering and opposition and death, than of a restraint of divine knowledge so as to allow of ignorance and perplexity, yet at bottom the problem is the same in each case. Our thoughts must be guided by moral rather than metaphysical considerations. Above all, we must be true to all the facts of the Gospel narrative.

In human knowledge we may distinguish two elements. First there is that knowledge which we acquire step by step—'discursive knowledge', as it is called—either by the operation of our mind, by processes of reasoning or argument, or else by receiving information from others. This includes all facts of history or natural science. Secondly, there is that knowledge which we call intuitive, gained not piecemeal, but by a direct and immediate perception. This includes all sensations as of colour or pleasure, or, again, all judgments of moral and spiritual insight. We see the truth, not as the conclusion of any argument or reflection, but with an immediacy and clearness that leave no room for doubt. When we turn to the Gospels, we find that in the first kind of knowledge our Lord, for all we can discover, shared all human limitations.[2] 'He grew in wisdom.' He used the ordinary methods of investigation. He asked questions to get information. He could be surprised at unforeseen events. The uncertainty of the future lay dark upon His soul. He expressly declared that He did not know the day of His coming to judgment. So, too, He accepted the current Jewish opinions about physical science or the books of the Old Testament, that He learnt from His human teachers.

---

[1] Cp. Moberly, op. cit. p. 167.

[2] Mk 11[1-4] (the instructions to find the colt) and Mk 14[13] (the man bearing a pitcher of water) were probably pre-arranged signals. Even if they were instances of unusual perception they could be paralleled from the lives of the prophets.

On all such points it would seem that He lived and thought as a Man of His own day.

But in the region of intuitive knowledge He showed a unique discernment. He claimed an unfailing insight into the mind of God and sympathy with His purposes, an unclouded vision of divine truth. He passed judgment on all questions of morality with the authority of one who saw the truth beyond dispute. He could read the thoughts and the hearts of friends and foes. He displayed an unerring perception of human character. The realm of moral and spiritual truth held no secrets from Him. His whole life and teaching were based upon this unique consciousness of God. He bore witness in His example and His discourses to what He knew. He revealed God by revealing Himself. Even here we may not draw a hard and fast line between the human and the divine. Among ourselves the power of moral and spiritual insight varies enormously. It depends not on education but rather on holiness of life. It is the pure in heart who see God. In the case of the Hebrew prophets and others we get instances of men endowed with powers of spiritual perception that the normal man does not possess, yet that in no way destroy their humanity. It is hard to set any limit to the moral and spiritual vision of a sinless human being. So in our Lord's case we may hold that here, too, the divine raised the human to its highest perfection. Even under the limitations of a human life He enjoyed a true and adequate perception of God and of His own relation to God. And this perception He imparted to His disciples so far as it could be expressed in the human language of His day.

We believe that our Lord came for a special purpose. He did not come to give us infallible information on questions of history, or criticism, or science. God has given us the ordinary methods of attaining to truth on such points, if we will only use them. Revelation is never given to save us trouble. Rather Christ came to bring men back to God. A real part of His saving work was to impart to men something of His own vision of the truth of God and to reveal the character of God and His purpose for man. The fulfilment of this mission demanded not omniscience but infallibility within the limits of the task entrusted to Him. Ignorance is one thing, error is another. If in His incarnate life He willed to submit to the limitations of human knowledge, yet He showed Himself aware of those limitations. On questions of moral and spiritual truth He spoke with the certainty of conviction: He claimed an infallible knowledge and appealed to His own life and character to prove the truth of His claim. 'Which of you convicteth me of sin? And if I say truth, why do ye not believe me' (Jn 8[46]). The power to live a life, faultless in its active performance of duty both towards God and towards man, carried with it the right to declare without contradiction, the secret source of strength, whence that power was derived. The truth of the life guaranteed the truth of the teaching.

There is, however, one point on which it has been maintained that our Lord showed not merely ignorance but error. He expected and taught others to expect His return to judgment and the end of the world within the lifetime of His own generation. Subsequent events have proved this teaching false. In support of this view the chief passages quoted are Mk 13³⁰, where 'all these things' that shall be fulfilled in 'this generation' at first sight would seem to include the final advent of the Son of Man predicted in vv. ²⁴⁻²⁷ (Mt 24³⁴ and Lk 21³² are parallel passages); Mt 24²⁹, where the final advent is foretold 'immediately after the tribulation of those days' *i.e.* the fall of Jerusalem (*n.b.* Mk 13²⁴ has 'in those days'). So, too, Mt 16²⁸ runs: 'There shall be some of them that stand here which shall in nowise taste of death, till they see the Son of Man coming in his kingdom' (Mk 9¹, 'till they see the Kingdom of God come with power'). At first sight these passages appear to suggest the fallibility of Christ. But a closer examination of the Gospels makes any such conclusion at least precarious.

(α) Our Lord expressly declared that as Man, He shared the ignorance of men and angels as to the time of His final advent (Mk 13³² and probably Mt 24³⁶).[1] It is therefore improbable that at the same time He should have predicted it as about to happen within a generation. Further, much of His teaching beyond dispute assumes a long interval before His last coming. The Gospel is first to be preached to all the nations (Mk 13¹⁰) and in the whole world (Mt 24¹⁴). In Lk 21²⁴ 'the times of the Gentiles' are interposed between the capture of Jerusalem and the coming of the Son of Man. We must not be too confident that we always know exactly what is meant by the 'coming of the Son of Man'. We are dealing not with English literalism but Oriental imagery. In one sense Christ most really came in judgment at the fall of Jerusalem. His words then received a first fulfilment in the lifetime of those who heard them. They await a further fulfilment whose date and distance are unknown. Above all, the primary aim of our Lord's eschatological discourses was not to give a detailed forecast of the future, but to rouse the disciples to the duty of watchfulness. They were to live as men in daily expectation of the Lord's return and prepared to render an account to Him.

(β) Here, if anywhere, we need to bear in mind that we have received our Lord's words through human agency. The discourse in S. Matthew is demonstrably a collection of speeches from different sources, probably not spoken at the same time but grouped according to subject-matter. The same is probably true of Mk 13. Hence, it is precarious to judge any saying by its present context. Again, the speeches have been translated from Aramaic into Greek. It is the

---

[1] We may not unreasonably suppose that the actual moment of the end of the world and the final Advent is contingent upon human conduct. Hence, inevitably, our Lord as man must be ignorant of its date (cp. also p. 285 ff.).

easiest thing for a reporter unconsciously to alter the exact wording, to add or subtract a shade of meaning, or to give precision to what was intentionally left vague. If our Lord's descriptions of His second coming were couched in dark and mysterious language, they may well have come down to us coloured by the presuppositions of those who heard them. If we compare Mt 16²⁸ with Mk 9¹, Mt 24³ with Mk 13⁴, and Mt 24²⁹ with Mk 13²⁴, we can see how the first evangelist has made more definite the vaguer expressions of S. Mark, so as to bring out his own belief that the final coming of our Lord would follow immediately after the destruction of Jerusalem. This definiteness demonstrates not the fallibility of Christ but of His interpreters. It is clear that the early Church, including S. Paul, lived in daily expectation of the Lord's return. This proves that His teaching did not exclude such an interpretation, but it does not prove that it was the true interpretation (cp. the misunderstanding recorded in Jn 21²³). It seems to have been our Lord's will that the Church should so live as to be prepared for His return at any moment. In a very real sense He 'came in power' in the coming of the Spirit at Pentecost. In another sense He came at the fall of Jerusalem.¹ In an equally real sense He comes in all times of crisis whether for the Church or for the individual. In every case His coming is a judgment, a blessing and an opportunity for those who are watchful, a condemnation of those who are not. In the fulness of time there will be a last coming and a final judgment.

(γ) We must also bear in mind that our Lord spoke as a prophet. He employs the imagery of ancient prophecy and contemporary apocalyptic. We must therefore take account of the perspective of prophecy. 'Long ages of the future are foreshortened in a series of pictures which seem to be immediate and simultaneous, until the course of events shows that they represent successive ages of long duration and slow development.'² Because this is so we do not dare to call the prophet mistaken. It may be that our Lord, as the last and greatest of the prophets, condescended to share their limitations and their mental outlook. He has told us expressly that He, as Man, did not know the day or hour of His return. But He had a clear vision of the certainty of that return, and that clearness He expressed under the symbol of nearness. His utterances must be judged by the standard of prophecy, and as such they have in part received and in part await fulfilment.†

(ii) In the Epistle to the Hebrews (4¹⁵) our Lord is stated to have been 'in all points tempted like as we are, yet without sin'. It has often been objected that such a statement is self-contradictory. With us

---

¹ We can hardly imagine all that the fall of the city and the abolition of the Temple meant to a Jewish Christian. It was a very shaking of heaven and earth and the fall of all that seemed most permanent. It was the dawn of a new world.

² Kirkpatrick, *Doctrine of the Prophets*, p. 407.

the sting of temptation lies not only in the solicitation from without but in our own inward affinity to evil. It is the traitor within the camp that betrays us. In the case of an unfallen human nature and a will that had never been weakened by consent to evil, this last element would be lacking. How could evil make its full appeal? Further, if Christ could not sin, His battle with temptation was, so to speak, a sham fight. There was no fear of falling.

Such objections are often urged, but if analyzed they rest at bottom on a misunderstanding of the meaning of temptation.

When our Lord became man, He thereby rendered Himself subject to temptation. God in Himself 'cannot be tempted with evil' (Jas 1[13]). But in expressing Himself in and through the limitations of manhood and the feelings and conditions of finite human life 'He deliberately put on—not, indeed, the personal capacity of sinning, but at least (if we may use the expression) the hypothetical capacity of sinning, the nature through which sin could naturally approach and suggest itself. ... There was, so far, in His human nature, the natural machinery for, or capability of, rebelling, that the reiterated negative "not my own", "not myself", does deny something.'[1] All free and finite existence contains the possibility of sin. Selfishness exists potentially as soon as there exists a self that can set itself up in opposition to the life of the whole. The fact of limitation carries with it the possibility of transgressing the limit.[2] Again, in virtue of His human nature our Lord possessed certain needs and desires common to all men: not only the elementary desires of the body, for food, drink, rest and the like, but also the desires of our higher nature, as for sympathy and companionship, and the more intellectual desire to explore all the manifold possibilities of life and to taste a full and rich experience. At any moment a being with such desires may find himself in circumstances when he has to choose between doing wrong in order to gratify them or leaving them ungratified. All such appetites, in themselves morally neutral, may become temptations to sin when their satisfaction would conflict with the known will of God. Here, too, our Lord was sensitive to temptation. The nature of His temptations in large part corresponded to His vocation. He was tempted to forward the Kingdom of God in ways that were not in accordance with the will of the Father, to do evil that good might come. He was tempted to escape the pain and shame of the Cross. He experienced the power of temptation in all its reality. In one sense, no two men's temptations are 'in all points' the same, yet they agree in containing the essential elements of temptation. No individual undergoes all forms of temptation. So our Lord's, though different in form very largely from our own, just because His work was unique, were as real and grievous to Him as our own are to us. His possession of unique

---

[1] Moberly, *op. cit.* p. 105.
[2] Cp. Westcott, *The Gospel of the Resurrection*, c. ii. § 24.

powers does not affect the point in question. The moral struggle is concerned with the use to which we put the powers, great or small, which we individually possess. Any power may be used either for the glory of God or for our own self-pleasing. Nor, again, does sinlessness affect the ultimate and essential nature of temptation. Our Lord, just because He was sinless, alone endured the full brunt of the assault. The man who yields to temptation has not experienced its extremest force. If, in God's providence, our trials are proportioned to our capacity (1 Cor 10¹³), our Lord's conflict may well have been sore beyond our imagination. Further, even in our own experience the temptations that come from sinless desires may be even more grievous than those that spring from our own past weakness.[1] Our own part in yielding to sin may alter the form of our temptation but it does not make it essentially different. A sinful disposition does make men more liable to fall, but it does not increase the pain of being tempted; rather it diminishes it, because it diminishes the antagonism to evil.

Again, when we say that sin was impossible to Him, we mean morally, not physically impossible. He could not sin, not because anything external prevented Him, but because He was Himself one in will with the Father. Temptation is not sin. It only becomes sin when the will fails to decide for the higher course or dallies with the temptation. Our Lord never consented to the suggestion of evil. By prayer and faith He overcame the tempter. He condemned sin, not only by suffering for it, but by personally resisting and overcoming it. His holiness was a real human holiness perfected through moral effort and conquest.[2]

Lastly, here as always, Jesus Christ is the great redeemer. What we need in our fight against sin is sympathy with us in all the pain and effort of resistance. That our Lord can give us, since He resisted 'even unto blood'. What our fallen nature craves is sympathy with us in our falls. That our Lord does not give, and it would be bad for us to receive it, since it would weaken us. Our Lord's true human sympathy is not lessened by His perfect holiness. He felt the strain, as none other has ever felt it, of directing His will unceasingly along the hard path of duty, at the cost of pain to body, mind and soul. It would seem that in the higher stages of the spiritual life, as evidenced by the saints, the pain of temptation lies less in the fear of defeat than in the hatred of all suggestion to evil. As men grow in holiness they grow in sensitiveness to the horror of sin. The more holy the soul the more painful is all such temptation. To our Lord it was more terrible than to others, just because He was sinless. Hence, He can indeed

---

[1] It has been suggested, for instance, that the thirst of the traveller in the desert, which arises out of a sinless human infirmity, may be more fierce than the drunkard's craving for strong drink.

[2] Cp. Gore, *The Incarnation of the Son of God*, pp. 165–167.

feel with us in our moral conflict. But though He can sympathize with us in our temptations, because He Himself was tempted, He can redeem us from sin just because He never sinned. 'If redemption is to be achieved the redeemer must stand free of moral evil. As the source of victorious spiritual energy He must Himself be in utter oneness with the will of God. The perfect moral health, the unstained conscience to which He is slowly raising others, must be present absolutely in His own life. . . . Like to His brethren in all else, yet He is unlike them here. Yet it is no paradox to say that such unlikeness makes His kinship perfect: for sin had made Him not more a man but less. Sin dehumanizes, and by its entrance the perfection of His vital sympathy would have been increasingly lost.'[1]†

(f) *The Virgin-birth.*—Our Article, following the Creeds, asserts that *The Son . . . took man's nature in the womb of the Blessed Virgin, of her substance.* The Church has always understood such words as these literally, as stating that our Lord was born of a virgin-mother, without the intervention of any human father. Strictly speaking, it was our Lord's conception, not our Lord's birth, that was miraculous. The term Virgin-birth would be more accurately styled the 'virginal conception'.[2] To-day this belief has been challenged by some who claim to be Christians. They hold that it forms no integral part of Christian belief, that there is no satisfactory historical evidence for it, that the statement of it in the Creed must be taken as symbolically, not literally true, that is, as an allegory, not an actual fact, and that in any case the belief in it as an historical event has no particular value for Christian faith. The main lines of argument in support of this contention may be summed up thus. S. Mark, S. Paul, and S. John are all silent about the Virgin-birth. This shows that it had no place in the earliest Gospel. The evidence of the two Gospels of S. Matthew and S. Luke proves on examination to be historically worthless. Similar legends told about great men can be quoted from other religions. This suggests that the idea was borrowed by the early Christians and consciously or unconsciously fashioned into a story to symbolize Christ's uniqueness. Further, it is more fitting, and in accordance with what we know of God's orderly working, that God's Son should sanctify the ordinary processes of human generation and birth by entering human life in the same manner as ourselves. Such a

---

[1] Mackintosh, *The Person of Jesus Christ*, p. 401; cp. Westcott's notes on Heb 7²⁶ and 4¹⁵.

[2] It is important to distinguish between the Virgin-birth and the 'Immaculate Conception'. They are often confused in popular thought. The 'Immaculate Conception' is the view that by a special miracle S. Mary was conceived and born free from any taint of original sin, that she might be the mother of Christ. Its aim is to secure her sinlessness. There is, however, no hint in Scripture or in any Father before S. Augustine that she was supposed to be sinless. Even he only supposed her to be free from actual sin. The doctrine stands on an entirely different footing from that of the Virgin-birth. It arose as a pious opinion, resting on a slender foundation of human logic. In the Roman Church it was elevated to the rank of a dogma in 1854.

miracle would place Him apart from us. By rejecting the historical truth of the story a spiritual faith is strengthened rather than weakened.[1]

In reply we maintain that this Article of the Christian faith cannot be so lightly swept away.

(i) There is a right order in approaching this question. We do not expect a man to believe in the Virgin-birth who does not believe in the divinity of Christ. As a matter of simple history men did not believe Christ to be God, because He was born of a virgin. Rather by a study of His life and character and by the experience of His redemptive power, they became convinced that He was a unique Person. Then, believing Him to be a unique Person, they were prepared to believe, when they were told it on good authority, that He entered the world in a unique way. We gather from the Acts and the Epistles of S. Paul that the apostolic preaching began with Christ crucified, risen and ascended. Then came the study of His human life. The apostles were primarily witnesses to what they had seen. It was only when men had accepted Him as their Saviour and proved for themselves the power of His risen life, that in due time they were bidden to learn how that earthly life began. Both then and now, the Virgin-birth came first in order of time but last in order of apprehension. Only so far as we have learnt for ourselves the uniqueness of Christ are we able to approach the evidence with the right presuppositions. This, then, explains in part the so-called silence of S. Paul and S. Mark. S. Mark's Gospel has preserved for us what is probably an outline of the earliest Christian preaching as given by S. Peter at Rome. To say that either the apostle or the evangelist did not know of the Virgin-birth is precarious. All that we have the right to say is that it was absent from the earliest preaching. Such silence is only to be expected, when we consider the reserve that always surrounds the mystery of birth. The blessed Mother would hardly have called public attention to such an event. It may be that in her lifetime the secret was jealously confined to a few. Again, when we consider the intimacy between S. Paul and S. Luke, it is hard to suppose that the former was ignorant of an event recorded by the latter. There is no occasion in his extant epistles when we can say that he must have mentioned the Virgin-birth if he knew of it. It may well have lain in the background of his mind, when he spoke of God as 'sending forth His Son born of a woman' (Gal 4^4) or of our Lord as the 'Second Adam', 'the heavenly man', the starting-point of a new humanity (1 Cor 15^{45-47}).

(ii) We must remember that the historical evidence for the event is more than that of two documents, the Gospels of S. Matthew and S. Luke. Behind them stands the witness of the Apostles and the whole of the early Church. It is incredible that if the Apostles had

---

[1] For a temperate statement of the case for rejecting the doctrine, see E. Brunner, *The Mediator*, pp. 322 ff.

taught or were teaching that our Lord was the son of Joseph, these two Gospels should have been accepted without a protest. No doubt, for a long time, the majority of Christians did not know of the Virgin-birth: many may have died without having ever heard of it. But by the time of Ignatius it was accepted without question from Antioch to Ephesus (cp. Ignatius, *ad Eph.* 19, *ad Trall.* 9, *ad Smyrn.* 1). He asserts the reality of our Lord's birth against the Docetists, though it is worth noting that an ordinary birth would have afforded a far stronger argument for his purpose, if he could have taught it. The story of the Virgin-birth must have been made known on very good authority to win so soon such unanimous acceptance. Later in the second century it has a place in the credal summaries which occur in the writings of Justin and Irenaeus. This by itself proves that the Virgin-birth was in full accord with the tradition of the early Church, and formed a part of its current catechetical instruction before the canonization of the Gospels.

When we turn to the two accounts in the Gospels we are struck by their independence. They agree in the main topic that they undertake to narrate, the Virgin-birth, but they differ in detail. There is no actual inconsistency between them, unless we read into either of them statements that are not there, but owing to our lack of knowledge it is not easy to piece all the details together. 'That an event is attested by two stories coming from different sources is usually regarded as affording a presumption of truth, not of falsehood.'[1] In this case we have two independent witnesses, and the source of each account seems to lie in the traditions of the Jewish Church anterior to the fall of Jerusalem.

Let us take S. Luke's Gospel first. With the possible exception of the governorship of Quirinius, we may say that the details of the framework of the story of the birth at Bethlehem have received support and illumination from modern archaeological discoveries.[2] This fact encourages us to trust S. Luke's evidence about the birth itself. It is agreed that behind his first two chapters lie very early sources, strongly Jewish in outlook, and showing no consciousness of the path of shame which Messiah had to tread. The whole tone of the narrative suggests that it came from S. Mary herself. The suggestion has been made to cut out 1^{34-35}, the verses that most clearly assert Mary's virginity. In defence of this excision there is no evidence whatever, internal or external.[3] It is a counsel of despair, only of importance as showing how far men will go to rule out evidence that conflicts with their own preconceived ideas about what the Christian faith ought to

---

[1] Armitage Robinson, *Some Thoughts on the Incarnation*, pp. 32–33; cp. the whole passage, pp. 31–41.

[2] See Ramsey, *Was Christ Born at Bethlehem?* and the commentaries on S. Luke by H. Balmforth (Clarendon Bible) and B. S. Easton (T. & T. Clark).

[3] A single Old Latin MS. (b) omits Mary's question and transposes the text. Cp. Box, *Virgin Birth*, pp. 223–225.

be. It still leaves unsolved the problem of the prominence of Mary throughout these chapters if Joseph was the father. Nor can we explain why she is so carefully styled virgin twice in v. 27.[1]

The account in the first Gospel is written throughout from the side of Joseph. It is Jewish in tone through and through. The writer is eager to search out Old Testament parallels to the events of the birth and infancy of One whom he regards above all as the Messiah. To our minds many of these parallels seem far-fetched. So much so, that it is clear that the writer did not invent the details of the story in order to fulfil Old Testament predictions. The Jews had no special reverence for virginity as such. Hence, it is impossible to explain the existence of the story unless it was believed to be literally true. It has been argued that the whole narrative is only an attempt to create a fulfilment for the prophecy of Isaiah 7[14]. The use of the Old Testament elsewhere by this writer lends no support to such a view. There is at present no evidence that the Jews either applied the passage to the Messiah or expected the Messiah to be born of a virgin. The Hebrew word in the text of Isaiah does not necessarily denote virginity.[2] Again, in 1[16] there are traces of a reading 'Joseph begat Jesus'. Even if this should be correct, the word 'begat' would be used in the same legal sense as elsewhere in the genealogy. Joseph acted as our Lord's legal father. He was known as Jesus son of Joseph. No alternative was possible.

As regards the Gospel of S. John, his silence is a token of consent. He certainly knew the synoptic Gospels, and at times corrects or explains or supplements them. If he had disapproved of the narratives of the Virgin-birth, he would have shown his disapproval. But is he silent? The language of 1[13] when he speaks of Christians as 'born, not of blood, nor of the will of the flesh, nor of the will of man, but of God', suggests an allusion. The Virgin-birth is both type and source of the spiritual new birth of the Christian. If we adopt the reading ὅς . . . ἐγεννήθη, following early Latin versions, the allusion becomes explicit.

Before we leave the evidence of the Gospels, it is well to ask, If we reject their account of the Virgin-birth, what is the alternative? Our opponents reply 'a birth in wedlock'. But that is an alternative for which we have no evidence whatever. The only non-miraculous birth for which there is any evidence at all is a birth out of wedlock. In later days the current Jewish slander was that our Lord was the illegitimate child of Mary. There are evidences for the existence of

---

[1] Cp. also Lk 2[49]. The first recorded words of Christ seem to be a correction of His mother's words, and imply that Joseph was not His father.

[2] The passage in Isaiah is one of the most obscure in the Old Testament. Possibly it rests on an old myth found also in Rev 12[1-6], in which at a time of crisis a deliverer miraculously appears. In this myth the mother may have been a virgin, and the LXX has παρθένος in the passage. But the whole emphasis is laid on the person of the deliverer, not on the manner of his birth. On the account in S. Matthew see McNeile's commentary.

this slander within the Gospels. Why did Mary accompany Joseph to Bethlehem? Why was she in her condition repelled from the inn? The whole story suggests something unusual. In the genealogy, Mt 1^{1-16}, we find the names of four women only, three of whom were of bad character. Their presence may well be a retort to current slanders about the birth of Christ. The Gospel begins with a refutation of the Jewish attack on the birth of Christ, as it ends with a refutation of the Jewish denial of His Resurrection. Again, in Mk 6^3, the people of Nazareth reject our Lord and say, 'Is not this the carpenter, the son of Mary?' The wording is altered in Mt and Lk. 'To designate anyone the son of his mother, whether his father were dead or alive, is almost unknown in the Old or New Testament, and hardly occurs, if at all, in Rabbinic writers. The words were clearly used by the people of Nazareth in an insulting manner; they were referring to rumours which existed as to our Lord's birth.'[1] The same is the simplest explanation of the Jews' retort in Jn 8^{41}, 'We were not born of fornication, we have one father even God.' Such an interpretation would suit admirably the irony of S. John. All the evidence points to something unusual in the birth of Christ. If this is admitted, the Christian conscience will not have much difficulty in deciding what is the true explanation.[2]

(iii) The alleged parallels from the legends of other nations usually break down on examination. Many are demonstrably later than the Gospel stories and are probably echoes of Christian teaching. Others are gross and carnal stories about the lusts of gods and heroes as different as possible from the Christian accounts. We really cannot compare the narratives of the Gospel with these silly tales. The prevalence of such legends does, indeed, witness to a widespread human instinct that the human race could not produce its own deliverer, but needed a divine impulse from above. They would then embody an unconscious feeling after the truth enshrined in the actual Virginbirth. As we have seen, the whole tone and outlook of the narratives is so Jewish that an admixture of pagan legend is incredible. It is equally impossible to find any adequate explanation in Jewish ideas. The only alternative is to regard them as an invention of Christian imagination. But from the first Christianity claimed, as against heathen religions, to be the truth. To suppose that Christians embodied their belief in the uniqueness of Christ in stories that bore the appearance of history, but were really only the work of pious fancy, is to charge them with an offence against one of the first principles of their religion. We do, indeed, find in the ridiculous stories of the

---

[1] Headlam in *C.Q.R.*, October, 1914. See pp. 23–26.
[2] The question has been raised, How could S. Mary have desired to restrain our Lord, as recorded in Mk 3^{31-34}, if she knew of all that is recorded in the stories of His birth? Her estimate of His Person could hardly have been higher than S. Peter's at Caesarea Philippi. Yet he vehemently rebuked the Master whom he had hailed as Messiah. She knew as yet nothing of the glory of the Resurrection.

Apocryphal Gospels the later attempts of Christian imagination to picture the birth and childhood of Christ, and the contrast with the canonical Gospels is most instructive. Such attempts were rejected by the Church as unhistorical. They are valuable only as showing what manner of stories Christians invented when they were unhampered by facts. In short, the Gospel stories cannot be treated as legends unconsciously imported or shaping themselves as the years went on. They are narrated as literal history in the lifetime of those who knew the Mother of Christ.

(iv) To assert that the story of the Virgin-birth may be treated as symbolic, is to misrepresent the place of symbolism. The clause 'born of the Virgin Mary' is in no way comparable to such a clause as 'He sat down at the right hand of the Father'. When we are attempting to describe something that is outside earthly experience we can only employ the language of symbol. We are driven to use metaphors borrowed from this lower world. It is apparent that words which have been coined to express earthly things are inadequate to express heavenly things. In picturing our Lord's ascended life, we can only do our best with human ideas and language. The clause 'He sat down at the right hand of the Father' is only our effort to portray the truth that the highest place of honour in heaven belongs to Him. But when we are dealing with the Virgin-birth we are dealing with an event that, on its physical side, lies within human experience. Human language is as competent to express it as it is to express anything. The language of the first century A.D. was as adequate as our language to-day. To say that the birth-narratives of the Gospels are only symbolic is in effect to say that they are untrue: it is not to reinterpret them but to deny them. As a matter of fact, the Virgin-birth can be supported by analogies from nature far more close than those that can be adduced in the case of some other miracles. Parthenogenesis—to use the scientific term—i.e. birth from a female without the intervention of a male, is not an unknown phenomenon. 'The latest investigations show that parthenogenesis can be artificially produced by an appropriate stimulus in many animals in which it does not naturally occur.'[1] Even among mankind there is evidence of a certain tendency to parthenogenesis. Such scientific facts do not, indeed, abolish the uniqueness of the Virgin-birth, but at least they show that its principle is not incredible. They in their measure support the literalness of the story.

(v) The question, however, still remains, What is the spiritual value of the Virgin-birth? What moral need of man does it satisfy?

Let us begin by admitting that we must not make a priori assertions about it. We do not dare to say that such a birth was the indispensable condition of an Incarnation, or that by no other means could the entail of sin be broken. All we claim is that the Virgin-birth is in

[1] Harris, Pro Fide,[2] p. xl. For evidence of science, see pp. xxxviii–xli.

the fullest accord with the revealed purpose of Christ's coming and with our own highest insight into that purpose.

We may illustrate this by a comparison between the birth of our Lord and the birth of John the Baptist. John's was essentially a birth from the past. In every sense he was a child of old age. His parents were of priestly family, stricken in years, righteous in works of the law. He summed up in himself and his mission both the strength and weakness of the Jewish nation. Theirs was a work of preparation. By the Law was given a knowledge of God's righteousness, a conviction of sin, but not the power to live up to such knowledge. So John could convict men of sin and baptize them with the baptism of repentance, but he could do no more. He waited for one mightier than himself who should baptize with holy Spirit, the breath of new life. But the birth of Jesus Christ of a young maiden of the tribe of Judah by the overshadowing of God's power was in all ways the opposite of the birth of John. Jesus Christ was neither physically, morally, nor spiritually the product of the past. The physical fact was a parable and pledge of the moral and spiritual fact. He brought into humanity what humanity could not achieve for itself, a new and undefiled stream of human life. The entail of weakened will and perverted desire was broken. The alleged parallels from other religions, so far as they really apply, witness to a dim consciousness of this need. Men aspired to be liberated from the fetters of their past and to rise above their inheritance of weakness and shame. Jesus Christ was the starting-point, the re-creation of a new humanity, and not merely the summit of past evolution. We dare not, indeed, affirm that without the Virgin-birth this influx of new life would have been impossible. But we can see how the creative act of God in the physical world was a most fitting counterpart of His re-creative act in the spiritual world.

Again, if Jesus Christ was the natural offspring of Mary and Joseph, it is hard to see how we can regard Him as other than an individual human person. In accordance with ordinary laws of nature the product of such union is in each case a single finite human personality. Christ would therefore be at best an individual man exceptionally favoured by being taken into a unique relation with God. In other words, we find ourselves face to face with a Nestorian Christ, who, as we have seen, cannot be the divine Redeemer known to Christian experience. Again, we find Christ not simply a Son of Man but the Son of Man. His humanity was a universal humanity raised above the limitations of sex and country. He realized the ideal of East and West alike. He combined the most opposite virtues. In other words, the Virgin-birth stands for this, that God did not simply reveal Himself through a single human Person, a Jew, but 'that God once for all and completely incarnated Himself in humanity as His Son, and in that all-comprehensive act made all men His sons—potentially.'[1]

---

[1] Du Bose, *The Gospel in the Gospels*, p. 217.

That is, Jesus Christ is not simply a unique example of manhood outside ourselves, to be admired from afar, but He is the truth of each one of us. We may each find in Him our true self and the power of becoming our true self. Once again, we do not assert that this was not possible without the Virgin-birth; we are content to point out its moral fitness. The spiritual and moral miracle of the existence of Jesus Christ demands an act of God not less unprecedented than the physical miracle.

Lastly, our opponents claim that since a full Christian faith was possible in the earliest days without a belief in the Virgin-birth, it is possible to-day. But it is one thing to be ignorant of a spiritual truth, quite another thing deliberately to reject it, when it has been brought to light. Undoubtedly individuals may abandon a belief in the Virgin-birth and yet retain faith in our Lord's divinity, but it is very questionable whether large bodies of people or the Church as a whole could do so. The experience of the last century tends to show that when men give up a belief in the Virgin-birth of Christ, they pass on to a view of His Person that is not that of the Catholic Church: it may be an up-to-date form of Nestorianism or an open Unitarianism. It is significant that the only opposition to the Virgin-birth in ancient days came from Ebionites and Gnostics, who refused to advance to the Catholic estimate of our Lord's Person. The real central miracle of Christianity that staggers the imagination is the Incarnation. If we once believe that God Himself entered into human life and passed through a human experience, then a belief in the Virgin-birth follows naturally and brings no new difficulty. The historical Incarnation involves a break with the past and a new and unprecedented divine activity, beside which the wonder of the Virgin-birth sinks into insignificance.†

§ 2. The Article then proceeds to affirm the reality of the atoning work of Christ, '*Who truly suffered, was crucified, dead and buried, to reconcile His Father to us, and to be a sacrifice not only for original guilt, but also for all actual sins of men.*'

(*a*) In any endeavour to enter into the meaning of the Atonement we must distinguish between the fact of the Atonement and attempted explanations of the fact or theories about it. It is the fact that is of primary importance. Through Christ crucified, Christians have found peace with God: they have tasted the joy of forgiveness for past sin: they have received new life and strength for the future. 'Being therefore justified by faith, let us have peace with God through our Lord Jesus Christ' (Rom 5[1]); 'Herein is love, not that we loved God, but that he loved us and sent his Son to be the propitiation for our sins' (1 Jn 4[10]); Christ 'his own self bare our sins in his body on the tree, that we, having died unto sins, might live unto righteousness' (1 Pet 2[24]). These are three typical statements from the New Testament, all bearing witness to a common experience. Christians were convinced

that through Jesus Christ they had passed out of darkness into light.
The old sense of condemnation had passed away (Rom 8[1]). They had
received a new capacity for righteousness and love and a new hope in
living (1 Cor 6[9-11], Eph 2[12-13], I Jn 3[14], etc.). Further, they were no
less convinced that this experience might be shared by all men who
would come to Christ in faith and repentance. That this vivid conviction of new life in union with God was no passing fancy of the
imagination was proved by their changed conduct and by the mutual
love and holiness of the Christian fellowship. This is the fact of the
Atonement. Through Christ crucified men of all ages have been
brought into union with God. The Gospel is in the first instance a
proclamation of facts, the invitation to share the pardon and peace
won by the Cross of Jesus Christ. At the same time, Christians have
quite rightly sought to understand the meaning of the Atonement.
As rational beings we are bound to think about what interests us
most. Hence the attempts to interpret the saving work of Christ in
terms of human life and thought. Such attempts are necessary that
the Atonement may make its deepest appeal to the whole of our
nature. Just because it is a revelation of God, shedding light both
upon the character of God and upon the needs and nature of man,
we must strive to grasp the truth that it reveals and bring it home to
ourselves.[1]

(b) In Scripture the atoning work of Christ is most often expressed
in language borrowed from the sacrifices of the Old Covenant. There
is probably no subject on which our ordinary ideas need a more
drastic revision than on the meaning of sacrifice. Modern research
has shown that the fundamental idea of sacrifice is that of fellowship
with God.[2] Sacrifice is found all over the world and seems to spring

---

[1] The word 'atonement' by its derivation means simply at-one-ment, the bringing
together of two parties that have been estranged. (It is so used by Shakspere, e.g.,
Richard III, Act i. Scene 3.) But in modern English, atonement has come to acquire
the meaning 'reparation' or 'making amends': so to our ears it tends to denote the
means by which reconciliation is made possible, rather than the reconciliation itself.
In the A.V. 'atonement' occurs only once in N.T. (Rom 5[11]) as a translation of καταλλαγή. The R.V. substitutes 'reconciliation'. In the O.T. the R.V. retains 'atonement'
in many passages. The word so translated rather means 'propitiation'. The verb
'kipper' comes from a root that means to 'wipe clean'. It is, however, always used
figuratively. Thus, it is used of propitiating a person, where the original idea may have
been wiping clean a face that is blackened by displeasure. It is also used in the passive
of sin being 'wiped out' or cancelled. Elsewhere it is used of God wiping clean either
the offence or the offender, where it practically equals forgiving. In a legal sense it is
used of a priest making propitiation (or atonement, R.V.) for a person or thing, i.e.
wiping it clean by a propitiatory act. In this last sense, at least, it comes to mean the
process by which propitiation is made rather than the propitiation itself, that is, it
corresponds with the modern use of 'atonement' rather than with its original meaning.
(See Driver, Article 'Propitiation' in Hastings' D.B. Since this was written, discoveries
in Babylonia have made it clear that the root-meaning of 'kipper' is to 'wipe clean'
rather than to 'cover' as used to be supposed. Cp. e.g. Dr. Burney, J.Th.S., April, 1910,
or C.Q.R., April, 1915, p. 55.)

[2] Cp. S. Augustine's definition of sacrifice: 'Omne opus quod agitur ut sancta
societate inhaereamus Deo.' See the whole passage, De Civitate Dei, x, 5 and 6.

out of a universal human instinct. Its original meaning is still a matter of dispute.[1] From the nature of the case we cannot now discover who offered the first sacrifice or what he meant by it. The practice may have originated independently at more than one place and not had the same meaning in every place. All that we can do is to note the diverse ideas underlying it as found in historical times. All evidence goes to show that sacrifice has no necessary connexion either with suffering or sin. In the case of friendly gods it was often a simple offering of food made as a tribute of respect or gratitude to the god, as to the head of a tribe. In the case of unfriendly powers it may have been regarded as a bribe to go away and do no more mischief. Again, primitive men claimed to hold communion with the god of their tribe by means of a banquet. Religion, it must be remembered, in primitive times was a purely social concern. The god was the god of the tribe or clan, not of the individual as such. According to primitive ideas communion with the god was effected by eating with him at a common meal. The god, like all the other guests, had his portion of food, which, it may be, was burnt that it might ascend to him. In certain countries the food thus eaten—usually food of a special kind—came to be identified with the flesh of the god himself. The vital union between the tribe and their god was renewed and strengthened by a physical feeding upon the life of the god. These sacrificial meals were occasions of joy and boisterous merriment.[2] Such festal meals are prominent in the earlier parts of the Old Testament. But as the sense of sin grew, men felt that before communion with their god could be attained, the sin or defilement, often in primitive times regarded as physical rather than moral, must be expiated. So the idea of sacrifice as a propitiation, an idea probably present in some degree from the first, was brought to the front. Accordingly, in the later religion of Israel the sin-offering came to be the most prominent. The awakened conscience felt that sin had come between the soul and God and must be removed before communion could be restored. Even so, the older forms of sacrifice, the 'burnt-offerings', which primarily though not exclusively expressed gratitude or homage, and the 'peace-offerings', which concluded in a social meal, still survived. And up to the end certain sacrifices were retained which did not require the death or destruction of any victim such as the meal-offering or the show-bread. In the light of such knowledge we can understand that since Christ by His death had made communion with God possible, that death was inevitably interpreted in the language of sacrifice. Christ had achieved perfectly and for ever all that the old sacrifices had attempted to achieve. In all ancient religions stress was laid on action rather than on belief. What was done and the manner in which it was done was all that

---

[1] Cp. E. O. James, *The Origins of Sacrifice*.
[2] Cp. Robertson Smith, *Religion of the Semites*, Lect. VII, esp. pp. 254–263.

mattered. No doubt certain general ideas lay behind the external rites
of sacrifice, but they were vague and disconnected. Sacrifice was
offered to attain certain recognized ends, but there was no definite
theory of sacrifice. Hence the use of sacrificial terms to express the
Atonement does not involve any single and complete theory about
the Atonement. It is as true to say that for the first Christians the
full meaning of the ancient sacrifices was interpreted by the death of
Christ as that the meaning of His death was interpreted by them.

(c) Turning then to Scripture, we find our Lord not only predict-
ing His death and passion but regarding them as the climax of His
work. He never viewed them as a failure or even as an interruption
to His activity. They had an essential place in His mission. He came
not to live only, but to die (e.g. Lk 12⁵⁰, Jn 12²³⁻²⁴). He always looked
through death to the Resurrection (Mk 8³¹, 9³¹, 10³⁴, etc.). He was
constrained to die not by outward compulsion but by inward necessity. The Scriptures declared His death to be the will of God (Mk 8³¹,
notice δεῖ, 9¹², 14²¹ and ⁴⁹, Lk 24²⁵⁻²⁷). We ask to what passages of
Scripture He referred. Probably certain of the psalms, such as those
on which He meditated upon the Cross. Probably, too, the spiritual
significance of the Old Testament sacrifices as ordained in the Law.
But the clearest passage is that of the Suffering Servant of Jehovah in
Is 53. The Servant takes upon him the sins of others (v. ⁶): his death
is a sin-offering (v. ¹⁰), making reconciliation for many (vv. ¹¹⁻¹²),
and is followed by a resurrection. In Lk 22³⁷ He applies to Himself
words from the description of the Suffering Servant. It is in this
sense, too, that 'The Son of Man came not to be ministered unto but
to minister' (i.e. as a servant) 'and to give his life a ransom for many
(λύτρον ἀντὶ πολλῶν)',[1] i.e. to buy back lives forfeited by sin (Mk 10⁴⁵,
cp. 1 Tim 2⁶). After His Resurrection in the first days of the Church
our Lord is explicitly identified with the Servant (Acts 3¹³ and ²⁶,
4²⁷ and ³⁰, cp. Mt 12¹⁸). His death upon the Cross is explained as the
fulfilment of Is 53 (Acts 8³²⁻³⁵). This reinforces the evidence of the
Gospels as showing that this interpretation of His Cross rests on our

---

[1] Λύτρον in LXX is used of the price paid to redeem a first-born son, whose life
belonged to Jehovah (Num 3⁴⁶), or a slave (Lev 25⁵¹), or a captive (Is 45¹³). We may
compare the teaching of Mk 8³⁷. When a man's life is forfeited, he has nothing to give
in exchange wherewith to buy it back. The Greek word λύτρον may be the equivalent
of either of two Hebrew words, one of which has definite sacrificial associations, being
the substantive from 'kipper'.

The dominant theory of the Atonement in the Church until the time of Anselm, so
far as it had one, was based on this metaphor of 'ransom'. The death of Christ was
viewed as a ransom paid to the Devil. This presses the metaphor too hard. The word
'ransom' is symbolical of the truth that Christ's death has freed us from slavery, and
that this freedom was purchased at a great cost. But when we go on to ask, to whom
was the ransom paid, we are pressing the metaphor beyond the limits of the truth that
it was selected to express. No answer can be given. Israel was often said to have been
ransomed or redeemed from Egypt. Such language laid stress on the mighty exhibition
of God's power and the cost of redemption. But obviously no ransom was paid to
Pharaoh. (Cp. Westcott, Hebrews, p. 297 ff.)

Lord's own teaching. The vision of the Transfiguration suggests that it was through meditation upon the Law and the Prophets that our Lord in His human consciousness learnt the divine necessity of His death (Lk 9³⁰⁻³¹). At the Last Supper in the institution of the Eucharist our Lord clearly attaches a sacrificial value to His death. He views it as inaugurating a new covenant between God and man by which remission of sins was secured to many (Mk 14²⁴, Mt 26²⁸, cp. Exodus 24⁸). He is in some sense the true Paschal Lamb. As the blood of the Paschal Lamb protected Israel from the angel of death, so His atoning blood averts God's judgment from those who take refuge in it.

In the Epistles our Lord's death is at once compared and contrasted with the leading forms of Jewish sacrifice. In Eph 5² the completeness of His self-sacrificing love is expressed under the imagery of the Burnt-offering. In 1 Cor 10¹⁶⁻²¹ and probably Heb 13¹⁰ the simile is rather that of the Peace-offering. Christ the Victim is the food of His people. More often His death is likened to the Sin-offering (Rom 3²⁵ and 8³, where περὶ ἁμαρτίας, according to the constant use of LXX, is the technical term for a sin-offering. 1 Pet 2²⁴ and 3¹⁸, 1 Jn 4¹⁰, and Heb 13¹¹⁻¹², an isolated passage standing apart from the general argument of the Epistle). Throughout Hebrews it is interpreted by the sacrifices on the Day of Atonement. Elsewhere He is regarded as the Lamb of sacrifice (1 Pet 1¹⁹, Rev 5⁶, etc., cp. Jn 1²⁹) and explicitly as the Passover Lamb (1 Cor 5⁸, cp. Jn 19³⁶). Further, the many passages that speak of the 'blood' of Christ imply a similar idea of sacrifice (Rom 5⁹, Col 1²⁰, Eph 1⁷ and 2¹³, 1 Jn 1⁷, Rev 5⁹, etc.). In short, the whole of the New Testament is permeated by sacrificial thought and language, unfamiliar to our modern minds. We need to get behind it to the ideas of universal human interest that it embodies.

(d) When we consider the Old Testament sacrifices, three leading general ideas stand out and find fulfilment in the atoning death of Christ.

(i) These sacrifices rest upon divine appointment. They are means ordained by God Himself by which His people may be brought back into communion with Him or may realize such communion (cp. 2 Sam 14¹⁴). They are never viewed as a means of overcoming God's reluctance to forgive, or as earning God's favour. So, in the New Testament the Atonement from first to last proceeds from the love of God. 'God was in Christ reconciling the world unto himself' (2 Cor 5¹⁸⁻¹⁹). 'It was the good pleasure of the Father . . . through him to reconcile all things unto himself' (Col 1¹⁹⁻²⁰, cp. Eph 2⁴⁻⁶). The Father is always represented as 'sending' the Son to be the Saviour of the world (1 Jn 4¹⁴, cp. Jn 3¹⁶). It was God who set forth Christ as propitiatory (Rom 3²⁵). Any theory of the Atonement that misrepresents it as an appeasing of an angry Father by a merciful Son not only breaks up the Persons of the Trinity, but contradicts the whole

tenor of Scripture. The initiative of the Atonement is always represented as lying with the Father (cp. Rom 5[8]).[1]

(ii) We may divide the process of Old Testament sacrifice into
three main portions, (a) The bringing of the victim to the altar,
(β) The death of the victim, (γ) The presentation of the blood before
God.

(a) The victim was brought by the offerer to the place of sacrifice.
It must be without blemish (Lev 1[3], etc.). There the offerer laid his
hands upon the victim's head, perhaps to signify a very intimate connexion between the offerer and the victim, and made confession of
sin. In the case of our Lord these preliminary actions fairly correspond to His life viewed as the approach to Calvary. His life of
obedience was, as it were, the bringing of the victim to the door of
the tabernacle. He came to do the Father's will. For that end a body
was prepared for Him (Heb 10[5]). By His conquest of temptation He
proved Himself a Lamb 'without blemish' (Heb 9[14], 1 Pet 1[19]). He, as
it were, laid His hand upon His own life by submitting to the discipline of suffering (Heb 5[8]). What in the case of the animal victim
was involuntary and unconscious, was in Him voluntary and conscious. Whereas in the old sacrifices the union between offerer and
victim was no more than outward and conventional, Christ was Himself both offerer and victim. Of His own will He gave Himself up to
die. His death came to Him in the path of duty and He accepted it as
the Father's will.

(β) The victim was slain, not necessarily by the priest at all, since
the slaying of the victim was not essentially a priestly act. Perhaps
the sole object of this was the setting free of the blood, 'which is the
life,' so as to be available for presentation to God. Very possibly it
contained also the acknowledgment that sin deserved death.[2] Here,
too, the New Testament draws the contrast between the involuntary
suffering of an irrational animal and the perfect obedience of the
Cross. The death of Christ was the climax of filial obedience (Heb
5[7-9], Mk 14[36], Phil 2[8], Rom 5[19], etc.). Our Lord voluntarily identified
Himself with men, and willed to endure death on their behalf (Gal 1[4],

---

[1] It has been often urged that in parables such as the Prodigal Son forgiveness is in
no way connected with the death of Christ. We may reply: First, Christ, like any good
teacher, teaches one point at a time. Secondly, in such parables He was addressing men
who were approaching God through Himself. He could speak of the Father's forgiveness unconditionally, because He had come from the Father to be and to do all that
was needed to make possible that forgiveness. We must remember that in the Epistles
stress is laid above all on the Cross and Resurrection, and in the Gospels a very large
proportion of space is given to the story of the death and passion.

[2] Probably a majority of modern scholars would dispute this, and hold that there
was no idea of transference of sins to the victim and of the victim suffering death as the
penalty of sin. Such an idea of penal substitution was certainly not carried through
consistently, but very strong arguments can be adduced in its favour. Some such
thought underlies Is 53 (cp. 2 Cor 5[21] and 1 Pet 2[24]), and is found in later Judaism. See
H.D.B. 'Sacrifice', pp. 340 and 342b, and Mozley, *The Doctrine of the Atonement*,
p. 14 ff.

2²⁰, etc.). As the representative of mankind He offered to the Father a perfect human obedience. Obedience could do no more than die. He made a perfect confession of sin and submitted to death as the due penalty of sin (2 Cor 5²¹). All that the old sacrifices prefigured, He perfectly and in actual fact fulfilled.

(γ) Then, when the blood was shed, the culmination of the sacrifice was reached in the manipulation of the blood by the priest. In the sin-offering it was sprinkled on the horns of the altar. On the Day of Atonement it was carried by the High-priest within the veil and sprinkled on and before the mercy seat. This was the essential act of sacrifice and could only be performed by the priest. It signified not the infliction of death but the offering of life. 'The life of the flesh is in the blood: and I have given it to you upon the altar to make atonement for your souls: for it is the blood that maketh atonement by reason of the life' (Lev 17¹¹). The killing of the victim was a necessary means to this end, but still a means (cp. Heb 9²²). Through the life thus liberated by death propitiation was made. The sin was wiped out and communion with God restored. The New Testament prefers to say that we are saved by the 'blood' of Christ rather than by the 'death' of Christ. That is, we are saved by the life of Christ that was surrendered to God in death, and thus set free to be the means of our atonement. Christ's redeeming work did not end on the Cross. It was consummated when as our high-priest He entered into Heaven to present His life to the Father. 'While the thought of Christ's blood (as shed) includes all that is involved in Christ's Death, the Death of Christ, on the other hand, expresses only a part, the initial part of the whole conception of Christ's Blood. The Blood always includes the thought of the life preserved and active beyond death.'[1] This thought will be developed when we come to the Ascension. We must not isolate the Cross from the Crucified if we wish to understand the meaning of the Atonement. The Cross was indeed the necessary means of our salvation. Only as having been slain, could Christ's life become available for us. But we are saved by a living Christ, not merely by something that He once did. Here again the 'blood' of Christ stands in contrast with the blood of victims. The life of the victims was only conventionally alive after death. But the life of Christ through death is a glorious reality. He has become all that He now is through the Cross. His 'blood' is Himself, His own life. As the 'Lamb that hath been slain' He is the 'propitiation for our sins' (1 Jn 2²).

(iii) The purpose of the Old Testament sacrifices was not exhausted by the removal of the sin. The people were restored to full communion with God in order that they might continue in His service. So the object of our Lord's atonement includes far more than a bare

---

[1] Westcott, *The Epistles of S. John*, Note on 'The idea of Christ's Blood', pp. 35–36. Cp. Milligan, *Resurrection*, Note 56.

forgiveness of sins. We are saved in order that we may serve, and in God's service find our true satisfaction. We are redeemed from evil that we may become something good. Through an abiding union with God made possible by Christ we are to live henceforth our true life as Sons of God. Christ is to be to us day by day a living Saviour imparting to us through the Holy Spirit His own life. As redeemed we are progressively to appropriate all the blessings of God's people (1 Pet 1⁴, cp. Rom 8¹⁷). No view of the Atonement can be satisfactory that ignores the work of the Holy Spirit in us, transforming us into the very likeness of Christ and sanctifying all our life. We are to do all things 'in Christ'. As members of Christ we are to share the joy and peace that the Spirit brings (cp. Gal 5²²⁻²³, Rom 14¹⁷). The Christian life here and hereafter is the goal for which we were saved. 'If while we were enemies, we were reconciled to God by the death of his Son, much more being reconciled, shall we be saved by his life' (Rom 5¹⁰).

(e) How then, it may be asked, can the Article speak of Christ dying 'to reconcile the Father to us'? Such language suggests that the Atonement wrought a change of mind in God towards us. We must admit that in all the passages in Scripture in which the word 'reconcile' is employed in connexion with the work of Christ, the fact is expressed the other way round. We are said to be reconciled to God, not God to us. That is to say, the change, according to our use of the term, is said to be wrought in us, not in Him (Rom 5¹⁰⁻¹¹, 2 Cor 5¹⁸⁻²⁰, Eph 2⁶, Col 1¹⁹⁻²²). But even if the form of expression in the Article is not scriptural, the truth that underlies it is. The Greek word (καταλλάσσω) translated 'reconcile' simply means to re-establish friendly relations between persons.[1] On which side the hostility exists is not determined by the word itself. Thus in Mt 5²⁴ the grievance is on the side of the brother of the man who is about to offer a sacrifice. Yet it is the man himself who is bidden 'to be reconciled'. In English idiom we should say that the brother needed to be reconciled. The moment that we grasp that the Atonement is at bottom a personal matter, we can see that a change on one side inevitably carries with it a change on the other. Further, we hear much in Scripture of the 'wrath' of God, as a present and not only a future attitude towards sinners (e.g. Rom 1¹⁸, Eph 5⁶, etc.). So, as unredeemed, men are said to be ἐχθροί 'hostile' to God. In some passages this may have a purely active sense, 'hating God,' but in Rom 11²⁸ it is certainly passive, being opposed to ἀγαπητοί, 'beloved,' and this suggests that a passive meaning cannot be entirely excluded elsewhere (e.g. Col 1²¹, Jas 4⁴). Again, it is true that the New Testament never speaks of 'propitiating God'. 'The propitiation is spoken of as being made in the matter of sin or the sinner. . . . That is, the

---

[1] Cp. Bengel on Rom 3²⁴ καταλλαγή est δίπλευρος et tollit (α) indignationem *Dei* adversum *nos* 2 Cor 5¹⁹, (β) *nostramque* abalienationem a *Deo* 2 Cor 5²⁰.

sin is regarded as an obstacle to communion, which alienates man
from God and is removed by the propitiation.'[1] On the other hand,
such words as propitiation (ἱλασμός) imply a person in the background. Someone must be propitiated, and who, if not God?[2]

But the real question goes deeper. Since God is holy, His relation
to sin must be one of active hostility, not of passive dislike. It is
impossible to think of God as not filled with unceasing energy against
all that is evil. That is the meaning of the 'wrath of God'. We are too
apt to limit our picture of the divine wrath by the analogy of human
wrath. In the case of men anger has almost always an element of
selfishness. It springs not from a pure love of good and hatred of evil,
but from mixed motives, pride, malice, and the like. It is often
arbitrary and personal. But even so a true zeal for righteousness involves a certain fierceness against wrong. 'Neither doth he abhor anything that is evil' is a terrible condemnation of a man's character.
In God His wrath is not a burst of feeling that overcomes Him and
leads Him into actions inconsistent with His character. It is rather
one aspect of His abiding love, as it deals with the sin that opposes
and wars against that love. It is the reaction of God's holiness against
transgressions. It is quite true that God's love never changes. But
love that is incapable of moral indignation against all that violates
and opposes love, or that is slow in putting forth a destroying energy
against it, falls short of the highest love. The Atonement does not
create God's love: as we have seen, it starts from that love. But it does
enable that love to act differently towards us by removing the sin that
has impeded its free activity. By repentance we do not change God's
will towards us, but we are changed ourselves, so that God can treat
us differently; hence, from our point of view and in relation to us
the attitude of God appears to change. The principle on which He
treats us is unchanged, but the treatment itself changes. The mind of
God toward sin is unaltered—it is our mind towards sin that has to
be transformed, not His—but the change in ourselves makes possible
a new personal relationship. To say that He is reconciled to us represents a real fact of personal experience. It expresses in the language
of human friendship the conviction that through the Cross of Christ
we have passed into the full light of God's favour.

(*f*) The question is often raised, Is the Atonement 'subjective'[3] or
'objective'? That is, does its efficacy lie in the appeal of the Cross
to our heart and conscience, or in some work that Christ did outside
us? The only true answer is that the Atonement must be both subjective and objective. On the one hand we must remember that the
problem of Atonement is very largely a moral problem. If men are to

---

[1] See Westcott, *Epistles of S. John*, p. 87. Cp. C. H. Dodd, *The Bible and the Greeks*, c. v.

[2] Cp. Sanday and Headlam, *Romans*, p. 91.

[3] For a discussion of the application of the word 'subjective' to theories of the Atonement, see K. E. Kirk in *Essays Catholic and Critical*, p. 255.

be brought into full union with God, their characters must become such that they are capable of entering into this life. The estrangement due to sin is not the result merely of a number of acts of sin, but of the state of mind and soul which issued in these acts. Our Lord died not simply to save us from the penalty of sin but from sin itself. Only men who have learnt to will what God wills, love what God loves, and hate what God hates, are able to enter into the fulness of the divine life. Just as no friendship is possible between men of utterly divergent tastes and ideals, so fellowship with God is impossible so long as we are alienated from Him in our wills and affections. The Atonement, therefore, must certainly be subjective in that it effects an entire change in us. But we must also maintain that the Atonement is also objective. By our sinful acts we have set free forces of desolation and disorder in the world. The evil consequences of our acts are not limited to our own characters. Mere penitence in us cannot undo the past. Hence, a true atonement must not only change us, but, as it were, provide healing and restorative power by which the evil consequences·of our sins in others and in the world at large may be repaired. Again, though the Atonement is primarily a moral problem, as between persons, still we should hesitate to say that it was only a moral problem. Our relation to Almighty God is more complex than our relation to our neighbour. He is our Creator and Preserver and King, with an unconditional claim upon our whole lives. Sin as against Him is something at once more rebellious and more unnatural than as against even the closest or the most authoritative of our fellow-men. Human analogies at their highest go a very long way in attempting to understand the meaning of the Atonement, but it is rash to assume that they go the whole way.

(i) Scripture quite recognizes the subjective value of the Atonement. In Rom 3^{25} ff. the Cross is viewed as the demonstration of the seriousness of sin. It has made it possible for God to forgive us without the danger of seeming to be indifferent to sin (cp. 2^4). It is an exhibition of the righteousness of God, bringing home to our conscience the awfulness of sin and showing up its blackness. Elsewhere Scripture speaks of the Cross as manifesting the infinite self-sacrifice of God's love (Rom 5^8). We see God on the Cross bearing the sins of men (cp. 1 Pet 2^{21} ff.). Calvary is the disclosure in time of the wounds that our disobedience is ever inflicting upon the heart of God. There we see the effect of our sins on the love of God laid bare. In the light of such a revelation we cannot continue to go on wounding one who bears our blows so unresistingly and meekly. His patient love must win our hearts and smite our consciences with shame. By every sin that we commit we crucify Christ afresh (cp. Heb 6^6 and 10^{29}). Thus the Cross leads us to repentance. It arouses in us new and deeper sorrow for sin. The love of the Crucified melts the stubbornness of our hearts. The Cross is at once the declaration of God's eternal willingness to bear with men and to forgive the penitent sinner and also the means of awakening penitence in us. The Cross has proved itself able to draw out love and penitence and so to make men at one with God. For the Cross is the supreme example of the purifying energy of self-sacrificing love.[1]

(ii) On the other hand, the above view of the Atonement does not express the whole truth. It does not do justice to all the language of Scripture. From first to last Scripture grounds our acceptance with God not simply on what Christ was or taught, but on what He has done. No doubt it is true that He could only do all that He did by being what He was. But it is no less true that He has become the Saviour that He is to-day, by doing what He did upon the Cross. All the language of sacrifice, all the phrases about the 'blood' of Christ involve the belief that His death opened up new possibilities, and that on the Cross He achieved an atoning act in some sense independent of its apprehension by us. The Atonement is the divine counterpart in action to the 'wrath of God', which wrath a merely subjective view is obliged to minimize or explain away. God is indeed love, but He is holy love, and such love when faced with sin can only issue in active antagonism. Christ on the Cross is not only the patient sufferer, but by His acceptance of death acknowledges the justice of the divine wrath. The death of Christ has a Godward as well as a Manward aspect, though we may find difficulty in entering into its meaning.

From another standpoint the merely 'subjective' view fails to satisfy the demands of our moral nature. We need something deeper than even the fullest disclosure of God's love; we need a transformation of the entire man from within, the infusion of new life and strength. Though we may hesitate to set a limit to the redeeming influence of love, our mind and conscience demand that any revelation of love shall be in the closest relation to our own moral needs. We feel that the Cross is more than a bare exhibition of divine love. Why should the exhibition of love take that form?[2] At present in many quarters there is a prejudice against any doctrine of substitution. Doubtless there have been gross and immoral doctrines of substitution. Men have supposed that so much suffering was the penalty for sin and that the penalty was paid by our Lord's suffering on the

---

[1] Cp. Dinsmore, *The Atonement in Literature and Life*, pp. 232–233. 'As the flash of the volcano discloses for a few hours the elemental fires at the earth's centre, so the light on Calvary was the bursting forth through historical conditions of the very nature of the Everlasting. There was a cross in the heart of God before there was one planted on the green hill outside of Jerusalem. And now that the cross of wood has been taken down, the one in the heart of God abides, and it will remain so long as there is one sinful soul for whom to suffer.'

[2] 'To die in order to display love, if there were no other adequate cause for dying, would be to reduce the Atonement to a mere pageant.' *Life of Bp. Edward Bickersteth*, p. 408.

Cross, or that the Father was pleased by the mere quantity of suffering, not by the obedience perfected through suffering. They have forgotten that Christ died not merely to save us from the punishment of sin but from sin itself. But there is also a true and most valuable doctrine of substitution. Scripture teaches most clearly that Christ came to do for us what we could not do for ourselves. As our representative He offered to the Father the homage of a perfected human life, obedient even unto death, a full confession of the sinfulness of sin, and a willingness to endure that death which is its punishment.[1] He did all this 'on our behalf', not that we might continue to be disobedient and impenitent, but that through Him we might have the power to do as He did. He created a new possibility of human' obedience and penitence which He imparts through the Holy Spirit to His members. Thus His obedience and hatred of sin are not a substitute for our own in the sense that we need not trouble to acquire them. But they are a substitute for our own in the sense that we could never have achieved them by ourselves, and only through Him are we now able to begin to achieve them. As we shall see, God accepts us here and now in Christ, since, in Christ, there is the possibility of our becoming all that we ought to be. Our present peace with God depends not upon the emotions aroused in us by the Cross of Christ, nor even in the promptings after holiness that the love of God awakens in us, but on what Jesus Christ is now and became through the Cross. In a very real sense He was there made sin for us (2 Cor 5[21], 1 Pet 2[24]). He paid the price of our redemption, that through Him we might be reconciled to God.

Note on the 'Victory' theory.—Dr. Aulen's book, *Christus Victor* (English translation 1931), drew fresh attention to this aspect of the Atonement. He maintains that the theme of Christ's work as *God's victory* over sin, death, and the devil dominates the thought of the New Testament and the Patristic Age on redemption. This may therefore be called the 'classic' theory of the Atonement. In contrast to this S. Anselm in the early Middle Ages for the first time gave a clear formulation of the 'Latin' theory of a *just satisfaction* offered to the Father by Christ *as man* through His death. In reaction to this Latin theory, based on legal ideas of justice and penitential works, there arose the Abelardian or 'subjective' view of Christ's death as God's appeal to man to repent. The characteristic defects of these two lines of thought do not appear in the victory theory, which makes no use

---

[1] Cp. Sparrow Simpson, *Reconciliation between God and Man, e.g.* 'The heavenly Father heard something entirely new upon the earth. It was a human voice pronouncing perfect judgment on human sin; perfectly concurring in the judgment of the Father upon sin; gathering up and pressing into one and perfecting all the earth's imperfect reparations; and offering a perfect sorrow for the sin of the world' (p. 128). It is this truth that Article 31 and the Prayer of Consecration express, when they say that Christ made 'satisfaction' for the sins of the world. The term 'satisfaction' is not scriptural but it represents an essential part of the teaching of Scripture on the death of Christ.

of legal views of sin and satisfaction, and at the same time sees redemption as an objective work of the divine power and love.

The merits of the 'classic' theory as expounded by Aulen are clear.
It undoubtedly reproduces much of the thought of the New Testament and the Fathers. It does not isolate the death on the Cross from
the victory of the Resurrection. It takes into account the corporate
character of sin. It insists that the work of redemption was initiated
and carried through by God, who by Christ's death and resurrection
achieved the eschatological victory over all the powers of evil. Room
must be found for the element of victory in any complete view of the
Atonement. Our Lord's perfect obedience was achieved at the cost of
conflict. Moreover, redemption conceived as the coming of the Kingdom of God, necessarily involved conflict with and triumph over
sin, death and the devil, which all contradict the divine sovereignty
(cp. Mt 12[28]). The Lord's resurrection was thus the first-fruits of the
victorious new creation of the last days; to participate in this new
creation is for Christ's members their eschatological hope, partially
realized here and now in the life of grace. No doctrine of Christ's
redeeming work can afford to neglect these points.

But against Aulen it must be noticed that Anselm's doctrine contained a truth, whatever defects may be found in his presentation of
it. The primitive conception of redemption included the idea of a
sacrificial offering 'for sin', made to the Father by Christ as man's
Head and Representative[1] *from within the human race*. Just as no
sacrifice for sin could be perfect without the conquest of sin, so the
conquest of sin on behalf of mankind could not bring back man to
God without a sacrificial acknowledgement of sin made by the Son
of Man to the Father. By itself the victory theory is therefore incomplete, and in some forms of its emphasis on a *divine* victory it is in
danger of minimizing the significance of our Lord's self-identification with man in the Incarnation.†

[1] For a note on Christ as 'man's Representative' or 'inclusively Man', see *Essays
Catholic and Critical*, p. 277.

THE RESURRECTION, THE ASCENSION AND THE JUDGMENT

ARTICLE III

Of the going down of Christ into Hell	*De descensu Christi ad Inferos*
As Christ died for us, and was buried : so also it is to be believed that he went down into Hell.	Quemadmodum Christus pro nobis mortuus est et sepultus, ita est etiam credendus ad Inferos descendisse.

The need of a separate Article to deal with this portion of the Creed was due to the many and violent controversies that raged around it about the time of the Reformation. Our present Article dates from 1563. The previous Article of 1552 was more definite. It clearly interpreted the descent as meaning that 'The body lay in the sepulchre until the resurrection : but His ghost departing from Him was with the ghosts that were in prison or hell, and did preach to the same, as the place of S. Peter doth testify.' Thus the Article took sides in the controversy by laying down a fixed interpretation of the clause in dispute. Though this interpretation is undoubtedly right, it was thought wiser to leave the precise meaning of the descent undefined.

ARTICLE IV

Of the Resurrection of Christ	*De resurrectione Christi*
Christ did truly arise again from death, and took again his body, with flesh, bones, and all things appertaining to the perfection of Man's nature, wherewith he ascended into Heaven, and there sitteth, until he return to judge all men at the last day.	Christus vere a mortuis resurrexit, suumque corpus cum carne, ossibus, omnibusque ad integritatem humanae naturae pertinentibus, recepit : cum quibus in coelum ascendit, ibique residet, quoad extremo die ad judicandos homines reversurus sit.

One of the Articles of 1553. Practically unchanged since. It is worded so as to assert not only the fact of the Resurrection, but also the reality of our Lord's risen and ascended Manhood in opposition to a form of Docetism, revived by the Anabaptists, which regarded our Lord's Humanity as absorbed into His Divinity after the Resurrection.

§ 1. In the A.V., unfortunately, the same word 'hell' is employed as the translation both of the Hebrew 'Sheol' or Greek 'Hades', the place of departed spirits, and also of 'Gehenna', the place of torment. In the R.V. this has been corrected. 'Sheol' or 'Hades' is in itself a neutral term.[1] By the time of our Lord popular Jewish belief had indeed come to regard it as a place of moral distinctions and as divided into two parts,[2] the one 'Abraham's Bosom' or 'Paradise', the abode of the righteous, the other the abode of the wicked. But generally speaking this last was distinguished from Gehenna.[3] In the book of Enoch, for instance, a composite work dating largely from the second century B.C., Gehenna is clearly a place of final punishment for the wicked, who are at present afflicted in a part of Hades until the day of judgment.

Accordingly, by the 'descent into Hell' we mean that our Lord's human soul, after its separation from His body by death, passed into that state of existence into which all men pass at death. In speaking about life after death at all we are driven to resort to symbolical language. We know that the body remains, but that the real self is no longer active through it. We naturally speak of the separation of the soul and body. The men of our Lord's day regarded Hades as a place situated underneath the earth, and the soul as literally going down to it. By us such language can only be used metaphorically. Whatever the mode of life be that is enjoyed by the self after death, we cannot help speaking of it in such metaphors as are derived from our present life in space. We are compelled to imagine Hades as a 'place'. Since our Lord was truly Man, after death He shared man's condition then no less than during His life on earth. That is the only point on which we can be definite. Thus in Lk 23[43], using current Jewish language, He promised to the penitent robber 'Verily, I say unto thee, to-day thou shalt be with me in Paradise.' He pledged His word that He and the robber would be sharing a common life, a life in which personality would not be obliterated, but 'I' would remain 'I' and 'Thou' remain 'Thou', and in which recognition and fellowship would be possible. He spoke of Himself and the robber as both alike enjoying one and the same 'Park of God'. Again, S. Peter applies to our Lord the words of Psalm 16[10] 'Thou wilt not leave my soul in Hades, neither wilt thou give thy holy one to see corruption' (Acts 2[27]). After showing that they received no fulfilment in David himself, he finds their fulfilment in the Resurrection of Christ (v. [31]). It is clear that he regards our Lord as having been in Hades between His death on Good Friday and His Resurrection on the third day. In S. Paul's Epistles a probable allusion can be found in Eph. 4[9], 'Now that he ascended, what is it also but that he descended into the lower parts

---

[1] The Latin translation 'Inferi' or 'Inferna' is similarly neutral. So was 'Hell' in mediaeval English.

[2] Our Lord employs this imagery in the parable of Dives and Lazarus (Lk 16[22]). We must not, however, claim His authority for the literal truth of the details.

[3] See Salmond, Article 'Hell', Hastings' D.B. vol. ii.

of the earth? (εἰς τὰ κατώτερα μέρη τῆς γῆς). He that descended is the same also that ascended far above all the heavens, that he might fill all things.'[1] Others, however, refer the words to the descent to earth at the Incarnation. But the most difficult passage still remains. In 1 Pet 3[18] we read 'Christ also suffered for sins once, the righteous for the unrighteous, that He might bring us to God, being put to death in the flesh, but quickened in the spirit' (πνεύματι i.e. our Lord's human spirit; there is no reference to the Holy Spirit as the A.V. mistranslation suggests): 'in which' (i.e. in His human spirit thus quickened at the moment of death) 'also he went and preached unto the spirits in prison, which aforetime were disobedient, when the long-suffering of God waited in the days of Noah.' Again, in 4[6] 'For unto this end was the gospel preached even unto the dead, that they might be judged according to men in the flesh, but live according to God in the spirit.' These two passages must be taken together, and so taken, they leave very little room for doubt as to S. Peter's meaning. He teaches that at the moment of death our Lord's human spirit went to Hades, and during His stay there preached salvation 'to the spirits in prison', i.e. the souls of dead men, in a like mode of existence to His own. In 3[20] special mention is made of those who rejected the warnings of Noah and perished in the flood (Gen 7[23-24]). But in 4[6] the 'dead' must be the same as the 'dead' in the previous verse, and include all who are not living. Why then are the men before the flood specially mentioned? Probably because they were typical of stubborn sinners; and there is some evidence that their salvation was a subject of discussion in the Jewish schools.[2]

The earliest Christian tradition, probably quite independent of this Epistle, supports the above interpretation.[3] This picture of Christ ministering to the departed made a great appeal to primitive Christian imagination. Allusions to it are found as early as Ignatius, Hermas and Justin Martyr. Till the time of S. Augustine no other interpretation was attempted. In his earlier writings he accepted the

---

[1] In the LXX of Psalm 63[10] τὰ κατώτατα τῆς γῆς is used of 'the lower parts of the earth', i.e. Hades. So in the LXX of Psalm 139[16] the same Greek is used to translate 'the lowest parts of the earth' used metaphorically of the womb. It is therefore at least possible that S. Paul is using a very similar phrase in the same sense and is referring to the descent into Hades as a proof of our Lord's sovereignty over the underworld (cp. Phil 2[10]). See Armitage Robinson, ad loc. 'The descent is to the lowest as the ascent to the highest, that nothing may remain unvisited.' Probably in Rom 10[7] S. Paul is adapting the language of Deuteronomy to express this same idea. 'The abyss' would include Hades. See Sanday and Headlam, ad loc.

[2] See Bigg. ad loc. 'In the Book of Enoch . . . will be found obscure and mutilated passages which may be taken to mean that the antediluvian sinners, the giants and the men whom they deluded, have a time of repentance allowed them between the first judgment (the Deluge) and the final judgment at the end of the world.' See also his note on 4[6].

[3] The earliest allusion to 1 Pet 3[18] and 4[6] seems to be in a saying of 'the Elders' quoted by Irenaeus (iv. 27, 2). See Swete, *Apostles' Creed*, pp. 57–60.

current teaching, though he wrongly identified Hades with Gehenna.[1] Later, in a letter to Evodius, Bishop of Uzala,[2] he explained S. Peter as meaning that Christ was in spirit in Noah, when Noah preached repentance to the men of his day. His authority lent great weight to this view in the Western Church, and it was adopted by Thomas Aquinas and many of the Reformers. It was often combined, as even by Bishop Pearson, with the view that Christ having died 'in the similitude of a sinner' went to Gehenna. But it is unnatural and quite indefensible. The interpretation that Christ preached to the dead fits in admirably with contemporary Jewish ideas and alone does full justice to the two passages taken together. The only other possible interpretation of the 'spirits in prison' would be to suppose that fallen angels are meant (cp. 2 Pet 2[4], Jude [6]), but this introduces an idea quite alien to the context and breaks the connexion between 3[19] and 4[6], besides using the word 'spirit' in a different sense from the previous sentence (3[18]).[3] Still less can be said for Calvin's idea that the descent into hell meant that in Gethsemane and on the Cross our Lord suffered all the agonies of the lost. This confuses Hades and Gehenna, and supposes that the Incarnate Son of God was personally exposed to the wrath of the Father.[4]

The fact conveyed in the clause 'He descended into hell' must be acknowledged by all who allow that our Lord was and is truly Man and that He really died. The further interpretation of His Descent as a mission to the unseen world rests on the evidence both of Scripture and independent primitive tradition. From the nature of the case too exact definition is impossible. We can only speak of life beyond the grave in picture language. The ministry to the departed cannot be attested by the evidence of eye-witnesses. The only historical evidence that can lie behind our records and the tradition of the Church, would be words of our Lord Himself. In the word from the Cross at least we get a revelation of the nature of the future life by one who claimed to know. But the words of S. Peter hint at possibilities that must appeal to the highest in us. The Descent into Hell stands for the truth that whatever condition awaits us after death, our Lord has been there before us and consecrated it by His presence. It suggests that bodily death may be the moment of quickening into a more vigorous life and opens up vistas of a ministry for His faithful servants in the world beyond the grave more fruitful even than any ministry here. Above all, it harmonizes with the instinctive belief of our hearts that Christ will in His own way reveal Himself to

---

[1] E.g. de Gen. ad litt. xii. 61.   [2] Aug. Ep. 164.
[3] See, however, E. G. Selwyn, *The First Epistle of S. Peter*, esp. Essay I, for a different view. This essay gives a full discussion of the evidence and of the points at issue in the interpretation of these passages of 1 Peter.
[4] Cp. Pearson's criticism: 'There is a worm that never dieth which could not lodge within His breast; that is a remorse of conscience, seated in the soul, for what that soul hath done.'

those who have had no opportunity of knowing Him in this life. Though a formal statement of this Article of the faith was absent from the earliest creed-forms, we may believe that the Western Church was rightly guided in including it in her developed statement of the faith.

§ 2. (a) The Christian Church owes her existence to the Resurrection. The Risen Christ is the centre of her life and teaching. The Apostles were chosen above all to be witnesses of the Resurrection (Acts 1^8, 2^{32}, 3^{15}, $4^{2 \text{ and } 33}$, 10^{41}, 13^{31}, etc.). For this task they were fitted by character and condition of life. Their very limitations, their slowness of mind and lack of imagination rendered them all the more reliable as witnesses. Their matter-of-fact outlook and practical turn of mind enabled them to give a straightforward and unanimous testimony to what they had seen. They had neither the inclination nor the ability to construct theories or to adapt facts to suit preconceived ideas. They impressed the world as having an intense belief in the truth of their message, based on their own observation. So only an eye-witness could be selected to fill the place of Judas (Acts 1^{22}). S. Paul, too, rested his apostleship in large part on the fact that he had seen the risen Christ (1 Cor 9^1, 15^{8-9}). It is abundantly clear that the earliest apostolic preaching centred in the Cross and Resurrection, as interpreted by the Christian Church.

In Scripture the chief lines of thought may be summed up thus:

(i) In the early speeches in the Acts the Resurrection is regarded as the divine reversal of man's judgment and as vindicating the Messiahship of Jesus of Nazareth (Acts $2^{32 \text{ and } 36}$ 'God hath made him both Lord ($\kappa\acute{\nu}\rho\iota\sigma$) and Messiah ($\chi\rho\iota\sigma\tau\acute{\sigma}\varsigma$), this Jesus whom ye crucified'). In the light of the prevalent interpretation of Deut 21^{23} the Cross was regarded as a sign of God's malediction. To the Jew, therefore, it was a clear disproof of His claims. It declared 'Jesus accursed' (cp. 1 Cor 12^3). The thought of a crucified Messiah was self-contradictory. Hence the Resurrection was proclaimed as proving the Jewish idea false: it was God's public attestation of the claims of the crucified (Acts 5^{30-31}). To the apostles it was also the fulfilment of our Lord's own predictions about Himself, thus proving His claims true (Mk 8^{31}, 10^{34}, etc., cp. Jn 2^{22}, 10^{18}). So to S. Paul the Resurrection is the ground of assigning to our Lord full Messianic authority (Rom 1^4, cp. Acts 13^{33}).

(ii) The Resurrection certified our Lord's death as redemptive. The apostles were able, out of the Jewish Scriptures, to explain the meaning and necessity of the death of the Messiah as foretold by the prophets. They identified our Lord with the 'suffering servant' of Is 52–53 (Acts 3^{26}, $4^{27 \text{ and } 30}$, $\pi\alpha\hat{\iota}\varsigma$ 'Servant' R.V., not 'child' as A.V.). The rising from the dead marked the acceptance of the sacrifice of the Cross. It is, as has been well said, 'the Amen of the Father to the "It is finished" of the Son.' The same thought of the Resurrection as the seal of our Lord's atoning death is found in S. Paul (*e.g.* Rom 4[25], 5[10], 6[4], 1 Cor 15[17], 1 Thess 1[10], etc., cp. Heb 13[20]).[1]

(iii) The Resurrection is regarded as the pledge of man's resurrection (1 Cor 15[12] ff., Rom 8[11], 1 Thess 4[14]). Not only do Christians here and now receive new life (Eph 2[5-9], Col 3[1]) as sharing the life of the Risen Christ, but from the first (Acts 4[2]) the Resurrection has been proclaimed as the assurance of a resurrection from the dead that will quicken the whole man and that is yet to come (cp. 2 Tim 2[18]).

(*b*) Our belief in the Resurrection of our Lord depends upon three main lines of evidence:

(i)   The appearances of the Risen Lord to many persons of different kinds, at different times and under different conditions.
(ii) The empty tomb.
(iii) The living experience of the Christian Church.

(i) The earliest witness in writing is that of S. Paul. In 1 Cor 15[3-8] he gives what is perhaps an official list of appearances. Behind S. Paul is the witness of the whole Church. He and all Christians were alike in their belief. In fact the very existence of the Church at all presupposes the existence of a belief that Christ was risen. The Resurrection had been put in the forefront of the apostolic preaching from the first. It is implied in all S. Paul's epistles. In all four Gospels we have an account of the finding of the tomb empty. S. Mark is unfortunately mutilated, but there can be no doubt that it went on to describe appearances of the risen Lord similar to those in the other gospels. It is not easy to fit together all the accounts of the appearances on Easter morning. There are apparent differences of detail. This, however, increases rather than diminishes the value of the evidence. It shows that we have the faithful testimony of independent witnesses, not the blind repetition of an official tale. Witnesses of any event, especially when it was observed in a moment of intense excitement, tend to vary in detail. Any judge would view with suspicion a too exact correspondence. Equally important, too, is the evidence of the Acts. The early chapters bear traces of a very primitive Christology. We see the Church, as it were, feeling her way towards a fuller understanding of all that the Resurrection meant. In 1 Pet 1[3] we seem to get a personal reminiscence of S. Peter's own mind.

(ii) All the Gospels record that the tomb was found empty. Like the Passion narrative, the story of the Resurrection must have been put into shape in the oral stage of the tradition at a very early date. In the written Gospels we can trace here and there embellishments of the narrative, notably in S. Matthew (*e.g.* the earthquake at the descent of the angel, the guard at the tomb, the resurrection of the saints). But the discovery of the empty tomb on the third day is a

---

[1] Cp. Westcott, *The Gospel of the Resurrection*, c. i. § 56–59.

basic element in the tradition. Moreover, it is attested by independent and earlier evidence supplied by S. Paul, who in 1 Cor
15³ f. reproduces the statement which he had himself received, *viz.*,
'that Christ died . . . that he was buried, and that he was raised on
the third day . . . ' This formal pre-Pauline statement, going back to
a very few years after the events, implies by its reference to the burial
that the Resurrection involved the empty tomb.[1] Like the Gospels it
refers to the 'third day'. We have in fact no trace of any primitive
account of the Resurrection and its immediate sequel in the appearances which does not include a reference to the disappearance of our
Lord's body from the tomb. The fact that the Gospels do not
attempt to describe[2] the event of the Resurrection itself supports the
veracity of this testimony about the discovery made by the women on
Easter morning.

(iii) From the first, Christians have manifested in their lives the
power of the risen Christ. It is clear that something remarkable must
have happened to change the timid and weak disciples of Good
Friday into the dauntless and courageous leaders of the Church that
we discover in the Acts. The apostles themselves ascribed their
transformation to the power of the Resurrection. So, too, we find
the Christian Church observing the first day of the week as a memorial of the rising from the dead. Sunday is a new institution. It was
not, it has never been and never can be the Jewish Sabbath. In origin
and meaning it is a purely Christian festival, a weekly remembrance
of the Resurrection. And the Christian service, the 'breaking of
bread', was not a sad commemoration of a dead and absent Master,
but a thanksgiving for the blessings imparted by a living and triumphant Saviour. Christian Baptism again loses its distinctive meaning
if Christ is not raised.[3] The continued existence and vitality of the
Church, her survival not only of attacks by enemies from outside,
but of sloth and dissensions among her own members, prove that
her life does not spring from a delusion. In every age the enemies of
our religion have always declared that it was about to pass away, but
their expectations have never been fulfilled. Once more Christians in
all ages have claimed to hold communion with a living Lord and to
receive from Him cleansing and strength. It may be argued that the
inner religious experience of Christians carries conviction only to
those who share it, and they may be mistaken in their explanation of
it. But apart from the widespread consensus of testimony from men
and women of every rank and class and country, we may point to a
definite and persistent type of character produced in the lives of

---

[1] Since the statement is not S. Paul's own, its interpretation is not affected by any
view which he may be supposed to hold about the relation of the risen body to the
fleshly body.

[2] The second-century apocryphal Gospel of Peter does not hesitate to describe the
emergence of the risen Lord from the tomb.

[3] Cp. Rom 6⁴, where the whole symbolism of baptism is worked out in connexion
with the Resurrection.

those who claim to depend on Christ. The Christian character entered into the world as something new. It startled and attracted Jews and heathen alike by its humility and joyousness, its new standard of values, and its reinterpretation of all human existence. We do not appreciate the moral results of the Christian faith, because we have always lived in the midst of them. But if we study pagan life as recorded in heathen literature or as found to-day in the Mission-field, the contrast between the Christian and the non-Christian outlook on life is undeniable. We may well ask whether those who are able to produce a new type of life and character, have not the right to say on what discovery it is based. Christians have always pointed to the Risen Christ as the source of all their strength. The world becomes an insoluble riddle, if the blessings of Christian faith are based on a fraud or a misconception.

(c) Taking then the narratives of Scripture as they stand, what conception can we form of our Lord's Risen Body? It is obvious that our only evidence is the Gospels. S. Paul's language in 1 Cor 15 suggests that he possessed similar accounts. His teaching on the nature of our own spiritual bodies is based on the nature of the Lord's Risen Body. Since the Resurrection is a unique event in human experience, there are no other instances with which to compare it.

(i) The Resurrection was not simply the resuscitation of the body laid in the grave. Our Lord did not return, like those whom He raised from the dead, to the old life. Nothing has done more to hinder a belief in the Church's doctrine of the Resurrection, than the idea that it teaches a mere reanimation of the material body. For this erroneous idea Christians have been largely responsible. The doctrine has often been stated in such a way as to imply a mere return to the old physical life. In early and mediaeval times such a conception was natural and caused no difficulty. We reject it not only because it conflicts with modern ideas but because it is inconsistent with the facts of the Gospel narrative. These, when interrogated, make it clear that 'the body with which our Lord rose from the grave though still a true body was not the same as that with which He died.'[1] A spiritual change had come over it. It was no longer subject to our wants and limitations: it could pass through doors and disappear at will. The door of the tomb was opened not to let the Lord out but to let the women in. There was no witness of the actual resurrection. If the implication of S. John's record of the tomb be accepted, there would have been nothing to witness. At the same time, though not subject to the limitations of our present life, the risen Lord could at will conform to them. He walked and spoke, and even ate and drank (Lk 24, Mt 28, Jn 20[11] ff., cp. Acts 10[41]).

So in the appearances of the Risen Lord we have a revelation of another life, a manner of existence of a higher order than our own.

---

[1] Milligan, *The Resurrection of our Lord*, p. 31.

By the Incarnation God no longer instructed men through prophets and teachers about the meaning and purpose of human life, but Himself entering into humanity wrought out the perfect human example and disclosed the possibilities of man's life on earth: in the same manner our Lord did not simply teach the immortality of man, but during the forty days actually manifested something of the glory of man's future life by living it before men so far as earthly and temporal conditions allowed. Thus the Resurrection is a new fact added to the sum-total of human experience. 'The life which is revealed to us is not the continuation of the present life, but a life which takes up into itself all the elements of our present life, and transfigures them by a glorious change, which we can only regard at present under signs and figures.'[1] A change had passed over the body, by which it had become wholly subject to the spirit, spirit-ruled and spirit-guided. We know how in our present life the body constrains and hampers our spirit. It grows weary and is not perfectly responsive to our will. It ties us down to the laws of space and of this material world. From all such limitations the Risen Christ is free. He can express Himself perfectly through His body, as and when and where He wills. He has not laid aside His manhood, but manifests within the circle of human experience a higher mode of human existence, hitherto undiscovered and unknown.[2] 'The risen body of Christ was spiritual . . . not because it was less than before material, but because in it matter was wholly and finally subjugated to spirit and not to the exigencies of physical life.'[3]

The precise relation of the risen body to that which was placed in the tomb, we cannot know. The material particles that form our bodies are ceaselessly changing. The identity of our bodies lies not so much in physical continuity as in the abiding relationship to the personality as its organ in the physical world. What persists is not the matter of which the body is composed but the formula or law of which the body is the outward expression. We believe that our Lord's Resurrection is the pledge of our own. As in His case, nothing that belongs to the perfection of our human nature will be lost. All that our present body stands for, will still be ours. We shall possess an organism adapted for life under future conditions as the body is adapted for life under earthly conditions. Our Lord's body

---

[1] Westcott, *op. cit.* c. ii. § 21.

[2] Cp. Westcott, *The Revelation of the Risen Lord.* 'Christ was changed. . . . As has been well said, "What was natural to Him before is now miraculous; what was before miraculous is now natural." Or to put the thought in another form, in an earthly life the spirit is manifested through the body; in the life of the Risen Christ the body is manifested (may we not say so?) through the Spirit. . . . The continuity, the intimacy, the simple familiarity of former intercourse was gone. He is seen and recognized only as He wills and when He wills. In the former sense of the phrase He is no longer with the disciples.' p. 8.

[3] Gore, *Body of Christ*, p. 127.

still bears the marks of the wounds (cp. Rev 5⁶). In Christ as in ourselves, the past still lives on in its permanent effect on what He is.
So we believe that all that we have become through moral effort in
this life will endure in the life that is to be ours hereafter.[1]

(ii) The question still remains, do not the words of our Article,
'*took again His body with flesh, bones and all things appertaining to the
perfection of man's nature*,' imply a very materialistic view of the
Resurrection? 'Flesh and bones' suggest a physical resuscitation.
The answer is that the words are based on the words of the risen
Lord in Lk 24³⁹ 'A spirit hath not flesh and bones as ye behold me
having'. The Article, therefore, must be interpreted by Scripture and
does not lay down any theory on the nature of the Risen Body. At
the same time, if it had been written to-day, it would probably have
avoided taking such an expression of Scripture in isolation from
other statements of Scripture that qualify it. The purpose of the
words is admirably summed up in the following phrase 'all things
appertaining to the perfection of man's nature'. The Risen Lord was
not less perfect Man than before.[2]

Before we leave the question of the Resurrection we must bear in
mind two great considerations:

(a) The evidence for the Resurrection must be considered not in
the abstract, but in the light of the character and claims of Christ.
Men sometimes speak as if the Resurrection of Jesus Christ would be
on a level with the resurrection, let us say, of Julius Caesar or Judas
Iscariot. That is profoundly untrue. To put it on the lowest level, we
are dealing with One who has lived in the fullest union with God,
who had done nothing amiss and who had trusted to God to vindicate Him openly. If we accept the uniqueness of Christ, we shall be

---

[1] It is true that from about the time of S. Augustine onwards down to quite recent
days, both in East and West, a materializing view prevailed. The resurrection was
taught to include a reassembling of the physical particles of the body. But the Church
has never formally defined its teaching on the subject and such a view can be reconciled
neither with S. Paul nor with many of the earlier Fathers. The retention of Origen's
phrase, 'The resurrection of the dead,' as a substitute for the resurrection of the flesh,
and the rejection in Western Creeds of 'The resurrection of this flesh' are witnesses to
a more spiritual view. Further the insistence by many writers on the complete restoration of the body laid in the grave is coupled with an equal insistence on the wonderful
change which will have come over it, which is really inconsistent with the idea of
physical restoration. This inconsistency is partly due to the clash between the intellect
and the imagination. The former demands a spiritual transformation. The latter can
only picture it in materialistic terms. We repeat that the final court of appeal is to
Scripture. (For a complete study of patristic teaching, see Darragh, *The Resurrection of
the Flesh*.)

[2] It is worth noting that the words are 'Flesh and bones' not 'flesh and blood'. Bp.
Westcott could write 'The significant variation from the common formula 'flesh and
blood' must have been at once intelligible to Jews, accustomed to the provisions of the
Mosaic ritual, and nothing would have impressed upon them more forcibly the transfiguration of Christ's Body than the verbal omission of the element of blood which was
for them the symbol and seat of corruptible life' (*The Gospel of the Resurrection*,
c. ii. § 20 note). If this distinction holds, we may compare 1 Cor 15⁵⁰. See also Milligan,
op. cit. pp. 241–242.

prepared to believe in His Resurrection, if there is good evidence for it.

(β) Everything depends upon the presuppositions with which we approach the evidence. Our final decision will rest on moral rather than on purely intellectual grounds. No amount of merely external evidence can ever compel belief. It is always possible in the last resort to evade or explain away the evidence for any historical event. Much more is this true in the case of such an event as the Resurrection. It is significant that all the appearances of the Risen Lord were made to disciples. Our Lord did not reveal Himself to Caiaphas or Pilate. As always, He would never compel belief by a miracle. Such an appearance would have contradicted the whole principle of His earthly ministry. Again, if the Resurrection was a fresh revelation of new life, such could only be given to those who were spiritually capable of receiving it. Only believers had the power to apprehend its true meaning. So to-day belief in the Resurrection depends not only on intellectual appreciation of the evidence but on moral sympathy with the life and teaching of Him who rose.[1]†

(d) We may now examine explanations of the facts that contradict the Christian tradition. Few to-day would support the 'thief theory' that the disciples stole the body (cp. Mt 28[13]). The very existence of this theory among the Jews is an interesting piece of evidence in support of the empty tomb. But it is psychologically absurd. The whole conduct of the apostles forbids us to regard them as conscious imposters. Why should they persist in a deception that brought them nothing but loss and danger? Such a plot is always betrayed in the long run. Wilful fraud is utterly inconsistent with their holy lives.

Fewer still would accept the 'Swoon theory', that Christ was not really dead, but swooned and recovered. This makes not only the disciples but our Lord deceivers. It is hard to see how a fainting and wounded form could convey any suggestion of a resurrection to a new and glorious life. And what became of the recovered Christ? When did He die?

More plausible is the suggestion that the disciples were sincere, but were the victims of hallucination. But this will not really stand close scrutiny. Such hallucinations, as far as we can discover, obey

---

[1] Cp. Mozley, *On Miracles*, Preface to Third Edition, p. xxiv: 'The truth is, no one is ever convinced by external evidence only; there must be a certain probability in the fact itself, or a certain admissibility in it, which must join on to the external evidence for it, in order for that evidence to produce conviction. Nor is it any fault in external evidence that it should be so; but it is an intrinsic and inherent defect in it, because in its very nature it is only one part of evidence which needs to be supplemented by another, or *a priori* premiss existing in our minds. Antecedent probability is the rational complement of external evidence, a law of evidence unites the two; and they cannot practically be separated.' The whole passage is worth reading. It was the fault of much eighteenth-century writing to assume that the mind could be compelled to believe in the Resurrection by a careful marshalling of external evidence.

certain general laws. For instance, they imply expectation. All the evidence shows that our Lord's friends, so far from expecting a resurrection, were preparing to embalm His corpse. The appearances were most unexpected and were received with incredulity. Such a lack of faith is hardly likely to be an invention. It cannot be said that modern psychology lends any support to this view, when the facts are tested. As a rule, when visions and illusions once begin to get a hold, they tend to spread. All the evidence goes to show that the appearances ceased abruptly at the end of forty days. In short, even apart from the empty tomb, the 'illusion theory' does not explain the facts.

The most popular alternative to-day to the traditional teachings of the Church is the view that regards the Resurrection as a 'purely spiritual truth'. The disciples saw visions. These visions were real— 'telegrams from Heaven'—sent by God to assure His disciples that the Lord was alive, and to implant in them faith in victory of life over death. The empty tomb and any idea of a bodily resurrection are unhistorical, the invention of pious fancy or materializing imagination. Our Lord's body went to dust in the tomb, as our own will. His spirit survived as ours will survive. Thus the Resurrection was entirely spiritual, to be discerned by the eye of faith. There was no miraculous breach of the natural law, such as the ordinary view supposes. On this view it is claimed that all that is of value for faith is retained, and Christian truth is lifted above any objections from the side of science or criticism. Jesus Christ lives: that is all that we need to know.[1]

Such a view may be stated so as to come very near the teaching of the Church. But it falls short of the fulness of the Gospel.

(i) We know of no preaching of the Resurrection in apostolic days that did not include the raising of our Lord's Body. The Gospels attest the universal outline of Christian preaching. So, too, S. Paul quite clearly knew of the empty tomb. S. Luke can put into his mouth an express allusion to it (Acts 13[29 and 35–36]). It is probable that this application of Ps 16[10] 'Thou shalt not suffer thy Holy One to see corruption' was a commonplace of apostolic preaching (cp. Acts 2[27–31]). The same knowledge of the empty tomb is implied in 1 Cor 15[3–4]. S. Paul proclaimed 'that Christ died . . . and that he was buried . . . and that he hath been raised on the third day'. The mention of the burial here and elsewhere (e.g. Rom 6[4], Col 2[12]) is gratuitous unless the resurrection is regarded as the reversal of the burial no less than of the death. 'The Death, the Burial and the Resurrection of Christ claim to be facts in exactly the same sense, to be supported by evidence essentially identical in kind, and to be bound together indissolubly as the groundwork of the Christian Faith.'[2]

---

[1] For this view see: Kirsopp Lake, *The Resurrection*, or Streeter's essay in *Foundations*.
[2] Westcott, *The Gospel of the Resurrection*, § 3.

Just as the death and burial were historical events happening in the world of sense, so was the Resurrection.[1] The attempt has been made to invert S. Paul's argument. He treats the risen Christ as 'the first fruits of them that are asleep' (v. [20]). In our own case our bodies perish, yet our risen bodies are regarded as in a real sense continuous with them (vv. [42] ff.). If the corruption of our present bodies does not destroy the continuity in our case, why is the risen Lord's possession of a spiritual body inconsistent with a belief that His natural body went to dust in the grave? This objection forgets that at the stage at which this Epistle was written, S. Paul still expected the Lord's return during the lifetime of most of those to whom he wrote. In his view the majority of the Corinthian Church would not taste of death at all. At the Lord's coming their present natural body would be transformed into a spiritual body. So in their case as in our Lord's their natural body would not see corruption. The difficulty at Corinth had arisen about those who died. As a result of their death, their condition was so obviously different from our Lord's. Men asked how, if the natural body perished, it could ever be transfigured into a spiritual body. The analogy with the Risen Lord seemed to be broken. The very existence of this perplexity points to a universal belief in the empty tomb.

(ii) Any view that denies the bodily Resurrection is faced with the difficulty of accounting for the complete disappearance of the crucified body. That this difficulty was felt early is shown by the Jewish story in Mt 28[11] ff. If the body of Christ could have been produced by the Jews or Romans, the whole Christian movement would have collapsed. If the body was not in the tomb, it must have been removed either by friends or foes; there is no alternative. Either explanation involves us in a tangle of difficulties. We may be perfectly certain that the authorities made every possible effort to discover the body and discredit the apostles. The body would be recognizable for a considerable time and there would be the evidence of those who removed it. It has indeed been supposed that the women went to the wrong tomb and found it empty. The disciples apparently were sufficiently simple to neglect any further investigations, and the Roman and Jewish authorities too incompetent to make the slightest attempt to clear up the mystery. Apart from other objections, any such theory that allows the finding of an empty tomb but holds that the Lord's body went to corruption elsewhere, lands us with a very

---

[1] It has been objected that the view of our Lord's Risen Body taken in these pages is no less contradictory to the main stream of Christian teaching than the Vision theory. The later Fathers and mediaeval teachers unanimously taught the resuscitation of our Lord's dead body. A sufficient answer is to point out that our view is at least consistent with the facts of the Gospel story. In the light of our modern knowledge we have been driven to reinterrogate Scripture, with the result that we have obtained from it a more spiritual view of the Resurrection. On the other hand, the Vision theory is compelled to reduce the Gospel evidence to mere legend. Our appeal is not simply to Christian tradition, but to Christian tradition as interpreting Scripture.

serious moral problem.[1] We are asked to suppose that the empty tomb had in the workings of providence an important place in convincing the world of the truth that Christ was alive, yet the belief in its emptiness was the result of mistake or fraud. Our conscience revolts from the thought that God employs such means to impress upon the world a new and vital revelation. No doubt illusion has its place in the divine economy. But this would be no mere illusion due to the infirmity of the human mind or imagination, it would be, so to say, a deliberate deception on the part of the divine providence.

(iii) On this view there was no Resurrection, only a survival. Death conquered the body and death kept what is conquered. There was no real victory over death, but merely a persistence through death. Such would be a redemption not of the whole man, but only of his spirit. The resurrection of the body assures us that all our being is redeemed and redeemable. No element in our nature is lost. The early Church rightly appealed to the bodily resurrection of Christ as setting forth the worth and dignity of the human body.[2] It has a glorious future in store for it and therefore must not be defiled. We know of no human life apart from the body. The bare survival of the spirit is not the Christian doctrine of immortality. Further, if Christ's body did not rise, the resurrection—such as it was—took place not on the third day, but on the afternoon of the death. In fact it was completed at the very moment of death.[3] Christians were wrong in supposing foolishly that they kept Sunday as the weekly memorial of the Resurrection: they only kept it as the memorial of the first vision. The persistent tradition of the 'third day' merely shows the inexactitude of the Christian mind. The true Easter-day is Good Friday.

(iv) We thankfully allow that it is quite possible for men to-day born and bred in a Christian atmosphere to reject the bodily resurrection of our Lord and yet retain a true faith in Him as a living Saviour. But it is very doubtful whether the first generation of Christians could ever have attained to such a faith, if His body had remained in the grave. It is equally doubtful whether simple people to-day could do so. There cannot be two creeds, one for the educated and one for the uneducated. If we allow that the apostles and others saw visions and heard voices, how are we to test their validity? We, indeed, after

---

[1] Many who accept the 'objective vision' theory confess that they cannot account for the disappearance of the body, and plead that so long as they accept the truth of the appearances, they are not called on to do so.

[2] The New Testament also hints at the 'cosmic' significance of the Resurrection of our Lord's body. It stands for the first instalment of the redemption of the material creation, the pledge that the whole creation shall be brought back into harmony with God's purpose. We see in the Risen Lord matter fulfilling its true purpose as the vehicle of spirit (cp. Rom 8[19-23], Eph 1[10], Col 1[20]).

[3] Incidentally the whole of the descent into Hades must be dismissed as not only mythical but meaningless.

nearly two thousand years of Christianity can appeal to a wide Christian experience and to the moral fruits of a faith in the risen Christ. The apostles could not do so. The empty tomb supplied just that corroboration in the region of external historic fact, that was needed. And to-day the plain man attaches most importance to historic facts. That a thing happened gives it in his eyes a superior kind of truth. He is not much attracted by bare ideas. One great reason for the spread of Christianity among men and women of every class and condition, civilized and savage, educated and ignorant, is that it claims to rest on historic fact. Destroy this foundation of historic fact and Christian faith might survive for a time, but it would not survive for long. Once again it is claimed on behalf of the vision-theory that it preserves the truth of the Resurrection and at the same time escapes the difficulty of supposing a break in the continuity of nature. Is this claim true? If the appearances were real and divinely caused, then they were miraculous. The miracle is removed from the physical to the psychological sphere, that is all. We are still left with a supernormal event, not the less so because it is in the region of mind and not of matter. We may even go so far as to doubt whether, since all mental activity is conditioned by processes of the brain, the perception of such visions would not necessitate a unique and direct action of God in the physical sphere. In short, the idea of a purely spiritual resurrection solves difficulties of imagination rather than difficulties of reason. To the man who starts from an *a priori* view that miracles do not happen, it is as impossible as the traditional view. It involves a very grave departure from the apostolic teaching.

§ 3. *Christ . . . took again His body, with flesh, bones and all things appertaining to the perfection of man's nature, wherewith He ascended into Heaven and there sitteth.*

(*a*) There is no certain allusion to the Ascension in the Synoptic Gospels. It is interpreted in the language of theology in the later appendix to Mk (16[19]). The exact meaning of Lk 24[51] is doubtful. The words 'and was carried up into Heaven' are omitted in ℵ D and the earliest Latin versions, and therefore probably formed no part of the original text. If they are omitted the verse only describes a disappearance of our Lord similar to His disappearance from the disciples at Emmaus (24[31]).[1] S. Luke preferred to reserve his narrative of the Ascension itself for his second volume. He regarded it rather as the preliminary to the descent of the Spirit than as the final

[1] If the words be retained, the Gospel appears at first sight to place the Ascension on Easter Day. This, however, is not a necessary inference. S. Luke has little sense of time and there may have been a considerable interval between vv. [43] and [44] or again vv. [49] and [50]. The same difficulty occurs in the Epistle of Barnabas (15[9]) which asserts 'We keep the eighth day as a day of joy, on which Jesus both arose from the dead and after being manifested, ascended into heaven.' This is probably a mere piece of clumsiness in expression. Even the Creed runs 'the third day He rose again according to the Scriptures, and ascended into Heaven.'

episode in the earthly life of Christ (cp. Acts 2^{33-34}). His Ascension is foretold by our Lord Himself in Jn 6^{62} and again after His Resurrection in Jn 20^{17}. Only in the Acts is the visible act of final withdrawal described (1^{9-11}). In the Epistles the Ascension is assumed rather than directly asserted. For instance, in Eph 4^{8-10} the words of Psalm 68^{18} are paraphrased with reference to the gifts of the Spirit, 'When he ascended on high, he led captivity captive and gave gifts unto men. . . . He that descended is the same also that ascended far above all the heavens that he might fill all things.' So, too, the quotation from an early Christian hymn given in 1 Tim 3^{16} concludes with 'received up in glory'. Again, in 1 Pet 3^{22} we find an unmistakeable allusion to the Ascension: 'Jesus Christ, who is on the right hand of God, having gone into heaven.' Further, the Ascension is presupposed in every mention of our Lord's priestly work and of His exaltation at God's right hand (e.g. Phil 2^{9-10}, Eph 1^{20}, Rev 3^{21}, etc.).

(b) In considering the Ascension we must distinguish between the outward and visible act of departure and its spiritual significance. The outward event is narrated in Acts 1^9. 'As they were looking, he was taken up and a cloud received him out of their sight.' We need not imagine that the Lord's body rose aloft visibly into the sky and disappeared slowly into its depths, as Christian art has depicted it. All that the narrative requires is a cloud hanging on the hillside a short way above where He and His disciples were standing, into which He rose. We may contrast the story of the Transfiguration. Then our Lord entered into the cloud and the cloud passed away leaving Him on earth. Now He passed into the cloud and did not return.[1] The whole constituted a sign marking this departure as different from His previous departures and expressing its finality. Some visible sign was needed to assure the disciples that they were to look for no more manifestations of the Risen Lord. Such an expectation would have distracted them from their work. During the forty days they had been trained to live in the knowledge that at any moment He might appear among them. Now that stage of their education was finished. They had been made ready to go forth and wield authority. The work for which they had been trained was about to begin. The sign was understood by the disciples. The expectation of any further visible manifestations of the Risen Lord ended abruptly. They were content to await the descent of the Holy Spirit and to find in Him the pledge of the invisible presence of their ascended Lord.

But this outward event was but the setting-forth of a great spiritual truth, in the only manner intelligible to men of that day. 'The

[1] Rackham, Acts, p. 8: 'In the Old Testament the incomprehensibleness of the divine nature was typified by a cloud which hid Jehovah from human view: so now the human body of Jesus is concealed by the same cloud which is the cloud of the Shekinah or divine glory. He is now "in glory".'

physical elevation was a speaking parable, an eloquent symbol, but not the truth to which it pointed or the reality which it foreshadowed. The change which Christ revealed by the Ascension was not a change of place, but a change of state, not local but spiritual. Still from the necessities of our human condition the spiritual change was represented sacramentally so to speak, in an outward form. . . . The Ascension of Christ is, in a word, His going to the Father—to His Father and our Father—the visible pledge and symbol of the exaltation of the earthly into the heavenly. It is emphatically a revelation of heavenly life, the open fulfilment of man's destiny made possible for all men.'[1] Doubtless the Apostles regarded the earth as flat and heaven as a place above their heads. They supposed that our Lord travelled there through space. Such a mental picture was consistent with itself and for many centuries presented no difficulty to reason. To-day such a naïve conception is impossible, nor is it in the least a vital part of the Christian faith. Our Lord's entrance into the fulness of His heavenly life obviously transcends all possible human experience. It can only be depicted in metaphor and symbol. The visible sign of His departure can be adequately described in earthly language and does not need restatement. Its spiritual truth must be reinterpreted in the best language that we can find. Difficulties about the Ascension arise not when we employ the simple realism of the first Christians, nor yet when we are whole-heartedly philosophic, but when we attempt to piece together fragments of the two positions. We must not be 'philosophic in patches'. Heaven is a state of being, not a locality. The inner meaning of the Ascension is not a removal to another part of the universe infinitely remote, but rather the final withdrawal into another mode of existence. Just as the Incarnation did not involve a physical descent, so the return to the Father did not involve an upward movement in space.[2]

(c) The language of Scripture suggests that the Ascension brought about no change in the condition of the Risen Lord. He was glorified not at the Ascension but at the Resurrection. The Ascension was a last farewell to the apostles, not a first entry into glory. In Scripture the Resurrection and Ascension are always viewed in the closest possible connexion (Acts 2$^{32-33}$, 5$^{30-31}$, Rom 6$^{8-10}$, Eph 1^{20}, Col 3^1, Heb 1^3, 1 Pet 1^{21}, 3$^{21-22}$, etc.). 'No sooner did He shake off the bonds of earth and take His place in the higher spiritual world to which He was ever afterwards to belong, than He may be said to have ascended into

---

[1] Westcott, *The Revelation of the Risen Lord*, p. 180.

[2] Swete, *The Ascended Christ*, p. 8. 'A conception which limits His ascent to any region however remote from the earth, or locates His ascended life in any part of the material universe, falls vastly short of the primitive belief; no third heaven, no seventh heaven of Jewish speculation, no central sun of later conjecture, meets the requirements of an exaltation to the throne of God.' The language of Scripture is worth noting. In Eph 4^{10} He is said to have ascended 'far above all the heavens', in Heb 4^{14} to have 'passed through the heavens' (cp. 7^{26}). So in Jn 16^{28} He declares that He is about to leave the world (κόσμον, the world of created things).

heaven. When for a special purpose He again appeared to His disciples as they had known Him during His earthly ministry, He may be said to have descended out of heaven. Wherever He was in that glorified condition which began at His Resurrection, there Heaven in its Scripture sense also was.'[1] This helps to explain the absence of reference to the Ascension in the Gospels. It was not separated in thought from the Resurrection.[2] When we have once grasped the nature of our Lord's spiritual body, the thought of the Ascension as from one point of view the counterpart of the Resurrection involves no new difficulty.

(i) Obviously we can know nothing of the condition of our Lord's manhood in His heavenly life. All that we are concerned to maintain is that He is still fully Man. As such He is the 'Mediator between God and man' (1 Tim 2^5 R.V.). 'He has entered upon the completeness of spiritual being without lessening in any degree the completeness of His humanity. The thought is one with which we need to familiarize ourselves. We cannot, indeed, unite the two sides of it in one conception, but we can hold both firmly without allowing the one truth to infringe upon the other.'[3] Nothing has been laid aside or lost which appertains to the perfection of man's nature. At the time of the Reformation Luther and certain of his followers maintained that as a result of the Ascension our Lord's humanity had become omnipresent. Against this doctrine known as 'Ubiquitarianism' the wording of our article was devised as a protest. A humanity that is of itself and unconditionally omnipresent would hardly be human any longer. As part of the created world it could scarcely attain to an attribute essentially divine. Rather we may picture to ourselves our Lord's humanity as a faculty that He possesses and through which He can still act in our world of space and time, whenever and wherever He wills so to do. For us our body represents the organ through which we act upon our present environment. Our Lord's spiritual body was employed by Him during the forty days as the perfected instrument of His will through which He manifested Himself to the senses of His disciples and assured them of His personal identity. Now, as ascended, He possesses all that the body stands for, inasmuch as He can still render His humanity active in our lower world at will. Through it He disclosed Himself to S. Stephen (Acts 7^{55}) and apparently to S. Paul (Acts 9^{3-5}, cp. 1 Cor 9^1) and to S. John (Rev 1^{13}). The Church has never had any difficulty in conceiving of Him as acting through His humanity in

---

[1] Milligan, *The Ascension of our Lord*, p. 26. Cp. Westcott, *The Revelation of the Risen Lord*, pp. 23–26.

[2] For an attempt to distinguish between the Resurrection and Ascension, see Denney, Art. 'Ascension' in *Hastings' D.B.* vol. i. There is no evidence whatever for a view that has been put forward at times, that our Lord's body was being progressively spiritualized during the forty days.

[3] Westcott, *Historic Faith*, Lect. VI.

the Holy Eucharist in many places at the same time. But this is not ubiquitarianism. His manhood is not regarded as, so to speak, automatically omnipresent. Rather in each case His activity is a direct act of will in fulfilment of His own promise and in answer to the prayers of the Church.

(ii) The ascended Christ is both priest and king.[1] As we saw[2] the culmination of the act of sacrifice was not the death of the victim, but the presentation of the blood 'which is the life' before God. So our Lord's atonement was completed by the Ascension. As on the great day of atonement the high-priest entered within the veil to offer the blood (cp. Lev 16[12-16]) Christ at His Ascension 'entered not into a holy place made with hands, but into heaven itself, now ($\nu\hat{\nu}\nu$, emphatic) to appear in the presence of God for us' (Heb 9[24]). He is still engaged in His priestly task and the Church awaits His return from within the veil (9[28]). 'The entrance was made, as the sacrifice was offered, once for all : the whole period of time from the Ascension to the Return is one age-long Day of Atonement.'[3] So our Lord, by His presence within the veil, is now making atonement for us. As the high-priest uttered no spoken prayer but by his presentation of the blood made reconciliation for Israel, our Lord as our representative, clothed in our nature, having become all that He now is through His Cross and Passion eternally presents Himself to the Father. He has, indeed, 'somewhat to offer' (Heb 8[3]). He is Himself both priest and victim. In the language of Rev 5[6] He is eternally 'the Lamb as it had been slain'. Our Lord is an abiding priest and an abiding sacrifice. He pleads for us, not by anything new or supplementary that He now does, but by what he has become through His death. The complete self-oblation of Himself once for all made on Calvary, lives on in His living unity of will with the Father.[4] He ever lives unto God (Rom 6[10], cp. 5[10], 'We are saved by his life,' cp. 1 Pet 3[21]). He is a priest for ever, not simply by commemorating a death that is past, but by the eternal presentation of the life that died. As such by His

---

[1] Our Lord's priesthood is not after the manner of Aaron, but of Melchizedek (Heb 6[20-7]). The difference does not lie in the function. *Qua* priesthood, the two are identical. Nor yet is the chief mark of difference that the kingship and priesthood are combined in one Person. This is secondary. Rather it is to be found in the fact that the one 'abides continually' (7[3]). His priesthood is eternal and ideal. The Aaronic priests are men that die : their priesthood is transitory. Christ is a priest 'for ever'.

[2] Pp. 86, 87.

[3] Swete, *op. cit.* p. 42. For a careful exposition of the symbolism see Gayford, *J.Th.S.* vol. xiv. p. 459 ff.

[4] 'It is not the death itself which is acceptable to the God of life : but the vital self-identification with the holiness of God. . . . It is the life as life, not the death as death ; it is the life which has been willing to die, the life which has passed through death and been consecrated in dying, the life in which the death is a moral element, perpetually and inalienably present, but still the life, which is acceptable to God.' 'In that eternal presentation Calvary is eternally implied. Of that life . . . the 'as it had been slain' is no mere past incident, but it has become, once for all, an inalienable moral element.' Moberly, *Ministerial Priesthood*, c. vii. pp. 245 and 246.

very presence in our human nature He intercedes for us (Heb 7[25], Rom 8[34]). 'The intercession of the Ascended Christ is not a prayer but a life.'[1] Through Him we have an abiding access to the throne of grace (Eph 2[13], Heb 4[14–16], 10[19] ff.). His death and entry into Heaven took place once for all: as historical events they lie in the past and can never be repeated (Heb 7[27], 9[28], 10[12], etc.). But the great priestly appeal lasts on. The whole life and ministry of the Church proceed from the priestly life of the living and ascended Christ.

(iii) Our Lord in Heaven is described as 'sitting at the right hand of the Father'. Such language is clearly metaphorical. God's right hand is the highest place of honour in Heaven. The symbolism was borrowed from Ps 110[1], 'Jehovah saith unto my lord' (*i.e.* an earthly king whether actual or ideal), 'Sit thou at my right hand, until I make thine enemies thy footstool.' The verse had been quoted by our Lord Himself to bring home the inadequacy of the current conception of the Messiah, as the 'Son of David', *i.e.* a merely earthly king (Mk 12[36]). Before Caiaphas He claimed that He Himself would fulfil it (Mk 14[62] where it is combined with imagery from Daniel). The Psalm in its original context is addressed to a Jewish king (perhaps Judas Maccabaeus or more probably an ideal figure of the Messianic king) who is bidden to share the throne of Jehovah. Later on (v. [4]) this king is declared to be by divine decree 'a priest for ever after the manner of Melchizedek'. The early Church from the first seized on this psalm and its phrases, sanctioned by the use of our Lord Himself, as being the least inadequate to describe the glory and functions of the Ascended Christ. It is quoted by S. Peter on the day of Pentecost (Acts 2[34]), and the symbolism takes its place henceforth as a part of primitive Christian theology (*e.g.* Rom 8[34], Col 3[1], Heb 10[2], [Mk] 16[19], etc.). Only in Acts 7[55] is the imagery modified. S. Stephen cries 'I see the heavens opened and the Son of Man standing at the right hand of God'. Christ is regarded as having risen up to succour His servant. 'Sitting at the right hand of the Father' clearly denotes authority and triumph. God 'made him to sit at his right hand in the heavenly places far above all rule and all authority and power and dominion and every name that is named not only in this world but also in that which is to come: and he puts all things in subjection under his feet' (Eph 1[20–22], cp. Mt 28[18], Heb 12[2], Rev 3[21], etc.). 'Sitting' has also been taken to denote 'rest'. To this we may demur as an undue pressing of physical imagery. The idea of rest is entirely absent from the psalm. If the Ascended Christ rests it is only in the sense in which God rested from His labours on the seventh day, when He ceased to create. Such rest was not incompatible with unceasing work (Jn 5[17]). The toil and sorrows of Christ's earthly life, the Cross and Passion were indeed ended. But the true antithesis to the pain and weariness of labour is not mere repose but a free and unfettered

---

[1] Swete, *op. cit.* p. 99.

activity. The life of the Ascended Christ is certainly not one of in-activity. He 'must reign till He hath put all enemies under His feet' (1 Cor 15²⁷). He sits 'expecting till his enemies be made the footstool of his feet' (Heb 10¹³). 'Our Lord's victory over the world in the days of His flesh was but an earnest of the longer warfare and the more complete conquest which are the work of His ascended life. When He sat down at the right hand of power, it was not for a brief cessation from warfare, but for an age-long conflict with the powers of evil. Sitting is not always the posture of rest. Some of the hardest work of life is done by the monarch seated in his cabinet and the statesman at his desk; and the seated Christ, like the four living creatures round about Him, rests not day nor night from the unin-termitting energies of heaven.'[1] As King, He reaps the fruits of His victory over sin and death through the battle that is being waged on earth against the forces of evil by His body the Church.

§ 4. *Until He return to judge all men at the last day.* (i) The idea of a future judgment was perfectly familiar to our Lord's contempor-aries. The prophets from Amos onwards had taken up and purified the popular expectation of the 'Day of the Lord', a day in which Jehovah would intervene to vindicate Israel and scatter their enemies and His. They had taught that such a coming must mean judgment. It would be a day of condemnation of all that was unrighteous both in Israel and outside. The same idea held a prominent place in the anonymous apocalyptic literature that had so large an influence upon Jewish thought between the cessation of prophecy and our Lord's day. The extent of this influence we are now only beginning to appreciate. All such literature was inspired by the hope of the restor-ation of Israel and the establishment of the Kingdom of God, through the direct and catastrophic intervention of God Himself. Though there is considerable variety in detail, all such pictures in-clude a judgment as a necessary prelude to the new era of happiness. Usually the judge is God Himself. Sometimes more than one judg-ment is described and the Messiah has a part in their execution. In a portion of one of these apocalypses, the Book of Enoch the universal judgment is assigned to a supernatural pre-existent Person 'the Son of Man', who acts as God's agent. The importance of these facts is that they help us to reconstruct the background of popular religion in our Lord's day. We have to face the fact that the language of our Lord Himself and of the writers of the New Testament is largely the language of this apocalyptic literature. When our Lord spoke of His return to judgment, He employed phrases and symbolism already familiar to many of His hearers. He made use of current ideas and metaphors to describe His mission far more than we used to suppose. Due allowance must be made for this when we attempt to understand their meaning. We cannot suppose that popular expectations were

[1] Swete, *The Ascended Christ*, p. 14.

embodied in a single consistent scheme. Doubtless they varied enormously in different circles and were often loose and fragmentary. But there did exist a definite circle of ideas in the popular mind, and prominent among these was that of a future judgment, ushering in the Kingdom of God.

This same idea appears in the teaching of S. John Baptist. In some sense he combined prophecy and apocalyptic in one. He revived the personal appeal of the prophet, but the form of his teaching was in large part that of the apocalyptic writings. He took the message that was stored up in the symbolic pictures of apocalyptic literature and by his preaching made it a living expectation in the hearts and minds of ordinary men. He proclaimed the immediate approach of the Kingdom of God (Mt 3²) and the advent of one mightier than himself who would execute the preliminary judgment (Mt 3⁸⁻¹², Lk 3¹⁵⁻¹⁷).

(ii) The new feature in our Lord's teaching is that He claims that He Himself will return in glory to be the judge. This claim permeates all His teaching. It cannot be denied or explained away. He proclaims that all men, Jew and Gentile alike, will give account to Him for their life here. They will be judged by His standard. Often this claim to judge is connected with the title Son of Man (*e.g.* Mk 8³⁸, Mt 25³¹, 13⁴¹, 24³⁷). This title is probably used in an apocalyptic sense taken from the book of Daniel or the book of Enoch. But it also includes the thought that it is in virtue of His humanity, as one who knows human nature from within, as 'representative man', that He will judge mankind. The Father 'gave him authority to execute judgment, because he is Son of Man' (Jn 5²⁷). This truth is represented under a great variety of symbolism. We have a whole series of parables, found chiefly in the first Gospel, emphasizing the certainty of His return and the need of preparedness. His return to judgment is likened to a flood (Mt 24³⁷⁻³⁹, cp. Mt 7²⁴) or a harvesting (Mt 13³⁰ and 41–43). His coming will be sudden and unforeseen yet visible to all (Mt 24²⁷⁻²⁸), enemies as well as friends (Rev 1⁷). He likens Himself to a thief (Mt 24⁴³, Lk 12³⁹), a bridegroom (Mt 25¹), a master of a household suddenly returning (Mt 24⁴⁴ ff., 25¹⁴ ff., Mk 13³⁴, Lk 12⁴²). Elsewhere He employs symbolical language borrowed from the Old Testament and frequent in later apocalypses, to describe the upheaval of the present order preparatory to His return and to picture the scene of judgment (Mk 13, Mt 24, 25³¹ ff.). The very wealth of illustration warns us against any too literal interpretation of details. Many of the scenes are incompatible, if viewed as literal predictions, but each brings out some feature in the final catastrophe. Beneath them all the claim to be the supreme and final judge of the world stands out clear. Our Lord proclaims that He will return in the glory of the Father, in such a manner that none can escape or evade His coming and that all human life will be tested by His presence.

(iii) In the earliest preaching the Lord's return held a foremost place (Acts 10[42], 1 Thess 1[10], 4[14-17], 2 Thess 2[2] ff., etc.). The news of judgment to come was an essential part of the Gospel that the Apostles proclaimed (cp. Acts 17[31], 24[25], Rom 2[15-16], 1 Cor 4[5], 2 Cor 5[10], Heb 6[2], 1 Pet 4[17], etc.). The early Church believed that the Lord's coming was to be expected very quickly, within the lifetime of many then living. We can see the value of such a belief, in the providence of God. Not only did it stimulate moral and spiritual earnestness. Ultimate values and eternal issues were not obscured by the claims of earth, since this earth was held to be about to pass away. But also it governed the development of Church organization. The apostles had no conception that they were laying down rules or planning a constitution for a Church that was to last for some two thousand years. All their administration was guided by the needs of some immediate demand or difficulty. Hence the elasticity and adaptiveness of Christianity was preserved. The Church was saved from a minute and rigid organization based on precise apostolic commands and therefore regarded as inviolable. Such an organization, however perfectly suited to the needs of the apostolic age, would have been an intolerable burden to any succeeding age. All through the New Testament we find broad principles laid down rather than detailed and formal rules. 'It may seem a paradox, but yet it is profoundly true, that the Church is adapted to the needs of every age, just because the original preachers of Christianity never attempted to adapt it to the needs of any period but their own.'[1]

Within the teaching of S. Paul himself we can trace a change of tone on the subject of the Lord's return. In his later epistles he dwells less upon the immediacy of His coming. He seems able to contemplate a considerable delay. He himself may expect to die first (cp. Phil 1[21-24], and contrast 1 Cor 7[26-31] and 1 Thess 4[15] 'we which are alive'). He dwells more upon the building up of the Church. So, too, in S. John's Gospel we find a marked absence of definitely eschatological teaching. Its place is taken by the thought of the coming of the Spirit. Even so, however, both in S. Paul's latest epistles and in S. John the thought of a final judgment by Christ is never let go (2 Tim 4[1] and 1[18], Jn 5[27-29], I Jn 4[17], etc.). This suggests that our Lord's teaching contained from the first certain elements which were appreciated more fully after a time and which tended to modify the expectation of His immediate return.

(iv) If we ask how we are to conceive of the return of Christ and the final judgment, and what the 'advent hope' means to us to-day, we must admit that as soon as we go outside the main truth, nothing is clear-cut. The important fact for our present life is that we shall have each personally to render an account of our lives to Jesus Christ. The standard by which we shall be judged is His and not the world's.

[1] Sanday and Headlam, *Romans*, p. 381. The whole note, p. 379-381, should be read.

The language of Scripture certainly suggests that this final judgment takes place not on the death of the individual but at 'the last day', after the general resurrection, and that it is shared by all mankind. But though this may be the best way that we can express the truth for ourselves, we must remember that it may be hopelessly inadequate. The varied symbolism in which the judgment is depicted in Scripture is at best an attempt to suggest to the mind spiritual realities that lie beyond our present human experience. The whole question of time comes in. Words like 'before' and 'after' may have no meaning in the life after death. The apparent interval between death and the final judgment may have no real existence. We cannot dogmatize on such points. It is well, however, to bear in mind certain facts.

(a) The imagery of Scripture is more consistent than we sometimes suppose. The impossibility of imagining a gathering of all mankind at one place is obvious. But though Scripture suggests this, it at the same time teaches that we shall all possess risen and spiritual bodies, raised above the limitations of space. The two thoughts must be taken together.

(β) The judgment will not be the arbitrary assignment of future destinies. Rather it will be the final and public declaration of what men have made themselves. In His earthly life, as S. John's Gospel makes clear, our Lord by His very presence among men as a Saviour, judged them. He acted as a touchstone of character. By their attitude to Him men showed themselves to be what they really were. This same judgment or division is made at every great crisis or opportunity that befalls either nations or individuals. Then in a real sense Christ comes and men reveal themselves by their behaviour towards Him. Such an experience cannot leave man unchanged. By their response they make themselves either better or worse. Salvation rejected is condemnation. If, then, this process of judgment is, so to say, automatically going on day by day, it leads us to expect a final judgment. All men must by acts of choice be building up a character of some kind. The coming of Christ in glory is a last great opportunity, that none will be able to escape. It will divide men by revealing what they have become. In one sense Christ will judge. In another sense men will judge themselves, in so far as they are prepared or not prepared to meet Him. The justice and inevitableness of the sentence will be apparent. The judgment will not change men. It will show them to be what they are.

(γ) By this judgment the individual is assigned his place in the new order of things in accordance with his character and capacity. From first to last Scripture speaks of men as divided into two classes, the saved and the lost.[1] It declares that at bottom all men must decide either for God or against Him. At the same time our Lord seems to

---

[1] Mysterious as this is it seems to correspond with the facts of human life. See Martineau, *Types of Ethical Theory*, vol. ii. pp. 65–69.

speak of gradations of reward and punishment (Lk 12^{47–48}, 19^{17–19}; cp. Jn 14² 'many mansions'). Every man is given that position in the new age which he has made himself capable of filling by his life in this age.[1]

(v) *The last day.*—The conception of a last day which ends time and history raises many difficulties.[2] But it stands for important Christian convictions. The created world as we know it had a beginning and will have an end. Moreover, its end will not be a mere ceasing of existence. Since it is God's creation, He will bring it to its final end and purpose. The 'last things' will be a consummation of the present order in a new world in which God's Kingdom is fully manifested. For this day the Creation is 'waiting' (Rom 8¹⁹); it cannot come until the 'sons of God' are 'manifested' in their resurrection glory. 'The last day' therefore means also that there will be a fulfilment of God's redeeming purpose in human history, which must run its appointed span in time until that purpose is complete and all the souls whom God intends to create have been through their earthly probation. The end is a consummation both of nature and history in an eternal order. To express these convictions we cannot dispense with the conception of 'the last day'. It stands for the seriousness and reality of all that happens in time, and also for the truth that the movement and meaning of all history cannot be understood from within history itself. The 'end' of history is in 'the life of the age to come', which is God's fulfilment of His creation in 'this age'. To Christian faith the nature of the divine judgment and salvation which this fulfilment will bring are already known in Christ. The Christian lives now as one who by his incorporation into Christ has entered on that eternal life which will be fully manifested when He 'comes again with glory'.[3]†

---

[1] Heaven and Hell must be regarded as spiritual states with an environment which completely corresponds to them. The secret of the bliss of Heaven is in the perfection of the soul's relation to God. An unholy man would find life in Heaven intolerable. He could have no sympathy with it. Hence the unavoidableness of Hell. The essential nature of Hell would seem to be the failure to attain Heaven. It is eternal loss, rather than eternal punishment. The fires of Hell are those that are to be found within the human heart, anger, bitterness, self-will and the like, and the lusts that survive after the power for finding pleasure in their satisfaction has for ever departed. Above all just as the joy of Heaven will consist in that full union with God for which we were made, so the loss of Hell is the loss of that union with God, for which sin and self-will incapacitate us (cp. 2 Thess 1⁹, Heb 12¹¹). Cp. von Hügel, *Essays and Addresses* (First Series), c. vii.

[2] For a discussion of the nature of Time see F. H. Brabant, *Time and Eternity in Christian Thought,* and on the Biblical doctrine, see art. 'Time' in *A Theological Word-Book of the Bible* (S.C.M. Press).

[3] For a valuable study of some questions relating to the Christian conception of history, see Quick, *The Gospel of Divine Action.*

THE HOLY SPIRIT

ARTICLE V

Of the Holy Ghost	*De Spiritu Sancto*
The Holy Ghost, proceeding from the Father and the Son, is of one substance, majesty, and glory, with the Father and the Son, very and eternal God.	Spiritus Sanctus, a Patre et Filio procedens, ejusdem est cum Patre et Filio essentiae, majestatis, et gloriae, verus ac aeternus Deus.

One of the new Articles added in 1563 by Archbishop Parker, based upon the Lutheran Confession of Würtemburg. Its addition may be due to the revival of ancient heresies by the Anabaptists, or simply to a desire for greater completeness.

§ 1. As we have seen, in the Old Testament the Spirit of God is simply God in action. His distinct personality is not yet fully recognized. The Old Testament conception has hardly been transcended in such passages as Lk 1[35] 'The Holy Ghost shall come upon thee and the power of the Most High shall overshadow thee', and the teaching of John Baptist (Mk 1[8], etc.) 'He shall baptize you with the Holy Ghost'. But in the teaching of Christ and of the New Testament generally language is used which implies clearly that He is both Divine and a Person. His divinity can hardly be questioned. 'Blasphemy against the Holy Ghost' is the sin that 'hath never forgiveness' (Mk 3[29], etc.). To 'lie to the Holy Ghost' is to 'lie to God' (Acts 5[3-4]). It is the presence of the Spirit that makes the Christian the temple of God (1 Cor 3[16] and 6[17]). On the other hand His personality was less quickly grasped. The word $\pi\nu\epsilon\hat{u}\mu\alpha$[1] in itself may mean 'wind', or 'spirit' or 'spiritual influence'. It is used alike of the Person of the Holy Spirit and of the gifts that He bestows. It is employed also of a man's 'spirit', which is a part or aspect of his personality. Further, its use in the Old Testament and in popular heathen religious thought tended to a certain vagueness.[2] In its current use it might mean no more than a divine influence or endowment or one of the minor deities of polytheism. But the language of Scripture goes beyond this. It speaks about Him as a Person. Christ can designate Him 'another Advocate' comparable to but not identical with Himself (Jn 14[26], 15[26]). He is to perform personal actions, to 'teach' and 'bear witness'. So in S. Paul's writing He 'maketh intercession with groanings that

[1] The attempt to distinguish between $\tau\grave{o}$ $\pi\nu\epsilon\hat{u}\mu\alpha$ as meaning the Person and $\pi\nu\epsilon\hat{u}\mu\alpha$ without the article as meaning His gifts or operation, though great names can be quoted in its favour, seems to have no real foundation.

[2] See C. H. Dodd, *The Interpretation of the Fourth Gospel*, pp. 213 ff. for the use of the term in Greek thought.

cannot be uttered' (Rom 8²⁶⁻²⁷). He 'divides gifts severally as He will' (1 Cor 12¹¹, cp. the whole passage). He can lead men (Gal 5¹⁸) and be grieved (Eph 4³⁰). Further, in baptismal formula (Mt 28¹⁹) and Trinitarian passages (cp. 2 Cor 13¹⁴) He is placed on a level with the Father and the Son, in a way that would be impossible, if He were no more than a divine influence. We could not speak of 'The Father, the Son and the Wisdom' or 'the Power'. The substitution of any such divine attribute shows at once the Personality of the Spirit.

§ 2. When we turn to the early Church, the general mind of the Church is perfectly clear. We find a vigorous belief in the Holy Spirit expressed in her life and worship. She baptized in the three-fold Name and required of candidates for baptism an acknowledgement of the Holy Spirit no less than of the Father and the Son. She included the Holy Spirit in her doxologies. In the hymn of praise that is put into the mouth of the martyr S. Polycarp, glory is given to the Holy Spirit, together with the Father and the Son. Whether actually spoken at the time of martyrdom or not, the words probably represent a familiar eucharistic thanksgiving. At the same time the doctrine of the Holy Spirit was not yet formulated in the language of theology. The presence and power of the Holy Spirit was a fact of Christian experience rather than an object of study and definition.[1]

So we are not surprised to find that in the first attempts to think out the position of the Holy Spirit there is not only a certain vagueness and indecision but also a real confusion of thought and the employment of language that in a later age would have been condemned as heretical. Thus Hermas appears to identify the Holy Spirit with the preexistent divine nature of Christ.[2] The apologists, Justin and Aristides, in their anxiety to emphasize the doctrine of the Logos, minimize the work and place of the Spirit.[3] Origen's speculations show how the Church was feeling after a clearer understanding of the mode of the Spirit's existence but had not yet attained it.[4]

---

[1] Cp. Swete, *The Holy Spirit in the Ancient Church*, p. 159. 'The devotional language of the early Church was in fact on the whole in advance of its doctrinal system. Men like Origen still had intellectual difficulties in reference to the relation of the Spirit to the other Persons of the Holy Trinity; but they could nevertheless associate His name in their prayers and praises with those of the Father and the Son. The worship of the Trinity was a fact in the religious life of Christians before it was a dogma of the Church. Dogmatic precision was forced upon the Church by heresy, but the confession and conglorification of the Three Persons arose out of the Christian consciousness, interpreting by its own experience the words of Christ and the Apostles and the primitive rule of faith.'

[2] *E.g.* Sim. IX. i. 1. *Pneuma* and *spiritus* are freely used by the Greek and Latin writers of the second and third centuries to denote the divine nature in itself.

[3] *E.g.* Justin assigns the miraculous conception to the Word Himself, *Apol.* i. 33.

[4] Origen raises the question in this form. Is the Spirit to be regarded as ἀγέννητός like the Father, or γεννητός like the Son, or is He to be ranked among the γεννητά, that is, the beings who have come into existence through the Logos? He is feeling his way to the later doctrine that the Holy Spirit is not like the Father the source of Godhead, nor like the Son 'begotten of the Father', but proceeds from the Father through the Son. As yet he had no technical language in which to express his thought. In placing

Montanism in the latter half of the second century with its revival of prophecy brought to the front the reality of the Person and power of the Holy Spirit. The movement was an exaggeration of a neglected truth. It is significant that Tertullian, perhaps under Montanist influence, was the first to formulate the relation of the Spirit to the Father and the Son in language approaching that of later theology. He even speaks of 'One substance in three who cohere together'.[1] But here as in his general manner of formulating the doctrine of the Trinity, Tertullian was in advance of his age.

§ 3. The final statement that the Holy Spirit is 'of one substance with the Father and the Son' was a secondary product of the Arian controversy. If the Son was, as Arius taught, a creature and not divine in the full sense, the Holy Spirit whom He sent must be even more creaturely and less divine. But for the time the Arians did not press this point. The centre of controversy was the Person of the Son. The Council of Nicaea was content only to reaffirm belief in the Spirit. But in 359 news was brought to Athanasius of certain Arians who had come to accept the Nicene doctrine of the Son, but still regarded the Holy Spirit as a creature, 'one of the ministering angels and superior to the angels only in degree.' These men he named 'Tropici', because they treated as τροπαί or metaphors all passages of Scripture that contradicted their own view. He also speaks of them as πνευματομαχοῦντες whence they became commonly known as 'Pneumatomachi'. Against them he wrote the letters to Serapion setting forth the consubstantiality of the Spirit.[2] At the Synod of Alexandria in 362 an anathema was directed against those who 'say that the Holy Spirit is a creature and separate from the essential nature of Christ'. Meanwhile similar views were being put forth at Constantinople; about the year 360 Macedonius, the bishop of Constantinople, while accepting the divinity of the Son, denied that of the Spirit, saying that he was only a minister and a servant. His followers became known by the name of Macedonians. For the time Macedonianism was a real danger to the Church. At a Roman Synod in 369 the appeal of the Macedonians was rejected and the full doctrine of the Trinity affirmed. In 381 at the Council of Constantinople Macedonianism was expressly condemned. This was an inevitable result of the defeat of Arianism. The controversy about the divinity of the Holy Spirit did not involve any fresh issue which had not been already considered. The doctrine of the Spirit was worked out by the Cappadocian Fathers. There had never been any real doubt as to His divinity in the Church at large. A creature would not be included in the Trinity. Christians were convinced that His working

the Spirit in the third class, among the γενητά, he laid himself open to the charge of ranking Him among the creatures. His tentative speculations became dogmas with some of his followers in the fourth century. See Swete, op. cit. pp. 127 ff. and pp. 163 ff.

[1] 'Unam substantiam in tribus cohaerentibus,' Adv. Praxeam, c. 12.

[2] See C. R. B. Shapland, The Letters of S. Athanasius concerning the Holy Spirit.

within their own souls proved Him to be not less than divine. But the Church did not wish to speculate. Even S. Cyril of Jerusalem, writing about 348, after a full exposition of the work of the Holy Spirit discourages all speculation about His Person. 'Be not over-curious about His nature or hypostasis. Had it been revealed in Scripture we should have spoken of it; what is not written, let us not venture to touch. It is sufficient for salvation to know that there is a Father, a Son, and a Holy Spirit.'[1] The Macedonian controversy that began not many months later obliged the Church to formulate her position.†

§ 4. What then is meant by the language of the Article, which speaks of the Holy Spirit as *proceeding from the Father and the Son*? The technical term 'proceeding' is used, simply because it is the language of Scripture.

(i) In Jn 15[26] Christ says 'When the Advocate is come, whom I will send unto you from the Father, even the Spirit of truth which pro-ceedeth (ἐκπορεύεται) from the Father, He shall testify of me.' Even under the Old Testament revelation men would have been prepared to assert that the Spirit of God in some sense proceeded from God. But the New Testament makes it clear that the gift of the Holy Spirit at Pentecost was a gift of the Ascended Christ. He was sent not only by the Father but by the Son. 'I (ἐγώ) will send unto you' (cp. 16[7], Acts 2[33]). Further, Scripture calls Him not only the Spirit of God but the Spirit of Christ Himself (Rom 8[9], Gal 4[6], Phil 1[19], 1 Pet 1[10-11]), and even the Spirit 'of Jesus' (Acts 16[7]), using our Lord's human name. In the coming of the Holy Spirit Christ Himself comes. Through the Holy Spirit, Christ dwells in the Church and in the hearts of believers (Jn 14[16-18], Eph 3[16b-17]). It is through the reception of the Spirit that Christians are 'in Christ'. This truth, that the Holy Spirit is the Spirit not only of God the Father but of Christ lies be-hind the difficult passage 2 Cor 3[17-18]. 'Now the Lord is the Spirit: and where the Spirit of the Lord is, there is liberty. But we all with unveiled face reflecting as in a mirror the glory of the Lord, are transformed into the same image from glory to glory, even as from the Spirit which is the Lord' (R.V. mg. καθάπερ ἀπὸ Κυρίου πνεύματος). The presence and power of the Spirit known in the Church since Pentecost are the very presence and power of Jesus Christ. In other words the new revelation of the Spirit is made as a sequel of the In-carnation. 'The Holy Ghost is mainly revealed to us as the Spirit of the Incarnate.'[2] He is not simply the Spirit of God in His absolute and eternal existence, nor the Spirit of God as putting forth the energy of creation, He is the Spirit of God Incarnate. Through Him

---

[1] *Cat.* xvi. 24.
[2] Moberly, *Atonement and Personality*, p. 194. Cp. the whole passage, pp. 194–205. See also L. S. Thornton, *The Incarnate Lord*, c. xii, for a discussion of the distinction between Christ and the Spirit.

we share the saving power of Christ's victorious humanity. By His coming the perfect human life of our Ascended Lord is bestowed upon us. This great truth is safeguarded by the assertion that He proceeds not from the Father only but from the Father and the Son.

(ii) But the words as used in the Article mean more than this. So far we have thought only about the 'Economic Trinity', *i.e.* God as active in redemption, God in His dealings with the world. But we cannot but believe that the 'Temporal Mission' of the Holy Ghost, as it is called, *i.e.* His descent as the Spirit of God Incarnate, corresponds to something within the 'Essential Trinity', that it rests upon and springs out of a relation within the eternal being of God. About the eternal life of God we can know nothing except in so far as it is outlined in the Incarnation. But we feel that the historical revelation of God through Jesus Christ as Father, Son and Holy Spirit, must depend upon distinctions and relations within the being of God. When we strive to express such distinctions and relations we can only do so in language borrowed from the manner of the Incarnation. Thus we speak of the Second Person of the Holy Trinity as Son, and the Third as Spirit. Further, if in time the Holy Spirit proceeded from the Father and the Son, we can only express His relationship to the Father and the Son in eternity by the use of the same language. For we have and can have no other. Accordingly, Catholic theologians have always taught that the Father is alone the underived source of Godhead (ἄναρχος) and the Son derives His being by eternal generation from the Father. Further, from the first it was held that the procession of the Spirit, like the generation of the Son, refers not only to His mission but to His essential life, that He derives His being from the being of God. Some theologians taught that the Spirit like the Son received His Godhead immediately from the Father alone. But the majority saw that just as His temporal mission was from the Father through the Son, just as the Holy Spirit who descended at Pentecost was the Spirit not only of the Father but of the Son, so within the eternal life of God He received His being not directly from the Father, but mediately through the Son. The Divine Essence was conceived as eternally passing from the Father through the Son into the Spirit. We may doubt whether there is any primary reference to this in Scripture at all. The words of Jn 16[14] where the Spirit is said to receive the things of Christ, just as Christ received all that is the Father's, would seem to refer primarily to the economic Trinity, though no doubt they hint at an eternal relationship.

(iii) The dispute between East and West has centred not on the fact of the 'double procession' but on the manner in which it is expressed. S. Augustine formulated it in the words 'proceeding from the Father and the Son' and this became the common language of the West. The Constantinopolitan Creed—our so-called Nicene Creed—had always said only 'Who proceedeth from the Father'. The Church of Spain, in its conflict with Arianism on the one hand and Sabellianism on the other, was the first to introduce S. Augustine's language into confessions of faith. The words 'Proceeding from the Father and the Son' had appeared in a profession of faith put forth by a Council of Toledo in 447. It used to be supposed that they were first inserted into the Creed at the Council of Toledo in 589. This, however, is doubtful. Those who denied the double procession were indeed anathematized, but evidence seems to show that the text of the Creed was kept pure by the Council. Their interpolation into the actual Creed was probably the work of copyists, under the influence of the anathema. For a long time the addition remained unobserved and awakened no controversy. It did not become a matter for public debate till the time of Charles the Great. Even then Pope Leo III, though he accepted the double procession, deliberately rejected the addition to the Creed and set up in S. Peter's copies of it without the addition.

It is clear, however, from the protests of the Franks that the interpolated form had spread to Gaul and the question of the procession had begun to arouse controversy. A dispute had arisen at Jerusalem between Greeks and Latins over the use of the new form of the Creed. Rome herself did not accept the addition till after the final breach between East and West. It is usually supposed that it was introduced by the influence of the Emperor Henry II, in 1014, along with the custom of repeating the Creed at Mass. The arguments of the Eastern Church against the language 'from the Father and the Son' were partly theological, partly historical. It has been argued that it implies two independent sources of Godhead and so breaks up the unity. This is untrue. The Western Church means no more by it than Eastern theologians mean when they use the language 'from the Father through the Son'. S. Augustine was most careful to guard against any violation of the unity of the Godhead. Again, it has been objected that it was inserted irregularly. This is partly true. We may reply, however, that the insertion was originally quite accidental and was very useful in dealing with heresy. To set it aside now would run the risk of appearing to deny the truth that it protects. All that the Western Church claims is to repeat the clause in a sense that is perfectly orthodox. We do, however, admit that the clause has not Catholic authority: that it is unfortunate that any addition was made and still more unfortunate that, if any addition was judged to be necessary, it was not made in the form that would have been acceptable to East and West alike, namely 'from the Father through the Son'.[1] In itself it is certainly inadequate to justify any rupture between East and West. We must remember, however, the real causes of division are to be found elsewhere, in political rivalry and jealousy between Rome and Constantinople.†

[1] Certain modern Greek theologians, however, would seem to be unwilling to use the words to denote more than the temporal mission from the Son.

THE SCRIPTURES

ARTICLE VI

Of the Sufficiency of the Holy Scriptures for Salvation

Holy Scripture containeth all things necessary to salvation: so that whatsoever is not read therein, nor may be proved thereby, is not to be required of any man, that it should be believed as an Article of the Faith, or be thought requisite or necessary to salvation.

In the name of Holy Scripture we do understand those Canonical Books of the Old and New Testament, of whose authority was never any doubt in the Church.

Of the Names and Number of the Canonical Books

Genesis,
Exodus,
Leviticus,
Numbers,
Deuteronomy,
Joshua,
Judges,
Ruth,
The I Book of Samuel,
The II Book of Samuel,
The I Book of Kings,
The II Book of Kings,
The I Book of Chronicles,
The II Book of Chronicles,
The I Book of Esdras,

De divinis Scripturis, quod sufficiant ad salutem

Scriptura sacra continet omnia, quae ad salutem sunt necessaria, ita ut quicquid in ea nec legitur, neque inde probari potest, non sit a quoquam exigendum, ut tanquam Articulus fidei credatur, aut ad salutis necessitatem requiri putetur.

Sacrae Scripturae nomine, eos Canonicos libros Veteris et Novi Testamenti intelligimus, de quorum auctoritate in Ecclesia nunquam dubitatum est.

De nominibus et numero librorum sacrae Canonicae Scripturae Veteris Testamenti

Genesis,
Exodus,
Leviticus,
Numeri,
Deuteron,
Josuae,
Judicum,
Ruth,
Prior liber Samuelis,
Secundus liber Samuelis,
Prior liber Regum,
Secundus liber Regum,
Prior liber Paralipomenon,
Secundus liber Paralipomenon,
Primus liber Esdrae,

The II Book of Esdras,
The Book of Esther,
The Book of Job,
The Psalms,
The Proverbs,
Ecclesiastes, or the Preacher,
Cantica, or Songs of Solomon,
Four Prophets the Greater,
Twelve Prophets the Less.

Secundus liber Esdrae,
Liber Hester,
Liber Job,
Psalmi,
Proverbia,
Ecclesiastes vel Concionator,
Cantica Solomonis,
IV Prophetae majores,
XII Prophetae minores.

All the books of the New Testament, as they are commonly received, we do receive, and account them Canonical.

Novi Testamenti omnes libros (ut vulgo recepti sunt) recipimus, et habemus pro Canonicis.

And the other books (as Hierome saith) the Church doth read for example of life and instruction of manners; but yet doth it not apply them to establish any doctrine. Such are these following:

Alios autem libros (ut ait Hieronymus) legit quidem Ecclesia ad exempla vitae et formandos mores; illos tamen ad dogmata confirmanda non adhibet: ut sunt:

The III Book of Esdras,
The IV Book of Esdras,
The Book of Tobias,
The Book of Judith,
The rest of the Book of Esther,
The Book of Wisdom,
Jesus the Son of Sirach,
Baruch the Prophet,
The Song of the Three Children,
The Story of Susanna,
Of Bel and the Dragon,
The Prayer of Manasses,
The I Book of Maccabees,
The II Book of Maccabees.

Tertius liber Esdrae,
Quartus liber Esdrae,
Liber Tobiae,
Liber Judith,
Reliquum libri Hester,
Liber Sapientiae,
Liber Jesu filii Sirach,
Baruch Propheta,
Canticum trium puerorum,
Historia Susannae,
De Bel et Dracone,
Oratio Manassis,
Prior liber Machabaeorum,
Secundus liber Machabaeorum.

This Article received its final form in 1571. The first paragraph is based on a similar statement in the Article of 1553. The remainder of the Article was added in 1563, being based on the Confession of Würtemburg, except that the list of the Apocrypha omitted 'The rest of the Book of Esther', 'Baruch,' 'The Song of the Three Children,' 'Bel and the Dragon,' and 'The Prayer of Manasses'. It was completed by the addition of these books in 1571. Its immediate object was to state the position of the Church of England with reference to the use and extent of Scripture, against Anabaptists on the one hand and Rome on the other.

(i) Certain among the Anabaptists regarded all Scripture as unnecessary. An Article of 1553 describes them as those 'who affirm that Holy Scripture is given only to the weak and do boast themselves continually of the Spirit, of whom (they say) they have learnt such things as they teach, although the same be most evidently repugnant to the Holy Scripture.' In other words if men claim to be under the immediate guidance of the Holy Spirit, and to have received a personal revelation, does not this supersede Scripture? Such a view implied a plenary inspiration of individuals, and opened the way for a chaos of interpretations, each claiming the authority of the Holy Spirit.

(ii) The ambiguous language of the Council of Trent had appeared to regard Scripture by itself as insufficient, and to place tradition on a level with it as an independent source of doctrine. In a decree published in 1546, and therefore before the compilers of this Article, it speaks of the 'truth and discipline . . . contained in the written books, and in the unwritten traditions, which, received by the Apostles from the mouth of Christ Himself or from the Apostles themselves . . . have come down to us. . . . We receive and venerate these traditions, whether they refer to faith or to morals, with the same (*i.e.* the same as Holy Scripture) devotion and reverence inasmuch as they were dictated either by word of mouth by Christ Himself or by the Holy Spirit, and have been preserved by unbroken transmission in the Catholic Church'. Such language at least suggested that part of the faith was to be found in Scripture and part in tradition. Further, the same decree of the Council of Trent includes within the canon the majority of the books of the Apocrypha (Tobit, Judith, Wisdom, Ecclesiasticus, Baruch, I and II Maccabees, and the additions to the books of Daniel and Esther) and regards them as of authority in matters of doctrine.

This Article is not intended to stand alone. It gives no answer to the vital question, Who is to decide what can be proved from Scripture? This is answered in Art. 20. Again, it deals only with the question of doctrine: questions of authority in matters of custom or ceremonies or organization are dealt with in Art. 34.

ARTICLE VII

Of the Old Testament

The Old Testament is not contrary to the New, for both in the Old and New Testament everlasting life is offered to mankind by Christ, who is the only Mediator between God and Man, being both God and Man. Wherefore they are not to be heard, which feign that the old Fathers did look only for transitory promises. Although the Law given from God by Moses, as touching Ceremonies and Rites, do not bind Christian men, nor the Civil Precepts thereof ought of necessity to be received in any commonwealth; yet notwithstanding, no Christian man whatsoever is free from the obedience of the Commandments which are called Moral.

De Veteri Testamento

Testamentum Vetus Novo contrarium non est, quandoquidem tam in Veteri, quam in Novo, per Christum, qui unicus est Mediator Dei et hominum, Deus et homo, aeterna vita humano generi est proposita. Quare male sentiunt, qui veteres tantum in promissiones temporarias sperasse confingunt. Quanquam lex a Deo data per Mosen, quoad caeremonias et ritus, Christianos non astringat, neque civilia ejus praecepta in aliqua republica necessario recipi debeant, nihilominus tamen ab obedientia mandatorum quae moralia vocantur nullus quantumvis Christianus est solutus.

This Article forms a sequel to the previous Article. It was formed by Archbishop Parker out of two of the earlier Articles of 1553, with slight modifications. It is directed against two opposite errors, both maintained by sections of Anabaptists.

(i) Some rejected the Old Testament entirely, and claimed, in virtue of their illumination by the Spirit, to be superior even to the moral law contained in it.

(ii) Others maintained that Christians were under obligation to obey the whole law contained in it, civil and ceremonial, as well as moral. We read of strange attempts to set up a literal 'New Jerusalem' in Westphalia. The Calvinists were not entirely out of sympathy with this idea, as was shown by Calvin's rule at Geneva.

Against both these views the Article insists that the Old Testament represents a preparatory stage in one divine revelation and must be interpreted as such, in relation to the whole scheme of revelation.

§ 1. The sufficiency of Scripture

The position of the Church of England laid down in this Article is quite clear. She does not require of a man as a condition of membership belief in any truth which is not contained in or cannot be proved from Scripture. In the ordering of priests the question is asked: 'Are you persuaded that the Holy Scriptures contain sufficiently all doctrine required of necessity for eternal salvation through faith in Jesus Christ and are you determined . . . to teach nothing as required of necessity to eternal salvation, but that which you shall be persuaded may be concluded and proved by the Scripture?'[1] We are bound to be faithful in declaring to men the 'whole counsel of God' (cp. Acts 20[27]) and to hold fast all that God has revealed (cp. 1 Tim 6[20]), not leaving out or slurring over any truth that is inconvenient or unpopular. But we are no less bound to respect the limits of divine revelation. On many points it is quite possible for good Christians honestly to hold different opinions. Ministers of the Church have no right to force upon men what are only conjectures. To require men to accept as authoritative teaching for which there is no real evidence is to strain and weaken faith. If men are asked to accept indiscriminately anything that individuals choose to teach, the inevitable result is that as soon as they learn the precariousness of part of the teaching, they reject not that part only but the whole. The Church of England, therefore, holds up the Bible as the sufficient standard of Christian teaching and as the embodiment of all those truths to which the Church was formed to bear witness. How can this position be justified?

(a) We must never forget that the Church existed and was at work

---

[1] What is meant by 'necessary to salvation'? The phrase is intended in this context to refer to those who have a desire to hold and live by the Christian faith. For them it is precarious to assume that they can obey the will of God and attain to eternal life with Him, if they are unwilling to accept in faith the truth that He has revealed. To them the teacher is bound to set forth the whole Gospel as 'necessary to their salvation', as that which 'a Christian ought to know and believe to his soul's health'. We need not take the phrase as settling questions about the destiny of the heathen who have not heard the Gospel or of those who are 'invincibly ignorant' of it or conscientiously reject it.

in the world for many years before any single book of the New Testament was composed. These books were written by members of the Church for members of the Church. They pre-suppose a certain knowledge in those who read them, based upon oral instruction (cp. Lk 1^4, Rom 1^{6-7}, 1 Cor 11^{23}, 15^3, Heb 5^{12-13}, 1 Jn 2^{12}). They were written not to create but to strengthen and educate faith. No single book of the New Testament was intended in the first instance for unbelievers. So to-day Scripture cannot be our earliest teacher. It is the Church that points us to the Bible as differing from all other books and that gives us that elementary instruction by word and example in the Christian life without which the Bible would be largely unmeaning. 'For whatsoever we believe concerning salvation by Christ, although the Scripture be therein the ground of our belief; yet the authority of man is, if we mark it, the key which openeth the door of entrance into the knowledge of the Scripture. The Scripture could not teach us the things that are of God unless we did credit men who have taught us that the words of Scripture do signify those things.'[1] To most of us the beginning of our religion is the teaching of the Church as represented say by a parent. In the earliest days preaching depended on the eye-witnesses and actual hearers of Christ. The first Christians did not test what they heard by the New Testament, for that did not yet exist. Rather as the books of the New Testament came one by one into their hands, they tested them by their conformity to the teaching of the apostles and those who heard them. S. Paul did not go with a Bible under his arm and quote proof texts in support of the Resurrection. Human nature, especially Greek human nature, was not one bit less inquisitive than it is to-day. Questions would be asked, and he would answer them by relating the testimony of eye-witnesses: 'Peter said this, John told me that.' So we must not place the Bible in a false position of isolation and divorce it from the continuous life of the society within which it was written. Behind the books of the New Testament stands the life and witness of the early Church illuminating and confirming them. The great failure of much negative criticism to-day is caused by treating the books of the New Testament as if they came to us from some unknown source. Passages which taken out of their context may be interpreted in more than one way, can only receive one interpretation when they are studied, as they were meant to be studied, in the light of a Christian life. Since the New Testament was written for Christians only Christians can fully understand it. Bible and Church must go hand in hand. The statement has been made that 'the Bible and the Bible only is the religion of Protestants'.[2] Apart from the fact that a book cannot be a religion, it denies the intimate connexion between the written word

---

[1] Hooker, ii. c. 7, § 3.
[2] It is inscribed on the tomb of Chillingworth. It is only fair to add that he did not use it in the misleading sense popular among the less educated Protestants of to-day.

and the Christian community. Like any other book, the Bible can only be interpreted aright by those who approach it with the right presuppositions, and those can only be attained by sharing in the life of Christian fellowship.

(b) Christianity is not the religion of a book but of a Person.[1] 'Christianity is Christ' in a way that Buddhism is not Buddha or Mohammedanism Mohammed. The centre of our faith is not the teaching of Christ but Christ Himself. Behind Church and Bible alike stands the living Saviour. Why then is the Bible placed in this supreme position? The answer lies in its special relation to Christ. The Old Testament is the record of the preparation of the world for His coming. It shows the choice and education of the Jewish people. They were called by God to a special task, and given a vision of His purpose which Christ alone could fulfil. The Old Testament is the book on which His own religious life was nourished. He reverenced it as the word of God and found Himself there. So in the New Testament we have on the one hand a fourfold picture of the earthly life of Christ, a selection of His teaching and mighty works, the story of His death and resurrection, all given to us on the authority of eye-witnesses and approved by the consent of the early Church as correct. We have further the earliest and most authoritative teaching of the Church itself. The Epistles show us the Gospel as it was proclaimed in apostolic days, and all that the Ascended Christ proved Himself to be to the first generation of Christians. They attest all unconsciously the fulness and vigour of the new life and hope that He had brought. The Apostles are obviously witnesses of special importance. They were trained by Christ Himself (Mk 3^{14}): they were promised special guidance by the Holy Spirit to remember and interpret His teaching (Jn 14^{26}, 16^{13-14}). So the New Testament possesses a unique value from its close relationship to the earthly life of Christ, from the character and position of its writers and its intimate connexion with the life of the early Church. 'It is self-evident to the mind that takes it in as a whole that the New Testament is a single movement of spiritual and Christian thought and life, and that it is complete and sufficient in itself. It is equally certain that neither the succeeding nor any subsequent age had in it either the plastic capacity or the creative power to take for itself a living form such as Christianity easily, freely and naturally assumed in its initiative stage. And therefore it was, to say no more, an act of practical wisdom to accept that first embodiment and expression of itself as in principle at least and in substance final and irreformable.'[2]

(c) The question still remains, can we do what the Article assumes, be assured that it contains all necessary teaching? May not some part have been omitted? We can hardly appeal for an answer to any

---

[1] Cp. Gore, *The Incarnation of the Son of God*, Lect. i.
[2] Du Bose, *Ecumenical Councils*, p. 25.

definite text of Scripture itself. The very idea of such a collection of Christian writings did not yet exist when any one of them was being composed. Each was written to meet a particular need at a particular time. But we can fairly appeal to the feeling in Scripture itself of the greater security of the written word. Christ habitually speaks of the Old Testament in such a way as to suggest that it is the adequate and authoritative embodiment of God's revelation to the Jewish Church. He finds in it the expression of the Father's will (Mt 4⁴, ⁷, ¹⁰). He proves His own teaching from it (Jn 10³⁴, Mk 12²⁶⁻²⁷). He appeals to the written law as against unwritten tradition (Mk 7¹⁻¹³). Again, in his preface to the Gospel, S. Luke refers to the greater certainty of the written word (Lk 1⁴, cp. Jn 20³¹). The New Testament from end to end assumes that the revelation of God in Christ is final and complete. Heb 1¹ ff. contrasts the fragmentary revelations of old times with the fulness of revelation in Christ. It is 'the faith once for all delivered to the saints' (Jude 3). There cannot be a second Christ or a second Gospel (cp. 2 Cor 11⁴, Gal 1⁶⁻⁸, etc.). That this message is adequately embodied in our Scriptures is shown by the testimony of the early Church. It was the Church that gradually decided the canon of the New Testament, and we find no consciousness at any time that any part of its message had been omitted or misrepresented. The Church did not in any sense create the Gospel. It is always God's word and not man's, but the Bible is the Church's record of it. This view of the sufficiency of Scripture is for questions of doctrine the unanimous view of the early Fathers. We can only give a few examples here. 'If any thing remains which Holy Scripture does not determine, no other third scripture ought to be received to authorize any knowledge, but we must commit to the fire what remains, that is, reserve it unto God' (Origen, *Hom. V. in Lev.*). 'The holy and divinely-inspired Scriptures are of themselves sufficient to the enunciation of truth' (Athanasius, *Contra Gentes*, 1). 'In these alone the doctrine of salvation is contained. Let no man add to or take from them' (*Festal Epistles*, ii). 'Believe those things that are written: the things which are not written, seek not' (Basil, *Hom.* 29). 'In those things which are plainly laid down in Scripture, all things are found, which embrace faith and morals' (Augustine, *On Christian Doctrine*, ii).¹ The position taken up by this Article is in effect a return to antiquity. It is supported both by the intrinsic nature of the New Testament writings and by the unanimous witness of the early Church. We may add that if we believe that the Holy Spirit guided the Church in the selection of these books, we must believe that no vital part of the revelation in Christ was suffered to be lost. The Apostles could hardly understand the importance of their witness for future ages. They expected the immediate return of the Lord. But their witness is all the more valuable because

---

¹ A long list of references could easily be compiled. See Harold Browne on Art. 6, p. 141 ff.; Palmer, *On the Church*, c. ii.

it is unpremeditated. Just because they built primarily for their own time, they built the better for all time. By the providence of God the Church was provided with a means of testing its faith. It can return again and again to Scripture as the standard expression of its own life, formulated in times of the greatest vitality.

(d) On the other hand, as we have already seen, Scripture needs the Church for its interpretation. Not only is much of it hard to understand (Acts 8[31], 2 Pet 3[16]), but its leading truths are not arranged in any definite order. We need the right point of view. One of the uses of creeds is to supply a simple scheme of truth. From the first the Church has always attached great importance to tradition, not as alternative to Scripture, but as a means to its correct interpretation. Tradition shows how the words of Scripture have been understood by the Church. Thus, S. Vincent of Lerins ends his *Commonitorium* with the words: 'We said above that this has always been, and even at this day is, the custom of Catholics to try and examine the true faith by these two methods: first, by the authority of the divine canon; secondly, by the rule of the Catholic Church; not because the canonical Scripture is not as to itself sufficient for all things, but because very many, expounding God's word at their own will, do thereby conceive divers opinions and errors. And for this cause it is necessary that the interpretation of the heavenly Scripture be directed according to the one only rule of the Church's understanding; only, be it observed, especially in those questions upon which the foundations of the whole Catholic doctrine depend.' It is in the same spirit that the canon of 1571 bids the clergy in their preaching 'see that they never teach ought in a sermon, to be religiously held and believed by the people, except what is agreeable to the doctrine of the Old and New Testaments, and what the Catholic Fathers and ancient bishops have collected from the same doctrine.'[1] The well-known saying 'The Church to teach and the Bible to prove' sums up the position of the Church of England on this point.[2]

§ 2. *The Canon of Scripture*

(a) The distinction made in this Article between canonical and non-canonical books raises in an acute form the whole question of inspiration. We shall shortly give some account of the history of the formation of the Canon, but the deeper question still remains: does this historical distinction depend upon any intrinsic quality in the books themselves? What is inspiration and how is it present in a unique form in the Bible?

(i) We may begin by drawing a distinction between 'Revelation' and 'Inspiration'. All knowledge implies both something to be known

---

[1] See Gee and Hardy, *Documents Illustrative of English Church History*, p. 476.
[2] On the Roman Catholic view of the authority of unwritten tradition, see Salmon, *The Infallibility of the Church* (1952 edition) c. v.; R. Hanson and R. Fuller, *The Church of Rome*, cc. iii and iv.

and a mind that can know it. Revelation and inspiration correspond to these two sides of knowledge. Revelation means the uncovering by God of some spiritual truth that man's mind may apprehend it. Inspiration means the quickening of the human mind and soul to perceive and understand what has been unveiled. 'In the act of revelation God unveils that which He desires men to know: in His act of inspiration He opens the eyes of men's minds to see that which He has unveiled.'[1] The truth which is given and the power of grasping it both alike come from God.

(ii) Neither the Bible nor the Church has ever defined inspiration. It can be recognized rather than defined. The nearest approach to any statement is in 2 Pet 1[20] 'No prophecy of scripture is of private interpretation. For no prophecy ever came by the will of men, but men spake from God, being moved by the Holy Ghost.' In 2 Tim 3[16] the word θεόπνευστος is applied to the Scriptures, *i.e.* the Old Testament, and the passage should probably be translated 'Every inspired scripture is also profitable for teaching, for reproof, for correction, for instruction which is in righteousness, that the man of God may be complete, furnished unto every good work.' These passages suggest on the one hand that the writers of the Scriptures were directly moved by the Holy Spirit, and on the other hand that this inspiration was given to enlighten and instruct men in the way of obedience to the divine will. Where spiritual truth is concerned God makes a revelation and inspires men to apprehend it in order that they may hear and obey His Word. We shall therefore not look to inspired writings for infallible information on questions of science and history. We have our natural powers of intelligent enquiry by which to investigate and obtain light on these questions. God's revealed and inspired Word is not intended to do for us what His natural gifts to us enable us to do for ourselves. Moreover, in the context of a large group of writings such as the Bible we shall not expect that any one member or part of the group will give us the whole content of God's revelation. The form and content of the inspired message are limited by the capacities of those to whom it is in the first instance given; the individual writer will have his proper place with others who have also received illumination. Thus we believe that four writers were each moved to compose a Gospel and so to give in different ways a fourfold witness to the truth of the Incarnate Life, and in the Old Testament 'the Law, the Prophets, and the Writings' together preserve God's revelation of Himself to His ancient people.

(iii) All forms of inspiration pre-suppose two factors, and this is particularly true of all inspired religious insight. There is first an inheritance of knowledge already embodied in some kind of corporate tradition. The individual is born into a community which

---

[1] Quoted by Watson, *Inspiration*, p. 24.

possesses a religion and he is taught its beliefs and customs. He starts from the common consciousness, however much he may later modify or correct what he has received. Secondly, within a living religious tradition there may arise from time to time individuals who with special gifts and prophetic insight permanently deepen and enrich the tradition or even by their influence turn it in new directions. In the course of time what they first perceived may become part of the common stock of knowledge in the community and receive embodiment in newly-shaped customs and institutions. This general picture is true of the working of inspiration in the biblical writers, but here it takes on a special form. Regarded from a purely historical point of view, the whole of the Bible is the literary deposit of the religious experience of a community with a continuous history and identity. There are crises in the history, above all the crisis of the coming of the Messiah, and each crisis leaves a mark upon the tradition, but there is continuity too from the earliest to the latest of the biblical documents. At each crisis appear prophetic figures. In the Old Testament Moses and the canonical prophets are pre-eminent in the crises of their day, and they are followed by the law-givers, the priests, the prophetic historians and the wise men, who embody the prophetic insight in laws, cultus, wise sayings, and historical tradition. So far the biblical tradition in its various phases is generally comparable to the history of other religious traditions. But in fact the continuity and the movement here take on a form which is not paralleled elsewhere, and that in two particular respects. First, the continuity exhibited in the Bible is not simply that of the story of a single nation with the phases of its religious experience, for the nation was destroyed in A.D. 70 and the continuity remained unbroken. Nor is it that of a developing idea or complex of ideas, for the movement does not depend on the work of a series of great thinkers. Rather the Bible claims to record a continuous and consistent series of divine acts specially related to the history of a chosen people, together with the interpretation of those acts which God made known to those whom He 'called' or 'raised up'. The basic continuity lies on the divine side, in God's will and purpose manifested in acts. On the human side the continuity is not that of steady and consistent development and response; Israel often rejects the divine revelation and learns as a nation only when it has passed through judgment (*e.g.* the Exile). Finally it rejected the Messiah when He came, but the divine purpose continued. Secondly, the determining form of inspiration in the Bible is of a kind which demands a more exact description than 'insight into spiritual truth'. The prophets, for example, did not conceive their function as the preaching of higher spiritual ideas to their contemporaries. They recalled them to knowledge of what God had done in and for Israel in the past; they discerned His present acts; and they announced that which He would do. In all this they were aware of a consistent divine character and purpose; God's acts revealed for them what He is and what He demands of His people. In so far as they teach truths about the nature of God and the duties of man these truths are derived from an understanding of God's covenant with Israel and are not separable from that understanding. Similarly in the New Testament apostolic inspiration is the gift of insight into the supreme divine act in the life and death and resurrection of Christ. For the apostolic writers everything turns on knowing and obeying the Word of God made flesh. Throughout the Bible we have the record of God's witness to Himself in the events of a particular history, interpreted and set down by minds which He enlightened to understand and expound it. This is the kind of authority which the Bible itself claims.

(*b*) We may now try to state more exactly what Christians mean by the unique inspiration of the Bible and by describing it as the 'Word of God'.

(i) Even the unbeliever can discern special qualities in the biblical books. As literature they hold a high place among the great books of the world. The philosophical moralist will find much to admire in many passages of the Bible, though some parts of its teaching on conduct may strike him as strange or even perverse. Again, if placed beside the classical scriptures of other faiths and studied by the comparative method, the Bible will hold its own; its place after such a comparison may appear pre-eminent even to some non-Christian minds, if they have been nurtured in our Western tradition. Yet none of these approaches will legitimately yield the conclusion that its authority for us is unique. A comparative consideration of the merits of the Bible as literature, as morals, and as a great religious classic is useful for some purposes and perfectly legitimate; it may for some minds open the way to a more profound insight into its meaning. But ultimately the inspiration of the Bible, as Christians understand it, can only be perceived and apprehended from within Christian faith.

(ii) The reason for this lies in the nature of the contents of the Bible. Its unity is found in its unique relation to Christ. The Incarnation is for Christian faith the central and supreme event in history, and the New Testament records both the facts of the Incarnate Life and their revealing significance. As described in the New Testament the life and work of Jesus Christ cannot be understood except as the climax and fulfilment of a preparatory revelation made to Israel and set forth in the Old Testament. The whole Bible reveals one moving and consistent divine activity of revelation culminating in the Word Incarnate. This unity is perceptible only to those who receive Christ in faith. To them the Bible reveals the story of the divine self-disclosure in a particular history, as its meaning was interpreted by prophets and apostles standing within the actual course of that history. Thus the Bible gives a knowledge of God which can be found nowhere else, for there is no rival account of what the Bible describes; and it conveys a truth, which, once it is recognized as such, must take a supreme place in the mind and heart of the believer.[1] The Scriptures are the unique Word of God because they are the only vessel containing this divine truth of which the centre and fulness is Christ. Faith in Him as Lord and Saviour is inseparably bound up with the divinely-ordered testimony of the Bible. As the permanent witness to God's truth, declared in God's historical self-disclosure, the Bible in its parts and as a whole has been formed by the creative and illuminating work of the Holy Spirit, whose function it is to bear witness to Christ. The claim that one canon of sacred writings bears unique testimony to God's revelation is a challenge to faith. But it is congruous with the divine choice of one people and the divine way of redemption by particular events.

(iii) The Church reads and hears the Scriptures not only as the record of that which has been revealed, but as the Word by which God speaks here and now to His people. When the divine Word took flesh in Christ He came to judge and to save. So the Word of God received and communicated by prophets and apostles before and after Christ was effective for God's saving purpose. By it the minds and consciences of those whom it reached were brought into a new relation with Him for judgment and salvation. The written Word remains the permanent instrument by which God guides and renews His Church. Through the inspired Scriptures the Holy Spirit to-day instructs, admonishes, and strengthens His people in that faith and life which He has created in them. The Word in the Bible is made contemporary and living when the Church hears, studies and preaches it with a desire to receive and obey it. So in her central act of worship the Church first hears the Scriptures and sums up their message in the Creed before proceeding to the sacramental celebration of Christ's saving work. In the doctrine and the life of the Church the Scriptures have manifestly been the constant source of reformation and renewal by recalling her to her fundamental faith and mission. We must therefore believe that in the divine purpose the Scriptures were formed by the Holy Spirit to be an enduring organ of His guidance of the Church in all ages. Without them the Church

---

[1] This does not mean that the truth given in the Bible is out of relation with other forms of truth. As the Bible teaches, God is the author of Creation as well as of Redemption. Our 'natural' knowledge of our world and of ourselves, so far as it is accurate and complete, is a true knowledge of His creation and it comes to us through faculties which He has created. But natural knowledge, *e.g.* scientific and historical, is never complete and is always in process of development. We must not therefore, expect that at any particular time every problem of its relation to Biblical truth can be solved. But at all times the central truths of revelation and redemption will throw light on other forms of knowledge, and these truths themselves, having been grasped, by faith, need to be interpreted and set in order by the powers of our understanding.

would be in danger of becoming separated from its roots. At the same time it is true that the Scriptures are, now as in the past, addressed to the living community which is God's people in Christ. Outside the life of that community they may lose the power to convey the wholeness of their message to the separated individual or group.

(iv) The inspiration of the Bible does not imply either that its meaning is self-evident or that it cannot be made the subject of thorough historical investigation. Within the Bible itself we find its writers studying and pondering over the words of earlier prophets and teachers. In the primitive Church of the New Testament period the Jewish scriptures were searched for their testimony to Christ, and ancient words took on a new significance. The utterances of the prophets expressed in limited and often material images could now be understood in their last and final meaning in Christ. The early Church put a considerable intellectual effort into the work of interpreting the Scriptures. In every age the Church must study and teach as well as read the Scriptures, for the divine Word does not operate automatically in a quasi-magical way on minds unwilling to devote themselves to thought and investigation. Again, the historical study of the Scriptures by the best critical methods available is legitimate and ultimately profitable for their understanding. The historical origin of the books of the Bible is relevant to their interpretation, and so too is the manner in which they were composed or compiled, their relation to one another in sequence, and the similarities and differences of their expression, outlook and purpose. It is part of the 'historical' character of the Bible that its books were written at various times over a long period and bear the marks of the different circumstances of their origin. Belief in inspiration does not give us any right to pre-determine how the Holy Spirit must have operated, particularly in the Old Testament, to enlighten men's minds 'by diverse portions and in diverse manners'. The theory of 'verbal' inspiration was the result of such a dogmatic pre-determination. New critical methods and a more intimate knowledge of the ancient world have tended in some phases of modern investigation of the Bible to produce results which appear destructive. The original meaning of important passages is seen to differ from their traditional interpretation; doubt may be thrown on the trustworthiness of important statements of fact. On the whole it may be said that what appeared to be the more destructive results of some of the critical work of the last hundred years were ultimately due not so much to the assured conclusions of scholarship as to the theological pre-suppositions of the critics. The work of analytical criticism is now more often combined with recognition of the underlying theological unity of the Bible, which stands out no less clearly when its books are studied in their setting in the ancient world. The Christian critical scholar who approaches the Bible with intellectual integrity will often find that he comes upon baffling problems, but without denying the problems or forsaking the method he will have an eye prepared to see the signs of one Spirit informing the whole Scripture.†

(c) How was the 'canon' of Scripture formed? Some account is needed to explain the position of the 'apocrypha'.

(i) The exact sense in which the term 'canon' was first applied to the Scriptures is disputed. Some have held that the word was used in the sense of 'rule of life' (cp. Gal 6¹⁶) and the books were called canonical as forming a rule of faith or life. More probably the word simply denoted the 'list' by which the contents were defined and 'canonical' simply meant 'on the list'. κανονίζειν is applied not only to the books as a whole but to a single book. But the other idea, if not present from the first, was soon suggested, and the Canon of Scripture came to be regarded as a standard to which an appeal could be made. The whole conception is Christian rather than Jewish. We must beware of arguing as if the Jews regarded their Scriptures as canonical in quite the same sense as the Christians.¹

(ii) The Jews divided the Old Testament into three great divisions: (i) The Law; (ii) The Prophets (these included the 'Former Prophets', *i.e.* the historical books of Joshua, Judges, Samuel and Kings, and the 'Latter Prophets', *i.e.* Isaiah, Jeremiah, Ezekiel and the Twelve); (iii) The Writings (these included the Psalms, Proverbs and Job, Daniel, Ezra, Nehemiah and Chronicles and the five 'rolls', *i.e.* the Song of Songs, Ruth, Lamentations, Ecclesiastes and Esther). It is usually supposed that these three divisions correspond to three more or less distinct stages in the formation of the Old Testament Canon. The traditions found in 2 Esdras 14 and 2 Macc 2¹³ assigning the formation of the Canon to Ezra and Nehemiah respectively are historically worth very little. The chief steps that we can trace in the process are these:

(a) The publication of Deuteronomy in 621 B.C. is the first great landmark (2 Kings 23¹⁻³). 'We have here a solemn religious act by which the king and people alike . . . accept the book read before them as expressing the divine will and take its precepts as binding upon themselves. This is the essential meaning that, as applied to a book, is contained in the epithet "canonical", which means "authoritative", and authoritative because in its ultimate origin Divine.'²

The Law promulgated by Ezra and Nehemiah was substantially our present Pentateuch, with the possible addition of the book of Joshua (Neh 8–10). If we allow for certain minor editorial changes and additions, the whole Law was probably canonical by then, *i.e.* 440 B.C. It is significant that the Samaritans accepted only the Law as canonical. The simplest explanation is that at the time that they

---

¹ The substantive κανών is found first in the writings of Amphilochius (380). Athanasius in his *Festal Epistle* (367) speaks of the books of Scripture as κανονιζόμενα.
² Sanday, 'Bible', *E.R.E.* ii. 565b.

formed their separate community the Canon of Scripture contained nothing else.

(β) No doubt the collection of prophetical writings began quite early. On the one hand, the failure of Chronicles, Ezra and Nehemiah to find a place in this section of the canon suggests that when they were composed, it was at least on the way to being closed. On the other hand, the Chronicler treats the text of Samuel and Kings with great freedom, which equally suggests that by 300 B.C. they were not canonical in the full sense of the term. The strange variations in the LXX version of Samuel seem to carry this condition of things down even to a later date. The earliest references to the 'prophets' as a definite collection are found soon after 200 B.C. In Ecclus 49^{10} (180 B.C.), the 'twelve prophets' are referred to as parallel to Jeremiah and Ezekiel. So, too, Dan 9^2 (168 B.C.) quotes Jeremiah as authoritative. The prophetic canon was therefore probably closed about 200 B.C.

(γ) The formation of the third section of the Canon is more obscure. The earliest mention of any such collection is the prologue to Ecclesiasticus (130 B.C.), which alludes to 'The Law, the Prophets and the other writings'. The very vagueness of the language employed suggests that this last division was not as yet clearly defined. On the one hand, the book of Daniel and certain psalms which are probably Maccabaean were admitted into it. On the other hand, the so-called 'Psalms of Solomon', composed 70–40 B.C., failed to find admittance. We may conclude, therefore, that this section of the Canon was closed about 100 B.C. It is worth noting that in 1 Macc 7^{17}, Psalm 79 is quoted as Scripture. But in any case the Psalms were the earliest of these writings to gain their position in the Canon.

(iii) Among the Jews of Palestine the Canon of Scripture was thus practically closed during the first century B.C. Edifying books were still composed and widely used and quoted, but there had grown up a refusal, at least on the part of the Rabbis, to place them on a level with the Scriptures. Discussion as to the right of certain books to a place in the Canon went on into the second century A.D. The most disputed were the Song of Songs, Ecclesiastes and Esther. The idea of canonicity was expressed in Jewish language by saying that the Scriptures 'defiled the hands', *i.e.* rendered those who handled them ceremonially unclean, the object of this rule being to prevent irreverent handling. The final stage in the settlement of the Jewish Canon was reached at the Council of Jamnia held about A.D. 90. After the fall of Jerusalem Jamnia became the centre of Palestinian Judaism. There the Canon of the Old Testament was for all practical purposes determined, and it included all the books in the English Old Testament and no others.

But meanwhile from the middle of the first century B.C. the Hellenistic Jews, especially the Jews of Alexandria, did not follow the

Palestinian Rabbis in the limitation of the Canon and the general treatment of the Old Testament. Not only did they adopt a different arrangement of the books, but they interspersed among the older books many later writings. These included books originally composed in Hebrew, such as 1 Maccabees, Ecclesiasticus, Tobit, Judith and Baruch and also books composed originally in Greek, such as Wisdom and 2 Maccabees and expansions of canonical books. So the Alexandrian Canon was much wider than the Palestinian, and it has even been argued that the Alexandrians recognized no fixed canon at all. They were ready to admit whatever they judged to be edifying.

Accordingly the Christian Church found itself faced both with a larger and a smaller Canon. When the first Christians broke away from Judaism they did not take with them a well-defined Bible. It would seem that on the question of the canonicity they were content to defer to the judgment of Judaism. Even as late as A.D. 170 Melito, Bishop of Sardis, travelled to Judaea to make a special list. Within the New Testament itself all the books of the Old Testament are quoted as authoritative except Ecclesiastes, Canticles, Esther, Ezra and Nehemiah. On the other hand, none of the apocryphal books is mentioned by name, though their language is in some cases undoubtedly in the mind of New Testament writers. But the book of Enoch, which lies outside even the Apocrypha, is quoted as Scripture in Jude [14]. The main body of the Church went on using the Greek Bible and the Alexandrian Canon. It was recognized, however, especially by learned men who were in touch with Judaism, that there was a more limited Jewish Canon. S. Jerome, for instance, who knew Hebrew, took over the canon of his Jewish instructors. Through his influence the knowledge of the difference between the Hebrew and Greek Bibles was kept alive. The influence of S. Augustine on the other side obtained for the apocryphal books a definite footing. Still all through the Middle Ages the more learned scholars drew a clear line between the Jewish Canon and the apocryphal books. At the Reformation the Council of Trent abolished every shade of distinction between the books.[1] Luther, following S. Jerome, separated the canonical from the apocryphal books, but gave the latter a place as 'useful to read'. Our Article, quoting S. Jerome, does the same. The Calvinists rejected the Apocrypha entirely, and the English Puritans wished the Church to follow their example.[2]

---

[1] The fact that the Roman Church does not include in its Canon some of our apocryphal books (1 and 2 Esdras and The Prayer of Manasses) illustrates the point that 'the Apocrypha' is not an undisputed and clearly-defined whole, like the Old and New Testaments.

[2] A relic of this Puritan tendency survives in the exclusion of the Apocrypha from all use in the Irish Church and in the inability of the British and Foreign Bible Society to supply complete Bibles. They are forbidden to include the Apocrypha by their constitution. The apocryphal books, since 'the Church doth read' them, should be included in complete editions of the Bible. The lectionary of 1922 and its more recent successors include lessons from the Apocrypha.

The word 'apocrypha' is one that has had many meanings. Originally it simply meant 'hidden', and 'apocryphal' books were books containing esoteric teaching known only to the few. The idea of such books was increasingly repugnant to the Christian Church and the word acquired a secondary meaning of 'heretical' or 'spurious'. In the fourth century the word is applied in a different sense by S. Jerome, and comes to mean simply non-canonical. 'Quicquid extra hos' (*i.e.* the Hebrew Canon) 'est, inter ἀπόκρυφα esse ponendum.' He uses it to include both those books that had previously been termed 'ecclesiastical' and also those usually styled 'apocryphal'. It is from S. Jerome that the title 'apocrypha' as we use it to-day comes.

(iv) The formation of the Canon of the New Testament, like that of the Old, was a gradual process. We may summarize its chief stages as follows:

(α) The earliest stage was the informal collection by local Churches of writings of spiritual value. These would include letters from Apostles and other leaders and probably collections of our Lord's sayings and perhaps records of His life and death, that were recognized as coming from reliable sources. A church like Corinth would preserve letters from S. Paul for future guidance. Then local churches would interchange letters and writings. 'Ephesians' was probably in origin a circular letter with the name of the local church left blank to be filled in. The words 'at Ephesus' in 1¹ are absent from the two oldest MSS. ℵ B. There is some evidence that Romans was also used as a circular letter without the addition of the last chapters. In Col 4¹⁶ the Colossians are bidden to hand on the Epistle to be read at Laodicea and in turn to read 'the Epistle from Laodicea', *i.e.* probably the Epistle to the Ephesians, which had been sent there first. We can see then how the germ of a canon arose. Churches compared notes about the sacred writings that they treasured. They interchanged copies, and so in a sense each church came almost unconsciously to form its own canon.

It is most difficult to ascertain how early the books of the New Testament won general acceptance in any given region. Our earliest evidence is that of quotations. In the earliest days we can hardly expect exact quotations from N.T. writings. They had not yet attained their unique position. Stress was still laid on oral tradition. Phrases from set catechetical formulas still lingered in the memory of the writers. There was as yet no conception of the duty of exact quotations from books that were not yet in the full sense canonical. So it is most difficult to be sure what N.T. books were known to early Christian writers. Our evidence does not become clear till the end of the second century.

(β) The earliest definite mention of anything like a canon of Scripture is found in the case of the heretic Marcion (A.D. 140). He formed a collection of S. Paul's Epistles, rejecting the Pastorals, and added a mutilated version of S. Luke's Gospel. These alone he accepted as authoritative. About A.D. 200 we find the Muratorian Canon, a fragment containing a list of books recognized as authoritative at Rome. This is the earliest list of the kind that has survived: it need by no means be the earliest that was formed. At the close of the second century we find in several writers the conception of a New Testament as a companion to the Old, and books from this new collection are cited as Scripture. This does not necessarily imply that the limits of this collection were as yet fixed. The Muratorian Canon includes the four Gospels, Acts, all the Epistles of S. Paul, the Apocalypse, two Epistles of S. John, S. Jude, and the First Epistle of S. Peter. The Second Epistle of S. Peter is treated as doubtful. 'Some of the members do not wish it to be read in the church.' It omits Hebrews, S. James, and one of S. John's Epistles, presumably the third. Hermas is to be read privately, but not in church.[1]

(γ) By A.D. 400 the Canon of the New Testament had for all practical purposes become fixed. Early in the fourth century Eusebius gives a list of books as accepted by his contemporaries.[2] He divides them practically into three classes: (1) the 'acknowledged' books (ὁμολογούμενα), (2) the 'disputed' books (ἀντιλεγόμενα), and (3) the 'spurious' books (νόθα). In the first class he places the four Gospels, Acts, the Epistles of S. Paul, the First Epistle of S. Peter and the First Epistle of S. John. The Apocalypse he places with hesitation in this class, though he afterwards includes it with a similar hesitation in the second class. It would also seem that he includes Hebrews among S. Paul's Epistles as he does elsewhere, though he allows that its authorship is disputed by the Roman Church.[3] In the second class he places, as 'recognized by most', the Epistles of S. James, S. Jude, 2 and 3 John and 2 Peter. Among the 'spurious' he includes the Acts of Paul, Hermas, the Apocalypse of Peter, the Epistle of Barnabas, the so-called 'Teaching of the Apostles', and also perhaps the Apocalypse of John. The Canon of S. Cyril of Jerusalem[4] (A.D. 340) is the same as our own except for the omission of the Apocalypse. The Canons of Athanasius[5] (A.D. 307) and Epiphanius[6] are identical with our own. At this time the chief point of difference was the acceptance of the Apocalypse. It was rejected, e.g. by Gregory of Nazianzum and Amphilochius of Iconium. A Synod of Carthage formally ratified a list identical with our present canon. Its date may be either 397 or 419 and its authority extended beyond Africa. This decision was confirmed by the Trullan Council in 692. But in actual fact the final determination of the New Testament canon was prob-

[1] The Muratorian fragment is given in Gwatkin, *Selections from Early Christian Writers*, p. 82 and Kidd, *Documents Illustrative of the History of the Church*, vol. i, p. 166.
[2] Eusebius, *H.E.* iii, 3 and 25, quoted Gwatkin, pp. 33 ff., Kidd, p. 235.
[3] *H.E.* iii. 3.
[4] *Catechetical Lectures*, iv. 33.   [5] *Festal Epistle*, 39.   [6] *Heresies*, c. 76.

ably due to other causes than the decisions of Synods. In the West the influence of the Vulgate and in the East the agreement of a few leading and learned authorities carried great weight. The decisions of Councils did but ratify current usage.

So then we may sum up the history of the Canon by saying it was the gradual work of the collective consciousness of the Church guided by the Holy Spirit. It was a task not only of collecting but of sifting and rejecting. There was a real 'inspiration of selection'. 'What a number of works circulated among churches of the second century all enjoying a greater or less degree of authority, only to lose it! ... It is certainly a wonderful feat on the part of the early Church to have by degrees sifted out this mass of literature: and still more wonderful that it should not have discarded, at least so far as the New Testament is concerned, no single work which after generations have found cause to look back upon with any regret.'[1] It was a work in which all members of the body played their part. The devotional taste of the multitude was guided and corrected by the learning and spiritual enlightenment of its leaders. Their decisions approved themselves to the mind and conscience of the whole Church. In the recognition of these books as forming an inspired Canon the belief that they were composed by Apostles or their disciples played a part. The Church attempted to make historical judgments because her faith is based on history. Not all books claiming to be by Apostles were accepted (*e.g.* The Gospel of Peter). The final test was whether the book was recognized to bear the stamp of apostolic truth and to set forth the apostolic gospel. This consideration applies to books which are now believed not to be directly apostolic in origin, *e.g.* S. Matthew's Gospel.[2]†

(*d*) The relation of the Jewish Law to the Christian Church was an early problem. On the one hand, Jewish Christians were reluctant to allow that even the regulations of the old law concerning food, etc., were no longer binding. On the other hand certain Gnostics and the Marcionites rejected the Old Testament altogether, partly on the ground that its morality was un-Christian. The Church refused to abandon the Old Testament and in various ways set about making a

---

[1] Sanday, *Inspiration*, pp. 27–28.

[2] The language of our Article is apparently inconsistent. It first defines as 'Canonical' those books 'of whose authority was never any doubt in the Church', which if strictly interpreted would exclude the 'Antilegomena'. Then it gives a full list of N.T. and says 'All the books of N.T., as they are commonly received, we do receive and account them for canonical.' Westcott suggested that a distinction was purposely made between 'Canonical' Books and such 'canonical books as have never been doubted in the church'. This would allow room for the opinions of reformers who rejected certain books, *e.g.* Luther rejected the Epistle of S. James. More probably the language is simply careless and we may fairly hold that the appeal is made to the judgment of the whole Church as expressed in the final form of the Canon. The disputed books were at most rejected by parts of the Church and their opinion was finally subordinated to the judgment of the Church as a whole.

reply to Marcion. Thus Irenaeus expounded the view that God's revelation and commandments had been given to men by stages according to their capacities and needs. He and other teachers developed the typological interpretation already begun in the apostolic Church, and by some, as by Origen and his school, allegorization in the manner of Philo was carried to extreme lengths. At the time of the Reformation the new emphasis on the authority of the Bible revived the whole question of the Old Testament. Some rejected it entirely 'as a book nothing necessary to the Christians which live under the Gospel'. Others again insisted on the obligation of the whole Jewish Law upon Christians. Article VII replies by laying down (i) that the O.T. is not to be rejected as contrary to the New; (ii) that it looks forward to Christ. God's promises to the Jews are more than transitory; (iii) that we must draw a distinction between the civil and ceremonial law which are no longer binding and the moral law which remains binding.

(i) 'The Old Testament is not contrary to the New' because it is an earlier and preparatory stage in one single divine revelation. To say that it is 'not contrary to', does not mean that it has the perfection of the New. In earlier times God allowed and even enjoined much that is imperfect and even, in the light of the higher standard of later days, wrong (cp. Lk 9⁵⁴ and the Sermon on the Mount). He taught men gradually, as they were able to receive it. We always need to remember that the Church does not accept the Old Testament by itself but only as fulfilled and supplemented by the New Testament. Nearly all the popular objections to Bible morality are based on the fallacy of taking the Old Testament apart in isolation from its fulfilment and correction in the New Testament.

(ii) It is perfectly true to say that the Old Testament offers salvation through Christ, though in a different way from the New Testament. Although in the light of our modern knowledge the history of the Messianic hope has needed to be rewritten, yet it remains as real and true as ever. The prophets and writers of the Old Testament voiced ideals and aspirations that they felt sure that a loving and righteous God must one day fulfil, just because He was loving and righteous. They were inspired to feel their need of a Saviour. This Messianic hope developed on several independent lines. At one time it took the form of an ideal king of the house of David whom God would raise up to do the work that the actual kings were doing so badly (cp. Is 9⁶, Ezek 34²³, etc.). At other times it was a vision of God Himself coming to judge the earth, to overwhelm the enemies of Israel and establish a reign of perfect justice (cp. Ps 50, Is 59¹⁶ ff., Mal 3¹, etc.). Elsewhere it appeared in the shape of the 'suffering servant', an idealization of a perfect Israel fulfilling God's destiny for itself and so by its sufferings redeeming the world (Is 53). In short, while other nations were content to look back to the past for a golden age, Israel was inspired to look for it in the future. This glorious picture they attempted to portray in the highest terms that they knew. In the hands of Israel's prophets it took many shapes, a restored and perfect Jerusalem, a new and painless earth, a kingdom of perfect justice, an age of plenty. The Messianic hope expressed itself in many ways, but all looked forward to the establishment of the Kingdom of God. In this sense certainly '*the fathers did not look only for transitory promises*'. These hopes and aspirations for the complete manifestation of His righteousness and sovereignty they were convinced that God must some day fulfil, because He was God. In a very wonderful way they all met and were fulfilled in Christ. The Old Testament promised a deliverer, the New Testament records His coming.

Again, the faith of Israel really carried with it a belief in a future life. No doubt any such clear and definite belief only appears quite late in Jewish writings. At first it would seem that the Jews regarded life in Sheol as a vague and shadowy existence, hardly worth being called life. The proof of God's favour was to be found in long life and prosperity in this world rather than in any reward in the next. But quite early writings bear witness to a faith in God that was bound to issue ultimately in a belief in a future life worth the name. In Mk 12^{26-27} Christ shows that the language of early times carried with it implications that were only partially understood by those who employed it. What the pious Jew really desired was life in union with God. Such life possessed a positive character independent of time altogether. Hence it is most difficult to be sure how much is meant by the language of many of the psalms. Such psalms as the 16th and 17th, for instance, contain the principle of eternal life in conscious fellowship with God, but it is doubtful if they imply anything like a personal resurrection. At the same time a belief that death could not destroy such fellowship was a deduction that faith in God must ultimately make and it is implicit in the psalmists' language. In the famous chapter of Ezekiel (37) the resurrection of dry bones signifies primarily the resurrection of the nation, not of the individual Israelite. But Israel could not contemplate a future reign of God upon earth to be enjoyed only by that generation of Israelites then alive. Therefore they were led to the belief that dead Israelites would be raised up again to share it. The Messianic hope must be for the whole nation, not for one part. This idea of a resurrection of the dead is found quite clearly in the late passage Is 26^{19} and again in Daniel 12^2. It is, as it were, being worked out in the book of Job (cp. 19^{25-27}). Though it was rejected by the Sadducees, it formed a part of common Jewish belief in our Lord's day. So we may say that the Jews only gradually came to hold explicitly a full belief in a future life beyond the grave, but that such a belief was contained from the first in their knowledge of God and God's character.

(iii) The difficult question of the O.T. Law is solved by making a distinction between the ceremonial and civil law on the one hand and the moral on the other. The distinction is useful and no doubt corresponds with the decision of the Church made at the Council of Jerusalem, but we need to remember that it is utterly alien to the Jewish mind. There is not one trace of it in O.T. itself. To the Jew all alike was the Law of God: each part was equally divine and equally sacred. If the first disciples more or less explicitly tolerated any such distinction it was because part of the law had been definitely abrogated by an act of God Himself, namely by the teaching of Jesus the Messiah, God's authorized representative. As such He had instituted a New Covenant by His death, under which Jew and Gentile can be saved not by obedience to the law but by faith in Jesus the Messiah. Accordingly, as the Council of Jerusalem and the teaching of S. Paul in his Epistles, especially Galatians and Romans, show, the ritual and ceremonial law was regarded as abolished by One who had authority to abolish it. The one sacrifice of Christ had made the ancient sacrifices superfluous and impossible; the New Israel under the New Covenant had its own rites of cleansing and initiation by which new members were incorporated into Christ. The ceremonial law of the Old Testament could no longer be regarded as God's command for Christians. The civil law was the law of Israel as a nation. In part it had fallen into disuse as a result of changed circumstances. But in any case it was superseded by the law of the New Israel. National distinctions were done away with. Hence the civil law of the Jewish nation was binding at most on Jews. There could be no longer any need for a Gentile to become a Jew in order to enter into God's chosen people. Faith in Christ was the sole essential condition for membership of the New Israel. The case of the moral law was different. It was an embodiment of God's will for all men, a partial disclosure of the law of man's true being. As such Christ did not abolish but rather deepened and enforced it (cp. Mt 22³⁷). The righteousness of His disciples was to exceed that of the Scribes and Pharisees as being righteousness of heart and will and not only of act (Mt 5²⁰). Further, Christians have a new motive, no longer a forced obedience to a law imposed from without, but a free and willing obedience springing from within, from a heart filled with the love of God. This new motive demands an even more complete submission to the will of God than the old. Accordingly we find in the Epistles abundant exhortations to Christians to live worthily of their profession by obedience to the moral law. Rom 13⁹, Eph 6², Jas 2¹⁰, etc.†

THE CREEDS

ARTICLE VIII

Of the Three Creeds	De tribus Symbolis
The three Creeds, *Nicene* Creed, *Athanasius'* Creed, and that which is commonly called the *Apostles'* Creed, ought thoroughly to be received and believed; for they may be proved by most certain warrants of Holy Scripture.	Symbola tria, Nicaenum, Athanasii, et quod vulgo Apostolorum appellatur, omnino recipienda sunt, et credenda, nam firmissimis Scripturarum testimoniis probari possunt.

One of the Articles of 1553, slightly altered. It was composed as a protest against Anabaptists, who rejected all creeds.

§ 1. *The origin of Creeds*

(*a*) From the first the Church required from all who wished to become her members, some public profession of faith in Christ. Men whose hearts were touched by the apostolic preaching were urged to repent and believe and be baptized (*e.g.* Acts 20[21]). S. Timothy, probably at the moment of his baptism, had confessed a good confession in the sight of many witnesses (1 Tim 6[12]). In the Bezan text of the Acts we find such a confession put into the mouth of the Ethiopian Eunuch: 'See, here is water; what doth hinder me to be baptized? And Philip said, If thou believest with all thy heart, thou mayest. And he answered and said, I believe that Jesus Christ is the Son of God' (Acts 8[36-37]). The last two sentences formed probably no part of the original text as written by S. Luke, but they are quite early[1] and illustrate the practice of the Church at least in sub-apostolic times. So, too, S. Peter speaks of the 'interrogation' ($\epsilon\pi\epsilon\rho\omega\tau\eta\mu\alpha$) in connexion with Baptism (1 Pet 3[21]).

(i) When we wish to go a step further and ask in what form such belief was expressed, the evidence is less clear. Probably some quite short and simple form of words was in use, such as 'I believe that Jesus is Lord'. The primary aim of the earliest apostolic preaching was to create the conviction that Jesus of Nazareth who had been crucified was the Christ. Men already possessed a belief in a Messiah: they were now bidden to identify the Messiah whom they expected with Jesus. The use of some such simple formula is implied in passages of S. Paul. 'No man can say that Jesus is Lord save in the Holy

---

[1] They were known to Irenaeus (180).

147

Ghost' (1 Cor 12³). 'If thou shalt confess with thy mouth Jesus as Lord and shalt believe in thine heart that God hath raised him from the dead, thou shalt be saved. For with the heart man believeth unto righteousness and with the mouth confession is made unto salvation' (Rom 10⁹⁻¹⁰, cp. Phil 2¹¹). The same custom is also suggested by the First Epistle of S. John. 'Whosoever shall confess that Jesus is the Son of God, God abideth in him and he in God' (4¹⁵. Notice the aorist, denoting a single definite act of confession.) So, too, in 5⁵ the context quite clearly points to a connexion between the confession that 'Jesus is the Son of God' and the coming by water, *i.e.* baptism (cp. also Heb 4¹⁴). The language of S. John suggests an alternative form of baptismal confession, 'I believe that Jesus is the Son of God', the phrase 'Son of God' having primarily a Messianic meaning. In short, all the evidence goes to show that from the earliest days Baptism in the name of the Lord Jesus was accompanied by a public acknowledgement of His lordship by the recipient. Matthew 28¹⁹ shows that before the end of the first century the confession of the three-fold Name accompanied baptism at least in some parts of the Church. The earlier confession of Jesus as Lord or Son of God was thus embodied in a fuller formula which was everywhere adopted in the second century. In these primitive confessions are contained the germs of our later Creeds.

(ii) One of the connecting links between our fully developed creeds and the short and simple formulas of the apostolic Church may probably be found in the questions and responses that formed a part of the service of baptism. The earliest precise evidence we possess about this service shows that these questions and answers were the form in which the threefold Name was invoked *at the moment of baptism.* This may be illustrated from the rite as described in the *Apostolic Tradition* of S. Hippolytus of Rome (A.D. 220).

'And when he who is to be baptized goes down to the water, let him who baptizes lay hand on him saying thus, "Dost thou believe in God the Father Almighty?" And he who is being baptized shall say, "I believe." Let him forthwith baptize him once, having his hand laid upon his head. And after this let him say, "Dost thou believe in Christ Jesus, The Son of God, Who was born by the Holy Spirit from the Virgin Mary, Who was crucified under Pontius Pilate and died, and rose again on the third day living from the dead, and ascended into the heavens, and sat down on the right hand of the Father, and will come to judge the living and the dead?" And when he says, "I believe," let him baptize him the second time. And again let him say, "Dost thou believe in the Holy Spirit, in the holy Church, and the resurrection of the flesh?" And he who is being baptized shall say, "I believe." And so let him baptize him the third time.'

This form of rite consisting of questions and answers at the

moment of baptism was not a peculiarly Roman custom. The evidence
points to the conclusion that it was normal in both East and West in
the first four centuries. Thus Tertullian in Africa writes 'We are thrice
immersed giving a somewhat fuller answer than the Lord laid down in
the Gospel.' In the fourth century S. Cyril of Jerusalem describes the
act of baptism by saying 'ye were led by the hand to the holy font of
the divine baptism . . . and each one was asked whether he believed
in the Name of the Father and of the Son and of the Holy Ghost and
ye confessed the saving confession'. There is no suggestion here that
the candidate for baptism himself uttered a credal statement in or at
the font. The question of the minister with the assent of the candidate
constituted both the invocation of the threefold Name and the saving
confession of faith. In the questions we have a tripartite *interrogatory*
creed forming part of the actual rite of baptism.

But, if at the crucial moment of the baptismal rite there took place
this process of definite questioning, this clearly pre-supposed some
considerable instruction of the candidates. It is in this preliminary
instruction that we find the origin of the fully developed creed-
forms. In reading the Acts of the Apostles we cannot but be struck
by the apparent scantiness of the teaching given to candidates for
baptism. Partly no doubt this was due to the inchoate form of the
Church's belief. She was only making clear to herself, as the result of
her growing experience, all that was contained in her belief in Jesus
as Lord. Moreover the first converts came almost entirely from Jews
or from those under Jewish influence, to whom the fundamental
truth of the Unity of God and His creation of the world would be
already familiar. But even within the New Testament we find hints of
a more or less regular outline of Christian instruction. The Roman
Christians had obeyed the 'form of doctrine unto which ye were delivered', *i.e.* as unto a guardian (Rom 6^{17}). S. Paul exhorted S. Timothy to 'hold fast the form of sound words, which thou hast heard of
me' (2 Tim 1^{13}, cp. also 2^{8}). We may be sure that some statement of
the main facts about the life and death of the Lord Jesus was always
given, where necessary, before Baptism. The early chapters of the
Acts suggest that the Church possessed a common store-house of
proof-texts from the Old Testament, used to reconcile the Jewish
mind to the unwelcome fact of a suffering Messiah. In 1 Cor 15$^{3-7}$
we have something approaching an official list of Resurrection
appearances (cp. also the later summary given in [Mk] 16^{9} ff.). In
1 Tim 3^{16} we have a fragment of an early Christian hymn. 'He who
was manifested in the flesh, justified in the Spirit, seen of Angels,
preached among the nations, believed on in the world, received up in
glory.' In the New Testament generally we find abundant evidence of
a tendency to crystallize fundamental points of belief in summary
statements. Sometimes, as in 1 Cor 15$^{3-7}$, Phil 2$^{5-11}$, 1 Pet 3$^{18-22}$,
these statements are purely Christological in content; others, as in

1 Cor 8[6], 1 Tim 6[13], 1 Pet 1[21] (cf. the opening greeting of some of the epistles) are bipartite in form. In other passages, such as 1 Cor 12[4-6], 2 Cor 13[14], 1 Pet 1[2], there is evidence of an underlying threefold structure. None of these are creeds in the sense of a fixed official and exactly worded formula; they all exhibit patterns of formulation which played a part in the final shaping of the creeds. We must note that, then as now, similar patterns of statement would occur in the liturgical prayers of the Church. By the second half of the second century we find these summaries tending to settle into one predominating form, namely, that with which we are familiar in the Apostles' Creed, with an opening section on God the Father, a central and rather longer section on Jesus Christ and the events of His life, and a third section on the Holy Spirit, the Church and eternal life. There is, however, no evidence that in the second or even in the early third century any one such profession of faith with a precise and sacrosanct wording was the officially recognized formula in any local church.[1] This stage was reached at some time in the third century. During this century the course of instruction of catechumens took on a more settled sequence. A few days or weeks before baptism the candidates were taught the words of the creed and its contents were expounded to them. This was the *traditio symboli*. Shortly *before* the baptismal service came the *redditio symboli*, when the candidate gave back the creed by repeating it in the presence of the Bishop or some other teacher. In East and West alike with variations in detail this procedure was general in the fourth century. The imparting and rendering of the official *declaratory* creed ('I believe'), with its careful and exactly preserved wording was thus the culminating point in the *preparation* of the candidate for baptism; in the rite of baptism itself the *interrogatory* creed retained its central place. The two forms of creed must have influenced one another in ways which we cannot follow in detail. No doubt the declaratory creed ultimately took its tripartite shape because the baptismal questions were naturally constructed on the threefold Name.

(iii) Accordingly we find in the fourth century the established use of official creeds in all the principal churches. The wording of many of them can be reconstructed with reasonable accuracy and in a few cases they are exactly quoted. Their general structure as developed out of the Trinitarian formula is identical; their details vary at different dates and places. There is nothing to suggest that before the rise of the Arian controversy the local creeds were formulated, revised or supplemented with a view to excluding heresy. Their purpose was to set forth positively the fundamental elements of the Christian faith for those who were entering on the Christian life in baptism.

[1] The variations in the creed-like formulas found in authors of the second century are not due to reluctance to quote the exact words of an existing official formula. The rule of secrecy about the creed came in later with the practice of the *traditio* and *redditio symboli*.

We can distinguish two main types of creed, Eastern and Western, corresponding in large measure to the difference between the Eastern and the Western mind. The West was always practical, interested in facts rather than ideas. The East was speculative, interested in ideas rather than facts. The West was unable to speculate for itself and unwilling to pay great attention to the speculations of others. It opposed error less from the love of truth in the abstract than from motives of practical Christianity and the wish to be free from the confusion and distraction of controversy. The East delighted to think out the intellectual content of the Christian faith. Hence, inevitably Eastern Christianity produced a crop of home-grown heresies, side by side with those heathen and gnostic errors that from the first had been the common enemy of the whole Church. These characteristics are reflected in the later development of the creeds. Western creeds are as a rule short, straightforward recitals of fact. Eastern creeds add dogmatic explanations and interpretations. The Western creeds on the whole remain closer to the original purpose of creeds, namely, to state positive truth. The Eastern creeds necessarily betray a more obvious desire to exclude heresy and error. Taking our so-called Apostles' Creed as a typical Western creed and our so-called Nicene Creed as a typical Eastern creed, we may illustrate from them these tendencies:

(α) We find the Eastern creeds giving the reason for certain facts, where the Western creeds are content simply to state the facts, even where there is no theological question at stake. The Apostles' Creed recounts our Lord's birth. The Nicene adds that it was 'for us men and for our salvation'. The Apostles' Creed records the Resurrection on the third day, the Nicene adds that it was 'according to the Scriptures'. The Nicene explains that baptism is 'for the remission of sins'. Similarly Eastern creeds alone have 'shall come again with glory'.

(β) Again, the Eastern creeds tend to greater theological precision. The Nicene, like other Eastern creeds, has 'One' before God, and adds 'Maker of heaven and earth'. Though our Apostles' Creed contains the latter clause, it was, as we shall see, a late addition, and the Nicene Creed amplifies this by adding 'and of all things visible and invisible'. It is characteristic of Eastern creeds to dwell on the life and work of our Lord before the Incarnation. 'The only begotten Son of God,' 'Begotten of His Father before all worlds,' 'Through whom all things were made.' Clause is added to clause in order to insist upon His Divinity. The Nicene addition 'of one substance with the Father' was added only to Eastern Baptismal creeds. The West felt no need of it. In contrast with this the Western creeds go straight on from the mention of our Lord to the fact of His Incarnation and His death. The theological interpretation of His death, 'He suffered' though present in Eastern creeds from the first in order to exclude Docetism, was a late addition in the West. The Nicene Creed further adds 'Whose Kingdom shall have no end' to refute the heresy of Marcellus, and emphasizes the Divinity of the Holy Spirit 'The Lord and the Giver of life' as against Macedonianism. The only additions found exclusively in the West are 'He descended into Hell' and 'the communion of Saints'.

(*b*) Hitherto we have dealt with creeds as local variations of a common type, framed for the sole purpose of the instruction and initiation of learners in the Christian faith. At the Council of Nicaea we find the first instance of the employment of a creed for an entirely different purpose, as a test of orthodoxy for teachers. No doubt in earlier days from time to time appeal had been made to the creed as the rule of faith and as the evidence of conformity to primitive and apostolic teaching. But such a use was only secondary and incidental. At the Council of Nicaea we find for the first time a creed deliberately constructed for use as a test of right teaching. This new creed was not intended to supersede existing creeds: it was called into existence for a new purpose. Accordingly we get from this point onwards a new class of creeds, 'conciliar' as opposed to 'baptismal'. The baptismal creed as being the personal confession of faith made by the individual, is naturally in the singular 'I believe'. The conciliar creed, as expressing the faith of an assembled body, is naturally in the plural 'We believe'. The employment of the singular is not a mark of Western as opposed to Eastern creeds, but is found in all baptismal creeds. The distinction between conciliar and baptismal creeds is not absolute. The former were built on the foundation of the latter. The threefold structure is always retained and a conciliar can be adopted as a baptismal creed by the change of the plural into the singular. But the action of the Council of Nicaea marks a revolution in the use of creeds.[1]

A third type of creed deserves mention, namely, private or individual theological confessions. Such sit more loosely to the creed-form and have in themselves no authority but that of the individuals who composed them. We shall see that our so-called Athanasian really belongs to this third type. The object of their existence is to state certain aspects of Christian truth which made a special appeal to their authors.

§ 2. *The Apostles' Creed*

(i) We may now turn to the history of '*that which is commonly called the Apostles' Creed*'. Put shortly, the Apostles' Creed as we use it, is

[1] This is why we meet with 'anathemas' for the first time at the end of the creed of the Council of Nicaea. 'The anathemas are there because and only because the creed is no longer the layman's confession of faith but the bishop's. The old principle that the profession of belief of catechumens should be positive in character is not infringed: the Council has not even in view the case of the clergy, still less that of the faithful laity: to bishops alone belonged the office of deciding in the last resort what was Christian and Catholic and what was heretical, and therefore bishops alone should be called upon to guarantee their soundness in the faith by formal and solemn anathema of error,' Turner, *History and use of Creeds*, p. 28.

an enlarged form of the Baptismal Creed of the Roman Church. This 'Old Roman Creed' is first found in Greek in a letter written by Marcellus of Ancyra about A.D. 340 to the Bishop of Rome and preserved in the writings of Epiphanius. Marcellus had been accused of a form of Sabellianism. In order to prove his orthodoxy he left with the Bishop of Rome a formal statement of his faith. This was in reality the Baptismal Creed of the Roman Church, which we find some sixty years later described in the commentary of Rufinus. It runs as follows:

1. I believe in God (the Father) almighty
2. And in Christ Jesus, His only Son, our Lord,
    Who was born of the Holy Spirit and the Virgin Mary,
    Crucified under Pontius Pilate and buried,
    The third day He rose from the dead,
    He ascended into Heaven,
    Sitteth at the right-hand of the Father,
    Whence He cometh to judge quick and dead.
3. And in the Holy Ghost,
    Holy Church,
    Remission of sins,
    Resurrection of flesh.[1]

The Latin version of the Old Roman Creed first appears in the commentary of Rufinus (A.D. 400), in which he compares the creed of his own Church of Aquileia with that of Rome. This then we can take as our starting-point. By the middle of the fourth century the Old Roman Creed was in use in the form given above. Two questions still remain. How much further back can it be traced? By what process of development did it assume the later form that we commonly call 'the Apostles' Creed'? It was maintained by Burn and others that the Old Roman Creed went back to the early years of the second century. There is nothing in its teaching to render this early date

---

[1] Our present text of Marcellus omits 'the Father' in the opening clause and adds 'eternal life' at the close. These changes were probably due to the mistakes of copyists. The Latin of Rufinus has 'the Father' and omits 'eternal life', and Jerome expressly tells us that the Roman Creed ends with 'Resurrection of flesh'. Other authorities support this version.

THE OLD ROMAN CREED
Credo in Deum patrem omnipotentem, et in Christum Iesum filium eius unicum, dominum nostrum, qui natus est de Spiritu Sancto et Maria virgine, crucifixus sub Pontio Pilato et sepultus; tertia die resurrexit a mortuis, ascendit in caelos, sedet ad dexteram patris, unde venturus est iudicare vivos et mortuos. Et in Spiritum Sanctum, sanctam ecclesiam, remissionem peccatorum, carnis resurrectionem.

THE LATER APOSTLES' CREED
Credo in Deum patrem omnipotentem, creatorem caeli et terrae, et in Iesum Christum filium eius unicum, dominum nostrum, qui conceptus est de Spiritu Sancto, natus ex Maria virgine, passus sub Pontio Pilato, crucifixus, mortuus et sepultus; descendit ad inferna, tertia die resurrexit a mortuis, ascendit ad caelos, sedet ad dexteram Dei patris omnipotentis, inde venturus est iudicare vivos et mortuos. Credo in Spiritum Sanctum, sanctam ecclesiam catholicam, sanctorum communionem, remissionem peccatorum, carnis resurrectionem, vitam aeternam.

improbable, but in view of what has already been said about the development of credal forms in the second century we could hardly date the composition of this creed much before the end of this century, and perhaps it was only in the next century that it became the sole official creed of the Roman Church. By the fourth century it was certainly well established, for its influence on the formation of other local Western creeds is apparent.

Harnack and Kattenbusch held that the Old Roman Creed became the direct parent of the Eastern Creeds. These, it was argued, could be traced back to a single model in the creed of Antioch, and this in turn depended on the Old Roman Creed which was introduced at Antioch after the deposition of Paul of Samosata in 272. More probably the local Eastern Creeds developed in the second and third centuries independently of Rome and out of the same fundamental needs and practices of the Church. In any case, the important fact is that they exhibit a similar outline of teaching with those of the West, though with some characteristic features of their own.

(ii) When we contrast the Old Roman Creed with our present 'Apostles' Creed' we find that it has been enlarged by the following additions:

'Maker of heaven and earth'
'Who was conceived'
'Suffered'
'Dead'
'Descended into hell'
'God ... almighty' (On the right hand of God the Father Almighty)
'Catholic'
'The communion of Saints'
'The life everlasting.'

Of these some appear in use in local creeds earlier than others. 'The life everlasting,' as we learn from Cyprian, had its place in a baptismal interrogation used in the Church of Africa as early as the middle of the third century. The creed of Milan had 'suffered' instead of 'was crucified' by the close of the fourth century, when S. Augustine was baptized. 'Descended into hell' is found in the creed of the Church of Aquileia by the time of Rufinus (A.D. 400) and had previously appeared in an Arian creed drawn up at Sirmium in 359 and accepted at Ariminum. The majority of the additions are found in the creed used by a certain Niceta or Nicetas, Bishop of Remesiana in the Balkan peninsula at the close of the fourth century. His creed contained 'maker of heaven and earth', 'suffered', 'dead', 'catholic', 'communion of saints', 'life everlasting'. His diocese lay on the borderland between East and West, on the high road between Constantinople and Milan, then the chief city of the West, and we may reasonably suppose that these additions were in part due to Eastern influence. Again, a creed-form has recently been discovered which is probably a personal confession of faith sent by Jerome to Cyril of Jerusalem. It contains practically all the additions in our present Apostles' Creed or some equivalent expression. Jerome came from much the same region as Nicetas, namely, Pannonia, and his creed forms a link between the Old Roman Creed and our present form. Again, we find most of the additions more or less current in Gaul between the middle of the fifth and the opening of the sixth century. We have sermons composed by Faustus, Bishop of Riez, for a time abbot of the great monastery of Lerins and by Caesarius, Bishop of Arles (died 543), and a letter written by Cyprian, Bishop of Toulon. From these we gather that by the close of the fifth century the Gallican Church used a creed that differed from our Apostles' Creed only by the omission of 'maker of heaven and earth'. It has been conjectured that the additions had travelled westwards from Pannonia through Aquileia and Milan to the south of France. There they became diffused through the influence of the school of Lerins. The Apostles' Creed in the precise form in which we now repeat it is first met in a treatise of Priminius, a missionary bishop who had been for a time abbot of the Benedictine monastery of Reichenau and worked in France and Germany about 750. But there are certain earlier creeds found in the Gallican Missal and the Gallican Sacramentary and employed in Gaul before 700 which contain all the additions but are marked by certain slight variations from our present form.

If we ask the further question, how came our Apostles' Creed to be substituted for the Old Roman Creed throughout the West and even in Rome itself, no certain answer can be given. It is a surprising fact (for a fact it appears to be) that from the sixth until at least the ninth century Rome abandoned her own ancient creed and substituted the Nicene Creed in the instruction of her catechumens.[1] At some time between the ninth and the twelfth centuries Rome resumed the use of her ancient formula, now in the expanded form of the Apostles' Creed, which was already prevalent in the Franco-German Church. Having given her creed to the West in early days, the Roman Church took it back again, enriched by additions made by the Christian piety of others, and thus ensured its universal acceptance in the West as the sole baptismal creed.[2]

---

[1] The interrogations at the moment of baptism remained unaltered, as the Gelasian Sacramentary shows, and closely resembled the Old Roman Creed, though in an abbreviated form.

[2] The only addition that needs explanation is 'the communion of saints'. The Latin 'sanctorum communionem' is ambiguous. Sanctorum may be either masculine or neuter. Probably it is masculine, as it is so taken in the sermon of Nicetas, where the addition first occurs. He explains the clause as the fellowship of holy men in one church. 'Saints' means 'Christians'; it must not be limited to specially famous Christians, but includes living and departed alike. It we take sanctorum as neuter, the 'holy things' mean 'sacraments'. The fellowship in holy things is a visible sign of the communion of saints.

(iii) In what sense, then, may our creed rightly be styled 'Apostles' '? It clearly cannot have been drawn up by the apostles themselves. It is found in a less fully developed form long after the death of the last apostle and its development into its present form can be traced. It is true that Rufinus supposed that the Old Roman Creed was put together by an assembly of the apostles before leaving Jerusalem and had remained unaltered; but there is no trace of any such belief in other writers, earlier and wiser than Rufinus,[1] including, for instance, S. Luke. Still less credence can be given to the legend, found first in Priminius, that assigned the composition of our present creed to the twelve on the day of Pentecost, distributing with some difficulty a fair portion to each apostle. It is possible that a belief of this kind gave rise to the title. More probably, however, the name 'symbolum apostolicum' or 'symbolum apostolorum' is used in a wider sense. It means no more than that the creed is a faithful summary of apostolic teaching and that its substance came from the apostles. In an uncritical age the title was perverted to mean that the actual creed came ready-made from the lips of the apostles. Another possible explanation of the name is that it was the creed of the Roman Church, the one and only apostolic see of the West; hence the creed of the apostolic see came to be called the Apostolic Creed.

(iv) The Apostles' Creed has been for a thousand years the Baptismal Creed of the whole Western Church. It has never been used in the East. In our Prayer Book it is found in two slightly different forms. First the ordinary form recited at Mattins and Evensong, found also in the Catechism. Secondly, an interrogative form found in the Baptismal service and the Visitation of the Sick. This last differs from the first in speaking of the 'Resurrection of the flesh' instead of the 'Resurrection of the body' and in adding 'after death' to the last clause. The Latin is 'carnis resurrectionem',[2] of which the 'resurrection of the flesh' is the more correct translation. The phrase is not Scriptural, but is quite early. 'After death' is an addition found in certain Gallican creeds, which failed to win a place in the final form of the Baptismal Creed.

§ 3. *The Nicene Creed*

Our so-called 'Nicene' Creed has a long and complicated history. We may best begin with some account of the Council of Nicaea itself.

(i) Our information about the proceedings of the Council is very

---

[1] A similar belief in direct apostolic authorship is found in Ambrose and possibly in Jerome, who speaks of 'symbolum . . . ab apostolis traditum'. Ambrose first applies the title 'apostles' ' to the Old Roman Creed.

[2] 'Huius carnis resurrectionem' is even found in some early forms, but happily was not adopted. The earliest Eastern creeds may have contained the phrase 'the resurrection of flesh'. But later Eastern creeds, perhaps under the influence of Origen, prefer 'the resurrection of the dead', as being closer to Scripture. We may wish the West had followed their example. Cranmer's translation of 'carnis' by 'body' may have been deliberate, to bring the phrase nearer to Scripture. See Swete, *J.Th.S.*, Jan. 1917.

inadequate. In a letter to his own church written shortly after the event Eusebius of Caesarea related that he had produced to the Council a statement of faith which he quotes. Included in this statement is what was evidently the baptismal creed in use at Caesarea.[1] The letter, after saying that this profession of faith was received as orthodox, appears to suggest that the emperor wished the Council to make the statement its own, with the one addition of the word *homoousios*, though Eusebius, when he goes on to quote the Creed eventually formulated by the Council reveals the fact that this differed from his own in a number of other clauses. Until recently it was generally held on the strength of Eusebius' letter that the Creed of the Council was in fact a revised form of the Caesarean creed. The key phrases 'that is of the substance of the Father' and 'of one substance with the Father' had been added to exclude Arianism, and a number of other changes had been made to give further anti-Arian emphasis. It is, however, by the most recent investigators regarded as unlikely that the Council arrived at its own formulation by taking this creed as its basis. Eusebius had a personal reason, not revealed in his letter, for presenting to the Council a statement of his faith; his orthodoxy had been seriously called in question by a Council held at Antioch a few months earlier. The Creed of Nicaea differs from the Caesarean formula in a number of incidental and comparatively unimportant phrases which can hardly have been the result of deliberate alterations. Probably the Council took as the basis of its new formula a baptismal creed from some Syrian or Palestinian church, closely resembling, but not identical with, that of Caesarea.

The Creed of the Nicene Council runs thus:

'We believe in one God, the Father almighty, maker of all things visible and invisible;

'And in one Lord Jesus Christ, the Son of God, begotten from the Father, only-begotten, that is, from the substance of the Father, God from God, light from light, true God from true God, begotten not made, of one substance with the Father, through Whom all things came into being, things in heaven and things on earth, Who because of us men and because of our salvation came down and became incarnate, becoming man, suffered and rose again on the third

---

[1] This creed is an important instance of a local Eastern baptismal creed in use before the Council of Nicaea. It runs as follows:

'We believe in one God, the Father almighty, maker of all things visible and invisible;

And in one Lord Jesus Christ, the Logos of God, God from God, light from light, life from life, Son only begotten, first-begotten of all creation, begotten before all ages from the Father, through Whom all things came into being, Who because of our salvation was incarnate, and dwelt among men, and suffered, and rose again on the third day, and ascended to the Father, and will come again in glory to judge living and dead;

We believe also in one Holy Spirit.'

day, ascended to the heavens, and will come to judge the living and
the dead ;

'And in the Holy Spirit.

'But as for those who say, There was when He was not, and, Before
being born He was not, and that He came into existence out of
nothing, or who assert that the Son of God is of a different hypostasis or substance, or is created, or is subject to alteration or change
—these the Catholic Church anathematizes.'[1]

This creed decisively excluded Arianism. The two phrases relating
to the divine substance meant that the Son shared in the being of
the Father; 'begotten, not made' ruled out the Arian assertion that
our Lord was a creature. It should be noted that the anathemas are
an integral part of the Council's statement, which thus differs in
form from a baptismal creed though it is based on one.

(ii) It will have been observed that there are important differences
between this creed put out by the Council of Nicaea and our own so-
called Nicene Creed. The latter is usually known as the Constantinopolitan Creed (C), because at the Council of Chalcedon (451) it
was quoted as 'the faith of the 150 fathers', *i.e.* the bishops assembled
at the Council of Constantinople (381). Since such records as we
have about the proceedings at Constantinople are scanty and do not
suggest the promulgation of any new creed, the connexion of C with
this Council is very obscure. The prevailing view in this country has
been that C was already in existence before 381 and was not, therefore, *composed* at the Council. This was held to be proved by the fact
that in the *Ancoratus* of Epiphanius, written in 374, a creed is quoted
which is practically identical with C. It was further maintained by
Hort[2] that Epiphanius obtained this creed from Jerusalem. When
Cyril, Bishop of Jerusalem, returned from exile in 362 he revised the
baptismal creed of his Church and took the opportunity to insert
into it some phrases from the Creed of Nicaea. How then did C,
originally emanating from Jerusalem, become associated with the
Council of Constantinople? It was suggested that Cyril, who was
present at the Council, produced C in defence of his own orthodoxy,
and his creed, having obtained the approval of the assembled bishops,

---

[1] Πιστεύομεν εἰς ἕνα Θεὸν Πατέρα παντοκράτορα πάντων ὁρατῶν τε καὶ ἀοράτων
ποιητήν·

καὶ εἰς ἕνα Κύριον Ἰησοῦν Χριστὸν τὸν Υἱὸν τοῦ Θεοῦ, γεννηθέντα ἐκ τοῦ Πατρὸς
μονογενῆ τοῦτ' ἐστὶν ἐκ τῆς οὐσίας τοῦ Πατρός, Θεὸν ἐκ Θεοῦ, Φῶς ἐκ Φωτός, Θεὸν
ἀληθινὸν ἐκ Θεοῦ ἀληθινοῦ, γεννηθέντα, οὐ ποιηθέντα, ὁμοούσιον τῷ Πατρί, δι' οὗ τὰ
πάντα ἐγένετο τά τε ἐν τῷ οὐρανῷ καὶ τὰ ἐν τῇ γῇ, τὸν δι' ἡμᾶς τοὺς ἀνθρώπους, καὶ διὰ
τὴν ἡμετέραν σωτηρίαν, κατελθόντα, καὶ σαρκωθέντα, καὶ ἐνανθρωπήσαντα, παθόντα
καὶ ἀναστάντα τῇ τρίτῃ ἡμέρᾳ, ἀνελθόντα εἰς τοὺς οὐρανούς, ἐρχόμενον κρῖναι ζῶντας
καὶ νεκρούς

καὶ εἰς τὸ Ἅγιον Πνεῦμα.

Τοὺς δὲ λέγοντας Ἦν ποτε ὅτε οὐκ ἦν, καὶ Πρὶν γεννηθῆναι οὐκ ἦν, καὶ ὅτι Ἐξ οὐκ
ὄντων ἐγένετο, ἢ Ἐξ ἑτέρας ὑποστάσεως ἢ οὐσίας φάσκοντας εἶναι ἢ κτιστὸν ἢ τρεπτὸν
ἢ ἀλλοιωτὸν τὸν Υἱὸν τοῦ Θεοῦ, τούτους ἀναθεματίζει ἡ καθολικὴ ἐκκλησία.

[2] In his *Two Dissertations*.

was henceforward associated with them. A further conjecture was that when Nectarius, an unbaptized layman, was elected Bishop of Constantinople during the session of the Council, this creed was employed as his baptismal confession and was then adopted as the baptismal creed of the imperial city.

In this reconstruction of the history of C there is one point which is not likely to be shaken. This creed is not an expansion of the Nicene formula, though from the time of Chalcedon onwards it was referred to as such; it has been formed by adding to some other baptismal creed certain Nicene phrases and some new clauses relating to the Holy Spirit. Whatever was the place and occasion of its origin, C is a baptismal creed supplemented by Nicene phrases and in its third section expanded to combat Macedonian views. Considerable doubt has, however, been cast on a vital point in the rest of the reconstruction outlined above. The creed which originally stood in the *Ancoratus* of Epiphanius in the place now occupied in the existing manuscripts by C was most probably not C but the Creed of Nicaea. If so, there remains no evidence to necessitate the view that C existed before the Council of Constantinople and the Jerusalem theory loses its main support. Moreover, between 381 and the Council of Chalcedon there is no clear and certain reference to this creed, though references to 'the faith of Nicaea' are frequent. We might infer from this that C was a local baptismal creed first brought into prominence at Chalcedon and then first attributed to the 150 fathers of Constantinople. This, however, would carry scepticism too far. No-one at Chalcedon disputed the assertion that C had been put out by the 150 fathers. This fact alone makes it virtually certain that the Council of 381 in some way gave its authority to this creed. Moreover, the apparent silence about C between 381 and 451 is not necessarily so profound as at first sight it appears to be. Dr Kelly observes[1] that in this period 'the description "the faith of Nicaea" or "the faith, symbol or *ekthesis* of the 318 fathers" was not necessarily applied solely to N (*i.e.* the Creed of Nicaea) in its pure authentic form. It could equally well be used of a creed, local or otherwise, which was patently Nicene in its general character, while differing from N in much of its language.' When the fathers of Constantinople are said (at Chalcedon) to have 'set their seal to the same (Nicene) faith' they may well have done so by including in their doctrinal statement (which we do not possess) a creed which both contained the vital Nicene phrases and also amplified the doctrine of the Holy Spirit. We may sum up by saying that recent investigation has renewed confidence in the ancient view that the Council of Constantinople promulgated and gave its authority to C. Whether the Council composed the Creed[2] or, as Dr Kelly thinks more probable, adopted an existing liturgical formula is a question which must be left open.

[1] J. N. D. Kelly, *Early Christian Creeds*, p. 323.   [2] Badcock, *History of the Creeds*, c. xiii.

In any case, after Chalcedon C rapidly won its way in all the orthodox parts of the Eastern Church and even everywhere took the place in the baptismal rite which had previously been occupied by local creeds. This position it owed partly to its intrinsic merits but largely perhaps to its connexion with the now dominant see of Constantinople. Just as the West received its baptismal creed from Rome, so the East received its baptismal creed from the New Rome.

But this is not the most familiar use of the creed. To the modern Christian the Creed of Constantinople is above all the creed of Eucharistic worship. As we have seen, it sprang out of instruction given to candidates for baptism: it was deliberately amended to become a test of orthodoxy. From the sixth century it has been used for a new purpose, as 'the continuous doxology of the faithful, Sunday by Sunday', in the Eucharist. 'To this position no other form of the creed ever aspired than that of Constantinople. Alike in the Greek, the Latin and even the Coptic Churches, its majestic rhythm and its definite but simple and straightforward theology have marked it out as the creed of Christian worship.'[1] It is true that the beginning of this custom was not altogether happy. It was introduced at Constantinople by the Monophysites, in protest against the definition of Chalcedon as a novelty infringing the sufficiency of the all-sufficient creed. But the custom commended itself to the mind of the Church and spread throughout the Churches of the East. Thence it extended gradually to the Churches of Spain, Ireland, and Gaul. But it was not adopted at Rome until 1014, when Pope Benedict VIII was prevailed on by the Emperor Henry II to assimilate the use of Rome to that of Germany and the rest of Christendom. Accordingly the creed, with the addition of the words 'and the Son', for the first time appeared in the Mass at Rome. We can see the appropriateness of our present Western usage. At the font the short and simple baptismal creed is sufficient: at the service which embodies the highest worship of baptized Christians there is a peculiar fitness in reciting the fuller confession of belief, which demands and is itself the product of a more matured faith, based upon a richer Christian experience.

Our English translation is not altogether satisfactory. (i) The word 'Almighty' as applied to the Father does not accurately represent the Greek 'παντοκράτορα', which means rather 'all sovereign'. The English 'almighty', which came in through the Latin omnipotens, as in the Apostles' Creed, suggests 'able to do anything'.

(ii) 'By whom all things were made' should rather be 'through whom' (δι' οὗ). 'By' in old English meant 'through'. The clause describes the Son as the agent of the Father in creation (διά as opposed to ὑπό) in accordance with the teaching of, e.g. Jn 1[3 and 10] and Heb 1[2b].

(iii) 'The Lord and Giver of Life' is an ambiguous rendering of the

[1] Turner, op. cit. pp. 46–47.

original, τὸ κύριον καὶ τὸ ζωοποιόν. 'The Lord' is a distinct attribute
and expresses the full divinity of the Holy Spirit. A better translation
would be 'The Lord and the Life-giver'; or at least a comma should
be inserted after Lord.

(iv) The word 'holy' was deliberately omitted by the reformers
before 'Catholic Church' not from any doctrinal reasons but because
they supposed that it was absent from the best texts. It is clear, however, that the omission is wrong, and 'holy' should be restored, as in
the Alternative Order of the Communion, 1928.†

§ 4. *The Athanasian Creed*

As we have seen, the Apostles' Creed was not composed by
apostles and the Nicene Creed did not originate at the Council of
Nicaea. So, too, 'Athanasius' Creed' is not the composition of
Athanasius. To begin with, it was beyond all doubt written in Latin,
while Athanasius wrote in Greek. Greek translations of it do indeed
exist, but the clumsiness of their language and the variety of their
renderings prove conclusively that they are translations and not
original. Further, the 'creed' shows close affinity with the writings of
the Latin fathers, Ambrose and Augustine. Its origins, therefore, lie
in the Latin-speaking church in a period subsequent to the death of
Athanasius. Again, strictly speaking, it is not a 'creed' at all. At best
it is an individual profession of faith, framed probably to be an instruction and later on used as a psalm or a canticle. It does not conform to the fundamental creed type arising out of the threefold
baptismal formula. It has not been expanded out of any simpler and
earlier creed. In doctrine it may be dependent on earlier creeds, but
not in form. The title of 'Symbolum' was not given to it in early MSS.
It was styled rather 'fides sancti Athanasii'. So, too, it is found at its
earliest appearance keeping company not with creeds but with the
psalter or with canons or with miscellaneous dogmatic formularies
to which were attached, with equal want of justification, the names of
great theologians. These last have all been forgotten: the 'Quicunque'
survives, and the reason may well have been, not only 'the survival of
the fittest', but its actual lack of creed-form. 'Other formularies
failed to live, because they perpetuated the structure and arrangement, while destitute of the authority, of the creeds. The "Athanasian" formulary lived on, because it put the old truths in a new and
effective setting: in other words, because it was a hymn about the
creed, and not itself a creed at all.'[1]

(i) What then can be said as to date and authorship?

The available evidence may be divided into two classes (α) internal, (β) external.

(α) The nature of the heresies combated in the second half of the
creed is consistent with an early date before Nestorianism or Monophysitism became prominent. The language used about the two

[1] Turner, *op. cit.* p. 70.

natures of Christ, *e.g.* 'Perfect God and Perfect Man of a reasonable soul and human flesh subsisting, equal to the Father as touching His Godhead, etc.,' is opposed to Arianism and Apollinarianism, both of which denied to Christ the possession of a 'reasonable soul'. There is nothing in the whole statement that directly hits Nestorianism. The language which insists upon the unity of the Person of Christ (*e.g.* 'not two but one Christ') can be found in the writings of S. Augustine and would be accepted by Nestorians in their own sense. No doubt Eutyches did 'confuse the substance', and much of the language employed would oppose his teaching; but it would be equally suitable to oppose the teaching of Apollinarius. In other words, no phrase in the whole creed compels us to suppose that the writer had ever heard of either Nestorianism or Monophysitism. It has further been argued, *e.g.* by Waterland, that, if Monophysitism had come into existence, the writer would have avoided the expression 'as the reasonable soul and flesh is one man, so God and man is one Christ', because this was precisely the illustration employed by the Monophysites. This argument, however, does not hold good, as a long list of Catholic writers can be compiled who all continued to employ the illustration even after the rise of Monophysitism. The internal evidence does not carry us very far. The argument from silence is always precarious. The author may have refrained from combating Nestorianism or Monophysitism, not because they did not exist, but because he and those for whose instruction he wrote were not particularly concerned with them. There is a limit to the number of heresies that can be controverted with profit in a single instruction. All that we can say is that the doctrinal content of the 'Quicunque' shows that the date of origin cannot be earlier than the last quarter of the fourth century, when Apollinarianism came under formal condemnation, and does not preclude, though it does not necessitate, a date earlier than the rise of the Nestorian controversy (428).

(*β*) The external evidence falls into three divisions: (*a*) quotations, (*b*) MSS., (*c*) commentaries.

(*a*) The earliest quotation from the 'Quicunque' which can hardly be disputed, is in a canon of the fourth Council of Toledo in 633, which quotes largely from it as a recognized authority. It is also quoted in a sermon found among the works of S. Augustine and for a long time attributed to Caesarius, Bishop of Arles (d. 543). It is now, however, considered that the attribution is doubtful, but even if the authorship is unknown, unless the sermon can be shown to be later, we still possess in it a quotation dating from the sixth century. Further, most authorities agree that there is a remarkable similarity between the undisputed writings of Caesarius and the 'Quicunque'. Again, we have the so-called 'Trèves Fragment', containing part of a sermon on the creed, which quotes from the 'Quicunque'. The Fragment was written about 730, but the sermon must be earlier, perhaps about 680, and therefore the 'Quicunque' must be earlier still. Other quotations can be found in anonymous sermons of the sixth and seventh centuries, but in all cases the exact date is uncertain.[1]

(*b*) The earliest MS. of the 'Quicunque' is the Codex Ambrosianus at Milan, written in an Irish hand. It is assigned by experts to the end of the seventh or beginning of the eighth century. Other early MSS. are the Codex Monacensis at Freising (eighth century), the Codex Petriburg at Leningrad (about 750) and Leidrat's MS. at Lyons (about 800).

(*c*) Besides these we have an independent source of evidence in early commentaries on the 'Quicunque', which witness to its existence in its present form. The earliest is the 'Fortunatus' commentary, which can hardly be later than 700 and may be much earlier, though our existing MSS. of the commentary are rather later. Other commentaries belong to the ninth and tenth centuries: some may be earlier. In any case the fact that the 'Quicunque' was thought worthy of such commentaries shows that it had been widely known and used for a considerable time. To sum up, our external evidence carries us back to the seventh century at the latest. If we place it side by side with the internal evidence we get a date for the origin of the 'Quicunque' between, say, 380 and 600. Neither on the question of date or authorship is any certainty attainable. All that we can do is to give some of the chief opinions that have been held.

Waterland, in his *Critical History of the Athanasian Creed*, published in 1723, laid the foundation of all future criticism. Mainly on internal evidence he held that the 'Quicunque' was composed in Gaul between 420 and 430, and he assigned it to Hilary, Bishop of Arles (d. 449), a pupil of Honoratus, the founder of the monastery of Lerins, the great centre of learning in south Gaul, and later Bishop of Arles. As we have seen, however, the internal evidence is perhaps less conclusive than Waterland supposed.

Burn[2] agreed with Waterland as to the early date of the creed, assigning it to Honoratus himself. He reinforced the previous arguments for an early date with strong arguments based on new evidence. He showed that the 'Quicunque' is exactly what would be needed against the teaching of Priscillian, Bishop of Avila in Spain (about 380). Writings of Priscillian were discovered in 1885 and they prove that what he taught consisted of a mixture of Sabellianism and Apollinarianism. These are just the two heresies that are most clearly opposed by the teaching of the 'Quicunque'. Further, he claimed that quotations from it occur in the writings of Avitus, Bishop of Vienne (d. 523), and of Faustus, Bishop of Riez (about 480). There are

[1] It is interesting to note that the 'Quicunque' had reached England by 798 since it is quoted by Denebert, Bishop of Worcester, on his election to the bishopric, as an authoritative formula.
[2] Burn, *Athanasian Creed*, pp. 30 and 33.

undoubted similarities of thought and expression between the 'Quicunque' on the one hand and the writings of Caesarius and Vincent
of Lerins (d. 450) on the other. So near do they come to it that each
of them has been suggested as its author. Two explanations are possible. Either such language was in the air and both avail themselves of
current theological phrases, which later on materialized into our
'Quicunque'. Or each was quoting from the 'Quicunque' which they
knew and respected as coming from an author belonging like themselves to the school of Lerins. Burn held that the latter is the true
explanation. He believed that it 'had been taught to him' (*i.e.*
Caesarius) 'from his early years and came as naturally to his lips as
the phrases of our Church Catechism rise to our lips', and that 'it is
easier to believe that Vincentius used the creed than that any one in
a subsequent generation or century, of less exact scholarship, picked
out his phrases and wove them into a document of this kind.' He
went on to point out that there are considerable parallels to the
teaching of the 'Quicunque' not only in S. Augustine but in S. Ambrose. That is to say, the elements out of which it is composed were
already present in the minds of the Church's teachers.

The great Benedictine writer, Dom Morin, proposed Caesarius
as the author on the strength of the close parallelism of style and
thought between the 'Quicunque' and his works. Dom Morin at one
time altered his opinion and regarded the 'Quicunque' as composed
not in Gaul but in Spain, by a certain Martin, Bishop of Braga, at
the close of the sixth century. He accepted no quotation from it
earlier than that in the canon of Toledo, and pointed to the existence
of a large number of anonymous formularies of Spanish origin dating
from the fifth century onwards, but he later returned to the view that
it was composed in Gaul.

In 1909 the Jesuit scholar, Heinrich Brewer, maintained that the
'Quicunque' was the work of S. Ambrose. This view has in recent
years found more support than when it was originally put forward,
and Burn himself in 1926 announced his acceptance of it.[1] The
'Quicunque', like the hymns of S. Ambrose, is anonymous. It may
have been intended for antiphonal singing which he introduced at
Milan. Its style and many of its expressions can be closely paralleled
in his known works. Certain of its phrases may go back to a letter
addressed to Ambrose and others by the Bishops assembled in Constantinople in 382. Brewer's argument in favour of the Ambrosian
authorship of the 'Quicunque' is weighty, but it cannot be said to
have closed the question, and some scholars still prefer to assign the
work to a fifth- or sixth-century composer.

(ii) The 'Quicunque' falls into three parts: (α) a summary of the
doctrine of the Trinity (vv. $^{3-25}$); (β) a summary of the doctrine of

---

[1] See *J.Th.S.*, vol. xxvii (1926) pp. 19 ff. But Burn doubts whether the creed can have
been intended by its author for antiphonal singing.

the Incarnation (vv. [28-38]); (γ) at the beginning and end, and in between these two large sections, we find warning clauses (vv. [1-2], [26], [27] and [40]). We may take these in order.

(a) This section on the Trinity is a summing up of the successive negative answers given by the Church to those attempts to explain the facts of the divine revelation in Christ, which she saw either to ignore or contradict some of those facts. The early heresies either 'confounded' (*i.e.* confused) 'the Persons' by practically denying the distinction between them or else divided the substance by introducing a form of tritheism or polytheism. As against Sabellianism v. [5] asserts the distinct Personality of the Father, the Son and the Holy Ghost. As against Arianism and Macedonianism, vv. [6-14] assert that whatever Godhead is, the Father, the Son and the Holy Ghost possess it equally: this is illustrated by selecting certain of the attributes of Godhead and assigning them to each Person in turn. In v. [9] 'incomprehensible' in the P.B. version, is a translation of the Latin *immensus* and means 'above the limitations of space'; the word probably came in to the English version through a Greek translation, $\dot{\alpha}\kappa\alpha\tau\dot{\alpha}\lambda\eta\pi\tau\sigma\varsigma$. In vv. [15-20] the Trinity of Persons is asserted side by side with the counter-truth of the Unity of Substance. In vv. [21-27] the modes in which the Three Persons possess the Godhead are set out in language taken from Scripture. All through the primary object is to say 'no' to ingenious speculations which explained away the mystery to mean either that the Three Persons are only three aspects of One God or that they are three separate divine Beings.

(β) The second section deals similarly with the Incarnation. vv. [30-33] emphasize alike Christ's true divinity and His true and full humanity as against Arius and Apollinarius. vv. [34-37] assert that the reality of His two natures did not destroy either the unity of His Person or the reality of either nature. Apollinarians in their wish to avoid a double Personality had 'confused the substance'. vv. [38-40] are a simple statement of the facts and issues of Christ's redemption. Once again we find not speculation, but the attempt of the Church to preserve the whole truth, by rejecting explanations that in reality were inconsistent with some of the facts.

(γ) The minatory portions require more explanation. Their interpretation depends upon the importance of the truth enshrined in the doctrines of the Trinity and the Incarnation. All Christians agree that Christ is the only Saviour. The doctrines of the Trinity and the Incarnation were only formulated to safeguard that conviction. The Church found in Christ the saving power of God Himself and hence was compelled to say 'no' to all explanations that must in the long run undermine that truth. Further, if we believe that Christ is the only Saviour, all who wilfully reject Christ, so long as they reject Him, cut themselves off from the only source of life and health and therefore incur the risk of grave loss and injury. These 'damnatory' clauses are primarily a warning of the terrible consequences that must follow the rejection of Christ.

Viewed in this light they are capable of a perfectly charitable interpretation, though it must be admitted that the English translation is inaccurate and harsher than the Latin original. In the first verse 'Whosoever will be saved', which suggests to modern ears 'Whosoever is going to be saved', should be translated 'Whosoever wishes to be sound' or 'healthy'. (Quicunque vult salvus esse.) The Latin 'salvus' may refer either to a present state of salvation ($\sigma\omega\zeta$-$\acute{o}\mu\epsilon\nu os$) or to the final issue. Examples of either sense can be quoted from contemporary ecclesiastical writers. Again, 'hold' (Latin *teneat*) would be better rendered 'hold fast', and in the following verse 'keep' (Latin *servaverit*) would be better rendered 'preserve'. So the opening would run: 'Whosoever wishes to be in a sound state, before all things it is necessary that he hold fast the Catholic faith: which except he preserve whole and undefiled, etc.' This makes it clear that the clause does not invoke damnation on heretics or heathen, but is a warning to those who possess the Catholic faith not to let it go through indifference or slackness. The words cannot apply to heretics or heathen who cannot hold fast or preserve what they have not got.

Again, in v. [26] 'He therefore that will be saved, must thus think of the Trinity' is not a fair rendering of the Latin 'Qui vult ergo salvus esse: ita de Trinitate sentiat.' 'Must' in the sixteenth century meant little more than 'should' and the whole sentence would more accurately run: 'Let him then who wishes to be in a healthy state, thus think of the Trinity.' In the following verse an even more serious mistranslation occurs. 'It is necessary to everlasting salvation that he also believe rightly the Incarnation of our Lord Jesus Christ.' 'Rightly' came into our version through a Greek translation, which apparently the reformers took as the work of Athanasius himself! This had $\acute{o}\rho\theta\hat{\omega}s$, whereas the true Latin original has 'fideliter', 'faithfully.' To 'believe faithfully' is not the same as to 'believe rightly'. It involves the will and heart and conscience and is a moral act of the whole personality, not merely an affair of the intellect. Once again it is an appeal to the Christian to be faithful to the light that he has received.

So, too, v. [40], 'This is the Catholic faith, which except a man believe faithfully, he cannot be saved' (or rather be in a sound state), is no more than the assertion that without Christ the truest kind of life is impossible.

What then are we to say of heretics and heathen who do not possess the Catholic faith? On the interpretation given above they are not under consideration at all. Christ is the only Saviour, but we believe that many who do not consciously believe in Him as yet, are unconsciously following His guidance. Since He is the light that 'lighteth every man', all that is good and true in the world comes from Him. Those men who follow the light that is given to them and live up to the best that they know are in reality disciples of Christ, though they may never have heard of Him (cp. Mt 25³¹ ff., which would seem to refer to the judgment of the Gentiles, τὰ ἔθνη). All that the Church teaches is that without Christ a man cannot be his best self. We are sure that every man whom God has created and for whom Christ has died will have an opportunity of knowing Christ, if not in this world then in some other. Whether that opportunity has yet been given in the case of any particular individual, we cannot say. We dare not say of any man, even the worst, that he has rejected Christ. It may be that in spite of a Christian home and education, Christ has been hidden from him by the sins and inconsistencies of Christians. The Church has her calendar of saints: she has no roll of the lost. God alone knows the secret of a man's heart and whether Christ has really been presented to him. Again, acceptance of Christ is far more than acceptance by the intellect of certain theological statements about Him. The 'Quicunque' itself makes this quite clear. It exhorts us not to understand but to 'worship' the Unity in Trinity and the Trinity in Unity. It warns us that we shall be judged at the Last Day for our works. 'They that have done good, shall go into life everlasting.' Its exhortations and warnings are addressed less to the mind than to the conscience and the will. Experience shows that on the whole the greatest hindrance to the acceptance of Christ and His claims is not intellectual difficulties, but moral indifference and sloth or the cherishing of unlawful desires.

But this position carries with it the conviction that the rejection of Christ involves loss. Whether finally any will reject Christ altogether is a question to which Scripture hardly gives a definite answer. While we dare not say dogmatically that any individual is finally lost, the teaching of Christ strongly suggests that there is such a possibility as that of final separation from Christ. He could say of Judas Iscariot 'It were good for that man, if he had never been born' (Mk 14²¹). So the language of the 'Quicunque' 'they that have done evil' shall go 'into everlasting fire' and 'he shall perish everlastingly', if we substitute 'eternal' and 'eternally' (Latin 'aeternum' and 'in aeternum') is simply a repetition of the language of Scripture. Christ pictures Himself as bidding those on His left depart into 'eternal fire' Mt 25⁴¹ (πῦρ αἰώνιον), and He explains this in v. ⁴⁶ as 'eternal punishment'. The phrase 'perish eternally' occurs in Jn 11²⁶ (cp. 2 Thess 1⁹, 'Eternal destruction from the face of God'). Whatever Scripture means, the 'Quicunque' means the same. The whole teaching of Christ insists upon the importance of life on earth and on the far-reaching results of our conduct here. Our mind rightly revolts from the thought of useless tortures prolonged through all eternity and from the pictures of the torments of hell to be found in mediaeval pictures. But such conceptions are no essential part of the doctrine of eternal punishment.[1] Some have thought that all will ultimately become reconciled with God and be saved—the doctrine known as universalism. But this lacks positive evidence in Scripture, and indeed is hardly consistent with certain statements in it. Others, again, hold that since Christ is the source of all life, final rejection of Him must involve as its consequence, annihilation. This view of 'conditional immortality' can be supported by very strong arguments and to many minds appears the most probable answer to the problem; but it can hardly be proved from Scripture. A view perhaps more consistent with Scripture is to suppose that there are, as it were, 'degrees of salvation'. It may well be that through suffering after death men will be brought to repentance, but that the consequences of their past will remain. They will be in a lower state than they might have been, but yet they will accept their condition as just. Punishment so accepted is still 'eternal punishment', but yet it has ceased to be torment.[2] But on such matters we can do little more than wonder. God has not given us any answer to the many questions that we would wish to ask. It may well be that our minds are as yet incapable of grasping the conditions of another world that lies wholly outside our present experience.

Lastly it may be urged that though the 'Athanasian Creed' may be interpreted in this sense, that was not the sense in which it was originally composed. That may well be true. It is quite possible that the author meant by 'salvus' final salvation, and that he believed in the eternal damnation of all heretics and heathen and even rejoiced in such belief. A cruel and barbaric age found small difficulty in cruel and barbaric ideas about God. But even if this is so the words of the formula admit of a perfectly Christian interpretation and we are not tied down to sixth century ideas about God. The clauses rest on Scripture, and if our interpretation of Scripture has changed, then we can with perfect honesty change our interpretation of these clauses too.

(iii) As regards the authority of this formula, let us frankly admit that it does not possess the same oecumenical authority as the Apostles' and Constantinopolitan Creeds. It has never been formally accepted by the Orthodox Church of the East. It is found (of course without the words 'and the Son') in modern editions of the Horologion placed apart from the Hour offices, possibly because these were first printed at Venice under Western influence. In the Russian service books it has been placed at the beginning of the psalter, perhaps since the middle of the seventeenth century. But it never has been recited at any office and is at best treated as an estimable theo-

---

[1] Cp. Illingworth, *Reason and Revelation*, p. 120.

[2] In defence of mediaeval pictures of hell, we must bear in mind that it was only through such gross and literal representations of the consequences of sin that spiritual truth could be brought home to rough minds.

logical exposition. Even its acceptance in this form would appear to be due to the belief that it was the work of Athanasius himself. In the West it came to be recited at Prime, on Sundays according to the Roman use, daily according to the use of Sarum. In the later middle ages Prime was frequently said by accumulation with other offices under the general title of Mattins. The more devout lay people would attend Mattins on Sundays and holy days. They would therefore be present at the recitation of the 'Quicunque'. How far they would attempt to join in or understand it is a different question. Few would understand Latin and the poor could not afford a Breviary. They would probably be occupied with their own private devotions. Hence it was a great change when in 1549 the 'Quicunque' appeared in English for recitation by the priest and people at Mattins on certain days, followed by the Apostles' Creed. In 1552 the number of days on which it was to be recited were increased. In 1662 it was definitely made a substitute for and not an addition to the Apostles' Creed. Its repetition was required some thirteen times a year at Mattins. This position assigned to it by the Reformers was due to the belief that it was a Greek Creed and the work of Athanasius. Owing to the position which Mattins came to hold in the life of the ordinary English layman, the 'Quicunque' assumed a prominence which was never intended and which has no parallel in any other part of the Church.

The new rubrics relating to the use of the 'Quicunque' in the revised Prayer Book of 1928 probably reflect with sufficient accuracy the present mind of the Church on this subject. Its use becomes on all occasions permissive. The first rubric says that it 'may be sung or said' at Morning or Evening Prayer on Trinity Sunday, the Sunday after Christmas, and the Feast of the Annunciation, or else that the section relating to the Holy Trinity may be used on Trinity Sunday and the second section relating to the doctrine of the Incarnation on the other two occasions. A further rubric suggests other feasts on which it may be used, and a revised translation is provided which takes account of the linguistic and textual points mentioned above. Permission is given to omit the 'damnatory' clauses at the beginning and the end when the new translation is used. To some these relaxations of the 1662 rubric may be welcome because they sympathize with the modern tendency to dislike dogma; the majority will think them right on broader grounds of liturgical and pastoral expediency. We may believe that every clause in the 'Quicunque' can fairly be interpreted in a sense agreeing with Scripture, and yet take account of the fact that its recitation has proved a stumbling-block to many devout Christians. It may not be wise to enjoin the frequent public use of a document which requires so much explanation and which, at the same time, cannot claim either the oecumenical authority of the Nicene Creed or an established place in the liturgy like that of the Apostles' Creed, the ancient baptismal confession of faith. The faithful adherence of the Church of England to the doctrines of the Trinity and the Incarnation is fully expressed in other liturgical forms; it remains an obligation on her pastors to teach and expound the truths set out in the 'Quicunque'. As a summary for the use of the teacher it is of outstanding and permanent value.†

THE NATURE OF MAN

ARTICLE IX

Of Original or Birth Sin

Original sin standeth not in the following of *Adam*, (as the *Pelagians* do vainly talk); but it is the fault and corruption of the nature of every man, that naturally is engendered of the offspring of *Adam*; whereby man is very far gone from original righteousness, and of his own nature inclined to evil, so that the flesh lusteth always contrary to the Spirit; and therefore in every person born into this world, it deserveth God's wrath and damnation. And this infection of nature doth remain, yea, in them that are regenerated; whereby the lust of the flesh, called in Greek Φρόνημα σαρκός, which some do expound the wisdom, some sensuality, some the affection, some the desire, of the flesh, is not subject to the law of God. And, although there is no condemnation for them that believe and are baptized, yet the Apostle doth confess, that concupiscence and lust hath of itself the nature of sin.

De peccato originali

Peccatum originis non est (ut fabulantur Pelagiani) in imitatione Adami situm, sed est vitium, et depravatio naturae, cujuslibet hominis ex Adamo, naturaliter propagati: qua fit, ut ab originali justitia quam longissime distet, ad malum sua natura propendeat, et caro semper adversus spiritum concupiscat, unde in unoquoque nascentium, iram Dei atque damnationem meretur. Manet etiam in renatis haec naturae depravatio. Qua fit, ut affectus carnis, Graece Φρόνημα σαρκός, (quod alii sapientiam, alii sensum, alii affectum, alii studium carnis interpretantur), legi Dei non subjiciatur. Et quanquam renatis et credentibus nulla propter Christum est condemnatio, peccati tamen in sese rationem habere concupiscentiam, fatetur Apostolus.

Almost unchanged since 1553. The words 'which also the Anabaptists do nowadays renew' were originally present after 'as the Pelagians do vainly talk'. This sufficiently shows the object of the Article. It is directed against the Pelagian views of Anabaptists.

ARTICLE X

Of free will

The condition of man after the fall of *Adam* is such that he cannot turn and prepare himself, by his own natural strength and good works, to faith and calling upon God: Wherefore we have no power to do good works, pleasant and acceptable to God, without the grace of God by Christ preventing us, that we may have a good will, and working with us, when we have that good will.

De libero arbitrio

Ea est hominis post lapsum Adae conditio, ut sese naturalibus suis viribus, et bonis operibus, ad fidem et invocationem Dei convertere ac praeparare non possit. Quare absque gratia Dei (quae per Christum est) nos praeveniente, ut velimus, et cooperante, dum volumus, ad pietatis opera facienda, quae Deo grata sunt et accepta, nihil valemus.

The latter half of the Article comes from an Article of 1553 and is based on S. Augustine. The first half was added in 1563 from the Confession of Würtemburg.

The title appears at first sight unsuitable. The Article does not deal with free-will but asserts the need of grace against Pelagian Anabaptists. But in reality the connexion is very close (*v.* below).

ARTICLE XV

Of Christ alone without Sin

Christ in the truth of our nature was made like unto us in all things (sin only except), from which he was clearly void, both in his flesh, and in his spirit. He came to be the Lamb without spot, who, by the sacrifice of himself once made, should take away the sins of the world, and sin (as S. *John* saith), was not in him. But all we the rest, (although baptized, and born again in Christ), yet offend in many things; and if we say we have no sin, we deceive ourselves, and the truth is not in us.

De Christo, qui solus est sine peccato

Christus in nostrae naturae veritate, per omnia similis factus est nobis, excepto peccato, a quo prorsus erat immunis, tum in carne, tum in spiritu. Venit ut agnus absque macula esset, qui mundi peccata per immolationem sui semel factam tolleret, et peccatum (ut inquit Johannes) in eo non erat: sed nos reliqui etiam baptizati, et in Christo regenerati, in multis tamen offendimus omnes. Et si dixerimus, quia peccatum non habemus, nos ipsos seducimus, et veritas in nobis non est.

This article dates from 1553. Its exact object is not certain. Probably it was directed against certain Anabaptists who denied our Lord's sinlessless. Others have held that it was aimed at the belief in the immaculate conception of the Blessed Virgin. This is unlikely. The belief was not yet *de fide* in the Roman Church. The Articles usually are perfectly straightforward in their attack on views that they do not accept. A much shorter and more definite Article would have sufficed. Further, the Blessed Virgin was never 'baptized and born again in Christ'. Hence the former view is preferable.

ARTICLE XVI

Of Sin after Baptism	*De peccato post Baptismum*
Not every deadly sin willingly committed after Baptism is sin against the Holy Ghost, and un-pardonable. Wherefore the grant of repentance is not to be denied to such as fall into sin after Baptism. After we have received the Holy Ghost, we may depart from grace given and fall into sin, and by the grace of God we may arise again, and amend our lives. And therefore they are to be condemned which say, they can no more sin as long as they live here, or deny the place of forgiveness to such as truly repent.	Non omne peccatum mortale post Baptismum voluntarie per-petratum, est peccatum in Spiri-tum Sanctum, et irremissibile. Proinde lapsis a Baptismo in peccata, locus poenitentiae non est negandus. Post acceptum Spiritum Sanctum possumus a gratia data recedere atque pec-care, denuoque per gratiam Dei resurgere ac resipiscere; ideoque illi damnandi sunt, qui se, quam-diu hic vivant, amplius non posse peccare affirmant, aut vere re-sipiscentibus veniae locum dene-gant.

This Article dates from 1553 with slight changes. The present title is the third. It is aimed at Anabaptist errors.

§ 1. *The true nature of man*

It is characteristic of the age in which our Articles were written that they hasten at once to speak of '*the fault and corruption*' of man's nature. '*Man is very far gone from original righteousness*,' *i.e.* as the Article of 1553 stated, 'his former righteousness which he had at his creation.' But we cannot understand man's present condition unless we know something of man as he is in himself. What is meant by that 'original righteousness' which man has lost? What is man's true nature and what is his relation to God?

(*a*) The phrase in the Article is an allusion to the picture of man's life given in the opening chapters of Genesis. The compilers of our Articles, no doubt, like all other men of their day, regarded these chapters as literal history, and Adam and Eve as historical persons. Such a view to-day is impossible, but the religious value of these chapters has been increased rather than diminished by modern know-ledge. The Jews inherited from their ancestors a stock of common Semitic traditions about the origin of the world and of mankind. As these were handed down from generation to generation, they were taken up by the prophets and under the guidance of God purged of their grosser elements and transformed into a vehicle of moral and spiritual truth. In their present form these chapters come not at the beginning but rather towards the close of God's revelation to Israel. They are, as it were, the summing up of those great truths about the nature and purpose of human life that God had been teaching the people by His prophets through the centuries. Israel had risen to a higher conception of human nature than that attained by any other pre-Christian religion. God had given to the prophets a unique insight into the meaning of man's relation to God, and into the true goal and purpose of our earthly life. In Genesis we find these truths that God had revealed set forth in an ideal picture of man living as God made and meant him to be.

Scripture, like science, represents man as the 'roof and crown' of God's creation (Gen 1^{26}, 9^{1-7}, Ps 8, etc.). He is the link between nature and God, God's vicegerent in the world. On the one hand he possesses a body akin to that of the beasts and made, like theirs, of the dust of the earth (Gen $2^{7 \text{ and } 19}$, etc.). Modern science tells us that our bodies are the product of long ages of evolution and are derived by physical descent from animal life. They are not one bit the less either human bodies or the creation of God because they have come to be what they are as the climax of a long process and not as the immediate result of the creative word of God. On the other hand, man is created 'in the image of God' (Gen 1^{27}) by a special in-breathing of divine spirit (2^7). No words could bring out more clearly the dignity and possibilities of human nature made 'but little lower than God' (Ps 8^5, R.V.).[1] It is in virtue of this 'image of God' in him that man is able to know and love God. Like can only know like. More particularly this image of God includes the possession of reason and will. Man is able to do what the animals cannot do, understand and co-operate with the divine purposes.[2] Further man was made for social life and development. All these elements of human life have their place in the picture of the Garden of Eden. Man is depicted as God meant him to be, at peace with himself, his neighbour, the world and God. By congenial employment in active fellowship with God his faculties are trained and developed. Did such a state of things ever exist in actual fact on this earth? We do not know. We may regard these chapters either as containing an allegorical account of human life as it once actually was, or as an

[1] The superiority of man to the animals is shown in Gen 2^{18-20}. Not one of the animals is found able to share Adam's life and be a 'help meet' for him. Cp. also 1^{28} ff.

[2] The possession of reason and will is implied by the imposition of a definite command and prohibition (2^{15-17}). No animal is treated in this way. Further, Adam learns to exercise his reason as infants to-day begin to exercise theirs by distinguishing things and giving them names (2^{19}). The social nature of man is shown in vv. $^{18-25}$. The family was to be the school of love, in which man was to learn to develop his social nature. It has often been pointed out that in Scripture man begins in a garden and ends in a city.

allegorical description of man's life as God meant it to be, though His purpose was never historically realized.[1]†

(b) But for the Christian the supreme revelation of the divine purpose for man is to be found in Jesus Christ. As Man He exhibited in their completeness all those powers that Adam is represented as exhibiting in some small and preparatory degree. He lived in unbroken fellowship with God. He displayed a perfect sympathy with the divine will and a perfect obedience. He lived His human life as Son of God because man was created to live as son of God. His human faculties were developed by the discipline of the home. He displayed an unfailing love to all men. Since man is made in the image of God, and God is love, man must be love too. In His teaching He interpreted human life from within. He knew what was in man, because He knew what was in Himself. His perfect humanity held no secrets from Him. The full meaning of 'original righteousness' may be studied in Jesus Christ. He alone fulfilled the destiny intended for man on this earth. Further He recognized in every human being the capacity for this same life. Alike in His teaching and in His behaviour He asserted the value of every human soul, just because it was human (cp. Mt 6^{26}, 12^{12}). Christ came to bring light and salvation because man was made for light and salvation. Because man was created in the image of God, he was called to live up to his position. Finally, by His resurrection and ascension Christ became the first-fruits of a redeemed humanity and revealed man's nature as destined for eternal life with God.

(c) This Scripture doctrine of 'original righteousness' rules out as un-Christian many widespread views of man's nature. It insists that every part of it is 'very good'. There is no necessary conflict between the lower and higher elements. We can glorify God in our bodies no less than in our spirits (1 Cor 6^{20}, cp. Rom 12^1). Even our highest activities are conditioned by bodily functions. Every natural desire has a purpose to fulfil. Man has been endowed with reason by which to guide his desires and with will by which to control them. A holy life is not a life in which the body is neglected or ignored. It is rather one in which all the powers of the body are subordinated to a single purpose, the will of God. Our Lord's example shows us a human body fulfilling its true function as the organ of a life consecrated to God. Accordingly, the man who indulges any passion is not being 'manly' in the true sense.[2] True manliness consists in subduing all

---

[1] 'Whether or not the corrupted state of human nature was preceded in temporal sequence by an incorrupt state, this is the most vivid and natural way of exhibiting the truth that in God's primary purpose man was incorrupt, so that evil in him should be regarded as having a secondary or adventitious character. Ideal antecedence is, as it were, pictured in temporal antecedence.'—Hort, *Life and Letters*, vol. ii. p. 329.

[2] It is specially necessary to insist that sins of the flesh are not 'natural' to man. They are a violation of his true nature. Impurity, for instance, is in the strict sense of the term 'abnormal', not because it is uncommon but because it destroys the balance of man's constitution. It violates the law of his being. It is also anti-social.

desires to the will. Christian asceticism aims not at annihilating such desires but at reducing them to order (1 Cor 9²⁷). The true Christian is not the man who has learnt to desire nothing, but the man who has learnt to desire the right things. We must regard our bodies neither as evil nor as negligible. Our Lord never belittled the dignity of the body or despised its needs. A large part of His ministry was taken up in healing it.

§ 2. While the study of man's nature in the light of Scripture discloses such magnificent possibilities, his actual condition is very different. He is at peace neither with God nor with the world, nor with his neighbour, nor with himself. This disordered state of his nature is what is meant by *original sin*. Before we can discuss the meaning of such a phrase or the account of it given in the Article, we must understand the meaning of the word 'sin'.

(*a*) No term is more frequently misused than 'sin'. The essential nature of sin depends upon our relation to God. An act that is morally wrong, if viewed as committed against the laws of the state, is a crime: viewed as an offence against our neighbour, it is an injustice or an injury: viewed as offence against our own well-being, it is an act of folly or a piece of damage. Only as committed against God is it a sin. To an atheist the word sin has no meaning whatever. Since the state has divine authority a crime is almost always a sin. Since we are commanded to love our neighbour, to injure him is to disobey God's command. Since God's law for us is not in any sense arbitrary, but expresses at once His will and the condition of our own highest welfare, an act committed against our own self is a sin. But in every case sin involves a reference to God. We may define sin as 'personal hostility to the will of God'. It is setting our will against His: actively disobeying His command or refusing Him the love and submission that we owe. 'Sin is lawlessness' (1 Jn 3⁴). The effect in ourselves is a dislocation of our inner life, a destruction of the balance and unity of our nature. Sin issues in a divided self. In relation to our fellow men sin is selfishness. The law of God represents the common welfare of all men. Disobedience results from the desire for some personal or private gain. By setting aside God's will we impair not only our own soundness but the soundness of the society in which we live. So, then, sin is primarily disobedience to the known will of God, either by doing what we ought not to do or leaving undone what we ought to do. It is often pictured as a disease, or a burden, or a stain, or again as an enemy attacking us. All these metaphors express a truth, but they are far too external. Sin is a condition of our own wills and so of our inmost selves. The definite acts of sin that we commit are evidence of and spring out of this inward disposition, a heart turned away from God and a will divided and impaired.

(*b*) How did sin originate? To-day we should confess that we find no ultimate answer to this question in Scripture. Scripture represents moral evil as not originated by man or confined to him. The compilers of our Articles no doubt regarded Gen 3 as a historical account of the commission of the first sin. This has coloured the language employed, '*The condition of man after the fall of Adam . . .*' (Art. X). They regarded all men as literally the *offspring of Adam*. To-day such a view is impossible. In this, as in the preceding chapters, we have an old myth that has passed through the hands of the Hebrew prophets and been transfigured so as to teach in the form of a story the meaning of sin. It gives us not a historical account of the origin of sin but an inspired analysis of its meaning. Its value lies not in its historical but its spiritual accuracy. Through their own experience and the experience of the nation, the prophets had been led to see that sin is essentially disobedience to God. This is wonderfully brought out in the picture of the taking of the forbidden fruit.[1] Though no certain reference to this chapter occurs in the rest of the O.T. this same conception of sin is implied throughout. The story awakens an echo in our own experience. All we can say is that whatever the first sin was, in order to be sin at all, it must have involved, first a knowledge of a higher law binding on the will, and then the conscious choice of a lower course, by one who knew it to be the lower. Our Lord in His teaching accepts and deepens the O.T. doctrine of sin. He assumes sin but never explains its origin. He calls us to deal in a practical manner with the sin in ourselves, by repentance and obedience. It is more important for us to recognize the unsatisfactoriness of our present condition and the remedy for it than to know how it originated. Jesus Christ came to save men from sin and to impart new life. Through the obedience of His Cross He restores that fellowship with God which our disobedience has impaired.

(*c*) This then is 'actual' sin, personal antagonism to the known will of God. But our Article speaks in the main of '*original sin*'. The phrase is not Scriptural, but was used first by Tertullian. It denotes not an act or habit but a condition of our nature. '*Original sin*' is at bottom the attempt to express the fact that all men fall into sin. 'Original sin is, fundamentally, simply universal sin. This is the fact which is at once the evidence and substance of it. We know that if sin is universal, and if there is no instance of a human being without it, universal sin must receive the same interpretation that any other universal does, namely, that it implies a law in consequence of which it is universal. Nobody supposes that anything takes place universally by chance, accident, or what we call curious coincidence. . . . This consequence applies just as much to the fact of sin in the human

---

[1] We notice first the recognition of God's command by Eve as binding (v. ³), then the temptation that is allowed to find a response within. The appeal is made to all sides of their nature. The fruit is 'good for food'—the lust of the flesh; 'pleasant to the eye'—the lust of the eyes; 'to be desired to make one wise'—the longing for a richer and fuller experience at all costs.

race if it is universal and this law we call "original sin".[1] Our Article appears definitely to associate this universal tendency to sin with the fall of Adam. '*Original sin standeth not in the following of Adam*' (*i.e.* does not consist in the universal imitation of Adam's bad example), '*but it is the fault and corruption of the nature of every man, that naturally is engendered of the offspring of Adam; whereby man is very far gone from original righteousness and is of his own nature inclined to evil.*' As we have seen, we no longer believe in the historical existence of Adam, and such phrases sound strange to our ears. But the truth of original sin is not in the least affected by any view that we hold about the historical value of Genesis. The whole religious experience of Israel bore witness to the sinfulness of the human heart, and this fact of universal conviction of sin shaped the story of Genesis. The story did not create the conviction, but the conviction the story. A deeper insight into the holiness of God was always followed by a deeper sense of human unworthiness (Is 6^{1-5}, Jer 17^9, etc.). Many passages in the Old Testament attest the universal sense of alienation from God (Ps 51^5, 14^3, Job 14^4, etc.). So, too, in the New Testament, our Lord assumes the universal sinfulness of man (Mt 7^{11}). He places in the universal prayer the petition 'Forgive us our trespasses'. He has no message for the 'righteous' (Mk 2^{17}, etc.). In order to enter the Kingdom of God repentence is always required (*e.g.* Mt 4^{17}). Men need not simply to be made better but to be born 'anew' or 'from above' (Jn 3^1 ff.). The Cross is the remedy for sin. Our Lord died to give His life as a ransom for those who had forfeited their lives by disobedience (Mk 10^{45}, etc.). 'If we say that we have not sinned we make God a liar' (1 Jn 1^{10}, cp. 1^8), because all His dealings with us imply our need of a Saviour from sin. The apostolic call for repentance receives its universal authority from the fact that 'Christ died for our sins'. It is true that S. Paul twice connects our sin with the fall of Adam (Rom 5^{12-15}, 1 Cor 15^{22}) following contemporary Jewish teaching. But the theory did not create the facts: the facts demanded a theory. S. Paul saw everywhere in the world of his day, among Jew and Gentile alike, the ravages of the sin that he knew in his own heart. The teaching that 'all have sinned' (Rom 3^{23}) was not due to a too literal interpretation of a Jewish allegory. It was the result of his own observation, sharpened by the knowledge that God had set forth Christ crucified as the universal remedy for sin.[2]

(*d*) Again, just because Jesus Christ is the revelation to us of what man was made to be, so He is also the final argument for the unnaturalness of our present condition. He convicts of sin those who come to Him. By placing their lives side by side with His, they realize the gulf between what they are and what they were meant to be. The

---

[1] Mozley, *Lectures and Theological Papers*, p. 136. The whole paper deserves most careful attention.

[2] See Sanday and Headlam, *Romans*, p. 136 ff.

victorious sacrifice of the Cross and the Resurrection is the judgment as well as the salvation of the world. '*Christ in the truth of our nature was made like unto us in all things (sin only except) from which He was clearly void both in His flesh and in His spirit. He came to be the Lamb without spot, who by the sacrifice of Himself once made should take away the sins of the world*; and sin (as S. John saith) was not in Him' (1 Jn 3⁵). This is the unanimous teaching of Scripture (Heb 4¹⁵, 7²⁶⁻²⁷, 9¹⁴, 1 Pet 2²², 2 Cor 5²¹).[1] The strongest argument is not the assertions of N.T. writers nor even isolated texts from the Gospels (*e.g.* Which of you convicteth me of sin? Jn 8⁴⁶, cp. 14³⁰), but the whole impression that He made on others, the claims that He made publicly for Himself and the glimpses that we are allowed to catch of His inner consciousness. He preserved an unbroken union with the Father (Jn 10³⁰). As a rule it is the holiest men and those living most closely to God who are most conscious of their sinfulness and most deeply penitent. He taught others to pray for forgiveness, but never did so Himself. Even on the Cross, when His whole life seemed ending in failure, He utters no prayer for pardon. He perceived that forgiveness was needed for His murderers, not for Himself. Two passages have been quoted on the other side. (i) 'Why callest thou me good? None is good save one, even God' (Mk 10¹⁷). Our Lord's apparent refusal of the title 'good' seems at first sight to imply a consciousness of sin. But in the Greek the emphatic word is not 'me' but 'good'. He was rebuking an emotional young man who was using extravagant language without thinking what it really meant, and had no true appreciation of the meaning of goodness. (ii) The cry from the Cross 'My God, why hast thou forsaken me?' (Mk 15³⁴). Here the Greek would more accurately be translated 'Why didst thou leave me?' It was no random cry, but a definite quotation from a particular psalm. It must be interpreted in the light of its context. This psalm is the only one of its class that contains no personal confession of sin and it ends in a song of triumph. The words imply unbroken trust in God and are an appeal that His help is long delayed. They are evidence of our Lord's unbroken faith, preserved even amid great darkness of soul. The Resurrection was the divine affirmation that He had made the complete and acceptable sacrifice of the 'Lamb without spot'.

(*e*) Our Article goes on to describe '*original sin*' as '*the fault and corruption of the nature of every man*'. It explains the fact that all men sin by laying down that all men inherit a common human nature that is corrupt inasmuch as it possesses a positive downward tendency to evil. This statement can only be understood in the light of previous theological discussion. No attempt was made to give any

---

[1] In Rom 8³ He is said to have come in the likeness of sinful flesh. 'The flesh of Christ is "like" ours inasmuch as it is flesh "like" and only "like" because it is not sinful.'— S. and H. *ad loc.*

formal account of original sin until the time of Augustine. The first traces of any controversy on the subject are to be found in the different views taken as to the origin of the human soul. The Eastern Fathers and Jerome and Hilary in the West taught that each soul was created out of nothing by God and joined to a body derived from its parents. This is known as 'Creationism'. It seems to reduce the 'solidarity' of the human race to a merely physical fact. Original sin on this view would lie in the body. The Western Fathers and Gregory of Nyssa in the East taught that the human soul was derived from its parents. Thus the first man contained within him all mankind. On this view a transmission of a tendency to sin is intelligible. The 'vitium originis'—to use Tertullian's phrase—necessarily affects all who are born of the common stock.[1] We may fairly hold that both views express a real truth. In some sense every human being is created by God. Each human life is His gift, none the less His because mediated by human action. Every man can say 'God made me'. On the other hand, no human life is an isolated unit: it would not be human if it were. And that common humanity which we share with others includes far more than merely physical attributes. It includes those moral, intellectual and spiritual capacities that distinguish man from the beasts, and can only be developed in society.

Again, the early Fathers, Eastern and Western alike, took a hopeful view of human nature.[2] They laid no very great stress upon the 'Fall' and its consequences. They had no very clear or unanimous teaching about the origin of sin. So far as they dealt with the results of the 'Fall', they held that man lost then a supernatural bias towards righteousness, comparable to the bias towards righteousness that follows from a good character. Man was left weak but fundamentally sound. Thus 'original sin' would be a loss of higher goodness, a 'privatio naturae'. But with S. Augustine a darker view of the results of the 'Fall' won considerable though by no means universal acceptance in the West. Augustine regarded man's original bias towards righteousness as natural. Hence Adam fell below the level of his true nature and corrupted his entire posterity. We inherit a nature that is not indeed entirely corrupt but yet has a positive inclination towards evil. The result is more than a mere 'privatio naturae': it is 'depravatio naturae'. This teaching of S. Augustine was partly drawn out in conflict with Pelagius. Pelagius denied any corruption of human nature at all. He held that Adam's sin injured no one but himself. As we should expect, he was a creationist. The widespread existence of sin he attributed, as our Article says, to the following of Adam's bad example. He was prepared to allow that some men even before the coming of Christ had lived free from sin. Thus the existence of

[1] Origen explained original sin by the theory of pre-existence. Men are really fallen spirits who fell in another world. This view won little acceptance in the Church and lies outside the main stream of Christian thought. It is maintained by theosophists.
[2] See N. P. Williams, *The Ideas of the Fall and of Original Sin*, Lect. iv.

'original sin', so far as he allowed that it existed at all, was due to purely external causes, bad environment, bad example and education and the like.

At the Reformation these questions were again debated with great vigour. Hence our present Article. Mediaeval teaching on the whole had taken a moderate view of the effects of the 'Fall'. The Council of Trent was content to speak of 'the loss of holiness and righteousness'. On the other hand, Calvinists and many Lutherans pushed the teaching of S. Augustine so far as to assert the total corruption of human nature. Our Article adopts a mediating position. On the one side it clearly takes a gloomier view of man's present position than the Council of Trent. It follows S. Augustine so far as to speak of '*the fault and corruption* (depravatio) *of the nature of every man, that naturally is engendered of the offspring of Adam, whereby man is very far gone from original righteousness, and is of his own nature inclined to evil.*' It definitely repudiates the Pelagian idea that the 'Fall' had no effect on man at all. On the other side it carefully avoids the Calvinistic extravagance of saying 'Tota depravatio'. This would be obviously untrue. If man were wholly corrupt he could not be aware of his corruption. There would be no moral struggle within, no discontent with self or desire for better things. The spirit would not lust against the flesh, as S. Paul tells us that it does (Gal 5[17]).[1] Nothing has done more to create a prejudice against the doctrine of original sin, than the idea that it means the total badness of human nature.[2]

How can we regard the teaching of the Article to-day? In the light of modern knowledge much of the old language seems unreal. We begin by pointing out that 'original sin' is not altogether a happy phrase. If sin means a will hostile to God, sin in the strict sense can only be predicted of a person and not of a nature. No part of our nature, no faculty that we possess can in itself be 'sinful'. It only becomes sinful when we exercise it unlawfully. No created thing in God's universe is evil in itself. It only becomes evil when it is misused by a being who has free-will. We must avoid any mental picture of original sin that would represent it as an evil substance transmitted by inheritance in the same way as physical peculiarities are transmitted. Hence the statement of our Article that original sin '*deserves God's wrath and damnation*' is open to serious criticism. Neither charity nor common-sense allow us to suppose that an infant who cannot choose between good and evil is personally exposed to the wrath of God because it will commit actual sin when it grows up. The words of the Article are only true if we look at the matter in an

---

[1] So, too, our Lord appeals to the natural affection of parents for children and the like. He rouses men to use their natural powers of reason and will. Cp. also Rom 2[14-15].

[2] For a discussion between two modern theologians in the Calvinistic tradition of the question, how far the *imago Dei* remains in fallen man, see E. Brunner and K. Barth, *Natural Theology*, esp. pp. 22 and 40. Cp. also D. Cairns, *The Image of God* and Quick, *The Gospel of the New World*, pp. 34 ff. (a brief and illuminating discussion).

entirely abstract way.[1] No doubt S. Paul calls us 'children' (*i.e.* simply 'objects') 'of wrath'[2] (Eph 2[3]), because apart from Christ we cannot live up to the standard of a holy God. But Scripture adds what the Article does not, that 'original sin' is an appeal not only to God's wrath but to God's pity (*e.g.* Lk 19[10]). The mind of God is to be seen in Christ, who hated sin and loved the sinner. The Article does, indeed, say that it is the 'nature' rather than the person that deserves God's wrath. But a nature apart from a person is a mere abstraction.

On the other hand if we reject illustrations drawn from heredity in the physical world as misleading, the great fact of the solidarity of human nature still remains. The unity of the race is moral and spiritual, not only physical. Mankind is one in sin.[3] Moreover, though we cannot inherit 'sin', experience shows that we do inherit dispositions and tendencies that easily become sin. Children resemble their parents in certain tastes and characteristics which we label good and bad in themselves, apart from the actions in which they may or may not issue. Further, in the moral and spiritual life it is by no means easy to draw a hard and fast line between heredity and environment and to say when the influence of one begins and the other ends. In any case human nature does not come to us ready-made. It begins as a bundle of possibilities that need the life of the community for their development. A purely individual human life is an impossibility. If 'original sin' seems unfair, we need to remember that the good tendencies and good dispositions of our nature come down to us by inheritance as well as its deficiencies. The unity of race that conditions original sin, conditions also salvation through Christ.[4]

---

[1] The best defence is that given by Dean Church, *Life and Letters*, pp. 294–295. 'The fact of what is meant by original sin is as mysterious and inexplicable as the origin of evil, but it is obviously as much a fact. There is a fault and vice in the race, which, given time, as surely develops into actual sin as our physical constitution, given at birth, does into sickness and physical death. It is of this inherited sin, looked upon in the abstract and without reference to concrete cases, that I suppose the Article speaks. How can we suppose that such a nature looks in God's eyes according to the standard of perfect righteousness which we also suppose to be God's standard and law? Does it satisfy that standard? Can He look with neutrality on its divergence from His perfect standard? What He may do to cure it, to pardon it, to make allowances for it in known or unknown ways, is another matter about which His known attributes of mercy alone may reassure us; but the question is, How does He look upon this fact of our nature in itself, that without exception it has this strong efficacious germ of evil within it, of which He sees all the possibilities and all the consequences? Can He look on it even in germ with complacency or indifference? Must He not judge it and condemn it as in itself, because evil, deserving condemnation?'

[2] Armitage Robinson, *Ephesians*, pp. 49–50. The phrase contains no idea of inheriting God's wrath, and 'children' has nothing to do with infancy.

[3] In all its forms Pelagianism is hopelessly individualistic. It is contradicted to-day by our sense of corporate and national sin, as a spiritual force hostile to God, lying behind the sins of individuals, yet in some sense independent of them.

[4] It is a question whether S. Paul in Rom 5[12–21] asserts the transmission of a sinful nature from Adam. 'The view taken of the sin of Adam is not so much that thereby human nature was infected in itself, but rather that thereby sin, an alien power, got a

But we have hardly yet got to the bottom of the problem. The difference between sin and righteousness is in the last resort one of personal relationship to God. As we saw, man cannot live his true life apart from that union with God for which he was made. We cannot draw hard and fast distinctions between the natural and supernatural elements in man's nature, simply because man's essential nature is to live in fellowship with God. By sin that fellowship has been impaired. Hence man's whole constitution has become disordered. Apart from God the heart becomes cold, the will enfeebled, the mind darkened. The result is that selfish desires lack control and the body tends to become master rather than servant. We are unable to resist evil suggestions from without. This would seem to be the root of original sin. We are born into a condition of life in which our full union with God is broken. To use the old language, original sin begins with a 'privatio', a cutting-off of the needed light and strength, and inevitably ends in a 'depravatio', a positive alienation of mind and heart from God.[1] For this condition we are not personally responsible. Original sin in itself does not involve personal accountability. We believe in original sin, not original guilt.[2] As we have seen, it appeals to God's pity. It only becomes actual sin when of our own will we yield to temptation and choose the wrong.

The latter part of the Article deals with a question that arose out of the discussion about the results of the 'Fall'. Experience shows that sinful desires remain even in the Christian after Baptism. How far are these 'true and proper' sin? The Calvinists naturally said that concupiscence was sin. The Council of Trent said that it was not 'truly and properly sin but . . . is of sin and inclines to sin'. Our Article is purposely vague. The allusion seems to be to James 1[14–15]. But the Apostle is clearly S. Paul. The most probable reference is to 'Rom 7[17] as expounded by S. Augustine.'[3]

(*f*) The question still remains: 'Is this view of sin consistent with the assured results of modern science?' 'Has it not been shown that man has risen, not fallen?' It has been argued that so-called 'original sin' is no sign of any estrangement from God or any corruption of our

---

footing in the world, and, involving all men in actual sin, brought death upon all. This is very far short of the Augustinian doctrine of original sin, which appears to be a development of 2 Es 3[21], 4[30], rather than of anything to be found in N.T. The language of S. Paul ("sin came into the world," Rom 5[12]), leaves room for the communication of a sinful tendency, not only by heredity in the strict sense of the word, but also by all that interpenetration of the individuals by the race which makes it impossible to regard them as isolated atoms dependent only on birth for their characteristics.' E. R. Bernard, art. 'Sin', *H.D.B.* iv. pp. 534*b*–535*a*.

[1] Cp. the insistence of Aquinas (*S. Theol.* II, I, cix.) that man is not only *spoliatus gratuitis*, but also *vulneratus in naturalibus*.

[2] For the meaning which may be attached to 'original guilt', see *Doctrine in the Church of England*, p. 63.

[3] Kidd, *Thirty-nine Articles*, p. 127.

nature. Rather it is a necessary product of man's upward development. It is the survival in us of passions and desires derived from our animal ancestry. It is the 'ape and tiger' within us. Our consciousness of a divided self is only due to the fact that these animal instincts, once useful and necessary at an earlier stage for the preservation of life, are in process of being moralized. If there has been 'a fall' at all, it has been a 'fall upwards'. That is to say there came a time when man first exchanged the life of merely animal contentment and harmony for the life of moral struggle and effort. He began to be aware, however dimly, of the distinction between a higher and a lower course of action. He learnt to contrast his gross animal habits with the idea of what he ought to be and might become. This new-born dissatisfaction with his former self was proof not of a fall but of an advance. It marked the 'passage from a brute life unconscious of moral distinctions to the spiritual consciousness of right and wrong'. There are as many 'falls' as 'souls'. It has been asserted : 'Man never possessed the original harmony of his whole being such as the doctrine of an unfallen state requires. . . . Sin is derived solely from the individual will and cannot be inborn; and the discord between flesh and spirit, lower nature and higher, animal propensity and rational morality, is no sign of a bias to evil but the inevitable outcome of man's development.'[1]

Others, from a slightly different standpoint, would argue that sin is a necessary phase in the evolution of mankind, which is being outgrown. No doubt we must admit that many sins are voluntary and deserve blame. But sin is primarily a mistake. The sinner is really seeking for God, but he is seeking for God in the wrong way. Sin is only a temporary error. Man finds out his mistake by the unsatisfactory consequences that follow his action. He learns to condemn himself. His higher self passes judgment on his lower self. He turns again to the right road having learnt the lesson. The 'relics of our brute ancestry' in us, that is to say, the tendency to seek our own selfish ends instead of the common good are being gradually purged away as civilization and culture advance. 'Slowly, very slowly, the race is climbing the steep ascent.' Ultimately in every member of the human race the ideal life will be attained. Some such view of sin not formulated or put into words is exceedingly common to-day. It may be stated in forms that, as far as they go, are perfectly Christian. But the question is whether it accounts for all the facts of the moral life as we observe it in our own hearts or in the history of the world.

(i) We may doubt whether the results of physical science throw any real light upon the problem of sin. We have to deal with man as he now is, not with man as he once was. We may recognize the continuity of all life on this earth of ours, but the fact still remains that

---

[1] Tennant, *Original Sin*, p. 31. For a full statement of this view see his larger book, *Origin and Propagation of Sin*.

man is no longer an animal. We cannot interpret human life in terms
of animal life. That would be to interpret the higher by the lower. All
sound philosophy allows that a thing's nature must be estimated not
by what it once was but by what it by becoming has become. An oak
must be studied as an oak and not as an acorn. We can speak of a
baby as a little man but not of a man as a big baby. At whatever
stage distinctively human life first appeared, just because it was
human life and no longer animal, new factors that were absent in
animal life intervened. Hence statements and conclusions that were
valid on the lower level are no longer valid on the higher. Take the
case of the individual man. As an infant he has no moral life: he is
not morally responsible for his behaviour. Yet when he comes to
manhood he has become a rational and moral being. We may not be
able to put our finger on a definite moment of time and say that then
moral life begins. But the change has taken place. The man is no
longer an infant. His adult life cannot be explained or expressed in
terms of infant life. No knowledge, however exact, of infant life, can
be applied to adult life, because the new factors of reason and conscience have now intervened. So in the development of the human
race, we cannot draw a hard and fast line as to where human life first
began. It is enough to know that man has become a moral being.
The conclusions of physical science are absolutely valid within the
sphere of facts that physical science studies. But when we get to the
moral life, new influences and powers appear, with which from its
abstract character physical science can have nothing to do. In this
higher region its conclusions no longer possess unconditional
validity. Sin belongs to this higher region. Physical science may
explain whence we derive our animal desires and passions, but it can
do no more. Its authority stops short just where the real problem of
sin begins.

(ii) Sin in its true sense was not possible until man had reached the
level of moral and rational life, however undeveloped he still was.
Man did not become conscious of sin when he first looked upon his
former animal behaviour and marked its unsatisfactoriness in comparison with the new and higher ideal that was dawning upon his
consciousness. Rather he first became conscious of sin when he recognized the good and chose the bad instead. We should agree with
S. Paul that 'sin is not imputed when there is no law' (Rom 5¹³). The
fractiousness and cryings of an infant are not sinful or proofs of a
fallen nature as S. Augustine supposed.[1] Science tells us that they are
the natural result of evolution. The child is not responsible for them.
A child can only commit actual sin when he has become conscious
of some law as binding upon him and disregards it. By this time he
has ceased to be a subject that can be adequately studied by physical
science alone. The problem of original sin is the problem of universal

[1] Cp. Aug. *Confessions*, i. c. 7.

sin. Why is a wrong choice always made? Not, how or why did we get the materials out of which to make it? The difficulty is not that man possesses animal passions and desires that need strict control, but that these are perverted and misused as they are not in the case of animals, and that the will does not control them. Universality of sin cannot be explained by universality of animal inheritance.[1]

(iii) The unsatisfactoriness of the attempt to account for sin as a by-product of man's evolution is seen more clearly when we consider those sins which are not sins of his animal nature at all. To say that the drunkard and the profligate are really seeking for God though they are seeking for Him in the wrong place, has a certain air of plausibility. In some sense they are seeking, or at any rate began by seeking, a satisfaction of self in their vices. But when we turn to sins of pride and calculated cruelty, the plausibility disappears. Is it possible to say that, for instance, a solicitor who deliberately schemes to take advantage of a client's ignorance to steal his money, is doing no more than making a mistake in his quest for God? To quote Dean Church again: 'It is important to bear in mind that in speaking of sin and sinners we are apt to take as our type one particular class of sin, the sins of the "publican and the harlot". It is natural that revolting, ruinous and flagrant as they are, they should represent sin to our minds. Yet there are sins more malignant and more difficult to conceive cured. I can conceive of many of those poor creatures whom the world speaks of as lost blindly "seeking after God". It is difficult to me to conceive this of those who with full knowledge and all advantages prey on human happiness in one way or another, the selfish seekers of their own interest and pleasure.' 'Men forget the sins of character, of the Pharisees and of the wicked, wise conspirators against human good and happiness, who are eminently the Bible type of the sinners who have everything to fear.'[2] If men are honest with themselves they must allow that there have been times when they saw the good and knew it to be the good and wilfully chose the evil. That is no mere survival of animal instinct nor any error of judgment, it is deliberate rebellion against God. Further, if Scripture is right in assigning the highest eminence to such virtues as faith, hope, charity, humility, meekness, purity of heart and the like, it follows that the contrary vices to these are the most grave, that is, those vices such as pride which have the least intimate connexion with our animal nature at all. We need to keep holy not only our bodies but our spirits. Spiritual sins are as real as and more deadly than bodily sins.

(iv) To say that man has risen, not fallen, involves serious con-

---

[1] It is significant that in his last book, *The Concept of Sin*, Dr Tennant was driven to what is essentially the Pelagian position, namely, the denial of the universality of sin (p. 268). His view of sin is far too individualistic.

[2] *Life*, p. 317.

fusion of thought. No doubt man has made immense advances in material prosperity, and in knowledge and culture. But such progress is not moral and spiritual progress. In the picture of God's purpose for man given in the opening chapters of Genesis, Adam is depicted as a naked savage, uncultured and undeveloped, but made for development in dependence upon God. He is further depicted as innocent rather than holy: since holiness can only be attained by the conquest of temptation. He is only making the first steps in the moral life, but as far as he went he was sound. Goodness does not depend upon civilization or knowledge, nor yet upon the possession of any complex moral ideal. It depends rather upon obedience to the will of God, so far as it is known. A child or a savage may be on the road to holiness, by living the life that God means him to live under his present circumstances. A learned and cultured professor may be unholy, simply because he does not live up to the best that he knows. Neither Scripture nor science suggests that primitive man was perfect in the sense of fully developed and possessing great powers of will and intellect. The idea, popular in the eighteenth century, that Adam in virtue of his unbroken communion with God was endowed with all knowledge, is wholly foreign to Scripture. Rather man is represented as undeveloped, but all that he ought to have been at that particular stage of his development. So far his nature was healthy. He was advancing on the right lines. He was beginning to attain holiness by obedience to the commands of God and the deliberate pursuit of good. Man's progress in the mastery of the world and in knowledge of many kinds has not been forwarded but hindered by sin. We need only reflect how to-day man possesses the knowledge and the means to put an end at once to much of the misery and disease and vice of the world. What is lacking is the will to make the effort and to endure the discomfort and trouble that the needful self-sacrifice would involve. Throughout history man's upward progress has been hampered by ineradicable selfishness and sloth. Man has indeed risen but not with that uniform and rapid progress that we should expect. God's providence may overrule men's sins and turn them to a good end. Yet 'there never was an evil action performed but a good one in its place would have led to better results'.[1] Further, man's moral and spiritual progress has lagged behind his advance in material prosperity. Civilization has brought with it new evils and new sorrows.[2] Every fresh discovery may be used either for the welfare or for the injury of mankind at large. All depends on the moral character of those who use it. Such knowledge in itself is non-moral.[3]

[1] Dinsmore, *Atonement in Literature and Life*, p. 244.
[2] Cp. Tyrrell, *Christianity at the Cross Roads*, pp. 120–122.
[3] In modern warfare we have seen all the resources of science being used for the destruction of human life. Their perversion is due not to any external compulsion, but to the uncontrolled passions within man's own heart. War has only revealed on a large scale man's inability to govern himself.

We do not wish to deny that there has been a real progress in moral ideals outside as well as inside the Jewish and Christian revelations. But there has not been a corresponding increase in the power or the will to live up to them. The sins of to-day may be less brutal and more refined, but they are sins none the less. Our ideals may have become more elaborate, but we have not become more holy. Our union with God is still broken. The human race shows no sign of outgrowing its sin.

(v) The question is often raised, If man's nature was ever perfect in the sense of all that God wished it at that time to be, how did temptation find any response within him? We have already seen that all human existence must from its very nature include the liability to temptation. Further, man was made in the image of God to render to Him a free love and obedience. If then man was not to be a mere conscious machine, he must in some sense be free to refuse that love and obedience. A love that is compulsory is not love at all. Thus the creation of a being endowed with free will, must, as far as we can see, include at least the possibility of the misuse of that will. If holiness can only be attained by the deliberate choice of good and the deliberate rejection of the lower, then the possibility of holiness includes within itself the possibility of something like a 'Fall'. The 'Fall' may well have been a process, rather than a single act. Further, Scripture and the teaching of Christ always suggest that behind the world lies a background of spiritual influences, good and bad alike. Our Lord quite definitely speaks of personal agencies of evil, external to man but able to influence him. Such ideas may not be popular to-day, but it is very doubtful whether we can explain the facts without them. No doubt this does not solve the problem: it only pushes it a stage further back. If we ascribe the first human sin to the suggestion of the Devil there still remains the question 'Who tempted the Devil? Whence did his temptation to sin come in the first instance?' Here again we can only conjecture that the creation of any form of free and finite being, must involve the possibility of an attempt to win a false independence of God. That is probably as far as human reason can go in attempting an intellectual solution of the problem of evil.[1]

(vi) Lastly neither experience nor Scripture lend any support to the view that the progress of the human race is inevitable and necessary, or that it is in any degree assured apart from our own moral efforts. History teaches us that nations, like individuals, do not necessarily grow better as they grow older. There is no uniform advance towards perfection. Sin does not only retard progress but brings down and degrades those who commit it. The world is strewn with the wreck of nations that have fallen into decay and dissolution. Christ teaches

[1] Cp. Sanday and Headlam, pp. 145–146; and A. W. Robinson, *God and the World*, p. 63 ff.

most plainly that the loss of present opportunities may involve not a mere temporary postponement of success, but a loss which is irretrievable. He speaks of an 'eternal sin' (Mk 3²⁹), a time when 'the door was shut' (Mt 25¹⁻¹³). He warns men in terrible language borrowed from the Old Testament of the worm that dieth not and the fire that is not quenched (Mk 9⁴³⁻⁴⁸). Present acts of choice carry with them results that endure far beyond this life. We must 'strive', not only 'seek', to enter in by the narrow door (Lk 13²⁴⁻²⁵) and there are few that find it (Mt 7¹³⁻¹⁴). The language may be metaphorical, but it must not, therefore, be explained away. If language has any meaning at all, it shows that salvation is no easy or obvious thing. Again, the New Testament never looks forward to a time when by gradual upward development this present world shall have become perfect. Our Lord can contemplate the possibility that when the Son of Man comes He will not find faith on the earth (Lk 18⁸). Rather His teaching points forward to some sudden and violent catastrophe that shall usher in the new age and abolish sin. The coming of God's Kingdom in all its stages (and first of all in His own earthly ministry) involves a tremendous struggle with powerful forces of evil (the 'kingdom' of Satan) which will cease only at the day of His final *parousia*. That day is known to the Father alone (Mk 13³²). The pictures of an ideal world whose fulfilment Old Testament prophecy located on this earth are in the New Testament transferred to a new heaven and a new earth. The Christianity of the New Testament is *not* a 'Christianity whose optimism is begotten of faith in this world ... whose courage and hope is maintained by the belief that the schism between the ideal and the actual will eventually be healed through an inherent *vis medicatrix naturae*, that the Kingdom of God is the natural term of a process of moral and social development.'[1] Moral goodness can never be the product of any mere necessity. Spiritual progress can only be won by effort. Such has always been the distinctively Christian belief and it is through such a belief that the victories of Christianity have been won. If men come to believe on any large scale that sooner or later perfection must come automatically, that men by their sins can only delay the full realization of the purpose of God for the world, human nature being what it is, it is safe to predict that men will relax their efforts to do right and reform the world. We can see the havoc wrought in the world by a view of sin other than that of Scripture. Christian teaching has proved its truth by its practical results. Christian leaders of all ages and classes have always insisted that repentance must be the foundation of a Christian life. If sin is something less than disobedience to God, if there is no need to worry about our sins, then repentance is needless and indeed unmeaning. Man needs at most an example or a teacher,

---

[1] Tyrrell, *Christianity at the Cross Roads*, pp. 118–119.

not a Saviour, and historical Christianity has from first to last been based largely on error.†

§ 3. (*a*) Grace[1]

'*We have no power to do good works*; *without the grace of God.*' In the language of theology grace means the power of God at work in ourselves (cp. Eph 3[7] 'the gift of that grace of God, which was given to me according to the working of His power' and Eph 3[20] 'the power that worketh in us'). The Greek word χάρις began by meaning either 'attractiveness' in an object or subjectively 'favour', 'good-will', as, *e.g.* of a superior towards an inferior. In the New Testament, especially in the Epistles of S. Paul, it acquires the additional meaning of 'unearned favour'. In Eph 2[3–7] God's 'grace' or 'favour' is contrasted with His 'wrath'. It is often used to emphasize the free bounty of God's gifts. In Rom 4[4], 11[6], etc., that which is given by God's 'grace' is compared with what we earn by our efforts, that which is a debt or deserved. The word is further extended to mean 'the state of favour' which the Christian enjoys by God's free mercy (Rom 5[2], 2 Cor 6[1], etc.) and even particular gifts (2 Cor 8[6–7], Eph 3[8], etc.). It is thus in the New Testament well on its way to its later theological meaning of the power of God bestowed on us. Grace is not something apart from God but is God Himself at work in us. The opening words of the Article need explanation: '*The condition of Man after the fall of Adam is such that he cannot turn and prepare himself, by his natural strength and good works, to faith and calling upon God: wherefore we have no power to do good works pleasant and acceptable to God without the grace of God.*' This might suggest that grace is only necessary because of the 'fall'. No doubt as sinners we need God's grace in a special way. But from the first man was absolutely dependent upon God. As we have seen, the weakness of will that these words lament is due to the separation from God that sin brought. In our whole life, physical and moral and spiritual alike, we are entirely sustained by Him. All the powers that we possess are His.

The Article speaks of grace under two aspects:

(i) We need '*the grace of God by Christ preventing us that we may have a good will*'. This is usually called 'prevenient' grace, *i.e.* grace that goes before (*praevenire*) or prevents us. We may compare the collect that begins 'Prevent us, O Lord,' *i.e.* start us. The actual term 'prevenient' comes from S. Augustine and was suggested by the Latin of Ps 59[10], 'Deus meus misericordia eius praeveniet me.' We need the prompting of God even to wish to do right. All holy desires and aspirations are due to the work of the Holy Spirit within our hearts. 'It is God that worketh in us both to will and to work, for His good pleasure' (Phil 2[13]). Our Lord Himself said 'No man can

---

[1] This section should be read with that on Sanctification, p. 209. 'Sanctifying grace' is a comprehensive term for the redeeming work of God *in us* through Christ and the Holy Spirit.

come to me, except the Father which sent me, draw him' (Jn 6[44], cp. Acts 16[14], James 1[17]).[1]

(ii) We need God's grace *'working with us when we have that good will'*. We pray to God not only to 'prevent us with his gracious favour' but to 'further us with his continual help'. This is usually called 'co-operating grace'. This term again comes from S. Augustine. It is based on such phrases as 'Domino cooperante' in the Latin of Mk 16[20]. Not only does God's favour show itself by 'putting into our minds good desires' but also by continually helping us to 'bring the same to good effect'. Our need of co-operating grace is shown by such words of our Lord as 'Abide in me', 'Apart from me ye can do nothing'. S. Paul can say 'By the grace of God I am what I am: and his grace which was bestowed upon me was not in vain; but I laboured more abundantly than they all, yet not I, but the grace of God which was with me' (1 Cor 15[10], cp. 2 Cor 3[5-6], 1 Pet 5[10]).[2]

(*b*) *Free-will*

God's grace needs to be met by man's free-will. What do we mean when we claim that man's will is free?

(i) The popular idea of free-will is that it means 'I am equally able to do either of two opposite actions. I can equally, *e.g.* speak the truth or tell a lie. The more undecided that I am the more free I am.' A little consideration shows that this idea is ludicrously false. We are not really free when we are in a state of weakness and indecision. The man who is not quite sure beforehand whether he can resist any given temptation, is not really free. S. Paul describes such a state in Rom 7[15-24], 'That which I do I know not: for not what I would that do I practise; but what I hate that I do. But if what I would not that I do, I consent unto the law that it is good. So now it is no more I that do it, but sin which dwelleth in me. For I know that in me, that is in my flesh, dwelleth no good thing: for to will is present with me but to do that which is good is not. For the good which I would I do not: but the evil which I would not that I practise, etc.' (cp. Gal 5[16-17]). But S. Paul does not call this state of vacillation and uncertainty 'freedom', he calls it 'the body of this death' (Rom 7[24]).

(ii) So we can see that our wills are only really free when we can do what we wish. True freedom is to have such mastery over myself that, *e.g.* I can always speak the truth. Every time that we commit an act, our act helps to form a habit. Our aim is by a constant repetition of acts to form the corresponding habit. We are then really free. We speak indeed of slavery to habits, but we mean by that slavery to bad

---

[1] Varied and remarkable expression is given to the doctrine of grace in many of the Prayer Book Collects, *e.g.* Easter II and V, Trinity VII, XII, XVII, XIX and XXV.

[2] The Article is not directly concerned with the 'good works' of the heathen, but its references to 'faith' and to 'the grace of God by Christ' would naturally suggest that 'good works pleasant and acceptable to God' cannot be produced by non-Christians. This was the view generally taken by S. Augustine on whose writings the Article is based. See Art. XIII.

habits. The power of forming habits, which is the condition of our freedom, may be equally the condition of our bondage to evil. It is obvious that freedom is not to be attained by the acquiring of the power to do any kind of actions but only right actions. We are really free, when we have built up habits of acting in accordance with the will of God which is equally the law of our own nature. We start with a certain indecision of the will—something like freedom in the sense that we discarded—in order that by repeated acts of right choice we may become free in the true sense. 'Our wills are ours we know not how, our wills are ours to make them thine.' The saint is the freest person on earth, not because he can do good and bad equally at will, but because he has fixed his will in harmony with God's will and is realizing the purpose of God for his life. A man is free when he is able to do that in which alone he can find true satisfaction.

(iii) When we speak of ourselves as free, we mean that we are the ultimate and responsible authors of our own conduct. All political and social life rests upon the assumption of this responsibility. Our sense of shame when we are caught doing wrong, our feeling of personal responsibility for our actions, our attempts to influence others for good by argument and appeal to their better selves, our efforts to improve the world, the system of punishment for crimes, all these have no meaning if man is simply part of a great machine. No doubt strong scientific and philosophical arguments can be adduced in support of the position that man is the victim of his environment and that all his actions are really determined by external forces. But the moment that we turn to practical life, by our judgments on others and by our own personal behaviour, we deny the validity of these arguments. Of course our power of choice is limited at any time by many things, our environment, our training, our past actions, bad habits, inherited weakness and the like. Nor is it claimed that we can act without motives of some kind. All that we maintain is that man has the power of selecting and making his own motive and following it and that he is not simply the passive victim of the most violent desire.

(c) *The relation of grace to free-will*

In the true life of man there is union of the grace of God and human free-will. Each is necessary. Without grace the will to do good would lack strength. Without the man's free-will the action would not be the action of the man himself at all. Grace and free-will are not in any sense opposing forces. Rather grace is the source and condition of all true freedom, enabling man to realize his true self. In the actual life of the Christian the grace of God and our own natural powers are so united that we cannot separate in our consciousness what is due to the one from what is due to the other. All that we can say is that all good thoughts, desires or actions involve both. We may go further and say that 'the very freedom of choice which grace affords can be used for the purpose of rejecting grace'. The grace of God places new possibilities within our reach but it remains with ourselves whether they shall be actualized or not. We possess 'the melancholy power of baffling the divine good-will'. Grace has been compared to true charity, that does for men just what they cannot do for themselves and no more. It does not pauperize us, but challenges us to do our utmost to respond to it. Grace is never given to save us trouble. God does nothing for us that we can do for ourselves. He 'helps those that help themselves'. Grace releases the will from bondage and warms the heart and enlightens the mind, but we must trust to it and use it. We are bidden to work out our own salvation with fear and trembling, for it is God that worketh in us (Phil 2^{12-13}). It is I who labour, yet not I, but the grace of God that is with me (1 Cor 15^{10}). That is the paradox of the Christian life: like our Lord Himself it is both human and divine. As the Article says the grace of God works '*with us*' not instead of us. The position may be summed up in two sayings: 'Qui fecit te sine te, non salvabit te sine te,' 'Man without God cannot, God without man will not.'

According as either side of the truth is exaggerated we get two opposite tendencies of thought. The first dwells so exclusively on the share of God in our salvation, that it practically denies human responsibility altogether. The second exaggerates the human side so as to put our need of God into the background.

(i) The extreme form of the first error is what is known as Calvinism. In the time of Elizabeth Calvinism was almost the dominant creed of the clergy of the English Church. Its doctrines have had an enormous influence on our Articles both in what they say and in what they do not say. Calvin himself did little more than push to its logical extreme one side of the teaching of S. Augustine. S. Augustine, like S. Paul, had experienced a sudden and violent conversion. Hence, inevitably, he was more conscious of the power of God in his own life and laid less stress upon the need of human effort. He felt that God Himself had intervened to save him and had bestowed upon him a salvation that he could never have achieved by his own struggles. God had entered into his life, rescued him from his former sinfulness and filled his heart with a passionate love of God that left no room for any lower desires. It seemed to him that God had done all: he had done nothing. This experience colours all his writings.[1] Calvin, taking hold of this side of his teaching, elaborated it into a formal system. He taught that man in himself is wholly corrupt, possessing no moral freedom. Till God's grace comes, all our desires and acts are inevitably sinful. When God's grace comes its action is irresistible. We do nothing at all, God's grace does the whole work. Why then

---

[1] See Williams, *The Ideas of the Fall and of Original Sin*, Lect. V. For the problem of grace and freedom in S. Augustine, see K. E. Kirk, *Vision of God*, pp. 335 ff.

are only a few transformed by God's grace? The only possible answer is that God by His own inscrutable and irresistible decree has chosen out from all eternity some men for salvation. This choice is quite independent of any goodness or merit on man's part. Those upon whom God's grace comes, the 'elect', must be saved: they cannot finally fall from grace. The rest are left to their sin and its eternal consequences. As a result of the 'fall' all mankind deserved damnation, but by God's free love 'the elect' are redeemed from this. Christ died not for all mankind but only for the elect.[1]

We must not shut our eyes to the merits of Calvin's system. It at least realized the sovereignty of God and the utter dependence of all human excellence upon Him. It emphasized the truth that all good has its source in God. It was logical and offered an explanation of certain problems in life, *e.g.* why some men are religious even under the greatest difficulties, while others who have every apparent advantage, are not. Further, it gave to the men who felt that they were among the elect an extraordinary strength and confidence. They were convinced that they had behind them all the resources of God, that God's plan for their lives could not be thwarted. They were ready to face death and danger in dauntless confidence, knowing that they were in the hand of God. But these advantages were purchased at a terrible cost. Calvinism forgot and allowed men to forget that God is essentially love rather than power. It treated divine justice as something different from human justice. It led inevitably to fatalism. As we shall see, Scripture never teaches us that grace is irresistible or that we cannot fall from a state of salvation, and it always assumes that God wishes all men to be saved. It has been well said, 'The more grace that a man receives the greater becomes his capacity for doing right. But it is always he who perceives

---

[1] Compare the Lambeth Articles which the Puritans desired to inflict upon the Church of England:

I. God from eternity has predestined some to life, and some He has reprobated to death.

II. The moving or efficient cause of predestination to life is not the foresight of faith, or of perseverence, or of good works, or of anything which is in the persons predestinated, but it is the sole will of God who is well pleased.

III. The number of the predestinated is predefined and certain, it can be neither increased nor diminished.

IV. Those who are not predestinated to salvation, of necessity will be damned on account of their sins.

V. True, living, and justifying faith, and the sanctifying Spirit of God, is not extinguished, falleth not away, vanisheth not away in the elect, either finally or totally.

VI. A man truly faithful, *i.e.* endued with justifying faith, is certain with the full assurance of faith, of the remission of his sins, and his eternal salvation through Christ.

VII. Saving grace is not given, is not communicated, is not granted to all men, by which they may be saved if they will.

VIII. No man can come unto Christ unless it shall have been given to him, and unless the Father shall have drawn him. And all men are not drawn by the Father, in order that they may come to the Son.

IX. It is not placed in the will or power of each man to be saved.

and desires what is right. . . . Grace is the perfection of individuality and not its abolition: the source of freedom and not its
negation.'[1]

Further, Calvinism cast a gloom over the whole of human life.
All purely human activities, such as literature, art, science and the
like, were discouraged as being tainted by the wickedness of man's
fallen nature. Being treated as corrupt, they tended to become corrupt. All the innocent gaiety of human life was not only ignored but
condemned. Religion was too often identified with dulness. There
was no grasp of the truth that the Incarnation has sanctified the
whole of human life. Calvinism was the doctrine of the Scotch Presbyterians and English Puritans. After their failure to enforce it on the
Church of England many of the latter separated from the Church because it was not Calvinistic. Similar teaching has been maintained by
many within our own Church and in the Roman Church. In its completeness it would now be defended by very few, but traces of its
teaching still haunt popular theology. What is really Calvinistic
teaching has often been confused with Christian teaching. Many who
have attacked or separated from Christianity have really attacked or
separated from Calvinism. To-day it influences religion mainly by
way of reaction. We are tempted to ignore those truths about God
that Calvinism distorted and placed in a false isolation.

(ii) At the other extreme stands 'Pelagianism'. Pelagius was an
excellent monk, by birth a Briton, who had always lived a decent life
and known no great moral crisis. He was offended by the prayer of
S. Augustine 'Give me the power to do what thou commandest and
then command what thou wilt.' 'Give the power,' he cried: 'Why!
you have the power.'[2] From the best of motives he endeavoured to
rouse men to a sense that everything depended on their own moral
efforts. He dwelt upon all that God expected from them. But he was
led into an extreme and quite indefensible position. He taught that
Adam's sin had injured no one but himself. Our will remained un-
affected not only by original sin but even by our own past sins.
Infants at birth were in the same condition as Adam before his fall.
At any time our wills can resist sin. Even before the coming of Christ
there had been men who had used their free-will so as to lead sinless
lives. So far as he acknowledged grace he identified it with our own
human powers and such external forces as the example of Christ and
the formal gift of pardon when we had sinned. Universal or almost
universal sinfulness was due only to the following of Adam's bad
example. Pelagius' view was perfectly logical, but he went upon ideas
without considering facts. He relied upon man's bare sense of ability
as if it were an infallible footing for the most complete conclusion.[3]

[1] Chandler, *Spirit of Man*, p. 154.
[2] *Confessions*, bk. x. c. 29, 31, 37, 'Da quod iubes et iube quod vis'; cp. *de Dono Perseverantiae*, c. 53.
[3] Mozley, *Augustinian Doctrine of Predestination*, p. 64.

He never got really down to the root of the question. The difficulty is not simply 'I want to be good and I can't': it is rather 'I know that I ought to do this: I feel that I could do it if I wanted to do it: but then unfortunately I don't want to do it or at least a large part of me does not want to do it.' Pelagianism, however, is very common to-day. It flourishes especially upon its own native soil. The ordinary respectable Englishman is often a Pelagian at heart, though he has never heard of Pelagius. Partly he has very little idea of God's intense holiness and the absolute consecration and self-sacrifice that God requires of him. He confuses the standard of Christ with the standard of decent society. Virtues such as meekness and patience lie entirely outside his vision. He does not even desire to acquire them. Those qualitites that he most admires, courage, fair play, truthfulness, he supposes that he can achieve by himself, if he will only make the effort to do so. As soon as a man awakens to a sense of the meaning of holiness as opposed to respectability, he learns his need of God's help and ceases to be a Pelagian.

(iii) Since this is the relation of grace to free-will it follows that a man may fall from a state of grace either through sloth or active disobedience. From quite early days some held that any man who fell into 'deadly sin' after baptism, was guilty of 'sin against the Holy Spirit'. Such sin our Lord pronounced to be unforgivable. They argued therefore that a man who fell into deadly sin not only could not be restored to communion by the Church (*locus paenitentiae*), but also could not expect forgiveness from God (*locus veniae*).[1] This teaching was revived by the Anabaptists and is directly contradicted by our Article.

The distinction between 'venial' and 'deadly' sin rests on I Jn 5$^{16-17}$. S. John, while insisting that 'all unrighteousness is sin', speaks of 'a sin unto death'[2] as contrasted with 'a sin not unto death'. This distinction was already familiar among the Jews. Originally the phrase meant quite literally a sin punishable with physical death, such death being a final exclusion from Israel. Then it came to be used of any offence that morally deserved similar punishment. Hence S. John employs the phrase for sin that excludes a man from fellowship in the Divine society. As thus separated from the Body of Christ, he can no longer be prayed for as a fellow Christian.[3] The distinction between 'deadly' and 'venial' sin has a practical value, but we cannot draw a hard and fast line between them. What is venial for one man under certain circumstances, may be mortal for another under other circumstances. Only God can know the full measure of guilt that

---

[1] Views of this kind were held among others by the Montanists, Novatianists and Donatists. Some held that though the Church could not restore to communion those who had once lapsed, still God might finally grant them His forgiveness. That is, they allowed to them a *locus veniae* but not a *locus paenitentiae*.

[2] ἁμαρτία πρὸς θάνατον, *i.e.* a sin, the natural issue of which is death.

[3] C. H. Dodd, *The Johannine Epistles, ad loc.*

attaches to any particular act of sin. It is not the outward act by itself but the motive and character lying behind it that count. On the other hand, common sense tells us that in the abstract certain sins are more serious than others.

Our Lord's teaching on 'sin against the Holy Ghost' has been the cause of much misunderstanding. In Mk 3$^{28-30}$, Mt 12$^{31-32}$, the Pharisees who deliberately assigned Christ's works of mercy to Beelzebub, are warned of the danger of 'blaspheming against the Holy Spirit'. Those who commit this sin, are 'guilty of an eternal sin' (Mk 3^{29}, R.V.) and never have forgiveness. In Lk 12^{10} similar language is used, but the context is entirely different.[1] In their present context the words about blasphemy againt the Holy Spirit can only refer to Christians who publicly deny Christ under fear of punishment. In each case the sin is not simply a single act, still less a sin of the tongue, but a state of mind. It would seem to be the wilful refusal to recognize and welcome goodness, when it is seen to be goodness. The assertion that Christ's works of mercy were due to Beelzebub was evidence that the Pharisees were in danger of falling into such a state. So, too, the public repudiation of Christ by Christians would equally be evidence of the beginning of such a state. Unless there is a change of mind the position must become hopeless. If men see and know the good and from hatred or cowardice deliberately call it evil, no more can be done. If such conduct is persisted in, the whole moral nature is warped and the power to discern truth is forfeited. So a character is formed that from its very nature renders forgiveness impossible. If this account of 'sin against the Holy Ghost' is true, it is clear that '*not every deadly sin after baptism*' even approximates to it.

There are, however, certain passages in the Epistle to the Hebrews that were taken, *e.g.* by Origen, to teach that those who had fallen into deadly sin after baptism could not be restored to communion by the Church. The most important is 6$^{4-6}$, 'For as touching those who were once enlightened' (*i.e.* probably baptized, φωτισθέντας) 'and tasted (γευσαμένους) of the heavenly gift and were made partakers of the Holy Ghost and tasted the good word of God, and the powers of the age to come, and then fall away (παραπεσόντας), it is impossible to renew them again unto repentance, the while they crucify to themselves the Son of God afresh (ἀνασταυροῦντας) and put him to an open shame (παραδειγματίζοντας)' (R.V. mg.). Here a study of the tenses employed brings out the meaning of the passage. So long as men go on crucifying the Son of God afresh and putting Him to an open shame, in spite of their past baptism and Christian privileges, nothing can be done to renew them again unto repentance. But there is not a word to say that if they forsake their

---

[1] For a commentary on these passages see C. K. Barrett, *The Holy Spirit and the Gospel Tradition*, pp. 103 ff.

sin and turn to God they may not be renewed unto repentance.[1] The same holds good in reference to 10[26-29]. Here also the 'fearful expectation of judgment' applied to those who after knowing the truth and having rejected Christ, go on sinning (ἁμαρτανόντων). Nothing is said of the impossibility of repentance. So, too, in 12[14-17], as the R.V. makes clear, what Esau sought diligently with tears and failed to find is not a 'place of repentance' but the 'blessing'.[2] These passages, in short, are not an assertion that no forgiveness is possible for post-baptismal sin, but an exhortation not to put off repentance too late. The failure to find pardon depends not on God's unwillingness to grant it, but on the sinner's refusal to comply with the conditions necessary for obtaining it.

Again, it follows from a right understanding of grace that '*After we have received the Holy Ghost we may depart from grace given and by the grace of God we may arise again and amend our lives.*' The Calvinists taught that a man who had once received grace, even if he fell away for a time, must in the end arise again and amend his life. This was known technically as a belief in 'indefectible' grace. Such teaching is plainly contrary to Scripture and to experience. S. Paul had beyond dispute received the Holy Ghost, but he never supposed that his position was therefore secure apart from his own moral efforts (cp. 1 Cor 9[27], Phil 3[12]). The grace of God may be received in vain (2 Cor 6[1], Gal 5[4], Heb 12[15]) or even resisted (Acts 7[51], Mt 23[37]). So, too, Saul in the Old Testament certainly received grace, but ultimately fell away (cp. 1 Sam 10[6-9] 'God gave him another heart'). Our Lord also taught that the salt may lose its savour (Mt 5[13]) and the good seed begin to grow but be choked (Mk 4[19]), and the branch in the vine bear no fruit and be burnt (Jn 15[6]). We may rejoice that the efforts of the Calvinists to change '*may*' into 'must' were unsuccessful.†

---

[1] Cp. Westcott, *ad loc.*, 'The apostasy described is marked, not only by a decisive act but also by a continuous present attitude, a hostile relation to Christ Himself and to belief in Christ; and thus there is no question of the abstract efficacy of the means of grace provided through the ordinances of the Church. The state of the men themselves is such as to preclude their application.'

[2] For a different interpretation of the passages in Hebrews, see K. E. Kirk, *The Vision of God*, Lect. iii. section v. See also Lect. iii and iv for evidence that in the early centuries certain sins were considered to be irremissible by the Church, *i.e.* to involve life-long penance and exclusion from communion. Even when the rigid discipline applied to these sins was modified in the third century, it remained for a long time the general rule that a second penance was life-long.

SALVATION

ARTICLE XI

Of the Justification of Man

We are accounted righteous before God, only for the merit of our Lord and Saviour Jesus Christ by Faith, and not for our own works or deservings. Wherefore, that we are justified by faith only is a most wholesome doctrine, and very full of comfort, as more largely is expressed in the Homily of Justification.

De hominis justificatione

Tantum propter meritum Domini ac Servatoris nostri Jesu Christi, per fidem, non propter opera, et merita nostra, justi coram Deo reputamur. Quare sola fide nos justificari doctrina est saluberrima, ac consolationis plenissima, ut in homilia de justificatione hominis fusius explicatur.

In its present form this dates from 1563 and is much fuller than the corresponding Article of 1553. Many of its phrases are borrowed from the Lutheran Confession of Würtemburg, others from the earlier Confession of Augsburg. Hence the avoidance of Lutheran exaggerations is remarkable. It avoids saying that a man is justified when he believes himself to be justified. *N.B.* 'by' = 'through' (Latin *per*). There is no 'Homily on Justification'. The real title is a 'Homily of Salvation'.

§ 1. '*Justification by faith*'

(*a*) The source of such words is to be found not in any abstract theological attempt to analyse the spiritual life but in the living experience of S. Paul.

(i) He uses such words as 'justified by faith' in order to describe to others the change that had taken place in his own life. As a pious Jew he had striven for years to win peace with God by his own efforts. He had tried to fulfil God's will by a complete obedience to the Jewish Law as the revelation of that will. Outwardly he had succeeded. He can write 'if any other man thinketh to have confidence in the flesh, I yet more . . . a Hebrew of the Hebrews; as touching the law a Pharisee . . . as touching the righteousness which is in the law, found blameless' (Phil 3⁴⁻⁶, cp. Gal 1¹⁴). But he did not find peace. The more earnestly that he strove to earn God's favour, the more conscious he became of his inability to satisfy the demands of an all-holy God. A perfect obedience to the law of God required absolute holiness not only in outward act but in inward motive and thought. The law could not help him to attain but could only convict him of not having attained it (cp. Rom 7⁷⁻⁸). God seemed to him to

199

stand over him as a taskmaster or judge, whose just demands he
could never satisfy. He felt himself always condemned as coming
short of God's standard. Just because he was honest with himself and
unwilling to be content with a low standard, he felt that through the
law God was bringing home to him the fact of his sinfulness (Rom
5[20], Gal 3[19]). However hard he tried, his best endeavours fell short of
what God commanded (Rom 3[19-20], 4[15], 7[9] ff.).[1] After his conversion
an utter change came over his life. Through his surrender to Jesus
Christ and his acceptance of His free offer of salvation, he found
peace with God. 'There is now no condemnation to them that are in
Christ Jesus' (Rom 8[1]) was an echo of his own experience. He felt
himself no longer condemned by God but 'justified' or acquitted.
He no longer strove to earn or deserve his own salvation by 'works of
the law', but accepted it as a free gift of God's grace won by Jesus
Christ and offered freely to all who would commit themselves to Him
(Rom 5[1-11], 8[1-17], Gal 2[16]). He knew himself to be no longer a slave
toiling at the impossible task of attaining a perfect holiness, but a
son of God (Gal 4[28]-5[1]). His acceptance rested not on his own efforts
but on the work of Christ. His religion was based not on what he
had done and was to do for God, but on what God in Christ had
done for him. There was no waiting. God accepted him just as he
was: he had closed with God's offer of forgiveness. His pardon was
not made conditional on future improvement. His acceptance was
free and immediate and complete. Henceforth it was his duty to live
up to the position that had been bestowed upon him.

The best illustration of the experience that S. Paul wishes to
express is the parable of the Prodigal Son (Lk 15[11] ff.). The Son is not
only received back but freely forgiven and treated with all honour.
He is not placed in any ambiguous position until it is seen whether
his repentance is genuine and lasting. The Father assumes that it is
both, because that is the best means of ensuring that in actual fact it
will be both. What matters is the change of attitude on the part of
the son: his willingness to return, to trust himself to his father's
mercy and to close with his offer. He is restored to the position of son
and called to live up to that position. He has not to earn it, but the
restoration is the free act of his father's love. In S. Paul's language
the son is 'justified', *i.e.* forgiven and accepted, acquitted and treated
as righteous.

(ii) We may now turn to examine the actual language used by
S. Paul. In the opening words of the Article it is assumed that to
'justify' ($\delta\iota\kappa\alpha\iota o\hat{\upsilon}\nu$) means to account righteous. It is properly a legal
or 'forensic' term, to 'acquit' and in itself says nothing about the
actual state of the person acquitted. He is 'treated as righteous'
whether in point of fact he is righteous or not.

---

[1] It is possible that S. Paul became clearly conscious of his true spiritual state under
the Law only after he had accepted the Gospel.

(α) In the LXX δικαιοῦν is used to translate a Hebrew word which means 'to do justice for a person', 'to treat him with justice' (e.g. 2 Sam 15⁴), and so, on the assumption that he is in the right, to 'acquit', e.g. in Exod 23⁷ God says 'I will not justify', i.e. acquit, 'the wicked'. In Is 5²³ the prophet reproves those 'which justify the wicked for a reward', i.e. receive bribes to acquit the guilty. It is also used in a wider meaning of showing or proving righteous. In Jer 3¹¹ 'Israel has shown herself more righteous' than Judah (cp. Ezek 16⁵¹⁻⁵²).

(β) So, too, in the New Testament the word is used with the same meaning, e.g. in Mt 11¹⁹ and Lk 7³⁵ 'Wisdom is justified of her children' or 'her works' = wisdom is vindicated or proved to be righteous by them. In Mt 12³⁷ 'By thy words thou shalt be justified' is opposed to 'By thy words thou shalt be condemned'. In Lk 10²⁹ the lawyer wished to 'justify' himself, i.e. to vindicate his position. In Lk 18¹⁴ the word is used almost in a Pauline sense. The publican goes home 'justified', i.e. forgiven by God and accepted.

(γ) The word is most common in S. Paul, being used, as we have seen, to express his own inner feeling of acceptance with God as contrasted with his former feeling of condemnation. In his Epistles there is no instance where the word must mean 'make righteous' and several where the context proves that it means 'acquit' or 'treat as righteous'. Thus, in 1 Cor 4⁴ he writes, 'I know nothing against myself, yet am I not hereby justified: but he that judgeth me is the Lord.' Again, in Rom 4⁵ we find: 'But to him that worketh not, but believeth on him that justifieth the ungodly, his faith is reckoned for righteousness.' Here it is expressly stated that the person justified has nothing to show in the way of meritorious acts: his one asset (so to speak) is faith, and this faith is taken as an 'equivalent for righteousness'.

So then from the point of view of scholarship the meaning of δικαιόω is quite clear.[1] It is a forensic term, used to express the initial act by which God pardons and accepts a man.

Yet at the time of the Reformation the meaning of to justify was hotly disputed, and to-day the official theology of the Church of Rome holds it to mean 'to make righteous'. The words of our Article show that the Church of England on this point takes sides with Luther against the Council of Trent. 'We are accounted righteous before God' is taken as the equivalent of 'We are justified by faith'. In the earliest days of the Church no controversy arose about this point. The question of justification first came into prominence in the Pelagian controversy. S. Augustine, writing against Pelagius, asserted that all man's holiness was due to the free grace of God. He used

---

[1] We may add that while verbs in -οω that are derived from adjectives with a physical meaning, have the sense of 'making', as e.g. χρυσόω = I make golden, verbs derived from adjectives with a moral meaning, have the sense of 'accounting as' or 'treating as', e.g. ἀξιόω, I account worthy, not I make worthy. Thus the sense of δικαιόω is naturally I account righteous.

justification to mean not only man's forgiveness and acceptance with God, but also an actual infusion of righteousness. 'It is true . . . that S. Augustine in one place admits the possibility of interpreting it either as "making just" or "reckoning just" (*De Spiritu et Litera*, § 45). But though he admits the two interpretations as far as concerns the words, practically his whole theory is that of an infusion of the grace of faith, by which men are made just.'[1] This erroneous view was no doubt assisted by the form of the Latin word 'iustifico'. In mediaeval theology justification was regularly taken to include an infusion of grace, and this view was confirmed by the Council of Trent. So in the interpretation of the Church of Rome justification includes not only free acceptance by God but also the first stage of sanctification, an imparting of actual righteousness. Our contention is that in Scripture it simply means being placed by God in a right relation to Himself. This is no doubt only a beginning. It is to be followed by sanctification, the actual impartation of holiness. It may be argued with truth that justification and sanctification can only be separated in thought rather than fact: that in actual experience God's word of pardon coming as an unspeakable surprise and striking home to the soul does quicken the possibilities of good that a man possesses. But the distinction is not only theologically sound but practically valuable. The moment that we open the door to the idea of a man's own actual righteousness having any place in God's act of forgiveness we are preparing the way, as mediaeval theology shows, for a return to those ideas of earning salvation by good works against which S. Paul's language is a protest. We are making God do what the Prodigal's Father did not do, give a place to some actual attainment of righteousness, however small, as a condition of acceptance.

(iii) Again, what does S. Paul mean by faith? The Greek word πίστις may be used either in an active or passive sense. It may mean either 'trustfulness, the frame of mind which relies on another' or 'trustworthiness, the frame of mind which can be relied on'.[2] In the LXX the verb πιστεύειν is used to translate the Hebrew verb 'to trust', as *e.g.* in the text often quoted by S. Paul 'Abraham believed in the Lord: and he counted it to him for righteousness' (Gen 15[6]), while πίστις is used in the passive sense as = trustworthiness. It is not used in the active sense, as Hebrew possessed no corresponding word for trustfulness. Only in S. Paul's other favourite text 'The just shall live by his faith' does the active idea seem to become blended with the passive. 'Constancy under temptation or danger with an Israelite could only spring from reliance on Jehovah.'[3] In the New Testament though the passive sense is found, the active predominates. It is used in many shades of meaning, just as πιστεύειν may be used in different senses. With an accusative (πιστεύειν τι) it means to believe

[1] Sanday and Headlam, p. 150.   [3] Lightfoot, *Galatians*, pp. 152–153.
[2] Lightfoot, *Galatians*, pp. 152–153.

that a thing is so. With a dative of a person ($\pi\iota\sigma\tau\epsilon\acute{\upsilon}\epsilon\iota\nu$ $\tau\iota\nu\acute{\iota}$) it means to believe what a man says. With $\epsilon\acute{\iota}s$ or $\dot{\epsilon}\pi\acute{\iota}$ ($\pi\iota\sigma\tau\epsilon\acute{\upsilon}\epsilon\iota\nu$ $\epsilon\acute{\iota}s$ $\tau\iota\nu\acute{\alpha}$ or $\dot{\epsilon}\pi\acute{\iota}$ $\tau\iota\nu\iota$) it means to believe in a person.[1] So $\pi\acute{\iota}\sigma\tau\iota s$ may have every shade of meaning between bare intellectual assent to a proposition and unconditional self-surrender to a person. In S. Paul's own writings it has many meanings. In its highest sense it means not only belief in God's promises but enthusiastic self-committal to a person. It is above all a personal relationship, the attitude of a child to his father. The true son not only believes his father's promises, but, accepting all that his father has done for him in the past and relying upon the same love for the future, desires to respond to all the claims that his father's love makes upon him. That was the attitude of Abraham towards God (Rom 4³) and of the Saints of the Old Covenant (Heb 11³ ff.). In the case of the Christian it is mediated by Jesus Christ. S. Paul calls it either 'faith in Jesus Christ', Rom 3²², ²⁶ (cp. 1 Jn 5¹³, etc.), or faith in God the Father who raised Him from the dead, Rom 4²⁴, Eph 1²⁰ (cp. 1 Pet 1²¹).

We can see now why S. Paul speaks of being justified by (*i.e.* through) faith. Religion is a personal matter between the soul and God. 'Faith' is the one possible attitude for intercourse between the soul and God, just as it is for intercourse between the child and his father. It involves the looking towards God in Christ, the trustful acceptance of His free pardon and the desire to live a life of fellowship with Him. It is far more than the assent by the intellect to certain truths. It involves the whole man. It demands a venture of the will, the readiness to throw in our lot with Christ 'to be ruled as well as to be saved by Him'. By our act of self-surrender we are placed in the right relation to God, that of sonship. From another side, faith is, so to say, getting into correspondence with Christ, reaching out the hand to receive the gift that He has won and is waiting to bestow. It is like the action of the woman with the issue of blood (Mk 5²⁵⁻³⁴). The healing power was there but it needed her own act to get into touch with it. It was an act of belief in Him. So it is in virtue of this turning to Christ, this personal relation to Him begun by our act of surrender that we are justified or accounted righteous.

(*b*) The objection may be raised: 'if we are justified by faith, if God treats us as righteous though we are in real fact far from righteous, is not there a touch of unreality about it? Is not our salvation made to depend on a legal fiction?' We must remember in the first place that though 'justification' is no doubt a legal term in origin, it is only used by S. Paul because it corresponded with an experience common to himself and to his converts. They felt that through Christ they had passed from the darkness of God's condemnation into the sunshine of God's favour. Again, it may be said that all forgiveness contains an element of fiction. Forgiveness means that the man who forgives

---

[1] See Moulton, *Grammar of N.T. Greek*, pp. 67–68.

treats the offender as better than he really is. It also rests on the assumption that the person forgiven can be changed. The moment that we pass from the relation between persons as it is felt to be in actual life, and try to express the act of forgiveness in legal or any other language, it tends to appear unreal if not actually immoral. Further, the sense of unreality in 'justification' tends to disappear when we bear in mind that justification is only the beginning. The new relationship to Christ begun by our act of self-surrender is not any passing or momentary fact. It is a relationship that we are to maintain all through our lives. We have by a deliberate act of our whole being put ourselves into touch with the one Saviour, the one cure for our disease. Justification through faith might with equal accuracy be styled justification through union with Christ. So long as we remain in union with Him our progress in holiness is assured. Through Him we shall one day become all that we ought to be. But —and here comes the grand news of justification—God does not wait till all this has been accomplished. He accepts us here and now, just as we are. He treats us as righteous in anticipation of the day when we shall be righteous. He sees us not as we are but as we are becoming. 'Deus patiens quia aeternus.' Justification is only the beginning, but since it is God who begins, the result is assured and only human wilfulness can hinder it. So it is that S. Paul after dealing with justification in the first chapters of the Epistle to the Romans, passes on to the 'mystical union' of the Christian with Christ in chapter 6. The story of the Prodigal Son closes with the readmission of the wanderer to his home and his restoration to all the privileges of sonship. But we cannot suppose that the Father is indifferent to his son's future behaviour. It is assumed that he is to live and grow in that home life to which he has been readmitted. '*There is no condemnation to them that believe and are baptized,*' as Art. IX says, even though they are far from holy, not because God has favourites or passes over in one man what He condemns in another. It is rather that penitence and faith represent a new attitude of the person to God. If we have repented of our sins and are honestly trying in dependence upon Christ to overcome them, we have done all that we can. Our dependence on Christ is the guarantee that we shall one day be perfect. The merits of Christ could have no possible influence on God's view of us, if we were separated from Him. But so long as we are living 'in Christ', *i.e.* in vital union with Him, His merit has everything to do with us. He is in a real sense responsible for us: we have handed ourselves over to Him.

This doctrine is, as the Article says, *a most wholesome doctrine and very full of comfort*. If our acceptance with God depended upon our having attained to a certain standard of holiness, we could never be quite sure that we had reached it: God would always seem to be standing over us as a critic and a judge. But the knowledge that God justifies us saves us both from hard thoughts of God and from morbid brooding over our own weakness and failures. It bids us look not at our very unsatisfactory selves, but at God and God's love and mercy as manifested in Christ. This attitude is the only sure foundation of a joyous and happy faith. Much of the gloominess of religious people is due to a neglect of 'justification by faith'.

(c) Our Article states that we are justified '*by faith only*'.[1] The exact phrase is not in Scripture, but it must be taken to mean just what S. Paul means when he says that men are justified by 'faith apart from works of the law' (Rom 3^{28}). We have indeed an apparent contradiction between the teaching of S. Paul and S. James on this point. S. James can write 'What doth it profit . . . if a man say he hath faith, but have not works? can that faith save him?' (2^{14}). 'Faith if it have not works is dead in itself' (v. [17]). 'By works a man is justified and not only by faith' (v. [24]). Both argue from the same text (Gen 15^6) with apparently opposite conclusions. S. Paul finds in Abraham an example of one who was justified by his faith in God : S. James the example of one 'who was justified by works in that he offered up his son Isaac upon the altar'. There is evidence that the text about Abraham was a standing subject for debate in Jewish schools. But when we get below the surface it is clear that the real difference between them is small. They were in temperament and outlook very different types of character, as the whole tone of their writings shows. Further, they were dealing with different types of error from a practical point of view. Thus to S. James 'faith' meant 'intellectual assent'. 'Thou believest that God is one : thou doest well, the devils also believe and shudder' (2^{19}). Faith here corresponds to what S. Paul calls knowledge in 1 Cor 8^1. But faith to S. Paul means, as we have seen, personal adhesion. Again, when he speaks of 'works', S. James is thinking of Christian activities, what S. Paul calls 'good works' (*e.g.* in Eph 2^{10}). S. Paul is always ready to admit that faith if genuine will show itself in acts of love and service. He speaks of faith as 'working' or 'active through love' (Gal 5^6). On the other hand, when he speaks of 'works', S. Paul means 'works of the law', *i.e.* works done to earn God's favour and viewed as deserving a reward. Again, both use 'to justify' in a forensic sense, but S. James has in view the final judgment (*e.g.* 2^{14}), S. Paul the initial act by which the soul is placed in right relation to God. Both have a practical end in view. S. James wishes to rebuke a barren orthodoxy, divorced from life; S. Paul is opposing a Jewish legalism, the spirit of the Pharisee who supposed that by the excellency of his works he could earn

---

[1] 'Sola fide' may suggest two erroneous ideas. (1) That faith can exist in isolation from any other Christian virtue or spiritual act. But faith in Christ's saving work cannot exist without some beginning of repentance for sin, of desire for sanctification and of love for God. (2) That life in the Church and the use of the sacraments may be superfluous or dispensable. But the New Testament assumes that faith, baptism and incorporation into Christ in the Church are inseparable aspects of one spiritual fact.

God's favour. In view of the familiarity of the question as a subject of discussion among the Jews, we cannot be sure that either had read the other's epistle. It is not certain which is the earlier. Either might quite well be rebuking a perversion of the other's teaching. There is no real contradiction between them.

This doctrine of justification by faith, almost forgotten during the middle ages and rediscovered at the time of the Reformation, was inevitably exaggerated and distorted in the reaction from mediaeval theology. The language of our Article is most cautious and avoids all exaggerations.

(i) There was a tendency on the part of the Lutherans, in their desire to exclude all human merit, to fall into what is known as 'solifidianism', and to argue that man is saved by 'faith only' in the sense that good works are not only unnecessary but positively harmful. They stated that a man was justified if he believed himself to be justified. To look for any fruit in a changed life was to deny the truth. That this is not the meaning of 'sola fide' in Article XI is shown by the following Article. This declares that *'good works . . . do spring necessarily of a true and lively faith; in so much that by them a lively faith may be as evidently known as a tree discerned by the fruit.'*

(ii) Again, we must notice the careful distinction in prepositions. Faith is the instrument or means of justification. We are justified *per fidem* or *fide*. But we are justified *propter meritum Christi*; the work of Christ is the ground of our acceptance with God. The doubled preposition (*propter meritum Christi non propter opera et merita nostra*) makes it clear that the Article contrasts the merit of Christ with our own works. Luther pushed his teaching so far as to say we are justified, 'propter fidem'. But God does not account us righteous as a reward of our faith any more than as a reward for any other excellency that we display. That would be to return to salvation by works. The saving power of faith resides not in the man who believes, but in the object of the faith, namely, Jesus Christ, the Almighty Saviour on whom it rests. Further, S. Paul teaches us that faith itself is God's gift (Phil 1[29]), and we should thank Him for it (Col 1[3-4]).

(iii) The mediaeval theologians had distinguished between *fides informis*, i.e. a bare intellectual belief, and *fides formata*, i.e. a faith informed or quickened by love. Accepting the distinction Luther argued that the first was sufficient for justification: the Council of Trent naturally argued for the latter. The Article ignores the whole question. The moment that we grasp that faith is faith in a person the difficulty disappears. In actual practice as between persons, we can hardly separate faith and love (cp. Gal 5[6]). Faith brings out more fully the side of trust and dependence. But in actual life we cannot trust ourselves wholly to a person whom we do not love, and love must involve trust.

(iv) Again, Luther in his attempt to explain justification spoke of 'an imputed righteousness'. God, he laid down, can treat us as righteous because Christ's righteousness is imputed to us and our sins are imputed to Him. This is a 'legal fiction', and happily our Article, like Scripture, is silent about it. Language is still used, *e.g.* in some of our hymns, that speaks of us as 'clothed with Christ's righteousness' as with a garment. The metaphor is an attempt to picture the truth that at any moment in our lives we fall short of God's perfect holiness; we must trust not in our own achievements, but in God's mercy through Christ. He represents what we still wish to be rather than what we actually are. The metaphor expresses a real truth, but is far too external. We cannot put on righteousness like a garment.†

ARTICLE XII

Of Good Works	*De bonis operibus*
Albeit that Good Works, which are the fruits of Faith, and follow after Justification, cannot put away our sins, and endure the severity of God's Judgment: yet are they pleasing and acceptable to God in Christ, and do spring out necessarily of a true and lively Faith; insomuch that by them a lively faith may be as evidently known as a tree discerned by the fruit.	Bona opera, quae sunt fructus fidei, et justificatos sequuntur, quanquam peccata nostra expiare, et divini judicii severitatem ferre non possunt; Deo tamen grata sunt, et accepta in Christo, atque ex vera et viva fide necessario profluunt, ut plane ex illis, aeque fides viva cognosci possit, atque arbor ex fructu judicari.

One of the four new Articles added by Parker in 1563. It aimed at striking a mean between

   (i) Roman over-estimate of good works as earning merit and forgiveness;

   (ii) Lutheran under-estimate of good works, leading to 'solifidianism' and 'antinomianism'.

'Solifidianism' is the belief that we are saved by a bare faith. 'Antinomianism' is the assertion that the Christian is free from any restraint even of the moral law.

N.B.—'Good works' is a technical term for Christian activities.

ARTICLE XIII

Of Works before Justification	*De operibus ante justificationem*
Works done before the grace of Christ, and the Inspiration of his Spirit, are not pleasant to	Opera quae fiunt ante gratiam Christi, et spiritus ejus afflatum, cum ex fide Jesu Christi non pro-

208 ARTICLE XIII

God, forasmuch as they spring not of faith in Jesus Christ, neither do they make men meet to receive grace, or (as the School-authors say) deserve grace of congruity: yea rather, for that they are not done as God hath willed and commanded them to be done, we doubt not but they have the nature of sin.

deant, minime Deo grata sunt, neque gratiam (ut multi vocant) de congruo merentur. Immo cum non sunt facta ut Deus illa fieri voluit et praecepit, peccati rationem habere non dubitamus.

Unchanged since 1553. Its object was to condemn the scholastic theory of congruous merit.

It is important to notice that the title does not correspond with the opening sentence. 'Works before justification' is not equivalent to 'works done before the grace of Christ and the inspiration of the Holy Spirit'. The title must give way to the text of the Article. There is abundant evidence in Scripture that God's grace is given to men before justification. God's grace was at work in the hearts of those who heard S. Peter on the day of Pentecost (Acts 2^{37}) and in the heart of S. Paul when he was converted (9^{11}). But in each case justification came later (cp. 2^{38}, 9^{17-18}). So, too, in the case of Cornelius, the workings of God's grace preceded by a long interval of time his acceptance of Christ (cp. 10^2 ff.). Hence works 'done before the grace of God' is much narrower than 'works done before justification'. The real difficulty of the Article lies in the addition 'forasmuch as they spring not of faith in Jesus Christ'. This seems to rule out the efforts of good and conscientious non-Christians. The following answer was suggested in a letter of Dr Hort. 'The principle underlying Article XIII seems to me to be this, that there are not two totally different modes of access to God for men, faith for Christians, meritorious performance for non-Christians. There is but one mode of access, faith; and but one perfect, and, as it were normal faith, that which rests on the revelation in the person of Jesus Christ. But faith itself, not being an intellectual assent to propositions, but an attitude of heart and mind, is present in a more or less rudimentary state in every upward effort and aspiration of men. Doubtless the faith of non-Christians (and much of the faith of Christians, for that matter) is not in the strict sense "faith in Jesus Christ"; and therefore I wish the Article were otherwise worded. But such faith, when ripened, grows into the faith of Jesus Christ; as also it finds its rational justification in the revelation made through Him. Practically the principle of the Article teaches us to regard all the good there is in the world as what one may call *imperfect Christianity*, not as something essentially different, requiring, so to speak, to be dealt with by God in a wholly different manner.'—(*Life and Letters*, vol. 2, p. 337.)

It is, however, doubtful whether Hort's answer meets the difficulty. The 'works' of which the Article speaks must be such as are *prima facie* 'good'; otherwise there would be no point in insisting that they are nevertheless not 'pleasant to God' and do not deserve grace. If we say that all the good works or aspirations of both Christians and non-Christians spring in some sense from faith, no works done 'before the grace of Christ' would be left for the Article to refer to. The Article seems in fact to be stating the normal view of S. Augustine that good works which do not spring from explicit faith in Christ are 'empty' and as he says in one passage, *in peccata vertuntur, omne enim quod non est ex fide peccatum est* (*Contra duas Ep. Pelag.* IV, 14. Cp. *Enarr. in Psalm.* 31, 2, 4).

W. Temple, *Nature, Man and God*, p. 417 f., after saying that this Article is 'unfortunately, even calamitously expressed', gives a constructive statement.

ARTICLE XIV

Of Works of Supererogation

Voluntary Works besides, over and above God's commandments, which they call Works of Supererogation, cannot be taught without arrogancy and impiety. For by them men do declare, that they do not only render unto God as much as they are bound to do, but that they do more for his sake, than of bounden duty is required; whereas Christ saith plainly, When ye have done all that are commanded to you, say, We be unprofitable servants.

De operibus supererogationis

Opera quae supererogationis appellant, non possunt sine arrogantia et impietate praedicari. Nam illis declarant homines, non tantum se Deo reddere, quae tenentur, sed plus in ejus gratiam facere, quam deberent, cum aperte Christus dicat; Cum feceritis omnia quaecunque praecepta sunt vobis, dicite, Servi inutiles sumus.

Almost unchanged since 1553.
Object: to condemn 'works of supererogation'.

§ 2. *Sanctification*

(*a*) In our Articles there is no direct teaching on Sanctification. There is no mention of the continuous work of the Holy Spirit in us after justification nor of the practical holiness of life that God requires. So the doctrine of justification is left unfinished. Art. XII comes nearest to any teaching on this subject, and Arts. XIII and XIV deal with certain difficulties connected with it.

God's ideal for us is absolute holiness. 'Ye shall be perfect, as your Heavenly Father is perfect' (Mt 5[48] R.V.). Nothing short of that is the object of Christ's redemption. While we are justified by faith at the beginning of our Christian life, we shall be judged by our works at the end (2 Cor 5[10], etc.). Good works are the necessary fruit of that life lived in union with God of which justification is the initial act (cp. Mt 7[16-30], etc.). If faith is all that S. Paul means by it, it must expand into action. A man who has accepted forgiveness through Christ, out of very gratitude to His Saviour, must try to serve Him and by serving Him to become like Him. We are to 'follow after . . . the sanctification without which no man shall see the Lord' (Heb 12[14]). Justification apart from sanctification remains incomplete.[1]

---

[1] It is significant that at the beginning of Rom 6 S. Paul assumes that those who are justified will have been baptized. Baptism is for him the sacrament both of justifying faith and sonship and also of our incorporation into Christ, by which we die to sin and rise to new life in Him. (Cp. Gal 3[25] [26].) We enter on the justified and the sanctified life at the same moment. Compare Hooker, *Eccl. Pol.* V, lvi, 11, 'Thus we participate Christ partly by imputation, as when those things which he did and suffered for us are imputed unto us for righteousness; partly by habitual and real infusion, as when

Any teaching on the Atonement that regards it merely as a work wrought by Christ outside ourselves is grievously inadequate. Nothing has caused more misunderstanding about this doctrine than the neglect in popular preaching of the truth of our union with Christ and the resulting work of His Holy Spirit within ourselves, as an essential part of His Atonement. As the hymn says 'He died that we might be forgiven', but it goes on to add 'He died to make us good'. The latter is as essential as the former. Christ did not die only to save us from the punishment of sin, but from sin itself. He came to deliver us from the weakness of our fallen nature and from slavery to bad habits. He is the source of new life. Through the Holy Spirit He imparts to us His own perfect human nature—that perfect humanity which He built up by His life of obedience and consummated by His death. The will of God is our sanctification (1 Thess 4^{1-8}), the complete subjection of all our powers of will and heart and mind to God's Holy Spirit.

Accordingly, in our Christian life everything turns upon our realizing our membership with Christ, on our self-identification with Him. We are to do all things 'in Christ'. Our growth in holiness may be called equally either the work of Christ or of the Holy Spirit. The Holy Spirit did not come to take the place of an absent Christ, but in His coming Christ Himself comes too. 'I will pray the Father and he shall give you another Advocate that he may be with you for ever, even the Spirit of truth. . . . I will not leave you desolate, I come unto you' (Jn 14^{16-19}). It is through the Spirit that the Ascended Lord dwells in the Church and operates in believers (Rom 8^{1-11}). The gift of the Holy Spirit is the seal of membership in Christ and acceptance by God (Eph 1^{14}, 4^{30}, etc.). The presence of the Spirit is the presence of Christ (cp. 2 Cor 3^{17-18}). 'We know that he (*i.e.* Christ) abideth in us by the Spirit which he gave us' (1 Jn 3^{24}). It is through the coming of the Holy Spirit at Pentecost that the Atonement is to be not an act outside ourselves, but a real transforming of our personality within, 'Calvary without Pentecost is not yet Calvary in vital relation to ourselves.' We may view the work of the Holy Spirit within us in two ways.

(i) Through Him we daily die to sin. The whole life of Christ was a dying to sin: this attitude to sin was perfected and consummated on the Cross. By that death He revealed and identified Himself with the mind of God towards sin. His whole attitude to sin was the perfection of that attitude to sin which God requires in us. Only the sinless can have a perfect antagonism to and hatred of sin. Every sin that we commit blunts our capacity for seeing sin in its true light and hating it as we ought. Our sins become a part of ourselves. It is 'I' who chose

grace is inwardly bestowed while we are on earth, and afterwards more fully both our souls and bodies made like unto his in glory.' The whole passage from which these words come deserves study.

and enjoyed the thing that was evil and there still remains in me the latent capacity of enjoying the evil thing. The Cross of Christ stands for that utter abhorrence of and resistance to sin which God requires in us, but to which we cannot attain. Our penitence in order to be perfect must rest upon and include such a complete antagonism to sin.[1] That is just what we cannot achieve. So we reach the position, that God requires of sinners true penitence, and just because we are sinners we are incapable of true penitence. Here we need the power of the Holy Spirit. He brings into our life a new capacity for penitence. Through the Holy Spirit we are to die to sin. Our sinful self is to be done to death. S. Paul speaks of us as crucified with Christ. 'I have been crucified with Christ' (Gal 2[20]). As members of Christ we share His Cross. 'Our old man was crucified with him' (Rom 6[6]). Through the Cross of Christ 'the world has been crucified unto me and I unto the world.' 'They that are of Christ Jesus have crucified the flesh with the passions and the lusts thereof' (Gal 6[14], 5[24]). Crucifixion is a slow and painful process. Our old sin-loving self was, so to speak, nailed to the Cross when we first believed in Christ and accepted Him as our Saviour. But it is not yet dead, and like a crucified man will take a long time to die. But its death is assured, so long as we do not take it down. Christ has nailed it to the Cross and it cannot survive. So through the indwelling power of the Holy Spirit our old self is slowly being crucified or done to death. We are 'becoming conformed unto his death' (Phil 3[10]). Christ's attitude to sin is being made our own, we are learning to hate sin as He hated it. We look forward to the day when the old self will be actually dead, slain by the power of the Cross of Christ infused into us through the Holy Spirit and made our own.

(ii) But there is also the positive side. It is not enough to be perfected in penitence, to grow into the mind of Christ towards sin. We must also be perfected in holiness. As the old self dies, the new self—the Christ-self—is being built up. We are not only to die with Christ but also to rise with Him (cp. the whole passage, Rom 6[1–11]). We are to realize in ourselves 'the power of His Resurrection' (Phil 3[10]). The death of Christ was the consummation of His filial obedience to the Father. He 'Through the eternal Spirit offered Himself without blemish unto God' (Heb 9[14]). All through His earthly life, by repeated and unfailing acts of obedience and right choice, He had built up a perfect human character. He had grown 'in favour with God' (Lk 2[52]). 'Though he was a Son,' yet He 'learned obedience by the things which he suffered.' That is, as His life continued, new opportunities were given and new temptations overcome. He was

---

[1] Dr Moberly speaks of Christ as 'the perfect penitent', *i.e.* as realizing that attitude towards sin which in us would be penitence. He maintains that only the sinless can be perfectly penitent. The difficulty in this use of the term is that 'penitence' in ordinary usage implies the sense of personal responsibility for sins committed. See, however, W. H. Moberly's Essay in *Foundations*.

ever learning the fulness of perfect obedience (Heb 5^{8-10}, cp. 10^{8-10}). On the evening of His Passion He could say 'I glorified Thee on the earth, having accomplished the work which Thou hast given me to do' (Jn 17^4). The Cross represented the climax of human obedience, the utter submission to the Father's will, the complete surrender of self. 'He humbled himself, becoming obedient even unto death, yea, the death of the Cross' (Phil 2^8). So through the Holy Spirit we are to be built up into the likeness of His perfect obedience. Christ is to be found in us. We are to learn to say with S. Paul 'I have been crucified with Christ; yet I live; and yet no longer I, but Christ liveth in me' (Gal 2^{20}). When sanctification is complete, the old self will be dead and the new man will be found in the image of Christ (Rom 8^{29}). We shall have become our true selves in Christ. The secret of the Christian life is 'Christ in you the hope of glory' (Col 1^{27}).

As we have seen, God does not wait until this has been accomplished. He accepts us here and now. But so long as our union with Christ is maintained, the end is certain. Seeing that it is God 'which began a good work' in us, we may be confident that He 'will perfect it until the day of Jesus Christ' (Phil 1^6). Hence S. Paul can look forward and speak in anticipation of it as already accomplished. Thus he can write, 'If any man is in Christ, he is a new creature; the old things are passed away; behold they are become new' (2 Cor 5^{17}), though it is clear that in actual fact a great deal of the old man was still left in the Christians of Corinth. So, too, in Col 3^{1-4} he tells the Colossians in the same breath 'ye died and your life is hid with Christ in God', and also that, as having been raised with Christ, 'they must seek those things that are above.' So in Eph 1^3 God has 'blessed us with every spiritual blessing in the heavenly places in Christ'. That is to say, God views us and we are to view ourselves as identical with the perfected saints that we hope one day to become.

Our final destiny is to enjoy God for ever and to be made like Christ when 'we see Him as He is' (1 Jn 3^2). So the new life, born in baptism and growing in Christ by grace, is to reach its fulfilment in the resurrection life of the age to come, for the resurrection too will be the work of God's 'Spirit that dwelleth in us'. The Christian will then have become all that he was 'made' in baptism, 'a member of Christ, the child of God and an inheritor of the Kingdom of Heaven' (The Catechism). By incorporation into Christ through the Holy Spirit we are, S. Paul says, already the children of God and joint-heirs with Christ. In the life to come we shall receive our full adoption and inherit the glory of those who are conformed to the image of God's Son (Rom 8^{11-30}). The salvation or supernatural end of man in God's purpose is the life in which sin and death are finally conquered and God's people are gathered to Him in the heavenly Jerusalem. This is only another way of saying that the members of Christ's body are to be made like Him, that by adoption in Him and union with

Him they are to be raised to the glory which His own victorious humanity now enjoys in heaven.

(*b*) We have already seen that 'good works' are the necessary fruit of 'a lively faith'. As representing our best efforts to please, God accepts them though Christ. The kindness of the Philippians to S. Paul is 'an odour of a sweet smell, a sacrifice acceptable, well-pleasing to God' (Phil 4^{18}). We are 'created in Christ Jesus for good works, which God afore prepared that we should walk in them' (Eph 2^{10}). Titus is bidden to show himself 'an ensample of good works' (Tit 2^{7}). S. Paul always appeals to the commonsense of his converts against the perversion of his teaching known as 'antinomianism', that is, the doctrine that since our salvation from first to last depends on the grace of God, we need make no effort to observe the moral law. 'The more that we sin, the more opportunity for the grace of God to forgive' (cp. Rom 6^{1} ff.). This error reappeared at the Reformation. Our Article employs needlessly harsh language about good works. It may be perfectly true in the abstract that '*good works which are the fruits of faith and follow after justification cannot put away our sins and endure the severity of God's judgment*'. Since we are imperfect, our noblest actions bear the mark of our imperfection. As being tainted by sin they cannot endure the judgment of an all-holy God (Rom 3^{23}, cp. Is 64^{6}). But religion is a personal matter. God is our Father. To use the best illustration, the presents that a small child brings to his parent may be intrinsically worthless, but are very precious to the parent as tokens of the child's wish to please him. So our good works may be full of imperfection but yet acceptable to God as an expression of our desire to serve Him. Of course they cannot earn or deserve our forgiveness.

(*c*) As we saw, our salvation can only be realized by the co-operation of our wills with the grace of God. Our own effort, therefore, plays a real part in obtaining it. Further, all salvation is social. The right use of grace benefits not only the user but his fellow men. The saint saves not only his own soul but forwards God's purpose for mankind. Under God he is a real means of saving others. Humanly speaking, if he had failed to do his part, not only he but others would have suffered loss. Hence, from one point of view, salvation is acquired as the result of 'good works' and holy living, in the sense that without them it would not have been acquired. The Church, as a whole, has won through the labours of the saints blessings that without them she would never have enjoyed. This truth is fully recognized in Scripture. The welfare of one member of Christ affects all the members (1 Cor 12^{26}, cp. Rom 12^{5}). It is the supplication of a 'righteous' man that avails much (Jas 5^{16}). S. Paul speaks of his work and sufferings as being endured for the salvation of others (2 Cor 1^{6}, cp. 12^{15}, Eph 3^{13}, 2 Tim 2^{10}). Further, in Col 1^{24} he writes, 'I rejoice in my sufferings for your sake and fill up on my part that which is lacking of the afflictions of Christ in my flesh, for his body's sake, which is the church.' These words mean more than that he suffers as Christ suffered, or even that Christ in a real sense suffers in His members' sufferings on earth (cp. Phil 3[10] and 2 Cor 1[5]). They mean what they say. S. Paul asserts that his own sufferings have a real place in affecting the salvation of the world. In the case of the individual Christ's sufferings need to be filled up by our own self-identification with them (cp. 1 Pet 4[1] with Bigg's note). We must take up our Cross and be crucified with Him. So in the case of the world, Christ's sufferings need to be filled up by the sufferings of His members. As Christians can forward the salvation of others by their intercessions, so they can by their sufferings.[1] As prayer for another is no substitute for his own personal faith and repentance, but rather a means of forwarding them, so the sufferings of the saints are not a substitute for the penitence of sinners, but a means through which such penitence may be brought about. There is such a thing as vicarious suffering, but never vicarious sanctification. But without vicarious suffering there would be little sanctification in the world. It is these two truths, first, that our sanctification demands our own effort, secondly, that by our efforts we can help forward the sanctification of others, that, however distorted, underlie the whole doctrine of merit as held in mediaeval times, and attacked in Articles XII–XIV.

(i) The idea of 'merit' is found quite early in the writings of Tertullian.[2] He taught first that a man could 'satisfy' God by doing what he knew to be His will and by not doing what God has forbidden, or, in the case of falling into sin, by voluntarily taking upon himself an equivalent amount of punishment. In this latter case the 'satisfaction' may be attained by alms, fasting, or the like, and above all by martyrdom. Such suffering is of the nature of an expiatory sacrifice. It balances the debt due to God. Further, if this suffering exceeds the amount required, the superfluity counts as 'merit'. It is reckoned as a 'good work' and so to say places God in our debt. Secondly, he taught that in many matters God has left man free to choose between a higher and a lower course. No man may do what God has forbidden, but if he takes advantage of God's permission to follow his natural inclinations he does not commit sin. If, on the other hand, he does not take advantage of God's permission and takes the highest course of all—what God wills, instead of what God merely allows—then he earns merit in the sight of God. This teaching was carried a step further by Cyprian. He held that in certain

---

[1] Bp. Lightfoot, in his note on Col 1[24], distinguishes between Christ's sufferings as 'satisfactoriae' and as 'aedificatoriae'. He maintains that we fill up the sufferings of Christ merely in forwarding His Kingdom, not in any sense in making atonement. Such a distinction is quite arbitrary and implies a view of the atonement as a transaction effected entirely outside human life. Cp. Chandler, *Cult of the Passing Moment*, p. 106 ff.

[2] See Bethune Baker, *Christian Doctrine*, pp. 353–355.

cases it is possible to acquire an amount of merit more than sufficient to deserve even the highest reward of heaven. In that case, the surplus may be passed on to benefit others, through an act of God's grace done in answer to the prayers of the saint, though the benefit is always conditioned by the state of the recipient. In these ideas we have in germ the mediaeval teaching on merit, on works of supererogation and on indulgences.

(ii) In mediaeval times it had come to be accepted that in some sense good works carried 'merit': further, that the merits of the saints were available to make up the deficiencies of others. This being the current belief and practice of the Church, the duty was laid upon the Schoolmen or School-authors mentioned in Art. XIII, to place the whole system on a rational basis. The Schoolmen were the systematic theologians of the middle ages.[1] Their object was with the aid of the newly discovered philosophy of Aristotle to reconcile faith and reason. Taking the doctrine and discipline of the Church as they found them, without questioning their origin or validity, they strove to present them as a symmetrical whole, agreeable to reason no less than to faith. Their task was not criticism nor the discovery of new truth, but the harmonization of the old. Their achievement took the form of 'sums of theology', weaving into a consistent and orderly system, complete even in the minutest detail, all that the Church had seen fit to say or to do.[2]

The Schoolmen explained the idea of merit by a distinction. They argued that the case of Cornelius showed that human free-will could go a certain way in its own strength in turning towards God. Such an effort done by man's unaided power did not indeed deserve a reward, but it was fitting that God's liberality should reward it. In technical language it earned merit not as a matter of debt, but 'of congruity' (*de congruo*), *i.e.* 'of fitness'. This is repudiated in Art. XIII. On the other hand, good works done by the aid of grace deserved a reward. They earned merit 'de condigno', as a matter of debt.[3] This is attacked in Art. XII.

Before we criticize the whole idea of merit, it is only fair to remember that the scholastic doctrine of merit can only be fully understood and judged as a part of a very complex and intricate system of

---

[1] The Schoolmen were the successors of the Fathers. Usually S. Bernard (d. 1115) is styled the last of the Fathers and S. Anselm (d. 1109) the first of the Schoolmen. The change of name marks a very real change of aim. 'Doctores they claimed to be, not Patres; not, as fathers, productive; not professing to bring out of their treasures things new, but only to justify and establish things old.' See Trench, *Mediaeval Church History*, Lect. XIV.

[2] The most famous is the *Summa* of S. Thomas Aquinas (1270), still the standard work of theology on the whole in the Roman Church. Scarcely less famous in their day were the writings of Albertus Magnus (1280), Bonaventura (1274) and later William of Occam and Duns Scotus.

[3] We may compare the illustration that is often given. 'A servant deserves his wages *ex condigno*: he may deserve support in sickness or old age *ex congruo*.'

theology. It is there balanced by statements of a very different nature. But popular religion is unable to make subtle distinctions. What is attacked in our Articles is the use made of the scholastic teaching in popular religion.

The mediaeval idea of merit is abstract and artificial. Our Lord in His teaching no doubt uses current Jewish language about the rewards given by God to those who serve Him. But in so doing He transforms the whole idea of reward. It becomes qualitative rather than quantitative. 'Since opportunities are a divine gift (Mt 25^{14}), service is a mere duty which cannot merit reward (Lk 17^9 ff.). Reward, therefore, becomes free undeserved grace and is pictured as great out of all proportion to the service rendered (Mt 19^{29}, 24^{47}, 25^{21}, etc.). This teaching really eliminates the idea of reward altogether.'[1] In other words the reward is not something external that can be abstracted from the man who receives it. It is primarily an inward quickening of soul, a new capacity for service and a closer union with God. Further, the whole idea of 'merit', in the sense of running up a debtor and creditor account with God, is utterly unChristian. 'Merit lives from man to man, and not from man, O God, to Thee.' For our whole life, for every power that we possess as well as for every opportunity of exercising it, we are utterly dependent upon God. He has an absolute claim upon all our life. Nothing that we can do can give us a claim against Him. Hence not only is the 'reward' that we receive from Him non-transferable, but from the nature of the case even the holiest saint can never possess any 'merit' that belongs to him, as it were, in his own right and can be transferred to another's account. Our personal relationship to our Heavenly Father cannot be expressed in terms of arithmetic.

The theory of congruous merit attacked in Art. XIII does indeed represent in a distorted form the great truth that any effort that we make will be met by God with an ever-increasing supply of grace. It is most surely congruous with the character of God to bestow more abundant grace on those who are unconsciously striving to serve and know Him. But this, like all God's gifts, is freely given. His grace is so magnificent a gift that we could never deserve it by the excellence of our own efforts. Further, the scholastic theory is frankly semi-Pelagian. It denies the need of prevenient grace. This is illustrated by the case of Cornelius. His prayers and alms were certainly good works done before justification. But equally certainly they were not done apart from God's grace. From first to last his salvation was due to divine grace. The whole idea of having to earn God's grace by making a good start in our own strength flatly contradicts S. Paul's teaching on Abraham (Rom 4$^{1-4}$, cp. 9$^{11-13}$).

So, too, with the idea of 'merit *de condigno*'. As we saw above,

[1] McNeile on Mt 5^{12}: The whole note deserves reading in this connexion. On the motive of reward in the Gospels, see K. E. Kirk, *Vision of God*, Lect. III, Sect. iv.

even our best efforts come far short of perfection. They cannot 'deserve' or 'earn' our acceptance or anything else. At the same time, it is sure at all times that the more fully we respond to God's calls, the more grace He bestows. But the right to expect this grace depends on the unfailing generosity of God, not on any excellence residing in our own works.

At the Council of Trent the phrases 'merit *de congruo*' and 'merit *de condigno*' were entirely avoided. The need of prevenient grace was clearly asserted. On the other hand, the assertion that 'all works done before justification . . . are truly sins or deserve the hatred of God' was anathematized. Still the idea of 'merit' was retained, and to-day, in spite of the balanced statements of her theologians, the Church of Rome in her ordinary teaching and practice never seems able to get away from the idea of accumulating merit by good works. There are large portions of S. Paul's Epistles which find no place in her teaching. On this point her teaching is un-Catholic. Popular Protestantism, with its insistence—often exaggerated insistence—on the freeness of God's salvation, bears witness to a portion of Catholic truth that Rome ignores.

(iii) In close dependence on mediaeval views about merit came the idea of 'works of supererogation',[1] *i.e.* '*voluntary works over and above God's commandments*'. We have seen that as early as Tertullian a distinction was drawn between what God 'permits' and what God 'wills'. It is not sin to do what God permits, but it is meritorious to do what God wills. In defence of this distinction the chief passage alleged is 1 Cor 7. Here S. Paul permits marriage, but 'by reason of the present distress', encourages celibacy. 'Concerning virgins I have no commandment (*praeceptum*) of the Lord, but I give my judgment (*consilium*)' (cp. also 2 Cor 8[8 and 10], where we find a similar contrast between 'commandment' and 'judgment'.) On the basis of this text a formal distinction was made between 'precepts' and 'counsels'. 'Precepts' were commands of God binding upon all men, which it was sin to disobey. 'Counsels' or 'Counsels of perfection' were, as it were, recommendations, which it was not necessary for a Christian to follow. Such refusal was not sinful. Such 'counsels' would include poverty, celibacy, the monastic life and the like. The performance of these, as being over and above God's commandment, would earn merit for those who performed them.[2]

The words of our Article on this subject are perfectly justified. No one can render to God more than he is bound to render, for God has a claim on the whole life of man. There is a very real truth that underlies the distinction between 'precepts' and 'counsels'. Some

[1] The term 'supererogation' comes from the Latin versions of Lk 10[35]. *Quodcumque supererogaveris*=ὅ τι ἂν προσδαπανήσῃς. *Erogare*=to disburse money; *supererogare*, 'to pay over and above.'
[2] On 'precepts and counsels' and 'the double standard', see K. E. Kirk, *op. cit.*, esp. Lect. V.

laws of God are binding upon all Christians without exception, as Christians. But there are other duties to which all Christians are clearly not called, as, for instance, the ministry. Those, however, who receive a call from God to one of these special duties, are bound to obey at the peril of their souls. The 'counsel' has become a 'precept' for them. They do not earn merit by complying, but they would disobey God by refusing. This principle is clearly seen in the case of the rich young ruler (Mk 10^{17-30}). The command to sell all that he had was clearly not a command to do 'a work of supererogation'. 'One thing thou lackest' shows that his life still came short of God's purpose for him. Further, the command was an 'ad hominem' command. Our Lord did not give it to all His disciples. By refusing it the man did not simply fail to earn merit, but he endangered his entrance into the Kingdom of God at all (v. ^{23}).[1] Neither in S. Paul nor in the Gospels can any basis be found for 'works of supererogation'. Lk 17^{10} quoted in the Article is perfectly clear.

ARTICLE XVII

Of Predestination and Election

Predestination to Life is the everlasting purpose of God, whereby (before the foundations of the world were laid) he hath constantly decreed by his counsel secret to us, to deliver from curse and damnation those whom he hath chosen in Christ out of mankind, and to bring them by Christ to everlasting salvation, as vessels made to honour. Wherefore, they which be endued with so excellent a benefit of God be called according to God's purpose by his Spirit working in due season: they through Grace obey the calling: they be justified freely: they be made sons of God by adoption: they be made like the image of his only begotten Son Jesus Christ: they walk religiously in good works, and at

De praedestinatione et electione

Praedestinatio ad vitam est aeternum Dei propositum, quo ante jacta mundi fundamenta, suo consilio, nobis quidem occulto, constanter decrevit, eos quos in Christo elegit ex hominum genere, a maledicto et exitio liberare, atque (ut vasa in honorem efficta) per Christum, ad aeternam salutem adducere. Unde qui tam praeclaro Dei beneficio sunt donati, illi spiritu ejus, opportuno tempore operante, secundum propositum ejus vocantur, vocationi per gratiam parent, justificantur gratis, adoptantur in filios Dei, unigeniti ejus Jesu Christi imagini efficiuntur conformes, in bonis operibus sancte ambulant, et demum ex Dei misericordia pertingunt ad sempiternam felicitatem.

---

[1] In S. Matthew's account of this incident (19^{16-21}) a distinction appears to be made between what is required for 'entering into life' and for 'being perfect,' *i.e.* a 'double standard' is suggested. See K. E. Kirk, *op. cit.*, p. 69.

length, by God's mercy, they attain to everlasting felicity.

As the godly consideration of Predestination, and our Election in Christ, is full of sweet, pleasant and unspeakable comfort to godly persons, and such as feel in themselves the working of the Spirit of Christ, mortifying the works of the flesh, and their earthly members, and drawing up their mind to high and heavenly things, as well because it doth greatly establish and confirm their faith of eternal salvation to be enjoyed through Christ, as because it doth fervently kindle their love towards God: so, for curious and carnal persons, lacking the Spirit of Christ, to have continually before their eyes the sentence of God's Predestination, is a most dangerous downfall, whereby the Devil doth thrust them either into desperation, or into wretchlessness of most unclean living, no less perilous than desperation.

Furthermore, we must receive God's promises in such wise, as they be generally set forth to us in holy Scripture: and, in our doings, that Will of God is to be followed, which we have expressly declared unto us in the Word of God.

Quemadmodum praedestinationis et electionis nostrae in Christo pia consideratio, dulcis, suavis, et ineffabilis consolationis plena est vere piis, et his qui sentiunt in se vim spiritus Christi, facta carnis, et membra, quae adhuc sunt super terram, mortificantem, animumque ad coelestia et superna rapientem; tum quia fidem nostram de aeterna salute consequenda per Christum plurimum stabilit atque confirmat, tum quia amorem nostrum in Deum vehementer accendit: ita hominibus curiosis, carnalibus, et spiritu Christi destitutis, ob oculos perpetuo versari praedestinationis Dei sententiam perniciosissimum est praecipitium, unde illos diabolus protrudit, vel in desperationem, vel in aeque perniciosam impurissimae vitae securitatem; deinde promissiones divinas sic amplecti oportet, ut nobis in sacris literis generaliter propositae sunt, et Dei voluntas in nostris actionibus ea sequenda est, quam in verbo Dei habemus, diserte revelatam.

An Article of 1553 with slight alterations. The whole question of Predestination was a burning question at the time. The most important point to notice is that it keeps to the language of Scripture throughout. The similarity between the Latin of the Article and the Vulgate is especially close. The chief passages on which it is based are Rom 8^{28-30}, 9^{21} and Eph 1^{3-11}.

ARTICLE XVIII

Of obtaining eternal Salvation only by the Name of Christ

They also are to be had accur-

De speranda aeterna salute tantum in nomine Christi

Sunt et illi anathematizandi,

sed that presume to say, that every man shall be saved by the Law or Sect which he professeth, so that he be diligent to frame his life according to that Law, and the light of Nature. For holy Scripture doth set out unto us only the Name of Jesus Christ, whereby men must be saved.

qui dicere audent unumquemque in lege aut secta quam profitetur esse servandum, modo juxta illam et lumen naturae accurate vixerit, cum sacrae literae tantum Jesu Christi nomen praedicent, in quo salvos fieri homines oporteat.

Unchanged from 1553 except in the form of the title. The 'et' in the opening sentence was omitted in 1563 and restored in 1571. It would seem to connect it with the last clause of Art. XVI.

§ 3. *Predestination and Election*

(*a*) Under these theological terms there lie two great problems.

(α) How can we reconcile God's omniscience with man's responsibility? If God when He creates a man foreknows that he will go wrong, is not God responsible for his sin in creating him? How can a God of love create a man who will never enjoy that happiness and union with God for which mankind was made?

(β) What do we mean when we speak of God's elect or God's chosen? To what are they chosen, some privileged position or eternal life? Has then God got favourites? Why are others not elect? Are they outside God's love?

The questions were violently debated at the time of the Reformation. In some form they exercise the minds of all men. Historically, three main solutions have been given.

(i) S. Augustine in his controversy with Pelagianism formulated his views on this question. In dealing with him we need to remember that they are coloured by his own strong religious experience. He felt that quite apart from any merit of his own God had called him. God's grace had come into his life, bringing with it a new power to love and serve God. He was convinced that God had a purpose of love for him from all eternity and that God's grace was enabling him to fulfil it. In the light of this he faced the question 'Why is the gift of this transforming grace given to some and not to others?' His own case showed that it was not earned by any goodness. Hence he answered that we cannot know. It depends on God's will alone. By God's decree, without any reference to future conduct, some are chosen as 'vessels of mercy' to redemption, others are simply left as 'vessels of wrath'. He himself went no further, but some of his followers carried his views to the logical conclusion that these last were definitely predestined to sin and evil. God's elect are kept faithful to Him by fresh supplies of grace, which endow them with the gift of 'perseverance'. This again is a mystery beyond human comprehension. Perseverance to the end is a sign that a man is predestinated to eternal life. The purpose of God for His elect cannot fail. S. Augustine had to explain away such texts as 'God willeth that all men should be saved' (1 Tim 2⁴), as meaning only that God, as no respecter of persons, willed some men of every age and class to be saved.

(ii) Calvin did little more than systematize this view and draw out its full implications (*v.* above). This doctrine—apart from personal experience—is based upon one side of S. Paul's teaching especially Rom 8 and 9, such as 8^{28-30}, 'We know that to them that love God all things work together for good, even to them that are called according to his purpose. For whom he foreknew, he also foreordained to be conformed to the image of his Son, that he might be the first among many brethren: and whom he foreordained, them he also called: and whom he called, them he also justified: and whom he justified, them he also glorified.'

Again, in discussing why Jacob was chosen and Esau rejected even before they were born and had done anything good or bad (9^{11}), and pointing to it as evidence of the freeness of God's choice, he adds, 'What shall we say then? Is there unrighteousness with God? God forbid. For he saith to Moses, I will have mercy on whom I will have mercy and I will have compassion on whom I will have compassion. So then it is not of him that willeth, nor of him that runneth, but of God that hath mercy. For the scripture saith unto Pharoah, For this very purpose did I raise thee up, that I might show in thee my power and that my name might be published abroad in all the earth. So then he hath mercy on whom he will and whom he will he hardeneth. Thou wilt say then unto me, Why doth he still find fault? For who withstandeth his will? Nay but, O man, who art thou that repliest against God? Shall the thing formed say to him that formed it, Why didst thou make me thus? Or hath not the potter a right over the clay, from the same lump to make one part a vessel unto honour and another unto dishonour? What if God, willing to show his wrath and to make his power known, endured with much long-suffering vessels of wrath fitted unto destruction: and that he might make known the riches of his glory upon vessels of mercy?'

The general impression gained by reading such a passage in isolation at first sight is favourable to something very like Calvinism. Exclusive stress seems to be laid on the power of God and the mysteriousness of its working. But a closer study corrects any such impression. S. Paul is speaking here primarily of nations, not individuals. Jacob stands for the nation of Israel and Esau for Edom (cp. 9^{25} ff.). Again, S. Paul avoids saying that God Himself prepared vessels of wrath unto destruction: he only says that 'God endured vessels of wrath fitted into destruction'. He does say explicitly that 'God prepared vessels unto glory' (v. 23). But no doubt from one point of view he would even say that God formed vessels unto wrath, just as he says above that God 'hardened Pharaoh's heart'. In such language, he speaks as a Jew. The Jews, ignoring all intermediate causes,

Q   B.T.A.

assigned all that happened to its ultimate cause, *viz*. God. A Jew would say equally that God hardens a man's heart or that a man hardens his own heart; that God fits a man for wrath or a man fits himself for wrath. For the process of hardening is due to one of God's laws, the law of character, and in this sense is the work of God. The man acts, and his actions produce the result that God's law renders inevitable. Even so it is worth noting that God's delay in manifesting His power in punishment is due to His 'long-suffering' (cp. Rom 2^4). More important still, these passages cannot be taken by themselves. They represent only one side of S. Paul's teaching. Elsewhere He speaks of God's love for all men and of the natural love in man for what is good. His exhortations assume the truth of man's responsibility. We cannot isolate one step in a long and involved argument such as that of the Epistle to the Romans and base a complete theology upon it.

(iii) In opposition to Calvinism, Arminius, who taught at Leyden about 1604 (and therefore after the date of this Article), formulated views previously held by many. He taught that God predestines to eternal life certain men because He foresees that they will use their free-will aright and be faithful to the grace that is given them. This view is called 'praedestinatio ex praevisis meritis'. A very similar view was held by many of the Fathers; in fact, so far as any doctrine on the subject was formulated at all in the Church, it was Arminian even in the West until the time of S. Augustine. In the East Augustinianism never won general acceptance. The only text that offers any support to such a view is Rom 8^{28-29}. The great majority of Greek commentators take 'according to his purpose' to refer not to God's purpose but to man's purpose 'in accordance with man's free act of choice'. This is impossible.

Again, the word 'foreknew' in the next verse has been pressed in an Arminian sense. But the word must be understood in accordance with Biblical usage, and means 'took note of', 'fixed His regard on' with a view to selection for some special purpose. The strong point of the Arminian view is that it lays stress on human responsibility, and on the truth that sufficient grace is given to all. Its weak point is that it appears to make God's election not a free gift, as S. Paul tells us it is, but a reward earned in advance by man's own efforts. Further, it does not really escape the harshness of Calvinism. Predestination according to foreseen merit logically implies condemnation according to foreseen failure.

(*b*) We need to bear in mind that Scripture insists upon three great thoughts. (i) God has an eternal purpose of love for all nations and individuals whom He has made. (ii) Salvation and grace are from first to last the gifts of God's free bounty. (iii) Man is responsible to God for his conduct.

(i) Whatever God has done or is now doing for us, He eternally intended to do. The Gospel is the mystery or secret 'which hath been kept in silence through times eternal, but now is manifested' (Rom 16^{25}). God 'called us with a holy calling, not according to our works, but according to his own purpose and grace, which was given us in Christ Jesus before times eternal but hath now been manifested by the appearing of our Saviour, Christ Jesus' (2 Tim 1$^{9-10}$, cp. Tit 1^2). God, by creating a human life, has in some sense made Himself responsible for it. A God of love and justice must have a purpose of love for every single being whom He creates, in the fulfilment of which the created being will find his true satisfaction. In this sense all must be predestined to life. It is this thought that, rightly grasped, has such great moral power. A man needs to feel that he has behind him not only his own efforts but God's eternal love: that God has a place for him to fill: that nothing can happen to him from outside without God's knowledge and permission: that it is God's will for him that he should do right and realize his best self. The success of our life must depend not simply on ourselves but on God's purpose of love.

(ii) God's purpose for us is to be realized through union with Himself. This union is brought within our reach through Jesus Christ. It was God's eternal purpose to sum up all things in Him (Eph 1^{10}). 'It was the good pleasure of the Father . . . through him to reconcile all things unto himself' (Col 1^{20}). His redeeming work was no after-thought. He was from all eternity God's elect or chosen (Is 42^1, 1 Pet 2^4), 'the Lamb that hath been slain from the foundation of the world' (Rev 13^8). When we are made members of Christ we share His election. We are '*chosen in Christ out of mankind*'. It is God's purpose to bring us '*by Christ to everlasting salvation, as vessels made to honour*'. 'He chose us in him before the foundation of the world . . . having foreordained us unto adoption as sons through Jesus Christ unto himself, according to the good pleasure of his will, to the praise of the glory of his grace, which he freely bestowed on us in the Beloved' (Eph 1$^{4-5}$, cp. 2$^{4-7}$). The glorious position, 'sitting in the heavenly places with him in Christ Jesus,' is, as S. Paul's language shows, not the reward of our own merit, but God's free gift. He chose us, not we Him. The initial act is God's, not our own (1 Pet 1$^{1-2}$). How is it then that all are not chosen or elect? The answer lies in the thought that God works out His purpose for the world gradually. No one can deny that spiritual graces and opportunities, no less than temporal, are unequally distributed (cp. Lk 12$^{47-48}$). Under the old Covenant Israel was by God's choice an elect nation. To them God granted a special revelation of Himself. They were His people (Deut 7^6, etc.). They had many spiritual advantages that the other nations did not have. So to-day the Christian Church is the new Israel (Gal 6^{16}, Phil 3^3): it has inherited the unique spiritual privileges of the old Israel. The Christian has spiritual advantages that those outside do not as yet enjoy (1 Pet 2$^{9-10}$, Heb 13^{10}). The Christian, like the Jew of old, is elect, or, to put it in modern English, selected, not because

God arbitrarily saves one man and passes over or condemns another, but because God's plan is to save men through men. The privilege of being elect carries with it the duty of using the advantages bestowed for the good of others. Abraham was chosen that ultimately in him 'all the families of the earth might be blessed' (Gen 12³). Israel was chosen to do a work for God for the ultimate benefit of the whole world (Is 49⁶, 60). Every Christian is called upon to say with our Lord Himself 'For their sakes I sanctify myself' (Jn 17¹⁹). The Church is the Body of Christ through which the world is to be won back to God (cp. Eph 3⁸⁻¹¹).

(iii) Accordingly, either a nation or an individual may at this moment not be elect for one of two reasons. (a) Their opportunity may not yet have come. As the Article says, God's spirit works *in due season*. (b) Their opportunity may have come and been rejected (cp. Acts 13⁴⁶). In Scripture the 'reprobate' are not those doomed to eternal damnation by some arbitrary decree of God, but those who disobey the light that is given to them (Rom 1²⁸, 2 Cor 13⁵). Thus Scripture seems to show that election is primarily to privilege, but such, if rightly accepted and used, is the means to eternal life. God's purpose is that it shall be so used. There is the very closest connexion between election and salvation. We are chosen according to God's purpose, not to any merely earthly destiny. But whether we attain it or no depends upon ourselves. Such election is God's method of leading us to salvation, but it needs to be made sure by our own efforts to live up to it (2 Pet 1¹⁰, cp. Col 3¹²). Attempts have been made to show that election is necessarily to eternal life. Our Lord's words are quoted 'Many are called but few chosen', where 'called' refers obviously to privilege and 'chosen' to final salvation, and the two are distinguished. But there is nothing in this contrary to what we have said above. Everything depends on the context in which the terms are used. In 2 Pet 1¹⁰ they are identified: here they are contrasted, and 'chosen' refers not to this life but to the day of judgment, when God's award depends upon the right use of the opportunities bestowed upon those who are called. No doubt it is God's purpose of love to bring those who are chosen in Christ to salvation: only our own sloth or wilfulness can thwart this. But as long as we live here we need care and watchfulness (cp. 1 Cor 9²⁷).

(c) We may ask, Is this the teaching of the Articles? There is nothing in the Articles that contradicts it, but the general impression produced is not the same. The reason is that the Articles give only one side of the teaching of Scripture. They deal with salvation entirely from God's side and ignore man's co-operation. The complementary side of the teaching of Scripture is passed over in silence. Our relation to God is a very complex one. If we consider all the metaphors by which our Lord illustrates it, we get a very long list. God is our King, our Master, our Judge, our Shepherd and above all our Father. To gain a true proportion we must take into account all these. This group of Articles is practically based upon one and one only, and that the most severe. God is viewed above all as 'a Lord Chief-Justice' or a 'moral connoisseur'. His Fatherly love for the souls whom He has made, His personal dealings with us, our response and all the nobler side of human nature are ignored. Hence the chilly and unreal feeling of these Articles. There is nothing untrue in them, but rather a want of proportion.

(d) Behind all these questions lies the problem of the relation of God's omniscience to man's free-will. This in turn is only one part of the standing mystery of the relation of the finite to the infinite and time to eternity. A definite solution is obviously impossible. Even if the human mind were competent to grasp truth, a large portion of the facts obviously lie outside any human experience. On such questions moral insight can go further than merely intellectual skill. The teaching of Scripture on such points can hardly be reduced to a system. It is always practical rather than speculative. Scripture holds before us two great counter-truths—first, God's absolute sovereignty (cp. Rom 9²⁰ ff.), and secondly, man's responsibility. Our intellects cannot reconcile them. So far as we can reconcile them at all it is by right action and vigorous moral life. Each truth finds its complete fulfilment in the moral life of Jesus Christ. We must not shut our eyes to either side of the truth, because it conflicts with our theories. The difficulty reaches its climax in such a case as that of Judas Iscariot. He was elect (Jn 6⁷⁰). We cannot but suppose that our Lord called him, because he had certain powers that he might have employed in the work of an apostle and that there was a work in the purpose of God waiting for him to do. On the one hand Christ has the moral insight to foresee his coming fall and its awful consequences (Mk 14¹⁸ ff.). On the other hand Judas is regarded as personally responsible. Up to the end Christ does all in His power to save him (Mt 26⁵⁰, Lk 22⁴⁸). We may not think that such efforts were in any sense unreal or that it was not God's purpose that he should live up to his privileged position.

Most theologians, no doubt, have held that God's omniscience is such that He possesses an accurate knowledge of every detail of the future and can foresee who will use the grace given to them. Others, however, hold that though God is indeed omniscient, He can only know what is knowable, and that by creating man with free-will He Himself introduced a certain element of contingency into the course of the world's history. For instance, Martensen writes:

'The contradiction which has been supposed to exist between the idea of the free progress of the world and the *omniscience* of God, rests upon a one-sided conception of omniscience, as a mere knowing *beforehand* and an ignoring of the *conditional* in the divine decrees. An unconditional fore-knowledge undeniably militates against the freedom of the creature, as far as freedom of choice is concerned; and against the undecided, the contingent, which is an idea inseparable from the development of freedom in time. . . . But such an unconditional fore-knowledge not only militates against the freedom of the creature, it equally is opposed to the idea of a freely working God in history. A God literally foreknowing all things, would be merely the spectator of events decided and predestined from eternity, not the all-directing governor in a drama of freedom which He carries on in reciprocal conflict and work with the freedom of the creature. If we would preserve this reciprocal relation between God and His creatures, we must not make the whole actual course of the world the subject of His foreknowledge, but only its essential import, the essential truth it involves. The final goal of this world's development, together with the entire series of its essentially necessary stages, must be regarded as fixed in the eternal counsel of God; but the practical carrying out of this eternal counsel, the entire fulness of actual limitations on the part of this world's progress, in so far as these are conditioned by the freedom of the creature, can only be the subject of a conditional foreknowledge, *i.e.* they can be foreknown as possibilities, as Futurabilia, but not as realities, because other possibilities may actually take place. . . . While God neither foreknows nor will foreknow what He leaves undecided, in order to be decided in time, He is no less *cognizant* of and *privy* to all that occurs. . . . His knowledge penetrates the entanglements of this world's progress at every point; the unerring eye of His wisdom discerns in every moment the relation subsisting between free beings and His eternal plan; and His almighty hand, His power, pregnant of great designs, guides and influences the movements of the world as His counsels require.'[1]

We may compare with this a passage from James' *Will to Believe* (p. 181).

'Suppose two men before a chess-board—the one a novice, the other an expert player of the game. The expert intends to beat. But he cannot foresee exactly what any one actual move of his adversary may be. He knows however all the *possible* moves of the latter; and he knows in advance how to meet each of them by a move of his own which leads in the direction of victory. And the victory infallibly arrives, after no matter how devious a course, in the one predestined form of checkmate to the novice's king.'

It may be that such mental pictures are as near as we can get to a systematized understanding of God's plan as it is revealed in Scripture and experience. We must maintain God's sovereignty. He knows all the possibilities that His universe contains. He is always able to overrule history to His purpose. But it may be that it rests with human choice and effort to determine by which of many possible roads the goal shall be reached. Modern thought is increasingly

---

[1] Martensen, *Dogmatics*, pp. 218–219.

dissatisfied with the idea of life as the mere unrolling of a previously determined system and insists on the part played by the free exercise of rational purpose. Choice has in a very true sense a creative power, since it determines the line along which evolution shall go forward. No doubt when acts are past we can trace them back to the causes that produced them: as we look back on them now they seem to be the one and inevitable result of those causes. But that does not show that the possibility that was actually realized was the only possibility before us at the actual time of choice. Our consciousness seems to point the other way. We must believe, however, that God's infinite love and power and wisdom can never be baffled or defeated in the final issue.

(e) The moral effect of the doctrine of Predestination

The meaning of the second paragraph may be put thus:

(i) On the one hand a knowledge of God's eternal purpose for us is a challenge to us to live up to it (cp. the closing sentence of the first paragraph). As Dr Mozley says, 'The sense of predestination which the New Testament encourages is connected with strength of moral principle in the individual. . . . No idea can be more opposed to Scripture or more unwarrantable than any idea of predestination separate from this consciousness and not arising upon this foundation.'[1] Again, God's election is a call to us to pass through those stages of the moral life which are the appointed road to sanctification and to use the means of grace that God has ordained. As Hooker says, 'There are that elevate too much the ordinary and immediate means of light, relying wholly upon the bare conceit of that eternal election which notwithstanding includeth subordination of means, without which we are not actually brought to enjoy what God secretly did intend: and therefore to build upon God's election, if we keep not ourselves to the ways which He hath appointed for man to walk in, is but a self-deceiving vanity.'[2]

(ii) The second half of the paragraph points out the dangers of brooding over the idea of predestination, dangers that were only too apparent at the time of the Reformation. If a man believes himself to be eternally lost by God's decree, then he may either be led to despair and possibly suicide, or he may decide that as he is to be damned anyhow, he may as well deserve it by having a good time during his life here. We hear of men taking their lives out of 'desperation'. Others, again, who believed themselves to be saved by the decree of God, claimed to live a life of unbridled license since nothing could destroy their election. Thus, whether a man felt himself to be lost or saved he might be thrust '*into wretchlessness (i.e.* recklessness) *of most unclean living*'.

(f) If the opening paragraph of the Article might suggest a Calvinistic interpretation, the last two sentences effectually dispel it. They

---

[1] *Augustinian Doctrine of Predestination*, pp. 44–45.   [2] Hooker, V. c. 60 § 3.

deny the Calvinistic doctrine of 'particular redemption', *i.e.* that Christ died for the elect only. '*We must receive God's promises in such wise as they are generally* (*i.e.* universally, for all men) *set forth in Holy Scripture.*' The reference is to such passages as 1 Tim 2[4]. The second sentence runs '*In our doings that will of God is to be followed, which we have expressly declared to us in the word of God.*' This rules out a view current at the time among certain Anabaptists that God had a secret will besides His will revealed in Scripture, and that this secret will might cancel the revealed will. Thus God's promises of salvation offered to all might not ultimately be valid.[1]

Art. XVIII at first sight seems hardly consistent with this last statement. It appears to deny salvation, *e.g.* to the heathen and those who have never heard of Christ. But this was not in the mind of those who composed it. It is aimed at a particular set of people at a particular time. The Latin title 'De speranda aeterna salute' shows that it is aimed at those who have the opportunity of being Christians. Two alternatives are possible: (i) That it was aimed at those who hoped to win salvation by joining some religious order (here called a law or sect), and observing its rule of life.[2] (ii) That it is aimed at Anabaptists, who rejected Christ as Saviour and treated any definite Christian belief as unimportant. In any case it raises a wide question: if belief in Christ is essential to salvation, what are we to say of good heathen or those among ourselves who reject the Christian faith. The answer is this: Christ claims to be the one and only Saviour (cp. Acts 4[12]). 'God gave unto us eternal life and this life is in his Son. He that hath the Son hath the life and he that hath not the Son of God hath not the life' (1 Jn 5[11-16]). But the Church never dares to say of any man that he is finally lost. Those who do not yet know Christ or who die without knowing Him will not '*be saved by the law or sect they profess*'. There is no Saviour but Christ. But we trust that in His own way and at His own time, He will make Himself known to them. Those who are faithful to the highest that they know are unconsciously serving Him even now. There are many unconscious Christians (cp. Jn 10[16]). Christ is the 'Saviour of all men, specially of them that believe' (1 Tim 4[10]).[3] In the parable of the sheep and the goats, those who have observed simple moral duties of love and kindness have really been doing them to Christ, and they seem to be the heathen (τὰ ἔθνη, Mt 25[32]). All that we must insist on is that men are bound to do their utmost to attain to further truth, and, when it is found, to live up to it and to the claims that it makes upon them (cp. Jn 7[17]).†

---

[1] It is worth noting that to-day the moral difficulty for most men lies not in the apparent inequality of opportunities for attaining heaven, but rather in the inequality of opportunities in this present life. The centre of gravity has shifted from the other world to this.

[2] See Dixon, vol. v. p. 397.

[3] On the question of the operation of the grace of Christ outside the visible economy of the Church, see E. L. Mascall, *Christ, the Christian and the Church*, p. 149.

THE CHURCH

ARTICLE XIX

Of the Church

The visible Church of Christ is a congregation of faithful men, in the which the pure Word of God is preached, and the Sacraments be duly ministered according to Christ's ordinance in all those things that of necessity are requisite to the same.

As the Church of *Jerusalem*, *Alexandria*, and *Antioch* have erred; so also the Church of *Rome* hath erred, not only in their living and manner of Ceremonies, but also in matters of Faith.

De Ecclesia

Ecclesia Christi visibilis est coetus fidelium, in quo verbum Dei purum praedicatur, et sacramenta, quoad ea quae necessario exigantur, juxta Christi institutum recte administrantur. Sicut erravit Ecclesia Hierosolymitana, Alexandrina, et Antiochena; ita et erravit Ecclesia Romana, non solum quoad agenda, et caeremoniarum ritus, verum in his etiam quae credenda sunt.

Almost unchanged since 1553. Its object was to give such a definition of the Church as would:

(i) Exclude various Anabaptist sects.

(ii) Deny the claim of Rome to be the only Church.

The latter section justifies the breach with Rome by denying her infallibility. As she has erred in the past, so she may err again at the Council of Trent. The allusion is to such events as the acceptance by Pope Liberius of an Arian creed, the acquittal of Pelagius by Pope Zosimus and the lapse of Pope Honorius into Monothelitism.

N.B.—A comparison of the title with the opening words shows that the Church and the visible Church are the same. The adjective is virtually a predicate.

§ 1. The Article starts off with the assumption that the Church of God is a visible society, *The visible Church of Christ*.

The Church as it appears in the New Testament is the successor or rather the continuation of Israel in the Old Testament. Among all primitive peoples religion is essentially social. The God is above all the God of the tribe. The individual worships Him as a member of the tribe. Only slowly does the idea of personal religion emerge. Israel is no exception to this rule. Jehovah made His Covenant with the nation as a whole. The individual Israelite shared its blessing as a member of the nation. To be cut off from Israel was to be cut off from Jehovah (cp. Gen 17¹³⁻¹⁴). The nation as a whole was God's son (Hos 11¹, Ex 4²²) and God's servant (Is 49³⁻⁶). The idea of personal responsibility and personal salvation did not become prominent till the time of Jeremiah and Ezekiel (Ezek 18). It was indeed only too obvious that the greater part of the nation proved unfaithful to its call. The prophets taught that God's purpose would be fulfilled through the faithful few (Is 6[13], Amos 9[8], etc.). But this faithful remnant was the true representative of Israel (cp. Rom 9): it was to form the centre of the coming Messianic Kingdom. The unfaithful were to be purged away, but it was still the visible nation of Israel, thus purified, that was to inherit the Kingdom. Fellowship with it was always the condition of sharing its glorious future.

That was the idea from which our Lord started. He purified the current conception of the Kingdom of God from many false and gross perversions. He insisted on the need for personal penitence. Mere physical descent from Abraham was not enough. But we find nowhere any hint that His Kingdom was not to be a visible body, just as Israel had been. He twice employs the word 'ecclesia'. In itself the word simply means a body of people gathered together. It was used, e.g. of the assembly at Athens (cp. Acts 19[38]). But in the LXX it was used to translate a Hebrew word that meant the nation of Israel as called forth ($\dot{\epsilon}\kappa\text{-}\kappa\alpha\lambda\epsilon\hat{\iota}\nu$) from their tents to an assembly for purposes of worship. In this sense it is used in Acts 7[38] and Heb 2[12]. The clearest translation of Mt 16[18], where our Lord employs the word of the Christian Church, would be: 'On this rock (i.e. on S. Peter as the first to confess faith in Himself as Messianic King or Christ) I will build my new Israel.' The sense in which He employed it in the second passage (Mt 18[17]) is less clear.[1] Dr Hort held that it there means the local Jewish community. But in any case it means a visible assembly. Again, Christ's whole action is in accord with this. He attached to Himself a recognized band of disciples (Acts 1[21–22]). He chose the Apostles and trained them to be the leaders of the new Israel. He instituted Baptism as a visible means of entrance into His Church, and the Holy Communion as the common meal of its members. So, too, throughout the New Testament the Church appears as a visible society in the world. S. Paul puts on a level 'the Jews', 'the Greeks' and 'the Church of God' as definite bodies of men (1 Cor 10[32]). He can speak of the distinction between 'those within' and 'those without' (1 Cor 5[12–13], cp. 7[12ff. and 39] and 14[23]) as something perfectly familiar. 'The Church' as used in the New Testament means sometimes the whole Christian society (e.g. 1 Cor 12[28], Eph 1[22], 5[23] ff.). Sometimes it is used for the body of Christians in a particular place which represented the Church of Christ, just as, e.g. the Roman citizens in a place represented the Roman Empire, e.g. Acts 8[1], 1 Thess 1[1]. It is even used of particular congregations of Christians worshipping together in someone's house (Rom 16[5], 1 Cor 16[19], Philem[2], Col 4[15]). But the individual Christian is always addressed as being a member primarily not of any local Church but of the one universal Church (Col

---

[1] See McNeile, who, however, regards the passage as a later addition.

3^{15}). We do not find a number of independent preachers converting men to Christianity and then those men forming themselves into a local Church or community. Rather they are made members of the one Church, and this Church necessarily has its local branches. These local Churches stand out like islands in an ocean of heathenism. But they are all parts of one universal Church (cp. Acts 20^{28}. The 'bishops' are appointed to feed not the Church of Ephesus but the Church of God.)

The Church of the New Testament is then a society (*coetus fidelium*).

(*a*) On the one hand she existed in the world as a visible society. Like other societies she had a form of admission; she had officers with recognized authority to execute certain functions relating to her corporate life; her members were subject to certain obligations and possessed certain privileges. The story of her origin and growth could be traced by human observation and recorded as part of human history. Even an unbeliever could perceive her existence as a society with a definite membership and a nascent institutional life. There is no trace in the New Testament of the idea that the true Church consists of a number of elect individuals whose identity is known to God alone.

(*b*) But the Church believed that her nature and existence were based on invisible realities. She was not the result of the convergent purposes of a number of human wills. Her existence was due to the will and action of God. What then was the place of the Church in the divine purpose? Primitive Christians certainly believed themselves to be living in the 'last days'. The Lord's coming to bring in the new age was generally expected in the near future. Christians are those who wait for God's 'Son from heaven' and 'are guarded through faith unto a salvation ready to be revealed in the last time'.[1] This expectancy of the Church, its faith and hope that it would inherit the blessings of the new creation in a new heaven and earth in which God's Kingdom had finally destroyed sin, death, and the powers of evil, was bound up with the belief that it was the new Israel, the final heir of all the promises of God. But the expectancy of the Church was quite different from that of the Jews who still hoped for the Messianic Age. For Christians the Messiah had not only come but had performed a work which meant that the new age had already dawned. His resurrection and the outpouring of the Spirit were events which by their very nature belonged to the End; what happened after them could be no more than the unfolding of all the consequences. In His risen humanity the conquest of sin and death was complete, and therefore in Him the Kingdom of God was fully manifested. But for two facts it might have been theoretically possible for those who knew of the resurrection of Christ to spread the news of the event and call upon individuals to wait with repentance

---

[1] Cp. 1 Thess 1^{10}, 1 Pet 1^5.

and trust for His return, when they would be gathered into God's new Israel and enjoy with the Messiah the blessings of the new world and the resurrection life. The first fact was that the Lord chose His Twelve Apostles during His ministry, commissioned them both before and after His resurrection as men who were sent by Him, and at the Last Supper incorporated them into the New Covenant in His sacrificed humanity. This meant that a visible Israel was to enter here and now on the benefits of His sacrifice. The other fact was that the Holy Spirit came and manifested the active presence of the risen Christ in those who accepted the Gospel. They shared in one Holy Spirit. Though unseen, the heavenly Lord was no absent exemplar of redemption, nor only its future minister. His salvation was a present reality. His coming in glory would crown and complete that which He was already doing in the common life of His faithful people. Moreover, the terms in which the New Testament understood our Lord's person and work all point to the existence of the Church as necessarily bound up with Him. If He is the Messiah, the anointed King, the Lord, the final Priest and Sacrifice, the Shepherd, the Bridegroom, the new Adam,[1] then there must be corresponding to Him a people, an *ecclesia*, a flock, a bride, and a new race, created through Him and for Him as the divinely willed end of His coming. He had realized all the Old Testament types and images and they carried with them a Church as part of that fulfilment.[2]

S. Paul described Christ and His people as one body (1 Cor 12, Rom 12) or Christ as the Head and His people as His body (Col 1, Eph 1).[3] This description does not stand alone, for it has parallels in the image of the Vine and the branches (Jn 15) and that of the bride (Eph 5, Rev 21[2], 22[17]). But it enables S. Paul to bring out points of importance with peculiar force. The intimacy of the relation between Christ and His Church could not be more forcibly expressed than by calling it His body. Again the description links the Church with Christ's own concrete historical life. It is the fulfilment of His own humanity and it is sustained in its true nature by the communion of His body in the Eucharist.[4] The diversity of functions and spiritual gifts in His people corresponds to the diversity of functions in a living organism. The Church as the body is a real community of persons in which divine gifts are variously bestowed for the benefit of the whole. The indispensable gift for each and all is *agape*.[5]

---

[1] The list could be extended. For the corporate reference of the title 'Son of Man' compare Dan 7 and the exposition in A. M. Farrer, *A Study in S. Mark*.

[2] Cp. essays ii, iii and vi in *The Root of the Vine* (essays in Biblical Theology by Swedish scholars).

[3] Cp. J. A. T. Robinson, *The Body* (S.C.M. Press).

[4] In his essay in *Mysterium Christi* Dr Rawlinson maintains that the description of the Church as the Body of Christ is derived from the Eucharist. Note that S. Paul does not describe the Church as 'a body of Christians' (which would have been an ordinary use of current language) but as '*the* Body of *Christ*'.

[5] Chapter xiii of 1 Cor must be read in close connexion with chapter xii.

But to do justice to the New Testament conception of the Church we must interpret the analogy of the body rightly. It has its own special application. For first, the heavenly Christ, His promises and His gifts can be perceived and received only through faith. The Church and its members are what they are by the 'hearing of faith', which is a door for the entry of the Spirit. Every act of the Church and its members pre-supposes their humble acceptance of the re-deeming acts of God for man in Christ. The Body of Christ has no life which works with the automatic and unconscious co-operation of the parts of a healthy physical organism. Secondly, Christ's humanity has its present glory by having suffered death. As S. Paul expounds baptism, a man who becomes a member of Christ's living body must first undergo death with Him. This death having happened once sacramentally is a constant state. It must be perpetually actualized in 'putting to death the deeds of the body', in the self-abnegation which is one aspect of *agape*, and in the conflict and suffering which arise from any presence of Christ in a sinful world. So the life of the heavenly Christ in His body is the power to die with Him in order to be in Him.

The Church, therefore, does not yet possess her true life as she will possess it in the age to come. Then conflict and death in all its forms will be overcome, the resurrection bodies of her members will be the perfect instruments of the Spirit, and the fellowship of her members in Christ and with one another will be secure and complete. Now the Spirit is present as a first instalment or pledge of what is to come. His presence is real; His creative work is wrought out in human lives and in an observable human fellowship, so that even the world can know the disciples of Christ (Jn 13[35]) and recognize the presence of the Spirit's gift of *agape*. But the Spirit's victories in the Church and in Christian lives must still be won by conflict and 'dying', and the Church 'walks by faith and not by sight'.

(c) Such according to the New Testament are the divine and invis-ible realities which create the Church and make it a divine-human fellowship existing in history. Because it exists in history it must, as a society of human persons, have certain institutional characteristics to preserve and express its common life. But because this common life is divine-human, its essential and characteristic institutions cannot be its own creation as a human society. First, therefore, the object of its faith is God's gift, namely Jesus Christ and His work. The sub-stance of this faith and its meaning must be continually renewed and handed on by the Church in its preaching and teaching, and even-tually also in its Scriptures and creeds. Secondly, it received from Christ two sacramental rites, baptism and the eucharist, to be acts of the society but also to be Christ's acts in it. The divine-human character of the Church is nowhere more clearly seen than in the sacraments. Thirdly, the apostles were appointed and sent by Christ, as He was sent by the Father, to gather His people and to shepherd and serve them. The fact that the Church is the communion or common life in the Holy Spirit in no way contradicts or conflicts with these institutional marks of its corporate life. For the Spirit's work is not that of free and boundless inspiration; His work is that proper to the Body of Christ; He comes to take the things of Christ and show them to the Church, and the things of Christ are given in a definite historical revelation which is the object and sphere of the Spirit's work.[1] The institutions of the Church are marked out by Christ as the organs through which His Spirit will work in the whole body.

§ 2. In its brief statement on the visible Church the Article refers to the institutional characteristics which, as we have seen, are determining in the corporate life of the Church according to the New Testament, namely, the preservation and teaching of the faith contained in the 'pure Word of God', the due administration of the sacraments according to Christ's ordinance, and all things that are necessary to that administration.[2] In the last phrase we must see a reference to the ministry. For the full interpretation of the Article there must be taken into account what is said in other Articles on the Church, the sacraments and the ministry, as well as the contents of the Book of Common Prayer and the Ordinal. For our present purpose the description of the Church in the Nicene Creed as 'One, Holy, Catholic, and Apostolic', the only oecumenical statement on the subject, will serve to call attention to further important points.

These four 'notes' are intimately connected with one another and depend upon the truth that the Church is the Body of Christ. In considering them we must remember that the Church as it exists at any particular moment on earth is only a part of the total reality. The Communion of Saints includes the body which is 'militant here in earth' and also the faithful dead who are at rest. The individual enters into the common life of this total body and is in Christ with all its members living and departed. Moreover, the true character of the Church as she now exists on earth cannot be understood apart from what she will be according to the divine redemptive purpose. Her members are 'sealed unto the day of redemption', and are nourished here in the eternal life which they will inherit at the last day. To understand the Church in the light of her final destiny in the glory of the Kingdom no doubt implies the hope that in the course of her earthly history she will continually grow in the 'fulness of Christ'. But it also means that we must see her now with all her imperfections as the company of those whom Christ is preparing for 'the freedom of the glory of the sons of God'. The point may be put

---

[1] Cp. 1 Jn 4².
[2] For an illuminating comment on the Article see C. H. Smyth in *The Parish Communion*, p. 293.

in another way. It is quite incorrect to say that the Church *is* the Kingdom of God. The divine sovereignty, as Scripture makes clear, will be fully manifested only when all His enemies have been put under Christ's feet in a new heaven and earth, and that is not yet actual. But in Christ's own ascended humanity the Kingdom is actual, for He is the new creation in which sin and death have already been overcome. The Church, His body, participates in this new creation in the limited manner which is possible in a world still subject to sin and death. We partake of Christ both by way of gift and by way of promise. The Kingdom is manifested in the Church but not yet as it is in its fulness in the ascended Christ. We shall not be made like Him until 'we see Him as He is'. Nevertheless, to the Church the promises are made. It is the Father's good pleasure to give the Kingdom to this flock. We must not, therefore, separate the Church as she is from the Church as she is to be. She has the promise that she will finally inherit the new world and in the light of that divine appointment she strives to enter more fully on that newness of life which she already possesses in the Spirit.

(*a*) What then is the unity of the Church in which we believe? That the Church has a unity follows from its being in Christ, for He cannot be divided. Yet strictly speaking every sin of every member of the Church is a breach of spiritual unity in Christ. The New Testament was well aware of this. In extreme cases the sinning member was excluded lest his sin should damage the whole body. 'The unity of the faith and of the knowledge of the Son of God' was still in some respects an object of corporate attainment, however truly the one body already existed (Eph 4¹⁻¹³). But that did not lead the Apostolic Church to despise the unity of a disciplined society. It took an instinctive concern in maintaining relations of visible fellowship in one society between the scattered local communities of which its totality was composed.[1] The word *koinonia*, 'communion', is used in the New Testament both of the visible community of persons and of the common participation in the invisible realities by which that community is sustained. In the Church of the early centuries the organization of its outward life grew and was elaborated to express and preserve unity. Schisms were frequent. Some of them were healed after a comparatively short duration without the setting up of any rival organization. Others, like the Donatist schism, produced a rival Church in the same area and led to mutual declarations that the other body was not a true part of the Church at all. In spite of these schisms, it was possible in the creative period of the patristic age to identify the Catholic Church with the great majority of Christians in communion with one another, and to regard schismatic bodies as

[1] Thus S. Paul took care to obtain the agreement of the Jerusalem apostles to his mission to the Gentiles, and was anxious that the Christians of Macedonia and Achaea should contribute to the relief of 'the poor among the saints that are at Jerusalem'. (Gal 2¹⁻¹⁰, Rom 15²⁶, 1 Cor 16¹⁻⁴, 2 Cor 8 and 9).

minorities who by the fact of their separation from the main body were outside the unity of the Church. Thus S. Augustine could say that concerning the true nature of the Donatist schism *securus judicat orbis terrarum*, 'the judgment of the whole (Christian) world can be confident'. But the patristic Church was aware too that Christian unity was in its deepest sense derived from the unity of Christ with His Church. The Christian entered the Church by a sacramental rite which incorporated him into Christ and bestowed the gifts of forgiveness and regeneration in response to a confession of the common faith, and in sacramental communion the unity of Christians with one another was not only expressed in a corporate ritual act such as any society might perform, but it was *given* by the common participation in the sacrament of Christ's body. As the New Testament clearly shows, this invisible life of the Church in her divine Lord has its proper counterpart in the outward community of all its members in one visible organization. And if the sacraments are corporate acts it must be true that outward unity and inward life cannot but be closely related. Yet S. Augustine found himself maintaining that the Donatists had valid sacraments and yet were not part of the true Church, and a century earlier there had been general recognition of the validity of the baptism of at least some heretics and schismatics. In some sense, therefore, it was possible to be in Christ and yet outside the one visible community of the Church. The relation between the two aspects of unity, that of outward fellowship and organization and that of sacramental incorporation into the one divine Lord, already presented a problem. The great schism which eventually took place between East and West has hardened in the course of nine centuries. The Latin Church regards Eastern orthodox Christians as outside the unity of the Church, but admits the validity of their sacramental life. In the West the events of the Reformation increased confusion, and the tendency of Protestant Christianity to produce new sub-divisions is apparently not yet exhausted in some parts of the world. In these circumstances it is unlikely that we shall be able to give any perfectly simple account of our belief in *one* Church.

(i) The Roman Church nevertheless offers a simple account. It regards visible oneness as essential to the nature of the Church. Not only ought not this unity to be broken; it cannot be broken. The Pope is the Vicar of Christ on earth and from this it follows that the true Church must consist only of those Christians in full communion with him. If only a handful remained faithful to him they would be the true Church and its unity would remain unimpaired. The papal theory will always be attractive to many minds. It offers a clear and simple account of unity, and can appeal to such powerful considerations as the probability that our Lord made some definite provision to guard against division in His body. But the claims of the papacy as they have developed in mediaeval and modern times cannot be substantiated from the evidence of Scripture and primitive tradition. Universal jurisdiction over the Church, and the infallible judgment on faith and morals which has eventually been seen as its natural corollary, were not functions which any individual professed to exercise in the Church of the New Testament or for many centuries afterwards. Only the clearest evidence of our Lord's will could justify such a tremendous claim.[1] These claims are sometimes supported by *a priori* arguments. The Church, it is said, being a visible community of men must have a visible human head. Whatever superficial appeal to logic this argument may possess, it ignores the consideration that our Lord Himself is the Head of the Church in virtue of His glorified humanity. Moreover, the whole body consists not only of the Church militant here in earth, but also of the faithful who are at rest. 'We as little expect to find part of a body possessing a head as we anticipate that a whole body will be without one.'[2] The claim for the papacy must ultimately rest, as Roman Catholics would generally acknowledge, on historical evidence of divine appointment. Nor can we accept the argument that our Lord cannot have allowed the visible unity of His Church to be broken. It is at least possible that some breaches of unity should be regarded as having the nature of a divine judgment on the sins and shortcomings of the Church in a particular age, though if so it is clearly our duty to see that the failures and errors which have caused division are overcome and to work for the restoration of visible unity. Thus the divine judgment will fulfil its purpose by bringing Christians to repent of their sins and errors and to think more deeply of the nature of their unity in Christ. We are bound to say that the papal dominion over the Western Church in the middle ages, exercised as it was through an increasing legalization of the whole system of Church life, was precisely one of the errors, though not the only one, which brought about division.

(ii) At the opposite extreme stands a view which has been characteristic of many Protestant nonconformists. They hold that the one thing that matters is for a man to have his heart right with God and have faith in Christ as his Saviour. He thus belongs to 'the true Church', 'the invisible Church of all true believers'.[3] It is no doubt desirable for Christians to associate themselves into societies or churches for practical purposes. But it is of comparatively little importance to which of these bodies a man belongs. He may belong to any or none or change his Church as often as he changes his coat. His general principle of choice is his liking for a preacher or his wish to go where he gets most good. On this view outward unity is of little or no importance. Multiplication of sects may be regarded as a sign

[1] For a review of the evidence, see pp. 342 ff.

[2] Darwell Stone, *The Christian Church*, p. 198, where these points are further developed.

[3] Cp. Hobhouse, *Bampton Lectures*, p. 388.

of vigorous life. All true believers in Christ are fundamentally at one: the essential point is personal faith and self-consecration. Such a view is not Scriptural. The theory of an 'invisible' Church contains the truth that God alone knows who are His, and that His true servants may be found in all Christian bodies and indeed outside them. But the word 'church' has in Scripture a definite meaning. As we have seen, it denotes a visible body. We have no right to take and use it in a quite different sense. Further, it inverts the true relation of the Church to the individual believer. The teaching of the New Testament on this point may be expressed in the words of Archbishop Frederick Temple: 'Men talk sometimes as if a Church could be constituted simply by Christians coming together and uniting themselves into one body for the purpose. Men speak as if Christians came first and the Church after: as if the origin of the Church was in the wills of the individual Christians who composed it. But on the contrary, throughout the teaching of the Apostles, we see that it is the Church that comes first and the members of it afterwards. Men were not brought to Christ and then determined that they would live in a community. Men were not brought to Christ to believe in Him and His Cross and to recognize the duty of worshipping the Heavenly Father in His name, and then decided that it would be a great help to their religion that they should join one another in that worship and should be united in the bond of fellowship for that purpose. In the New Testament on the contrary the Kingdom of Heaven is already in existence and men are invited into it. . . . Everywhere men are called in: they do not come in and make the Church by coming.'[1]

Again, on this view of the Church, just as on the Roman view, its unity cannot be destroyed. You cannot divide an invisible body. Yet S. Paul speaks of it as divided (1 Cor 1^{10}, Rom 16^{17}, cp. 1 Jn 2^{19}, Jude ^{19}). For one great value of the unity of the Church is that it is a school for Christian character. Fellowship in the Church is always regarded as a moral discipline. The effort to live and grow in unity calls for humility and self-suppression. Christians are bidden to live not as isolated individuals but as members of one body (cp. Phil 2^1 ff.). If a Christian who is offended or finds his fellow-Christians distasteful can immediately go off and start a Church of his own, the healthful discipline of a common life is evaded. We see how strenuously the Apostles and especially S. Paul contended for the outward unity of the Church. The modern idea of separate free 'Churches' ministers to the desires of our fallen human nature by providing a means of escape from the need of self-control. Lastly, the Church exists to carry on the work of Christ in the world, and that work is hindered by open divisions among Christians. Our Lord's will is that Christians should be manifestly one, so that the world may believe in His divine mission (Jn 17^{20-23}).

[1] Sermon preached at the consecration of Truro Cathedral.

To complete this account of Protestant views we must, however, add that in the last half-century the theological ideas of many leading thinkers in Continental and British Protestantism have undergone a notable change on the subject of the Church. This is due to a number of convergent causes which we shall notice in discussing reunion. But among them must be mentioned here the scientific study of the New Testament, which has reaffirmed from many different points of view that the Church was, and is, an essential element in the whole Gospel. At the same time there has been a renewed study of the classical theologies of the Reformation. Calvin, and to a lesser degree Luther, accepted the idea of the necessity for a visible organized Church and and of the duty of the individual Christian to belong to it. The English Nonconformists of the seventeenth century were bodies of Christians with a developed corporate life and strict discipline. It is therefore realized by leading Protestant theologians of the present day that on their own scriptural principles and in loyalty to elements in their own history they must acknowledge that the Church belongs to the centre and not to the periphery of Christian faith. They are taking a leading part in the Ecumenical Movement and other discussions concerning Christian unity. Serious theological discussion about unity is only possible among those for whom the visible Church is a serious concern. The movement of thought about the Church we have just described is therefore an important and necessary stage in any advance towards reunion. But difficult problems remain about the nature of the unity which ought to be achieved. And it is perhaps a significant fact that in spite of their friendly relations with one another and the existence of a large area of common principle and practice, the Free Churches in England appear still to be content to remain as separately organized bodies.

(iii) It has never occurred to the Church of England, even after its vast extension into the Anglican Communion, to claim to be the whole Church of Christ. At the Reformation she claimed no more than to be a local and national part of the Church, reforming herself in accordance with Scripture and primitive tradition. The English Reformation involved the rejection of the papal jurisdiction and ultimately schism with all that part of the Church which remained obedient to the Pope. But in spite of the definite condemnation of some Roman doctrines by the Articles and by the implications of her practice, the Church of England has never denied that the Roman Church is part of the Catholic Church.[1] By this fact alone, even if no others were concerned, we should be committed to the view that the visible Church can be divided and the resultant parts can still remain within the Church. As it is now often expressed, there can be 'internal

---

[1] The evidence is fully stated in Gibson, *The Thirty-Nine Articles*, pp. 506 ff. The fact that Roman priests who enter the Church of England are accepted as priests and are not re-ordained is in itself conclusive. Article XIX states the fact of error and fallibility. Its authors did not lack language to say more if they had intended to do so.

schism' *i.e.*, the kind of schism which does not necessarily involve the consequence that the true Church must be identified with one or other of the parties to the schism to the exclusion of the other. During and after the sixteenth century, in England and elsewhere, further divisions have taken place among Western Christians, and in any general view of Christendom the Eastern Church has remained an important fact to be taken into account. In this complicated situation it becomes a matter of considerable delicacy to define the attitude of the Church of England towards the various forms of division. It is unlikely that any single account will do full justice to all the known facts or be acceptable to all anglicans who think about the subject. The Church of England is not in the habit of making explicit and detailed pronouncements on such matters until a situation arises in which a decision is unavoidable. Nevertheless some facts and some of her principles are reasonably clear.

The claim of the English Church after, as before, the Reformation to be the Catholic Church in this land has naturally caused her to take a serious view of schisms at home. From the first movement of reform in the reign of Henry VIII some individuals and groups in England remained loyal to the Pope. Their break with the Church of England did not become formal and official until the Pope in 1570 excommunicated Queen Elizabeth and forbade them to attend the worship of the English Church. From that time onwards Roman Catholics in England have been in schism with us, and until 1829 suffered considerable civil disabilities as a result. In 1850 the present Roman episcopate in England was established by Pius IX, not without strong protests from the Church of England, and the fact of schism thus received expression in a rival hierarchy. To Roman Catholics in England we still have to address the claim that the English Church is the historic Church of the nation. In the reign of Henry VIII it was reformed, or rather its reformation was begun and continued until the final settlement in 1660. Reformation was no new thing. The Church had been reformed before and doubtless will be reformed again. No new body was created by Act of Parliament or in any other way. No date can be pointed out when the old Church was dissolved and a new Church formed to take its place. We do not claim that the Reformation was perfect, but some drastic change was certainly needed. The Roman Church itself was reformed very soon after by the Council of Trent. All that we claim is that we had the right to reform ourselves without forfeiting our identity. The Church of England, as reformed, asks of its members belief in nothing that cannot be proved from Scripture and therefore has not belonged to the Christian faith from the earliest days. It has preserved the historic Creeds as a key to the interpretation of Scripture. It has maintained the historic ministry. Thus the *pure Word of God is preached* among us and *the Sacraments duly administered*. This is our claim to faithful continuity with the whole Catholic Church of the past. We admit many imperfections, but no departure from any part of the faith or any of the means of grace which the Church has always believed to be essential to her character as the Body of Christ. Bitterness, hatred and ignorance have disfigured our inevitable controversy with Rome in the past. It is at least an advance towards Christian unity that to-day these unpleasant features are much less in evidence. Impartial study of history does not permit us to take unlimited pride in the persons and policies involved in the Reformation movement. In modern times, when the attempts of states to bring Churches into subjection for their own political purposes have caused so much suffering and led to such heroic resistances, we are better able to enter with some sympathy into the feelings of those Roman Catholics who in the sixteenth century would not accept the idea of a national Church with a Tudor sovereign as its supreme Governor. Again we recognize that the missionary zeal of the Roman Church is by itself a testimony to her spiritual vitality. But if our controversy with Roman Catholics has lost much of its old ignorance and prejudice, union with them remains at present impossible. We cannot join them without professing our belief in certain doctrines which certainly formed no part of primitive Christianity. Before a man is admitted into the Roman Church he has to profess his belief in the supremacy of the Pope and to repudiate all Christian bodies not in communion with him. Further, three new doctrines have in recent years been solemnly proclaimed to be dogmas divinely revealed and therefore essential to true Christian faith, namely, in 1854 the immaculate conception of the Blessed Virgin Mary, in 1870 the infallibility of the Pope, and in 1950 the assumption of the Blessed Virgin Mary. Unity is of great importance, but the importance of truth is supreme. On the other hand, Roman Catholics cannot worship with us because the whole status of the Church of England rests upon the repudiation of papal jurisdiction which is the keystone of their position. If the Roman view of the Pope is right their position is perfectly logical.

Conformity to the Church of England was never complete even among those English Christians who rejected the Pope. Those who were thorough-going Calvinists could not be content with the doctrine, worship, and discipline of the Church of England. In the course of the sixteenth and seventeenth centuries they emerged as organized bodies separated from the Church. They rejected episcopacy and set up new ministries of their own, with an 'independent' form of Church order in which power rested with the local congregation. The present Baptist and Congregational Unions are the heirs of these movements. In the eighteenth century the Methodists began as a group of religious societies within the Church. John Wesley himself was on many points of doctrine a 'high churchman'. His conduct was inconsistent. On the one hand he repeatedly asserted his wish that his followers should not separate from the Church, and he died an English churchman. On the other hand, at the close of his life, he claimed that bishop and priest were in origin the same order and that as a priest he had authority to ordain others and he actually did so. From this has sprung the present Methodist ministry. More and more the religious life of the Methodists found its centre not in the Church but in their own societies. When the strong personality of John Wesley was removed, there was no bond strong enough to stay the separation.

There were anglican divines in the seventeenth century who with slight reservations regarded the Protestant Churches of the continent as parts of the true Church in spite of their lack of bishops, but they were not able to take the same favourable view of the Protestant Nonconformists at home. The Canons of 1604 speak of them roundly as schismatics, who set up 'their pretended Church' and 'separate themselves from the Communion of Saints as it is approved by the Apostles' Rules, in the Church of England.'[1] In the nineteenth century the considerable growth of the Nonconformist Churches brought into prominence the social and political factors which have from the first played a part in these divisions. To-day these factors are much less powerful and have largely ceased to operate as real causes of division because such existence as they still have is allowed for and discounted. Much misunderstanding and irrelevant opposition has thus been removed. But the divisions remain.

As regards individual Nonconformists we cannot lightly accuse them of being personally guilty of the sin of schism. If they have been duly baptized they are members of the Catholic Church and their separation from the Church is usually due to no fault of their own. They were brought up in some separated body: they have found in it the centre and support of their religion. It has been a real spiritual home, the scene to them of their deepest spiritual experience. They cannot be expected to leave it for the Church, about which they know very little and whose spiritual superiority is by no means overwhelmingly apparent. Others again have left the Church, not because they possess a schismatical spirit or are hostile to the real mind of the Church, but because that particular part of the Church to which they have belonged has repelled them by its spiritual deadness and want of sympathy, or because its representatives have obscured the presence of Christ by the slovenliness or wickedness of their lives. Again, in different places and at different times vital truths of the Christian faith have become obscured and neglected, whether it be the need of personal conversion, or the spiritual independence of the Church or the right place of the sacraments. Those who have awakened to the

[1] Canons 9 and 10.

value of such truths and whose desire to live up to them has been treated with coldness, have naturally turned to another body in whose life such truths appeared to find better expression. Moreover, at some periods in its history members of the Church of England and their official representatives, under the influence of a deeply Erastian view of the relations of Church and State, have spoken and acted as though the existing social and political order was as immutable and divinely ordained as the Gospel itself. The Nonconformist Churches have stood consistently for the spiritual independence of the Church and for its right to judge all things in the light of the truth committed to it. If our divisions are to be overcome we shall have to admit that much in our own history has contributed to their existence.

(iv) The question of a restoration of unity between the Church of England and Protestant Nonconformists at home has, however, now become part of a much larger question. The Free Churches of England have spread widely over the world as a result of their missionary zeal. Moreover, the last half-century has witnessed an increasing desire among Christians everywhere to take steps to restore broken unity. This desire has arisen from a number of converging causes and motives. Among them the most obvious are the inconvenience and scandal of our divisions as they have become apparent in the mission field, and the need for united Christian action in an increasingly godless society. But with these contemporary problems of the work of the Church has come also the widespread recovery of the idea of the Church as an essential part of the Gospel and as a community which, by its very nature and place in the divine purpose, ought to be visibly one. It is impossible to trace here the outline of events and movements which have resulted from this new desire for unity.[1] Some local reunions have already taken place. But the most considerable result has been the series of conferences and discussions which constitute the Ecumenical Movement, with the formation of the World Council of Churches. The Roman Church has taken no part in these conferences, but all the principal non-Roman communions, including the Eastern Orthodox Church, have been represented.

We cannot fail to recognize that this movement, however imperfectly, bears witness to a repentance for the sin of division and to a desire to move towards unity which spring from the deepest Christian motives. The most hopeful feature about it is that it has discovered how difficult the problems are. It has been obliged to engage in serious theological discussion. Any approach to unity raises the whole question of the nature of the Church. In the present phase of the Ecumenical Movement the participants have found themselves forced to consider more deeply the meaning of their own traditions,

---

[1] See G. K. A. Bell, *Documents on Christian Unity* (three volumes), and the Reports of the Lambeth Conferences of 1920, 1930 and 1948.

and to see that their understanding of the Church is bound up in many respects with their whole understanding of the Gospel; it is not in its essential features a convenient or accidental piece of organization attached to their fundamental faith. Though the Protestant Churches represented have much in common, they differ from one another in significant points of emphasis. But the most serious line of division is still that between 'catholic' and 'protestant' views of the nature of the Church. The continuity of historical and sacramental life, which to the 'catholic' is embodied in the continuity of the episcopate and is one important aspect of the continual abiding of the Church in Christ, is unintelligible to the 'protestant', who finds continuity in the faithful acceptance and preaching of God's Word and believes that a group or body of Christians which is faithful in this way may legitimately set up its own form of ministry.[1] For this and other reasons there is no general agreement as to the shape of the visible unity towards which Christians should move. 'Organic unity' is by no means universally accepted as its proper description.

Through its Bishops assembled in successive Lambeth Conferences the Anglican Communion has made clear its desire and intention to take a full part in the work for unity.[2] The traditional order of ecclesiastical life with its emphasis on the sacraments and the threefold ministry, which we have inherited and maintained, makes it impossible for us to regard the visible unity of the Church as of secondary importance. We have consistently maintained that this unity will not be reached without the general acceptance, as its basis, of the Scriptures, the faith of the Nicene Creed, the sacraments of Baptism and Holy Communion, and the episcopate with its historic functions and continuity.[3] For the non-episcopal communions this anglican approach raises hard questions about the nature of the Church and the Ministry, not least the question of the status and authority of their own existing ministries and their own status as Churches. A minimizing view of the importance of episcopacy would no doubt make possible a large measure of immediate inter-communion, but such a step if taken would give rise to new divisions and also render our present divisions more easily tolerable than they ought to be. If episcopacy has the functions and significance which the whole Church attached to it from primitive times and which remained unquestioned until the sixteenth century,[4] some degree of negative judgment on those bodies of Christians which are non-episcopal

---

[1] For a review of the problems concerning the nature of the Church as they have emerged in these discussions, see the Report entitled *The Church* issued by the Faith and Order Commission of the World Council of Churches (S.C.M. Press, 1951).

[2] Cp. the Appeal for unity issued by the Lambeth Conference of 1920.

[3] Successive Lambeth Conferences since 1888 have maintained these principles which are sometimes known as 'the Lambeth Quadrilateral'. They were first stated in a declaration on unity issued by the General Convention of the Protestant Episcopal Church in the U.S.A. in 1886.

[4] See what is said on the Ministry of the Church below, pp. 322 ff.

seems inevitable. Their ministries, created at the time of their separation and continued in various ways, cannot be said to be one with the ministry of the whole Church of the past, derived from and perpetuating the ministry of the Apostles of the Incarnate Lord; their eucharists must lack the sure and fully corporate character which an episcopal ministry alone could give them. With this judgment, however, should go the recognition that wherever a body of baptized Christians possesses a corporate life of devotion and service, based on faith in the deity of our Lord and His redeeming work, they have a share in the life of the Body of Christ and its spiritual riches.

It may well be true that 'the edges' of the visible Church 'are blurred'[1] and will always remain so in this world. Nor can we afford to forget that the results of our divisions have affected us all and have in varying ways impaired our hold on the fulness of Christ's life and truth. Meanwhile the Church of England is bound to work with faith and repentance for the restoration of visible corporate unity. We hold that that common life will find its true and complete expression only when there is one faith, one baptism, one eucharist, and one ministry, as the way of corporate communion in one Lord.

(b) We also profess our belief that the Church is 'holy'. This mark of the Church too, is a gift, an achievement and a promise. Thus, in the New Testament, Christians are frequently described as ἅγιοι, 'holy', though their moral and spiritual perfection is far from complete. But S. Peter can exhort them to 'become holy in all manner of living' because 'He who called' them 'is holy', and S. Paul can speak of Christians knowing what are the 'riches' of the glory of His inheritance in the saints, i.e. the glory of the eternal future which is God's promise to all His sanctified people (1 Pet 1[15], Eph 1[18]). In the Old Testament the root idea of holiness is 'separation'. At first its sense was primarily ceremonial or physical; but it gradually acquired a spiritual meaning. That which was set apart for God must be free from blemish, in the first instance physical blemish, and later, as the sense of morality developed, moral blemish. So Israel is a holy nation separated from the other nations by God for His purpose (Ex 19[6], Lev 11[44] and 20[36], etc.), and therefore called to live up to this vocation. Our Lord is the 'Holy One of God' (Mk 1[24]) called and set apart to do the Father's will (Jn 10[36]). The language applied to the old Israel is applied to the Church as set apart in Christ (1 Pet 1[15–16], 2[5–9]). Christians are saints, ἅγιοι, as members of the new Israel. They have been sanctified by the washing of baptism; the Holy Spirit is at work in and among them; they partake of one spiritual meat and drink. In all these respects they are a holy people. But the actual

[1] The expression is taken from an article by a Roman Catholic writer in *Blackfriars*, September 1941, 'Membership of the Church' by V. White, O.P.

sanctification of the Church, like that of the individual Christian, is a slow process demanding continuous watchfulness and effort. At present the Church is incompletely responsive to the Divine will. But God sees her not only as she is but as she is to be. This does not mean that we are to acquiesce in her present imperfection. Though it is true that the Church is a refuge for the penitent and is God's home for those who wish to be good rather than are good, still, it is the Church's duty to exclude those who persist in wilful and deliberate sin and show no signs of penitence (cp. 1 Cor 5$^{1-8}$). Dr Gibson has shown that the Article includes such an exercise of discipline in the due administration of the Sacraments.[1] Conversely, though we must strive to forward the actual holiness of the Church, we must not make the Church's slowness of attainment an excuse for separating from her. In all ages there have been men who have desired to realize here and now the ideal of a Church consisting only of the actually holy. That was the aim of the Donatists and the Puritans. They left the Catholic Church because she contained good and bad Christians and joined other societies which were to consist only of the good. But the Puritan ideal has always failed in practice. Sooner or later the old inconsistencies reappear in the separated bodies and the logical result is further separation. Moreover, Puritanism is associated not altogether unfairly with hypocrisy and sanctimoniousness. Nothing could be further from the example of Christ, who chose as His disciples not the righteous but penitent sinners. It is through the Church that God's Holy Spirit sanctifies men. The Church's holiness to-day is but an earnest of the holiness that is to be hereafter. That final holiness of the Church is portrayed for us in Rev 21^{9}-22^{5} in the image of the holy city Jerusalem into which are gathered all the people of God and from which the glory of God's presence excludes all that is unclean.

(c) We believe in the Catholicity of the Church. In itself the term 'Catholic' simply means 'universal'. It is first applied to the Church in the letters of S. Ignatius, who contrasts the one universal Church with the many local bodies of which it is composed. Later on, as meaning the Church throughout the world, one in discipline and doctrine, it was used to mark the contrast with heretical bodies that were local, peculiar and isolated in their views. As such the word contains two main thoughts.[2]

(i) Since Christ is the one Saviour of the world, the Church is to include men of all classes and nations. The Gospel is to be preached

---

[1] Gibson, *Thirty-nine Articles*, p. 495.

[2] 'The Church is called Catholic because it extends throughout all the world, and because it teaches universally and completely all the doctrines which ought to come to the knowledge of men . . . , and because it brings into subjection to godliness all the race of mankind, governors and governed, learned and ignorant; and because it treats and heals every class of sins that are committed in soul and body, and possesses in itself every form of virtue which is named, both in deeds and in words and in every kind of spiritual gifts' (S. Cyril of Jerusalem, *Cat.* xviii, 23).

to the whole world (Mt 28[19], Acts 1[8]). Every man and people will find in Christ what they need. In Christ distinctions of race and position are abolished (Gal 3[28], Col 3[10-11]). Not only do all men need the Church, but the Church has need of them. Every race has its contribution to make towards the interpretation of Christ. Christ is being fulfilled in proportion as the nations bring in their gifts to the Christian Church (Eph 1[23], with Armitage Robinson's note, cp. Rev 21[24]). Though the Church is universal in idea and in purpose she is far from universal in fact. Whole races at present lie outside her. The Chinese and the Indian have hardly begun to make their contribution to its fulness—a contribution that may well be no less valuable than that already made by the Greek and the Roman. The Church's Catholicity has been retarded by her slackness in missionary endeavour. In the Church all nations are to be united in the fulness of a common life. The Catholic Church can be content with no purpose short of that.

(ii) The Church exists to teach the whole truth in its fulness and proportion. So Catholic teaching comes to be opposed to teaching that is defective or one-sided. The truly Catholic-minded man is one who rises above the limitations of his age or class or country or temperament. In his zeal for one aspect of the truth he does not ignore or deny another. A heretic, on the other hand, isolates and exaggerates·a truth to such a degree that it becomes almost untrue, and shuts his eyes to other parts of the truth. The popular antithesis of Catholic and Protestant is often misconceived. All true protest against error is based on a knowledge and love of truth. A Catholic love of truth is bound to protest against all error that limits or denies the truth. In a sinful world every man should wish to be at once both a Catholic and a Protestant. One of the worst effects of division in the Church is that each of the divided parts tends to emphasize its distinctive features over against those of the others and so in one way or another all tend to endanger the proportion of Catholic truth. The breaches of unity at the Reformation were the result of one-sided developments, that is, of a failure of Catholicity in the mediaeval Western Church, and these breaches in turn have given rise to other fragmentations or distortions of the truth, which in isolation have become more fixed and intractable. The desire for unity must be a desire for a renewed Catholicity, in which all partial truths and forms of Christian life are brought together into wholeness. In this task the providence of God has given the Church of England a special responsibility and opportunity. From the movement of protest at the Reformation she took certain insights forgotten or obscured in the mediaeval Church, and tried to integrate them with a form of life which was Catholic in the sense that it was inherited from the universal Church of the past. This work of integration in her own body is a perpetual task of the Church of England. Her successes and failures in the task may have significance for Christians at present divided from her.

The realization of the full Catholicity of the Church is therefore a goal that is set before us to be attained by prayer and effort. We need greater missionary zeal. We need greater earnestness and humility in searching for and welcoming new or forgotten truths. Only so will the Church be truly Catholic, and all nations will find in her Gospel that for which they are seeking.

(d) The Church is apostolic. Not only is she derived by historical descent from the twelve Apostles, but she exists to carry on the work for which they were sent forth. She represents Christ to the world. She is built upon the foundation of the Apostles (Eph 2^{19-20}, Mt 16^{18}, Rev 21^{14}), since they were, so to speak, the first stones laid in her building. Her faith is derived from their preaching (Jn 17^{20}). Every single Christian community was either founded by an Apostle or goes back to one so founded. The ministry of the Church hands down the commission given to the Apostles. Thus, so far as she is faithful to her mission, the Church is apostolic in her aim, her teaching and her ministry. She fails to be apostolic when she ceases to 'go and make disciples of all the nations'.†

THE CHURCH'S AUTHORITY IN DOCTRINE

ARTICLE XX

Of the Authority of the Church

The Church hath power to decree Rites or Ceremonies, and Authority in controversies of Faith: And yet it is not lawful for the Church to ordain any thing that is contrary to God's Word written, neither may it so expound one place of Scripture that it be repugnant to another. Wherefore, although the Church be a witness and a keeper of Holy Writ, yet, as it ought not to decree any thing against the same, so besides the same ought it not to enforce any thing to be believed for necessity of Salvation.

De Ecclesiae auctoritate

Habet Ecclesia ritus sive caeremonias statuendi jus, et in fidei controversiis auctoritatem; quamvis Ecclesiae non licet quicquam instituere, quod verbo Dei scripto adversetur, nec unum Scripturae locum sic exponere potest, ut alteri contradicat. Quare licet Ecclesia sit divinorum librorum testis et conservatrix, attamen ut adversus eos nihil decernere, ita praeter illos nihil credendum de necessitate salutis debet obtrudere.

Except for the opening clause (The Church . . . faith) this was taken from the 42 Articles. The opening clause first appears in the Latin edition of 1563 and was probably added by the authority of the Queen. It was ratified by Convocation in 1571, if not earlier, and so the whole Article possesses equal authority.

Its object is to define the authority of the Church against
  (i) Puritans who minimized it, in matters of ceremonial;
  (ii) Papists who exaggerated it, in matters of doctrine.

§ 1. Before we can discuss the nature and extent of the authority of the Church, we must form some idea of what we mean by 'authority'.[1] The ultimate ground of all human authority lies in the social nature of man. The laws of the State represent, in idea at least, the general welfare of the community. The individual submits to them even at his personal inconvenience, as representing the will of the society, whose life and benefits he shares. The same is true when we turn to smaller

---

[1] The idea of the Latin word 'auctoritas' from which 'authority' is derived, may best be rendered by 'weight'. A command or an opinion comes to us with more or less authority according to the 'weight', moral or intellectual, of those who issue it.

societies. Ideally the rules are framed in the interests of the whole society, to forward the carrying out of the purpose for which the society exists. As contrasted with the will of the individual member, they stand for the welfare and the wisdom of a wider whole. There should be no conflict between authority and freedom. The individual can only realize himself through social life. The true well-being of any society should include the well-being of each and all of its members.

When we turn to questions not of conduct and practice but of belief and knowledge, the same distinction holds good. All knowledge of what is true must be based on experience, my own or that of others. I know that a thing is true either because I have seen it for myself or because someone else, whom I can trust, has seen it and told me. That is to say, my knowledge may be either first hand or based on the authority of another. In this case clearly 'authority' represents an experience wider than my own, whether it be the experience of a single teacher or a body of experts or the community at large. The possibility of knowledge resting not on personal investigation but on authority depends upon the sharing of a common human nature. We assume that what is true, is true for all minds. These principles hold good when we consider the place of authority in matters of faith. The child accepts on the authority of his parents certain statements about God, our Lord, the Bible and so on. He says his prayers because he is told to do so. A child's religion must begin by being second-hand, based not on experience but on authority. As he grows, he begins to verify for himself what he has been taught. This verification is not only intellectual but moral and spiritual. He learns the reasons for the beliefs that he has accepted on authority. He studies Scripture and is taught the nature and value of the evidence contained in it. Side by side with this there should be a growth in the personal knowledge of our Lord. He comes to know that Jesus Christ is a Saviour, because he has proved Him to be so. He prays, no longer because he is told to, but because he has found the value and power of prayer. So, too, the orderly system of Christian doctrine awakens a response not only in the mind but in the heart and will. The great Christian truths shine largely by their own light. This progressive verification of the Christian faith by the individual is a very complex process. It must vary enormously both in thoroughness and extent according to the education and capacities and opportunities of the particular person. There will always remain large tracts of Christian truth that no one individual can fully explore for himself. For his belief about these he will necessarily be dependent on the authority of the Church. This authority, as we have seen, represents primarily the collective and corporate experience of all Christians, not only the living but the departed. In believing what the Church teaches, we are only acting as we act in all other spheres of practical life, artistic and intellectual. Everywhere the individual must start from the common stock of knowledge. He must largely be dependent upon his teachers. All through, his limitations and eccentricities need to be supplemented and corrected by the corporate mind of the community.

This conception of 'authority' does not in the least impair the unconditional authority that we feel to belong to a revelation made by God or to the teaching of our Lord. Since God is perfect Wisdom and perfect Truth, to refuse belief in any truth that He has revealed would be not only presumptuous but unreasonable. The real difficulty is to prove the genuineness and accuracy of what is claimed to be a revelation from God.[1] We believe Christ to have possessed a perfect insight into the things of God and to have expressed the truth that He saw, not only in His teaching but in His conduct. Since divine truth cannot change, His revelation cannot become out of date. At the same time we notice our Lord's use of authority. He did not enjoin belief in His teaching under severe penalties. Rather He left it to make its appeal to the conscience and reason of men, backing it by the example of a perfect human life. That is, He encouraged men to verify its truth from their own experience.

§ 2. We may now turn to the authority of the Church on questions of order and doctrine.

The distinction between the two is well drawn in Art. XX. '*The Church has power to decree* (ius statuendi) *Rites or Ceremonies and authority* (auctoritatem) *in controversies of faith.*'[2] That is to say, the Church's power in matters of 'rites and ceremonies' is legislative. She has power to decree new ones, to modify or abolish old ones and to enforce obedience upon her members. Her power in such matters is legislative, the power to make laws, as Parliament makes laws for all Englishmen. This power is limited only by Scripture. '*It is not lawful for the Church to ordain anything that is contrary to God's word written.*' That is to say, there is to be nothing in such rites or ceremonies that is forbidden by Scripture or expressive of teaching that is contrary to Scripture. We might give as instance the use of some substance other than water in Baptism or the introduction of the worship of Angels into public services. The claim here made for the Church is only the claim that any society would make for itself, to manage its own affairs, so far as is consistent with its own first principles. This right is implied in the teaching of Christ. 'Whatsoever

---

[1] Cp. Salmon, *The Infallibility of the Church* (1952 edition), p. 92. Speaking of the claim of the Roman Church to be the medium of new revelations which it is treason to God not to accept, he writes: 'Should I account it a compliment if any one told me that he would not only believe anything I said but anything that anyone said I said?'

[2] It is assumed that 'the Church' spoken of in this Article is the whole Body, the Church universal. The problems raised by the divisions of the Church and by the existence of national churches are dealt with later. The general principles that govern the life and action of the Church are stated first. The application of them to present conditions can only be made when they have already been stated.

ye bind on earth, shall be bound in heaven, and whatsoever ye loose on earth shall be loosed in heaven' (Mt 18[18], cp. Mt 16[19]). To 'bind' and to 'loose' meant in current Jewish speech to 'declare forbidden' and to 'declare allowed'. Christ was only bestowing upon the new Israel the same authority that He recognized in the old. 'The Scribes and Pharisees sit on Moses' seat: all things therefore whatsoever they bid you, these do and observe' (Mt 23[2-3]). We find the Church putting this power into practice. S. Paul in 1 Cor gives quite definite regulations for the conduct of divine worship. Men are to pray and prophesy with their heads uncovered, women with their heads covered (11[4-5]). There are to be rules about speaking with tongues and prophesying (14[26] ff.) and the conduct of women (14[34], cp. 1 Tim 2[12]). Since we possess bodies as well as souls, our worship is bound to clothe itself in at least a minimum of outward form. Common worship, if it is to be orderly, needs some regulation, whether this be by definite rules or by the growth of recognized custom. The aim is, 'Let all things be done decently and in order' (1 Cor 14[40]). Rites and ceremonies at their best and highest are the expression of reverence and devotion in the presence of God.[1] Modern psychology tells us that the attitude of our bodies has a far greater influence on the vigour and attention of our minds and the concentration of our wills than might be supposed. The danger in the case both of churches and individuals is that the outward acts in which devotion was embodied in times of special fervour and spiritual zeal may survive as a hollow form when the spirit of devotion has declined, and so may become a hindrance rather than a help to true and spiritual worship, a substitute for, rather than a realization of heartfelt service. But as members of a society, in questions of public worship we are bound to yield obedience to the common rule. If we dislike a custom or a ceremony we may agitate in all lawful ways for its alteration, but till it is altered it is our duty to submit for the sake of unity. Such submission is a part of the self-subordination that unity involves. This power of the Church is, as we have seen, limited by Scripture, and so long as the Church is governed by the Spirit of Christ, she will use it with all due consideration for tender consciences and for the manifold varieties of human nature. The Puritans demanded that the Church should enforce no rite or ceremony,[2] however harmless in itself, unless it received positive support from Scripture. They objected to, e.g. god-parents or the ring in marriage, as not being commanded in the Bible. The Article is aimed at them. Their objection rested on a misapprehension of the purpose of

[1] Cp. Moberly, *Ministerial Priesthood*, pp. 54–55.

[2] It is worth noting that 'a Rite is a service, a Ceremony is any action accompanying it, either necessary or subsidiary to it. This distinction was obscured in the sixteenth century and the two terms were constantly used as synonymous: e.g. in the Acts of Uniformity, or title page of the Prayer Book. . . . The confusion of language is still a common one, and cannot be defended.' Proctor and Frere, *History of the Book of Common Prayer*, p. 17.

Scripture, which was given not to be a handbook of ceremonial but an instructor in moral and spiritual truth. They took a purely individualistic view of the Christian life. If the Church is faithful to Scripture, she may be trusted under the guidance of the Holy Spirit to work out for herself in each age that system of common worship which is best able to express her devotion and her obedience, and she can claim from her members their loyal adherence to it. S. Paul's final rebuke to the discontented members of the Church of Corinth is 'If any man seemeth to be contentious, we have no such custom, neither the Churches of God' (1 Cor 11[16]).

§ 3. In matters of faith the case is different. The Church exists to propagate certain beliefs. As we have seen, all that she teaches is centred in Christ, and her message is sufficiently set forth in Scripture. Hence, in all her teaching she must be faithful to the message that she was founded to proclaim. Her primary function is that of *witness*. She is to bear witness before the world to the truth. Christianity claims to be the absolute religion. Christ is Himself the Way, the Truth, and the Life. In Him God's revelation is final and complete. Hence, the Church's duty is to 'guard the deposit' (1 Tim 6[20]). Her members are to 'contend earnestly for the faith which was once for all delivered unto the saints' (Jude [3], cp. 2 Jn [2]). Her aim is to protect her beliefs from diminution or from accretion (cp. 2 Jn [9]). In any merely human system of truth such changes are necessary and beneficial. Obsolete ideas are discarded: new ideas are incorporated in the light of fresh discoveries. But no part of the divine revelation can ever become out of date, nor does it need to be supplemented from outside. Hence the place assigned to Scripture. '*Although the Church be a witness and keeper of Holy Writ: yet ... besides the same ought it not to enforce anything to be believed for necessity of salvation.*' As keeper of holy writ, she is responsible for preserving her sacred writings entire and free from contamination, and for handing them on to future generations. As witness, she cannot alter or add to the truth: she is the servant and not the mistress of her message.

(*a*) But controversy forced upon the Church a new function. She was called on to play the part not only of witness but of judge. She had to decide between conflicting interpretations of her message and to say no to false speculations. We saw that Article VI left open the important question, who was to decide in case of dispute what Scripture does teach on any given subject. Art. XX supplies the answer. '*The Church hath ... authority in controversies of faith.*' This authority is an extension of her function of witness. It is judicial, not legislative. It differs from her power to decree rites and ceremonies. A judge has not authority to make laws, but only to determine what the law is and to apply it to the particular case before him. So the Church has no authority to decree new doctrines, but simply to declare what the truth is and always has been. The Church's judgment in controversies of faith is primarily one of recognition. She judges an opinion true or false because it agrees with or differs from a pre-existent standard. She bears witness that this teaching is or is not in harmony with the message that she lives to proclaim.

The difference between the legislative power of the Church in the case of rites and ceremonies and her judicial authority in matters of faith is well illustrated by the decrees of the Council of Nicaea as quoted by Athanasius. The Council had before them a question of church order, the date of keeping Easter, and also a doctrinal question, namely, the teaching of Arius. 'With reference to Easter,' he says, 'such and such things were determined (ἔδοξε and at such a date), for at that time it was determined that all should obey a certain rule; but with reference to the faith they wrote not "such and such things were determined" but "this the Catholic Church believes", and they added immediately the statement of their faith, to show that their judgment was not new but apostolic, and that what they wrote was not any discovery of theirs, but was what the Apostle taught.'[1] In other words, the Church is not the organ of a new and growing revelation but a witness and interpreter of a revelation once given.

(b) Are we then to say that there is no development in the Church's teaching and in the knowledge of divine truth? The answer to this question turns on what we mean by development. If by development we mean the addition of new doctrines implying a positive increase in the content of divine revelation: if such development requires that the Church should be considered not simply as a witness to the faith once given, but as the organ of a fresh revelation from God, then we deny that there is any development in this sense, and we claim in support of our denial both Scripture and the teaching of the Fathers. Nothing is clearer than that the Church in early days did not claim any power of adding to the faith: novelty was a sign of heresy. At her synods and councils she sought to declare not some new truth but what the Church had always and everywhere believed. As S. Vincent of Lerins wrote:[2] 'We within the Catholic Church are to take great care that we hold that which hath been believed everywhere, always and by all men (ubique, semper, ab omnibus) . . . and that we shall do, if we follow universality, antiquity and consent. Universality we shall follow, if we confess that one faith to be true which the whole Church throughout the world confesses: antiquity, if we depart in no wise from those truths, which it is plain our holy forefathers held: and consent, if in this antiquity itself we follow the definitions and sentences of all or practically all the priests and doctors together.' As we shall see, the early writers found in the apostolic succession of the ministry a guarantee of the continuity of apostolic doctrine. The Fathers are never tired of referring men back to Scripture as the touchstone of genuine Christian teaching.

[1] *Ath. de Synodis*, 5, quoted Gore, *R.C. Claims*, c. iii.   [2] *Commonitorium*, c. 2.

On the other hand we do admit development in another sense. There is a progressive understanding of the faith delivered to the saints. The truth does not grow, but we grow into it. The revelation has been there all the time, but we had not eyes to see all that it means and we are only slowly coming to comprehend its full beauty and significance. And this development of our knowledge takes place in two chief ways.

(i) Through controversy the Church is compelled to mark off certain lines of teaching as false, and therefore asserts the opposite teaching to be true. So what was before implicit in her belief, becomes explicit. No new truth is added, but she comes to a clearer consciousness of what she believed all the time. Just as nothing does more to clear up our minds on a subject than being obliged to answer questions on it, so the Church, through being cross-questioned about the belief to which she bore witness, came to a more thorough comprehension of its meaning. In this sense the Athanasian Creed is the development of the teaching of the Gospels and S. Paul. It is an instance of what S. Vincent expresses thus:[1] 'When she was roused by the novelties of heretics, the Catholic Church, by the decrees of Councils, has ever affected this and nothing more—that she should consign to posterity in the security of a formal document, what she had received from her ancestors by mere tradition, summarizing great matters in a few words, and generally, with a view to greater clearness, stamping with the speciality of a new term an article of the faith which was not new.' The technical language is indeed new, but S. Paul would have no difficulty in accepting the theology of the Athanasian Creed, if it were explained to him. We may say that there is a development in the statement of truth but not in the substance of it. S. Peter's knowledge of the Catholic faith included all that the Church teaches to-day.

(ii) Secondly, not only words but ideas and modes of thought change. Accordingly the faith has to be interpreted to each age in the language of that age. Our mental vocabulary has been enormously enlarged by the growth of science and psychology, etc. Conceptions like 'evolution', 'natural selection' and the like were unknown to our forefathers. Our whole idea of personality has been deepened by modern research. If we take up and read a book written a hundred years ago we feel as if we were moving in a different world. So the faith, if it is to be intelligible to our age, must be translated into terms of current thought. As Bishop Westcott wrote:[2] 'As the circumstances, of men and nations change materially, intellectually, morally, the life will find a fresh and corresponding expression. We cannot believe what was believed in another age by repeating the formulas which were then current. The greatest words change in meaning. The formulas remain to us a precious heritage, but they require to be

<hr>

[1] op. cit., c. 23.   [2] Westcott, Gospel of Life, p. 281.

interpreted. Each age has to apprehend vitally the Incarnation and the Ascension of Christ.' So there is development in this sense, development of expression. The essence of the faith to which the Church bears witness is not changed, but the form in which it is presented does change. Further, new circumstances arise and call for a new application of the old truths. Each age has its own problems, social, moral and religious, and turns to Christ to find the remedy for its distress. So new depths of meaning are called out which hitherto had lain unnoticed or obscured. No new Gospel is proclaimed, but the old Gospel is applied to new conditions, and so new aspects of it disclosed. It is one of the glories of the Christian faith that it contains an answer for every human need. Here again there is a development of truth, a fuller entering into the wisdom of God, a wider sympathy with the mind of Christ, through practical obedience to the faith once for all revealed. In these senses we do allow development of truth. What was implicit becomes explicit: truths are not changed but translated into new forms so as to correspond to new needs, intellectual, moral, and practical.†

(c) Here we find ourselves face to face with one of the burning questions of the day. How are we to distinguish between legitimate development and illegitimate? Where can we draw the line between the reinterpretation of the old facts and the addition of new facts? It is hard to separate the fact from its interpretation or to decide at what point the attempt to express old doctrines in modern language passes into the assertion of something new and strange. All of us agree that the Church must present her teaching to the men of to-day in such a form that it may make its greatest appeal to them. Every endeavour to do this must claim our sympathy. But it is fatally easy in any such endeavour, while attempting to translate the faith into up-to-date terms, either to add to it or to diminish it. In the light of this problem we must consider (α) The Roman doctrine of development, (β) Modernism.

(α) The Church of Rome claims to be the Catholic Church. As such it claims that its whole body of teaching is and has always been both infallibly true and also identical in substance with the teaching of the Apostles. This position obviously needs defence. It is by no means apparent that the Church of the Apostles or of the Fathers believed in, let us say, the Treasury of Merit, or the Immaculate Conception of the Blessed Virgin, or the Infallibility of the Pope—to select three conspicuous instances of modern Roman teaching. The defence that the Church of Rome would prefer is that these doctrines are based on Scripture. The earlier Roman controversialists attempted to prove their position from Scripture with indifferent success. Isolated texts torn from their context and not always accurately translated are not formidable arguments. Modern scholarship and the growth of the historic sense have rendered the attempt even more hopeless. A second line of defence was to lay down that such doctrines as could not be proved from Scripture were part of an apostolic tradition handed down in secret. This secret primitive tradition was viewed as an independent witness to the truth. As we saw, any such view is contrary to patristic teaching, which unanimously held that Scripture contained a sufficient account of the divine revelation in Christ. Further, in early days this reliance on secret tradition was the weapon not of orthodoxy but of heresy.[1] It was the Gnostics not the Church who fell back on such authority. Writers such as Tertullian and Irenaeus insist that there is not and never has been any concealed element in the Gospel of Christ. Accordingly, a third line of defence has to be attempted. Most modern Roman writers, though not all, would maintain that the teaching of the Roman Church to-day is a development but still the true and legitimate development of the teaching of the Apostles. Cardinal Newman could write, 'Every Catholic holds that the Christian dogmas were in the Church from the time of the Apostles; that they were ever in their substance what they are now; that they existed before the formulas were publicly adopted in which as time went on they were defined and recorded.'[2] In other words, even the most modern dogmas were in some sense implicit in the primitive belief. Newman himself could write about the Vatican Council, that imposed the dogma of Papal infallibility, before it had given its decision, that if the definition should be made, it would turn out to be a part of the original deposit of belief.[3] Newman himself was responsible for placing the doctrine of development on a new basis. One modern Roman line of argument may be summed up as follows: A seed contains within itself a principle of growth. An acorn, for instance, has within it the potentiality of becoming an oak. Under suitable conditions by a gradual process of development this potentiality is realized: each stage of growth is determined by the law of its nature until it culminates in the full-grown oak-tree. So Christian doctrine started as a germ, containing within itself the power of growth. It was planted in the Church in order to grow. Through centuries of Christian life it has grown. Partly through controversy, partly by the arguments of theologians, partly by the Church's study of her message, the germ of apostolic doctrine has developed into the full modern doctrinal system of the Church of Rome. Every stage of development has been determined by the stage before and led on to the stage that followed. Under the guidance of the Holy Spirit the Church has been inspired to see and welcome the growth in truth, and in due time to proclaim it as a new dogma, an essential part of her teaching. So the dogmas of the Church of Rome to-day are the necessary evolution of the teaching of the Apostles. At

[1] Cp. Tert. *de Praescr.* c. 25–28, who expressly repudiates the idea of a secret tradition.
[2] *Tracts, Theol. and Eccl.* p. 287, quoted Gore, *R.C. Claims*, p. 39.
[3] Chandler, *Cult of the Passing Moment*, p. 57.

first sight we may indeed be struck by the difference between the elaborate formularies of to-day and the simplicity of the belief of earlier ages. The connexion between is no more obvious at first sight than that between the oak and the acorn. But the study of Church history will show us how the faith of the Apostles passed stage by stage into the faith of the Church of Rome to-day. There was no break in the process of development. By the Holy Spirit the Church was infallibly led on from step to step, until the latest discovery of divine truth made at the last Vatican Council was added to the formal Creed of the Church.

This view of development is an admirable defence of the Roman system of doctrine—probably the only possible defence to-day. But it is open to criticism on two main grounds.

(i) It assumes the very point that needs proof, namely, that the Church has been infallibly guided at every stage by the Holy Spirit and has never fallen into error. We do indeed allow that modern Roman doctrine is a development of apostolic teaching and that we can trace that development step by step during the Church's history. Further, we allow that we cannot, as it were, take a knife and say 'up to this point the development is sound; here error begins'. But we maintain that all development is not necessarily healthy development. Cancer is a growth, but it is an unhealthy growth. Because Roman teaching has as a matter of history developed in a certain direction, that is no proof that it is a right direction or the only direction. Lutheranism and Calvinism are in some sense developments of apostolic teaching. But we do not accept them on that account. We see that they are one-sided and need pruning. It is possible that the development of Roman theology may be no less one-sided and no less in need of pruning. The whole Roman argument from development presupposes that the Church of Rome both has the monopoly of the guidance of the Holy Spirit and also has been completely faithful to that guidance. We are not prepared to concede that either of these presuppositions is true. We claim to test the development of Roman doctrine and see whether it is healthy and whether indeed from its very nature it is not inconsistent with the Christian faith.

(ii) A second and equally serious argument is that this view too often tends to confuse logical and organic development.[1] Roman theologians as a rule try to show that their doctrines are a logical development of apostolic doctrine, and when this begins to fail, they insensibly pass over to organic development and metaphors borrowed from it. But logical development and organic development are two entirely different things. Truth grows in quite a different way from an acorn. Truth develops in one or two ways. Either new facts come within our experience; we receive a positive increase of

---

[1] Newman guarded himself against falling into this error. His followers have not always done so.

information. Or by the use of thought our minds draw out by closer examination or by analysis what is implicitly contained in our present knowledge. The books of Euclid are the best illustration of this last method of growth. But an organism does not grow by such means. An oak is not logically implicit in the acorn. We cannot deduce from a seed what will emerge from it. If Christian truth is to grow it must develop in accordance with the laws that govern knowledge and not those that govern acorns. If the Church of Rome to-day knows more about divine truth than the Church of the Apostles, such increase in knowledge must have come either from the receiving of additional information, *i.e.* by an additional revelation from God, or else from closer study of the apostolic faith and the thinking out of all that is contained in it. Again, this idea of the belief of the Church as an 'organism' treats the 'belief' as a thing with a life of its own, divorced from the minds that hold it. The mind develops its own ideas, the ideas do not develop themselves. We cannot abstract the idea of development of doctrine from the life of the Church taken as a whole, and the Church consists of men and women, in whose lives thought is only one element. The whole idea of the 'organic' development of doctrine is perfectly logical and perfectly consistent in the abstract, but it does not correspond with the facts of life and leaves out large and essential parts of human experience.

So we refuse to accept such doctrines as those of the Treasury of Merit or the Immaculate Conception or Papal Infallibility as true developments of Christian truth. They cannot be proved from Scripture. There is no evidence that they formed part of the belief of the Church in early times. Nor can they be logically deduced from apostolic teaching. Human logic is only valid when it has a complete and adequate knowledge of the facts from which it argues, but when it deals with divine truths about which our knowledge is limited, its conclusions are at best precarious. Logic is most triumphant in dealing with abstract or mathematical statements, in the form 'all A is B'. When we know the symbols A and B, we know at once all that there is to be known about them. They are the pure creation of the human mind. But we cannot detect in advance by logic the course of human history or the conduct of our friends. So to argue that our Lord's sinlessness and the holiness of the Blessed Virgin imply that she must have been conceived free from all taint of original sin, and to state this as a new dogma, that of 'the Immaculate Conception' is to strain logic. Such an argument would only be valid if we knew all about original sin and heredity and the manner of the Incarnation. Further, since the Blessed Virgin is a historical person we are justified in asking for historical evidence that she either claimed to be sinless or made the impression of sinlessness on others. In Scripture there are indications that at times she lacked the complete and immediate sympathy with our Lord's purposes which would be evidence of entire sinlessness. She is rebuked by Him once (Jn 2⁴) and even takes part in an attempt to restrain Him from His ministry (Mk3²¹ ᵃⁿᵈ ³¹ ff.)[1]. In the Acts, after the first chapter, she disappears. The whole idea of the 'Immaculate Conception' is the natural outcome of the place that she has come to hold in modern Roman devotions, not of the place that she held during her life on earth. Logic cannot create new facts, and the Roman developments of doctrine are not on the same level as the earlier developments of doctrine, such as we admit in the case of the formal statement of the doctrines of the Incarnation and the Trinity. They imply an addition from outside to the deposit of faith, and so demand in the last resort a fresh revelation. At best they are but pious opinions which grew up in the Church as the private beliefs of individuals and schools, and afterwards were exalted into dogmas. We fall back upon the test of Scripture as interpreted by the universal Church and by such a test they stand condemned.†

(β) Modernism is in itself, as the name implies, only the attempt to be modern—to re-state the Christian faith in modern language, in accordance with modern knowledge and modern modes of thought. Such attempts in themselves are wholly laudable: the only question is whether, in the desire to give an up-to-date presentation of the Catholic faith, some essential elements may not be omitted or ignored. Certain teachers, in their wish to make Christianity modern, have failed to keep Christianity Christian. So the term 'Modernism' denotes a tendency rather than a definite school of thought or body of teaching. It has been used in the most varied senses, favourable and unfavourable. A Modernist may suggest to one mind a man who is doubtful whether the book of Genesis came straight from the hand of Moses, to another mind a man who has dissolved the Christian faith into a beautiful legend. At the same time there are certain definite positions to which the name Modernism is usually applied, and with these we will deal.[2]

Modernism starts from the desire to get back behind all dogmatic statements to the actual experience which those who first used them were attempting to describe. It claims that such dogmatic statements are to be accepted only so far as they can be verified from the present experience of the Church, and are to be interpreted in accordance with that experience. On this view the Modernist is not concerned to deny development in doctrine or to maintain that the latest Roman

---

[1] For instances of the very strong language used by the Fathers in condemnation of her conduct, see Gieseler, *Ecclesiastical History*, ii. p. 35.

[2] 'Modernism' should, strictly speaking, be limited to the movement in the Roman Catholic Church led by Loisy, Tyrrell, etc. The majority of so-called Modernists in England are more accurately styled 'Liberal Protestants'. Liberal Protestantism is based on the attempt to get back to the 'Historical Jesus', and is essentially different in nature and purpose from Evolutionary Modernism. Both movements however agree in adopting certain advanced critical views.

dogma can be deduced from the teaching of the Apostles. Rather he says, that all doctrinal statements are only the attempts of each age to express the fulness of its own spiritual life in language proper to itself. Such are not to be taken as literal clear-cut statements of fact, but are symbolic statements, true in their own way, but not true in the same sense as mathematical statements or statements of historic facts are true. All alike are inadequate. Each generation must endeavour to get back to the common spiritual experience and to express its meaning anew in accordance with the current terms and ideas of the day. It is from this standpoint that we must view the doctrinal statements of the New Testament. No one can dispute that the Church of those days enjoyed a very real and vivid religious experience, connected with the coming of Jesus of Nazareth. Christians were conscious of a new insight into divine truth and a new energy of thought and action springing from a quickened vision of God. This experience they tried to portray and explain, using the only language at their disposal, the phrases and formulas of their own age. These in process of time became obsolete, and the Church was obliged to find new language in which to describe all that this Christian life meant to herself. This new language again in time became old and proved inadequate and was duly supplanted by a fresh dogmatic statement couched in the ideas and phrases of a later age. This process of development has continued down to to-day. The common experience of the Christian Church abides, but its intellectual expression has changed and must change as knowledge grows and new ideas become current.

In this spirit the Modernist approaches the Creeds of the Church. In so far as he identifies himself with the life of the Catholic Church through all the ages, he claims to be in sympathy with all for which the Creeds stand. But he claims, none the less, to interpret them in accordance with his own mental outlook. Taken as literal statements of fact they belong, he would say, to past ages, but taken as symbolic of spiritual truth they find a response in present Christian experience which is its own verification. Take, let us say, the statement of the Virgin Birth. If taken as a literal statement of historic fact, it becomes a question for literary and historical criticism, but if taken as representative of spiritual truth it awakens at once a response in the Christian consciousness. Whether Jesus of Nazareth was in actual fact born of a Virgin does not matter and cannot be proved, all that matters is to hold fast the spiritual truth enshrined in the statement, namely, the uniqueness and purity of the life and teaching of Jesus. So, again, it is irrelevant to the highest type of Christian faith to trouble about the details of the Resurrection or to discuss whether the appearances were more than a series of visions; the sole important truth for faith is that life is stronger than death, and this truth was admirably symbolized by the series of Resurrection narratives that we owe to early Christians. So, too, the question of the person and teaching of the historic Jesus of Nazareth is of quite secondary importance. We are to fix our attention on the Spirit of Christ at work in ourselves and in the Church. In the story of His life and death we find the highest ideal of humanity portrayed, but how far that story is historical we need not ask. Its spiritual truth and value are guaranteed by its appeal to the highest in us, and are in no way dependent on the accuracy of any documents. The miracles found in the New Testament are the endeavour on the part of simple folk of the first century to express, in accordance with the spirit of their own age, the incomparable power of goodness. With some exceptions they have no parallel within our experience, but their value lies not in their actual occurrence, as too many have supposed, but in their representation of the new and healing life that comes from God. So with the decisions of Councils and the later dogmas of the Church. These at best have a protective value. They bear witness to the inner life of the Church and are to be understood, as it were, from inside. We are to find their counterpart within our own religious life. Accordingly, spiritual religion is independent alike of historical facts and of doctrinal statements. As such it is raised above all possible objections whether from the side of historical criticism or physical science. It moves on a different plane. The proof of its validity is to be sought in the continuous experience of religious men. Such religion will and must clothe itself in dogmatic formulas, borrowing language from the things of earth. But the truth of such formulas depends solely upon their value for the religious life. Faith is essentially independent of all of them. Faith created them and faith can and must reinterpret them in accordance with its own inward vision. This is briefly the general position of the Modernist held with more or less consistency by different teachers.

Up to a point Modernism invites our sympathy. At least it is alive to the importance of keeping doctrine in the closest touch with life. Orthodoxy, Catholic and Protestant alike, is always tempted to regard doctrines as abstract statements of truth on a level with mathematical propositions or assertions of historical fact, revealed ready-made from Heaven and apprehended by the intellect. There has been a real danger that the appeal of Christian truth not to the mind only but to the conscience and affections should be ignored. Take, for instance, the Old Testament. This has been made to live again for us in recent years. We have come to regard it no longer as a mechanically dictated volume of supernatural truth, equally inspired in all its parts, but rather as record of human experience. We look within and we find portrayed the doubts and strivings of the human soul and the Spirit of God at work illuminating the hearts and minds of men as they wrestled with the problems of life. We search our own hearts and there we find similar doubts and strivings, and we feel that God is dealing with us as He dealt with them. Their experience awakens an echo in us. Modernism approaches Christian doctrine in this same spirit, regarding it as worked out in the lives of men. It can only have its full meaning for those who, as it were, know it from inside. Again, we cannot but sympathize with the attempts of Roman Catholic Modernists to free themselves from the vast and ever-increasing system of dogmatic utterances that are binding on members of the Church of Rome. This growth of infallible utterances on all manner of subjects is the inevitable fruit of the Roman theory of development of doctrine. The original revelation has been developed by the teachers of the Church, and especially the Pope, so as to cover questions of science and criticism. Successive Popes have declared certain opinions binding upon all good Catholics which every educated man in Europe knows to be false. Yet the theory of an 'infallible' Church prevents these errors from being openly repudiated. But the Modernist is able to say that these dogmatic utterances are true not literally but symbolically: their value lies not in their scientific or historical affirmations, which are those simply of one age, but in the spiritual truth that they enshrine. Each generation must interpret them anew in the light of its own knowledge. In this way awkward decisions can be explained away as passing stages in the expression of spiritual truth.

But Modernism pays too high a price for its gains. It ends by reducing Christianity to a mere religion of ideas, based on a vague sentiment. It makes all definite belief impossible.

From the first Christianity has claimed to be a historical religion, springing out of the life and teaching of a definite historical Person. The Christian has been called on to declare his belief in certain definite events, as actually having happened. The Apostles did not primarily regard themselves as the expounders of new ideas disclosed by a great teacher, but as eye-witnesses of definite historic events— the life, death and resurrection of Jesus the Messiah. His teaching and the example of His life had a place in their preaching, but a subordinate place. The centre of all Christian life was Jesus Christ Himself, crucified and risen. Now historic facts cannot be proved or disproved by any purely inward experience. They require historic evidence. No doubt this evidence is in its nature more complicated than at first sight appears. Much depends on the character of the witnesses. We are influenced in accepting their testimony by the self-consistency of their story and its agreement with what we know from elsewhere. The reason why, for instance, we reject without hesitation otherwise excellent evidence for some of the miracles of the middle ages is that they are childish and unworthy of the character of God. The value of historical evidence can only be determined by a great number of considerations. Our estimate of its value will depend largely upon our own presuppositions and sympathies. But that does not alter the fact that we cannot discover historical facts without it. The death and resurrection of Jesus Christ, for instance, which are the central articles of the faith cannot be proved or disproved by the inward religious experience of Christians. They may make a great appeal to our highest selves. We may find that by basing our lives upon them we gain assurance that they are true. But these inward feelings would not by themselves justify us in erecting them into facts of history. They may well incline us to accept the historical evidence for them, but they can never be a substitute for that evidence. We cannot create past history out of our inner consciousness. In other words the Modernist is false to Christianity when he makes religious experience the sole test of doctrine. Doctrines that assert historic facts need also historical evidence. Further, such events happened in one way and in only one. No amount of looking into our own souls will assist us to learn how they happened. We must depend for our information on eye-witnesses. The Modernist criterion of truth is insufficient.

Again, an enormous amount of haziness is covered by the popular phrase 'religious experience'. We are justified in asking 'experience of what?' The ultimate issue is whether the ideals and hopes of Christianity rest on a solid basis. It is a very interesting study to observe the process by which we come to hold them. Religious psychology is able to describe the laws that govern the religious emotions, but it cannot even touch the final problem, is religion in touch with anything ultimately real? Are its truths true for all minds? If Jesus Christ is no more than an ideal figure in which humanity has portrayed its highest aspirations, we are still compelled to ask how do we know that these aspirations are really the highest? If the truth of Christianity is to be verified by an appeal to Christian experience, how are we to know that this Christian experience is a valid experience? The Modernists can only reply that Christianity satisfies them. They have no answer to the man who retorts 'but it makes no appeal to me'. On the other hand the Church has always joined together inward experience with outward fact. She has claimed that the Christ who manifests Himself in our hearts and lives, manifested Himself also in an actual human life, lived on earth, and that the test of true religious experience is to be found in the revelation of God thus given. Christian experience is thus experience of One who lived as a figure in history. The Christian revelation was given in a definite place and at a definite time. So the facts of history and the daily experience of the Christian support one another. Without such a foundation in historic fact so called 'religious experience' may be no more than vague aspirations and sentiments. But historic fact is in some sense altogether independent of the merely human. There, if anywhere, we come into contact with a world that we find and do not make. In the historic Christ we have an assurance that our own best and highest ideals correspond with a reality not ourselves. Through Jesus Christ we are in touch with ultimate truth.

Again, Christianity as represented by Modernists is not traditional Christianity but something entirely different. In the ancient world Christianity conquered its rivals very largely because it was a religion based on certain facts of history. Christianity did not come to a world without religion: it came to a world full of religion. There was any amount of religious experience. But Christianity survived and the other creeds did not. Partly its survival was due to the fact that it combined spiritual experience with a pure and lofty morality and a strict monotheism. But one great cause of its victory was its historical character. In place of imaginary redeemers it offered to the world a Redeemer who had actually lived and died and risen again. Take, for instance, its most formidable rival, Mithraism. Mithraism offered men redemption and immortality. Its worshippers were united in a common brotherhood with sacraments and worship so similar to those of Christians that the Fathers assigned them to the imitation by the Devil of Christian rites. But all the devotion, all the pious longings after God and immortality that Mithraism aroused rested on no solid basis. 'There never was a Mithra and he never slew the bull.'[1] Mithraism failed largely because it rested on nothing more than 'religious experience'. But if Christianity conquered because it offered man a historical Saviour and a redemption wrought out by an actual death and an actual Resurrection, then we cannot set aside the historical grounds of our faith as unnecessary or optional. If the contentions of Modernists are true there is really no essential difference between Christianity and Mithraism: the Christian Creed is at best only a slightly more adequate symbol of spiritual truth than the legend of Mithra killing the bull: it produces not a Saviour, but an idea of a Saviour. But only a Saviour can save.

Further, Christianity claims to be a religion for all men, not only for the wise or the spiritually gifted, but also for the savage and the plain man. But a religion of ideas can only make a limited appeal. It has no message for the dull and uneducated. The average man is influenced by concrete facts. It is the actual death and resurrection of Jesus Christ that come home to his heart. If Jesus Christ be pronounced to be only a shadowy figure upon whom men have projected their ideals, if His resurrection is only an allegory of spiritual truth, then the saving power of the Christian faith disappears. We are left with nothing but human aspirations disguised. If Modernism is true, then Christianity can only be the religion of a few mystics, gifted with a keen insight into the unseen world. The ordinary man is not a mystic. He has neither the ability nor the time to become one. The opposition to Modernism in all its forms is not due simply to clerical

---

[1] Bigg, *Church's Task under the Roman Empire*, p. 52. Cp. also Mozley, *The Achievements of Christianity*, c. i.

prejudice or conservatism.[1] It arises from the conviction on the part of those who deal with the spiritual life of ordinary men and women, that in setting aside the historical ground of the faith, Modernists are undermining Christianity itself. If, as we saw, Modernism judges the truth of doctrines by their spiritual value, why does it shut its eyes to the spiritual value of historicity as such? We may doubt whether Modernism could ever arise except in an atmosphere created by generations of historical Christianity. It has yet to show that it can continue to maintain itself as Christian, while denying or belittling that belief in historical facts to which it owes its birth. All the evidence at present goes to show that Modernism, unless it is balanced by a due insistence upon the historic facts of the Incarnation and the Cross, gradually declines into a misty theism.

Lastly, we hold that Modernism has overlooked the real meaning and limitations of symbolism. As we have insisted, all that lies outside our present human experience can only be represented in symbol. We can only have symbolic pictures of heaven or the descent into hell. Such symbolism varies from age to age. Further, we must allow that our human language is unable to express adequately divine truth. The words in which the Church has attempted to state the doctrine of the Trinity are admittedly inadequate. But when we come to facts of ordinary human experience, the inadequacy of human language tends to disappear. It is being employed for the purpose for which it was formed. This applies especially in the case of events of history. Our contention is that if Jesus Christ was born of a virgin mother, if His body was raised from the dead and the tomb left empty, human language in the first century was as adequate to express these events as it is to-day. To treat these statements as not historically but only symbolically true is in effect to treat them as untrue. It is not reinterpretation but denial. It may be urged, however, that some of the Old Testament narratives which our forefathers treated as historically true, we are content to treat as only symbolical: and this change would include not only the opening chapters of Genesis and the book of Jonah, but also large parts of the historical books. In the book of Chronicles, to give an example, most students would allow that we find the ideas of a later age embodied in an imaginary narrative of past events: in other words, what is apparent history is in

---

[1] The blind acceptance of what is new is not always a sign of faith. An idea is not necessarily true because it is new, any more than because it is old. The attempt to contrast the 'faith' of Modernists with the 'fear' of conservative Christians, begs the whole question. 'Faith means not only trustfulness but trustworthiness, and in trustworthiness the fear of betraying trust forms an essential part. If we give to a friend a sum of money to hold in trust for our children, we do not praise the "faith" which invests it all in a gold-mine of dazzling promise and doubtful existence, but rather the "fear" which clings to the sober security of consols. What if the Church of England be a trustee to whom God has committed for future generations a revelation of Himself? May not some even of her institutions guarantee the safe-keeping of that trust?' Quick, *Essays on Orthodoxy*, Introduction.

reality true only symbolically. Our reply is twofold. First, the historical evidence for much of the Old Testament history is very different from that for the facts of the Creed. In the New Testament we get documents very close in time to the events that they record. In the Old Testament much of the evidence is centuries later, and some of the writings, from the very nature of the subject-matter with which they deal, must be symbolical. The New Testament has been through the fire of criticism and its substantial accuracy as history has become increasingly clear. Secondly, it is impossible to maintain that the literal accuracy of the whole of the Old Testament has at all times had a central place in the proclamation of the Gospel. But the historical facts of the Creed have from the first been an essential part of all apostolic preaching. The alleged comparison will not stand examination.

To sum up, we hold that the fundamental mistake of Modernism is that consciously or unconsciously it starts from an idea of development of doctrine which regards such development as the discovery of new truth. It ignores the primitive conception that the primary function of the Church is that of witness. It ends by producing a Christianity that is outside the range of criticism because it has abandoned nearly everything that is worth criticizing. It leaves men with a 'religious experience' that is an experience of nothing in particular. Modernism contains no Gospel.[1]†

ARTICLE XXI

Of the Authority of General Councils	*De auctoritate Conciliorum Generalium*
General Councils may not be gathered together without the commandment and will of Princes. And when they be gathered together, (forasmuch as they be an assembly of men, whereof all be not governed with the Spirit and Word of God,) they may err, and sometimes have erred, even in things pertaining unto God. Wherefore things ordained by	Generalia Concilia sine jussu et voluntate Principum congregari non possunt; et ubi convenerint, quia ex hominibus constant, qui non omnes spiritu et verbo Dei reguntur, et errare possunt, et interdum errarunt etiam in his quae ad Deum pertinent; ideoque quae ab illis constituuntur, ut ad salutem necessaria, neque robur habent, neque

[1] Modernism, as a movement common to a recognizable body of theologians, has been virtually extirpated in the Roman Church since the early decades of this century. In England, Liberal Protestantism has in the same period become a less well-defined and influential movement, at any rate in the minds and writings of theologians. The questions relating to history, experience and dogma discussed in the text above are, however, of permanent significance, and tend to recur in acute forms in any Church in which, as in the Church of England, freedom of historical enquiry and an element of liberalism in doctrine have a recognized and traditional place.

them as necessary to salvation have neither strength nor authority, unless it may be declared that they be taken out of Holy Scripture.

auctoritatem, nisi ostendi possint e sacris literis esse desumpta.

Practically unchanged since 1553. It is significant that the original draft had included the following clause: 'Kings and pious magistrates can without waiting for the decision or gathering together of General Councils, in their own state according to the word of God, decide about matters of religion.' Happily this was struck out before publication.

The Article from first to last is aimed at the Council of Trent. The Church of England declared in advance that she did not feel under obligation to accept its decisions.

§ 4. (a) If the Church possesses authority in controversies of faith, she must have some means of exercising that authority. What steps can she take to defend her faith from false interpretations and unauthorized additions or diminutions? The bishops are the normal organ of the Church's teaching power. They have authority to proclaim the truth in her name. We find this authority in the earliest days claimed and used by the Apostles. S. Paul or S. Peter bears witness to the faith as it is to be believed by loyal members of the Church. They do not claim to originate new truth but to hand on under the guidance of the Holy Spirit what they had received. So, too, Timothy and Titus are sent with like authority to teach in the name of the Church (1 Tim 4¹¹⁻¹³, 2 Tim 2¹⁵, 4², Tit 3¹⁰). In later days this duty passed to the bishops. But since this teaching authority is ultimately of the nature of witness, an individual bishop may from lack of knowledge or judgment fail to express the true voice of the Church. No one has yet maintained that omniscience or infallibility are among the gifts conferred by consecration. In such a case it is clearly incumbent upon the other bishops to correct him. The bishops are the guardians of the faith not only as individuals but as a body. We can find examples of such action within the New Testament. The action of S. Peter in eating with men uncircumcised was challenged and S. Peter made his defence before the Apostles and the brethren (Acts 11¹⁻³ and ¹⁸). Later at Antioch he was publicly rebuked by S. Paul for refusing to eat with Gentiles and apparently accepted the rebuke (Gal 2¹¹⁻¹⁴). The Council of Jerusalem originated in a dispute caused by the conduct of certain teachers at Antioch. The dissension was ended by the united action of the whole Church. The point at issue was a question of practice involving a question of doctrine, the relation of the Jewish Law to the Gospel. The Apostles and elders met together. S. James as president summed up the debate and proposed a motion. This was adopted and took the form of a letter. The decision of the Council was ratified by its acceptance on the part of the whole Church (Acts 15).

The later system of synods is the working out of this same principle. By the third century it had become part of the regular organization of the Church that the bishops of neighbouring Churches should meet together at least once a year for discussion.[1]

Probably the earliest meetings were chiefly for purposes of common action on matters of discipline, *e.g.* excommunications. In a missionary church then, as to-day, without such common action discipline would cease to exist. But their action soon was extended to 'deeper questions for the common good'.[2] Further, these synods tended to become no longer merely small local gatherings but to include a large number of bishops from a wide area.[3] From the first their decisions had taken the form of canons or laws. But the area of the jurisdiction of a synod remained for a long time quite vague, and its decisions needed to be recognized by the Churches to which they were addressed. The independence of the local bishops was only slowly checked. Again, just as the bishop might err, so the local synod might err. As in the case of bishops safety lay in corporate action and discussion, so in the case of synods security was sought by comparison of decisions and by intercommunication between synods. By this means the witness of distant parts of the Church was obtained, and certainty might be gained by collecting the testimony of many independent witnesses. By the growth of the local synod and the intercourse between different synods the Church was able to reach serious decisions on matters of faith. The vital importance of these synods is shown by the attempt of the Emperor Licinius to suppress them, as the surest means of damaging the Church.[4]

(*b*) With the appearance of a Christian Emperor a new era opened. Constantine was above all anxious to preserve the unity of the Church. Only a united Church could render the maximum of service to the empire. Accordingly he gladly accepted the appeal of the Donatists to settle their dispute with the Catholics. He nominated four bishops, including the Bishop of Rome, who with fifteen others held a council. The Donatists were condemned. At first Constantine rejected their appeal from the decision of the Council, but at length in his desire for unity he called together 'very many bishops from different and innumerable places' to meet at Arles. Here we find, for the first time, a synod fairly representative of the whole of the Western Church. This had been made possible by the assistance of the Emperor. The Donatists were again condemned.

So the way was prepared for the first 'General Council', that of Nicaea. The rise of Arian teaching in Egypt threatened to divide the Church. The Bishop of Alexandria had attempted to quell it, but without success. Constantine was obliged to resort to his old plan and summon a Council, this time from East and West alike. Hence

---

[1] Cp. C. H. Turner, *Camb. Mediaeval History*, vol. i. pp. 164–166.
[2] Tert. *On Fasting*, c. 13.
[3] *E.g.* sixty bishops met at Rome in 251 to condemn Novatian. Eighty-seven met at Carthage in 256, etc.
[4] Eusebius, *Life of Constantine*, i. 51.

T   B.T.A.

it is clear that the idea of a 'General Council' did not originate
spontaneously in the Church, but was introduced from without. As
has been well said, 'The conception of a General Council did not give
rise to Nicaea, but *vice versa*.' The idea struck the imagination of the
Church and commended itself to her as a visible realization of her
fellowship and as the crown of the synodical system. So Nicaea became only the first of a long series of Councils that claimed the title
of 'General'.

(*c*) The question arises, what is the test of a council's claim to be a
'General Council'? It was a question very much in evidence at the
time of the Reformation. The Pope had summoned the Council of
Trent as a 'General Council'. The King of England among other
Christian princes had been cited to attend. In actual fact it was
composed solely of bishops of the Roman Church. Not only was the
Eastern Church unrepresented, but the Reformers held aloof. Hence
the Church of England refused to acknowledge that its decisions
were necessarily binding on her. This explains the tone of Art. XXI,
with its want of enthusiasm for 'General Councils'. The writers had
in mind not the great General Councils of the past, whose decisions
they accepted with all reverence, but the Council then sitting at
Trent. When the Article speaks of 'General Councils' it means those
that make a claim to be general, as Trent did. We must balance the
language of the Article by the language of the Reformers elsewhere.[1]

Our Article makes three statements about such councils.

(*a*) '*General Councils may not be gathered together without the
commandment and will of Princes.*' This is a hit at Trent, which was
convened by the Pope. 'May not' (*non possunt*) means more than
'cannot as a matter of fact', though this is true enough. A Prince
could forbid his subjects to attend, or disperse a 'General Council' by
the use of force. 'May not' means rather 'may not lawfully'. As a
matter of simple history the first eight acknowledged 'General
Councils' were convened by the Emperor. As we saw, the very idea of
such originated with Constantine. He made its assembling possible
for the first time, not only by legalizing the position of Christianity,
but by offering free conveyance at the imperial cost to all the bishops.
So later councils were summoned not by the Pope but the Emperor.
Chalcedon, indeed, was summoned at the request of the Pope, Leo,
but by the command of the Emperor Marcian. Indeed, because of the
civil interests involved, it could not be otherwise. So the statement of
the Article is true historically. The Pope claimed the right of con-
vener in the sixteenth century, but such a claim is not in accordance
with antiquity and has been denied by many Roman authorities. If

---

[1] *E.g.* in a closely parallel passage the *Reformatio Legum Ecclesiasticarum*, speaking
of the four General Councils of Nicaea, Constantinople, Ephesus and Chalcedon,
writes 'magna cum reverentia amplectimur et suscipimus'. So one of the Homilies
speaks of Six Councils as 'received of all men'. Cp. also the language of Hooker,
I. x. 14, V. liv. 10, VIII. ii. 17.

we ask the further question, why should the State to-day be consulted about the holding of a council? would a council held without the sanction of the State be *ipso facto* irregular? We must remember that the Articles here, as elsewhere, assume that the Princes are Christians. The Emperor acted in his capacity as the first layman of the Church. The consent here required is a part of that 'royal supremacy' which is explained later. If the State has become secular, circumstances have altered and the wording of the Article no longer holds good. Even so the fact remains that the civil power can forbid its citizens to attend such a council or refuse to allow it to be held in its dominions.

(β) *'When they be gathered together (forasmuch as they be an assembly of men, whereof all be not governed with the spirit and word of God) they may err and sometimes have erred even in things pertaining unto God.'* This again is an appeal to history. No one can deny that councils which *a priori* would appear to have as good a claim to be entitled 'General' as any, from their size and representative nature, have fallen into error and their decisions have been reversed. For instance, the Councils of Ariminum and Seleucia decided in favour of Arianism. The Council of Ephesus, nicknamed 'Latrocinium' or the 'Robber-council', decided in favour of Monophysitism, and its decisions were reversed at Chalcedon. So again in the later Iconoclastic controversy, we find one set of councils deciding in favour of the use of images and another set reversing their decrees. With these facts before it our Article hints that the Council of Trent may likewise fall into error, for all its claim to be 'general'. The reason given is also in the fullest accord with the evidence. The conduct of the bishops at Nicaea was not perfect. At later councils it was positively scandalous. Even at Chalcedon there was intimidation and brawling. Such only showed that all those present were not entirely governed by the Spirit of God. Hence their decision might readily be swayed by passion or self-interest.[1]

(γ) *Things ordained by them as necessary to salvation have neither strength nor authority, unless it may be declared that they be taken out of Holy Scripture.* A General Council was summoned not to add a new doctrine to the substance of the Christian faith but to make plain what Christians had always believed and to say 'no' to novel interpretations that were inconsistent with it. Their duty was to witness to the faith once for all delivered. Hence the decision must be based on Scripture. To symbolize this a copy of the Gospels was

[1] Cp. the candid opinion of Gregory of Nazianzum in a letter of 382. 'If I must speak the truth, I am of a mind to shun every assemblage of Bishops, because I have never seen a good end to any synod, nor remedy of evils but rather an addition to them. There are always contentions and strivings for dominion (do not think I am using too strong language) beyond description' (Ep. 130, al. 55, cp. also Ep. 124 al. 84). Elsewhere he likens the younger bishops at the Council of Constantinople to wasps (*Carmen*, xi. l. 1686) and says it was a disgrace to be among such 'hucksters of the faith' (*Carm.* xii. l. 153). Cp. Turner, *op. cit.*, p. 166.

placed on a throne in the middle of the assembly. Hence the Church of England stated in advance that she was not bound to accept the decisions of Trent unless they were based on Scripture.

We are bound, therefore, to ask, how we can decide what councils that claim the title of 'General' are really 'General'. The only answer that meets all cases is that the oecumenicity of a council depends on the after-reception of its decisions by the whole Church. The decrees of even the largest and most representative council are not the Church's last word on the subject. They are an important stage in the Church's ascertainment of the true faith, but they need to be ratified by the general acceptance of the Church at large, not necessarily at the moment but after consideration. The reason why the Council of Nicaea is reckoned as general and the Council of Ariminum is not, is that in the long run the Church recognized the decrees of Nicaea as representing her mind. Accordingly we are prepared to find that different councils are accounted as 'General' in different parts of the Church. The English Church has recognized four—Nicaea, Constantinople, Ephesus and Chalcedon. To these are sometimes added two more, the second and third of Constantinople, which only ratified the decisions of previous councils. It is worth noting that at all six the Westerns were very inadequately represented. The Eastern Church would add those of Nicaea in 787 and Constantinople in 879. The Roman Church would add many others, though Roman historians are not always consistent with one another.

At the present day the divisions of Christendom render a 'general' council impossible. Great though the loss be, we must not exaggerate it. For the first three centuries no such council was practicable, but men could ascertain the mind of the Church as a whole by the comparison of local traditions and teaching. A verdict thus gained falls short of the deliberate and considered judgment of a council, but it is not to be despised. The question has often been asked, what right has, e.g. the Church of England to put forth an authoritative statement of belief such as these Articles. The Reformers made it clear that they only put forth these Articles, subject to an appeal to a free general council, when such could be held. They were put forth in an age of division and controversy, partly to declare the permanent adhesion of the Church of England to the Scriptures and the Catholic Creeds, partly to give a general statement of her attitude to certain questions hotly debated at the time. (See page 18). But the Church of England does not suppose that she has nothing to learn from other Churches. A statement of truth that is based upon the life and witness of the whole Church must possess an authority that one based on the life and witness of only a section of the Church can never possess.†

§ 5. What then is the relation of the authority of the Church to the judgment of the individual?

(a) If even a general council, fully representative of the whole

Church, may err, what guarantee do we possess that the whole Church may not fall into error on some point? The only possible answer is to refer to the doctrine of grace. What our Lord promised to His Church was not infallibility, but an infallible guide, the Holy Spirit. As we saw, in the case of the individual the grace of the Holy Spirit is not irresistible, it requires the co-operation of the human will. The same is true of the Church, which is composed of individual men and women. The guidance of the Holy Spirit is not irresistible: it is not a substitute for intellectual or moral effort. The Church may through sinfulness miss or reject it. Just because the Church is not perfectly holy, therefore she is not perfectly responsive to her infallible Guide. Thus even a decision that is issued by a general council is not infallible. The more general the council and the wider the acceptance of its decision, the more it represents the deliberate and considered opinion of the Church and the greater the authority with which it comes to us. But general councils are not an automatic machinery for turning out infallible utterances.[1]

On the other hand, we do believe in the perpetual guidance of the Holy Spirit and that He will not suffer the Church to go far astray without revealing the truth to faithful servants of God within the Church. An Athanasius is raised up to stand against the world. Thus the way is prepared for a return from error. Again and again truths that have been neglected or obscured have been recovered in such a way. A later generation is able to correct and revise the decisions of the earlier. Further, as we have seen, the more 'Catholic' the Church becomes, the better-proportioned her hold upon truth will be. As the Church pursues her task of evangelizing the world, the more completely she will understand her own nature and message. In proportion as the Church grows in holiness and in fulness of life, she will grow in the true knowledge of God.

(b) In the last resort the belief of the individual must depend upon those faculties for the discovery and recognition of truth with which God has endowed him. Our Lord did not shrink from appealing to man's power of choice. He did not demand a blind acceptance of His teaching, on penalty of condemnation. He asked for faith, which is an activity of the reason and the will. No one can shift the personal responsibility for faith on to the shoulders of others. This is true even of those who wish to hand over their responsibility for what they believe to an infallible Church or an infallible Pope. The initial act of surrendering their power of decision must be their own. So, too, the continuous acceptance of the decisions of such an external authority is an internal act of will, albeit of a slothful will. Even the most rigid system of authority cannot deny the need of 'private judgment', though it reduces it to the act of swallowing official utterances with the minimum of moral or intellectual digestion.

[1] Cp. a valuable passage in Rackham, *Acts*, pp. 266–270.

How, then, can the individual find out the truth? Not only is it hard to ascertain the mind of the Church on many points, but her witness is divided. We can only answer that in religion, as in all subjects, there is not and never has been any easy or obvious road to the attainment of a complete and unerring statement of truth. The individual will naturally start from the official teaching of that Christian body whose life he has shared. In so far as this life has satisfied his moral and spiritual needs, he will be disposed in favour of the doctrinal teaching that underlies it. We must not exaggerate the difficulty of his task. There is a large central body of Christian truth that is common to all Christians, enough to form a starting-point for a Christian life. The primary truths of the faith as summed up in the Creed are unmistakable. The real difficulties begin when we pass on to secondary truths. These include detailed explanations of primary truths and matters of Church order and discipline that involve questions of doctrine. In all such discussions a man must be guided by reason and spiritual perception. He has the right to demand the Scriptural basis of all teaching presented to him. Where the meaning of Scripture is not clear, he must turn to the tradition of the Church and to the decisions of councils when such can be had. Appeal must also be made to great teachers, ancient and modern. We need not only the exegesis of the Fathers, especially of those who spoke Greek as their native tongue, but the accuracy of modern scholarship and research. Where our various teachers disagree, we must use our reason to weigh the arguments on either side. The more that a teacher appeals to us by the holiness of his life, and the more that his words come home to us with spiritual power, the more ready we shall be to trust his judgment. We must always remember that the experts in the Christian religion are the saints, not the theologians. A saint may not be in the least qualified to give an opinion on the date of a book or the theological accuracy of a definition. On such questions we consult the scholar or the theologian. On the other hand, if the opinions of the scholar or the theologian are inconsistent with the experience of the saint, we may rightly hesitate to adopt them. The ascertainment of Christian truth calls for the effort of the whole man. It demands prayer no less than study. Spiritual vision is something deeper than intellectual vision.

We are bound then to hold together two principles. First, the need for authority arising out of the duty of the Church to teach and expound the Gospel. Secondly, the duty of the individual to enter upon Christian truth as a personal conviction of which he can give some account.

(c) In the Church of Rome the compelling power of authority is often isolated and distorted. The demand is made that the teaching of the Church should be accepted without enquiry. Where she has spoken, the use of reason is either superfluous or an act of rebellion.

Her exposition of any passage of Scripture forecloses all investigation into its meaning. Thus authority acquires a military hue. The individual's duty towards it is summed up in the one word 'obedience'. The idea of 'consentient witness' is abandoned. Against the official demands of the Church even conscience would seem to have no rights. The Church is viewed as an infallible guide on questions of morality and discipline, no less than of faith. Whether the Church has definitely pronounced on any given question is of course open to enquiry. Also, the exact meaning of official pronouncements may be disputed. But the general position is quite clear. The Church is inspired by God to declare truth. To question or reject her utterances is to doubt God. And for practical purposes 'the Church' tends to mean not the whole body of the faithful but the official teachers.

This attitude has more to say for itself than is often allowed. The ordinary man needs far more guidance than is often realized. He has neither the inclination nor the ability for independent theological enquiry. The authority of the Church gives him what he needs. Its doctrine is far more likely to be correct than his own, since it rests on a wider experience. The child needs instruction and the majority of men never rise beyond the stage at which continuous tutelage is necessary. On the other hand, the Roman use of authority differs from our Lord's use of authority. Reason and conscience cannot be treated like private soldiers. A growth in knowledge and experience stimulates a spirit of enquiry. This must be met, not stifled. The wish to understand is not wrong. If the dogmatic teaching has been true it has nothing to fear from investigation. The Church teaches her doctrines because she believes them to be true: she does not believe them to be true because she teaches them. An insistence on the blind acceptance of any teaching can only lead to scepticism or to the weakening of the spiritual fibre.[1]

(d) On the other hand, Liberal Theology and Protestantism isolate and exaggerate the claims of private judgment. Authority is regarded as an unreasonable tyranny, imposing upon the mind by an arbitrary decree statements of belief that are incredible. The individual is made the sole judge of truth. Every man is to be his own theologian. Such a view carried to extremes denies the corporate nature of all truth. It also rests on a false conception of authority. While we allow that if a man, after study and prayer, is in the end convinced that a doctrine is untrue, he is in duty bound to deny it and if need be sever himself from the Church that professes it as an integral part of her Creed, still he must remember that the probability is that on any given point authority is right and he is wrong. Authority represents a wider experience and an ampler wisdom. He is therefore bound to show good reason for his decision. Every man has the right to his own opinion, but his right carries with it the duty of taking the utmost

[1] Cp. Acton, *History of Freedom.*

pains to collect evidence upon which to form a sound opinion. Mere rebellion against authority is foolish. The indulgence of premature and hasty prejudices shows not a passion for truth but an intellectual arrogance. A home-made theology may be a very narrow theology. There are, indeed, too often occasions on which the principle of authority has been misused to suppress liberty of thought, but if rightly used authority is the minister and not the foe of true liberty. From the very nature of the case the Church is bound to exercise authority on matters of doctrine. We must not 'confuse the right of the individual to be free with the duty of the institution to be something'.[1]

§ 6. The limitation of the Church's authority in doctrine may be seen by certain examples in which the Church of Rome has added to the revelation in scripture.

ARTICLE XXII

Of Purgatory	*De Purgatorio*
The Romish doctrine concerning purgatory, pardons, worshipping and adoration, as well of images as of reliques, and also invocation of saints, is a fond thing vainly invented, and grounded upon no warranty of Scripture, but rather repugnant to the word of God.	Doctrina Romanensium de purgatorio, de indulgentiis, de veneratione, et adoratione, tum imaginum tum reliquiarum nec non de invocatione sanctorum, res est futilis, inaniter conficta, et nullis Scripturarum testimoniis innititur: immo verbo Dei contradicit.

Unaltered since 1553 except that in 1563 'The Romish doctrine' (doctrina Romanensium) was substituted for 'the doctrine of school-authors' (doctrina scholasticorum)—probably to bring the condemnation up to date.

N.B.—In the original draft of the Article 'the scholastic doctrines' condemned included that of prayer for the dead. This was struck out before publication.

(a) Purgatory

(i) Our Lord Himself scarcely can be said to make any direct revelation on the subject of the intermediate state. In the parable of Dives and Lazarus (Lk 16[19-31]) and again in His words to the dying robber on the Cross, He employs current Jewish language. Thus He seems to bestow His sanction upon the general principles of contemporary Jewish belief. More than this we cannot say. To press the details of the parable is hazardous. But our Lord's language does certainly imply a state of consciousness after death that is conditioned by our conduct here. He deliberately refutes the Sadducee's denial of a

---

[1] Arniel, quoted in Creighton, *Persecution and Tolerance*, p. 127.

future life (Mk 12²⁶). His profound reserve on such a subject about which curiosity is most active, is in striking contrast to the detailed pictures alike of Jewish apocalypses and of later Christian theology. His teaching throughout is marked by a stern insistence upon the eternal issues that hang upon our use of present opportunities. He discourages speculation about the future in the interest of moral earnestness about the present (cp. Lk 13²³ ff.). Above all He urges the duty of watchfulness.

In the Epistles the scantiness of references to the intermediate state is in part to be explained by the expectation of our Lord's immediate return. The majority expected to be alive at His coming. But the death of Christians at Thessalonica brought S. Paul face to face with the question. He lays down that the union of departed Christians with our Lord is not broken by death (1 Thess 4¹³⁻¹⁶). In 2 Cor 5⁶⁻⁸ and Phil 1²³ S. Paul seems to regard death as the entrance into a fuller union with Christ than is possible on earth. S. Peter's language about the quickening of our Lord's human spirit at death (1 Pet 3¹⁸) suggests that our own spirits may then receive a more abundant life and that like our Lord Himself we may be called to a new form of service in the world beyond the grave. In Heb 11¹⁶ ᵃⁿᵈ ⁴⁰ and 12¹ the departed saints of the old covenant are regarded as looking forward to sharing with us the consummation of God's purposes. In Rev 6⁹⁻¹¹ the souls of the martyrs are pictured as underneath the altar crying aloud in prayer for the final subjugation of evil and they are bidden to 'rest for a little time'. So, too, in 14¹³ the promise is given that they 'which die in the Lord from henceforth . . . may rest from their labours'.

But this intermediate state, though a state to be desired, is always viewed as an imperfect, temporary and preparatory state. Just as our Lord did not attain to the fulness of His glorified human life till the Resurrection, so, since the full life of man is one of body and soul united, there is still the Resurrection from the dead to look forward to. Thus S. Paul seems to regard the soul, when by death it has put off the body, 'the earthly house of our tabernacle,' as in some sense 'unclothed' and waiting for the resurrection body, 'our habitation which is from heaven' (2 Cor 5¹⁻⁴). He even speaks of it as 'absent from the body' (5⁸). In Phil 3²⁰⁻²¹ the Christian waits for a Saviour from heaven 'who shall fashion anew the body of our humiliation, that it may be conformed to the body of his glory.' This clearly happens not at death but at the appearing of Christ. So in 2 Tim 4⁶⁻⁸ S. Paul expects his 'crown of righteousness' not at death but at 'that day', *i.e.* the last day. In 1 Cor 15⁵¹ ff. the putting on of immortality and final defeat of death is assigned to the general resurrection at the last day (cp. Heb 9²⁸). The same thought is found in Rev 6¹¹ ('for a little while') and, indeed, throughout the book: whatever difficulties of interpretation there are, it is quite clear that the faithful departed have not yet attained to their full bliss. The New Jerusalem has yet to come down from heaven.

To sum up, we cannot but contrast the reticence of Scripture with the bold and confident assertions of too much later theology. At the same time, certain general principles are consistently laid down. There is a universal belief in an intermediate state, which will end with the coming of Christ and the final judgment. It is held that only through the resurrection will man attain to the perfection of his whole nature.

We must always bear in mind two points:

(a) It is probable that we are unable to receive any detailed teaching about our future life. The conditions under which it will be lived are so entirely different from those of earth that no description in human language is possible. ·

(β) There can be no doubt that the writers of the New Testament were largely influenced by Jewish ideas. It is not always easy to say how much is due to teaching taken over from Judaism and how much is definitely Christian. Hence we must be very cautious in pressing their language. As we have said before, the whole question of time comes in. It is very difficult, again, for us to conceive of a soul without a body, *i.e.* an organism by which it can enter into relation with its new environment. We may well suppose that the soul in some sense possesses the germ of a body even in the intermediate state.

(ii) We turn from Scripture to the belief of the early Church. We know of no time when Christians did not pray for the departed. Such prayers may well have been a part of the Church's inheritance from Judaism.[1] It is usually held that in our Lord's day the Jews were accustomed to pray for the dead. We read (2 Macc 12[39] ff.) that Judas Maccabaeus commanded prayers for the men who had fallen in battle and collected money for a sin-offering on their behalf. The apologetic tone of the writer suggests that his action needed defence, but it proves that such prayers were at least possible at that date (c. 100 B.C.).[2] Further, it is highly probable that the prayers for the dead in later Jewish worship go back to far earlier days and were in use in the synagogue worship that Christ attended. The New Testament is silent on the subject, except that S. Paul's prayer for Onesiphorus in 2 Tim 1[18], 'The Lord grant unto him to find mercy of the Lord at that day,' is quite possibly such a prayer: the context suggests that he was dead. As soon as we get a Christian literature, namely, the close of the second century, we find the practice established. Tertullian speaks not only of prayers for the dead but of the

---

[1] See Luckock, *After Death*, c. v.

[2] The men in question had fallen in battle, but under their coats were discovered things consecrated to idols. Hence their death was viewed as a punishment from God. The novelty may have lain not in prayer and sacrifice for the dead, but for the dead under such conditions.

offering of the Holy Eucharist on their behalf.[1] The only opponent of such prayers in antiquity was a certain Aerius in the fourth century. As he also took an Arian view of Christ and founded a schism, there is no reason to suppose that he spoke for anyone but himself. So, too, from the middle of the second century onwards, we find requests for prayers on tombstones, *e.g.* the tomb of Abercius, Bishop of Hierapolis, and sepulchral inscriptions in the Catacombs going back to quite an early date. By the fourth century there is clear evidence for the regular inclusion of intercession for the dead in the eucharistic liturgy in most parts of the Church.[2]

Such prayers imply a belief in progress after death, but that is all that we have the right to say. On examination, they go to prove that the early Church held closely to the teaching of Scripture.[3] The intermediate state was regarded as primarily a state of rest and refreshment and of closer union with Christ preliminary to the Resurrection. In the Eastern liturgies the requests are for such things as 'Rest', 'A place and a mansion in God's Kingdom,' 'The Resurrection of the Body,' 'That the sins of the departed may not be remembered.' These blessings, it is hoped, the faithful dead are already assured of and in part enjoy. In the West the earliest prayers are very similar.[4] But, as the West had always a deeper sense of personal sin than the East, such prayers tended to make more mention of sin, cleansing and forgiveness. Even so, the propitiatory aspect did not become dominant till after the time of S. Augustine, and even in mediaeval days something of the old spirit survived in the offices of the Church, in contrast to the current popular teaching on Purgatory.[5]

A similar change of tone shows itself in the writings of the Fathers. The idea of purification after death is found from quite early times. But until the time of S. Augustine it seems to be almost universally connected not with the intermediate state, but with the actual Day of Judgment. Tertullian, indeed, applies the words of Christ about 'paying the uttermost farthing' to punishment after death; but he

[1] *De Corona*, c. 3 'We offer on one day in the year, oblations for the dead, as birthday honours. . . . (c. 4) For these and such like rules, if thou requirest a law in the Scriptures, thou shalt find none. Tradition will be pleaded to thee as originating them, custom as confirming them, and faith as observing them.' Probably it is only the oblation that is rested on tradition, not Scripture.

[2] Cp. Srawley, *Early History of the Liturgy* (1947).

[3] Cp. Mason, *Purgatory*, pp. 58–77.

[4] Cp. the Roman Canon of the Mass, 'locum refrigerii, lucis et pacis.'

[5] At the Reformation all prayers for the dead as distinct from the living were removed from the Prayer Book, in the reaction against everything connected with purgatory. But the faithful departed were meant to be included in the prayer of oblation 'that we and all thy whole church may obtain remission of our sins'. It is important to notice that the condemnation of prayers for the dead that was included in an early draft of this Article, was deliberately withdrawn. The question was left open. It is true, indeed, that one of the Homilies forbids all such prayers, but it does so on the ground that at death all souls pass at once to their final condition, heaven or hell. This is not Scriptural, and if we deny the premisses we are not bound to accept the conclusion. Prayer for the dead is now regularly included in authorized services.

only suggests that the punishment for small offences will take the form of the delay of the sinner's resurrection.[1] There is no explicit suggestion of discipline during the time of waiting.[2] Clement of Alexandria, Origen and Gregory of Nyssa all speak of a fiery trial which awaits man after death. But this is conceived not as a prolonged discipline in the intermediate state, but as the day of judgment itself. At the appearing of Christ, the Christian who is in need of purification will be at once chastened and healed. The fire that cleanses is regarded not as the fire of purgatory but as the fire of hell, which it is supposed that all men in their measure experience and which is not only penal but remedial. For those who need it the trial will, indeed, be severe. The righteous will be purged by it, the wicked will hardly, if ever, escape from it. We must note that such teaching is based not so much on Scripture or Christian tradition as on heathen philosophy and speculation. There were indeed certain texts of Scripture which could be brought in to reinforce it, especially 1 Cor 3^{13-15}, but its real origin lies elsewhere. A similar belief was shared by Basil and Gregory of Nazianzum. In the West it was adopted by Hilary, Ambrose and Jerome. But after Gregory of Nyssa the subject was practically dropped in the East. Down to the Council of Florence in 1439 the Eastern Church had no doctrine of purgatory. There the Greek delegates, under great pressure of outward misfortunes, were induced to consent to the doctrine of Purgatory in a vague form.[3] But the East as a whole refused to accept the decrees. Since then the Eastern Church, though protesting against the Roman view of purgatory as an innovation unknown to Scripture and the Fathers, has come to teach a process of purification after death,[4] though it is not officially committed to any definite view about it.

In the West speculation about punishment after death found a more congenial home. S. Augustine is the real founder of a belief in a penal purgatory between death and judgment. This teaching is quite explicit in his latest work, the *De Civitate*. He combats the view that all punishment is remedial. 'Some endure temporal punishments in this life only, some after death, some both now and then, but all before the last and severest judgment. But not all who endure tem-

---

[1] *De anima*, c. 58.

[2] The *Acts of Perpetua*, dating from the close of the second century, probably does not imply a belief in any form of purgatory. Perpetua's little brother, Dinocrates, had died unbaptized. In a first vision she saw him in torment. She interceded for him, and in a second vision saw him released from pain. Her prayer had obtained for him the benefits of baptism. As unbaptized he was not in purgatory at all, but in a place of torment reserved for the heathen. Her prayer was irregular, and she only dared to attempt it because of a special revelation. As a rule such prayers were limited to Christians.

[3] 'If such as are truly penitent shall depart in the love of God, before they have made satisfaction for their deeds by worthy fruits of penance, their souls are purged after death by purgatorial punishments.'

[4] Cp. the reply of the Orthodox Church to the Encyclical of Leo XIII in 1895.

poral punishments after death come into the everlasting punishments
that are to follow that judgment. For we have already said that in
the case of some, what is not remitted in this world is remitted in the
world to come' (xxi. 13, cp. also c. 16 and c. 24 where he quotes
Mt 12^{32}, 'forgiveness in this world or in the world to come,' as proving that some will be forgiven in the next world). Later, in c. 26, he is
more cautious, 'If after the death of this body, until we come to that
last day of condemnation and reward, which follows the resurrection
of our bodies, in this interval of time the spirits of the departed are
said to endure fire of such a nature as not to be felt by those who have
not had such characters and desires in this bodily life as to require
the consumption of their wood, hay and stubble, but to be felt by
others who have carried with them building of this kind—whether
only there or here and there, or here and not there, their worldly
yet pardonable things are to find the consuming fire of transitory
tribulation, I do not dispute it for perhaps it is true.'[1] We cannot but
notice the very tentative and hesitating language. It is obvious that
there is no formal and authoritative Church teaching on the subject.
Augustine was feeling his way. He states his own opinion, but it is
only an opinion. Even so, his primary concern was not speculation
but insistence on a living faith. Such a purgatory, if it exists, as he
believes, is not any excuse for slackness here. It is only for Christians
who have at bottom remained true.

The great name of Augustine was sufficient to win general acceptance for his teaching in the West. But it remained still an opinion.
Not until the close of the sixth century do we find this doctrine of
purgatory endowed with any semblance of authority. In the *Dialogues*
of Gregory the Great the question is raised 'Are we to believe in a
purgatorial fire after death?' Clearly it was a legitimate subject for
discussion. The answer is given that 'a purgatorial fire before the
judgment for certain light faults is to be believed'. Such faults include
unbridled conversation, immoderate laughter, undue anxieties, mistakes due to ignorance, including adherence to the wrong Pope!
Gregory's teaching makes use of certain stock texts, as 1 Cor 3^{15},
Mt 12^{32}, but its real support is the series of 'thrilling ghost stories',
which form a large part of the *Dialogues*. In fact it was claimed that
a whole flood of new light had been shed upon the condition of the

---

[1] In his earlier writings we find a similar belief. In his homily on Ps 38, in expounding
v.^{1}, he quotes 1 Cor 3^{15}, and distinguishes between the fire 'that is to consume the ungodly for ever' and 'that which is to purge those that are to escape through the fire'.
Then to ensure that this fire shall not be lightly thought of, he adds, 'Though we should
be saved by fire, yet will that fire be more grievous than anything that man can suffer
in this life whatsoever.' This almost casual sentence did much to stimulate the gruesome
mediaeval descriptions of the torments of Purgatory. In his *De fide et operibus*, cc.
24–29, he again discusses S. Paul's language. He quite definitely places the purgatorial
fire as distinct from the fire of hell between death and judgment. Cp. *Enchiridion*, cc.
68–69. For a full discussion of his doctrine, see Mason, *op. cit.*

departed by recent revelations and apparitions. We need to remember that the mediaeval doctrine of Purgatory rested for the most part upon the visions narrated by Gregory, reinforced by fuller and later evidence of the same precarious nature. In plain English, an uncritical age was unable to distinguish between nightmares and revelations.

(iii) This conception of Purgatory as a place of fiery torment from which few of even the holiest Christians could hope to be exempt, came to be the dominant feature of mediaeval Christianity. As set forth by the Schoolmen it had become further corrupted by the new and terrible notion that punishment was satisfaction for sin. In order to place the current system on a rational basis, the distinction was elaborated between the guilt (*culpa*) and the punishment (*poena*) incurred by sin. Guilt, it was held, was forgiven in absolution, but the punishment that had to be borne still remained. In practice men came to think little of the guilt. That was forgiven through the merits of the Cross of Christ, and the slightest compunction, a tear or a prayer to the Virgin, were sufficient to procure the divine forgiveness through the Church's absolution. Then the sinner was safe from the eternal pains of hell. But Purgatory was more serious. The full measure of punishment had to be worked off, if not in this world, then in the next. God was bound to exact 'up to the last farthing', the retribution due to sin. Accordingly, the chief aim in life came to be to make provision against the torments of Purgatory. These could be reduced in advance by the performance of pilgrimages and other good works and by the purchase of 'Pardons'. Even after death the release of the soul could be hastened by prayers and Masses and the acquisition of pardons to be placed to the account of the departed. The whole matter was placed on a quantitative basis. The disciplinary aspect of purgatorial suffering had retreated to a secondary position. Hence the growth of solitary Masses and the springing up of the chantry system. Indeed, the chief value of the Mass came to be regarded as an insurance against the pains of Purgatory. The clergy became purveyors of salvation at a fixed tariff: the laity proved themselves eager customers. The doctrine was officially formulated for the first time in 1439 by the Council of Florence. We have travelled far, I will not say from Scripture, but from Augustine and Gregory.

We cannot wonder that the bitterest attacks of the Reformers were directed against Purgatory and everything connected with it, even the Mass itself. Purgatory seemed to have been invented to fill the coffers of the Church. The language of our Article is amply justified. Such doctrine was not only '*grounded upon no warranty of Scripture*' but '*repugnant to the word of God*'. Christianity had been degraded into a religion of fear, darker even than the terrors of pagan superstition. The Council of Trent fully admitted the evils. It forbade the discussion of 'the more difficult and subtle questions' in popular discourses. It commanded the bishops to prohibit as 'scandals and stumbling blocks to the faithful', 'those things which tend to a certain kind of curiosity or superstition or which savour of filthy lucre.' But it lacked the discernment or the courage to condemn the real root of the evil. It at least left open the view that the state of the faithful departed is chiefly one of suffering. It declared 'there is a purgatory and that the souls there retained are relieved by the suffrages of the faithful but chiefly by the acceptable sacrifice of the altar.' That is at present the official teaching of the Roman Church.[1] But the Catechism put forth by the Council goes further and speaks of a 'purgatorial fire' in which the souls are 'tormented' (*cruciatae*), and popular Roman teaching, approved by the highest authorities, is still further removed from the cautious assertion of Trent. No doubt the Roman doctrine may be presented in a most refined and spiritual way.[2] But we may fairly complain that no attempt is made to control extravagant and superstitious ideas. There is a wide gulf between the theological minimum defended by Roman apologists,[3] and the lucrative exaggerations of popular teaching.

(iv) What then can we say about the whole idea of purification through suffering after death? It is more than doubtful if the often-quoted passage in 1 Cor 3 [10-15] has any real bearing on the subject. S. Paul is referring to Christian teachers. Their work will be tested at the day of judgment. Only that which is built of the finest materials will be able to endure the test. All unworthy work will be destroyed, but the teacher himself, though he suffers the loss of his reward, will escape 'as through fire', a proverbial expression like 'a brand plucked from the burning'. There is no reference to the time between death and judgment and no mention of purification of character.[4] So, too, texts like Mt 5[26] 'till thou hast paid the last farthing' or 18[34] 'till he should pay all that was due', seem to picture rather an endless term of punishment. An infinite time is not sufficient in which to pay off an infinite debt. Nor again can we argue dogmatically that if a sin 'shall not be forgiven in this world or in that which is to come '(Mt 12[32]), therefore some sins must be forgiven in the next world. The emphasis is laid rather on the incurable nature of the particular sin. In short, even the doctrine of purgatorial suffering after death, in whatever form it is held, can hardly claim to be proved from Scripture, and the Church of England is therefore perfectly justified in refusing to enforce it as an article of belief.[5]

---

[1] See Möhler, *Symbolism*, vol. ii., pp. 138–139.

[2] As in the beautiful close of Newman's *Dream of Gerontius*, which should certainly be read.

[3] Cp. *e.g.* Chapman's reply to Bishop Gore, c. 3.

[4] See Goudge or Robertson and Plummer, *ad loc.* On the other side see Gayford, *The Future State*, pp. 44–46.

[5] To make belief in a purgatory of any kind a necessary part of the Christian faith can only be justified on the ground of some additional revelation. 'If the idea of a Purgatory had not got beyond a "perhaps" at the beginning of the fifth century, we are safe in

At the same time, as we have seen, such a belief has been widely held in various forms in all parts of the Church since the second century and it is entirely in accordance with reason. The language of Scripture bids us view the state of the faithful departed as primarily one of rest and refreshment. But when we consider the moral imperfection of so many who die in the faith of Christ and the impossibility of seeing God 'without sanctification' (Heb 12^{14}), it is almost impossible not to think that the life beyond the grave includes discipline through which the character is purified. Some form of purgatory is almost an intellectual necessity. Such would, indeed, involve suffering, but it would be suffering voluntarily accepted. We must also place side by side with it the purifying power of joy and thankfulness. Gratitude and happiness can elevate the character no less than pain and struggle. No doubt in the abstract God could make souls holy in a moment, and we dare not say what the very experience of death may be able to effect, but such an act of immediate and irresistible moral change contradicts all that we perceive of God's methods. We must be content to admit that we know very little, but we can believe that the growth in holiness begun on earth will be continued and perfected hereafter.[1]

(b) *The Romish doctrine concerning Pardons* or Indulgences[2] (*Indulgentiae*) is also declared both unscriptural and contrary to Scripture. The mediaeval system of indulgences has a long history behind it. We may pick out the following stages in its evolution.

(i) Indulgences first arose in connexion with the penitential system of the Church. In early days open and notorious sin cut off the offender from communion. The repentance by which he made his peace with God and was restored to communion included public confession of sin and the acceptance of discipline imposed by the Church. Sin was regarded not only as an offence against God but as a wrong done to the Christian society—the Body of Christ. The object of this discipline was twofold. First, it was a pledge of the reality of penitence. Secondly, it aimed at exciting and deepening penitence. But these pastoral aims were often, particularly in the West, over-

---

saying that it was not by tradition that the later Church arrived at certainty on the subject' (Salmon, *Infallibility of the Church* (1952), p. 58.) The Church of Rome largely bases her detailed knowledge of purgatory on a series of such revelations (cp. *op. cit.*, pp. 84 ff.).

[1] The word 'purgatory' by derivation simply means 'a place of cleansing', but it has evil associations and is perhaps best avoided. ' "Purgatory" is not a word that I should spontaneously adopt, because it is associated with Roman theories about the future state for which I see no foundation. But the idea of purgation, of cleansing as by fire, seems to me inseparable from what the Bible teaches us of the Divine chastisements; and though little is said directly respecting the future state, it seems to me incredible that the Divine chastisements should in this respect change their character when this visible life is ended. Neither now nor hereafter is there any reason to suppose that they act mechanically by an irresistible natural process, irrespectively of human will and acceptance' (Hort, *Life and Letters*, vol. ii. p. 336).

[2] The term 'indulgentia' was borrowed from Roman law. There it signified a remission of taxation or penalty.

shadowed and obscured by the view that penitential discipline was a penalty paid as a satisfaction for the sin committed, a penalty of which the Church had power to determine the details, but which was also due to God. In the third century, after the persecution of Decius, the African Church was faced with a great disciplinary problem. Many Christians had lapsed. Some had actually offered sacrifice, others had offered incense to heathen gods, others again had bought certificates certifying falsely that they had cleared themselves from the charge of Christianity by similar acts. Before the lapsed could be restored to communion, S. Cyprian justly imposed upon them a period of penitential discipline. Some of them, however, grew impatient and looked for some means of shortening this period. They asked the Confessors, *i.e.* men who had suffered torture or imprisonment for the faith, to intercede for them and obtain a remission of discipline. Some Confessors went further and, not content with intercession on behalf of the lapsed, claimed the right in their own name to restore to communion those under penance or even excommunicate. They gave them tickets of readmission (*libelli pacis*) which claimed to admit them and their friends to communion without having first accomplished the discipline imposed on them. This claim of Confessors to act in their own name was opposed by S. Cyprian. But the right of intercession was acknowledged. Here we find the germ of indulgences. The Church at the intercession of a Confessor remitted a part of the punishment imposed by herself. This, if wisely and justly done, was well within her own rights. She was doing no more than using her power of binding and loosing. We must remember, however, that behind Cyprian's action lay a definite theory of the transference of merit, by the intercession of those who possessed a superfluity of it, to the account of others whose moral condition enabled them to receive it.

(ii) An important step was taken when about the seventh century an indulgence passed from being a remission of an outstanding penalty to being the commutation of such a penalty for a payment of money. We find the system of 'Penitentials', *i.e.* the Church assessed the penance due for particular crimes at a certain rate, and by payment of the requisite sum of money remission of discipline could be purchased. Here again the system was probably unwise and led to disastrous results, but the Church can hardly be said to have exceeded her powers. What she bestowed for money was not God's forgiveness but remission of ecclesiastical penalty.[1]

A fresh step was taken at the Council of Clermont (1095). There a full commutation of penance was promised by Pope Urban II to all who would take part in a crusade. Henceforth we find the practice of remitting the temporal penalties of sin for all who would perform certain acts of devotion profitable to the Church, *e.g.* building

[1] See Strong, *Christian Ethics*, pp. 342–343.

churches, pilgrimages, etc. Men were naturally ready to substitute such special acts of devotion for a long and dreary period of penitential discipline. So long as it was recognized that what was commuted by such an indulgence was the performance of canonical penance no new principle was involved.

(iii) A more serious change was made when the growth of a belief in Purgatory extended the sphere in which satisfaction for sin could be made. As we saw, men came to believe that whereas the guilt (*culpa*) of sin was forgiven in absolution, a temporal punishment (*poena*) was still due, and this punishment must be worked off, if not in this life, then in Purgatory. Since Purgatory is in time and not in eternity, the power of indulgences was held to extend there too. Further, it was held that indulgences were transferable. They might be purchased for the benefit of the departed and added to his account. Since indulgences were granted 'a culpa et venia' and such phrases as 'venia peccatorum' were employed in connexion with them, we cannot wonder that the uneducated regarded them as affording remission not only of the penalty but of the guilt of sin. The Church was unwilling to clear up a misunderstanding so profitable to its own purse. The demand for indulgences was increased by the Act of Pope Boniface VIII, who decreed that those who visited Rome in the year 1300 and every hundredth year following should, if penitent and having made their confession, obtain the fullest remission of their sins (*plenissimam suorum veniam peccatorum*). This 'Jubilee' was an enormous financial success. So much so that later Popes found it advisable to shorten the interval between them.[1]

(iv) Indulgences existed, and it was the business of the Schoolmen to frame a theological defence for existing practice. This was done with the aid of the theory known as the 'Treasury of Merit', which was formally authorized by Pope Clement VI in 1343.[2] They held that in the sacrifice of Christ upon the Cross there was infinite merit, far more than was needed for the salvation of the world. This surplus, to which was added the merits of the saints acquired by 'works of supererogation', formed a spiritual treasure entrusted to the Church for the benefit of her members.[3] In practice the Pope, as having the power of the keys, was able to dispense this for the benefit of the faithful whether on earth or in Purgatory, so as to pay up whatever still remained of the satisfaction due as the penalty of sin.[4]

Such a theory is the barest guess-work, a proof of theological desperation. The Schoolmen were faced with a hopeless task. The

[1] For the growth of the system of indulgences see Creighton, *History of the Papacy*, vol. vi. pp. 68 ff.

[2] We find a strangely similar idea of the merits of the Fathers in later Judaism (cp. Gore, *Ephesians*, note c.).

[3] If the merits of Christ were infinite, it is not clear why the merits of the saints were required at all. Infinity cannot be increased.

[4] The indulgence was thus not only an *absolutio* (a remission) but a *solutio*, a payment from another source.

'treasury of merit' rests on a conception of 'merit' as something transferable and able to be added and subtracted by the rules of mathematics. The Communion of Saints, which rests upon unity of life, is coarsened and degraded by it into the likeness of a joint-stock company. Life cannot be expressed in terms of arithmetic. The whole idea is unscriptural and unspiritual. It obscures rather than illuminates the great truth of the union of all Christians living and departed in Christ. Further, it certainly cannot be proved from Scripture. Such a doctrine and the enormous claims built upon it can only be justified by a positive increase in revelation. If this increase has been made, when and to whom was the revelation given? From time to time protests were made by the best men, as, for instance, Dante, but the scandal was too profitable to be abated. As is well known, the protest of Luther, from which we may date the beginning of the Reformation, was occasioned by the traffic in divine forgiveness.

At the Council of Trent the abuses of the system were acknowledged. The Council claimed that power had been granted to the Church to confer indulgences. It anathematized those who asserted that they were useless or denied that the Church had such powers. But it went on to add 'The Council desires moderation to be used . . . lest by too great facility ecclesiastical discipline should be weakened'. It commanded that all base profits for their purchase whereby their illustrious name had come to be blasphemed, should be abolished. Every bishop was to search out abuses in his own diocese and bring them before the Provincial Synod, and so on. The decree is vague. The real cause of offence was not faced. The Church of Rome to-day retains indulgences and still represents them as more than a mere remission of ecclesiastical discipline imposed by the Church. She still teaches that they avail for souls in Purgatory. Theologians explain that they are only of avail 'per modum suffragii', but popular religion pays little heed to such distinctions. There is no point on which the modern Roman controversialist is less comfortable than that of indulgences.†

(c) *The Romish Doctrine . . . concerning Worshipping and Adoration as well of Images as of Reliques* is condemned on the same principles. In the earliest days of the Church neither pictures nor images had any place in Christian worship. Converts from Judaism brought with them their antipathy to all imitative art. Further, art had become identified with the idolatry and obscenity of a decadent pagan civilization. It was necessarily viewed with suspicion and banned from Christian use. There was need of a formal severance from the past before Christian art could be born.

(i) The first beginnings of a Christian art are to be found in the Catacombs. Symbolical paintings of very varied merit have been discovered dating from the beginning of the second century. The earliest example of any employment of art in church is the custom of painting the symbolical figure of the Good Shepherd on the chalice, mentioned by Tertullian.[1] At the beginning of the fourth century the building of more dignified churches had begun and it was natural that Christians should introduce into their churches the art that had beautified their tombs. In 305 the Synod of Elvira found it necessary to forbid the representation of objects of worship by paintings on the walls of the churches. Clearly these pictures were no longer only symbolic: they were intended to be portraits. But during the fourth century such pictures came to be generally admitted, in spite of occasional protests as that made by Epiphanius, who tore down a curtain in his diocese that bore a likeness.

Statuary, as being more closely associated with idolatry, became Christianized more slowly. Apart from sculptures on tombs we can find but the scantiest traces of Christian statuary during the first five centuries. Up to this day the Greek Church regards 'images' as a violation of the Second Commandment and employs only 'ikons', i.e. representations of our Lord and the saints in mosaic or painting. This, however, has made little difference in practice. In the West at the beginning of the seventh century Gregory the Great found it necessary to protest against the misuse of pictures and images.[2] In the East the scandal became so great that in the eighth century the Emperor Leo the Isaurian issued an edict for the destruction of all 'ikons'. From this started the iconoclastic controversy which lasted to the middle of the ninth century. Roughly speaking the Emperors were the champions of the party of destruction and the Popes of retention. The beginning of the end came with the Second Council of Nicaea in 787, which ultimately came to be accepted as the seventh general council by East and West alike. This decided in favour not only of images but of the veneration of images. It enjoined that they should be set up and 'treated as holy memorials, worshipped, kissed, only without that peculiar adoration ($\lambda \alpha \tau \rho \epsilon \iota \alpha$) which is reserved for the Invisible, Incomprehensible God.'[3] The controversy lasted on till 840, but in the end the decisions of the Council of Nicaea triumphed. Whatever sympathy the iconoclastic party must arouse by their zeal against abuses is more than counterbalanced by their fanaticism and want of religious earnestness. Further, the question had become complicated by the discussion about the permanence of our Lord's human nature. This was in effect denied by the iconoclasts in their arguments against representations of our Lord's human form. Their triumph would have been a disaster for Christian faith.[4]

---

[1] De Pudicitia, c. 10.

[2] Ep. 7. They are to be made and exhibited only to instruct the minds of the unlearned. Any worship or adoration is forbidden.

[3] $\tau \iota \mu \eta \tau \iota \kappa \dot{\eta} \pi \rho o \sigma \kappa \dot{\upsilon} \nu \eta \sigma \iota s$, which is to be paid to images, is not divine worship. The Council compares it with the veneration due to the Gospels. It is akin to the veneration shown to Emperors.

[4] The decisions of Nicaea did not win immediate acceptance in the West. All adoration of images was condemned by the 'Caroline' books edited by Alcuin about 790,

But, unhappily, the veneration of images in the West did not stay within the limits marked out for it by Councils. S. Thomas Aquinas in the thirteenth century advocated that 'latria', the highest form of worship reserved for God alone, be paid not only to Christ, but to images of Christ and even to the Cross. 'We also address and supplicate the Cross even as the Crucified Himself.'[1] If this was the teaching of the learned, we may be sure that the practice of the unlearned went considerably further. In 1408 Archbishop Arundel ordered that the clergy should preach and teach the veneration (*venerari*) not only of the images of Christ and of the Cross but of the saints, 'with processions, bendings of the knees, bowings of the body, incensings, kissings, offerings, lightings of candles and pilgrimages.' This was the deliberate encouragement of superstition. It opened the way for widespread fraud and lucrative miracle-mongering. Even the opponents of the Reformation admitted the existence of gross abuses. Such, indeed, is implied in the language of the Council of Trent itself, which commands the retention of images and that due honour and veneration should be paid to them, but utters very pointed warnings against superstition and lucre.[2]

(ii) The real question that underlies adoration of images is far more complex than at first glance appears.[3] What do we mean by 'worship' or 'adoration'? How does one set about worshipping an image? We all naturally treat the photograph of one we love with respect and reverence. Pictures and other objects become endeared to us by association and acquire a value that goes far beyond their intrinsic nature. In the case of religion we rightly treat with reverence a picture of our Lord or a crucifix. Such are often a real stimulus to our

---

so-called from their connexion with Charles the Great. In 794 the Council of Frankfort, acting probably under a misapprehension of the meaning of προσκύνησις, rejected the decrees of Nicaea. For an account of the controversy see Tixeront, *History of Dogmas*, III.

[1] *Summa*, iii. 25, Arts. iii. and iv.

[2] ' Not that any Divinity or virtue is believed to be in them on account of which they are to be worshipped : or that anything is to be sought of them : or that trust is to be placed in images, as in former days was done by the heathen, who placed their hope in idols : but because the honour which is shown to them is referred to the prototypes which they represent. . . . In the invocation of saints, the veneration of relics and the sacred use of relics let all superstition be taken away, all base gain be abolished, finally all lasciviousness avoided, so that images be not painted or adorned in wanton beauty and men misuse not the celebration of saints and visitation of relics to revellings and drunkenness' (Session 25).

[3] The Scriptural arguments used by Roman controversialists to defend image-worship hardly deserve mention. Any support drawn from the rendering of Heb 11[21] in the Douai version, 'Jacob adored the top of his rod,' rests on a mistranslation. The verse should run 'Jacob worshipped, leaning upon the top of his staff' (R.V.) So, too, Psalm 99[5] should be translated not 'Adore His footstool', but 'worship at His footstool'. The second commandment clearly forbids image-making for worship. But we are Christians, not Jews. Since in the Incarnation God was made man, the representation of our Lord does not infringe the spirit of the commandment or endanger a right belief in the nature of God. We may, however, regret that in most Roman catechisms the second commandment is combined with the first and so abbreviated as to obscure entirely the condemnation of image-worship. Attempts have been made to argue from David dancing before the Ark (2 Sam 6[14]). The weakness of the whole case is obvious.

imagination. They are a means of education and a help to devotion, at least to certain people and at certain times. It is no more wrong to treat them with reverence than to treat a Bible with reverence. But at what point does superstition begin? When does reverence pass into idolatry? That is a question not of outward act but of inner motive and intention. Official Roman theology has recognized this by the distinctions that it draws between various degrees of reverence. Latria is the supreme worship due to God alone. Hyperdulia, a degree of reverence due to the Blessed Virgin alone. Dulia that degree of reverence due to the saints and their images. These distinctions are excellent on paper, but have proved to be very difficult to observe in practice. There is no such thing as a devotional thermometer. No precise rules can be laid down. We cannot wonder that at the Reformation a clean sweep was made of all images. What has been profitable for education or devotion in one age may always become dangerous and unhealthy in the next. The appeal to the eye-gate into the soul of man cannot be ignored, but the methods by which the appeal is made must vary at different times. Superstition begins when the means employed to express and quicken devotion get in between the soul and God, when the means are erected into an end, when some inherent power, independent of God Himself, is supposed to reside in the means used or when they are treated as possessing a magical efficacy that relieves the user of them from the strain of moral earnestness. Against such dangers no rules can be a safeguard. The Bible no less than images has been used superstitiously. Puritanism has its superstitions. Human nature always desires a substitute for that 'worship in spirit and in truth' which alone God desires. The use of images in Churches is a question of discipline. Its expediency varies with the circumstances of the day. In our Article the Church of England rightly protests against their misuse. How far they shall be permitted is a question for a national Church to decide.

(iii) Closely connected with the question of images is that of relics. The natural reverence for the bodies of those dear to us was in the case of Christians heightened by the new respect for all connected with human body taught by the Incarnation. Such reverence was further increased by the honour that was felt to be due to martyrs. In the early days this instinct was satisfied by the careful collecting of their remains for burial, by assembling for worship and celebrating the Holy Eucharist at their tombs. It is sufficiently expressed by the letter from the Church of Smyrna recounting the martyrdom of S. Polycarp (155). They scornfully reject the insinuation that they worship any but Christ. 'Him being the Son of God we adore, but the martyrs as disciples and imitators of the Lord we cherish as they deserve for their matchless affection towards their own King and teacher.'[1]

[1] c. xvii. Lightfoot, *Apostolic Fathers*, part ii. vol. iii. p. 484. It continues in c. xviii. 'We afterwards took up his bones which are more valuable than precious stones and finer than refined gold and laid them in a suitable place; where the Lord will permit

But with the lowered tone of spiritual life that began in the fourth century, the purity of motive disappeared and reverence became mixed with superstition. The alleged discovery of the true Cross by Helena, mother of the Emperor Constantine, in 326 gave a great impetus to the downward movement. Relics became treated as valuable for their own sake and as instinct with supernatural power. It was believed that miracles were wrought through them. Nominal Christians, less than half converted from paganism, gave a hearty welcome to the cult. Throughout the middle ages relic-worship was unquestioned. After the crusades a most lucrative trade was plied with relics of all sorts from the Holy Land. Pilgrimages to the shrines of saints combining amusement with salvation were a marked feature of mediaeval life. At the Reformation, as was to be expected, there was a violent reaction. The Council of Trent did, indeed, retain the adoration of relics, with many cautions, as we have seen, that bear witness to the seriousness of the abuse. The general position is very similar to that in the case of images. No real arguments from Scripture can be adduced. The cures wrought by 'handkerchiefs and aprons' taken from the person of S. Paul (Acts 19^{12}) were sudden and spontaneous. There is no trace anywhere in the New Testament of the preservation of relics for worship. Here again the borderline between reverence and superstition is hard to define. We naturally treasure things as mementoes of those we love. From their associations they become invested with a new and most real value. Such a sentiment is right and natural so long as it does not pass into the ascription to them of any inherent power. Temperaments and ages differ, and what may be healthy and helpful to one man at one time is unhealthy and harmful to another man at another time. The decision must be left to reason and conscience. In the case of the Church as a whole the treatment of relics comes within the province of ecclesiastical discipline. At the time of the Reformation the Church of England judged very drastic action to be expedient. She was within her rights in doing so.

(d) *The Romish doctrine ... concerning invocation of Saints, is a fond thing, vainly invented and grounded upon no warranty of Scripture, but rather repugnant to the word of God.*

(i) It is not altogether clear what the Article intended to condemn under the title of 'the Romish doctrine concerning the invocation of saints'. There is a certain ambiguity both about 'Romish' and 'invocation'. Bishop John Wordsworth has argued that 'Romish' is simply synonymous with 'Romanist'.[1] It is quite a vague term for doctrines upheld by the favourers of the Pope, whether abroad or in England, selected because it was not abusive. Of such doctrines the Council of

us to gather ourselves together, as we are able, in gladness and joy, and to celebrate the birthday of his martyrdom for the commemoration of those that have already fought in the contest and for the training and preparation of those that shall do so hereafter.'

[1] *The Invocation of Saints and the 22nd Article*, pp. 44–48.

Trent was the formal exponent. The substitution of such a word for the earlier reference to the 'school-authors' was perfectly natural in 1563. The day of the latter was past. But there is evidence that the word may be used in many senses.[1] Again, 'invocation' may mean either of two things: the simple request to a saint for his prayers, 'ora pro nobis,' or a request for some particular benefit. In mediaeval times the saints had come to be regarded as themselves the authors of blessings. Such a view was condemned at the Council of Trent, but invocation in the former sense was defended and asserted. 'It is good and useful to invoke the saints as suppliants and to resort to their prayers, aid and help for obtaining benefits from God through His Son Jesus Christ our Lord, who alone is our Redeemer and Saviour.' The direct petitions to saints for blessings found in modern Roman devotions are always explained as no more than requests to the saints to pray to God that He will grant such blessings. The point at issue about our Article is this, Does it condemn both forms of invocation or does it only condemn requests for benefits?

In favour of the latter position it may be urged (α) Our Article cannot condemn the doctrine of Trent on this subject because that was not formulated till the close of 1563, whereas our Article had been issued in its present form by February of that year. (β) There is some evidence that the distinction between the two kinds of invocation was recognized at the Reformation. They were distinguished in the Bishop's Book and the King's Book. In the first of these books 'invocation' is quite definitely used of such prayer as should be made to God alone, and such invocation is contrasted with requests to the saints for their prayers.[2] In the second book the language is changed, but though this technical use of 'invocation' is withdrawn, the distinction between the two kinds is maintained.

On the other hand it has been replied: (α) Though the formal discussion of the question of invocation of saints at Trent is later than our Article, the Council's decision had already been anticipated in the decree 'De Sacrificio Missae', issued in September 1562. In this the duty of asking saints for their prayers was explicitly maintained. This decree may well have been known to Convocation when it met in January 1563, and the change to 'Romanensium' may be a reply to it. (β) The limited use of 'invocation' as found in the Bishop's Book is an isolated instance to which no real parallel can be quoted. The very fact that it was withdrawn in the King's Book suggests that it was felt to be unsatisfactory. 'This peculiar limit to the term "invocation", was in fact a transient usage, of which traces appear in some later English writers. But it was never accepted as the usual or

---

[1] Dr Darwell Stone in *The Invocation of Saints*[3] (p. 46) gives instances of its use for the Popes, Roman Catholics in general and the extreme party.

[2] 'To pray to Saints to be intercessors with us and for us to our dear Lord for our suits which we make to Him, and for such things as we can obtain of none, but of Him, so that we make no invocation of them, is lawful and allowed by the Catholic Church.'

established meaning of the word.'[1] (γ) Further, the Articles were revised in 1571 under the presidency of Parker, who had also presided in 1563. It is quite clear that by that time the only Romish doctrine worth considering was that of Trent. If our Article had been intended only to condemn popular superstitions, the phrase could hardly have been retained.

On the whole, then, we incline to the view that the Article condemns all kinds of invocation, though we allow that there is a loophole for maintaining the other view.

(ii) In the New Testament there is no allusion whatever to asking departed Christians for their prayers. The practice is neither allowed nor forbidden. In part this silence may be explained by the comparative absence of speculation about the future state due to the daily expectation of the Parousia. But if the practice were so vital to Christian faith as some have maintained, we might have at least expected, let us say, some allusion by S. Paul to the prayers of the Blessed Stephen.

The practice of invoking saints became officially countenanced in the Church during the fourth century. All authorities are agreed on this point. We find no invocations of saints in any Christian writer and teacher before the fourth century.[2] The question of popular devotions is more obscure. Inscriptions on tombstones containing requests to the departed are found in the Catacombs and elsewhere. Such form only a small proportion of the whole and their date is by no means certain. Few are earlier than 313. Some would understand them less as formal invocations than as parting requests to the dead to remember their friends in the Beyond. In view, however, of contemporary pagan customs they are probably to be regarded as invocations. They would form a starting point for the custom of prayer to martyrs at their tombs. In the fourth century the practice first received the encouragement of theologians. Such invocations are found in the writings of the Cappadocian Fathers, the two Gregories and Basil, in Chrysostom and Ephraem Syrus, and in Ambrose and Augustine. From the latter it is clear that in his day the practice was a popular one, sanctioned indeed by the authority of great teachers, but that such invocations were not yet admitted into the public services of the Church. A great impetus was given to the movement by the hymns of Paulinus of Nola and Prudentius. The first introduction

---

[1] Wordsworth, *op. cit.*, p. 60.

[2] A passage of Origen (220) sometimes quoted in favour of the practice refers not to saints at rest, but to saints still on earth. 'It is not improper to offer supplication, intercession and thanksgiving to saints: and two of these—I mean intercession and thanksgiving—not only to saints, but to mere men, but supplication to saints only, if any Peter or Paul can be found, that they may help us: making us worthy to enjoy the license which was granted to them for forgiving sins' (Quoted Luckock, *After Death*, p. 175, and examined pp. 187–188). The contrast is between holy men and men who are not holy. For the atmosphere in which the cult of the saints developed, see Bigg, *Wayside Sketches in Ecclesiastical History*, I–III.

of invocations to a saint (the Blessed Virgin) into public worship is said to have been made by Peter the Fuller, the monophysite patriarch of Antioch (*c.* 480). Before the middle of the eighth century they had made their way into Litanies. In the Middle Ages beyond all doubt saints were treated as direct authors of benefits spiritual and temporal. They had become for practical purposes departmental deities.[1] That this is pure heathenism all would allow; as the decrees of the Council of Trent show, no one could attempt to defend such a misconception. But the question still remains, 'Is it right to ask saints for their prayers?' This limited form of invocation is all that is permitted and defended officially, both in the Roman and Greek Churches, however little popular practice conforms to official theology.

In favour of the practice it is argued that the souls under the altar (Rev 6[9]) are engaged in prayer, and in Heb 12[1] the saints are called 'witnesses' of our race. It is inconceivable that holy souls should cease to pray for those whom they love on earth. S. Peter or S. Paul must continue to pray for the Churches that they founded or a mother to pray for her children. Again, if it is right to ask our earthly friends for their prayers, why is it not equally right to ask our fellow-Christians beyond the veil for theirs? We are still fellow-members of the Body of Christ and we may believe that if through death they have entered into a fuller union with Christ their power of prayer has become intensified. The practice of invocation makes the communion of saints a reality. It has been the unbroken custom of the Catholic Church in East and West alike since the fourth century at least.

On the other hand, there are very strong arguments that cause us to hesitate in adopting the practice and that justify the Church of England in banishing all invocations of saints from her public worship.[2]

(*a*) Such invocations rest upon the assumption that the saints can hear them: otherwise they are utterly unreal. This is a very large assumption and certainly cannot be proved from Scripture. The Fathers speak very doubtfully about the knowledge that the saints possess about the affairs of earth. If S. Ambrose in one place encourages men to implore the prayers of martyrs, in another place, addressing his own brother who was dead, he implies that the dead are unconscious of the sorrows of the living. S. Augustine practically denies that the dead know unconditionally what is happening on earth, though they may get to hear of it from those who join them from earth or angels may tell them what they need to know. Or,

---

[1] Cp. the words of Sir Thomas More: 'We set every saint in his office and assign him such a craft as pleaseth us: S. Loy a horse-leech, S. Ippolytus a smith, S. Apollonia a tooth-drawer, S. Syth women set to find their keys, S. Roke we appoint to see to the great sickness and S. Sebastian with him. Some saints serve for the eye only, others for a sore breast.'

[2] In the English Litany, published in 1544, the invocation of saints was confined to three clauses, only S. Mary being mentioned by name. In the 1549 Prayer-Book these were deleted.

again, they may come to learn what is needful by an exceptional and
direct revelation of God the Holy Ghost. He expressly leaves it an
open question how the martyrs are able to aid those whom they help.[1]
The saints may even be unconscious of the benefits wrought by God
in answer to requests made to them. This uncertainty could not continue. The practice was established and a theological defence for it
had to be found. By the time of Gregory the Great (c. 600) an
answer had been found. 'The saints inwardly see the brightness of
Almighty God, and therefore we cannot believe that they are ignorant
of anything outward.'[2] This is the explanation usually adopted. The
saints enjoy the vision of God, and as God sees all things they also
see them in God, as in a mirror. Even so Peter Lombard, the school-
man (1164), can speak of it as 'not incredible', and later Duns Scotus
is content to say that it is 'probable' that God reveals our prayers to
the saints. Even later Roman apologists have admitted that it is not
certain whether the saints are aware of our prayers. In short, the
whole theory that the saints possess all knowledge in the Beatific
Vision is a piece of pious speculation.[3] It was unknown to the Christian
Church for many centuries and if more than a speculation, must
have been revealed since: if so, when and where? Further, in Roman
theology a sharp distinction is made between the saints who have
been admitted to heaven and the rest of the faithful departed who
are elsewhere. Only the invocation of the former is enjoined; the invocation of souls in purgatory is tolerated but not encouraged.[4] This
distinction is most questionable. Scripture and the early Fathers
seem to know of no admission of any of the departed to the full
glories of heaven until after the resurrection of the dead: in this
Christians follow in the steps of Christ. The martyrs in the Revelation are 'under the Altar', and 'under the Altar' is not 'before the
Throne'. So Justin Martyr,[5] Irenaeus[6] and Tertullian[7] all make it
plain beyond any possibility of doubt that they believed that no soul

---

[1] See the full quotations from his *De Cura pro Mortuis* given and discussed in
Mason's *Purgatory*, pp. 145–153.

[2] Gregory, *Moral. in Job* 12[12].

[3] Heb 12[1] lends little support to the belief. μάρτυρες may be either 'witnesses' or
'martyrs': in any case the Christians are bidden to look not unto them, but 'unto
Jesus'. The runner in an earthly race fixes his eyes on the goal, not the spectators.

[4] The Eastern Church refuses to accept this sharp distinction and invokes all the
departed. Children invoke their parents, etc. Such invocation is far closer to that first
introduced into the Church, and is free from many of the objections that can be brought
against the Roman practice.

[5] *Dialogue with Trypho*, c. 80. Those who say 'that there is no resurrection of the
dead, but their souls are taken up to Heaven at the moment of death' are not to be
considered Christians at all. Cp. also c. 5.

[6] *Adv. Haer.* v. 31. It is following the example of the heretics 'to break through the
order in which the righteous are advanced' and 'say that as they are dead they pass
beyond the heavens'. Christians are in a place appointed by God for the resurrection
and only after rising with their bodies 'come to the vision of God'.

[7] *De Anima*, c. 55, 'Heaven is opened to none while earth remains.' The martyrs are
privileged at death to enter Paradise, but Paradise in Tertullian's view is not heaven.
For full quotations see Mason, *Purgatory*, pp. 78–86.

went to heaven at death but only after the resurrection of the dead at the Last Day, and such teaching lasted on for several centuries. Again, if saints can hear petitions addressed to them at any time or place, this means that, say, S. Mary or S. Peter can hear and intercede for thousands at the same time; such an infinite capacity trenches on the divine attributes of omniscience and omnipresence. To sum up, while it is possible that the saints can hear invocations, there is no sure ground for affirming it. The opposite opinion is at least equally tenable.

(β) Requests to the saints are not on a level with requests to our own living friends. The very fact of death removes the similarity and destroys the normal attitude of man to man. The danger is increased when only great saints are invoked. The practice seems to have begun with invoking relatives or close friends. The Fathers invoke their own teachers and companions. The earliest examples occur, as we should expect, in funeral orations and sermons on martyrs, and then are largely rhetorical. The next step was to invoke martyrs apart from their tombs, and other conspicuous saints. Finally, invocations were confined to canonized saints and the most primitive form tended to disappear. Thus the centre of gravity has shifted altogether. In the first six centuries, for instance, only one invocation of the Blessed Virgin is known, and the saints invoked are local saints. With the change the danger of reverence passing into worship is increased. Further, when requests are sung in public worship or said on bended knee, the feeling of worship is encouraged. The request will speedily become a prayer. Even S. John under similar conditions fell twice into error and was reproved (Rev 19[10], 22[8]). The custom of invocation first became prominent at a time when pagans in large numbers flocked into the Church, imperfectly trained in the doctrine of the one true God. They carried their heathen ideas with them. The pagans had been accustomed to inscribe upon their tombs invocations to the departed and to feast at their tombs on certain fixed days. The saints easily took the place of the many gods and spirits of heathenism. To say that invocation of saints is in origin largely pagan and a part of natural religion, is not necessarily to say that it is wrong. But it at least leaves it an open question whether it is Christian or in accordance with Christian revelation. Further, let us remember that what is defended is simply asking saints for their prayers. We may fairly ask if invocation has ever stopped there. In history request for prayers very rapidly passed into request for benefits. In modern Romanism the distinction is preserved only in the study of the theologian. If the Fathers could have seen the results that a few centuries later were to follow from their very tentative and often inconsistent teaching on the subject, we may believe that they would have shrunk from the steps that they took to encourage such invocations.

(γ) We need to be very jealous for the honour of God and the purity of worship. The saints have often been more popular than God, because they have been supposed to be more human and less severe towards sin. So fallen man obtains what he craves for, an object of worship that does not make too great demands upon him for holiness of life. Again, we need to insist on the true and perfect humanity of our Lord. The extravagant devotion to the Blessed Virgin has largely arisen from the obscuring of our Lord's humanity. As Son of Man He combines the strength of manhood with all the tenderness and grace of womanhood. There is no need to go outside Him for the fullest and truest human sympathy.[1]

(δ) The direct invocation of saints does at least bring into practical religious life certain great Christian truths, the reality of the communion of saints and the unseen world, the actuality of life after death and the like. We must admit that the Church of England has minimized these parts of the Christian faith in her life and teaching. Where Rome has erred by excess, we have erred by defect. The question is, can these truths have their due practical effect without resorting to invocation? An answer may be found in the ancient practice of 'comprecation'. 'Comprecation,' as opposed to 'invocation', is the practice of asking God Himself for a share in the prayers of the saints. This is a truly primitive and Catholic practice, found in the ancient Liturgies and open to no possible theological objection. It affirms the truth that the saints do pray for us, it meets the human need for active fellowship with the departed and it brings into the sphere of practical religion the communion of saints as including not only those on earth but those beyond the veil.[2]

Finally, we claim that the action of the Church of England in excluding all invocation of saints from public worship is in full accord with the principles for which she stands. She refuses to impose any teaching that cannot be proved from Scripture. To admit such invocation would be to affirm what Scripture has not affirmed, that the saints can hear our petitions. That is a point about which individuals are entitled to hold opposite opinions and our Church would be false to her own teaching if she curtailed this liberty by introducing invocations. She would, in effect, exclude those who are unable to accept the claims upon which such a practice is based. At the same time, individuals are left perfectly free to adopt such invocations in their own private prayers and to ask their dear ones who are departed to pray for them. There is a real distinction in principle. Our position is not in the least un-Catholic. It is true that for many centuries the Roman

---

[1] Cp. Fr. Benson, *Letters*, vol. i., p. 287.
[2] Cp. *e.g.* the words of S. Cyril of Jerusalem, 'Then we make mention of those who have fallen asleep before us, first of patriarchs, prophets, apostles, martyrs that God would at their prayers and intercessions receive our supplications.' In any case we must insist at all costs that we approach the saints through Jesus, and not Jesus through the saints.

Church and the Churches of the East have practised invocation of
saints in their public services. But the practice does not fulfil the test
of catholicity, *quod ubique, semper, ab omnibus*, since it was unknown
for at least two and probably three centuries. At the lowest estimate
it is a matter on which a national Church can legislate for herself.
We should not be right in refusing communion with a Church that
practised it, simply on that ground. But after all our appeal is not
simply to Catholic custom, but to Catholic custom as tested by Scripture. If we are loyal to this, our position is unassailable.†

THE CHURCH'S AUTHORITY IN DISCIPLINE

ARTICLE XXXIV

Of the Traditions of the Church

It is not necessary that Traditions and Ceremonies be in all places one, or utterly like; for at all times they have been diverse, and may be changed according to the diversity of countries, times, and men's manners, so that nothing be ordained against God's Word. Whosoever through his private judgment, willingly and purposely, doth openly break the traditions and ceremonies of the Church, which be not repugnant to the Word of God, and be ordained and approved by common authority, ought to be rebuked openly, (that other may fear to do the like), as he that offendeth against the common order of the Church, and hurteth the authority of the Magistrate, and woundeth the consciences of the weak brethren. Every particular or national Church hath authority to ordain, change, and abolish ceremonies, or rites of the Church ordained only by man's authority, so that all things be done to edifying.

De traditionibus Ecclesiasticis

Traditiones atque caeremonias easdem, non omnino necessarium est esse ubique, aut prorsus consimiles. Nam ut variae semper fuerunt, et mutari possunt, pro regionum, temporum, et morum diversitate, modo nihil contra verbum Dei instituatur.

Traditiones, et caeremonias ecclesiasticas, quae cum verbo Dei non pugnant, et sunt auctoritate publica institutae atque probatae, quisquis privato consilio volens, et data opera, publice violaverit, is ut qui peccat in publicum ordinem Ecclesiae, quique laedit auctoritatem Magistratus, et qui infirmorum fratrum conscientias vulnerat, publice, ut caeteri timeant, arguendus est.

Quaelibet Ecclesia particularis, sive nationalis, auctoritatem habet instituendi, mutandi, aut abrogandi caeremonias, aut ritus ecclesiasticos, humana tantum auctoritate institutos, modo omnia ad aedificationem fiant.

The last paragraph, 'Every particular, etc.,' was added in 1563. The remainder dates from 1553, and is largely based on the 13 Articles. The object is to defend the changes made at the Reformation against Roman attacks from without and disloyalty within.

§ 1. *The position of National Churches*

(*a*) We have already distinguished between the judicial authority of the Church in 'controversies of faith' and her legislative power in decreeing 'rites and ceremonies'. So far we have treated of the Church as a whole, as a single organized society. But in point of fact the one Catholic Church is represented in different parts of the world by local churches, possessing a life and individuality of their own. We find the beginnings of this even within the New Testament. The Churches of Corinth, Rome and Jerusalem, for instance, have their own character and their own problems of discipline and worship. It is evident, then, that in the working of the Church this fact must be taken into consideration. On questions of doctrine no fresh problems are raised. Truth must be one and the same in England and Germany, in Asia and America. As we have seen, practical difficulties arise about the expression of the one faith. The existence of different types of mind, progress in knowledge and education, the natural tendency of the human mind to one-sidedness, all bring with them their own problems. But these may arise equally even within a single local church. The existence of many local churches introduces no really new factor. Granted that there is such a thing as Christian truth, contained in Scripture, then the teaching authority alike of the whole Church and of local churches is limited by it. But when we come to questions of discipline and order, the case is different. As we have seen, Scripture lays down general principles and leaves it to the Church to work them out in her order and worship. This leaves open the door for considerable variety in administration and in practice. Disciplinary rules which the consciousness of the Church in one part of the world may feel to be necessary for the safeguarding of Christian morality or the propagation of Christian faith, may in another part of the world be unnecessary or even harmful. Again, the same spirit of devotion naturally clothes itself in very different forms of worship in the East and in the West. This is not to say that there are not right and wrong, better and worse forms of worshipping God. S. Paul, for instance, does not dismiss such questions as those decided in 1 Cor 11 as meaningless or trivial. He insists that Christian custom and ritual must really be in conformity with Christian spirit and Christian teaching. Due regard is to be paid to the customs and ritual of other Churches. But we are bound to recognize differences of race and temperament, of age and education. What was natural and seemly in the Middle Ages may be merely quaint to-day. What is supremely edifying in Honolulu may be grotesque in London: what is the worthy embodiment of English reverence and devotion, may be utterly meaningless in Timbuctoo. Hence '*It is not necessary that Traditions and Ceremonies be in all places one or utterly alike; for at all times they have been diverse and may be changed according to the diversities of countries, times and men's manners, so that nothing be ordained against God's Word.'* ... *'Every particular or national Church hath authority to ordain, change, and abolish ceremonies, or rites of the Church ordained only by man's authority, so that all things be done to edifying.'*

The phrase *'national Church'* requires some attention. Men sometimes argue that a national Church is only so many dioceses of the Catholic Church.[1] We allow, indeed, that it does consist of a given number of such dioceses, but it is far more than their mere collocation. Its unity is not simply a unity of addition. The Church of England, for instance, is bound together by the sharing of a common life and character peculiar to itself. It is foolish under the influence of a hard and abstract logic to attempt to shut our eyes to the influence of nationality upon the traditions and history of a Church. This principle of nationality the Church found already existing in the world: from the outset Christians belonged to some race or some State. The Church could no more evade or escape the fact of the nation than the fact of the family.[2] Nationality is a part of universal human nature. Here, as elsewhere, the Church is called upon not to abolish, but to discipline, purify and consecrate what is natural. We must admit that the Church has widely failed in her task, but the fact of nationality has, in all parts of the world, left its mark upon her history and organization.[3] In the case of the Church of England, the name represents far more than the Church of a particular geographical area. It is the Church through which during her history as a nation England has expressed her religious needs and aspirations. Our Church is not simply the Church of the majority of individual Englishmen, but its history and its character are intertwined with the history and character of the nation as a whole. Its order, its services, its formularies all reflect the strength and the weakness, the characteristics and the limitations of the English character.[4]

---

[1] Sometimes it is said with less accuracy that a national Church is only so many 'provinces' of the Catholic Church. The unit of the Church is the diocese, with the bishop at its head. The 'province' is primarily an aggregation of dioceses, not a subdivision of the Church.

[2] Cp. Mozley, *University Sermons*, 'On War,' esp. pp. 97–102.

[3] Even within the Roman Empire racial peculiarities tended to colour the life and theology of particular Churches. The limits of ecclesiastical dioceses came to conform to national or provincial boundaries. The broad distinction between East and West, so apparent in the history of the later Empire, has its counterpart in the doctrine and worship of the Church. In the West after the fall of the Empire the free development of national Churches was limited in varying degrees by the unifying policy of Rome. The Reformation was in part a revolt against such repression. To-day in Roman Catholic countries the spirit of nationality, which the Church has affected to ignore, has too often taken its revenge by banishing Christianity from the national life. In the East the course of history has been very different. The Nestorian and Monophysite schisms were caused by national antipathy to Constantinople more than by deliberate rejection of orthodoxy. Up to the present day the Churches of the East, whether orthodox or unorthodox, have tended to err in the direction of being over-national.

[4] For the specially English type of Christianity, see Collins's introduction to *Typical English Churchmen.*

The same is seen in a greater or less degree in other local or national churches.[1]

(b) Admitting, then, that the Catholic Church is represented in different parts of the world by particular or national Churches, which reflect in their traditions and customs racial and local peculiarities, we may ask, whether this power to *'ordain, change and abolish ceremonies or rites of the Church,'* or, we may add, rules of Church order and discipline, is unlimited. The Article appears to recognize only one ground of limitation, *'so that nothing be ordained against God's Word.'* So, too, in the preface to the Prayer-Book entitled 'Of Ceremonies, why some be abolished and some retained,' appeal is made solely to principles of expediency in dealing with such as 'have had their beginning by the institution of man'. That is to say, the Church of England claims unlimited power to alter or abolish rites and customs of the Church, however ancient or widespread, provided that they rest upon human institution.

Now to-day it is often asserted that there are certain 'Catholic[2] customs' which it is beyond the competence of any local or national Church, such as the Church of England, to alter or abolish. It is argued that when a rule or a practice can be shown to have been observed by the universal Church, such a rule or practice represents the mind of the universal Church and, therefore, can only be amended or repealed by the decision of the universal Church. A particular Church, as being only a part of the universal Church, has no authority to act in such case by itself. It is not a question whether such changes would be expedient or wise, but whether it is possible for a local Church to make them.

In order to answer this question we may begin by considering how those customs and rules came into being. In the main local customs originated not by any deliberate act on the part of the Church, but unconsciously and as it were automatically. Divine service was held. As in the presence of God, all was done in the spirit of reverence. Such reverence expressed itself in certain natural actions of the body and in orderly methods of procedure. The attempt was made to do everything 'decently and in order'. Hence, as in all common life, the habit grew up of doing certain things in a particular way and from repetition this habit acquired a new sanction, a sanction all the greater as it was felt to express the mind of the community. Later on such customs were often made into definite rules by local synods or councils. The actual form that these customs took depended very largely on local conditions, sometimes, indeed, on accidental material circumstances. In the formation of such customs we must not ignore

---

[1] On Christianity and Nationalism, see W. Temple, *Church and Nation*, Lect. II.

[2] In ordinary conversation the use of the term 'Catholic' is too often ambiguous. It may mean in the strict sense 'universally held and practised'. But it may only mean 'held and practised in some part of the Catholic Church', *e.g.* the Roman Church, or that part of it known to the speaker. The distinction is important.

the influence of secular life. 'We must remember that the religious life of such a region or such a Church rests upon the ethnic and social life prevalent there; its customs were based upon this and expressed in terms of ethnic and social life. In this or that ethnic life there was much that was local: Egyptian or Syrian, Greek or Roman, Gallican or Spanish. There was much that savoured of a particular time or phase of thought; much even that must be pronounced frankly pagan, although it long survived or reappeared at a later day in the Church of Christ. No view of the past can be adequate that fails to remember this.'[1] So, too, local bodies of Christians exercised the right of regulating the life and conduct of their members in accordance with Christian principles and of laying down rules for carrying out the Church's work in an orderly and effective manner. In the first instance these rules were decisions made for dealing with a particular case or a particular set of circumstances. When similar cases arose, they were naturally dealt with in a similar manner. So a customary method of procedure arose. Accordingly, in all Churches there arose customs about rites and ceremonies, traditional methods of working and regulations about Church order and discipline, resting for their authority upon the consent of the particular Church.

If this was the method in which Church customs and traditions arose, we should expect to find, as in fact we do find, very considerable variety among them. This diversity of custom is the natural expression of racial and local differences. Its prevalence is at all times in the Church's life the rule rather than the exception. Its existence is recognized and approved by many of the highest authorities in the Church. Thus, the Council of Nicaea decreed 'let the ancient customs prevail'. Augustine more than once explicitly commands the observance of local customs. His mother Monica was perplexed because the custom of the Church of Africa was to fast on Saturdays, but the custom of Milan was not to fast. He consulted Ambrose on the subject, who recommended conformity to local custom. 'When I am here I do not fast on Saturday; but when I am at Rome I do: whatever Church you may come to, conform to its custom, if you would avoid either giving or receiving offence.'[2] His own advice to others is the same as that of Ambrose. Difference of custom 'if it is clearly not contrary to the faith or to sound morality, is to be held as a thing indifferent and ought to be observed for the sake of fellowship with those among whom we live.' Historians like Socrates and Sozomen, both writing in the fifth century, describe at length the great variety of customs and Church orders to be found in different parts of the world without a hint that such variety was not desirable.[3] Again, Augustine

---

[1] Collins, 'Conditions of Church life in the first six Centuries,' *C.H.S.* Tract No. xcii. p. 33.

[2] *Ep.* 54, cp. also *Ep.* 36, § 32.

[3] Cp. Socrates, *H. E.* v, 22; Sozomen, vii. § 19.

of Canterbury put to Gregory the Great the question, 'Whereas the faith is one and the same, why are there different customs in different Churches? and why is one custom of Masses observed in the holy Roman Church and another in the Gallican church?' He received the reply, 'It pleases me, that if you have found anything, either in the Roman, or the Gallican, or any other Church, which may be more acceptable to Almighty God, you carefully make choice of the same, and sedulously teach the Church of the English, which as yet is new in the faith, whatsoever you can gather from the several Churches. For things are not to be loved for the sake of places, but places for the sake of good things. Choose, therefore, from every Church those things that are pious, religious and upright and when you have, as it were, made them up into one body, let the minds of the English be accustomed thereto.'[1] No doubt as time went on there was an increasing tendency to secure uniformity of custom, largely in order to strengthen the authority of Rome. But no one would maintain that local differences of custom are in themselves wrong or undesirable.

(c) If, then, it is granted that particular or national Churches may rightly institute and retain their own traditions and customs, it follows that they may no less modify or abolish them. This is indeed very necessary. Customs tend to increase in number. They spring up more readily than they die down. The danger is that the ever-increasing number and complexity of rites and traditions may become a burden and a hindrance. Customs that were in origin the spontaneous product of reverence and zeal survive long after they have exhausted their usefulness. They hinder rather than help devotion and retard activity. Sometimes a custom becomes so meaningless and obviously unnecessary that it is gradually and even unconsciously dropped: it is abrogated in the same way in which it grew up. Moreover, it has been generally held that even canon law may be abrogated by 'desuetude', that is, not simply by continued neglect but by the growth of a definite practice to the contrary. This is proof that the old law no longer represents the mind of the Church, but that new circumstances demand a new application of her principles. On the other hand, especially in matters of ritual, human nature is conservative. Old customs and ceremonies are retained even after their practical usefulness has ceased and their original purpose has been forgotten. New ones are constantly springing up and being added to the old. Hence, from time to time in the interests of simplicity and sincerity, a deliberate pruning and revision is called for. S. Augustine complained in his time that the Christian religion was being oppressed by the number of burdensome ceremonies that had grown up, till Christians were even in worse case than the Jews.[2] At the time of the Reforma-

---

[1] Bede, *E.H.* (Giles' translation), i. 27. Cp. also the answer of Anselm to Waleran quoted by Collins, *op. cit.* p. 19.

[2] *Ep.* 55, § 35.

tion matters had gone from bad to worse. As the Prayer-Book, after referring to S. Augustine, says, 'What would S. Augustine have said, if he had seen the ceremonies of late days used among us; whereunto the multitude used in his time was not to be compared? This, our excessive multitude of ceremonies, was so great and many of them so dark, that they did more confound and darken, than declare and set forth Christ's benefits unto us.' Plainly, then, in such cases the only hope is the deliberate abolishing of such customs and ceremonies as are no longer edifying.

We are now in a better position to face the question as to the existence of certain 'Catholic customs' which it is beyond the power of any particular Church to vary. We believe that our Article has taken up a perfectly sound position in asserting that the only ground for the retention or repudiation of any custom that is *ordained only by man's authority* by a particular or national Church is expediency, *'so that all things be done to edifying.'* Such language rules out any idea that a local Church is fettered in its liberty of action because a custom adopted by itself has been adopted by other local Churches or been generally adopted. Even where such a universal custom has been approved by a general council, we must remember that the decrees of a general council are subject to the approval of the whole Church: they have authority only so far as they represent the mind of the Church.[1] As soon as a particular Church repudiates a custom that has been hitherto universally observed, it is apparent that it no longer represents the mind of the whole Church, and therefore has lost the authority which it formerly possessed. The Catholic Church of one generation cannot bind the Catholic Church of the next generation in such matters. Life involves change and movement. The moment that we grasp that all tradition and custom, all rites and ceremonies, are valuable only so far as they minister to the truest self-expression of life, the reasonableness of this position is clear. Further, when we turn to history, we find that as a matter of fact customs that

---

[1] When long lists of conciliar decrees are hurled at our heads in order to induce us to adopt a certain custom as being 'Catholic', it is well to remember the following caution given by Dr. Collins:

'We must beware of *arguing that a thing was always done because a Canon was passed to say that it should be done.* . . . the first thing that the Canon shows is that at the time and in the region where it was passed the thing was *not* done, and that they who passed it wished that it should be done. No doubt, Canons were sometimes obeyed; perhaps usually so. Some of them . . . have inaugurated an entire change in the practice of the Church. But there are Canons . . . which might almost have been said to come into the world still-born and others which never seem to have been carried out in any real sense. And in general, whenever we find that the substance of a particular Canon is repeated over and over again elsewhere, the inference to be drawn is not that the matter was one upon which the mind of the Church has always been quite clear—else there would very probably have been no Canon on the subject in the first instance—but rather that the enactment was one which, rightly or wrongly, did not at that time commend itself to the Church at large; and that it was repeated simply because it could not be carried out.' He then goes on to point out that the really vital things in Church order, such as the ministry, do not rest on decisions of councils at all.

were once universal and had behind them the sanction of general councils, have fallen into abeyance without any definite abrogation by the whole Church. The Council of Jerusalem enjoined abstinence from blood. The rule is, we are told, still observed in the East: it has long been disregarded in the West. The Council of Nicaea forbade kneeling in Church during the season of Easter. Once again this is still observed in the East but not in the West. So, too, the Eastern Church has made certain innovations, such as the restriction of the choice of bishops to monks. All these are indisputable instances of changes made in Catholic customs by particular Churches. They may or may not be wise, but few would maintain that they were unlawful. Other instances will occur as we deal with certain other Articles. To maintain that there is any custom that a particular Church is unable to alter on its own authority, simply because it has at some period been observed by the whole Church, is to fly in the face of reason and history.[1]

No doubt the case is not so simple as it appears, so long as we are discussing the question quite generally. The moment that we deal with concrete cases other considerations than those of abstract right or pure theology come in. We should all agree that the more widely any given custom had gained currency, the more probable is it that it is valuable and therefore not lightly to be repealed. Nor do we wish to minimize the offence that may be caused to other particular Churches by the giving up of ancient traditions that are still venerated and retained among themselves. Nor can we pass over the question of motive. A change that in itself is unimportant may be the sign of an unchristian spirit or of perverted doctrine. Customs that originated with a purely utilitarian aim come in time to be invested with a doctrinal significance that was entirely absent from the minds of those who first practised them. Hence the abandonment or retention of such customs comes to be regarded as the public denial or affirmation of the doctrines popularly associated with them.[2] Again, not in-

---

[1] In 1947 the Report of the Archbishop's Commission on 'The Canon Law of the Church of England' was published (S.P.C.K.). It contains a review of the history of Canon Law with particular reference to the Church of England and the draft of a revised body of Canons. The proposals are under discussion by the Convocations. In this way it is hoped to provide the Church with a body of Canons recognized as expressing her mind and adapted to her present needs.

[2] An excellent instance of this is the matter of clothes. At the celebration of the Eucharist in primitive times the officiants naturally wore their best clothes, out of reverence to God and as expressive of festal joy. In course of time the fashion of clothes changed. In the West the barbarian type of dress supplanted the old Roman type of dress for ordinary life. But religion is naturally conservative. The Christian minister retained the old type of dress after it had been abandoned by the layman. He continued to celebrate the Eucharist in clothes that were no longer those of secular use. This beyond all possible doubt is the historical origin of Eucharistic vestments. In certain details they have been modified by ecclesiastical custom, but in their essentials they represent the ordinary civil costume of the well-dressed layman of the first century A.D. When they ceased to be the layman's ordinary dress they began to acquire a sacerdotal significance. Their unfamiliarity prompted various quaint and symbolical

frequently, when the special circumstances that gave rise to a ritual practice have passed away, the practice itself remains, and in order to justify it a new and mystical explanation is invented. It comes to be regarded as symbolical of some Christian truth or some pious fancy.[1] We must allow due weight, too, to the associations that come to gather round some practice that in itself is merely utilitarian. In such ways as these the unlimited right of a particular Church to change customs or ceremonies is in actual practice modified.[2]†

---

explanations of their meaning. In England they have come to be regarded by many as expressive of the Roman doctrine of the Eucharist. The precariousness of such a view is obvious when we remember that up to this day they are still retained by Lutheran Churches in Scandinavia, who find nothing in them that runs counter to the purest Lutheranism. Nor did the authors of the *Ornaments Rubric*, at any rate when it was first issued, see in them anything fundamentally opposed to the teaching of the Elizabethan Prayer-Book. It is probably a matter for regret that the Evangelical party have not adopted them *en masse*, as they adopted the surplice, so odious as a rag of Popery to their Puritan forerunners, and thus deprived them of any Roman significance. Putting aside the vexed question of obedience to the *Ornaments Rubric*, vestments are valued by very many to-day whose loyalty to Anglicanism is undoubted. They are visible symbols of the continuity of the Church. They are beautiful in form. It is not unreasonable that if the minister has a special vesture for taking public prayers he should have a different one for celebrating the Holy Eucharist. It is impossible to maintain that the wearing or not wearing of any particular kind of clothes affects the validity of sacraments. Their use is a matter of 'reverent and seemly order'.

[1] As we have said, ritual is primarily good manners. In the celebration of the Eucharist the officiant is the organ of the Church, which is represented by the assembled congregation. When he leads them in prayer or, as their minister, performs the various acts that the service requires, it is natural that he should stand, as it were, at their head. Hence under ordinary circumstances in England to-day we get the Eastward position. In primitive times the celebrant usually stood facing the people, at the other side of the Holy Table, with the other clergy ranged on either side of him, in imitation of our Lord and His Apostles at the Last Supper. The Pope still celebrates thus at S. Peter's. Thus, either the Eastward or the Westward position is natural. The position at the North end, as a piece of ritual, is perfectly meaningless. It is a survival from the days when the Holy Table was temporarily removed from the East end of our churches and placed lengthwise in the chancel or body of the church, so that the celebrant's position naturally turned with it and he found himself facing South instead of East. When the Table returned to its old position, altar-wise, the celebrant's position at the North end was quite illogically retained. It has now come to be regarded as symbolical of 're-formed doctrine'. On the other hand, if, when the celebrant acts as the minister of the congregation, it is natural that he should face East, it is equally natural that when he acts or speaks as God's minister to the congregation, he should turn to them, as in pronouncing the absolution or reading the Epistle and Gospel. It so happened that mediaeval books were bulky and not easily lifted. Hence the custom arose for the sake of convenience of not turning round to read the Epistle. As long as this was in Latin, not much was lost. But now that the books are light and the Epistle is read in English, it is absurd to continue to read it into the wall. The practice is defended as being Catholic, presumably because it is still continued in the Roman Church along with the use of Latin. But surely Catholicism is not incompatible with courtesy. The custom, which arose purely as a matter of practical convenience, is to-day no longer convenient or edifying.

[2] The question of 'Catholic customs' may be illustrated by the question of 'fasting Communion'. This was the custom by the time of Tertullian (*On Fasting*, c. 10), S. Augustine had never heard of a time when it was otherwise, and assigns it a command of S. Paul (*Ep.* 54 or 118). Beyond all doubt the custom was universal in East and West alike down to the Reformation. In primitive times the character of the day determined the time of the Eucharist. On Sunday when fasting was forbidden, it was early; on half-fasts, in the afternoon; in Lent, so as to end at nightfall. On the other hand, there is no command in Scripture on the subject. S. Augustine's statement is at best a

ARTICLE XXIV

Of speaking in the Congregation in such a tongue as the people understandeth	*De loquendo in Ecclesia lingua quam populus intelligit*
It is a thing plainly repugnant to the word of God, and the custom of the Primitive Church, to have public Prayer in the Church, or to minister the Sacraments, in a tongue not understanded of the people.	Lingua populo non intellecta, publicas in Ecclesia preces peragere aut Sacramenta administrare, verbo Dei, et primitivae Ecclesiae consuetudini plane repugnat.

Rewritten and strengthened in 1563. In the previous year the Council of Trent had anathematized those who said that 'Mass ought only to be celebrated in the vulgar tongue'.

§ 2. We may now turn to two definite instances in which the Church of England has used her authority to change previously existing custom.

(*a*) The language in which public services are to be conducted and the sacraments ministered is clearly a question that a particular or national Church has authority to determine. The Church of England, in returning to the vernacular, claims the support both of Scripture and the custom of the primitive Church.

The only passage of Scripture that bears directly on the question is 1 Cor 14. In this chapter S. Paul contrasts 'speaking in an unknown tongue', *i.e.* unintelligible ecstatic utterances, with prophesying, *i.e.* preaching. This by itself, however, is hardly to the point, as no one would be so foolish as to preach in a tongue not understanded of the

---

tradition unsupported by any evidence. In the earliest days the Communion was preceded by the Agape. It is at most, therefore, an ecclesiastical custom, venerable as representing the mind of the Church. Therefore a national Church has the right to change it. It is not mentioned in the Prayer-Book, and, though recommended and observed by individuals, has not been enforced for centuries in the Church of England. In 1893 a Report of the Upper House of Southern Convocation declared that to teach that it is a sin to communicate otherwise than fasting, is contrary to the spirit and teaching of the Church of England. Even the Church of Rome admits that the custom is of human institution, since the Pope has the right to dispense from it. We believe our Church to be quite right in leaving its observance to the individual conscience. Fasting is a means to an end, not an end in itself. Food is God's gift and cannot, as food, defile the man. On the one hand, fasting represents the share of the body in the self-preparation before communion. As such, it has a quasi-sacramental value. On the other hand, if it weakens our attention or unfits us for our work, it ceases to be a means to the true end. Social customs have changed and circumstances are very different from early days. Life in an English climate is far more strenuous. Perhaps what we most need is a new definition of fasting. (See, on the rigorist side, Puller, *Concerning the Fast before Communion*, 1891; on the other side, Dearmer, *The Truth about Fasting*, 1928. Also G. R. Dunstan in *Theology*, Jan. Feb., 1950, and following correspondence in April and May. For recent Roman relaxations of the rules, see *Acta Apostolicae Sedis*, vol. XLV. 16 Jan. 1953.)

people. But in v. [14] he proceeds to the question of prayer, 'If I pray in a tongue, my spirit prayeth, but my understanding is unfruitful.' Praying and singing are to be not only with the spirit but 'with the understanding also'. Further, prayer in a tongue excludes 'the unlearned'. As he cannot understand it, he does not know when to say 'Amen' at the end (v. [16]). 'Thou verily givest thanks well, but the other is not edified.' S. Paul lays down two principles. First, he deprecates any form of devotion in which the intellect has not its due place. Secondly, he lays down that the great aim must be the edification of the whole body. It is clear that prayers in a foreign tongue as compared with prayers in English, are far less in accordance with these principles. Not even the providing of translations makes the service equally real. In this sense the use of '*a tongue not understanded of the people*' '*is a thing plainly repugnant to the Word of God.*'

As regards the '*custom of the primitive Church*', the facts are beyond dispute. Primitive liturgies were always in the native tongue and such still exist in many languages. Rome itself originally used a Greek liturgy which was translated into Latin when the Church there became Latin-speaking. Latin only came to be used in public worship throughout the West as the language of the Empire. It continued to be used for reasons of convenience as being the common language of educated people. During the period of change and uncertainty this was an advantage, but in the present order of things this advantage is more than counterbalanced by its disadvantages.[1] The custom of the primitive Church no less than practical experience supports the change.

ARTICLE XXXII

Of the Marriage of Priests	*De conjugio Sacerdotum*
Bishops, Priests, and Deacons, are not commanded by God's Law either to vow the estate of single life or abstain from marriage. Therefore it is lawful also for them, as for all other Christian men, to marry at their own discretion, as they shall judge the same to serve better to godliness.	Episcopis, presbyteris, et diaconis nullo mandato divino praeceptum est, ut aut coelibatum voveant, aut a matrimonio abstineant. Licet igitur etiam illis, ut caeteris omnibus Christianis, ubi hoc ad pietatem magis facere judicaverint, pro suo arbitratu matrimonium contrahere.

This Article was written by Parker in 1563. Notice that 'sacerdotum' is the equivalent of priests. Deacons are clearly regarded as priests in the making. Bishops possess the priesthood in addition to their special authority.

[1] The Liturgical Movement which has in the last two or three decades gathered much strength in parts of the Roman Church seems likely to lead in the end to a demand for a liturgy in the vernacular. The congregation can take a full corporate part in the Liturgy only when it can hear and understand what the celebrant is saying.

(*b*) The Church of England has exercised her disciplinary authority on a second point, the marriage of the clergy. The first half of the Article is true beyond dispute. No passage of Scripture commands bishops, priests and deacons '*either to vow the estate of single life or to abstain from marriage*'. It is true that our Lord pronounced a blessing on those 'who made themselves eunuchs for the kingdom of heaven's sake' (Mt 19^{12}). S. Paul, too, regarded the celibate life as preferable, since it gave the opportunity for undistracted service of God; he did not forbid marriage, but discouraged it in view of 'the present distress', *i.e.* the threatening outlook for the Church at Corinth which he regarded as the prelude to the second coming of Christ (1 Cor 7).[1] On the other hand, we find throughout the New Testament the fullest recognition of the sacredness of marriage. The presence of Christ at Cana (Jn 2^1 ff.) and His teaching on divorce (Mk 10^5 ff., etc.) attest its sanctity. S. Paul in Eph 5$^{22-33}$ finds in marriage the most fitting symbol of the union between Christ and the Church. In 1 Tim 4^3 'forbidding to marry' is classed among the 'doctrines of devils'. So, too, in Heb 13^4 marriage is to be 'had in honour among all' (cp. also 1 Pet 3^7).[2] In 1 Cor 9^5 S. Paul claims the right to 'lead about a wife that is a believer, even as the rest of the apostles and the brethren of the Lord and Cephas.' This implies that the majority of the apostles and the brethren of the Lord were married men, as indeed we should expect, since celibacy was almost unknown among the Jews (cp. Mk 1^{30}). Again, in the Pastoral Epistles one of the conditions required of those to be ordained deacon (1 Tim 3^{12}) or bishop (1 Tim 3^2, Tit 1$^{5-6}$) is that they should be the 'husband of one wife'. There is no reason to suppose that S. Paul insisted on marriage as a preliminary to ordination: such a condition would have excluded himself. But it is evident that he expected that normally the clergy would be married men.[3]

Since, then, Scripture lays down no law of celibacy, the marriage of the clergy is one of those matters that a particular Church can decide for itself. The Church of England lays down no restrictions about the marriage of the clergy either before or after ordination. '*It is lawful also for them, as for all other Christian men, to marry at*

---

[1] In vv. $^{1-7}$ he seems to be answering a question of the Corinthians, 'Are the relations between married persons to continue after conversion?' v. ^{7} gives his answer. Continency is a special gift to the individual to fit him for a special work. Where it has not been given, normal relations must continue. In vv. $^{8-9}$ and v. ^{25} ff. he turns to the case of the unmarried. He regards it as best that if possible they should remain as they are, but the same principle holds good as before. His whole teaching is governed by his expectation of the Parousia. This would make the birth of children superfluous.

[2] The language of Rev 14^4 is metaphorical. See Swete, *ad loc.*

[3] The exact meaning of μιᾶς γυναικὸς ἀνήρ is disputed. Probably it means no more than 'faithful to one wife', a very necessary condition in those days. Others take it to mean that the man must not have married a second time. Certainly in later days there was a prejudice in the Church against second marriages, and in 1 Tim 5^9 ἑνὸς ἀνδρὸς γυνή clearly means a woman who has not married again. On the other hand, Gentile opinion disapproved of second marriages among women but not among men.

their own discretion, as they shall judge the same to serve better to godliness.' When we turn to the history of the early Church we find indisputable evidence for the ordination of married men, but little if any for marriage after ordination. Though we hold that a national Church is perfectly competent to make its own rules equally about either case, in studying history we must keep the two questions distinct.

During the first three centuries there is abundant evidence of the existence of a married clergy and of their continuing to have children after ordination. Indeed the sixth of the Apostolic Canons ordered the deposition of any bishop, priest or deacon who separated from his wife 'under the pretence of piety'. On the other hand, it seems to have been an unwritten custom of the Church that clergy should not marry after ordination. No undisputed instance of such a marriage can be produced. About 220 Hippolytus vehemently attacked Callistus for saying that any one of the clergy who married 'might remain in the clergy as not having sinned'.[1] Such a decision was clearly an innovation. Before the close of the third century the general custom of the Church found expression in the 25th of the Apostolic Canons, that forbade marriage after ordination to all above the order of subdeacon. At the Council of Ancyra (314) a special exception was made in the case of deacons who at the time of ordination gave notice of their intention to marry. At another council, held about the same date at Neo-Caesarea, a canon was passed deposing priests who married after ordination. The need of a special canon suggests that offenders were numerous.

In the fourth century we find the beginnings of the cleavage of custom between East and West. Partly owing to a development of S. Paul's teaching which regarded celibacy as a higher state, partly owing to a false dualism that viewed marriage as defilement,[2] partly owing to certain practical advantages, a feeling grew up in favour of celibacy, especially among the laity who did not have to practise it. It was part of a general movement that exalted asceticism. As so often, Spain led the way in advocating strictness of discipline. At the Council of Elvira (305) the excited feelings roused by the recent persecution of Diocletian led to the passing of a canon forbidding priests to live in wedlock with their wives. The Council of Nicaea was only preserved from passing a similar canon by the protests of the Egyptian Confessor Paphnutius, himself an unmarried man.[3] Henceforth the Eastern Church, with certain local and temporary exceptions, has maintained the traditional custom of the early Church.[4] The par-

[1] Ref. ix, 12, 22.
[2] This idea is found as early as Origen and is in flat contradiction to Scripture.
[3] See Socrates, *H.E.* i. 11.
[4] The Council of Gangra in Cappadocia (358) anathematized those who held aloof from the ministrations of married clergy. On the other hand, in the fifth century the clergy in Achaia, Macedonia and Thessaly were required to refrain from the use of

ochial clergy are men married before ordination.[1] Only monks are celibate. The only modification is that since the Quinisext Council (692) bishops have been definitely required to give up living with their wives, and in practice they are usually chosen from the monks. Even at the opening of the fifth century this was becoming the rule for bishops, and Synesius of Cyrene, who insisted on retaining his wife, was an exception to the general custom.

In the West clerical celibacy was enforced with greater strictness. The Popes used their influence in this direction. The first authentic decretal, issued by Pope Siricius in 385 to the bishop of Tarragona, forbade the marriage of priests and deacons. The same principles as those of Elvira are laid down by the Council of Carthage (390) and by later councils in France and Spain with varying strictness. Despite Papal decrees and decisions of councils the rule was far from universally observed. Gregory VII in 1074 found it necessary to reassert it with unprecedented severity, partly to forbid the enrichment of clerical families. In England the application of Gregory's rule was modified by the common-sense of Lanfranc. In future no married men were to be ordained, but married priests were not compelled to send away their wives. Not till 1102, under Anselm, did celibacy become the absolute and universal law of the English Church. But it is one thing to pass such laws, quite another thing to enforce them. 'Throughout the whole period from Pope Siricius to the Reformation . . . the law was defied, infringed, eluded. It never obtained anything approaching to general observance, though its violation was at times more open, at times more clandestine.'[2]

At the time of the Reformation the abuses of the system were so gross that no reform was more urgently demanded than the legalization of clerical marriage. The laity desired it in defence of their own families. Celibacy was, however, enforced during the reign of Henry VIII by the Six Articles and the King's Book, although Cranmer had recently married a wife. Not till 1547 did Convocation repeal all canons against such marriages. In 1549 Parliament definitely legalized clerical marriage. In 1559 Elizabeth's injunctions required the clergy to obtain the sanction of their bishops before marriage. At the Council of Trent strenuous efforts were made especially by the

---

marriage. This, however, did not affect the general practice of the Eastern Church. Even bishops had children after their consecration (Socrates, *H.E.* v. 22).

[1] In the Eastern Church it is part of the work of theological colleges to find wives for their unmarried students, usually from the daughters of the clergy. We are told that the arrangement works well.

[2] Milman, *Latin Christianity*, vol. 1, p. 160. Cp. vol. 3, pp. 440–441. The Church of Milan deliberately and openly retained a married clergy till 1058. Even the great Archbishop Heribert was married and after his death canonized! They claimed to continue the tradition of S. Ambrose, in independence of Rome. So, too, Bishop Wordsworth shows that there were eminent clerical families in England and that the Church in Wales hardly pretended to enforce celibacy (*The Ministry of Grace*, pp. 235–238).

Emperors to obtain a dispensation at least for the clergy in their own empire. These efforts failed and the Council of Trent forbade clerical marriage. By this rule the Church of Rome is still bound. She would seem to admit, however, that it is a question not of divine command but of ecclesiastical discipline. In the case of the Uniat churches, *i.e.* the Greek churches in communion with Rome, she allows a married clergy in accordance with the custom of the Eastern Church. Thus the points at issue between ourselves and Rome are really the right of a national Church to legislate for herself on such matters and also the expediency of such a change.[1]

The root of the trouble has been the failure to realize that the unmarried life is quite definitely a vocation, and that as being a vocation it comes from God to some people only and cannot be made to order. Protestantism as a rule has fallen into the opposite error of minimizing the need and the desirability of unmarried clergy or of bodies of men who have voluntarily bound themselves to live under rule in a community. But it is evident that there are certain types of work both at home and in the mission field that can only be efficiently carried out by such men. The slum parish, where a married priest can hardly live and bring up a family, often calls for unmarried clergy. So, too, abroad the missions of the Roman Church are often both more economical and more successful than non-Roman missions, because of the abundance of monastic orders and the enforced celibacy of the clergy. In some parts at least of the mission field married missionaries are at once less effective and more expensive. For the maintenance of Christianity in a settled country, professedly Christian, a married clergy is very often desirable. For aggressive work in a heathen or hostile land a celibate clergy is almost essential. The comfortableness of Anglicanism has seriously interfered with its missionary spirit. If, then, we believe that there is work that can only be done by celibate priests, we are bound to believe also that some are called by God to fulfil it. As S. Paul teaches, the vocation to a life of celibacy is a gift from God. With its hardships and temptations it is to be accepted as coming from Him. There will be those who will freely undertake it 'for the Kingdom of Heaven's sake'. By it they will be freed from worldly cares and ties and thus able to devote themselves unreservedly to special kinds of work. We may be thankful for the revival among ourselves of the monastic life. At the same time, even if we regard such a life as in a sense higher than that of the married priest, we must remember that only God can call to it. Vocations cannot be manufactured even at the bidding of the Church. For those who receive the call, it is God's

---

[1] There is, however, a certain ambiguity about the decree of the Council of Trent. Some have held that it makes the denial that clergy can marry a matter of faith and, therefore, irreformable. But the language is capable of a milder interpretation. See *C.H.S.* Lectures, vol. i. p. 69.

call to them and they are bound to believe that He will give them grace to fulfil it. To force celibacy on all who have a vocation to the priesthood is neither right nor wise. As is proved by the state of the Roman Church to-day, no less than by that of the Western Church in the Middle Ages, it opens the way to grave moral scandals. The best that can happen is that in place of clerical marriage there arises a more or less tolerated system of concubinage. We must not judge of the effects of compulsory celibacy by the state of the Roman Church in England, where it is seen at its best, but by its effects in other lands where it is comparatively free from criticism or competition. It is only one instance of the impossibility of making men holy by laws imposed purely from outside. No doubt a certain efficiency is gained by it. An unmarried clergy can live more economically, adapt themselves better to new circumstances and above all are more easily manoeuvred. It fits in admirably with the quasi-military organization of the Roman Church. But these advantages are gained at a terrible cost. On the other hand, the Anglican Church has yet to learn the due place to be given to celibacy.

At the same time we must recognize to the full that there is no less a vocation to the married life. In many parts of England and of the mission field what is sorely needed is the sight of Christian family life. The Christian home is one of the great advertisements of the Gospel. There is nothing in marriage that cannot be consecrated to the service of God. To maintain the opposite is not Christian, but Manichaean. If the existence of a married clergy has its dangers, the history of England shows that it also brings its blessings.[1] Neither Catholic custom nor commonsense contradicts the present rule of the English Church, which leaves the clergy free to marry or not '*as they shall judge the same to serve better to godliness*'. The Catholic Church needs the peculiar gifts and excellencies both of married and unmarried priests.†

ARTICLE XXXIII

Of excommunicate Persons, how they are to be avoided	*De excommunicatis vitandis*
That person which by open denunciation of the Church is rightly cut off from the unity of the Church, and excommuni-	Qui per publicam Ecclesiae denunciationem rite ab unitate Ecclesiae praecisus est, et excommunicatus, is ab universa

---

[1] It is one of the results of some four centuries of married clergy in England that in face of all evidence many to-day refuse to credit the stories of widespread moral corruption in the monasteries at the time of the Reformation. Cp. Coulton, *Mediaeval Studies*, 1st Series, i. and vi.

cated, ought to be taken of the whole multitude of the faithful, as an Heathen and Publican, until he be openly reconciled by penance, and received into the Church by a Judge that hath authority thereunto.

fidelium multitudine (donec per poenitentiam publice reconciliatus fuerit arbitrio judicis competentis) habendus est tanquam ethnicus et publicanus.

Composed in 1553.

§ 3. The Church of Christ exists for a definite purpose, to proclaim the truth as it is revealed in Christ, to minister the sacraments ordained by Him, and also to declare and interpret His will and enforce obedience to it upon her members. Therefore, like any other society she has the right to expel from her fellowship those members who wilfully set at naught her decisions or are disloyal to her principles.

(a) In the Old and New Testaments we find this right exercised by the Jewish Church. Whatever may have been the custom in earlier days the practice of excommunication is found quite early from the days of Ezra onward (Ez 10[8]). In the time of our Lord exclusion from the synagogue was the regular punishment for serious offences: by it the offender was deprived of all religious privileges. It is clearly alluded to in the Gospels (Lk 6[22], Jn 9[22], 12[42], 16[2]). Our Lord gave authority to His Church as the new Israel to 'bind' and to 'loose', i.e. in current Jewish language to 'declare forbidden' or 'declare allowed' (Mt 16[19] and 18[18]). This authority inevitably carried with it the corresponding duty of warning and, in the last resort, excluding those who refuse to accept such decisions. Like Israel of old, the Church is under obligation to enforce the divine law within her borders. In Mt 18[15-17] the offending brother in the last resort is to be brought before the ecclesia. If he refuses to hear the ecclesia he is to be treated 'as the Gentile and the publican', i.e. as one who by his own act has put himself outside the people of God. The meaning is perfectly clear, whether ecclesia in the first instance meant a local Jewish synagogue or the Christian Church. Our Lord lays down a general principle which the Christian Church has embodied in her system of discipline. She can only enforce obedience by spiritual penalties such as depriving the offender of certain privileges of membership. The final penalty is that of depriving him of membership altogether.

In the Epistles we find instances of the exercise of this power. The most important is that given in 1 Cor 5[1-7]. S. Paul first reproves the Church at Corinth for tolerating the presence of a member known to be guilty of grave moral sin (vv. [1-2]). He then, in virtue of his authority as an apostle in the name of Christ, declares him excommunicate and calls on the assembled Church to associate themselves with him in carrying out the sentence (vv. [3-5]). The object of this action is twofold: first the preservation of the whole body from moral infection—'a little leaven leaveneth the whole lump' (v. [6]); and secondly the ultimate salvation of the offender,—'to deliver such a one unto Satan for the destruction of the flesh, that the spirit may be saved in the day of the Lord Jesus' (v. [5]). The penalty is medicinal. The phrase 'deliver unto Satan' sounds strange to our ears. The meaning is that the Church is the covenanted sphere of God's blessing and protection, and therefore to be put out of the Church is to be put out into that sphere where the power of Satan is unchecked (contrast Col 1[13]).[1] Satan is expected to use his power and visit the offender with 'the destruction of the flesh', *i.e.* probably death. Through this judgment it is hoped that by God's providence the sense of his sin may strike home to the man's soul. There is evidence that in the early Church spiritual offences were expected to be and in point of fact were punished by sickness and death (cp. 1 Cor 11[30-32], where the profanation of the Eucharist has this result, and the cases of Ananias and Sapphira, Acts 5, and Elymas, Acts 13). Satan is regarded as inflicting such sufferings (cp. Heb 2[14], Acts 10[38], Lk 13[16], 2 Cor 12[7]). To hand a man over to Satan, then, is to expose him to them. We, today, rather lay stress on the hope that by loss of privileges the offender who is excommunicated may be brought to penitence.

A second case occurs in 2 Cor 2[5-11], referring almost certainly to an entirely different person. This man apparently had been excommunicated by the Church at Corinth in obedience to S. Paul's instruction ('this punishment which was inflicted by the majority,' v. [6], cp. v. [9]) for an offence against S. Paul himself (this seems implied in vv. [5] and [10]). The excommunication succeeded in bringing the offender to repentance, and S. Paul is now able to urge his complete forgiveness. Once again he claims to act 'in the person (or presence) of Christ', and Satan is mentioned as likely to gain an advantage (v. [11]) if the penitent is not brought back again within the safety of the Church.

A third case is that of Hymenaeus and Alexander, who 'made shipwreck concerning the faith', apparently by teaching 'that the resurrection is passed already' (2 Tim 2[18]): 'whom I delivered unto Satan, that they might be taught not to blaspheme' (1 Tim 1[19-20]). The further mention of Hymenaeus in 2 Tim 2[17-18] shows that the sentence had failed to bring him to repentance.

Other references to excommunication occur. Tit 3[10], 'A man that is heretical after a first and second admonition refuse.' 2 Thess 3[14], Rom 16[17], and 1 Cor 5[9-11] hardly go beyond forbidding friendship with the disobedient. 2 Jn [10-11] discountenances the reception of false teachers: this refusal of fellowship is practically excommunication. In 3 Jn [10] it would appear that Diotrephes had misused this same

---

[1] Cp. 'Let him be anathema', *i.e.* accursed in 1 Cor 16[21] and Gal 1[8-9], which seems to include both ecclesiastical censure and spiritual condition.

power against faithful Christians. In early days fellowship in the Church was all-important. A solitary Christian life in a pagan world was almost impossible. We must notice that in Scripture the grounds of excommunication include false teaching, immorality and insubordination. To draw distinctions between faith and morals and worship and to exclude any one of them from the discipline of the Church is contrary to all Bible teaching. In each case the Church exists to guard and propagate the teaching of Christ and she cannot refuse the duty. She has no authority to dispense men from obedience to the will of her Master.

(b) When we turn to the early Church we find the power of excommunication regularly employed.[1] Without it the Church could never have maintained her Christianity in the loose moral atmosphere of heathen society and amid the multitude of conflicting systems of religion, philosophy and magic. In the mission field to-day the same need for strict discipline is recognized by all Christian bodies. Accordingly, we find a regular course of procedure in order to prevent abuse. Offenders were not excommunicated unless they were convicted either by their own admission or by the evidence of trustworthy witnesses. A single witness, even if he were a bishop, did not suffice. For the first three hundred years the penalties of excommunication were purely spiritual, the shutting out from communion and from membership in the Church. Unhappily from the time of Theodosius onward, excommunication began also to involve certain civil penalties. The Church did not shrink from invoking the aid of the secular arm. So, too, in the Middle Ages, as a result of the confusion of Church and State, excommunication involved civil as well as ecclesiastical pains and penalties. Hence its true nature became obscured.

(c) It is clear, both from our Article and from the Prayer-Book, that the Church of England intended to retain excommunication. The service for the burial of the dead may not be used 'for any that die . . . excommunicate'. Excommunications are to be read out after the Nicene Creed. The rubrics before the Communion Office direct the curate to refuse communion to any who is 'an open and notorious evil liver, or have done any wrong to his neighbours by word or deed, so that the Congregation be thereby offended', or again in 'those between whom he perceiveth malice and hatred to reign'. The names of such persons are to be sent to the Ordinary. 'And the Ordinary shall proceed against the offending person according to the canon.' The canon in question is the 109th of the canons passed in 1604 ordering notorious crimes and scandals to be certified to the Eccles-

---

[1] E.g. Irenaeus, Haeres. iii. c. 3, 34, who tells the stories of S. John and Cerinthus and Polycarp and Marcion. Cyprian, Ep. 41, c. 2, and 59, cc. 1, 9, 10, 11, and De Oratione Dominica, c. 13, where he speaks of those who by the commission of any grievous crime are shut out from communion and forbidden the heavenly bread.

iastical Courts. Other canons of the same series deal with the excommunication of various types of offenders. The 68th forbids the reading of the Burial Service over those lying under 'the greater excommunication'. This shows that the law of the Church of England continues to recognize the old distinction, dating back to quite primitive times, between 'the lesser excommunication', *i.e.* the depriving of the use of the sacraments and exclusion from divine worship, and 'the greater excommunication', *i.e.* entire exclusion from the divine society, such as that contemplated in the words of our Article. Further, both the canons and the Article make it clear that sentence of excommunication is not to be inflicted or removed at the arbitrary will of any individual, even a bishop. In each case there is to be *'a judge that hath authority thereunto'*. It is presumed that, as in old days, the Church has her own courts in which she administers her own laws.

In actual practice the right of excommunication has almost entirely fallen into disuse. This is largely the consequence of the unhappy confusion between civil and ecclesiastical punishments. Quite rightly questions of marriage and wills and other matters that used to be decided in the ecclesiatical courts have now been withdrawn into the civil courts. Further, by an Act of George III, happily abolished, excommunication was enjoined as the punishment for contempt of court. But even though this same Act recognizes the right of ecclesiastical courts to continue to pronounce spiritual censures for ecclesiastical offences, the right sense of Church discipline has become impaired by its long admixture with secular legal processes. As a result the Church has largely become identified with the world. Her standard is supposed to be not the teaching of Christ and the law of God, but the conventions of society and the law of the State. Hence any attempt to enforce the rule of Christ where it goes beyond the civil law is viewed as sacerdotal interference. No doubt, on the whole, both the conscience of the individual and public opinion tend to keep persons, who are guilty of open profligacy, away from the sacraments and services of the Church. But there are other sins than those of the flesh which ought to be so intolerable to the conscience of the Church that she cannot endure the presence of those who wilfully persist in committing them. Such sins as those of making money at the cost of others' health and happiness, or dishonest methods in business ought to be branded as unchristian. We need a new recognition of the practical holiness demanded from all members of the Body of Christ. This is not to fall into the Puritan error of limiting the Church to those who are actually holy. So long as a man is making an effort after holiness, even with many lapses, there is room for him in the Church. But there should be no place for those who do not even desire to live up to the standard of Christ and who actively set at naught Christian principles. The power of excommunication has been abused in the past, but that is no reason why it should be neglected. What is needed to-day is an awakening to the sense that churchmanship carries with it definite obligations.†

ARTICLE XXXV

Of Homilies

The second Book of Homilies, the several titles whereof we have joined under this Article, doth contain a godly and wholesome Doctrine, and necessary for these times, as doth the former Book of Homilies, which were set forth in the time of *Edward* the Sixth; and therefore we judge them to be read in Churches by the Ministers, diligently and distinctly, that they may be understood of the people.

Of the Names of the Homilies

1. Of the right use of the Church.
2. Against peril of Idolatry.
3. Of repairing and keeping clean of Churches.
4. Of good Works; first, of Fasting.
5. Against Gluttony and Drunkenness.
6. Against Excess of Apparel.

7. Of Prayer.
8. Of the Place and Time of Prayer.
9. That common Prayers and Sacraments ought to be ministered in a known Tongue.
10. Of the reverent estimation of God's Word.
11. Of Alms-doing.
12. Of the Nativity of Christ.
13. Of the Passion of Christ.

De Homiliis

Tomus secundus Homiliarum, quarum singulos titulos huic Articulo subjunximus, continet piam et salutarem doctrinam, et his temporibus necessariam, non minus quam prior Tomus Homiliarum, quae editae sunt tempore Edwardi sexti: Itaque eas in Ecclesiis per ministros diligenter, et clare, ut a populo intelligi possint, recitandas esse judicavimus.

De nominibus Homiliarum

De recto ecclesiae usu.

Adversus idolatriae pericula.
De reparandis ac purgandis ecclesiis.

De bonis operibus. De jejunio.

In gulae atque ebrietatis vitia.

In nimis sumptuosos vestium apparatus.
De oratione sive precatione.
De loco et tempore orationi destinatis.
De publicis precibus ac sacramentis idiomate vulgari omnibusque noto, habendis.

De sacrosancta verbi divini autoritate.
De eleemosina.
De Christi Nativitate.
De dominica passione.

14. Of the Resurrection of Christ.	De resurrectione Domini.
15. Of the worthy receiving of the Sacrament of the Body and Blood of Christ.	De digna corporis et sanguinis dominici in coena Domini participatione.
16. Of the gifts of the Holy Ghost.	De donis Spiritus Sancti.
17. For the Rogation-days.	In diebus, qui vulgo Rogationum dicti sunt, concio.
18. Of the state of Matrimony.	De matrimonii statu.
19. Of Repentance.	De poenitentia.
20. Against Idleness.	De otio seu socordia.
21. Against Rebellion.	

Composed in 1563 and slightly altered in 1571.

§ 4. A temporary use of the Church's authority in discipline is seen in the Homilies. They were a product of the needs of the age. At the time of the Reformation all teaching was disorganized. Learned or capable preachers were few, and of those few a large part were hot-headed and violent. The government wished to suppress all teaching that was inconvenient or might lead to disorder. Hence preachers were licensed, and no unlicensed preacher might deliver a sermon. To take the place of sermons 'Homilies' were composed by well-known leaders, to be placed in the hands of the clergy for reading in church. This plan was first discussed in 1542. It was first put into practice in 1547 when the First Book of Homilies was produced and commanded by the authority of the King to be read every Sunday at High Mass (cp. the rubric after the Nicene Creed). Under Mary a new set of Homilies was proposed, but never carried out. Under Elizabeth the First Book was reprinted and a Second Book added to it. Our Article was amended in 1563 so as to include both sets. In 1571 the last Homily was added in view of the Northern Rebellion of 1569. As was natural, they were unpopular among many of the clergy, both Papistical and Puritan. Hence they read them unintelligibly. This is forbidden by the Article.

The Article only claims for them a vague and temporary authority. Happily we are not bound to accept every statement in them. They do not stand on a level with the Prayer-Book or the Articles. They came into existence for a special emergency which has now passed away.

ARTICLES XXIII AND XXXVI

THE MINISTRY OF THE CHURCH

ARTICLE XXIII

Of Ministering in the Congregation

It is not lawful for any man to take upon him the office of public preaching, or ministering the Sacraments in the Congregation, before he be lawfully called, and sent to execute the same. And those we ought to judge lawfully called and sent, which be chosen and called to this work by men who have public authority given unto them in the Congregation, to call and send Ministers into the Lord's vineyard.

De ministrando in Ecclesia

Non licet cuiquam sumere sibi munus publice praedicandi, aut administrandi Sacramenta in Ecclesia, nisi prius fuerit ad haec obeunda legitime vocatus et missus. Atque illos legitime vocatos et missos existimare debemus, qui per homines, quibus potestas vocandi ministros, atque mittendi in vineam Domini, publice concessa est in Ecclesia, cooptati fuerint, et adsciti in hoc opus.

The history of this Article is important. Its substance is derived from the 10th of the 13 Articles of 1538, the attempted compromise between Anglicans and Lutherans. This in turn was partly based on the Confession of Augsburg. Thus the history of the Article accounts for its vagueness. Both Lutherans and Anglicans wished to oppose Anabaptists, who held that an internal call to the ministry dispensed a man from the need of any external authorization whatever—a view that could only lead to ecclesiastical anarchy. Both parties agreed on the need of some external call, but any further agreement about the nature of the authority that could confer ordination, whether episcopal or presbyterian, could only be attained by vagueness. Even so, the language of the Article has been strengthened: 'legitime' was substituted for 'rite' and 'et missus' added after 'vocatus'. The words 'cooptati et adsciti' are also an addition. But its colourless tone and weakness in positive statement are corrected by the language of Article XXXVI and the preface to the ordinal. We must study all these together to learn the mind of the Church of England.

ARTICLE XXXVI

Of Consecration of Bishops and Ministers

The Book of Consecration of Archbishops and Bishops, and ordering of Priests and Deacons,

De Episcoporum et Ministrorum consecratione

Libellus de consecratione Archiepiscoporum, et Episcoporum, et de ordinatione Presbyterorum lately set forth in the time of *Edward* the Sixth, and confirmed at the same time by authority of Parliament, doth contain all things necessary to such Consecration and Ordering: neither hath it anything that of itself is superstitious or ungodly. And therefore whosoever are consecrated or ordered according to the Rites of that Book, since the second year of the aforenamed King *Edward* unto this time, or hereafter shall be consecrated or ordered according to the same Rites; we decree all such to be rightly, orderly, and lawfully consecrated and ordered.

et Diaconorum editus nuper temporibus Edwardi VI et auctoritate Parliamenti illis ipsis temporibus confirmatus, omnia ad ejusmodi consecrationem et ordinationem necessaria continet, et nihil habet, quod ex se sit, aut superstitiosum, aut impium; itaque quicunque juxta ritus illius libri consecrati aut ordinati sunt, ab anno secundo praedicti regis Edwardi, usque ad hoc tempus, aut in posterum juxta eosdem ritus consecrabuntur, aut ordinabuntur, rite, ordine, atque legitime statuimus esse et fore consecratos et ordinatos.

This Article in its present form dates from 1563, supplanting an earlier Article that was both wider and vaguer in statement. It asserted the validity of our Ordinal against (i) the Puritans, who regarded it as containing things 'superstitious or ungodly'. They objected not only to episcopacy, but to the formula 'Receive the Holy Ghost'; (ii) the Papists, who regarded orders conferred with the English Ordinal as invalid for various reasons, among which one was that it did not 'contain all things necessary to such consecration and ordering'.

§ 1. *The Christian ministry.*—The Church, like any other society in the world, needs some kind of organization. 'God is not a God of confusion' (1 Cor 14[33]). From her very nature she requires officers to perform certain functions on her behalf and as centres round which she may gather. A purely human society as a matter of course elects, appoints, and if need be dismisses its own officers. They owe their authority entirely to the will of the society. But the Church is not a purely human society. All would agree that her mission and authority rest not upon the will of man but on the will of God. Hence all Christians would be at one in asserting that for the call and appointment of her ministry, she is in some sense dependent on God. The question still remains, what constitutes a valid call and appointment? The Church of England insists upon:

(*a*) The inward call to the individual. This is not mentioned explicitly in the Articles, because all, including Anabaptists, agreed upon its necessity. In the ordering of Deacons the first question begins: 'Do you trust that you are inwardly moved by the Holy Ghost to take upon you this Office and Ministration?' The whole point of the Article is that, taken by itself, it is insufficient. If the individual is to be made the sole judge of his call, the Church would be placed at the mercy of any man who felt himself so called, whatever his life and teaching might be. The New Testament makes it quite clear that the judgment of the individual must in this as in all things be tested and confirmed by the judgment of the community (cp. *e.g.* the qualifications demanded in 1 Tim 3^{1-10} and Tit 1^{5-9} and the test implied in 1 Cor 12^{1-3}, 1 Jn 4^{1-3}).

(*b*) The inward call, therefore, needs to be supplemented by the outward call of the Church. Practically all organized Christian bodies would agree that '*It is not lawful for any man to take upon him the office of public preaching or ministering the Sacraments in the congregation, before he be lawfully called and sent to execute the same.*' So in the ordering of Priests the candidates are asked : 'Do you think in your heart that you be truly called, according to the will of our Lord Jesus Christ and the order of this Church of England?' The meaning of 'sent' may be explained as a reference to Jn 20^{21}, but more probably it is to be explained in the light of the Ordination Service, as the commission to perform the duties of the office in a particular sphere of work. The authority is given to minister 'where thou shalt be lawfully appointed thereunto'. Commonsense makes it evident that the officers of any society must not only possess authority from the society but also be given a sphere of work by the society.

(*c*) The real question of dispute is concealed in the words : '*Those we ought to judge lawfully called and sent, which be chosen and called to this work by men who have public authority given unto them in the congregation to call and send Ministers into the Lord's vineyard.*' Who have this public authority and whence was it given to them? Art. 36 and the Ordinal make it quite clear that the Church of England means by these, bishops. The inward call by God and the outward call of the Christian community are calls to seek ordination by a bishop, not to do without it. The word 'cooptati' implies that ministers must be 'chosen' by those who are themselves ministers. In practice the Church of England requires episcopal ordination for all who are to minister in its churches. Those who have received such in, *e.g.* the Church of Rome, are not reordained on joining the English Church. The ministers of nonconformist bodies who have not received episcopal ordination must receive it before they are allowed to minister. From the Reformation down to to-day episcopal ordination has been required. Cases may be found in times of disorder and confusion, when the Church's discipline was disorganized, in which a minister not episcopally ordained held a benefice, but such an act was utterly irregular and in defiance of the clear will of the Church.[1] The question, therefore, remains, What ground has the Church of England for insisting upon ordination by a bishop, as a condition of a

---

[1] The addition in 1661 to the Preface to the Ordinal of the words 'or hath had formerly Episcopal Consecration or Ordination' made the will of the Church clear beyond doubt.

valid appointment to its ministry? We must beware of putting the question in the form: Is the ministry from above or from below? All who recognize the Church's share in the appointment of ministers must agree that in one sense it comes from below. All again who recognize the need of a call from God, must agree that in another sense it comes from above. The question is what, if anything, does ordination by a bishop add to the inward call by God and the outward call of the Church? Is it true that in any sense it conveys a commission from Christ given in the first instance to the Apostles and handed down from them through those who have in turn received authority to transmit it?

§ 2. In answering this question we may begin by drawing a distinction between, first, 'apostolic succession' considered as a series of historical facts, and secondly, the various interpretations put upon these facts by the Church. As always, life came first and theology second: the Church acted first and thought afterwards. Under the guidance of the Holy Spirit the Church instinctively put forth certain orders of ministry to perform certain duties for the whole Body, just as a living organism puts forth organs for the discharge of certain functions necessary to its life. Later on men came to reflect not only on what had been done but on the manner in which it had been done. They saw that almost unconsciously the Church had acted on certain principles: these they began to examine and draw out, in order that they might discern all that they implied and the light that they threw upon the life of the whole body.

What then are the facts?

(a) The early Church lived in expectation of the immediate return of Christ. Hence she had no mind to make any detailed arrangements for her future organization. Our Lord had provided His Church with a ministry and His teaching made clear that this ministry would continue until His return (Lk 12$^{42-43}$, Mt 28$^{19-20}$). Whether other ministries besides the Twelve would be needed, remained to be seen. The New Testament insists upon the deliberate call and choice of the Twelve Apostles by Christ Himself (Mk 3$^{13-14}$, etc.). They were appointed to be with Him, and He imparted special teaching to them. Above all, they were to be the witnesses of the resurrection. The Mission of the Seventy attests the existence of a wider circle of disciples, entrusted with ministerial work, but there is no indication that they were appointed as a permanent body. The Twelve alone, it would seem, were present at the institution of the Eucharist (Lk 22$^{14 \text{ and } 28-30}$, Mk 14$^{17-20}$). It has been keenly disputed whether S. John represents the promise of the Spirit and the great commission as given to the Twelve alone or to the whole Church (Jn 20$^{22-23}$). The question is not of primary importance, as in any case they were given to a Church which Christ Himself had already provided with a ministry, through which the powers bestowed should normally be exercised. Taken by itself S. John's narrative leaves the question open.[1] But the story of Acts 2 seems to make it clear that only the Twelve received in the first instance the special outpouring of the Holy Spirit at Pentecost. This explains the filling up of the number of the Twelve by the election of Matthias compared with the failure to do so on the death of James.[2] The title 'Apostle' is applied in the New Testament to others besides the Twelve, *e.g.* Barnabas and Paul (Acts 14[14]), and apparently to James, the Lord's brother (Gal 1[19]), and perhaps others. Of these only S. Paul seems to be on a level with the Twelve (Gal 1[1] and 2[7-9], 2 Cor 11[5]). We must distinguish between the Apostles of Christ, those personally sent forth by Him, namely, the Twelve, and S. Paul and the 'apostles of the Churches' (2 Cor 8[23], Phil 2[25]), that is, men sent forth by some local Church to a particular work. S. Paul was counted an apostle in both senses (cp. Acts 13[2-3]), but Barnabas only in the second and inferior sense.

Pressure of circumstances compelled the Church to develop a ministry. The earliest indication of this is the appointment of the Seven (Acts 6[1-6]). In order to meet an urgent need, certain functions are delegated to them. They are elected by the Church at large (vv. [3 and 5]), but the Apostles ordain them (v. [6]). The extent of their commission is not clear, but the conduct of Philip at Samaria shows that it possessed quite definite limits. He is able to preach. He can take the decisive step of baptizing Samaritans into the new Israel, but he has no authority to lay on hands, and is compelled for that purpose to send to Jerusalem for Apostles (Acts 8[12-17]). The precise relation of these 'Seven' to the order of deacons is obscure. They are never called διάκονοι, though the word διακονεῖν is used in connexion with them.

The origin of the order of presbyters is nowhere described. It has been suggested that they were a deliberate imitation of the Jewish presbyters. More probably they were a purely Christian institution spontaneously created to meet a need of the Church. The name in itself is quite vague and may mean no more than 'elder men' (*e.g.* 1 Pet 5[5], 1 Tim 5[1-2]). More important than the name are the duties that they were commissioned to perform. Dr Hamilton holds that they were primarily ordained to break bread at the Eucharist. For such a function no remarkable spiritual or intellectual gifts would be required, but rather a good character and practical holiness of life. But if this is so, they almost immediately began to perform other duties as well, such as pastoral work, teaching and ruling (Acts 20[28], 1 Pet 5[1], 1 Tim 5[17]). The order seems to be universal (Acts 15[6] Jerusalem, 20[17] Ephesus, Tit 1[5] 'in every city of Crete', cp. James 5[14],

---

[1] On the one side, see Westcott, *Commentary on S. John*, and on the other side Gore, *Church and Ministry*, pp. 228 ff., and Hamilton, *The People of God*, vol. ii. Appendix i.

[2] Cp. also v. [7] which shows that they all were Galileans. This excludes at once the idea that the Spirit visibly came on the whole Church.

etc.). When we read in Acts 14[23], 'When they had appointed for them elders in every church . . . they commended them to the Lord', from what we know of S. Luke's method we may be fairly certain that he is giving a typical instance of S. Paul's practice on his missionary journeys. All the evidence that we possess goes to show that they were ordained either by Apostles or those sent by Apostles with authority to ordain (1 Tim 5[22], Tit 1[5]). We also hear of ἐπίσκοποι or bishops. The more probable view is that in Scripture this is simply another title for the same office, describing the general supervision that it carried with it. This is the natural interpretation of, *e.g.* Acts 20. In v. [17] the presbyters of the Church are called, in v. [28] S. Paul speaks to them as 'bishops', without the slightest indication that he is not addressing them all. So, too, in Tit 1[5–9], after telling Titus that he had been left in Crete to appoint elders, S. Paul goes on to describe the kind of man fit to be appointed as 'the bishop'. In Phil 1[1] 'bishops' and 'deacons' only are mentioned, when we should expect a mention of presbyters. A fair case, however, can be made against the identification.[1] If they are not one and the same, 'presbyter' was probably simply a title of honour rather than an office, and 'bishops' were appointed out of them. In that case we must translate Acts 14[23] as 'they ordained presbyters (or elder men) in every church' (to be bishops, understood)—a doubtful use of χειροτονεῖν. It is worth noting that 'deacons' are always mentioned in conjunction with 'bishops' and not with 'presbyters'. The probable explanation is that at first deacons existed to help the presbyters in those rather vague and indefinite duties which came under the heading of 'overseership'.[2] But in any case we need to remember that the important question is not of names, such as 'bishop' and 'presbyter', but of the authority which lay behind the names. It is quite conceivable that in the earliest days 'bishop' was an alternative title for 'presbyter' and later on was used to designate a wider and distinct office and authority. In our own Church, for instance, the titles of 'vicar' and 'curate' have, as it were, changed places. The curate was originally the 'man in charge', the vicar his substitute (*vicarius*).

But in the earliest days of the Church the possession of peculiar spiritual gifts by individuals made them conspicuous members of the local community. We find what is called a 'charismatic' ministry. The clearest instance is the 'prophets', men endowed with special gifts of vision and of declaring God's will (Acts 11[28], 13[2], etc.). They owed the gifts not to any human appointment, but to a special and direct endowment of the Holy Spirit. In 1 Cor 12[28] and Eph 4[11] they seem to be regarded as directly called by Christ. Hence the most that the Church could do was to regulate the use of their gift. In order to

---

[1] See *e.g.* Vincent (International Critical Commentary) on *Phil* 1[1].

[2] On the primitive presbyterate, see K. E. Kirk (ed.), *The Apostolic Ministry*, Essays iii, iv and v.

prevent imposture they needed to be recognized by the community as truly inspired by God (1 Jn 4^1 ff., 1 Cor 12^{1-3}). So, too, evangelists and teachers seem to have been marked out by the manifestation of peculiar spiritual gifts for their work (Eph 4^{11}, 1 Cor 12^{28}, Rom 12^6 ff.). The relation of this charismatic ministry to the presbyteral ministry naturally varied. They moved on different planes. There was no reason why a man should not belong to both. The possession of special gifts might well mark out a man as suitable to be appointed presbyter or deacon or 'an apostle of the Church'. They would assist him in many parts of his work. On the other hand their presence was not essential.[1]

Accordingly, the picture that Scripture gives us of the apostolic age is as follows. We see a number of local Churches possessing presbyters who ordinarily preside at the Eucharist, and also, it would seem, deacons. But behind all the life of the local Churches stands the Apostolic order. However much self-government they possessed, it was all exercised under the visitation and supervision of the Apostles (cp. 1 Cor 4^{21}, Acts 15^{36}, 3 Jn ^{10}, etc.). The case of the Church at Corinth shows that there at least very little organization even of small details was attempted by the local Church without S. Paul's advice and authority (cp. 1 Cor 7-8, $11^{2\text{ff and }34}$, etc.).[2] Further, from time to time they would be visited by delegates from other Churches, by prophets and other gifted men. Later on we find apostolic delegates like S. Timothy and S. Titus specially sent with authority to guard the faith, to ordain and to exercise discipline. In the New Testament Church, then, there existed a three-fold ministry of apostles, presbyter-bishops and deacons, and it also seems certain that outside the ranks of this ministry (as well as within it) there were men with recognized spiritual gifts, particularly that of prophecy, who exercised their gifts when the Church was assembled for worship. We have no right to expect absolute uniformity. In the freshness of the outburst of spiritual life that began at Pentecost, extraordinary gifts were displayed that did not permanently endure. The Church did not organize itself on any carefully prepared plan: rather under the guidance of the Apostles it evolved necessary officers to discharge practical duties. Passages such as 1 Thess 5^{12} and 1 Cor 12^{28-30} suggest that at first there was no great uniformity in titles and that offices may have existed which did not endure.

Outside Scripture we turn to what evidence we possess. Unfortunately the evidence for the period just after the Apostles is of the scantiest. In the West the earliest piece of evidence is the Epistle of S. Clement, written about A.D. 96, perhaps during the lifetime of

---

[1] On Harnack's theory of the 'charismatic ministry', see Kirk, *op. cit.*, p. 145, note i.

[2] The primacy of the Apostolate stands for the historical character of the Christian revelation. A primacy of 'free inspiration' would deny this, and so the message of the Christian prophet was subject to tests of its validity and the exercise of his gift was subject to apostolic direction (1 Cor 14.).

S. John. S. Clement wrote in the name of the Church of Rome in reply to a request from the Church of Corinth for advice. Disturbances had broken out there about the deposition of certain presbyters. In his reply he makes clear that he knows of two kinds of presbyters and two kinds only: first, those appointed by the Apostles themselves; secondly, those appointed by ἕτεροι ἐλλόγιμοι ἄνδρες, to whom the Apostles had given authority to appoint. The Corinthians had attempted to depose some of these presbyters and add a third kind: namely, those appointed by themselves. This action he regarded as sinful because the deposed presbyters 'were from the Apostles, the Apostles were from Christ and Christ was from God'. It was a breach of Church order, and that order was based on the will of God. Further, it seems quite clear that 'Presbyter' and 'Episcopus' are still used as titles of the same office. He can write in c. xliv, 'It will be no light sin, if we thrust out from the bishop's office (τῆς ἐπισκοπῆς) those who have offered the gifts unblameably and holily. Blessed are those presbyters who have gone before . . . for they have no fear lest any one should remove them from their appointed places.' On the other hand, we find an analogy drawn between the Christian ministers and the 'high priest', 'the priest' and 'the Levite' which may imply something like the later threefold ministry, or may only imply that the presbyters had a chairman. The position of S. Clement himself is not absolutely clear. At this date there may or may not have been a single 'Bishop' of Rome. At any rate he writes in the name of the Church as a whole, not in his own.[1]

In the East the letters of Ignatius (A.D. 115) give us a consistent picture of Church organization in Asia. The bishop has become as distinct from the presbyter as in later days. He is compared to Christ or God and the presbyters to the Apostles, an analogy probably suggested by his presiding at the Eucharist. 'Let no man do aught of things pertaining to the Church, apart from the Bishop. Let that be held a valid Eucharist which is under the Bishop or one to whom he shall have committed it.' Such is his invariable tone. No attempt is made to defend or explain the authority of the bishop. But everywhere insistence is laid on the practical duty of submission to him. He is the one centre of unity.

The *Didache*, a fragmentary document of uncertain date and place and of disputable value, is perhaps to be placed at the close of the first century and probably represents life in some obscure Church in an out-of-the-way part of Syria. In any case it lies off the main stream of development. We find mention of bishops, clearly presbyter-bishops, and deacons, as the local ministry. The chief place is held by travelling apostles and prophets of a decadent type, who need to be

---

[1] On Clement's Epistle see the editions by Lightfoot, W. K. Lowther Clarke (S.P.C.K.) and Harnack (*Das Schreiben der Römischen Kirche an Die Korinthische*, Leipzig, 1929).

carefully tested and watched (cc. 11–13) and may perhaps settle down permanently as teachers.[1]

By the time of writers like Irenaeus and Tertullian (A.D. 180) we find the regular threefold ministry. Bishops have taken the place of apostles, but are located in one place. Presbyters are as distinct from them as from deacons. Further, no recollection seems to be left of a time when it was otherwise. The charismatic ministry has practically disappeared. Its authority and influence have passed to the regular ministry. The exact process by which this later threefold ministry arose is a problem that at present is insoluble. How did the 'monarchical episcopate' arise? 'When we have explained how the supreme powers of the general ministry were made to devolve on an individual who belonged to the local ministry, we have explained the origin of episcopacy.'[2]

The only certain point is that there is no trace whatever of any struggle in the early Church by which episcopacy came into being. If presbyterianism had ever been established under apostolic authority, it would hardly have yielded up its power without a contest. History shows that presbyterianism is a very strong, stable and stubborn form of government. Clement of Alexandria and Tertullian both affirm and Irenaeus implies that the local episcopate was set up in Asia by S. John himself.[3] There is no reason to doubt this statement. It fits in admirably with the evidence of Ignatius. In the West it is very probable that the process was more gradual. There is some evidence that both at Rome and Alexandria the power to ordain was held not by any single individual but conjointly by a college of presbyter-bishops. If so, then it became gradually reserved for the chairman, and the time came when presbyters were ordained with limited powers.†

(b) Such, then, are the main facts. In face of dangers from within, the Church was compelled to reflect upon the meaning of her own action. She found in the apostolic ministry a safeguard against the perils that threatened her life.

(i) As we saw, Clement of Rome found in the orderly succession from the Apostles a pledge of unity. It was in accordance with the will of God. The breach of it was rebellion against duly constituted authority, and therefore against God. The particular danger of the day, as shown in the letters of Ignatius, was that the Church might break up, and especially break up into separate and rival gatherings for the Eucharist. Against this the one ministry formed the protection.

---

[1] The *Didache* is the only evidence for independent *travelling* prophets. Judas and Silas (Acts 15[32]) were delegates of the Jerusalem Church who were *also* prophets. We may equally suppose that the prophets of Acts 11[27] formed an authorized mission to Antioch.

[2] C. H. Turner, in the *Cambridge Mediaeval History*, vol. i., p. 145.

[3] Clement, *Quis dives salvetur*, 42; Tertullian, *Adv. Marc.* iv. 5; Irenaeus, *Adv. Haer.* iii. 3. 4.

(ii) To Irenaeus the chief significance of the apostolic descent was that it guaranteed the truth and purity of the Church's doctrine. 'We should hearken to those Presbyters, who are in the Church; those who have their succession from the apostles, as we have pointed out; who with their succession in the episcopate received a sure gift of truth (*charisma veritatis*), at the good pleasure of the Father: but the rest, who withdrew from the primitive succession and gather in any place whatever, we must hold in suspicion' (*Adv. Haer.* iv. 26, cp. iii. 2). The danger to the Church at this time was that the revelation in Christ should be lost amid the confusion of strange Gnostic teachings and similar heresies. The succession provided a test of the apostolicity of the doctrine.

(iii) In the time of Cyprian the unity of the Church was threatened by the secession of definite organized schismatical bodies. These were not all heretical in teaching. In the case of some of them the dispute was rather over questions of discipline. The Church seemed about to dissolve into a multitude of jarring sects. Under these circumstances Cyprian found in the historic episcopate the foundation of Church unity. 'The Episcopate is one, each part of which is held by each one for the whole,'[1] *i.e.* all bishops are independent and equal. Each possesses in himself the whole power of the episcopate, which is derived by descent from the commission of Christ given to the Apostles. Those who separate from the bishop, separate from the Church, and so place themselves outside the sphere of God's promises. Schismatical ministrations, such as baptism or absolution, are invalid, since they have not upon them the stamp of the authority of the Church, of which the bishop is the visible symbol. Such was the teaching of Cyprian.

(*c*) Our claim in the Church of England to-day is that we possess the historic ministry of the Catholic Church, coming down in historical descent from the Apostles. We lay stress upon it for several reasons.

(i) Regarded externally it is a visible and concrete link with the Church of the past and with the historic life of Christ on earth. It is a pledge that there has been no breach of continuity in the Church's life. Whatever authority Christ willed to give to His Church we possess.

(ii) It is the ministry not of a local Church but of the whole Catholic Church. Ideally all the ministrations of the Church are not the acts of any one part by itself but of the whole body of Christ. For instance, every true Eucharist is a Eucharist not just of the few Christians gathered within the walls of a building, but of the whole Church, of all the faithful living and departed. Hence the minister must possess authority to act not simply as minister of one part of

---

[1] *In solidum* (=for the whole) is a legal term. When two parties borrowed in common a sum of money, each was responsible *in solidum*, *i.e.* for the whole. See Cyprian, *de Cath. Eccl. Unitate* 5.

the Church but as the minister of the whole. The root idea of absolution is that of readmission to the fellowship of the Body of Christ; hence, one who bestows it must possess the authority of the whole Body. So in all his ministry and teaching the minister exercises his functions, not in virtue of any private and personal gift, not even as the representative of any local body of Christians, but as the instrument of the whole Body of Christ. It is not the minister as such who baptizes or ordains or blesses or absolves or celebrates the Eucharist, but the whole Church through him and Christ through the Church. Apostolic succession secures this Catholic as opposed to individual or local authority of the minister. The historic ministry is the ministry of the whole Church and not of any part of it.

(iii) As following from this we believe that the succession is the guaranteee of valid ministrations. Whatever gifts God may bestow outside it, we are assured that His grace is to be found within it. On the side of doctrine it is a pledge of Catholicity. It assures us that we remain in the fellowship of apostolic teaching and lose nothing of the fulness of the apostolic Gospel.

Two cautions, however, are needed.

(α) The question of apostolic succession and that of episcopacy are quite distinct. Historically, no doubt, the historic succession settled down into the form of Church government known as 'Monarchical Episcopate', in which a single bishop alone has authority to ordain. But there is reason for believing that at one time in certain Churches the authority to ordain was given not to a single bishop but to a college of presbyter-bishops or even possibly in some cases to a presbyter-bishop acting singly. This is no breach of principle. It is by no means essential that functions should always and everywhere be distributed in the same way. For instance, in the West to-day only a bishop has authority to confirm. In the East the priest confirms with oil blessed by the bishop for the purpose. The only necessary point is that no minister should go outside the limits of the authority entrusted to him. Conversely, the largest body of Methodists in America have decided that the episcopal form of government is the most desirable. Accordingly, they have appointed chief ministers who are styled 'bishops'. But these 'bishops' have no connexion with the historic ministry. They possess authority to act only for their own community.

(β) The doctrine of apostolic succession has often been degraded by being presented in a very inadequate and mechanical form. It must not be regarded as a bare transmission of certain quasi-magical powers from one individual to another. Neither the minister who ordains nor the minister ordained bestows or receives any power as an isolated individual. We must never separate ordination from the life of the Church as a whole. The bishop who ordains acts for

Christ in His Church; the minister who receives ordination is ordained from Christ in and for His Church.[1]

(d) This view may be seen more clearly by contrasting it with the view taken as a whole by Nonconformists. Their view of the ministry is based upon two great assumptions.

(i) Any group of Christians, or at least any 'organized' body of Christians, possesses and has always possessed the inherent right to elect and ordain ministers to perform certain functions on behalf of the community.

(ii) The authority of bishops themselves arose originally in this way. No doubt in the earliest days there was a travelling ministry of apostles, prophets, evangelists, etc., who did not derive their authority by delegation from the community. But in course of time these came to an end. Their functions were gradually taken over by the local ministry of presbyter-bishops and deacons. In time one of the presbyter-bishops, perhaps as a result of being chairman or correspondent for the local Church, perhaps in order to secure greater efficiency, came to be elevated above the rest and to be regarded as 'the bishop'. But in origin bishop and presbyter are the same office. The duty of ordaining came in practice to be restricted to the bishop as a general rule, but there is no evidence that this was always so. Accordingly, bishops are no more than glorified presbyters: their authority rests in the last resort solely upon the choice of the community. Apostolic succession means no more than that, as the Apostles and the charismatic ministry died off, the local ministry stepped into the vacant place.

The consequences of this view are plain. If each community of Christians possesses the inherent right of electing and ordaining ministers, then all such ministers are equal. What the community did once, the community can do again at any time. Nonconformist ministers who avowedly derive their orders from the laying-on of hands of men who represent their particular body, possess precisely the same validity as those ministers who have received episcopal

---

[1] 'When we go back to the first records of the Church we find neither a Ministry which called people into association with it, nor an undifferentiated fellowship which delegated powers to a Ministry: but we find a complete Church, with the Apostolate accepted as its focus of administration and authority. When the Lord's earthly ministry was ended, there was found in the world as its fruit and as means of its continuance this Body, in which the distinction of Ministry and Laity is already established. The Apostles were in no sense ministers of the Laity; they were ministers of Christ to the laity, and to the world waiting to be won. They took steps for the perpetuation of the ministry, and it has descended to ourselves. So when I consecrate a godly and well learned man to the office and work of a Bishop in the Church of God, I do not act as a representative of the Church, if by that is meant the whole number of contemporary Christians; but I do act as the ministerial instrument of Christ in His Body the Church. The authority by which I act is His, transmitted to me through His apostles and those to whom they committed it; I hold it neither from the Church nor apart from the Church, but from Christ in the Church.' Archbishop William Temple in a Presidential Address to the Convocation of Canterbury, May 1943.

ordination. For the authority of the bishops themselves, if we trace it back far enough, is derived from the same source. The sole and ultimate authority is to be found equally distributed in all Christians. The need of common action and common worship demands some kind of ministry, just as the need of government in England demands the election of representatives in Parliament. But the authority of the ministers, like the authority of members of Parliament, is wholly dependent on those whom they represent. Accordingly, the refusal of the Church of England to treat ministers who have not received episcopal ordination on an equality with those who have received it, is arbitrary and indefensible.

Two main lines of argument are adduced for the nonconformist view: first, historical; secondly, practical. The historical arguments can be summed up thus.

(α) Scripture and the earliest writings, especially the *Didache*, are entirely silent on the need or the existence of apostolic succession. The growth of the ministry can be traced, and it is due to purely human organization.

(β) We can point to certain definite instances which contradict the whole theory of apostolic succession. The *Didache* shows us prophets, who were not ordained, celebrating the Eucharist. The people are bidden to elect bishops and deacons to celebrate when the prophets are not there. Further, the Canons of Hippolytus[1] direct that the bishop, after election by the people, shall be consecrated by 'one of the bishops and presbyters'. Also, in the same canons a confessor who has endured torture is to be enrolled as a presbyter without ordination. The bishop is to pray over him, but omit the petition for the Holy Spirit. His conduct has shown that he has already received the Spirit. Further, a confessor is treated as possessing by the direct gift of the Spirit the power of absolution. Again, Jerome tells us that at Alexandria down to the third century 'the priests always elected one of their own number, placed him in a higher degree and called him bishop: just as if our army should make an emperor, or deacons elect one of themselves and call him archdeacon.' So, too, he tells us that churches at first were governed by 'the common council of priests', but for the sake of unity one was elected and set over the others. Hence the bishop is greater than the priest by 'custom' not the 'Lord's arrangement'.

(γ) We can never be sure that the succession has not been broken at some point, as we have not evidence of each and every ordination.

(δ) The whole idea of apostolic succession is to be connected with the development that began in the third century by which sacerdotalism invaded the Church. Bishops and presbyters became regarded as

---

[1] These Canons are, however, now recognized to be a late document, possibly of the fifth or sixth century. *The Apostolic Tradition* of Hippolytus himself (*circ.* A.D. 220) orders consecration of a bishop by a bishop only. Cp. Dix, *The Apostolic Tradition*, pp. lxxvi and 3.

'sacerdotes', no longer the representatives of the congregation, but mediators between them and God.

To these arguments we may reply as follows:

(α) The argument from silence is always precarious, especially when there are very few witnesses to be silent. Behind all documents is the continuous life and activity of the Church. Such silence as there is may well be explained by the fact that the principle of succession was unquestioned. It is not mentioned because there was no need for mention. It emerges into prominence as soon as attention is drawn to its importance by the needs of the Church. Further, we have very clear evidence of the ordination of presbyters either by apostles or apostolic delegates. In fact, we cannot point to any that we know not to have been so ordained. The one thing that seems beyond dispute is that in apostolic days the people did not ordain their own ministers. They elected them, in some cases, at least, but such election was a call to be ordained by the proper people (Acts 6[3 and 6], 14[23], Tit 1[5]). The nonconformist view of the early Church always ignores the apostolic background.

(β) No undisputed instance can be adduced of ordination by men who were off the line of apostolic descent. The evidence of the *Didache* is very precarious. Its date and value are disputed.[1] Even if genuine it shows us life in a Christian community off the main stream of Christian life. The people are bidden to elect ($\chi\epsilon\iota\rho\sigma\tau\sigma\nu\epsilon\hat{\iota}\nu$) bishops and deacons. This may well have been with a view to ordination by some competent authority. Nor, again, is it absolutely certain that prophets did celebrate the Eucharist. The language of the *Didache* may rather refer to the offering of thanksgiving after the Eucharist. The earliest ordination rite we possess confines ordination to a bishop.[2] As to the treatment of confessors, at most it represents a temporary exception to the regular Church usage. If such were appointed bishops, they had to be duly ordained.[3] No one would wish to doubt that there had been certain changes in the external form of the ministry. Even if we accept Jerome's statement, all that it shows is that in some places at one time the power of ordination was given to a college of presbyters. This may have been so in other places for a time. But because some presbyters once possessed authority to ordain, it does not follow that this authority is inherent in the office of presbyter always and everywhere. That would be to confuse names with the authority that lies behind names. It is one thing to possess authority to celebrate the Eucharist, or bless or absolve, as the Church's representative: quite another thing to be able to bestow this authority on another person to act in the name of the Church. So soon as the monarchical episcopate became established, and

---

[1] Some authorities now assign it to a late date in the second century. For a review of modern theories, see F. E. Vokes, *The Riddle of the Didache* (S.P.C.K., 1948) and also *J.Th.S.* xxxix, p. 370; xl, pp. 133, 258.

[2] Dix, *op. cit.*, p. 3.   [3] *Ibid.*, p. 18.

ordination was restricted to 'the bishops', presbyters would be ordained with diminished powers, such as they possess to-day. Non-conformists seem unable to realize that even if presbyters and bishop were at one time identical, that does not prove that every presbyter to-day is, as it were, a potential bishop, nor does it in the least destroy the meaning of apostolic succession.[1]

(γ) From the nature of the case we could not have evidence of every ordination. But if we believe that the ministry of the Church developed under the guidance of the Holy Spirit, we must believe also that God was able to preserve its validity. As soon as the Church became conscious of the significance of her acts, all steps would be taken to ensure valid ordinations. The main stream of the Church's practice is clear. From quite early days it has been the custom for a bishop to be consecrated by at least three bishops, though one would suffice. Any irregularity would thus soon be rectified.

(δ) In reply to the charge of 'sacerdotalism' we must plead that there is a true and a false sacerdotalism. Indisputably the whole Church is a kingdom of priests. But certain of the priestly functions of the Church are performed through duly constituted organs. The priesthood of the whole body is realized through its representatives. Therefore they can rightly be called 'priests' in a special sense. As priests they act not as substitutes for but as representatives of the whole body. It is a 'ministerial priesthood'. As priests they do not possess any magical powers inherent in their own individual persons, rather they possess authority to perform certain priestly acts in the name of the whole Church. The Church realizes her priesthood in and through them. The English word 'priest' is etymologically only an abbreviation of presbyter. But it has come to be the equivalent not only of 'presbyter' but of 'sacerdos'. Christian ministers are not called 'sacerdotes' or '$\iota\epsilon\rho\epsilon\hat{\iota}s$' in the New Testament or the earliest writings, to avoid confusion with the Jewish and pagan priesthood. But sacerdotal language is used in connexion with their duties (cp. Heb 13^{10}, Rom 15^{16}). So the *Didache* speaks of the Eucharist as $\theta\upsilon\sigma\acute{\iota}a$ and the prophets as $\mathring{a}\rho\chi\iota\epsilon\rho\epsilon\hat{\iota}s$. Clement of Rome uses even stronger language. As the danger of confusion passed away the title came to be used of Christian ministers. It was seen that all the truth embodied in the sacrificing priesthood of the Jews and heathen was fulfilled in the Christian ministry. A priest may be defined as one who represents God to man and man to God. The only priest in the full and perfect sense of priesthood is Jesus Christ. The Mosaic priesthood was partial and preparatory. Jews and pagans never attained

---

[1] A claim has been made on behalf of the Methodists that they possess the historic ministry, since their orders ultimately go back to John Wesley, a priest of the Church of England. But in ordaining ministers John Wesley went outside the commission that he had received. Even if priest and bishop were at one time identical they had long ceased to be so in his day. He could act for no one but himself. The English Ordinal with which he had been ordained makes quite clear what were the limits of his authority.

to the true ideal of priesthood. That was revealed in all its fulness for
the first time in Christ. Hence Christian priests are not the same as
Jewish priests. This does not prove that they are not truly priests, for
that would be to interpret the higher by the lower. Rather in their
measure they share the priesthood of Christ. At the Reformation the
Church of England deliberately retained the title 'priest', though in
mediaeval times its meaning had been perverted, because it contained
a real truth. Christ is the perfect priest. The Church is His body. The
organ of a priestly body cannot be less than priestly.[1]

The second or practical line of argument takes the form of the
assertion that Christian bodies who repudiate any idea of apostolic
succession show at least as much vitality as those who maintain it.
This is specially seen in the mission field.

We may reply that all bodies live and work in the power of the
truths that they hold. These Protestant bodies stand for definite
truths. They owe their power to the positive truth to which they bear
faithful witness. The same applies to the good works of Unitarians
and Agnostics. The test of visible spiritual results as applied by
Protestant Nonconformists may, if they are not careful, prove too
much. In any case we cannot measure real spiritual advance by outward results. The true measure of the life of a Christian body can
only be fully known by those who live in it. Further, Scripture shows
that God's gifts have often been concealed by man's sin and that
quite genuine authority may become obscured through the faithless-
ness and indolence of those who hold it. In a world of sin the outward
and the inward do not always correspond. But when we turn from the
consideration of Christian bodies taken individually to the Church
as a whole, there can be no possible doubt of the evils of disunion.
One great cause of the divisions and subdivisions of Christendom has
been the neglect to hold fast the historic ministry and the truth for
which it stands. We see a competition between a number of sects for
adherents, with a consequent lowering of the standard required for
membership. We see the energies of Christians expended not in a
united effort against the common foe, but in mutual wrangling and
conflict. The separate gifts that are all needed in combination for the
extension of the Kingdom of Christ are too often found parted among
the various Christian bodies. This weakness and failure is a proof of
the evils of disunion. In face of it we need to be not only destructive,
but constructive. If the principle of the historic ministry, as standing
for the ministry of the whole Church, is denied, what can be substituted for it as a centre of unity? No doubt from the nature of the
case the truth of apostolic succession, as a fact of history, can never
be decisively proved or disproved so as to convince all opponents.
But its moral and spiritual significance must surely be apparent to

---

[1] On the meaning of priesthood, see Moberly, *Ministerial Priesthood* and the essay
by A. G. Hebert in *The Apostolic Ministry*.

all. The bodies that have parted with the historic ministry have split and are still splitting into smaller fragments. The one possible centre of reunion is the historic ministry, which embodies an authority wider than that of any local or partial Church.

How, then, does the Church of England regard Nonconformist ministrations? Stress should be laid on the positive rather than on the negative side. We are bound to hold fast to our ministry to secure the validity of our own ministrations. But the true antithesis to 'valid' in such cases is not 'invalid' but rather 'precarious'. We are convinced that Nonconformist rites are irregular: they have not on them the stamp of approval of the whole Church. But we have no wish to dogmatize on their position in the sight of God or to deny that He employs them as means of grace. God is not limited to His ordinances, but we are. We believe that the maintenance of the succession is God's will for us and a real means towards the reunion of Christendom. Those who repudiate it we leave to God's judgment. There is abundant evidence that here, as elsewhere, God uses what is not wholly in accordance with His will. We do not deny or wish others to deny any spiritual experience that they have gained. But we believe that to loosen our hold on the historical ministry in the hope of attaining a rapid and partial unity would be to postpone any hope of a complete and lasting unity. It is recognized that in a re-united Church there must be 'a ministry acknowledged by every part of the Church'. This practical requirement can hardly be met by any ministry which stands apart from the apostolic succession.†

§ 3. The validity of our orders has constantly been denied by theologians of the Church of Rome on various grounds. The earliest and simplest line of attack was to assert that the line of succession had been broken. An absurd story commonly known as the 'Nag's Head fable' was fabricated.[1] This alleged that Archbishop Parker was not duly consecrated, but underwent a mock ceremony at the Nag's Head Tavern in Cheapside. This has long been abandoned by serious Roman controversialists, though traces of it still linger among the ignorant. A second attempt was made to show that Bishop Barlow, who was the principal consecrator of Parker, was himself never rightly consecrated. This objection too has failed. Three other bishops took part in the consecration, and we are told all laid their hands on his head and said the words. The position of Barlow did not really, therefore, affect the validity of the act. But there is no reason whatever to doubt Barlow's own consecration. It may also be observed that even if the English Church had lost her orders in the time of Elizabeth, she would have recovered them later through Laud. At the consecration of Laud there met not only the English but also

---

[1] 'It is so absurd on the face of it that it has led to the suspicion of Catholic theologians not being sincere in the objections they make to Anglican orders' (Estcourt, quoted by Brightman, *C.H.S. Lectures*, vol. i, p. 147).

the Irish and Italian lines of succession. All the bishops who survived in 1660 had been consecrated by Laud. As we shall see in the latest Papal pronouncement on our orders, the historical arguments are all tacitly dropped.

A second line of attack has been to argue that our orders are invalid owing to either 'insufficiency of form' or 'lack of intention'. These two arguments are closely connected, but ought to be kept distinct.

(a) As to 'insufficiency of form'. The Ordinal used in the consecration of Archbishop Parker was that of Edward VI, to which our Article refers. It has been maintained that the form of consecration and of ordination contained in it is invalid, on the ground that in the words that accompany the laying on of hands there is no specification of the order that is intended to be conferred. In the Ordinal, until it was revised in 1661, during the laying on of hands the archbishop was directed to say 'Take the Holy Ghost and remember that thou stir up the grace of God which is in thee by the imposition of hands, etc.' In the revision of 1661 the words were expanded into their present form 'Receive the Holy Ghost, for the office and work of a Bishop in the Church of God, now committed unto thee by the Imposition of our hands; In the Name of the Father and of the Son, and of the Holy Ghost. Amen. And remember, etc.' It has been argued that the earlier form was insufficient because the particular order was not specified, and, indeed, that this insufficiency was felt by the Church of England is proved by the subsequent emendation. This argument is not very strong. The very quotation from 2 Tim 1[6] is sufficient to show that the office to which the words refer is the same as that to which S. Timothy was himself consecrated by S. Paul, namely, the Episcopate. Nor is there any real doubt throughout the service what is taking place. Further, the Latin Pontifical is equally vague in its language, 'Receive the Holy Ghost,' the office for which the Holy Ghost is given being determined by the context. So, too, the form in the Ordinal of Edward VI for the ordination of priests ran originally, 'Receive the Holy Ghost: whose sins thou dost forgive, etc.' In 1661 the words 'for the Office and Work of a Priest in the Church of God, now committed unto thee by the imposition of our hands' were inserted. Here, too, the quotation from Jn 20[23], 'Whose sins thou dost forgive, etc.,' fixes the meaning. The insertions of 1661 were probably made in order to rule out the Presbyterian idea that bishop and priest were the same office. They must be viewed in the light of contemporary Church history.

A further objection now proved to be unsound must be mentioned. In the Western rite for the ordination of priests there had been introduced a ceremony known as the 'porrectio instrumentorum'. The bishop presented the candidates for ordination with a paten and chalice, saying, 'Receive authority to offer sacrifice to God and to

celebrate Masses as well for the living as the dead.' This was deliberately omitted in the second Prayer-Book of Edward VI. It was
argued, therefore, that this omission rendered the 'form' invalid. In
the seventeenth century a school of theologians had come to hold
that this particular ceremony, with the words that accompany it,
was the actual matter and form of ordination. In the fifteenth century
Pope Eugenius IV, in his letter to the Armenians which was appended
to the decrees of the Council of Florence, had definitely committed
himself to this view. Other controversialists were content to maintain that only certain powers of the priesthood were conveyed
through this ceremony. But in the seventeenth century, owing to the
researches of the Roman Catholic antiquarian Morinus, it was
established beyond all doubt that the ceremony had not existed during the first thousand years of the Church's life. It was purely Western
and Roman. If, then, it was essential for a valid ordination the
Church had possessed no valid orders for a thousand years. The
objection, therefore, in its old form, fell to the ground.

(*b*) The opponents of Anglican Orders have therefore fallen back
on the charge of 'lack of intention'.[1] This is the argument of the
Papal Bull 'Apostolicae Curae' issued in 1896, condemning our
orders as null and void. The Pope maintains that the Ordinal of
Edward VI and our present Ordinal are not so much absolutely and
in themselves inadequate, but that the changes made in them at the
Reformation are evidence of a change of intention on the part of the
Church. The deliberate omission of any mention of the sacrificing
power of the priesthood and of the 'porrectio instrumentorum',
which was the visible sign of the conferring of that power, show that
the Church of England does not intend to ordain a 'sacrificing priesthood'. Her offices betray a defective idea of the priesthood, and
therefore true priests cannot be made by them.[2]

In reply to this charge it has been pointed out that any explicit
mention of the sacrificial function of the priesthood is entirely absent
from several forms that Rome acknowledges to be valid, including
not only the Coptic rite but the ancient Roman rite. But this hardly
meets the objection. It is not at all the same thing never to have had
any explicit mention of the sacrificing power of the priesthood, as it is
to have cut it out after such mention has once been inserted. In order to
defend the action of the Church of England we must go back to first
principles. Here, as elsewhere, the Church of England desired to
return to antiquity. She appealed against one-sided and perverted
mediaeval ideas to Scripture and primitive tradition. In the later

---

[1] Nothing is more damaging to the Roman case than the constant shifting of argument to which they have been driven.

[2] This Bull is an official condemnation of Anglican Orders, confirming the previous
practice of the Church of Rome in refusing to recognize them. Dr Briggs, however,
was assured by Pius X that this decision of his predecessor was not infallible. See
Briggs, *Church Unity*, p. 121.

Middle Ages the function of offering the Eucharistic sacrifice had assumed such undue prominence in the popular idea of the priesthood, that there was serious danger of forgetting the ministry of the Word and the pastoral work that belong essentially to the office. The Reformers rightly desired to recall men to a truer, fuller and better-proportioned view of the ministry. Accordingly, in the Ordinal the comparatively late addition of the 'porrectio instrumentorum' and the singling out of the sacrificial function of the priesthood were omitted. This did not mean that the Church of England in any sense intended to institute, as it were, a new order. The preface to the Ordinal, composed in 1550 and continued in 1552, makes it as clear as human language is able to make it, that she intended to continue those orders which had been in the Church from the days of the Apostles, namely Bishops, Priests and Deacons, in the same sense as they had always existed.[1] When we turn to Scripture we find no stress laid upon the authority given to ministers to celebrate the Eucharist. It is preposterous to suppose that our Lord chose or ordained the Apostles chiefly or primarily to offer the Eucharistic sacrifice. In S. Paul's address to the presbyter-bishops of Ephesus, the stress is laid on the faithful preaching of the Word and the care of the flock (Acts 20[28-31]). In the Pastoral Epistles, in the choice of presbyters the emphasis is laid on the possession of qualities of character which are needed for pastoral supervision and teaching (1 Tim 3[1-7], cp. 5[17], Tit 1[7-9]). So S. Peter places in the forefront of the duty of presbyters the general oversight of the flock (1 Pet 5[1-4]). In such passages as these there is no explicit mention of the Eucharist. No one can doubt that it was the centre of Christian worship on every Lord's Day, nor that any one of the presbyter-bishops had authority, if need be, to preside. But when we compare the New Testament picture of the presbyters with the modern Roman idea of the priest, we feel the centre of gravity has shifted. So, too, in the early Church, the power to celebrate the Eucharist is not the predominant mark of the presbyter.[2] It is not isolated from his other functions. It is not singled out for special mention in primitive ordinals. It was only during the Middle Ages and as the result of a one-sided view of the sacrifice of the Eucharist that an equally one-sided view of the office of the

---

[1] 'It is evident unto all men diligently reading Holy Scripture and ancient Authors, that from the Apostles' time there have been these orders of Ministers in Christ's Church: Bishops, Priests, and Deacons. . . . And therefore to the intent that these Orders may be continued and reverently used and esteemed, in the Church of England; no man shall *be accounted or taken to be a lawful Bishop, Priest, or Deacon in the Church of England or suffered to* execute any of the said Functions, except he be called, tried, examined, and admitted thereunto, according to the Form hereafter following, *or hath had formerly Episcopal Consecration or Ordination.*' (Words here printed in italics were added to the Preface in 1661.)

[2] As we have said, the English word priest by derivation simply means 'presbyter'. But it has acquired the meaning of 'sacerdos'. The Christian presbyter in virtue of his office is a 'priest'. Priesthood is one of his functions.

priesthood came to be held. At the Reformation the Church of England of set purpose returned to the primitive conception of the ministry.

Again, it is untrue to say that the Church of England denies the Eucharistic sacrifice. She only repudiates any form of corrupt teaching that makes it in any sense a repetition of the sacrifice once for all offered on Calvary. In her service the Church of England makes it abundantly clear that her intention is to confer the orders which our Lord instituted and the Apostles conferred. Her purpose is shown by her use of the language of the New Testament throughout the Ordinal. She means her orders to be those of the New Testament. As such she confers upon her priests authority to 'minister the Holy Sacraments'. This includes the celebration of the Eucharist. Here again her intention is that the Eucharist shall be all that the Lord intended it to be. The sacrifice of the Eucharist is not something additional; it is the Eucharist itself in one of its chief aspects. Whatever it means, it is included in our Lord's words of institution. Hence, in conferring authority to minister the Sacraments, she confers authority to offer the Eucharistic sacrifice. Indeed, she cannot do otherwise. Even if the Church of England had denied the Eucharistic sacrifice, that would not render her orders invalid. For it is agreed, even by Romanists, that heresy does not render sacraments invalid. But she has not done anything of the kind. It is perfectly true that our Ordinal does not make explicit mention of 'the sacrifice of the Body and Blood of Christ', because it is unnecessary. The full meaning of the Eucharist depends on the Lord's command, not on our theology. Inasmuch as our priests receive authority to celebrate it, they receive authority to fulfil all that it means.

So, then, our real quarrel with the Church of Rome is at bottom about the meaning of priesthood and of the Eucharistic sacrifice.[1] We contend that Roman teaching on both is so out of proportion as to be almost untrue. If the Church of Rome chooses to say that we do not intend to make priests exactly in her sense of the word, we are not concerned to deny it. We are content to make priests in accordance with the ministry of the New Testament and the Primitive Church.

The Roman arguments rest upon two great assumptions. First, that Rome is at all times infallible, and therefore her teaching at any time about the meaning of priesthood must be accepted without question. Secondly, that Rome has a divine right to implicit and universal obedience, and therefore any change in the form of service without her consent shows a contumacious spirit. Neither of these assumptions can be granted, and without them the whole argument collapses.†

---

[1] See Chapman's *Reply to Bishop Gore*, c. ix. esp. § 1. He allows that we have orders in the sense in which we claim them.

§ 4. The real centre of our controversy with Rome has always been our repudiation of the Papal jurisdiction. Article XXXVII only repeats the declaration made by Convocation in 1534. 'The Pope of Rome hath no greater jurisdiction conferred on him by God in Holy Scripture, in this realm of England, than any other foreign bishop.' The questions at issue are partly historical, partly doctrinal.

(a) In Scripture the only Church that holds a pre-eminence is the Church of Jerusalem. There presided James, the Lord's brother: there the first council was held. Jerusalem was the scene of our Lord's death and the birthplace of the Christian Church, from whence the Apostles and others had gone forth. Its pre-eminence as the centre of Christian organization was natural. But in A.D. 70 the Church of Jerusalem was scattered by the destruction of the city. It was not until 66 years later that the new town of Aelia Capitolina was built on the site. The Church there was purely Gentile and never recovered its former position.

Meanwhile the predominantly Gentile churches had come spontaneously to group themselves round certain centres. These were selected according to two cross-principles, partly as having been founded by Apostles, partly as being the capitals of districts and provinces, and therefore the natural centres of organization. In the West, Rome was the single apostolic see and also the capital of the Empire: hence it attained a special pre-eminence. In the East, Alexandria and Antioch, which were also apostolic sees, and respectively the second and third cities of the empire, attained a like pre-eminence. By the time of the Council of Nicaea (325) their privileges could be recognized as 'ancient customs'.[1] Eighteen years later, at the Council of Sardica, a proposal was carried that bishops who had been condemned by provincial councils might appeal to Rome, and the Pope might enjoin a new trial.[2] The council was purely Western: its decrees were never accepted in the East. Indeed, there is no evid-

---

[1] The sixth canon of Nicaea runs: 'Let the ancient customs prevail, namely, those in Egypt, Libya and Pentapolis, that the Bishop of Alexandria have authority over all these, since this is customary for the Bishop of Rome also. Likewise both in Antioch and the other provinces, the privileges ($\pi\rho\epsilon\sigma\beta\epsilon\hat{\iota}a$) be secured to the churches.' The canon is silent about any jurisdiction of Rome over the whole Church. The nature of the authority belonging to the three Churches is the same, even if Rome is quoted as a precedent. At a later time it was found necessary to insert a spurious clause claiming that Rome always had the primacy. Exactly how far her jurisdiction at this time extended is doubtful, certainly not over all the West. (Bright, *Canons*, p. 20 ff.: Puller, *The Primitive Saints and the See of Rome*, pp. 138–139.)

[2] The decree was introduced very tentatively by Hosius. 'If it please you.' It was recognized as a new departure, not the confirmation of an ancient custom. The power of appeal was limited to bishops, and the object of the canon was to put a stop to the growing custom of appeals from church courts to the Emperor. In any case the Pope himself did not try the case. He could only order it to be reheard. The judges were to be bishops of a neighbouring province, or, if the accused specially desired it and the Pope consented, the Pope might send priestly delegates to act as assessors. The whole scheme shows no consciousness of any inherent power of the Bishop of Rome to be the final court of appeal.

ence that this canon was ever put into practice. Its main importance is that by accident or design the Church of Rome later on quoted the canons of Sardica as Nicene, and even after the error had been pointed out by the Church of Africa, continued to claim for them the oecumenical authority of Nicaea. Under their false title they proved exceedingly useful.

The grounds on which Rome enjoyed a privileged position were made clear at the Council of Constantinople in 381. The recognized order of precedence, resting on Imperial status, Rome, Alexandria, Antioch, was disturbed by the foundation of Constantinople to be the new capital of the Empire. In the third canon it was decreed 'that the Bishop of Constantinople have the precedence of honour after the Bishop of Rome, because it is new Rome.' This canon was ratified at Chalcedon, in spite of the protest of the Roman delegates.[1]

These two canons are quite incompatible with any recognition of modern Papal claims. They assert that the precedence accorded to Rome by general consent rested not on divine but on human appointment and depended on her Imperial position. So much so that when the new Rome was founded it was reasonable to grant her similar privileges. There is no mention of Rome's apostolic foundation. The primacy is given to the Church rather than the bishop.[2]

This view is supported by a famous passage of Irenaeus. As against the Gnostics he appeals to apostolic tradition. This is to be discovered by the consentient witness of Churches that possess the succession of bishops from the Apostles. To save time he appeals especially to the Church of Rome in the West. 'For to this Church on account of its more influential pre-eminence, it is necessary that every church should resort, that is the faithful who are from all quarters: and in this church the tradition which comes down from the apostles has always been preserved by those who are from all quarters.'[3]

---

[1] 'We, following in all things the determination of the holy Fathers and acknowledging the canon just read' (*i.e.* the third of Constantinople) '. . . do ourselves also have the same determination and decision concerning the privileges of the most holy church of Constantinople, new Rome. For the Fathers have naturally assigned its privileges to the see of the elder Rome, because that city is imperial. And being moved by the same consideration, the 150 most religious bishops' (*i.e.* of the Council of Constantinople) 'awarded the same privileges to the most holy see of the new Rome, judging with good reason that the city which was honoured with the sovereignty and senate and enjoyed the same privileges as the elder imperial Rome, should also in things ecclesiastical be magnified like her, holding the second place after her.' (See Puller, *op. cit.*, pp. 12–13; Bright, *op. cit.*, pp. 106 ff. and 219 ff.)

[2] No doubt S. Leo refused to accept the canon and the West as a whole rejected it. But in practice the East accepted it and obeyed it. Constantinople retained her rank and Rome had to recognize the existing facts. At the Quinisext Council (692) all the canons of Chalcedon were confirmed. In any case, the canon is clear evidence of the mind of the Church.

[3] *Adv. Haer.* iii. c. 3, § 2. 'Ad hanc enim ecclesiam propter potentiorem principalitatem necesse est omnem convenire ecclesiam, hoc est eos qui sunt undique fideles, in qua semper ab his, qui sunt undique, conservata est ea quae est ab apostolis traditio.' 'Convenire ad' cannot mean 'agree with'. Such a translation is doubtful Latin and makes nonsense of the context. If all Churches must agree with Rome, all that

These points are clear. Irenaeus appeals to the witness of the Roman Church as a whole, not to the infallible authority of its bishop. The value of this witness depended not simply on the inherent dignity of the Church, but on its central position. All roads led to Rome, and it became, as it were, a clearing-house of Christian tradition. The preservation there of the true apostolic tradition depended not simply on the Church itself, but on the constant stream of visitors from outside. The passage witnesses against any idea that supreme authority was inherent in the Roman see as such. Irenaeus then proceeds to appeal to the witness of the famous apostolic churches of the East, Smyrna and Ephesus.[1]

During the third century, however, the Church of Rome came to put forward a very different explanation of her primacy. She claimed that the bishop of Rome was the inheritor of the special authority given to S. Peter by our Lord. The earliest surviving evidence of this claim is in the letter written by Firmilian, Bishop of Caesarea, to Cyprian, criticizing a letter of Pope Stephen, who made extensive claims in the name of S. Peter.[2] Neither Firmilian nor Cyprian recognized his authority. But henceforward the See of Rome was prepared to put forward such claims to universal authority based on the succession from S. Peter and in later days backed by the canons of Sardica misquoted as Nicene.

The Church of Rome eventually succeeded in making good her claim to supremacy, at least over the West. But her success was not achieved in the first instance by convincing the conscience of the Church that she had inherited a divinely bestowed authority. It was secured by the legislative action of the State and a series of well-timed forgeries. About 370 the Emperor Valentinian I granted to the Pope certain rights to hear appeals in his own court and to call upon the civil power to compel submission to his authority. In 382 a council at Rome under Pope Damasus petitioned Gratian to enforce this law. Gratian granted a new constitution, assigning to the See of Rome jurisdiction over the western part of the Roman Empire. In effect it created a patriarchate of Rome. This new jurisdiction was

---

would be required against the Gnostic would be the utterance of Rome. The appeal to other Churches would be superfluous. 'Necesse est' means 'it is the inevitable result of Rome's central position'. Unhappily the Greek original of the whole passage is wanting.

[1] On the passage see Puller, *op. cit.*, pp. 19–35, and T. E. Jalland, *The Church and the Papacy*, pp. 109 ff.

[2] This letter is printed among S. Cyprian's, No. 75, see esp. § 17: 'Herein I am justly indignant at such open and manifest folly in Stephen, that he who so boasts of the seat of his episcopate and contends that he holds the succession from Peter, on whom the foundations of the Church were laid, introduces many other rocks and builds anew many churches, in that by his authority he maintains baptism among them.' 'Stephen who proclaims that he occupies by succession the chair of Peter.' The argument is not affected by the fact that the Western Church came to agree with Stephen that heretical baptism is valid, rather than with Firmilian and Cyprian, who maintained that it was not. The point at issue is the repudiation of the jurisdiction of Rome.

resisted in Gaul and Africa. More than one African council passed canons forbidding any appeal beyond the seas, *i.e.* to Rome. In Gaul the opposition of Hilary of Arles to Pope Leo I provoked the intervention of the Emperor Valentinian III, who bestowed upon the see of Rome not only judicial but legislative authority. The Popes were not unwilling to make use of the coercive powers given them by the State. They cloaked their action by appeals to the authority of S. Peter or the Sardican canons : but their real strength lay in the support of the State. So by a gradual process the primacy of Rome, which had been first a primacy of honour due largely to accidental and secular causes, was transformed into a monarchy. Certainly by the time of Leo the Great we can discern the germ of the modern Papacy. The Papal theory which began as the opinion of a school within the Church, came in time to dominate the Western Church and was exalted into a dogma. No doubt there was need of a strong central authority, and the Papacy met that need. The development was not due merely to the ambition of Rome. But the fact that Rome succeeded does not prove the truth of the arguments on which she based her claim to succeed.[1]

Special mention must be made of the effects of what are known as the 'Forged Decretals'. About 850 an unknown writer in Gaul, usually styled the 'Pseudo-Isidore', composed what professed to be a collection of decrees issued by Bishops of Rome, together with letters from famous ecclesiastics and acts of councils. It contained a certain amount of genuine material, but the bulk was deliberate forgery. His primary object was to strengthen bishops against the discipline of local councils and metropolitans. In his documents the authority of the Pope is exalted so as to make him in effect the only authority who can really deal with bishops. A Pope at a distance had fewer terrors than a lesser authority near at hand. These decretals appeared to show that the earliest Bishops of Rome had claimed the most extensive powers. The Western Church was deluded by these forgeries, and their effect was enormous. The principles laid down in them revolutionized the constitution of the Church. The compilers of the canon law drew largely upon the 'Forged Decretals'. The Church was persuaded that the Pope was, according to the will of Christ, absolute monarch of the whole Church and the fountain of all canon law, endowed with supreme judicial and legislative authority. That the decretals are spurious is acknowledged to-day even by the Church of Rome. But she still upholds and has even developed that conception of the Papacy which they were so largely instrumental in moulding and enforcing upon the Church.

In the case of England, the Church as a whole was neither more nor less Papal than elsewhere. In Saxon times Rome interfered very little

[1] For a very fair statement of early Church history from a Roman standpoint, see Duchesne, *Early History of the Christian Church.*

with her independence. The case of Wilfred shows that a Papal decree could be opposed successfully. After the Conquest England was inevitably drawn closer to the rest of Europe. There was a tendency for the Church to become increasingly subject to the Pope, to accept the theory that in some sense her bishops derived their authority from him. She could not be exempt from the influences of the time. The Papal power was at its highest in England during the miserable reign of Henry III. The scandalous schism in the Papacy itself, when rival Popes divided the allegiance of the Church, shook its position. There was a reaction towards a more primitive conception of episcopal and synodical government, in which England took her part. The Council of Constance (1414) clearly declared the Pope subordinate to a general council. But the conciliar movement failed to reform the Church. Its failure left the Papacy the stronger. But the need of reform became again urgent. The unspeakable moral corruption of the Roman court called for more drastic action. When the Church of England in 1534 repudiated the authority of the Pope, she reasserted an independence that belonged to her by inherent right.

The Council of Trent increased the power of the Papacy. At the close the council voted that they should ask confirmation from the Pope for all that they had decreed. Only one bishop opposed the suggestion. The Pope was declared supreme even over councils.[1] The development of the Papal power at the expense of the Church took a new start from Trent. The bishops were placed under stricter control. Finally, in 1870, at the Vatican Council, a belief in the infallibility of the Pope was made 'de fide'. In the decree 'Pastor Aeternus' it was asserted (i) that the Bishop of Rome has by divine right full and universal jurisdiction; (ii) that he is infallible when he speaks *ex cathedra*, *i.e.* when 'performing his office of pastor and doctor of all Christians, in virtue of his apostolic authority, he defines a doctrine concerning faith or morals to be held by the universal church.'[2]

(*b*) We may now examine the arguments by which this concentration of all authority, ecclesiastical and doctrinal, into the person of the Bishop of Rome, is defended. The chief arguments may be summarized thus. Our Lord gave the primacy to S. Peter. He came to Rome and was Bishop of Rome and deposited the primacy in the See of Rome. Hence, since the Bishop of Rome as the inheritor of his authority is the visible head of the Church, to break off communion with him is to place oneself outside the Catholic Church. It is admitted that there has been a certain development in the formul-

---

[1] This declaration was so framed as to exclude certain occasions on which a Pope had undoubtedly given erroneous decisions to local churches, *e.g.* the instructions of Pope Eugenius to the Armenians.

[2] As late, however, as 1682 the Gallican Declarations limited the Papal power by the assent of the Church.

ating of the doctrine of infallibility, but it is argued that it is a legitimate development, on a line with the development of teaching, say, about the Holy Trinity.

What evidence is there that our Lord granted any supremacy to S. Peter? The chief texts adduced are Mt 16$^{18-19}$, 'Thou art Peter, and on this rock I will build my church.' Lk 22^{32}, 'When once thou hast turned again, stablish thy brethren.' Jn 21$^{15-17}$, 'Feed my sheep.' At first sight these passages are certainly not very convincing. They do not exclude the granting of a supremacy, but they do not obviously imply it. S. Peter had been the first in time to grasp the truth of our Lord's Messiahship. As such he was the first member of the new Israel (ἐκκλησία) which was to be based on personal adhesion to Christ. 'This rock' is not S. Peter the individual, but S. Peter as being the first to confess Christ. The authority to 'bind' and 'loose' given to him was later extended to all the Apostles (Mt 18^{18}). If S. Peter was the first stone of the foundation, others were soon added to it (cp. Rev 21^{14} and Eph 2^{20}). The second passage, Lk 22^{32}, contains a special prayer for S. Peter, because of his special danger. There is no mention of a gift of leadership for all time. He is to strengthen his brethren by his recovery as he weakened them by his fall. So, too, in Jn 21$^{15-17}$, our Lord's solemn threefold repetition of the command is the public restoration of S. Peter to his apostolic position, forfeited by his threefold denial. It confers no mission beyond that given to the Apostles as a body (cp. Jn 20$^{21-23}$, Mt 28^{19}, Acts 1^{8}).

This interpretation of these passages is in the fullest accord with the whole evidence of the New Testament. The other Apostles up to the last appear totally unaware that the primacy has already been promised to S. Peter (Mk 10^{35} ff., Lk 22^{24}, etc.). In the Acts his conduct is not accepted without question and he is obliged to defend himself before the Church (Acts 11^{2}). The Apostles as a body send him on a mission (8^{14}). At the Council of Jerusalem his speech did not close the discussion. S. James presided, summed up, and gave the decision (ἐγὼ κρίνω, 15$^{1-22}$). S. Peter's name is not mentioned in the final settlement (vv. ^{22} ff.). Henceforward S. Peter drops out of the story and initiates nothing. Again, in Gal 2^{11} we find S. Paul rebuking him openly. So, too, in his First Epistle S. Peter's language does not hint at any special privileges bestowed upon himself (cp. e.g. 5^{1}). In short we do not find S. Peter recognized as the divinely appointed head of the Church. His authority is not invoked as final where on the Roman theory we should have expected it to be invoked. We do not deny that S. Peter was the spokesman of the apostolic band and their leader—for evil as well as good. In the beginning of the Church's life he plays a prominent part, as we should expect. But all this falls immeasurably short of the Roman contention of a supremacy conferred on him. He is always 'primus inter pares'. There is no hint that he is anything that the other Apostles are not. Passages such as 1 Cor

12^{28} and Eph 4^{11} are silent on any order of ministry higher than the apostolate.

Again, in interpreting the meaning of passages of Scripture we can rightly appeal for guidance to tradition. Tradition is almost universally unfavourable to the Roman interpretation of Scripture. In patristic commentaries of the first six centuries on Mt 16^{18} there is no fixed interpretation.[1] This lack of unanimity proves that no special importance was as yet attached to the passage. So, too, with the other passages. There is no hint that they attest the bestowal of a supremacy vital to the constitution of the Church.

Lastly, even if we were prepared to yield to the contention that Scripture affords evidence of a primacy over the whole Church bestowed by our Lord on S. Peter, no text can be quoted that even faintly suggests that our Lord also bestowed authority on S. Peter to transmit his primacy to others or that S. Peter ever intended to do so. S. Peter's privileged position, whatever it was, died with him.

That S. Peter visited Rome is most probable. It rests upon quite ancient tradition. 'Babylon' in 1 Pet 5^{13} is probably Rome (cp. Rev 14^8). But there is no real evidence that he founded the Church at Rome. It would seem that it grew up no one knows how by the confluence of individual Christians from other Churches.[2] In the earliest allusions S. Peter and S. Paul are recognized as joint and equal founders of the Roman Church.[3] This suggests that S. Peter was the founder only in the same limited sense as S. Paul. There is little reason to doubt that both Apostles were martyred there. But this is a very different thing from saying that S. Peter was first diocesan Bishop of Rome. The title is an anachronism. S. Paul was as much Bishop of Rome as S. Peter, and other Churches could claim to possess the episcopal succession from S. Peter as truly as Rome. The Church of Antioch might be styled, with equal accuracy, the See of Peter. But the whole idea of the Apostles as diocesan bishops presupposes a later development of Church organization.[4] Irenaeus distinctly teaches that Linus was the first 'bishop' of Rome and received his

---

[1] For the variety of patristic interpretations, see Darwell Stone, *The Christian Church*, p. 200.

[2] The belief in S. Peter's 25 years' episcopate at Rome rests on comparatively late evidence. If there is no evidence that 'another place' in Acts 12^{17} is not Rome, there is no evidence that it is. In Acts 15 S. Peter seems established at Jerusalem (cp. Gal 1^{18} and 2^9). If he went to Rome to escape from Herod, he went because it was the safest place of concealment. Rom 15^{20} is ambiguous. S. Paul's desire 'not to build on another's foundation' may be taken either as a reason for visiting Rome, since no Apostle had been there, or it may be an excuse for the delay in visiting Rome, since an Apostle had been there, and so the other regions had to be covered first. (Cp. S. and H., *Romans*, pp. xxv. ff.)

[3] *E.g.* Iren. *Haer.* iii. 3, §§ 2-3.

[4] 'If we call an Apostle bishop, because he exercised episcopal—nay more than episcopal—power, we must also hold that in apostolic times, one bishop might hold several sees, and one see have, at the same time, more bishops than one' (Salmon, *Infallibility of the Church*, 1952 edition, p. 142).

episcopal authority from S. Peter and S. Paul during their lifetime.[1] The exact order of the early bishops of Rome is somewhat obscure, but no writers for the first two centuries or more speak of S. Peter as first bishop. The story of his episcopate is probably derived from Ebionite literature composed in the name of Clement of Rome in order to vilify S. Paul. It possesses no evidential value, but it helped to shape the traditions of the early Church. All the genuine literature that we possess of the subapostolic age goes to show that the importance of the Bishop of Rome was merged in that of his Church. Ignatius sends his greeting not to the bishop, but to the Church at Rome. Clement writes his one genuine epistle not in his own name but in that of the Church. In short, all evidence goes to show that S. Peter was not in the technical sense Bishop of Rome and did not bequeath any unique authority to that see.[2]

Once again, there are certain facts in ancient Church history that are entirely inconsistent with the modern Roman theory of the Pope's infallibility and supremacy of jurisdiction. At the close of the second century Pope Victor excommunicated the Quarto-deciman Churches of Asia. His excommunication was disregarded. Even the other bishops of the West rebuked him. In the third century Pope Stephen excommunicated Cyprian and the Oriental Churches who agreed with him for refusing to recognize heretical baptism. Cyprian and Firmilian in reply asserted their episcopal independence, and posterity approved. Further, Meletius, Bishop of Antioch, who presided over the Council of Constantinople, was not recognized by Rome, who supported his rival Paulinus. During the council he died and was canonized. His name is to be found in the Roman Calendar to-day. But on the modern Roman theory, since he died out of communion with Rome, he died outside the Church altogether. Other equally important facts could be quoted, but these instances are sufficient to show that the early Church as a whole knew nothing of Papal supremacy.

No doubt passages can be quoted on the other side. Bishops who desired the support of Rome employed flattering language that fell short of strict theological accuracy, not more flattering perhaps than that which they applied to the Emperor. There was, as we have seen, a universal respect paid to Rome as the leading Church. Further, there is among the Fathers what may be called a Papal school who tended to exalt the prerogatives of the Bishop of Rome; but their opinion was at best the opinion of a party and was rejected by the greater part of the Church.[3] If it came to triumph in the West, the

[1] *Haer.* iii. 3, § 3.

[2] On S. Peter in Rome, see Jalland, *op. cit.*, Lect. iii, and O. Cullmann, *Peter, Disciple, Apostle, Martyr.*

[3] Among these we might place Cyprian. He certainly regarded the Roman see as a symbol of Church unity and used very high language about it. But his conduct towards Stephen interprets his meaning. He certainly did not hold that the authority of each bishop is mediated by that of the Bishop of Rome. His view was that the episcopate is one and shared by each bishop, like a property held in common. It is usually supposed

triumph was due not to the deliberate acceptance of the Papal claims by the reason and conscience of the Church, but partly to external circumstances and partly to calculated ambition backed by force and fraud. The East continued to bear witness to the primitive truth.

To sum up, the contention of the English Church is this. If the claims of the Pope to be the infallible head of the Church and the source of all ecclesiastical jurisdiction are well founded, then a right belief in them is an essential part of the Christian faith. We have the right, therefore, to expect to find clear proof of this in Scripture and primitive tradition. That is just what we do not find. On the other hand, there are facts of many different kinds that show that the early Church knew nothing of any such belief. We cannot suppose that God would have left His Church without as clear evidence for the supremacy of S. Peter's successors as for, *e.g.* the doctrine of the Trinity. The only possible line of argument in defence of the Roman position is that of development.[1] We are not concerned to deny that the Papacy is a development or that in the providence of God it played a most useful part in conserving the unity and discipline of the Church during times of general confusion when a strong central authority was required. But we may still ask whether the modern Papacy is a legitimate development, and are bound to test it, as we test other developments of Christianity, such as, for instance, the Salvation Army, by the rule of Scripture and tradition and the light of reason. The Roman and Catholic theories of unity are incompatible. On the Roman view the unity of the Church is based upon absolutism. Every kind of power is derived from a single head, the Pope. On the Catholic view the unity of the Church is that of one life in Christ which unites a variety of free and living wills. Every element in the Church has its part.[2] The Pope is only one among many of the bishops of the Church. On the Roman theory unity is, as it were, imposed from without by external authority; on the Catholic theory it grows from within, as the spontaneous product of the one life that works in all the members of the Body of Christ. We believe that neither historically nor theologically can the Papal theory of unity be justified by an appeal to Scripture, and therefore we are free to reject it without forfeiting our Catholic inheritance.†

---

that Cyprian's writings were afterwards interpolated to support the Roman view. (Cp. Puller, p. 49 ff., or Benson, *Cyprian*, c. iv. See, however, *J.Th.S.* (New Series) vol. v (1954), p. 19, where modern studies of this question are reviewed.)

[1] We may doubt whether this is really compatible with the Papal Bull that declares the infallibility of the Pope a tradition received from the beginning of the Christian faith. But see Dom Chapman, c. vi. § A.

[2] Cp. Gore, *R.C. Claims*, c. vii. 'The original idea of the Episcopate would have secured for the Church a duly representative government and would have provided, by the confederation of relatively independent Churches, a system of checks upon one-sided local tendencies. The Papacy represents the triumph of Imperial absolutism over representative, constitutional authority, and of centralization over consentient witness and co-operation.' The Eastern Churches on the whole stand for the older view of confederation.

THE SACRAMENTS

ARTICLE XXV

Of the Sacraments

Sacraments ordained of Christ be not only badges or tokens of Christian men's profession, but rather they be certain sure witnesses, and effectual signs of grace, and God's good will towards us, by the which he doth work invisibly in us and doth not only quicken, but also strengthen and confirm our Faith in him.

There are two Sacraments ordained of Christ our Lord in the Gospel, that is to say, Baptism, and the Supper of the Lord.

Those five commonly called Sacraments, that is to say, Confirmation, Penance, Orders, Matrimony, and extreme Unction, are not to be counted for Sacraments of the Gospel, being such as have grown partly of the corrupt following of the apostles, partly are states of life allowed in the Scriptures; but yet have not like nature of Sacraments with Baptism, and the Lord's Supper, for that they have not any visible sign or ceremony ordained of God.

The Sacraments were not ordained of Christ to be gazed upon, or to be carried about, but that we should duly use them. And in such only as worthily receive the same they have a

De Sacramentis

Sacramenta, a Christo instituta, non tantum sunt notae professionis Christianorum, sed certa quaedam potius testimonia, et efficacia signa gratiae atque bonae in nos voluntatis Dei, per quae invisibiliter ipse in nos operatur, nostramque fidem in se non solum excitat, verum etiam confirmat.

Duo a Christo Domino nostro in Evangelio instituta sunt Sacramenta: scilicet, Baptismus, et Coena Domini.

Quinque illa vulgo nominata Sacramenta: scilicet, confirmatio, poenitentia, ordo, matrimonium, et extrema unctio, pro Sacramentis Evangelicis habenda non sunt, ut quae, partim a prava Apostolorum imitatione profluxerunt, partim vitae status sunt in Scripturis quidem probati: sed sacramentorum eandem cum Baptismo et Coena Domini rationem non habentes, ut quae signum aliquod visibile, seu caeremoniam, a Deo institutam non habeant.

Sacramenta non in hoc instituta sunt a Christo ut spectarentur, aut circumferrentur, sed ut rite illis uteremur, et in his duntaxat qui digne percipiunt salutarem habent effectum: Qui

wholesome effect or operation: But they that receive them unworthily purchase to themselves damnation, as S. *Paul* saith.

vero indigne percipiunt, damnationem (ut inquit Paulus) sibi ipsis acquirunt.

This is one of those Articles in which large and important alterations were made in 1563. The first paragraph, based largely on the Confession of Augsburg, formed the last paragraph of the original Article of 1553. The second and third paragraphs were composed in 1563. The last paragraph of our present Article formed the first of the earlier Article, but has undergone two important alterations, (i) An opening clause consisting of a quotation from S. Augustine has been omitted, (ii) the condemnation of the theory of grace *ex opere operato* has been withdrawn.

Its object may be summed up thus:

(i) To condemn as inadequate teaching about the sacraments held by Anabaptists, Zwinglians and others;

(ii) To restore a sense of proportion in the view of sacraments by a reference to Scripture;

(iii) To make clear that they require a moral effort in the recipient.

N.B.—Allowed =*probati*, *i.e.* approved.

Duly=*rite*, *i.e.* with right matter and form and a duly authorized minister.

Worthily =*digne*, *i.e.* with right inward disposition.

ARTICLE XXVI

Of the Unworthiness of the Ministers, which hinders not the Effect of the Sacrament

Although in the visible Church the evil be ever mingled with the good, and sometimes the evil have chief authority in the Ministration of the Word and Sacraments, yet forasmuch as they do not the same in their own name, but in Christ's, and do minister by His commission and authority, we may use their Ministry, both in hearing the Word of God, and in the receiving of the sacraments. Neither is the effect of Christ's ordinance taken away by their wickedness, nor the grace of God's gifts diminished from such as by faith and rightly do receive the Sacraments ministered unto them; which be effectual, because of Christ's institu-

De vi institutionum divinarum, quod eam non tollat malitia Ministrorum

Quamvis in Ecclesia visibili, bonis mali semper sunt admixti, atque interdum ministerio verbi et Sacramentorum administrationi praesint; tamen cum non suo, sed Christi nomine agant, ejusque mandato et auctoritate ministrent, illorum ministerio uti licet, cum in verbo Dei audiendo, tum in Sacramentis percipiendis. Neque per illorum malitiam effectus institutorum Christi tollitur, aut gratia donorum Dei minuitur, quoad eos qui fide et rite sibi oblata percipiunt, quae propter institutionem Christi et promissionem efficacia sunt, licet per malos administrentur.

Ad Ecclesiae tamen disciplinam pertinet, ut in malos minis-

tion and promise, although they be ministered by evil men.

Nevertheless, it appertaineth to the discipline of the Church, that inquiry be made of evil Ministers, and that they be accused by those that have knowledge of their offences; and finally being found guilty by just judgment, be deposed.

tros inquiratur, accusenturque ab his, qui eorum flagitia noverint, atque tandem justo convicti judicio deponantur.

Practically unchanged since 1553. Taken mainly from the Thirteen Articles and through them based in part on the Confession of Augsburg.

Object.—To condemn the idea of Anabaptists that the personal holiness of the minister was a necessary condition for any valid preaching of the Word or ministration of the sacraments.

§ 1. The word 'Sacrament' has a long history.[1] In classical Latin 'sacramentum' meant 'a sacred pledge'. It was used for a soldier's oath or for caution money deposited to prevent frivolous suits. The word is first used in reference to Christians by Pliny in a letter to the Emperor Trajan. He writes that Christians bound themselves 'sacramento', not to commit some crime (as popular opinion supposed), but rather not to commit theft, robbery, adultery, etc. The word here, in the writing of a heathen governor, must still have its meaning of 'oath' or 'solemn promise'. Its appearance is almost accidental. Its first employment in any technical Christian sense was in the earliest Latin-speaking Church, that of North Africa. Here it was used to translate the Greek word μυστήριον. μυστήριον originally meant a secret (not anything 'mysterious' in our sense of the word). It is used, e.g. of State secrets. Hence it came to be applied to religious truths that were known only to the initiated or to acts 'where more was meant than met the eye or ear', and where the secret meaning was known only to those who had been taught it. Thus it had quite a wide range of meaning, and its Latin translation, sacramentum, had at first an equally wide range. Through the Latin versions of the New Testament it passed into the common vocabulary of the Latin-speaking Church. In the Fathers it is used in its old sense of oath or of any Christian truth or ceremony or ordinance.[2] But in quite early times we find a tendency to contrast the fewness of Christian with the multiplicity of Jewish ordinances.[3] Accordingly, the term sacrament

[1] Cp. Trench, Study of Words, pp. 138–139, and more recently E. Masure, The Christian Sacrifice (Burns Oates), pp. 79 ff., with the literature there referred to.

[2] E.g. Tertullian applies it to the baptismal vow. 'In Sacramenti verba respondimus.' He even speaks of Christians being accused 'de sacramento infanticidii'. Cyprian speaks of the Lord's Prayer as containing many great 'sacraments', of the three hours of prayer as 'a sacrament of the Trinity'. Pope Innocent can write of two sacraments in the Eucharist, the bread and the wine.

[3] S. Augustine wrote how under the new dispensation Christ 'has knit together His people in fellowship by sacraments which are very few in number, most easy in ob-

came to be limited to those rites which were commanded in the New Testament. The number of sacraments varied with different writers. The fixing of the number as Seven is assigned to Peter Lombard (d. 1164). It is accepted in a decree of the Council of Florence (1439), and finally ratified by the Council of Trent in 1547. Accordingly, at the time this Article was composed the idea of Seven Sacraments had long been familiar.

§ 2. In all teaching about sacraments we have to face an initial objection. Christianity, it is said, is a spiritual religion. God is a Spirit. We are spiritual beings. What God asks for in us is a right inward disposition of the will, namely faith, not the performance of specified ceremonies. We are told to worship the Father 'in spirit and in truth'. What place, then, can outward and material things have in the dealings of spirit with spirit? How can the pouring of water on a man's forehead or the tasting of bread and wine affect the soul's relation to God? History shows that the great danger of religion is that it should sink into substituting forms and ceremonies for spiritual obedience. It would therefore be well for Christianity to shun the danger altogether. Such objections are widespread. They rest not on mere prejudice, but often on a desire for reality. We must face them.

(a) Such objections often rest upon a view of material things and the external world that is not Christian at all. The Christian Church has always contended against the view that matter is intrinsically evil. All material things have their origin in God. The world as He made it is 'very good'. The statement that we are 'spiritual beings' is a half-truth. Man is not only spirit, but spirit linked to and realizing itself through a material body.

Our very thoughts and prayers are conditioned by certain bodily functions. Our whole spiritual activity is dependent upon the body. An injury to the brain will wreck the finest intellect. A bad headache will disintegrate the devotions of a saint. We cannot explain the relation of the spiritual to the material, whether in human life or in the world at large. It is an ultimate fact that we are compelled to admit, even though our finite understanding cannot grasp it. As Christians we hold that the material is not necessarily opposed to the spiritual. Rather matter fulfils its true purpose when it is subject to spirit and used as a means to the self-realization of spirit. On the other hand, our whole life in this world is mediated by matter. As Dr Moberly says, 'If a man is not spiritual in and through the body, he cannot be spiritual at all.' So the union of spiritual and material

servance, and most excellent in significance, as baptism solemnized in the name of the Trinity, the Communion of His Body and Blood and also whatever else is commended to us in canonical Scripture, apart from those enactments which were a yoke of bondage to God's ancient people, suited to their state of heart and to the times of the prophets and which are found in the books of Moses' (Ep. liv. 1 quoted in the earlier edition of the Article. Cp. also *Christian Doctrine*, iii. 9).

in the sacraments corresponds to and rests upon their union in man himself. Just as in man the material may overcome and degrade the spiritual, the body may become master instead of servant, so in the sacraments the outward side may win an undue predominance. It may become not a means but an end, not the expression of a spiritual state but a substitute for it. But just as the misuse of the body does not render it possible or even desirable for us to attempt to discard it, so the misuse of sacraments is an argument not for their abolition but for their right use. 'Corruptio optimi pessima.' The more that we insist upon the terrible results that follow from the misuse of the sacramental principle, the more we bear witness to its inherent power, and the more urgent becomes the call to claim and consecrate such a mighty possibility for the service of God.

(b) Sacraments are as old and wide as religion itself. We appeal quite rightly to the universal appearance of religion as a proof of its reality and importance. We may extend the argument and claim that the prominence and universality of the sacramental principle is a proof that it satisfies a legitimate and universal human need. In all parts of the world we find sacred ablutions. Partly they symbolize the desire for inward purification, partly they create a sense of purity in preparation for drawing near to God. Again, we find in most primitive worship sacred meals in connexion with sacrifice holding a central place. The original meaning of sacrifice is disputed, but beyond all doubt in historical times these sacrificial rites came to express the communion of the worshippers with their god and with one another. The language in which this idea is expressed is often crude. Sometimes the god was conceived in animal form, and the tribe who claimed kinship with him fed on the flesh of the sacred animal and thus were regarded as feeding on the life of the god. In more civilized tribes the communion was rather sought by sharing a common meal with him. Such rites, often crude, debased, and corrupt, must not be despised. They may claim to be taken at their best, as the efforts of primitive man to realize communion with God. They have their place in the preparation of the world for Christ. If we believe that from the first the Word of God was 'lightening every man that cometh into the world', we find in them a divinely prompted feeling after God, an inspired education of needs and aspirations that awaited their full satisfaction in Christ. Our Lord came to fulfil the highest ideals, not only of the Jews but of the heathen too. Their sacrifices, like the Jewish, were in their degree a preparation for Christ. By the deliberate institution of Christian sacraments our Lord drew men to find in Himself the satisfaction of those needs to which the persistence through long ages of such imperfect rites had borne witness. Christ did not originate but consecrated afresh the sacramental principle. Here, as elsewhere, He came not to destroy but to fulfil.

(c) Sacraments are often called ' an extension of the Incarnation'. Just as Christ took on Him a human nature that through it He might draw near to us, so He still draws near to us in things that we can touch and see. From His Birth to His Resurrection His earthly life was 'broad-based' on matter. The Atonement was wrought out on a Cross with material blood. In His miracles He employed material means as an aid to faith.

Again, in the Incarnation, God's dealings with the world took the form of definite outward historical events. The Atonement is not the less spiritual because it was achieved through certain acts in time to which we can give a date and place. So, too, in His Sacraments Christ still deals with His Church through outward events. While He moved on earth among men it needed faith to discern His authority. Only the eye of faith could discern in the death on the Cross more than the murder of an innocent man. So in the sacramental happenings of the Christian life faith is needed to discover and appropriate their inner meaning; but that does not make them the less real. In the moral and spiritual life, as elsewhere, it is the concrete and particular rather than the abstract and general that counts. The Devil has his sacraments. We all condemn love of money in the abstract. The test comes in the particular temptation to make money by means that our conscience condemns. The further we get down the scale, the more important the concrete becomes. A friend or a glass of beer, very definite and material facts, embody in themselves the spiritual conflict for many a human soul. Christianity is a universal religion, not only for the intellectual but for the plain man, not only for the spiritually gifted but for the dull-witted and the savage. For these spiritual truths need to be enshrined in concrete facts. Through sacraments the meaning of unseen realities is brought home to simple minds. Religion descends from the eternal and invisible to manifest itself in space and time, becoming not one bit the less spiritual in so doing. Just as 'the Word was made flesh', so the living Christ still condescends to the needs of men and makes Himself known to them in the actual and the detailed. Of themselves the water of Baptism or the bread and wine of the Eucharist can do neither harm nor good to the spirit of man—no more and no less than the sound-waves that underlie speech or the colours that form the raw material of the painter's art. But through the spoken word or the painter's scene our spirit can communicate to another something of its own life, thoughts and suggestions, whether of beauty or of shame. So through outward and visible signs Christ communicates Himself to us.

(d) Sacraments are a necessary condition of the social side of religion. If a man wishes to enter into any relations with his fellow-men he must employ material means. The use of a physical medium is the condition of all human intercourse. The glance of an eye, the utterance of the tongue, or whatever it be, all involve the use of matter. A purely spiritual life, if it were conceivable for a man, would be a life of isolation. The very nature of Christian sacraments emphasizes the social side of all true religion. They are 'a divine provision against spiritual individualism'. Their form is that of ceremonies only possible among members of a society. They remind us that religion includes not only our relation to God but our relation to our brethren. While corporate religion cannot exist without sacraments of some kind, the Christian sacraments are peculiarly expressive of this common life, and, indeed, demand it. A purely individual religion may be most spiritual, but it is not the religion of Jesus Christ.

(e) While all human life is in some measure patient of being brought within the range of sacraments, certain elements in it stand out as primary and fundamental. We can see why our Lord, as it were, focussed the sacramental principle on two great ordinances. He took the two most simple and universal needs, common to all mankind, the need of cleanliness and the need of food, and based on them the two sacraments of the Gospel. As Dr Illingworth says, 'He consecrates an ablution and a meal, the two necessities of our daily life, to be the witness through the ages of His spiritual presence among men.' We cannot limit the sacramental principle to these two rites, of unique authority though they be. They are but the supreme demonstration of the subjection of the material to the spiritual. Even the more private and individual acts of human life may afford the material for sacraments. But Christ ensured that no man should be outside the range of sacramental experience. He shows that sacramental life is not for a few but for all. Starting from the two great sacraments, men may learn to find in the whole of human life a parable of divine truth. Every act and need may be consecrated to the service of God. Human life will only become fully spiritual when it has become fully sacramental.†

§ 3. The Article gives four objects for which Christian sacraments exist.

(a) They are 'badges or tokens of Christian men's profession'. This view is true as far as it goes, but by itself is inadequate. It was specially emphasized by the Zwinglians. They are the means by which we publicly confess our allegiance to Christ and our membership of the Christian society. Such public confession is in Scripture demanded of Christians (Mt 10³², Rom 10⁹). In heathen lands baptism is recognized by all parties as the decisive act that marks allegiance to Christ. It often costs a man the loss of home and friends. As Article XXVII says, 'Baptism is . . . a sign of profession and mark of difference whereby Christian men are discerned from other that be not Christened.' At home the same is still true in the case of an adult. To be baptized or confirmed is an open act of allegiance. So, too, in many parts of England, to come to communion is to act differently from others.

The very act of coming is an act of witness to Christ. It is felt that a man is compromised by it in a way that he is not by mere attendance at Church. The Christian ought to be prepared to compromise himself publicly for Christ.

(b) *They be certain sure witnesses . . . of grace and God's goodwill towards us.* The fact that sacraments exist is an abiding proof that God in His love wishes to bestow grace on man. Our personal call to use them is a proof that God wills to bestow grace on us personally. They are witnesses of God's goodwill both for the past and the future. As the Catechism says: sacraments 'are a means whereby we receive' grace 'and a pledge to assure us thereof'. In the Holy Communion we thank God 'for that . . . Thou dost assure us thereby of Thy favour and goodness towards us; and that we are very members incorporate in the mystical body of Thy Son.' If we base our assurance of belonging to God only upon passing through certain religious feelings, then our sense of assurance shifts with our shifting feelings. But God's grace is wider and surer than man's emotions. Through a right use of the sacraments, as pledges of God's love, our certainty is made to depend upon definite outward facts about which there can be no doubt.

(c) *They are effectual signs of grace and God's goodwill towards us by the which He doth work invisibly in us.* An 'effectual' sign is a sign that is no mere parable, but conveys the blessing that it symbolizes. These words rule out the Zwinglian view of, *e.g.* the Eucharist as a bare memorial. As the Catechism says: By 'sacrament' 'I mean an outward and visible sign of an inward and spiritual grace given unto us . . . whereby we receive the same.' This efficacy of sacraments depends upon the ordinance of Christ. God is the efficient cause (*n.b.* Latin *per quae ipse in nobis operatur*), the sacraments are only instrumental causes. 'Christ is the chief and principal worker in all sacraments as a function of His everlasting Priesthood.'

(d) *By the which He . . . doth not only quicken but also strengthen and confirm our faith in Him.* Sacraments are an aid to faith. Just as in the Old Testament the Pillar of Fire and the Pillar of Cloud are represented as an aid to the faith of Israel, helping them to believe in a God whom they could not see, so Christian sacraments help our faith to lay hold on God. The use of such simple means helps us to realize both our own needs and the power of God. Our readiness to use them is a test of our belief in God's promise and power (cp. 2 Kings 5^{10-14}). Again, they offer definite opportunities for acts of faith. They set before us definite promises of God for faith to claim. Faith, like all our other faculties, needs exercise and grows stronger by use. There is often a danger that a newly awakened faith may waste itself in vague emotion. The sacraments afford definite objects on which to focus itself. They provide definite efforts for our wills to make, and thus have an important place in the education of Christian faith.

§ 4. The Article then goes on to deal with the number of sacraments. It places on a level by themselves the two sacraments of the Gospel. *There are two Sacraments ordained of Christ our Lord in the Gospel, that is to say, Baptism and the Supper of the Lord.* These will be considered under the later Articles. Then it proceeds *Those five, commonly called Sacraments, that is to say, Confirmation, Penance, Orders, Matrimony, and Extreme Unction, are not to be counted for Sacraments of the Gospel.* We notice that the Article does not deny to them the name of sacraments. 'Commonly called' is not in the language of the Prayer-Book necessarily derogatory. We find, *e.g.* 'The Nativity of our Lord, or the Birth-day of Christ, commonly called "Christmas Day".' All that the Article insists is that these rites are not to be counted equal to the other two. It then goes on to give reasons for this position. (i) On the positive side they are *such as have grown partly of the corrupt following of the Apostles, partly are states of life allowed in the Scripture*; (ii) on the negative side, *They have not any visible sign or ceremony ordained of God.* These reasons need some consideration. The sentences are not very exactly worded. Only Extreme Unction can really be said to have grown from the *corrupt following, i.e.* the bad imitation (*prava imitatione*) *of the Apostles.* The words can hardly apply to Penance with its mediaeval accretions, still less to the substitution of unction for laying on of hands in Confirmation. Again, Matrimony and Orders may fairly be called *'states of life allowed', i.e.* in the language of the time approved (*probati*) 'in the Scriptures', but neither of the positive reasons applies to either penance or confirmation. The negative reason, however, covers all five. Confirmation is really a part of Baptism, but we have no decisive evidence in Scripture that the laying on of hands was commanded by Christ (see, however, Heb 6[2]). Christ undoubtedly left with His Church the power to absolve sinners (Jn 20[23]), but He did not command any visible sign or ceremony in which that absolution should be embodied. The same is true of Orders (Jn 20[21-23]). We find laying on of hands employed in Scripture for ordination, but we possess no definite command of Christ. So with Matrimony. The most we can say is that Christ 'adorned and beautified' it 'with His Presence', as the Marriage Service says, and S. Paul calls it a μυστήριον (Eph 5[32]), but the word is not used in any technical sense. The same applies to unction. In neither case did Christ institute a sacrament.

The difference between ourselves and the Church of Rome in the number of sacraments is mainly a matter of words. The mediaeval number of Seven had certain practical conveniences. It met the great crises of life with appropriate sacramental ordinances. Moreover all of them could claim some authority from the New Testament. On the other hand, the Church of England bases the distinction that it makes on Scripture, and had good reason for doing so. It uses the word Sacrament in a narrower and in a wider sense. In the Catechism it declares that Christ ordained two sacraments only 'as generally' (*i.e.* universally) 'necessary to salvation'. Even the Church of Rome has never gone so far as to assert that the outward and visible sign of the other five was expressly given by Christ Himself, nor yet that all seven are on the same footing. The Council of Trent anathematized any who should say 'that these seven sacraments are equal to each other in such wise as that one is not more worthy than another'.

§ 5. Two of these sacramental rites call for special treatment here. (*a*) Penance: (*b*) Extreme Unction.

(*a*) The whole conception of Penance rests upon two main truths: (i) Sin, while in its essence it is an offence against God, is also anti-social. By our sins we injure not only ourselves but the society to which we belong. (ii) The visible sign of union with Christ is life in the fellowship of the Christian Church. No doubt this truth has become obscured by human sin, by the divisions of Christians and the failure of Church discipline. But ideally and, as it were, sacramentally membership in the visible Body of Christ is the normal means of sharing in the divine life of Christ.

When we turn to the Church as it is in Scripture we find that the duty is laid upon it of exercising judicial power over its members. From its very nature it not only possesses the right inherent in all societies of exercising discipline upon members who neglect or disobey its own rules, but it possesses special authority, arising out of its relation to Christ, in dealing with the sins of men. We find our Lord giving to S. Peter as the first member of His new Israel not only the power to 'bind and to loose', *i.e.* to declare forbidden or allowed, but also 'The keys of the kingdom of heaven' (Mt 16[19]). Again, S. John represents the Risen Christ as breathing on the assembled Church and saying 'Receive ye the Holy Ghost: whosoever sins ye forgive, they are forgiven unto them; whosoever sins ye retain, they are retained' (Jn 20[23]). We certainly find the Church acting upon this commission. The Church tests men before admitting them into fellowship. Faith and repentance were required of all candidates for Christian Baptism (Acts 2[37-41], etc.). It was the Church that claimed to judge whether they truly possessed them. And this claim to judge is not confined to the initial act of receiving into membership. The Church no less claims to judge those who are its members as to their fitness to remain such. 'Do ye not judge them that are within. . . . Put away the wicked man from among yourselves' (1 Cor 5[12-13]). Those who because of wilful and notorious sin were put out of the Church were regarded as delivered over to Satan (1 Cor 5[5], cp. 2 Cor 2[5-11], 1 Tim 1[20]). That is to say, the Church was regarded as the scene of salvation. To be cut off from the Church, as from Israel of old (cp. Exod 31[14]) was to be cut off, not only from a visible society, but from covenanted union with God. Outside God's Church Satan was regarded as having power to inflict special sufferings. Again, when the offender is penitent, the Church equally claims to be the judge of his penitence, and, if it thinks right, to readmit him to membership (2 Cor 2^{10-11}). In all cases alike the Church's judgment is dependent upon the guidance of the Holy Spirit, who in this as in all things is to guide men into all truth (Jn 20^{22}, cp. Jn 16^{13}). A judgment of the Church which was not inspired by the Holy Spirit would not be ratified by God.

Here, then, we find the origin of penance. Just as at the beginning of the Christian life sins are remitted to the unbaptized by baptism (Acts 22^{16}), so to the already baptized sins are remitted by absolution. Such absolution is primarily the Church's judgment that a man may be rightly admitted to full fellowship and especially to the Holy Communion, which is the supreme expression of Christian fellowship. The life of Christ is normally to be found within His Body, the Church. The Church remits sins by restoring a man to membership in His Body, and retains sins by refusing such restoration. Here, as elsewhere, the authority is that of the Church as a whole, but it is exercised by those who have been commissioned by Christ to act as ministers of the whole Church, e.g. the Apostles.

In Scripture and in the earliest days there is no evidence of private confession. Notorious offenders were required to make public confession before the whole congregation. Only after long and grievous discipline were penitents restored to communion. In James 5^{16} we find the command 'Confess therefore your sins one to another'. The 'therefore' connects it with the calling in of the elders of the Church to anoint the sick man with oil and to pray for him. There is no mention of formal absolution.

Auricular confession arose first as a preparation for public confession. It was obvious that those who were publicly convicted of sin were not necessarily the only offenders. A man might have fallen from Christ without the Church having become aware of his fall. Hence those who felt themselves in danger of being in this state, consulted privately some spiritual adviser about their true condition, with the object of making public confession and doing penance if such were judged advisable. Further, as primitive simplicity declined, public confession of sins began to be found undesirable. The young were familiarized with gross sins. It was a fruitful source of scandal and even made the basis of prosecution in the law-courts. Hence, the historian Socrates tells us, after the Decian persecution (A.D. 250), bishops in the East appointed a regular officer or 'penitentiary' to hear private confessions, impose suitable penance and grant absolution, where public confession was not judged necessary. In the West Leo the Great sanctioned a similar arrangement (A.D. 440). In this way private confession to a priest became the ordinary way of dealing with grave sins.[1] Where public scandal had been given, public penance was still enforced. In 1215 the Lateran Council made confession to a priest obligatory once a year. Disobedience rendered the offender excommunicate. As the custom needed defence, the Schoolmen used their ingenuity to provide one. Hence the elaborate mediaeval doctrine of the 'sacrament of penance'.

The mind of the Church of England on the subject of private confession is to be found in the Prayer-Book. Here, as so often, the Church of England has returned to primitive practice. Compulsory confession is abolished, voluntary confession is retained. In the first exhortation in the Communion office the conditions necessary for making a good communion are laid down. The duty is enforced of self-examination and repentance. Stress is laid on the absolute need of a 'full trust in God's mercy' and 'a quiet conscience'. Then it proceeds: 'therefore if there be any of you, who by this means cannot quiet his own conscience herein but requireth further comfort or counsel, let him come to me, or to some other discreet and learned Minister of God's Word, and open his grief; that by the ministry of God's holy Word he may receive the benefit of absolution, together with ghostly counsel and advice, to the quieting of his conscience and avoiding of all scruple and doubtfulness.' Again, in the Visitation of the Sick the rubric runs: 'Here shall the sick person be moved to make a special confession of his sins, if he feel his conscience troubled with any weighty matter. After which Confession, the Priest shall absolve him (if he humbly and heartily desire it), after this sort.' Then follows the form of absolution. 'Our Lord Jesus Christ who hath left power to his Church, to absolve all sinners who truly repent and believe in him, of his great mercy forgive thee thine offences: And by his authority committed to me, I absolve thee from all thy sins. In the Name of the Father, and of the Son, and of the Holy Ghost. Amen.' It is remarkable that the English Church retains the comparatively late form, 'I absolve.' If there could be any doubt that the Church of England intended to retain private confession, it is dispelled when we find the 113th Canon of 1603 warning clergy against revealing sins made known to them in confession. Further, it was widely practised in the reigns of Elizabeth, James I and Charles I, and again after the Restoration. The Prayer-Book makes clear two great points about it.

(a) There is no suggestion that we are not ordinarily able to prepare ourselves for Communion apart from auricular confession. Neither Scripture nor the Prayer-Book nor the Primitive Church asserts that 'mortal' sin cannot be forgiven on true repentance without private

---

[1] The origins of private penance present a complicated problem, which may be studied in K. E. Kirk, *The Vision of God*, Lect. v and R. C. Mortimer, *The Origins of Private Penance*. Its development was considerably influenced by the practice of private confession in the monastic life.

absolution. Such a statement is often made but never proved. Although there is no reason to credit the Lateran Council with any but the best motives in making confession obligatory, in actual practice it does not work. It does not make sufficient allowance for human nature. Forced confessions are often formal and not infrequently dishonest. Unless they are inspired by real penitence they are apt to become an easy way of salving the conscience. Sin is lightly regarded, as pardon for it can easily be obtained at the next confession.

(β) On the other hand, confession is not an end in itself but is a means to an end, namely, peace with God. A clear conscience is absolutely essential for a Christian life (cp. 1 Tim 1[5]). If a man cannot attain this by himself, confession is necessary for him. It is notorious that many are unable to quiet their own consciences. Some cannot feel that they are really sorry for their sin. Confession in the presence of another is a real help, since it enables a man to see his sins as others see them, and so is a step to seeing them as God sees them. Others cannot realize the fact of forgiveness. Here the personal absolution comes home in a way that general absolutions fail to do. There is no essential difference in quality between the two. Either avails for the true penitent and neither for the impenitent. There are not different brands of absolution. But it is a simple fact of experience that private confession is a real means to many souls of bringing home the fact of God's forgiveness through Christ. Further, penitence like faith demands self-expression. The self-humiliation of allowing another to overhear the penitent's confession to God, the receiving of a penance which is regarded not as any attempt to make up for the sins but as an expression of willingness to bear whatever punishment God is pleased to send, are all practical outlets of sorrow for sin by which that sorrow is deepened and made more real. However imperfect the penitence may still be, and true penitence is the work of a lifetime, the man still feels that he has tried his hardest. Lastly, auricular confession is a great opportunity of obtaining an independent opinion about our life from one who has had all the facts laid before him, so far as we can do so. Simple people need far more guidance in self-examination and dealing with temptations than is always realized.

Finally, Christianity is, above all, a social religion. Sin injures the whole body. Confession is a universal instinct of man, as a social being. These principles underlay the confessions that we find in the Old Testament (Lev 5[5], Num 5[6-7], Josh 7[19], 1 Sam 14[43]) and in the New (Mk 1[5 and 44], Acts 19[18]). In the development of the Church they have come to find expression in the sacrament of Penance. The priest's absolution is no charm uttered by one who is supposed to possess in his own person some magic power, nor yet is it merely the publication of a forgiveness that God has already bestowed. It is the receiving back by God's family into the Father's home of a brother who is conscious of having sinned not only against the Father's love but also against the peace and unity of the whole household.†

(b) Extreme Unction

Anointing the sick as a means of healing is a widespread custom. In Mk 6¹³ we read that the Apostles 'anointed with oil many that were sick and healed them'. The same custom prevailed in the early Church, as is shown in James 5¹⁴⁻¹⁵. 'Is any among you sick? let him call for the elders of the Church; and let them pray over him, anointing him with oil in the name of the Lord; and the prayer of faith shall save him that is sick, and the Lord shall raise him up; and if he have committed sins, it shall be forgiven him.' Such anointing must be taken in connexion with the gifts of healing spoken of in 1 Cor 12⁹. It was clearly for the healing of the body of the sick person, who, it was hoped, would recover. Later, when the gifts of healing had declined, it became known as *extrema unctio* (*i.e.* the last anointing after those at baptism and confirmation) and reserved for administration to those at the point of death. Thus *extrema unctio* came to be the equivalent of 'unctio in extremis', and, further, was viewed as bestowing primarily spiritual benefits. Even so the English rite still contained prayers for the sick person's recovery, and then, if the man recovered, it might be repeated. The earliest evidence of its appearance as a religious rite is a letter of Pope Innocent I early in the fifth century. He replied to a bishop who asked for information, that a bishop might certainly anoint the sick with oil, quoting S. James. Further, he made it clear that if the bishop blessed the oil, priests or even laymen might use it in the hour of need. Only those who were under exclusion from the sacraments might not receive it, since it is a kind of sacrament (*quia genus est sacramenti*). The fact that a bishop needed to ask such a question is clear evidence that the custom was not universal. The Pope's vague language shows that 'unction' was not yet an established 'sacrament'. Further, even a layman might administer it. No other reference to unction as a sacramental rite can be found till the time of Pope Innocent III in the twelfth century.[1] The subject was discussed at the Council of Trent. It was declared to be a sacrament, instituted by Christ, representing the grace of the Holy Spirit, cleansing away venial sins and comforting the infirm. The one trace of its primitive use is the statement that the sick man 'sometimes obtains bodily health when it is expedient for the welfare of his soul'. Accordingly, though it is primarily a 'sacrament of the dying' it may be repeated if the sick man recovered. In the First Prayer-Book of Edward VI a service of anointing was still retained 'if the sick person desire it'. In the Second Prayer-Book it was wholly omitted and has never been restored. The defence of the position of the Church of England is that there is no evidence either in Scripture

---

[1] But the considerable liturgical evidence may be studied in the article on the Visitation of the Sick in *Liturgy and Worship*, pp. 472 ff.

or the practice of the primitive Church that the rite is of universal and lasting obligation. Its use or disuse is merely a question of discipline. In quite modern times a desire for its revival has arisen in connexion with 'faith-healing'. It is a well-established fact that our minds and wills have greater influence over our bodies than at first sight appears. 'Suggestion' has great power for good in the case of nervous disorders and others that at first sight would not seem to come under that head. At the same time there would seem to be no reliable evidence at present that 'faith-healing' is of the slightest value against organic diseases. The use of unction, accompanied by prayer, would, it is claimed, afford a visible means of strengthening the will-power of the patient and give him the opportunity to exercise it. It would regularize the employment of powers of suggestion that beyond all reasonable doubts are genuinely possessed by certain persons and within certain limits efficient. The use of unction has been sanctioned for such purposes by certain bishops. It is a return to its primitive use. How far it is capable of such use depends upon the whole question of the scope of 'mental healing' which is at present under investigation.[1]†

§ 6. The final section of this Article deals with the right use of sacraments. '*The Sacraments were not ordained of Christ to be gazed upon, or to be carried about: but that we should duly use them.*' This sentence is not happily worded. 'The Sacraments' would naturally apply to Baptism and the Eucharist: but there is no evidence of any superstitious gazing on baptism, rather the reverse: superstitious ideas about baptism have been fostered by its being performed privately. Unless it is a mere slip, the plural must refer to the two elements in the Eucharist and the allusion is to Corpus Christi ceremonies and the like, referred to more explicitly under Article XXVIII. The remaining sentences follow from the nature of grace. If all grace needs the co-operation of our human wills in seeking and using it, sacraments as means of grace demand a right disposition in the recipient. They are not magical charms or mechanical devices that produce effects independently of our own faith and efforts. Such could have no place in a moral life. Hence '*In such only as worthily receive the same they have a wholesome effect or operation. But they that receive them unworthily, purchase to themselves damnation, as S. Paul saith.*' The allusion is to 1 Cor 11[29], 'He that eateth and drinketh (unworthily A.V.) eateth and drinketh judgment (damna-

---

[1] Since the above paragraph was written the question of the use of unction and the laying-on of hands for the sick has been further discussed. In 1924 there was published 'The Report of the Committee appointed in accordance with Resolution 63 of the Lambeth Conference, 1920, on *The Ministry of Healing*'. This Report was accepted by the Lambeth Conference of 1930 and in January 1932 the Convocation of Canterbury appointed a Joint Committee to draw up services (1) for Unction and Laying-on of Hands, (2) for Laying-on of Hands without Unction. The services drawn up by the Joint Committee were approved on 6 June, 1935 by the Convocation of Canterbury for provisional use in the province.

tion A.V.) unto himself, if he discern not the body.' The context makes it perfectly clear that S. Paul by judgment ($\kappa\rho\iota\mu\alpha$) means temporal chastisement sent by God in mercy to recall the careless to a sense of their sin (cp. v. [32], 'that we may not be condemned with the world'). 'Damnation' in modern English means eternal punishment, and here, as in the Prayer-Book, conveys to our ears an entirely wrong idea. In the sixteenth century its use was not necessarily so limited. The practical effect on uneducated people has been and still is to drive them away from Holy Communion. What the Prayer-Book means by 'worthily' receiving is explained by the sixth and last answers in the Catechism and the exhortations in the Baptismal and Communion offices.

The balance of this Article is further shown by the removal, in 1563, of a condemnation of the phrase 'grace *ex opere operato*'.

(i) Originally the phrase conveyed a true and valuable idea. 'Opus operatum' was contrasted with 'opus operantis', and implied that the efficacy of all sacraments depends upon the appointment of their author, God, and not on the merit of the officiant or recipient. In this sense it is used by the Council of Trent. It vindicates the important truth that grace is God's free gift. We do not earn or create it by our own faith or moral efforts.

(ii) This became corrupted into the idea, condemned in this Article, that sacraments conferred grace automatically, quite apart from the faith or penitence of the recipient. In this sense it was rightly condemned in the first edition of the Article. As we saw, the blessing that we personally receive must depend on our individual capacity for receiving it, namely, our true repentance, our real belief in Christ and His promises, our desire to surrender ourselves to Him and to employ the grace that He bestows. It has been said, 'The grace of Sacraments does not depend on our faith, but for its effect in us all depends on our faith'; and again, 'Grace without faith may come upon us, but it cannot make us holy.' This second truth was secured by the language of the Article, and the condemnation of the phrase was wisely withdrawn, since it contained a true meaning as well as a false.

The truth of Article XXVI follows from a right view of the nature of sacraments. Here, as in similar cases, we must distinguish between a man's personal character and his official capacity. The evil life of a Christian minister, as of any Christian, brings reproach upon God and His Church. Such, therefore, must be removed. On the other hand, the validity of his official acts is not affected. A bad judge, *qua* judge, must be obeyed, as the king's representative, no less than a good one. So in the sacraments the minister acts not as an individual but as the organ of the Church. God's promises are made not to him individually but to the Church as a whole. Therefore their fulfilment is not affected by his personal lack of faith. On any other supposition means of grace would always be precarious. So our Lord distinguishes between the official commands of Scribes and Pharisees who 'sit in Moses' seat' and their private conduct. He bids us obey the former, but not imitate the latter (Mt 23$^{2-3}$). Scripture often gives instances of God sending blessings through bad men, *e.g.* Saul in the Old Testament and Judas in the New. We have no reason to suppose that Judas' ministry was any less productive of good results than that of the other Apostles.

HOLY BAPTISM

ARTICLE XXVII

Of Baptism

Baptism is not only a sign of profession and mark of difference whereby Christian men are discerned from other that be not christened: but is also a sign of regeneration or new birth, whereby, as by an instrument, they that receive Baptism rightly are grafted into the Church; the promises of the forgiveness of sin, and of our adoption to be the sons of God by the Holy Ghost, are visibly signed and sealed: faith is confirmed: and grace increased by virtue of prayer unto God. The Baptism of young children is in any wise to be retained in the Church, as most agreeable with the institution of Christ.

De Baptismo

Baptismus non est tantum professionis signum, ac discriminis nota, qua Christiani a non Christianis discernantur, sed etiam est signum regenerationis, per quod, tanquam per instrumentum, recte baptismum suscipientes, Ecclesiae inseruntur, promissiones de remissione peccatorum, atque adoptione nostra in filios Dei per Spiritum Sanctum visibiliter obsignantur, fides confirmatur, et vi divinae invocationis gratia augetur.

Baptismus parvulorum omnino in Ecclesia retinendus est, ut qui cum Christi institutione optime congruat.

The main body of the Article dates from 1553. In 1563 the language on Infant Baptism was strengthened. The earlier Article had only said that the custom was to be 'commended' and 'retained in the Church'.

It is aimed at (i) the inadequate view of Baptism taken by Zwingli and the Anabaptists; (ii) the denial of Infant Baptism.

§ 1. Christian Baptism has a long history behind it.

(a) The use of ceremonial washings as preparatory to approaching God in prayer and worship is a common feature of many ancient religions. It was a natural symbol for that purification, however inadequately conceived, which the worshipper desired before coming into the presence of God. It corresponded to a universal human instinct. We find such use of water among the Jews. It is commanded in the Old Testament (*e.g.* Lev 8⁶, 14⁹, etc.). Further, by the time of our Lord the custom had arisen for proselytes to the Jewish faith to be not only circumcised but baptized. Proselytes so baptized were said by their entrance into Judaism to be 'born again'. A 'new creature' (καινὴ κτίσις), the phrase applied by S. Paul in 2 Cor 5¹⁷ to the Christian, as being in Christ by baptism, was a current Jewish term for a proselyte. The plunge beneath the water in baptism represented a death to the old life and the rising from the water a birth to the new life within the sphere of God's Covenant. The baptism of John can only be understood in the light of such contemporary Jewish custom. It differed from the ordinary ceremonial washings of the Jews because it was not repeated. It was preparatory for the coming of the Messianic Kingdom. In effect John treated the Jews as on a level with Gentiles: they needed to become, as it were, proselytes, in order to enter the Kingdom. Mere descent from Abraham was not enough. God required personal penitence, and such penitence must express itself in public submission to John's baptism (Mt 3, etc.). But John's baptism was only preparatory. It was only a 'water-baptism unto repentance'. Those who received it were at best placed in the closest relation to God that was possible under the Old Covenant. John himself looked forward to the coming of One who would 'baptize with Holy Spirit and fire' (3^{11}). Such baptism would bestow not only forgiveness for the past but new power for the future. Those who received it would enter into the Messianic Kingdom and all its blessings. We read, too, of baptism as practised by our Lord's disciples during His life on earth (Jn 4^{1-2}). This baptism would seem to be on a level with John's. It cannot have been full Christian baptism. Such was only possible after the Ascension, when Christ was glorified and the Spirit was given (cp. Jn 7^{39}). At its highest it was a mark of discipleship, not a means of membership of Christ.

(b) This practice of baptism, already familiar to the Jews and easily intelligible to the heathen, Jesus Christ took and made to be the visible mark of acceptance of Himself as Saviour and of membership in the Christian society. This is definitely asserted in Mt 28^{19}, 'Go therefore and make disciples of all nations, baptizing them into the name of the Father and of the Son and of the Holy Ghost.' But the belief that Christian baptism originated in the direct command of Christ does not depend on a single text. His own baptism at John's hands had consecrated the rite for Christians and given it a new Messianic significance. From first to last the New Testament knows of no other means of entrance into the Church. A Christian and a baptized person are synonymous terms. The universal practice of baptism in all churches, Jewish and Gentile alike, starting from the day of Pentecost (Acts 2^{38}) without any hint of questioning or debate, can only be explained by the fact that it was instituted by Christ Himself. Many writers have held that the language of Acts shows that baptism was at first administered in the name of Jesus only (Acts 2^{38} 'in the name of Jesus Messiah', 8^{16} 'into the name of the Lord Jesus', 10^{48}, etc., cp. also Gal 3^{27}, Rom 6^3). This is possible. There were some who held the name of Jesus Christ by itself to be sufficient, even as late as the fourth century. It was defended on the principle that baptism in the name of One Person of the Trinity implied baptism in the name of all. On the other hand, it is equally possible that the phrases of the Acts and Epistles are not intended to represent the actual formula used, but rather to distinguish Christian baptism from Jewish baptism or John's baptism. S. Paul, for instance, speaks of being 'baptized into Moses' (1 Cor 10[2]), with an implied contrast to being 'baptized into Christ', but this does not mean that the formula 'into Moses' was ever used.[1]

It is noticeable that the *Didache* both speaks of baptism 'into the name of the Lord'[2] and also gives the Trinitarian formula showing that the two are not in any way inconsistent or mutually exclusive. Attempts have also been made to show that the original text of Mt 28[19] ran simply 'Baptizing them in the name of the Lord', and was expanded later to correspond with ecclesiastical custom.[3] It is admitted that not one of our present MSS contains any hint of this alternative reading, but it is argued that Eusebius of Caesarea several times quotes the verse in its shorter form. He had access to many good and early MSS in the great library of Caesarea, and it is reasonable to suppose that he quotes it on their authority. On the other hand, he quotes the verse in full when he needs it, and it is equally reasonable to suppose that he abbreviated it for his own convenience. We are not greatly concerned to deny that baptism in the name of Christ may have once been common, but it certainly cannot be proved, and opponents of orthodoxy have no right to assume it as true. The language of 2 Cor 13[14] shows that S. Paul expected all Corinthian Christians to be familiar with the type of teaching that is summed up in the Baptismal formula and is strong evidence of its primitiveness.[4]

§ 2. What meaning is given to Baptism in Scripture? Primarily it signified the public acknowledgement of Jesus as Lord or Messiah and entrance into the new Israel. To-day this meaning is seen most clearly in heathen countries, but it must never be lost sight of. As the

---

[1] The 'name' in popular usage means much more than the 'title'. The name of a god or person was supposed to be, as it were, a real expression of himself. In any case, when our Lord spoke of baptism 'in the name' of the Trinity, He was not primarily giving a form of words to be used. He was expressing the nature of the life bestowed. Men were to be immersed into the full life of the Godhead, as He had revealed it. The Greek word βαπτίζειν is not such an exclusively technical word as our 'baptize'. It means 'immerse' in a general sense, and this wider meaning is never quite lost sight of in the New Testament.

[2] This may mean the Trinity, but the context favours Christ.

[3] On the one side see *E.R.E.* ii. 380 a. On the other side Chase, *J.Th.S.* 1905, pp. 481 ff.

[4] Cp. also Abrahams, *Studies in Pharisaism and the Gospels*, esp. pp. 45–46. There is a Jewish phrase, 'a proselyte to (or in) the name of heaven,' *i.e.* one who is baptized for God's sake and for no personal motive. In the Talmud there is another phrase, 'baptism in (or to) the name of freedom,' applied to slaves, who, on rising to the rank of freemen, were rebaptized. 'A fine contrast and complement of baptism in the name of freedom is the proselyte's baptism in the name of heaven, or in its Gospel form— baptism in the name of Christ.'

Article says, '*Baptism is not only a sign of profession and mark of difference, whereby Christian men are discerned from other that be not Christian*' (*a non Christianis*).[1] That, indeed, was the only meaning that the Zwinglians and Anabaptists would allow to baptism. It was quite true as far as it went, but inadequate, as the Article goes on to point out. Scripture makes it clear that baptism is not only a sign of profession but a means of grace.

(*a*) We turn first to the teaching of our Lord as given in Jn 3^{1-8}. The question may be raised how far we have here a literal record of His teaching. But in any case when the passage was written Christian baptism had long been established and even if the words are an interpretation of Christ's teaching rather than a record of it, the Church approved them as a true interpretation. Nicodemus apparently regarded himself as fit to enter the Messianic Kingdom just as he was. He had refused to submit to John's baptism as a preparation. He needed to be taught that a man must be 'born again' (or from above) before he can even see the Kingdom of God (v. [3]). He must be born 'of water and Spirit' before he can enter the Kingdom (v. [5]). In other words, the Kingdom of God is a spiritual kingdom and can only be shared by those who by receiving new life possess the capacity for sharing it. The reference to baptism is unmistakable. Nicodemus stands in the same relation to the new Israel as a Gentile to the old Israel. He must become a 'new creature'. But whereas Jewish baptism and even John's baptism was only with water, the baptism that admits into the Kingdom of God is 'of water and Spirit' (ἐξ ὕδατος καὶ πνεύματος—the preposition not being repeated binds the two words into a single phrase). This baptism not only symbolizes cleansing and new life, but bestows them. The water is at once the symbol and the channel of the Spirit. Some have seen an allusion to Gen 1^2. The new man rises from the water of baptism at the creative touch of the Spirit of God, even as the world sprang to life as He moved on the face of the waters at the first creation. The root idea is perfectly clear. At our first birth we receive the initial capacity for life in this present world: at our new birth the initial capacity for life in the Kingdom of God and 'the age to come'.

This same thought underlies the whole of the New Testament teaching on Baptism. S. Paul speaks of it as 'the bath of regeneration' (Tit 3^5). More often he expresses the same idea in a slightly different form. By baptism we are incorporated into the body of Christ and become His members (1 Cor 12^{13}, Gal 3^{27}). By our natural birth we are 'in Adam', *i.e.* we inherit a common human nature shared by our fellowmen: by our new birth in baptism we become in Christ (1 Cor 15^{22}). Christ is the new Adam, the source of a new and regenerate humanity. Henceforward the Christian is to live and do all

---

[1] Cp. the Baptismal office: 'Baptism doth represent unto us our profession: which is to follow the example of our Saviour Christ and to be made like unto Him, etc.'

things in Christ (Eph 1³, 2⁶, etc.). As members of Christ His life is within us (1 Cor 6¹⁵). It is the same relation to Himself as that which our Lord describes in the allegory of the vine (Jn 15¹ ff.). His life is to circulate in us, as the sap of the vine in the branches. Further, S. Paul develops this thought so as to bring out that the birth to the new life must involve a death to the old. In virtue of our union with Christ we share His death and burial, that we may rise with Him to newness of life (Rom 6³⁻¹¹, Col 2¹². Note the aorists in each case, referring to the single definite event of baptism). The symbolism of immersion admirably set forth this truth. The plunge beneath the water represented the death and burial of the old man, the rising from the water the birth to new life in union with the Risen Lord. Henceforth the baptized is to reckon himself 'dead to sin but alive unto God in Christ Jesus' (Rom 6¹⁰ ff., Col 3¹⁻³). Having been made a member of Christ, he is called to live as such (1 Cor 6¹⁵, Eph 5⁷⁻⁹, etc.). In 1 Pet 3²⁰⁻²¹ stress is laid on present salvation begun here and now through baptism. The Church is the ark in which safety may be found.

(b) The blessings of baptism mentioned in the Article are not a number of detached blessings, but flow from the union with Christ thus gained. Baptism is 'a sign of regeneration or new birth'. 'Sign' is clearly used in the sense defined in the previous Article as 'effectual sign'. That is, baptism not only symbolizes new birth but conveys it, since by it we are made members of Christ.[1]

Again by baptism 'as by an instrument, they that receive baptism rightly are grafted into the Church.' This simply expresses the same truth from another standpoint. The Church is Christ's body. The metaphor of grafting comes from Rom 11¹⁷; the Gentiles are like a wild olive grafted into the ancient stock of the true olive so as to be enriched by its life, the true olive being the Israel of God. The promises of the forgiveness of sin . . . by the Holy Ghost are visibly signed and sealed. It is as being in Christ that we are forgiven. We have entered into the new life and the stains of the old life have been washed away. In the New Testament baptism is always 'unto the remission of sins', i.e. not only an expression of repentance, but a visible sign and seal of God's forgiveness. On the day of Pentecost S. Peter bids the multitude 'Repent and be baptized each one of you in the name of Jesus the Messiah, unto remission of your sins and ye shall receive the gift of the Holy Spirit' (Acts 2³⁷⁻³⁸). Ananias called on S. Paul to 'be baptized and wash away thy sins, calling on the name of the Lord' (Acts 22¹⁶, cp. also 1 Cor 6¹¹, Eph 5²⁶). As Article IX puts it, 'There is no condemnation to them that believe and are baptized' (renatis et credentibus), not because God has favourites and arbitrarily passes over in one man what He condemns in another, but because those who repent and are baptized have faced their sin

---

[1] Cp. the opening of the Catechism, 'My baptism: wherein I was made a member of Christ, etc.'

in penitence and done their best to remedy it by coming to Christ to receive from Him that new life which alone can restore them to spiritual health. Their sins are forgiven them as being 'in Christ'. The actual cleansing of the body with the water is the 'sign and seal' of the inward purification and acceptance by God. A document is sealed when the donor who has promised a gift 'actually makes the thing promised over to the receiver and thereby assures the possession of it to him'.[1]

The promises . . . of our adoption to be the sons of God by the Holy Ghost,[2] *are visibly signed and sealed.* Again, it is as being members of Christ that we share His sonship. It is through Him we 'receive the adoption of sons' (Gal 4$^{4-5}$). So in Rom 8$^{15-17}$ S. Paul writes: 'Ye received not the spirit of bondage again unto fear; but ye received (ἐλάβετε, aorist) the spirit of adoption, whereby we cry Abba, Father. The Spirit Himself beareth witness with our spirit, that we are the children of God: and if children, then heirs; heirs of God and joint heirs with Christ' (cp. also Gal 3$^{26-27}$). The objection may be raised 'are not all men children of God? They do not need to be made so by baptism.' This objection confuses potential with actual sonship. God made men to be His children, but sin has come in between God and men. All men have by creation a capacity for sonship, but sin has blinded their eyes and warped their affections. By ourselves we cannot be all that God meant us to be. Can we say that a child is in any real sense a son to his father if he has never seen or known him or if he from the first has been alienated from him? Only Jesus Christ has ever lived on earth a human life as a true Son of God, and by baptism He imparts to us the power of His own human sonship. Only He can fully restore our capacity for filial love and obedience and take away the sin that has destroyed sonship. So, too, it is as members of Christ that we share His election and are among 'the elect people of God' (Rom 16^{13} and Eph 1^4) and are inheritors of His Kingdom. 'I was made a member of Christ, the child of God and an inheritor of the Kingdom of Heaven' (The Catechism). Baptism, therefore, like the Eucharist, has an eschatological reference; it is a pledge not only of the new life with and for God in this world but also of our final inheritance of eternal life at 'the manifestation of the sons of God', when we shall receive our 'adoption, namely, the redemption of our bodies' (Rom 8$^{19, 23}$).

Faith is confirmed: and grace increased by virtue of prayer to God. The exact meaning of this sentence is most obscure. The best interpretation seems to be that throughout this paragraph the Article has in view only adult baptism. Infant baptism is not dealt with till the

---

[1] Sadler, *Church Doctrine, Bible Truth*, p. 120.

[2] Dr Gibson, placing a comma before and after 'by the Holy Ghost', connects the words with both the forgiveness and the adoption. This was the punctuation of the earliest English editions. No question of doctrine is concerned.

second paragraph. In that case the 'faith' that is confirmed is the faith of the baptized. It is strengthened by exercising itself in the sacramental act. So, too, the grace increased is that of the baptized, and it is increased in answer to the prayers either of himself or preferably of the Church. The new life bestowed in baptism is God's gift in response to the prayers of the Church.[1]

(c) If, then, baptism conveys all these blessings, how is it that many baptized persons are living openly in sin? Our prisons, for instance, are full of baptized criminals. These facts, it is often urged, disprove any doctrine of baptismal regeneration. Such an objection misunderstands both the nature of grace and the true meaning of 'regeneration'. As we saw, God's grace will do nothing for us without our own co-operation. Baptism places us in a new relation to God: we, on our part, must respond to this and use it. Baptism brings within our reach new possibilities for holiness: we must realize them by the use of our wills. As baptized we have not only new claims upon God, but also new duties and responsibilities towards Him. As members of Christ, we are in touch with new forces for good, but they will only make us holy in so far as we work with them. The failure of many baptized persons does not show that baptism is valueless: it only shows that they have not responded to and used the benefits of baptism.[2]

Again, much confusion has arisen because the word 'regeneration' has been used in different senses. The Prayer-Book means by it simply incorporated into Christ. All baptized persons are 'regenerate' in this sense. On the other hand, Nonconformists identify 'regeneration' with 'conversion'. They mean by regeneration that spiritual renewal which membership of Christ results in, when it is rightly accepted and used. It includes the conversion or turning of the will to God and the personal acceptance of Christ. In this sense a baptized person who has made no effort to live up to his privileges is not 'regenerate'. If we use Prayer-Book language we say that regeneration needs to be supplemented by conversion. The actual renewal of the soul requires both the gift of the grace of God in baptism and also

---

[1] If the first section has in mind infant as well as adult baptism, the simplest interpretation would be to interpret the words as denoting an increased blessing won for the baptized by the prayers of the bystanders. Dr Gibson explains it in the light of the prayer in the Baptismal office, in which the minister in the name of all those present thanks God for their call to the knowledge of His grace and faith in Him, and then proceeds, 'Increase this knowledge and confirm this faith in us evermore.' On this view the words describe what takes place in the baptized subsequent to their own baptism, when they are reminded of their own baptism by witnessing another's. In any case the Latin 'vi divinae invocationis' hardly corresponds to the English 'by virtue of prayer unto God', and might be translated 'in virtue of the invocation of God', *i.e.* of the name of the Trinity.

[2] We may compare the gifts of baptism to a store of money lying at the bank. A man may possess such and yet be naked and starving because he has not claimed and used his money. His plight does not prove the non-existence of the money. So by faith and obedience we have to claim and use our baptismal grace.

the personal surrender of the will to that grace. A man should be both regenerate and converted. Regeneration is the work of God: it is accomplished in a moment: by it new powers are placed in our grasp. Conversion is our work in conjunction with God: it calls for effort and self-surrender. It may be either rapid or slow. In the Bible we have instances of both kinds. We may be able to point to a definite moment of conversion or not. Many Christians pass through more than one conversion. The important thing is that there shall be a thorough self-surrender to the divine will. Conversion may precede regeneration or follow it. In the case of children who are baptized as infants, it must necessarily follow it. In the case of adults from whom faith and repentance are required, it must have begun before baptism. But conversion is not a substitute for regeneration. It is a call to seek baptism, not to do without it (cp. the case of S. Paul, Acts 9[18], Cornelius and his friends, 10[47], the disciples at Ephesus, 19[5]). One of the proofs of conversion is the willingness to obey the command of our Lord by submitting to baptism and to confess Him by joining openly the Christian society of which baptism is the visible entrance. Whatever blessings God may bestow outside, by baptism we enter within the circle of God's covenanted mercies. No conversion, however complete, can of itself guarantee full and abiding union with Christ. The normal means of that union, where it can be had, is baptism, followed by a life lived in the fellowship of the Church.[1]†

It is only fair to mention another view of baptism held by many reformers known as the 'obsignatory' view. This view has its origin in Calvinism. Since God's grace is irresistible and given only to the elect, it follows that sacraments cannot in any real sense be 'means of grace'. Rather they are pledges or seals of blessings already belonging to the recipient as a child of grace. They assure him of the reality of the divine blessing. On this view baptism does not make us children of God, it only assures us that we are such or can be such when we fulfil the necessary conditions of faith and repentance, just as the coronation does not give the king his sovereignty, but is the seal of an already possessed sovereignty. This view is still held even by many who have abandoned the Calvinism that originally suggested it. It can hardly be reconciled with the language of the Articles about sacraments as 'effectual signs of grace'. It renders almost meaningless much of the baptismal service, e.g. the words in which after the baptism of the infant we thank God 'that it hath pleased thee to regenerate this infant with thy holy Spirit', and of the Catechism,

---

[1] A difficulty is often felt about the words of 1 Jn 3[9] and 5[18], 'Whosoever is born of God sinneth not' or 'doth not commit sin'. The difficulty is equally great whether 'born of God' means 'baptized' or 'converted'. No one could hold that a converted man never sins. The only answer lies in drawing attention to the present tense (ἁμαρτάνει) which refers to a habit of sin. S. John is assuming that the Christian is responding to the position given him as son of God (cp. Rom 8[14]). In so far as he does this and realizes the new life, he does not commit sin.

which declares that we were 'made' members of Christ by baptism. In the case of adults it reduces baptism to little more than an aid to faith. In the case of infants it is hard to see on this view that baptism has any value at all. It might just as well be deferred to a later age, when its meaning would be understood by the recipient.

§ 3. We can now turn to the question of infant baptism, always remembering that the Scripture language about baptism is coloured by the prevalent practice of adult baptism. So too, much of the language both of our Prayer-Book and our Article, which is based on Scripture, is applicable in its full sense only to adults. As applied to infants it requires a certain accommodation to new conditions.

(a) Historically there seems no reason to doubt that the practice of infant baptism dates from apostolic times. It is in the fullest accord with contemporary ideas on religion. 'The idea that a parent should enter a religion or covenant relation with God as an individual merely, i.e. by himself as distinct from his immediate family would never occur to the ancients, least of all to a Jew.'[1] Every Jewish boy was circumcised when he was eight days old and thus brought within the covenant. In the case of proselytes to Judaism, the children were baptized and, if males, circumcised. The practice was defended on the ground that 'one may act for another to his advantage though not to his disadvantage apart from his knowledge and consent'. We do not, indeed, find any positive mention of infant baptism in the New Testament, but we do not find the slightest hint of any age limit. Looked at in the light not of modern thought but the thought and custom of the first century, silence on the point is most readily explained by the supposition that infants were baptized. We have record of the baptism of the whole households (Acts 16[15], 1 Cor 1[16]). S. Peter can bid men repent and be baptized, 'for to you is the promise and to your children' (Acts 2[39]). So, too, S. Paul sends a message to children based on their membership in Christ's body (Col 3[20], Eph 6[1], n.b. 'in the Lord'). Infant baptism was certainly practised in the early Church.[2] The first known objector to it is Tertullian. His objection is based on the ground that infants may fall into sin later, and, since baptism cannot be repeated, such sin may fail to obtain forgiveness: hence it is wiser to delay. These words are evidence for the existence of the practice, and he does not oppose it on doctrinal grounds. Down to a much later date baptism was frequently postponed till the approach of death from a conviction of the unforgivableness of post-baptismal sin, and a desire to have a good time in the present world. But such a practice did not express the mind of the Church. On the other hand, the conditions of apostolic Church life were those of the mission field. And in the mission field then, as to-day, adult baptism is the rule and infant baptism the exception. Children are

---

[1] E.R.E. ii. p. 379.
[2] It is implied, e.g. by Justin Martyr and Irenaeus.

only baptized where both parents are Christian or where some very definite guarantee is given that the child both can and shall be brought up as a Christian. Further, in times of persecution parents might be afraid to have their children baptized.

(b) We cannot doubt that the Church was rightly guided and that 'The Baptism of young children is in any wise to be retained in the Church, as most agreeable with the institution of Christ.' The new covenant cannot be narrower than the old: the New Israel cannot put barriers where the Old Israel put none. It is often objected that infants cannot have faith and repentance. That is indeed obvious. 'Faith and repentance' are necessary conditions, when they can be had. But spiritual life is the free gift of God, and where there is no active disbelief or impenitence to oppose a bar to God's mercy, it does not need faith for its reception. We need not be consulted about our second birth any more than about our first. Children, when they come into the world, enter upon an inheritance tainted by sin. They should equally possess from the first that union with Christ which is the antidote to sin. After all few of us would refuse to pray to God to bless a child. We read of our Lord blessing children who were so small that He could take them up in His arms, and therefore were presumably incapable of faith (Mk 10$^{13-16}$). Our Lord always required faith for the reception of His blessings, where faith could rightly be expected, but in this case He expressly invited little children to come to Him. We cannot possibly tell what precise effect either His blessing or our prayers have on the infant life, but we cannot suppose that they have no effect. So, too, we may not be able to define the inward effect of bringing children to Christ in baptism: the infant cannot recount the story of its spiritual experience. All we can say is that we believe that they receive from Him the best that they are capable of receiving.

Further, infant baptism embodies a profound spiritual principle. Religion starts not with what we do for God but with what God does for us.[1] We do not have to climb up to God first, to earn His goodwill by so much repentance or faith or so many good works. God's love and His free gifts come first, and we are bidden to live up to them. Privilege comes before responsibility. The reverse view seems at first sight to be common-sense, but in practice it has always led to hard and gloomy views of God. We can never be sure that our faith or works have come up to His standard. The true view is an appeal to our trust and gratitude. Above all, it gives us a sure ground of approach to God. As baptized Christians we are God's children, even though we may be His bad children, and we can always fall

---

[1] Cp. the opening of the Church Catechism, which begins with what God has done for us and then goes on to point out what we are to do for Him. So, too, our citizenship and our home come to us unearned and we have to live worthy of them. We do not have first to deserve them.

back on the sonship that He bestowed upon us. The Prodigal Son
had not earned his position as son. He had received it, and used it
unworthily. But in the hour of distress he could fall back upon it as a
ground of appeal. Though a bad son, he could still cry 'Father'. So,
when children are baptized their baptism always remains as a ground
of appeal. We do not bid them be good and say that then, if we judge
them good enough, they will be baptized. Rather we say they are
Christians and therefore must live as Christians. Nothing could be
more Scriptural.

Lastly, many objections to infant baptism depend for their force
on a falsely isolated view of the sacrament. As we have seen, the
grace given in baptism does not transform us without our own effort.
It needs to be claimed and used. Accordingly, the child must be
taught that he is a member of Christ and all that such membership
involves. If he never learns his position as a child of God and makes
no effort to avail himself of the powers placed within his reach, that
does not show that infant baptism is of no value: it shows rather
that the divine gift is being left unused.[1] Further, life of all kinds can
only be realized by development, and that development needs the
right environment. By baptism infants not only receive the power of
a new life, but are placed in the Church in which this new life is to be
progressively developed. Our natural human life depends for its
growth upon fellowship. A child after birth needs to be fed and
clothed if it is to be strong and healthy. Later on it needs education
and instruction. So the baptized infant requires food and nursing for
its soul if it is to grow up spiritually sound. The Christian child is to
come to self-consciousness within the Church. He is to be taught all
that his life means and the grand possibilities that it contains. Hence
the need of godparents, who in the name of the Church promise to
train the child. Accordingly, teaching on baptismal regeneration
must never be separated from the thought of the Church as God's
family in which the new life is to be realized. The gift of God in
baptism implies as its background His gifts to the Church as a whole.
It is very doubtful whether it is right to baptize infants indiscriminately as is too often done to-day, when there is no real security that
they will be brought up as the Prayer-Book directs. God-parents are
too often selected not for spiritual but for worldly reasons. As a
result, baptism comes to be regarded either as a mere form or else as
having a vague magic efficacy. The failure to mark any difference in
later life between the baptized and the unbaptized is put down not to

---

[1] We may compare the case of the insincere adult who is baptized, without real faith
and penitence, e.g. Simon Magus (Acts 8[13] ff.). When his insincerity is disclosed he is
bidden to repent and amend his life: but there is no suggestion of rebaptism. We might
have supposed that his unbelief and sin would have hindered the reception of the gifts.
Rather the blessings of baptism have been given once for all and they await the will
that will use them. He is to obtain remission of sins in virtue of his relation to Christ
founded in baptism, not by a new baptism.

the failure of man's co-operation but to the absence of divine efficiency. Much as we deplore the refusal of the Baptists to administer baptism to infants, at least their position witnesses to the fact that Baptism means a great deal. That is a truth that the Church of England needs to restore to its due prominence.[1]

§ 4. What is the relation of Baptism to Confirmation? In apostolic times it would seem that Baptism included a laying on of hands (Acts 19[6], cp. Heb 6[2]) and possibly an anointing with oil (2 Cor 1[21-22], 1 Jn 2 [20 and 27]). The language about anointing may be purely metaphorical, but washing and anointing commonly went together. We find no explicit mention, however, of anything but baptizing with water in Acts 8[38] and 9[18]. In Acts 8[12-17] we find baptism distinctly separated from the laying on of hands and the gift of the Spirit connected with the latter. Philip clearly possessed only authority to baptize. The Apostles came to lay on hands. Beyond all doubt in the custom of the early Church Baptism, unction, and the laying on of hands formed a single sacrament, like the bread and wine of the Eucharist. Origen, for instance, can write, 'Through the laying on of hands the Holy Spirit was given in Baptism.' In the West the laying on of hands was restricted to bishops, and owing to the difficulty of obtaining a bishop became separated from Baptism. The title 'Confirmation' is late and purely Western. In the Greek Church the laying on of hands has dropped out. Infants are baptized and anointed with oil that has been specially blessed by the bishop for the purpose. That is, Baptism and Confirmation are still one. In the West, unction has been dropped by ourselves and the laying on of hands by the Roman Church. It is usually held that the 'form' of Confirmation is prayer for the gift of the Spirit. It is doubtful whether either unction or the laying on of hands can claim any higher authority than that of the custom of the Church. Many hold that the universal use of the laying on of hands by the Apostles from the first points back to a definite command of Christ, but that the command has not been preserved. In Heb 6[2] the 'laying on of hands' is included among the 'first principles of Christ'. Very possibly this implies that He Himself taught it. The arguments are strong but not absolutely conclusive.

In primitive times Confirmation, whatever the relative prominence of unction or laying on of hands in local practice, was part of a single sacrament of Christian initiation, by which the candidate was transferred from this world into the life of the Church, cleansed from sin, made a member of Christ, anointed with the Holy Spirit, and 'sealed unto the day of redemption'. Like baptism with water the Confirma-

---

[1] The importance of Baptism is also obscured by the custom, in defiance of all Prayer-Book rules, of administering it in a hole-and-corner fashion instead of in the presence of the congregation. The whole idea of admission to Christian fellowship loses its natural expression. We have substituted 'Private Baptism' in Church for Public Baptism.

tion part of the rite had the once-for-all character proper to initiation, and the intervention of the bishop as the chief pastor and priest further emphasized its initiatory significance. In the West the direct episcopal ministration of Confirmation has been fairly consistently maintained, but practical difficulties due largely in the first instance to the unprimitive size of dioceses led to the separation of the rite from baptism. This in turn raised the theological question of the relation of the gift bestowed in Baptism to that bestowed in Confirmation. The question was never a major issue in the patristic age, but where it is explicitly expounded or discussed, particularly in the third and fourth centuries, Confirmation is said to bestow the Holy Spirit. Side by side with this evidence the Fathers, following the apparent emphasis of the scripture references to Baptism, sometimes speak as though baptism with water was of sole importance. In the mediaeval West where the difficulty of administering Confirmation was acute the initiatory significance of the rite was largely lost and it became a separate and almost superfluous sacrament for 'the increase of grace', *augmentum gratiae*.[1] At the Reformation the Church of England retained the Western practice of separating Confirmation from infant baptism but restored its initiatory character in two ways. First, the close relation to baptism was brought into prominence by including in the rite the renewal of baptismal vows, and secondly it was re-affirmed that admission to Holy Communion was restricted to those who had been 'confirmed or were ready and desirous to be confirmed'.[2]

Modern discussions of the pastoral use and significance of Confirmation have revealed a general desire to retain traditional anglican practice. There remains the theological question of the relation of the gift in Baptism to that in Confirmation. Varying views are current in the Church of England. One emphasizes the need that persons baptized in infancy should, on arriving at years of discretion, explicitly assume the responsibility for obedience to the vows already made in their name. Through this personal act of faith and acceptance of responsibility the significance of Baptism comes to its fulfilment and in the Confirmation Service the whole act is supported and blessed by the prayers of the Church. This view has a continuous history since the sixteenth century. For another view, also widely held, the laying on of hands has a more sacramental character and is the means of a special gift of strengthening by the Holy Spirit, but no negative inferences about what is bestowed in Baptism are drawn. This view can claim considerable support from the Prayer Book

---

[1] Thomas Aquinas, *Sum. Theol.* III, lxxii. 6, 'ita se habet confirmatio ad baptismum sicut augmentum ad generationem.'

[2] The rubric (based on the Sarum Manual) at the end of the Order of Confirmation dates from 1549, except for the qualifying clause which was added in 1662. The modern Roman practice by which children are commonly admitted to Communion before they are confirmed continues to deprive the rite of its true initiatory character.

rites.[1] Another view, while accepting the value of the renewal of vows, regards Confirmation as a sacramental rite which completes the sacramental act begun in baptism and bestows the gift of the Holy Spirit.[2] Thus baptism *as a sacrament* is incomplete until Confirmation. As a corollary of this view it is usually denied that the Holy Spirit is given in baptism. This interpretation can appeal to evidence in Scripture and primitive tradition. So long as practice continues to be uniform and the traditional order of Baptism, Confirmation, and admission to Communion is maintained it may not become urgent for the Church as a whole to decide the problem of the respective parts played by Baptism and Confirmation in the total act of Christian initiation.[3]†

---

[1] In the baptismal service we pray 'Give thy Holy Spirit to this infant that he may be born again'. The Bishop prays that the confirmed 'may daily *increase* in the Holy Spirit'.

[2] The ancient prayer (from the Gelasian Sacramentary) which in our rite precedes the laying-on of hands still (in spite of the change of 'Send into them' to 'Strengthen them') appears to imply that the seven-fold gift is now to be given for the first time. Moreover, persons baptized as adults are not dispensed from Confirmation though they have 'answered for themselves' at baptism (see rubric following Baptism of Such as are of Riper Years).

[3] 'The existence of some questions which defy definition is the price we have paid for the great advantages of administering Confirmation at an age of discretion' (*The Theology of Christian Initiation*, p. 23). But plans for re-union which involve statements about the functions of bishops may make it difficult to avoid a decision on some issues concerning the theology of Confirmation.

THE HOLY COMMUNION

ARTICLE XXVIII

Of the Lord's Supper

The Supper of the Lord is not only a sign of the love that Christians ought to have among themselves one to another: but rather it is a Sacrament of our Redemption by Christ's death. Insomuch that to such as rightly, worthily, and with faith, receive the same, the Bread which we break is a partaking of the Body of Christ; and likewise the cup of blessing is a partaking of the Blood of Christ.

Transubstantiation (or the change of the substance of Bread and Wine) in the Supper of the Lord cannot be proved by Holy Writ; but is repugnant to the plain words of Scripture, over-throweth the nature of a Sacrament, and hath given occasion to many superstitions.

The Body of Christ is given, taken, and eaten, in the Supper, only after an heavenly and spiritual manner. And the mean whereby the Body of Christ is received and eaten in the Supper is Faith.

The Sacrament of the Lord's Supper was not by Christ's ordinance reserved, carried about, lifted up, or worshipped.

De Coena Domini

Coena Domini non est tantum signum mutuae benevolentiae Christianorum inter sese, verum potius est Sacramentum nostrae per mortem Christi redemptionis.

Atque adeo, rite, digne, et cum fide sumentibus, panis quem frangimus est communicatio corporis Christi: similiter poculum benedictionis est communicatio sanguinis Christi.

Panis et vini transubstantiatio in Eucharistia ex sacris literis probari non potest. Sed apertis Scripturae verbis adversatur, Sacramenti naturam evertit, et multarum superstitionum dedit occasionem.

Corpus Christi datur, accipitur, et manducatur in Coena, tantum coelesti et spirituali ratione. Medium autem, quo corpus Christi accipitur et manducatur in Coena, fides est.

Sacramentum Eucharistiae ex institutione Christi non servabatur, circumferebatur, elevabatur, nec adorabatur.

The original Article of 1553 on the Lord's Supper coincided with the low-water mark of sacramental teaching in the Church of England. It was contemporary with the Second Prayer-Book of Edward VI containing the 'Black Rubric', which in its original form denied any 'Real and Essential Presence of Christ's natural flesh and blood' in the sacrament. In its present form, as restored in 1662, it only denies the ' "corporal" presence of Christ's natural flesh and blood', a most important change.

So the third paragraph of the Article denied 'the real and bodily presence, as they term it, of Christ's flesh and blood, in the sacrament of the Lord's Supper'. In 1563 this Article was altered to correspond with the changes made in the Prayer-Book of 1559. The original third paragraph was struck out and the present one substituted. The author of our present paragraph, Bishop Guest, expressly stated that it was drawn up not to 'exclude the Presence of Christ's Body from the Sacrament, but only the grossness and sensibleness in the receiving thereof.' The rest of the Article remained unaltered, except that the second paragraph was strengthened by the addition of 'overthroweth the nature of a sacrament'.

The Article excludes:
   (i) Anabaptist views which made the Lord's Supper a mere love feast;
  (ii) Zwinglian views which made it a bare memorial of Christ's death;
 (iii) The Roman doctrine of transubstantiation.

ARTICLE XXIX

Of the wicked which do not eat the Body of Christ in the use of the Lord's Supper

De manducatione corporis Christi, et impios illud non manducare

The wicked, and such as be void of a lively faith, although they do carnally and visibly press with their teeth (as Saint *Augustine* saith) the Sacrament of the Body and Blood of Christ: yet in nowise are they partakers of Christ, but rather to their condemnation do eat and drink the sign or Sacrament of so great a thing.

Impii, et fide viva destituti, licet carnaliter et visibiliter (ut Augustinus loquitur) corporis et sanguinis Christi Sacramentum dentibus premant, nullo tamen modo Christi participes efficiuntur. Sed potius tantae rei Sacramentum, seu symbolum, ad judicium sibi manducant et bibunt.

Composed in 1563, but omitted before publication probably by the personal intervention of Elizabeth in order not to hurt the feelings of the Papist party. But it was passed by Convocation in 1571 and hence-forward is found among the rest of the Articles.

§ 1. All over the world men have expressed their fellowship with one another by a common meal. Further, these common meals have often had a religious significance. One of the earliest ideas underlying primitive sacrifice was that of communion between the god of the tribe and his people. The god was regarded as present as an honoured guest at the feast made upon the sacrificial victim. Among many tribes the god was also identified in some sense with the victim slain and it was supposed that by feeding upon the flesh of the god the divine life shared by him and the tribe was renewed and strengthened.

This idea of communion with God through a common sacrificial meal was not absent from the religion of Israel. After the exile, with a fuller realization of the holiness of Jehovah and a deeper consciousness of sin, this aspect of sacrifice became less prominent. Stress was laid more on the propitiation and atonement that was needed before communion with God could be restored than on the communion itself. But the older idea survived. So, too, among the Gentiles sacrificial meals were quite common. Other ideas of sacrifice, such as that of a gift to the gods, are found, but the conception of fellowship was never lost. In the world into which our Lord came the ideas of communion with God by a sacred meal, of the receiving of divine life through participation in the sacrificial victim, of the perfecting of human fellowship through such participation and the like were perfectly familiar. Just as Jesus Christ summed up in Himself the fulfilment of the highest ideals alike of Jewish prophecy and Gentile morality, so in the Holy Communion He summed up the fulfilment of the highest ideals of worship, both Jewish and Gentile.

(a) The institution of the Holy Communion is recorded by the three Synoptists and by S. Paul (1 Cor 11). The title 'Lord's Supper' comes from 1 Cor 11²⁰.¹ It is noticeable that the accounts of Mt and Mk contain no command for its repetition. In Lk 22¹⁹ the words 'This do in remembrance of me' are absent in the Western text and may have been inserted from the account in 1 Cor. So the only undisputed evidence in Scripture for our Lord's command to celebrate it is that of S. Paul. But behind his words there stands the universal and continuous practice and tradition of the Church. Attempts have been made to assign the repetition of the Eucharist either to the Church or to S. Paul. For such views there is no real positive evidence.²

(b) When we turn to the evidence of Scripture it is by no means easy to give any very certain account of the practice of the first Christians in reference to the Eucharist. In 1 Cor 11¹⁷⁻³⁴ it is clear that at Corinth it was celebrated after and in close connexion with a common meal. The word δεῖπνον may include both. There is no sug-

---

¹ It is questionable whether the phrase 'The Lord's Supper' was used by S. Paul as a formal title. On the one hand, the use of the adjective κυριακόν instead of τοῦ κυρίου suggests this (cp. κυριακή for Sunday in Rev 1¹⁰). On the other hand, the words in the context may only mean that where division and selfishness are, a supper may indeed be taken, but it will never be the Lord's.

² The words of 1 Cor 11²³ 'For I (ἐγώ) received of the Lord (ἀπὸ τοῦ κυρίου) that which I also delivered unto you ' hardly warrant us in supposing that S. Paul claims to have received a special revelation on the subject. If the emphatic ἐγώ might be taken to favour such a view, the use of ἀπὸ (not παρά) and the use of the words 'the Lord Jesus' no less forcibly suggest that he received his information mediately through the Apostles. In any case, it is incredible that the Church should have received a new sacrament from S. Paul without any hint of enquiry or opposition. He was not such a universally popular person, especially among Jewish Christians. Further, Acts 2⁴² and ⁴⁶ imply that the Eucharist was being celebrated at Jerusalem long before S. Paul's conversion.

gestion that this combination was wrong or an innovation on the part of the Corinthians. S. Paul's own words 'This do as oft as ye drink' (the Greek contains no 'it') may mean 'as often as ye hold a common meal together'. When we turn to the Acts we find evidence of a similar custom. The familiar title the 'Last Supper' reminds us that eating together had all through His ministry been a bond of union between our Lord and His disciples. At such common meals doubtless He was accustomed to break bread and give thanks even as He did at the feedings of the multitude (Mk 6[41] and 8[6]). His performance of these acts at the Last Supper was only in accordance with His regular habit. It was by the manner in which He performed these same acts, that He made Himself known to His disciples at Emmaus after His Resurrection, even though they had probably not been present at the Last Supper (Lk 24[30-31 and 35], cp. Jn 21[13]). So, after the Ascension, it was only natural that the disciples should continue to meet for the breaking of bread, the outward sign of fellowship. At first it would seem that the common meal of the Christian brotherhood was held daily. In Acts 2[42] we read that the first Christians 'continued stedfastly in the apostles' teaching and fellowship (or 'in fellowship' R.V. mg. καὶ ἐν τῇ κοινωνίᾳ) and in the (τῇ) breaking of bread and the prayers' (the Bezan text has 'the fellowship of the breaking of the bread'). Again, in v. [46], 'And day by day continuing stedfastly with one accord in the temple and breaking bread at home (κατ' οἶκον) they did take their food (τροφῆς) with gladness and singleness of heart, praising God and having favour with all the people.' The probability is that by 'the breaking of the bread' is meant a common meal held in conscious imitation of the Last Supper and concluding with the Eucharist. The mention of food (τροφή) in v. [46] shows clearly that a meal is meant. The use of the article (τῇ κλάσει) in v. [42] suggests that the phrase 'the breaking of the bread', in itself applicable to any meal, was beginning to acquire a technical meaning in the mouths of Christians. In such early days of Church life all was inchoate and unformed. The Church was feeling her way towards organized life and worship.

Such a daily common meal and Eucharist was not possible everywhere. It is doubtful whether it could have existed apart from the peculiar conditions of common life at Jerusalem. Accordingly, as the Church spread abroad such daily reunion was found to be impossible. The common meal became part of the distinctive worship of the first day of the week. It was doubtless so at Corinth. In Acts 20[7-13] this is expressly stated. S. Luke gives a typical instance at Troas. 'Upon the first day of the week when we were gathered together to break bread, Paul discoursed with them.' Then follows the incident of Eutychus. Finally, when Paul 'had broken the bread and eaten (γευσάμενος) and had talked with them a long while even till break of day, so he departed.' The order would seem to be a common meal, after which S. Paul took the opportunity of all the Christians being assembled to deliver a lengthy discourse, then the Eucharist (γευσ-άμενος, meaning, as we should say, 'having communicated'), followed by a final discourse.[1] The meal would thus be held on Saturday evening, since, according to the Jewish mode of reckoning, the first day of the week began at 6 P.M. on Saturday: the Eucharist would begin after midnight. We have only to imagine an interval for sleep between the two parts to get to the later custom of observing Saturday night as a preparation for Sunday and holding the Eucharist early on Sunday.

In Acts 27[33-36], just before the shipwreck, we find an account of a meal. 'When Paul . . . had taken bread, he gave thanks to God in the presence of all: and he brake it and began to eat. Then were they all of good cheer and began to eat.' The language is strangely Eucharistic, but the meal clearly did not include the Eucharist.[2] The company consisted almost entirely of unbelievers, and the confusion of a storm at sea is hardly the moment for such a celebration. The important point is that the passage shows that 'to break bread' could be used of an ordinary meal. In Jude [12] and the parallel passage in 2 Pet 2[13] we find the title 'Agape' or 'love-feast' definitely given, according to the best reading, to the common meals of Christians. These are in danger of being polluted by the presence of immoral members. Probably the misbehaviour of such and drunkenness (1 Cor 11) brought these love-feasts into bad reputation among the heathen. No light is thrown on their relation to the Eucharist. We conclude, then, that in apostolic times as a general rule the Eucharist formed the conclusion of a common meal or agape and was not sharply distinguished from it. The whole was considered sacred as being a representation of the Last Supper. Whether an Agape was ever held without a Eucharist or *vice versa* we cannot be certain. There is nothing improbable in such a separation. The phrase 'breaking bread' is in itself quite vague and might be applied either to a meal or to the Eucharist or to the combination of the two.

Outside Scripture the earliest evidence has been very differently interpreted. It is probable but not certain that in the *Didache* the Agape preceded the Eucharist, and indeed is included under the title εὐχαριστία. So, too, Dr. Lightfoot held that in the time of Ignatius the two had not yet been separated.[3] In his letter to the Smyrnaeans he writes, 'It is not permitted without the bishop either to baptize or hold a love-feast.' The Eucharist is clearly included under the title

---

[1] Others, however, hold that the Eucharist preceded the meal. On this view in v. [11] 'breaking bread' refers to the Eucharist and γευσάμενος to the meal. It is true that S. Luke uses γεύομαι in the sense of 'taking food' but the reversal of the order of the Last Supper is most improbable so long as the meal and the Eucharist were still combined.

[2] 'The similarity is due, not so much to the fact that the Holy Eucharist is a meal, as that every meal has a sacred character and food "is sanctified by the word of God and prayer" ' (Rackham, *Acts*, p. 490).

[3] Lightfoot, *Ignatius*, vol. ii. p. 313, and vol. i. p. 386.

Agape. It is inconceivable that it should be omitted, especially as it has been mentioned earlier in the letter. The first clear evidence for the separation of the two is in Pliny's letter to Trajan (*Ep.* 96).[1] This makes it clear that in Bithynia by A.D. 112 Christians had come to hold two meetings on Sunday (*stato die*). At the first they met 'before day and sang a hymn to Christ antiphonally as to a God and bound themselves by an oath (*sacramento*)' not to commit certain crimes. This seems to be a somewhat vague account of the Eucharist, possibly mixed up with a confused recollection of the baptismal vow. At the second meeting later in the day they met 'to take food' but that 'ordinary and innocent food' (*promiscuum tamen et innoxium*— a refutation of pagan slanders); but in consequence of Trajan's edict forbidding the existence of clubs or guilds, these last meetings had been abandoned. This last statement would refer to the Agape. Whether the separation of Eucharist and Agape had taken place before Trajan's edict or in consequence of it is not certain, but it is clear that the Eucharist had been transferred to the morning. Many authorities hold that the result of Trajan's edict was a general separation of the Eucharist from the Agape and a giving up of the latter as being unessential.[2] This need not have taken place everywhere at the same time. At any rate, Justin Martyr (150) describes the Eucharist without any mention of the Agape.[3] But the Agape still continued to exist. It tended to assume the character of a charity supper contributed by the rich: possibly from the earliest days it had been a means of providing sustenance for the poorer members of the society. It became increasingly distinct from the Eucharist and gradually lost its sacred character and became a common meal and nothing more. Hence by the canons of various councils it was forbidden to hold it in churches. It lingered on in Africa as late as the Trullan Council in 692.[4]

§ 2. We may now turn to the inner meaning of the Eucharist. This is determined by the position that Jesus Christ holds in the Church and by the closeness of union between Christians and Christ.

(*a*) As we have seen, eating together is everywhere a sign of fellowship. *The Supper of the Lord is ... a sign of the love that Christians ought to have among themselves one to another.* This meaning is included in the title 'Holy Communion'. No one has ever attempted to deny it. This unity is symbolized by the one bread[5] and the one cup.

---

[1] Lightfoot, *op. cit.* vol. i. pp. 52–53.

[2] S. Augustine held that the separation was one of the reforms introduced by S. Paul when he came to Corinth. It is most probable that abuses connected with the Agape favoured the separation.

[3] Irenaeus never mentions the Agape. Tertullian speaks of the Eucharist as celebrated before daybreak (*De Cor.* c. 3) and treats the Agape as quite distinct.

[4] This account in the main follows Lightfoot. For a more recent discussion of the early Agape and Eucharist, see Dix, *The Shape of the Liturgy*.

[5] The Eastern Church still preserves the full symbolism of 'one bread' by using one (leavened) loaf which is divided.

'Seeing that there is one bread (or loaf), we who are many are one body: for we all partake of the one bread' (1 Cor 10[16], R.V. mg., cp. Jn 13[35] and 15[12]). The name 'Agape' which could include the Eucharist, was probably derived from our Lord's command 'to love one another', given on the same night as the institution of the Eucharist.[1] The many clubs existing under the Roman Empire showed their unity by common meals. But just as the Church is more than a mere human society, so her common meal is more than a bare symbol of fellowship. Hence this view by itself is inadequate.

(b) Accordingly the Article proceeds: It is *not only* a sign of love; *but rather it is a Sacrament of our redemption by Christ's death.* As the Catechism says, it was ordained 'For the continual remembrance of the sacrifice of the death of Christ and of the benefits which we receive thereby'. It constitutes a proclamation before the world of the Lord's death (1 Cor 11[26]) and also a means of bringing it home to ourselves. Whether the Last Supper was in detail a Passover meal or not is doubtful. The evidence of S. John's Gospel makes it clear that it took place the evening before the actual Passover.[2] But it was in the closest connexion with the Passover and was instituted to take its place in the new Israel. The Passover was a means of keeping in mind and a public thanksgiving for Jehovah's redemption of Israel from slavery in Egypt. So the Eucharist was to be kept 'in remembrance of' Christ (1 Cor 11[25]), and as a thanksgiving[3] for the redemption wrought by His death. Further, the deliverance from Egypt was but the prelude to the renewing of the Covenant at Sinai. At the Passover-meal the individual Israelite claimed his share in the Covenant made by God with Israel. Christ's words 'This is my blood of the covenant which is shed for you' (Mk 14[24]) look back to Exodus 24[8] and suggest that a new covenant was about to be ratified by the blood of a better Sacrifice. Every Eucharist is a memorial of this new Covenant made by God with a new and greater Israel, and each Christian who partakes of the Eucharist claims his share in the blessings won by Christ's death. The very term for the Passover liturgy, Haggadah, or 'showing forth', is that used by S. Paul (1 Cor 11[26]). So, too, the 'cup of blessing' was the regular name for the third cup at the Paschal meal (cp. 1 Cor 10[16]), at least in later times.[4] In short, the Eucharist is the Passover of the Christian Church.

---

[1] Cp. the beautiful prayer in the *Didache* (9): 'As this broken bread was scattered upon the mountains and being gathered together became one, so may Thy Church be gathered together from the ends of the earth into Thy Kingdom' (Gwatkin's *Selections*, p. 21).

[2] But see J. Jeremias, *The Eucharistic Words of Jesus.*

[3] The actual title, εὐχαριστία, is not found in the New Testament, though it occurs in Ignatius and the *Didache*, but εὐχαριστεῖν is used of our Lord's own giving of thanks (1 Cor 11[24]). Possibly, too, in 14[16] εὐχαριστία is used of thanksgiving at the Lord's Supper.

[4] For an account of the Passover as now celebrated in a Jewish home, see Oesterley and Box, *The Religion and Worship of the Synagogue.*

(c) Insomuch that to such as rightly, worthily and with faith receive the same, the bread which we break is a partaking of the body of Christ; and likewise the cup of blessing is a partaking of the blood of Christ. This statement is based on 1 Cor 10[16], 'The cup of blessing which we bless, is it not a communion (κοινωνία) of the blood of Christ? The bread which we break, is it not a communion of the body of Christ?' It asserts the reality of the gift bestowed on those who receive the sacrament rightly (*rite*), worthily (*digne*), and with faith. The Holy Communion is an 'effectual sign', not only representing but conveying spiritual food. 'Rightly' here refers to the due observance of all that Christ commanded, the right matter and form. 'Worthily' refers to the right inward disposition of the recipient. It would include 'with faith'.

What is meant by partaking of the Body and Blood of Christ?

(i) We turn first to Jn 6. This was spoken exactly a year before the institution of the Eucharist, at the previous Passover. Moreover, by the time that the Gospel was composed, the Eucharist had been the centre of the life of more than one generation of Christians. Hence we can hardly exclude all reference to the Eucharist. The true relation between this discourse and the Eucharist would seem to be that in the former Christ speaks primarily of the gift of His own life which men needed and which was to be bestowed through the Eucharist: a year later He instituted the Eucharist to be the means of bestowing that life. The gift is spoken of as future, not present (6 [27 and 51]). Christ connects it with the time after His Ascension and the coming of the Spirit (vv. [62-63]). Throughout the discourse, step by step, greater stress is laid on the absolute need not only of Christ's teaching but of Christ's life. Our Lord begins with a contrast between the 'meat that perisheth', the ordinary food of the body, and 'the meat that abideth unto eternal life', which He will give (v. [27]). The condition of receiving it is faith (v. [29]). Such bread can only come, like the manna, by the direct gift of God (v. [33]), and He Himself is this bread (v. [33]). In v. [51] this bread is further defined as 'my flesh'. In v. [53] the objection of the Jews is met by an increased claim, 'Except ye eat the flesh of the Son of Man and drink His blood, ye have not life in yourselves. . . . For my flesh is meat indeed and my blood is drink indeed. He that eateth my flesh and drinketh my blood abideth in me and I in him.' With such language we compare 1 Cor 10[16-17] and 11[27]. Throughout, the thought is of identity of life between the believer and Christ. His 'body and blood' primarily represent His perfect humanity. The living Christ bestows upon His members the strength of a perfect human life, offered in sacrifice and triumphant over sin and death, in order to cleanse and refresh our weak and tainted lives. In eating and drinking by a deliberate and voluntary act we take into ourselves something that is outside ourselves, in order that it may become part of ourselves and so our bodies may be strengthened. So in the Holy

Communion by a deliberate and voluntary act we receive the life of Christ into our souls that it may become our life. The feeding of the 5000 which preceded the discourse was an acted parable of the spiritual truth laid down in the discourse. So in the Holy Communion our Lord took bread and wine, the typical ordinary daily food of the Galilean peasant, to be the outward sign of the normal food of the Christian soul. The visible reception is at once the parable and the means of the inward reception by faith. In each case the goodness is there first in the food outside ourselves and by the appropriate act we take it into ourselves. Again, all food corresponds to the nature of the life that it is to sustain. Our bodies can be strengthened by bread and wine, because bread and wine contain just those elements out of which the body is composed. In like manner the spiritual food of the Christian must correspond to the life of the Christian. But the life of the Christian is, as we have seen, none other than the life of Christ: we are members of His body, branches in the vine. So the food of the Christian must be Christ. The Christ-life can only be fed by new supplies of Christ. He alone can be the bread of life. Accordingly, in the Holy Communion the Christian, as a member of Christ, receives by faith through the outward and visible sign of the bread and wine the inward and spiritual grace of the perfect humanity of Christ. Partaking of the Body and Blood of Christ can mean no less than this.

(ii) The further question may be asked: 'Why are the body and blood spoken of in separation, and symbolized by the bread and the wine respectively?' The answer is that our Lord's language and that of S. Paul is borrowed from the picture of a sacrificial feast. The reference to the body and blood in separation recalls the act of sacrifice in which the blood was poured out. In the Holy Communion we feed on the life of the living and glorified Christ who has become all that He is through death.[1] He is eternally 'the Lamb as it hath been slain'. The life that He imparts to us is life that has passed through death. Hence it is fitly mediated through bread and wine.

(iii) As partaking of the perfect humanity of Christ, we also partake of all the blessings won by His sacrifice. 'What merit, force or virtue soever there is in His sacred Body and Blood, we freely, fully and wholly have it by this Sacrament.'[2] We enjoy the manifold privileges of the new Covenant ratified by His death (Mk 14[24]). So, by a right reception of the Holy Communion we are filled with all the fruits of His redemption. These blessings are not something apart from Christ, but in so far as our life in Christ grows, we enter more fully into their meaning.

§ 3. So far almost all Christians would agree. The language used

---

[1] We must resolutely put away the revolting idea that in any sense we feed on the body and blood of a dead Christ.
[2] Hooker, v. 67, § 7.

might vary, but all are at one in holding that through the Holy Communion our union with Christ is deepened and strengthened, by faith we receive new life from Him and enter into the fulness of the heritage won by His death. Controversy has arisen on the question of the relation of the inward gift to the outward elements. The first thing that we must grasp is that this further question is relatively less important. In an age of bitter controversy Hooker could write: 'Shall I wish that men would more give themselves to meditate with silence what we have by the Sacrament and less to dispute of the manner how?' 'What these elements are in themselves it skilleth not, it is enough that to me which take them they are the Body and Blood of Christ.' 'Let it therefore be sufficient for me presenting myself at the Lord's table to know what there I receive from Him, without searching or inquiring of the manner how Christ performeth His promise.'[1]

For 800 years there was no formal dispute on the subject. The earliest controversial treatise was by a certain Paschasius Radbert in 831, which was the beginning of a long and unedifying wrangle, leading up to the formal statement of the doctrine of transubstantiation at the Lateran Council in 1215. The attempts made to state the relation of gift in Holy Communion to the outward elements may be summed up as follows:

(a) The 'Receptionist' view. On this theory the bread and wine in the Holy Communion are merely tokens not channels of the inward grace that is given. They are like the water in baptism, outward signs ordained in order to assist faith, but brought into no vital relation to the divine realities that they represent. The devout communicant does indeed by an act of faith receive the body and blood of Christ at the moment that he receives the bread and wine, but in no real sense by means of them. Thus Christ is present only in the hearts of the faithful recipients. His coming is connected not with the consecration of the elements but with the reception. This view was taught by Calvin: it was the necessary corollary of his doctrine of grace. If grace is given only to the few elect, it clearly cannot be possible for all to receive it who receive the bread and wine. So its reception must be essentially independent of the reception of the visible elements. The theory has been largely held in the Church of England[2] and was ex-

---

[1] Cp. the whole passage, v. 67, §§ 5–7 and 12–13.

[2] Hooker is usually claimed as a receptionist. He certainly writes, 'The real presence of Christ's most blessed Body and Blood is not therefore to be sought for in the Sacrament, but in the worthy receiver of the sacrament' (c. 67 § 5). But other passages qualify this statement. He also writes, 'This bread hath in it more than the substance which our eyes behold' (c. 67 § 12), and 'The power of the ministry of God . . . by blessing visible elements, . . . maketh them invisible grace' (c. 77 § 1). Further, Hooker's great object was to allay contention by fixing the minds of all Christians on those great truths concerning the Eucharist about which they were all agreed. He refused to join in a bitter and barren controversy about the mystery of the Eucharist. Accordingly, as Bishop Paget wrote, 'He should have the credit of having really meant what he said. On the ground of some passages in his argument he is claimed as supporting one side

392 ARTICLE XXVIII

pounded at length by Waterland. It represents one side of the teaching of S. Augustine and can be supported by isolated sentences of other Fathers. It is perfectly tenable by loyal members of the Church of England. There is nothing in the Prayer-Book that definitely contradicts it. Quite rightly the Church of England excludes only a Zwinglian view of the Sacrament—a view, that is, which is not only inadequate, but positively denies a part of the truth.†

(b) The Real Presence. On this view we hold that we receive through the bread and wine the Body and Blood of Christ, because in answer to the prayers of His Church and in fulfilment of His own promise, He has brought the elements into a mysterious union with Himself. He has, as it were, taken them up into the fulness of His ascended life and made them the vehicle of imparting that life to His members. Thus He is in a real sense present not only in the devout communicant but in the consecrated elements. Of the manner of this union we affirm nothing. The Presence is spiritual, not material.

This, in some form, is the teaching of the Roman and Eastern Churches, of Luther, of the Fathers and early liturgies, and has always been held by many within the Church of England. It would appear to be the most consistent with Scripture and the tradition of the Church, and also to be a safeguard of certain great Christian principles.

(i) Let us turn first to Scripture. An enormous amount of labour has been wasted in attempting to get back to the actual words spoken by Christ and to interpret the meaning of 'is' in 'This is my body' and 'This is my blood'. In Aramaic the word 'is' might, or might not be definitely expressed. The important point is that S. Paul understood these words to contain a promise of a divine gift. He bases on them the solemn warning 'Wherefore (ὥστε) whosoever shall eat the bread or drink the cup of the Lord unworthily, shall be guilty of the body and blood of the Lord' (1 Cor 11²⁷). If the existence of the gift is made conditional upon the faith of the individual communicant, as receptionists teach, the unworthy recipient can hardly be said to be 'guilty of the body and blood of the Lord'. If the presence of Christ is to be sought only in the heart of the faithful recipient, there can have been no presence for him to profane. As being unworthy he has drawn near only to bread and wine. Further, if the words mean only 'This represents my body', we have only a parable, not a promise: they contain no pledge of any sacramental gift. The words are not really parallel to such allegorical statements as 'I am the bread' or 'the door'. These last couple together an idea and a concrete reality. But the words of institution couple together two concrete realities of the external world. Again, in 1 Cor 10¹⁶ S. Paul connects the 'com-

in the very controversy from which he urged men to refrain. . . . Those who know Hooker's ways and do him justice will not easily think him so careless or so disingenuous as to break the bounds which he was strenuously appealing to other men to keep' (see Paget, Introduction to Hooker, bk. v. p. 176).

munion of the body' and 'the blood' not with reception but with consecration. He speaks of 'The cup which we bless' and 'the bread which we break', 'we' being the minister as the organ of the assembled Church.

(ii) Again, if we turn to the Church as the interpreter of Scripture, the main stream of Christian teaching is quite' clear. We find a singular absence of theological controversy about the Eucharist, but the general line of thought may be exemplified by these words of Irenaeus, 'The bread which is of the earth receiving the invocation of God is no longer common bread but Eucharist, made up of two things, an earthly and a heavenly.'[1] No doubt certain individuals or schools of thought exhibit a tendency to lay a one-sided emphasis on particular aspects of the truth, as, for instance, to dwell on the Eucharist as imparting the gift of bodily immortality, but such teaching did not express the mind of the Church as a whole and was corrected by the corporate consciousness. The early liturgies all attest a belief in the Real Presence. There is a marked difference between the treatment that was accorded to the water in Baptism and the elements in the Eucharist. No special care was taken of the water. Indeed, baptism was often administered in streams. But the consecrated elements were by a natural instinct always treated with the utmost reverence.[2] In Baptism there are no words that in any way are the counterpart of the words of institution.[3]

(iii) The Sacraments are an extension of the Incarnation, in so far as through them the Incarnate Lord still offers His own saving grace to men. But the Incarnation was an event discerned by faith but in no way produced by faith. When Christ walked on this earth, those who discerned the divine in Him, discerned what was really there. Their faith enabled them to see and grasp the truth. It was quite possible for men to be blind to His divinity and to miss the blessings that He brought within their reach through lack of faith, but that does not prove their unreality. In other words, faith is a capacity for intuition or apprehension. It can recognize and respond, but not create. It can rest upon and surrender itself to what already exists, but it calls nothing into being. So with the gift promised in the Holy Eucharist. It is contrary to all analogy to make the existence of the gift in any

---

[1] Irenaeus, *Adv. Haer.* iv. 18, § 5.

[2] Cp. Gore, *Body of Christ*, p. 76 and note 5.

[3] It is worth noting that when the Fathers speak of the bread and wine as 'signs' or 'symbols' of the body and blood of Christ, they do not in any way imply a merely receptionist view. To us a 'symbol' at once suggests that the reality symbolized is absent. To them a 'symbol' was rather 'the evidence to the senses of a divine reality actually present'. 'The really heavenly element lay either in or behind the visible form without investing itself with it' (Gore, p. 89, quoting Harnack). The Fathers do indeed avoid any such language as would speak of Christ as present in or under the bread and wine. They rather speak of the bread and wine as 'types' or 'symbols' of spiritual realities invisible to the eye of sense, but most truly present. S. Cyril of Jerusalem, for instance, writes: 'Under the sign (ἐν τύπῳ) of bread is given thee the body, under the sign of wine is given thee the blood.' (*Cat.* xxii. 3.)

sense dependent on faith. Rather the gift is there, objectively: those who approach with faith discern and appropriate it, those who have not faith are, as it were, blind to the gift, and fail to claim it.[1]

Again, the Incarnation was God's gift to His people as a whole. Some availed themselves of it, others did not. So the Holy Eucharist, like all the blessings bestowed through Christ, is primarily a gift not to the individual Christian but to the whole body of Christ. The individual as a member of the body is bidden to claim and appropriate his share of it. This truth is of the highest value as emphasizing the corporate nature of all true Christianity. We may compare the coming of the Holy Spirit at Pentecost. The fire first appeared as one and then as 'tongues parting asunder'[2] (Acts 2³). The receptionist view weakens the social aspect of the Eucharist by making it a number of separate donations to individuals. The doctrine of the Real Presence vindicates the unity of life which is to be realized in brotherhood.

The opposition to any such phrase as 'real presence' is due in the main to the fear that it means presence in space and involves materialistic ideas. Let us admit that the primary idea of the Eucharist is that of Christ active rather than of Christ present, of Christ as bestowing a gift rather than of the gift bestowed. But it still remains true that our imaginations are unable to conceive of Christ as active unless He is in some sense present and of the gift as bestowed unless it is there to be bestowed. No doubt Christ is present always and everywhere, behind all the processes of nature and human life. But that was not inconsistent with a presence in a new way and for a new act of divine grace in the Incarnation. Again, Christ promised to be with His Church 'all the days' (Mt 28²⁰), yet He could say, 'Where two or three are gathered together in my name, there am I in the midst of them' (Mt 18²⁰). That promise does not imply a previous absence, but rather a presence in a special way and for a special purpose. So, too, in the Holy Communion Christ acts in fulfilment of a special promise and vouchsafes to His Church a special presence of Himself. Christ is still Man. He did not lay aside His human nature at the Ascension. Nor yet was His body then removed to an infinitely distant part of the universe, rather it was raised above the limitations of space altogether. It became the perfect self-expression of spirit. Heaven is a manner of life, not a place. So in His Heavenly life Christ still possesses all the capacities of perfect manhood. He can still render His humanity active at will and act through it in our world of space and time. Only the Lutherans have ever pictured Christ's manhood as, so to say, automatically and unconditionally omnipresent. It is nearer

---

[1] Cp. the words of Thorndyke, 'The eating and drinking of it' (*i.e.* the Lord's Body and Blood) 'in the sacrament, presupposes the being of it in the sacrament . . . unless a man can spiritually eat the flesh and blood of Christ in and by the sacrament, which is not in the sacrament when he eats and drinks it, but by his eating and drinking of it comes to be there.'

[2] Not 'cloven' as A.V., an impossible sense for the present participle.

to truth to assert that Christ can act through it at will, and make it a present power in the world wheresoever He is pleased to do so.

Now in the Holy Communion He gives us His Body and Blood. Here, if anywhere, He acts through His glorified humanity. We must try therefore to conceive of Him as present not only as God but as Man, present by an act of will to bestow upon us the gift of His own Manhood. This act, or this presence—in whichever way we view it, is no fresh humiliation. It is in no way on a level with the submission to the limitations of our present world made at the Incarnation. Rather it is on a level with the ascended life: it is Christ's very heavenly presence itself.[1] There is no opposition between a 'real' and a 'spiritual' presence. The most 'real' things are not those that belong to the material world. A 'spiritual' presence is presence in the manner of a Spirit, a manner outside our earthly experience, but not therefore imaginary or unreal, any more than Heaven is unreal.

The manner of this Presence and its relation to the outward elements we cannot define, except in so far as we reject certain attempts of our imagination to picture it. Thus, it involves in no sense a movement in space.[2] Nor is it in any sense comparable to the chemical changes to be viewed in our laboratories. It is rather analogous to the spiritual changes that take place in ourselves. If we say that Christ is present 'in' the sacrament, we use 'in' metaphorically, as when we say that Christ abides in the Christian and the Christian in Christ. Wherever we study the relation between spirit and matter, whether between God and the world, or our souls and our bodies or here, our reason and our imagination are always baffled. We can only speak in symbolical language borrowed from space. It is a real source of strength to the Church of England that she refuses to speculate on the question or to make the acceptance of human speculations a condition of membership.[3]†

---

[1] The early liturgies use language both about the Body and Blood of Christ as being present at our earthly altars and of our oblations of bread and wine as being carried up to the heavenly altar and there united with His Body and Blood. (Cp. Gore, *op. cit.* pp. 84–85, and Fr. Benson, *Letters*, vol. i. p. 273.)

[2] Cp. the words of Cardinal Newman (*Via Media*, vol. ii. p. 220): 'If place is excluded from the idea of the Sacramental Presence, therefore division or distance from heaven is excluded also, for distance implies a measurable interval and such there cannot be except between places. Moreover, if the idea of distance is excluded, therefore is the idea of motion. Our Lord then neither descends from heaven upon our altars, nor moves when carried in procession. The visible species change their position, but He does not move. He is in the Holy Eucharist after the manner of a spirit. We do not know how; we have no parallel to the "how" in our experience. We can only say that He is present, not according to the natural manner of bodies, but *sacramentally*. His Presence is substantial, spirit-wise, sacramental; an absolute mystery, not against reason, however, but against imagination, and must be received by faith.'

[3] Cp. the lines attributed to Queen Elizabeth:

His was the Word that spake it:
He took the bread and brake it:
And what that Word did make it,
I do believe and take it.

Indifferent poetry, but admirable theology.

(c) The Roman doctrine of 'Transubstantiation', condemned in our Article, is an attempt to define the relation of the gift to the elements in the Eucharist. As a formal definition it has its roots far back in Church history. Just as Monophysitism was the culmination of a tendency to exalt our Lord's divinity at the expense of His humanity and to reduce the latter to a mere semblance, so we find a tendency among certain early writers to exalt the divine gift in the Eucharist in such a way as to minimize or even explain away the reality of the bread and wine after consecration. This appears first in the East: in the West it was kept in check by the influence of S. Augustine, who unmistakably believed in the permanence and reality of the elements.[1] A new stage began with the treatise of Paschasius Radbert composed in 831. He taught beyond all doubt a doctrine of 'transubstantiation'. By consecration the natural substance of the elements is annihilated: there is on the altar 'nihil aliud quam corpus et sanguis Domini'. Only the appearance of bread and wine remains to test faith and afford a screen to the awful realities. This teaching was opposed at the time, especially by Ratramnus, a monk of Corbey, but the controversy died down for some two centuries. Then it was rekindled by the teaching of Berengar, Archdeacon of Angers, who attacked the crude popular language about the Eucharistic presence. He himself held the doctrine of an objective but spiritual presence in the elements. In 1059 Berengar was forced to recant, and the decree which was forced upon him at Rome in the presence of the Pope is sufficient evidence of the dangerously materialistic view taken by the Church as a whole at that time. He was made to assert that 'The bread and wine after consecration are not only a sacrament but also the true body and blood of our Lord Jesus Christ and are sensibly not only in sacrament but in truth touched and broken by the hands of the priests and bruised by the teeth of the faithful.' Berengar's opponents asserted even that the body and blood of Christ were physically eaten with the mouth.

But his protest had not been in vain. The gross and superstitious teaching was at once defended and refined by the teaching of the Schoolmen. They took advantage of the current philosophical distinction between substance and accidents[2] to formulate a theological statement of transubstantiation. The philosophy of the day held that our senses can only perceive the qualities or 'accidents' of things. Beneath these qualities or 'accidents' there is an underlying reality, the thing itself, to which was given the technical name of 'substance'. For instance, bread possesses certain 'accidents' of which our senses

---

[1] In the East it became common from the fourth century onwards to speak of the bread and wine as being 'changed into' the Body and Blood. This 'conversion' language appears in S. Ambrose, but did not come into general use in the West until much later.

[2] Berengar had known of this distinction and had combated in advance any use of it for this purpose. He held that 'accidents' could not exist apart from the 'substance' in which they inhered. That was also Wycliffe's argument.

inform us, hardness, colour, taste, smell, etc. But these are not the bread itself. Behind them is the 'substance' of bread in which they cohere. This 'substance' is beyond the range of all our senses, touch included. So the Schoolmen laid down that through consecration the 'substance' of the bread and wine was by the almighty power of God changed into the 'substance' of the body and blood of Christ. No change can be detected by the senses. The 'accidents' of the bread and wine remain in order to veil the divine gift.

No doubt this philosophical speculation does not necessarily involve a materialistic view of the sacrament. 'Substance', as so used, is intangible. But it could do nothing to correct the debasing influence of popular superstition, and there can be no denying that the ordinary view of transubstantiation in the Middle Ages was absolutely carnal and materialistic, as, indeed, it is in popular Romanism to-day. The actual word 'transubstantiation' is first found in use in the eleventh century. It received official sanction at the Lateran Council in 1215. It is employed however in a less definite sense than in Tridentine theology. Despite the obvious misunderstandings and abuses that attached to it, it was retained and re-asserted at the Council of Trent,[1] and has remained as an article of faith in the Roman Church.

Our Article rejects the doctrine on four grounds:

(α) *Transubstantiation* (*or the change of the substance of bread and wine*) *in the Supper of the Lord cannot be proved by Holy Writ.* Scripture knows nothing of any philosophical distinction between 'substance' and 'accidents'. The words of institution may reasonably be interpreted as the promise of a divine gift, but they throw no light whatever on the manner in which that gift is related to the outward sign. Roman controversialists have indeed admitted that transubstantiation cannot be proved from Scripture. It is at best one explanation of Scripture.

(β) It is *repugnant to the plain words of Scripture.* That is to say, Scripture speaks of the Bread after consecration as still bread (1 Cor 11[26 and 28]). We may add that the Canon of the Roman Mass does the same, since it goes back to an age that knew nothing of transubstantiation.

(γ) It *overthroweth the nature of a Sacrament.* In the words of the Catechism a sacrament has two parts: 'the outward visible sign,' here bread and wine, and the 'inward spiritual grace', the body and blood of Christ. But if, as on the Roman view, the substance of the bread and wine is annihilated, the reality of the outward sign is

---

[1] *E.g.* 'If anyone shall say that in the Holy Sacrament of the Eucharist the substance of the bread and wine remains together with the Body and Blood of our Lord Jesus Christ and shall deny that wonderful and singular conversion of the whole substance of the bread into the Body and of the whole substance of the wine into the Blood, the appearance only of the bread and wine remaining, which conversion indeed the Catholic Church most fittingly calls Transubstantiation, let him be anathema' (Council of Trent, Session xiii. Canon 2).

destroyed, *i.e.* the nature of the sacrament is overthrown as lacking one of its two parts.

(δ) It *hath given occasion to many superstitions.* As Dr. Gore has truly said, 'The atmosphere in which the doctrine of transubstantiation grows into a dogma is calculated to send a shiver through one's intellectual and moral being.' Paschasius Radbert drives home his teaching by recounting a series of miracles in which drops of blood flowed from the consecrated Host as the form of the infant Christ appeared. A similar miracle was opportunely registered in order to forward the institution of the Festival of Corpus Christi in 1264. The gross imagination of mediaeval theologians did not shrink from discussing the precise relation of the reception of the Lord's Body to the processes of physical digestion. In answer to the objections of opponents, miracles were lavishly postulated. It was supposed that the more contradictions that were offered to reason, the greater was the opportunity given for the meritorious exercise of faith.

As against the popular idea of transubstantiation as held and taught in the Roman Church both in the Middle Ages and to-day, these objections are conclusive. Attempts, however, are made by educated Romanists to escape them. They point to the fact that the Canon of the Mass calls the Host after the recital of the words of institution 'bread', as S. Paul does, and therefore claim that the Roman Church still in some sense recognizes it as bread. Again, they argue that the 'accidents' that remain are real and therefore constitute a true outward visible sign. Further, as we all should admit, the fact that anything has given rise to superstition is not conclusive against it. The Bible itself has given rise to many superstitions, but that is no reason for abolishing it or denying its value.

In this way it is possible to get a refined doctrine that is not open to the charge of materialism. But although it may be held in this form by subtle and educated minds, we must repeat it is not the ordinary teaching of popular Romanism. Further, it practically explains away the mediaeval doctrine altogether. 'Thus the modern Roman theologians allow to the consecrated bread and wine all the reality which anyone believes any bread and wine to possess, or, in other words, explain away transubstantiation, till it remains a verbal incumbrance due to an inopportune intrusion into Church doctrine of a temporary phase of metaphysics.'[1] Further, in however refined a form it is held it is open to very grave objections.

(α) It not only attempts to define what Scripture leaves mysterious, but binds men down to one particular form of philosophy. At best it is a pious opinion. We should not wish to condemn those who choose to hold it or to expel them from the unity of the Church. But the Church has no authority to add to the divine revelation a mere philosophical opinion.

[1] Gore, *op. cit.* p. 120.

(β) It 'detracts from the kingdom of nature in order to magnify the kingdom of grace'. On the Roman view the natural is destroyed to make room for the supernatural: the bread and wine are not really consecrated to be the vehicle of divine blessings, they are annihilated. Such a view as this is at bottom akin to Gnosticism, not Christianity. Christianity has always taught that the material attains to its highest end in becoming the means and expression of the spiritual. The supernatural completes and perfects the natural. In the Incarnation our Lord's manhood was not absorbed or destroyed by His divinity. Rather He alone was perfect man. In the controversies about the Incarnation the Fathers use the analogy of the Eucharist in order to prove this. According to the Roman doctrine the analogy of the Eucharist would prove just the opposite. 'Transubstantiation' is in its whole conception essentially unspiritual. It treats our Lord's ascended and glorified Humanity as on a level with the things of earth which must needs make room for its coming.[1]†

§ 4. The third paragraph affirms the great truth that safeguards and is the complement of the doctrine of the 'Real Presence'. *The body of Christ is given, taken and eaten in the Supper only after an heavenly and spiritual manner. And the mean whereby the body of Christ is received and eaten in the Supper is faith.*

Just as Christ's body and blood are present without being made subject to space and movement, so when we eat and drink them they are not made subject to any physical process. We can no more eat and drink them physically than we can eat bread and butter by faith. Each food, the natural nourishment and the spiritual nourishment, has its own means of reception. If, by faithful reception of the body and blood of the Lord, 'the body and soul' of the communicant are 'preserved unto everlasting life' such reception can be 'only after an heavenly and spiritual manner'.[2]

(*a*) This truth is further explained by Article XXIX, '*Of the wicked which do not eat the body of Christ in the use of the Lord's Supper.*' The phrase '*eat the body*' clearly refers to the spiritual eating spoken of in Article XXVIII. '*The wicked and such as be void of a lively faith, although they do carnally and visibly press with their teeth (as S. Augustine saith) the Sacrament of the body and blood of Christ; yet in nowise are they partakers of Christ, but rather to their condemnation*

---

[1] Some mention must be made of the unhappy doctrine maintained by Roman theologians of repute that the presence of Christ bestowed in the Eucharist is withdrawn as soon as the elements begin to be digested. By a second miracle transubstantiation is reversed. The 'substance' of Christ's Body is withdrawn. The 'substance' of the bread is replaced. So the coming of Christ is only a temporary visit, for about a quarter of an hour, not a permanent deepening of that union with Christ that only sin can weaken or destroy. This flatly contradicts the true Christian teaching as given by S. Augustine, 'What you see in the Sacrament passes away, but the invisible thing signified does not pass away but remains.' Christ abides in us and we in Him.

[2] For the meaning attached to this Article by its author, Bishop Guest of Rochester, see p. 383 above. His statements are quoted in full in Stone, vol. ii., pp. 210 ff.

do eat and drink the sign or Sacrament of so great a thing.' The wicked
and the faithful alike receive the elements that have been brought into
union with the body and blood of Christ. Neither wicked nor faithful
carnally and visibly press with their teeth more than the bread and
wine. But only the faithful receive the body and blood of Christ, since
only they possess that faith which is the indispensable means of receiving them. This Article does not in any way deny the 'real
presence', it only rules out any carnal view of it. To give an illustration: when our Lord was on earth He possessed healing power quite
independently of the faith of men: but only those who possessed faith
could get into touch with it. Many touched His garments, but only
the woman who had faith was healed (Mk 5³⁰ ff.). The healing power
was there: the touch of faith did not create it, but faith, as it were,
opened the channel to appropriate the blessing. So in the Eucharist,
Christ in all His saving power is present. The wicked are only capable
of receiving the visible and material signs of His presence. But those
who approach with faith can receive the inward grace and become
partakers of Christ by feeding on His Body and Blood. Attempts
have, indeed, been made to distinguish between 'eating the body of
Christ' and 'partaking of Christ'. It has been claimed that the wicked
do the former to their soul's peril, but cannot do the latter. No such
distinction, however, can be drawn, and Scripture seems to know of
no feeding upon Christ that is not unto life (cp. Jn 6⁵³ ff.). The wicked
only receive the outward 'sign or sacrament' that has entered into the
closest relation with the divine gift. The gift itself is withheld or
withdrawn, we know not how.¹

(*b*) *The Sacrament of the Lord's Supper was not by Christ's ordinance reserved, carried about, lifted up or worshipped.* This last section
of the Article is carefully worded. It is based on a sound and intelligible principle. The Holy Communion was given to us by Christ for
a definite purpose. We can only be secure of its blessings so long as
we respect the limits of that purpose. The faithful Christian is
assured that in receiving the Holy Eucharist he is brought face to face
with Christ. The Lord's presence is guaranteed by the Lord's promise.
But it is a spiritual presence: and a spiritual presence, however real,
is not necessarily controlled by the same laws as an earthly presence.
The appearances of our Lord after His Resurrection during the great
forty days did not obey the same laws as those that limit and govern
our present earthly humanity. Though He condescended to use
material means, He was not subject to them. So we must not presume to argue about our Lord's presence in the Eucharist as if it
were in any way an earthly presence. We are sure that He is present

¹ It is universally agreed that the unworthy communicant does not enter into that
union with Christ which is the ultimate end of receiving the sacrament. It might,
however, be held that S. Paul's reference to those who are 'guilty of the body and blood
of the Lord' and 'eat and drink judgment' to themselves (1 Cor 11¹⁷, ²⁹) suggests that
the unworthy receive a divine gift, but for judgment and not salvation.

to bestow His body and blood. We cannot be certain that that Presence abides when we use the consecrated bread and wine for a new and entirely different purpose, a purpose not ordained by Christ, but prompted by the fallible logic of human devotion. If our Lord could at will enter or withdraw Himself from the Upper Room, so at will He comes to fulfil His promise in the Eucharist and at will He can depart when that promise has been fulfilled. We cannot, as it were, bind Him to earth by our treatment of the elements. Such thoughts lie behind the very cautious statements of the Article. The practices mentioned are not condemned as sinful. No anathema is levelled at those who retain them. All that is asserted is that they are precarious, as going outside the ordinance of Christ.[1] The Church of England, therefore, was perfectly justified in abolishing them. At best they are practices enjoined by a part of the Catholic Church.

(i) Reservation purely for the communion of the sick or absent is thoroughly primitive and natural. It is in full accord with the spirit of Scripture and the revealed purpose of Christ and was the custom of the primitive Church. Justin Martyr tells us that a portion 'is sent to them that are absent, by the deacons'. In an age of persecution, and when perhaps the majority of Christians were slaves, members were often unavoidably prevented from being present. So, too, the Communion was sent to Christians in prison. Again, we read of Christians taking away the consecrated elements in order to communicate themselves at home during the week or carrying them with them when on a journey. Tertullian speaks of a Christian woman at home 'secretly, before all food' tasting the Lord's Body.[2] So, too, as late as the time of S. Basil the monks in the desert, where there was no priest, communicated themselves with the reserved sacrament. In times of persecution such a practice of private communion was necessary. But it was liable to abuse, and from the fourth century onward the Church took steps to suppress it.[3] We hear also of the Eucharist being sent as a sign of fellowship to distant churches. This custom was familiar to Irenaeus. In the East it was forbidden by the Council of Laodicea in 365, but lasted on longer in the West. Such practices did not commend themselves to the mature judgment of the Church. The practice of reservation continued, but under due restrictions in church. The canon law required that it should be kept under lock and key. According to the first Prayer-Book of Edward VI the sick

---

[1] Cp. the similar statement of Article XXV: 'The Sacraments were not ordained of Christ to be gazed upon or to be carried about.'

[2] 'Ante omnem cibum' must surely mean 'before all food', not 'before every meal', though great names can be cited to support the latter translation. There is no evidence for communicating ordinarily more than once a day.

[3] Was the sacrament always or ever reserved in both kinds? Probably, as a rule, only the Bread was reserved, but at the time of receiving a fragment was placed in a cup of wine, which was thus regarded as consecrated. This certainly was the usage in some places. (See Wordsworth, *Holy Communion*, p. 266 and the references to reservation in Dix, *The Shape of the Liturgy*.)

might be communicated with the reserved sacrament on the same day as a celebration in church. In the second Prayer-Book this permission was withdrawn: there was a very real danger of conveying the sacrament away and using it for superstitious purposes.[1] In 1662 the present rubric was added enjoining the consumption in church of all the consecrated elements at the close of the service. The primary object of this was to forbid not reservation but the irreverent carrying of the elements out of church for ordinary consumption, which the Puritans were quite capable of doing. But indirectly the rubric forbids all reservation, and even the primitive custom of taking away their portion to the sick. This is a real loss, since every communion of the sick involves a separate private celebration. Happily many bishops have allowed reservation for this purpose under proper conditions—a great relief in crowded parishes, especially as all sickrooms are not adapted for private celebrations.

The Article is aimed at reservation when practised not only for purposes of communion, but in order to provide a localized object of worship. This is a comparatively modern and entirely distinct practice. It is a use of the sacrament that diverges widely from the declared intention of Christ. It arose in the dark ages and received a great impulse through the assertion of Transubstantiation. The Pyx, or receptacle, at or above the altar containing the reserved sacrament, came increasingly to take a prominent place in the eyes of worshippers. In 1264 the festival of Corpus Christi was instituted and the Blessed Sacrament was exposed for worship. So the central act of the modern Roman service of Benediction is the blessing of the congregation by the priest with the consecrated Host.

(ii) Carrying about the Host in procession is only an extension of the same practice. Such a procession came soon to be one of the chief ceremonies of Corpus Christi, though it appealed too largely to the popular taste to be confined to that day.

(iii) The lifting up or elevation of the Host after consecration in order to be adored by the people was first introduced about A.D. 1100 and is on a level with the previous practices. This elevation must not be confused with the manual acts during the prayer of consecration, when the priest solemnly reproduces the action of Christ at the Last Supper and takes up the bread and the cup. Nor yet again has this elevation any connexion with that usually found in oriental liturgies, where, after the Lord's Prayer and before the Fraction, the priest lifts up the elements with the words 'holy things for holy men', as a preliminary to communion. Elevation for adoration was supposed to signalize the actual moment of consecration. It was expressly forbidden in the first Prayer-Book of Edward VI.[2]

---

[1] Cp. the last rubric at the end of the Communion Office of 1549.

[2] In the silent Canon of the mediaeval Mass the Elevation did at least direct the attention of the people to what was being done at the altar. But it gave rise to the unfortunate consequence that for the people the main motive of eucharistic worship

(iv) If Christ is present in the Eucharist, most certainly He is then as always to be adored. But this, as we have seen, is quite different from adoration of the Blessed Sacrament divorced from Eucharistic worship. We have no ground for believing that He gave us the Eucharist in order to dwell among us to-day by an abiding external presence as during His earthly life or to afford a visible object of adoration. Nor, again, are we justified in that absolute identification of our Lord with the outward sign that is implied in modern Roman devotions.

Finally, let us gladly admit that in these practices as allowed by the Church of Rome to-day we do find the expression of very deep and real devotion to our Lord. But we maintain that that devotion is purchased at a great cost.

Since there is a vigorous movement to introduce not only individual, but corporate devotions before the reserved Sacrament, including Benediction, into the Church of England, we will develop more fully the objections to such practices felt by many who believe wholeheartedly in the Real Presence in the Sacrament and are in full sympathy with the general Catholic position. These innovations are defended on two main grounds, first that they are a natural development of Reservation for the sick and have behind them the authority of the Western Church, and secondly that experience both on the Continent and in England shows that they promote devotion and win many to Christ.

In reply we protest that these practices are not so much practices of the Catholic Church as of the Counter-Reformation. They have no authority in Scripture or primitive custom. Even the learned Roman Catholic, Father Thurston admits that 'In all the Christian literature of the first thousand years, no one has apparently yet found a single clear and definite statement that any person visited a church in order to pray before the Body of Christ which was kept upon the altar.'[1] So, too, the Orthodox Churches of the East reserve the Sacrament, usually on the Altar, with a lamp burning before it. Not only does the intervention of the Screen and the Holy Doors shut it out from any possibility of adoration by the people, but even those who enter the Sanctuary make no sign of reverence as they pass before it. No one can deny the belief of the Eastern Churches in the Real Presence, but here, as so often, they preserve ancient tradition. Only in the West has the cult of the reserved Sacrament been developed. The beginnings of this are to be found in the Middle Ages, but the full growth was accelerated by reaction against the minimizing views of Protestant reformers in lands which did not accept the Reforma-

became the desire to see the Host. The Reformers rightly regarded this as a perverted piety.

[1] Note in Bridgett, *A History of the Holy Eucharist in Great Britain*, p. 170. On the case of Gorgonia (Gregory of Nazianzum, *Orat.* viii. 18), which Father Thurston regards as irrelevant, see *C.Q.R.*, April, 1918, p. 119 ff.

tion. Thus these practices are relatively a late development, at least in the form in which we are asked to accept them to-day, and the authority behind them is not that of the Catholic Church but of the Roman Church since the Reformation.

This is not in itself a ground of condemnation. They may be healthy and legitimate developments, a fresh adaptation of old forms of worship to meet new demands and circumstances. We must examine them in the light of reason and of the fruits that they produce.

Theologically it is hard to find a satisfactory defence. We hold that the Christian religion has a twofold foundation, Christian experience and historic fact. Both are necessary. Each reinforces the other. In order that experience may be kept Christian, it needs constantly to be tested by the New Testament. In support of the doctrine of the Eucharist, we can appeal not only to Christian experience throughout the ages and to the intrinsic moral and spiritual value of its symbolism, but also to the mind and promise of Christ as revealed in the historical facts of its institution. The sense of His presence and of the new life that He imparts is no mere product of collective imagination. It is guaranteed by His actual word and act. But there is nothing in His institution or in the outward signs to suggest in any way that He gave us the Eucharist in order that through the consecrated elements He might dwell among us to-day by an abiding external presence comparable to His presence during His life on earth. 'The Presence is given under a form which indicates that it is to be received.' Any other use is not only unauthorized and goes beyond the declared purpose of Christ, but is in danger of obscuring that purpose by suggesting that 'the value of the Sacrament is intended to reside in itself'.[1] No doubt certain critics hold that the Eucharist was not instituted by Christ Himself, but by the Christian Church, in imitation of mystery cults, though under the guidance of the Holy Spirit. On this view it is quite possible to argue that the Church may be equally inspired to adapt it to new uses, and the appeal to historic fact falls to the ground. Benediction may be defended, as it is by certain Modernists, as a piece of edifying symbolism, but no more. This is perfectly consistent Modernism, but will hardly commend itself to most advocates of these practices. It is precisely because we uphold both the importance of historic facts and also the objective nature of the Eucharistic Presence, that we hesitate to support these developments. In the Church of Rome they are defended by an appeal to the infallible authority of the Church. This is a dangerous argument for Anglicans, since the same authority pronounces that their orders are no orders and their sacraments are no sacraments. Judged by the principles for which the Church of England stands, the theology of these practices is precarious.

[1] W. Temple, *Christus Veritas*, p. 241.

Attention must be called to another theological danger. While it is plain that they do not necessarily presuppose transubstantiation, yet as a matter of history their development was largely due to the promulgation of that doctrine, and the arguments commonly used by Roman Catholics to urge their value are bound up with transubstantiation. The practice of visits to the Tabernacle is advocated on the ground that the Presence granted to the recipient in communion is withdrawn at a certain stage of the digestion of the elements. Thus a writer in the Month can say, 'Of course to have Him in our hearts in Holy Communion is more in itself than to have Him near to us in the tabernacle. But we have Him in Holy Communion only for a few minutes at a time, and in proportion as we believe this and take it to heart is our desire to seek His Presence in the tabernacle again and again.' Such theology is a denial of the truth that the sacred Humanity of Christ dwells in all true believers. It is a practical contradiction of the teaching of S. John's Gospel that union with the ascended Christ through the Holy Spirit maintained and deepened through the Sacraments is a better substitute for the relationship that the disciples enjoyed during His earthly ministry.

Again the Eucharist has many aspects. It embraces in one glorious complexity the many-sided richness of Christian grace and truth. It is the meal of God's family, the means of fellowship both with Christ and with one another through Him, the Christian sacrifice, the commemoration of His redeeming victory on the Cross and so on. It includes both the feeding of our souls and our self-oblation to the Father through Him. The extra-liturgical use of the Sacrament tends to abstract and isolate one element, the Presence of Christ, and to destroy the proportion of truth so as to suggest a local and material Presence. The whole conditions suggest a Presence on a level with the visible and material order. 'The Prisoner of the Tabernacle' is a phrase that sums up this tendency and is hard to reconcile with S. Paul's vision of a Christ who fills all things. The inevitable result of this emphasis is that a church where the Sacrament is not reserved is regarded as an 'empty' church, a place where prayer is less effective and God further off. All services, not only Mattins, but Evensong, which do not bear on the use of the Sacrament are to be depreciated. The divine omnipresence is in danger of being forgotten. It is one thing to regard the sacraments as the means by which One who is always present, becomes present in a unique and supremely characteristic manner for a special purpose. It is quite another thing to limit His effective presence to the Sacramental presence. There is a danger of encouraging a view of God which is less than Christian, and of ignoring His active presence in the universe. We must always remember that the most fundamental question of all religion is our idea of God.

When we pass on to the fruits of these practices in life and devotion, from the nature of the case the evidence is less clear. It cannot be denied that many find these forms of worship attractive, though their attraction seems to be limited to certain temperaments, and they repel many, where they are not enforced and where all criticism is not forbidden by the iron discipline of the Church of Rome. Even though piety is stirred and the love of Christ deepened, as indeed we should expect from any forms of devotion that led men to contemplate Him, this does not prove that they are the best way. History shows that the degradation of religion has often been the fruit of the surrender to the popular desire for forms of worship that roused the maximum of emotion with the minimum of moral and spiritual, not to say intellectual effort. When we turn to the wider results of Counter-Reformation piety, while we gladly find much to admire, we do not believe that the very limited type of Christianity that is produced represents the highest Christian ideal. One important and objective piece of evidence is the quality of the devotional literature that the cult has inspired. If we take away those forms that are in origin Eucharistic, it is strangely sentimental and childish. The worship of God demands all our faculties, reason included, and where reason is ignored poverty of worship must in the long run result. The whole devotional atmosphere of modern Romanism is too often alien from that of the New Testament. Not only do these innovations in worship tend as it were to swallow up and depreciate the recitation of the divine office until the whole of Christianity seems to centre round the Blessed Sacrament, but reason and conscience are starved. Just as theology, if it is to remain alive and human, must keep in the closest touch with devotion and practical Christian effort, so devotion if it is not to become one-sided and relaxed, must not be divorced from the activity of the mind and the moral sense.[1]

---

[1] The following considerations, among others, would probably now be urged by those who take a different view of extra-liturgical devotions from that maintained in the text. (1) In the later Middle Ages the desire to see the Host at the elevation and the extra-liturgical use of the sacrament became dominating elements in popular eucharistic piety and tended to displace completely the participation of the people in the whole eucharistic action, especially since the reception of Holy Communion was very infrequent. This represented a fundamental perversion of eucharistic doctrine and practice, and fully explains the strictures of the Reformers on any use of the sacrament outside the liturgy and their positive desire to insist on the participation of the people in the whole rite, to emphasize the reception of communion as integral to it, and to encourage more frequent reception. In the situation then existing these measures were salutary and necessary. (2) At the present day in the Church of England the question of extra-liturgical devotions arises in a context very different from that of mediaeval times. In quarters where the desire for such devotions exists, frequent communion is usual and is not, according to the evidence available, endangered where these devotions are practised. (3) If reservation be conceded, the devotional use of the reserved sacrament is not mainly, and certainly not exclusively, a doctrinal issue. 'The real question is, is the devotional use of the reserved sacrament a good and desirable kind of prayer?' Can it be so ordered as to promote a right total eucharistic practice and not to disturb its true balance? Much will depend not only on the whole context of teaching and practice in a particular parish in which the sacrament is used devotionally outside the liturgy, but also on the character of the prayers and hymns used in the

A distinct question is that of church discipline. Even if we grant that the extra-liturgical use of the Sacrament is desirable, it cannot be said that it is essential. It falls within the power of the local church to regulate it. All who by their own free choice are admitted to minister in the Church of England promise on oath to use only the services of the Book of Common Prayer or such as are ordained by lawful authority. By Catholic custom the use of the reserved Sacrament falls under the control of the Bishop. To hold Exposition or Benediction in defiance of the Bishop of the Diocese is an Anglican peculiarity for which there is nothing to be said from the standpoint of Catholic order. It is indeed often argued that the parish priest has the inherent right to reserve for the sick in virtue of ancient canon law which has never been repealed. Even this however is disputable in face not only of the long desuetude of the custom, but of the independent legislation in another sense, through the deliberate provision in the Prayer-Book of the office for private communion. Even here if we are to have reservation, it should be by the authority of the episcopate.[1]†

ARTICLE XXX

Of both Kinds	*De utraque specie*
The Cup of the Lord is not to be denied to the lay-people. For both the parts of the Lord's Sacrament, by Christ's ordinance and commandment, ought to be ministered to all Christian men alike.	Calix Domini laicis non est denegandus, utraque enim pars Dominici Sacramenti, ex Christi institutione et praecepto, omnibus Christianis ex aequo administrari debet.

Composed by Archbishop Parker in 1563.

§ 5. There is no evidence whatever to support the present Roman custom of denying the cup to the laity either in Scripture or in the use of the primitive Church. At the Last Supper those present all drank of the cup (Mk 14[23]). At Corinth all alike received in both kinds. S. Paul could write, 'Let a man prove himself and so let him eat of the bread and drink of the cup' (1 Cor 11[28]). The account of Justin Martyr is conclusive for the custom of the Church in the second century. Indeed, it is admitted by Roman theologians that

---

special service. If these are restricted to what is sound and healthy, it is unlikely that this form of devotion to our Lord can produce undesirable effects or lead to distorted views.

[1] Provision for reservation under severe restrictions was made in Proposed Prayer-Book of 1928 (cp. the Book as proposed in 1927). A parish priest who wishes to reserve continuously for the purpose of communion does not now in general find that episcopal assent is withheld.

till the twelfth century communion in Church was always given in both kinds.[1] The only possible exception was when the sacrament was reserved for the absent or the sick. But even here it is doubtful whether there is any decisive evidence for communion in one kind only. Justin Martyr makes it quite clear that in his day the deacons carried both elements to those who were not present. Jerome at the end of the fourth century speaks of a certain bishop who carried about 'The Lord's body in a wicker basket and His blood in a vessel of glass'.[2] Whether this refers to his practice when visiting the sick or when on a journey, we cannot tell. The more common custom was to consecrate wine afresh for the communion of the sick by adding to it a particle of the consecrated bread. Sometimes the consecrated bread that was reserved for this purpose had been moistened before reservation with consecrated wine from the chalice. More often it was reserved by itself.[3] But in either case the fresh wine was deemed to be consecrated by the intinction of the consecrated bread. Usually the sick man's communion was made in a single act. We find words of administration for this purpose, such as 'The Body and Blood of the Lord be unto thee remission of all thy sins'. It is going too far to say that we can prove that in early days communion was always given in both kinds. But the prevalence of such customs as these proves that such was the desire of the Church where possible. They have been retained in the Eastern Church.[4]

Further, communion in one kind, so soon as it appeared, was vigorously denounced by the highest authorities of the Church. In the middle of the fifth century certain Manichaeans refused to drink of the cup and Pope Leo commanded that they should be excommunicated. At the close of the same century Pope Gelasius, hearing that some after receiving the Body, from some motive not explained, 'abstained from the cup,' ordered that they should 'either receive the Sacraments entire or be repelled from them altogether because the division of the one and the same Mystery cannot take place without a huge sacrilege'. This utterance was inserted in Gratian's collection of canon law and at a later date had to be explained away. The Schoolmen were equal to the task, and Aquinas boldly refers it to the consecrating priest alone.

At the close of the eleventh century the custom of communicating in one kind only began to be adopted unofficially. The motive was probably convenience, the avoidance of any danger of spilling the wine. It was condemned by the Council of Clermont in 1095, and again by Pope Paschal II in 1118. But the practice spread during the next two centuries and was defended by ecclesiastical writers. The

[1] *E.g.* Cardinal Bona, quoted by Wordsworth, *Holy Communion*, p. 268.
[2] Ep. 125, § 20.
[3] See Freestone, *The Sacrament Reserved*, and the comments on his conclusions by Harris in *Liturgy and Worship*, p. 548.
[4] For evidence see Wordsworth, *Holy Communion*, p. 263 ff.

change was made gradually. Aquinas, who died in 1274, only speaks of it as the custom of many churches. Evidence of the survival of primitive practice is found as late as the middle of the fourteenth century. When the Council of Constance met in 1415 it was widely hoped that the abuse would be checked. Unhappily communion in one kind was formally adopted as the official practice of the Church. The Council claimed for the Church the power of ordering that the sacrament should be given to the laity in one kind only. 'Though in the primitive Church this Sacrament was received under both kinds, yet has this custom been introduced ... that it should be taken by the celebrants under both kinds and by the laity under the kind of Bread only. . . . Wherefore since this custom has been introduced by the ¡Church and the holy Fathers on reasonable grounds and has been very long observed, it is to be accounted for a law.'

The reason alleged for the denial of the cup to the laity was commonly the risk of irreverence. Another reason was the danger of giving the simple occasion to 'think that Jesus is not entire under each species'. When the practice had become general, this last was the theological defence attempted for it. It was held that 'as much is contained under either kind as under both', for the whole Christ, both body and blood, is received under both. This doctrine, known as 'Concomitance', is, to say the least, the purest speculation. It makes assertion about matters that are clearly outside our knowledge. It can claim no support from Scripture or early teaching.

At the Reformation the restoration of the cup to the laity was demanded in the Lutheran Confession of Augsburg. In England it was restored immediately after the death of Henry VIII. But the Roman Church refused to abolish the existing custom. At the Council of Trent the doctrine of 'Concomitance' was distinctly affirmed. It was asserted that communion in one kind was sufficient and that the Church had power to ordain it. All who denied these assertions were anathematized. It is true that a section was added to the canons on this subject promising that at the earliest opportunity the Council would consider whether some relaxation of the rule might be allowed. But the opportunity has never arrived. At this day the Church of Rome is fettered by the decrees of Trent.

The practice is utterly indefensible. Not only does it rest on a precarious theological speculation, but it is in open disobedience to the express command of Christ. It is defended as a useful ecclesiastical regulation. The Church has, indeed, authority to decree rites and ceremonies, but not in contradiction to Scripture and to our Lord's own words. It cannot be denied that the practice has a certain practical convenience. But we cannot set that against the plain direction of Christ. The danger of irreverence can be reduced to a minimum. The Church of England in company with the Churches of the East is content to hold fast to the primitive and Scriptural practice.[1] *Both parts of the Lord's Sacrament by Christ's ordinance and commandment ought to be ministered to all Christian men alike.*

ARTICLE XXXI

Of the one Oblation of Christ finished upon the Cross

The offering of Christ once made is the perfect redemption, propitiation, and satisfaction, for all the sins of the whole world, both original and actual, and there is none other satisfaction for sin but that alone. Wherefore the sacrifices of Masses, in the which it was commonly said, that the Priests did offer Christ for the quick and the dead, to have remission of pain or guilt, were blasphemous fables, and dangerous deceits.

De unica Christi oblatione in cruce perfecta

Oblatio Christi semel facta, perfecta est redemptio, propitiatio, et satisfactio pro omnibus peccatis totius mundi, tam originalibus quam actualibus. Neque praeter illam unicam est ulla alia pro peccatis expiatio. Unde missarum sacrificia, quibus vulgo dicebatur, sacerdotem offerre Christum in remissionem poenae, aut culpae, pro vivis et defunctis, blasphema figmenta sunt, et perniciosae imposturae.

In substance dates from 1553. Only slightly altered later. The decrees of Trent on this subject were not issued till 1562, hence the doctrine attacked is not official Roman teaching but popular mediaeval ideas. It asserts

(i) The uniqueness and all-sufficiency of the sacrifice of the Cross;

(ii) The falsity of any view that made each Mass a sacrifice independent of or additional to the sacrifice of the Cross.

§ 6. The Eucharistic Sacrifice

(*a*) The New Testament says very little in detail about the Eucharist as a sacrifice, but it leaves no doubt, wherever it is mentioned, that the Church regarded it as such. In 1 Cor 10[14-21] S. Paul's argument rests upon an identity of principle between the Christian Eucharist and the sacrificial meals of the Jews and heathen. He speaks of the 'table of the Lord', which in Old Testament language is simply a synonym for 'altar' (Mal 1[7 and 12], Ezek 41[22], 44[16]). In the Eucharist no less than in these sacrifices, those who eat, have communion with the altar, that is with God, who is represented by the altar. Hence the inconsistency of attendance at the Christian Eucharist and at idolatrous sacrifices. 'Ye cannot partake of the table of the Lord and of the table of devils.' So, again, in the Epistle to the Hebrews we read, 'We have

[1] To attempt to suggest what loss of grace the Church of Rome inflicts upon its laity would be to indulge in speculation as unprofitable and unprovable as that on which the doctrine of concomitance is based.

an altar whereof they have no right to eat, who serve the tabernacle'
(13¹⁰). A sound scholarship forbids us to limit 'altar' here to the
actual table. But the reference to the Eucharist is unmistakable, and
the words imply a sacrifice present comparable to those of the old
covenant, of which the members of the new Israel partake as Israel
after the flesh did of theirs. So, too, when we turn to the accounts of
the institution the whole tone and structure are sacrificial. It is true,
indeed, that the words 'Do this' (τοῦτο ποιεῖτε) in themselves mean
no more than 'perform this act'. Attempts have been made to press
the translation 'sacrifice this'. In the Septuagint ποιεῖν is undoubtedly
used in the sense of 'sacrifice' or 'offer'; but only when the context
demands it. In itself it is as vague as the English verb 'do'. None of
the early Fathers, with the single exception of Justin Martyr, understand the words here as meaning in themselves more than 'do this'.
Again, the word 'remembrance' (ἀνάμνησις) is employed in the Septuagint in a sacrificial sense (cp. Heb 10³). But in this case also the
word in itself is quite indeterminate. Who is reminded and of what
he is reminded, depend solely upon the context. The fact, however,
still remains that both the manner and circumstances of the institution leave no doubt of the sacrificial nature of the Eucharist. The
'Body' and 'Blood' mentioned in separation recall the pouring out of
the blood in sacrifice. They are given not simply 'to' you, but 'for
you' (ὑπὲρ ὑμῶν), i.e. on your behalf. It is clear that our Lord's Body
and Blood are not only our spiritual food: they are that because they
are first the sacrifice that prevails for us.[1] The words 'This is my
blood of the covenant' (Mt 26²⁸) or 'This is the new covenant in my
blood' (1 Cor 11²⁵) are an echo of the words of the covenant-sacrifice
of Exodus 24 (quoted Heb 9²⁰). The whole service is the Passover of
the new Israel.

In the early Church the Eucharist is from the first spoken of in
sacrificial language.[2] It is called the 'spiritual' and 'un-bloody'
sacrifice. It is viewed by Irenaeus and the Fathers generally as the
'pure offering' foretold by Malachi (1¹¹). The heathen world was full
of sacrifices. The Church could hardly have avoided explaining her
worship in terms of sacrifice. The question still remains in what sense
she employed them. Gradually the Church made clear to herself all
that was implicit in the Eucharist from the first. She found in it at
once the fulfilment and the correction of those imperfect ideas and
aspirations that were embodied in Jewish and heathen sacrifices.

(b) As we have already seen, several distinct ideas underlay the
sacrificial worship of the Jews and heathen, and these ideas were not
sharply defined. Sacrifice was a gift or tribute, an expression of
homage. It was also a means of propitiation and a means of com-

---

[1] The phrase the 'bread of God' (Jn 6³³) may in itself be sacrificial (cp. Lev 21⁶, etc.,
where it refers to the sacrifice as a whole, originally perhaps regarded as the actual
food of Jehovah).

[2] See, for instance, Gore, *Body of Christ*, p. 157.

munion. Through the common sacrificial meal the union between the worshippers and their God was strengthened. All these ideas run into one another and find their expression in the Christian Eucharist.

(i) What the Church offers to God in the first instance is simply bread and wine, as a token of homage and dependence upon Him, and an act of thanksgiving for His mercies of creation and redemption. In Old Testament sacrifices thoughtful Jews had come to discern that the worth of a sacrifice in the eyes of God lay not in its intrinsic value, as if God needed man's gifts, but in the spirit of the man who offered it (e.g. Ps 50$^{5-17}$, 51$^{16-17}$, 69$^{30-31}$). In early days the people brought their offerings to God in kind as an expression of thanksgiving. The bread and wine actually used in the Eucharist were taken from these offerings of the faithful. So to-day the oblations of bread and wine and the collection of money which takes place at the same point in the service are in origin and significance one and the same act. The connexion between them is preserved in so far as the bread and wine are the gifts of the whole congregation as being bought out of the alms.

(ii) Then in the prayer of consecration the Church in obedience to our Lord's command performs in remembrance of Him those acts that He Himself performed at the Last Supper. We pray that our earthly oblations of bread and wine may, by the power of the Holy Spirit, be united with the heavenly oblation of our Lord. God, so to say, shows His acceptance of our offerings by giving them back to us charged with the fruits of our Lord's passion, to be the spiritual food of His body and blood. In the early liturgies the effect of consecration is expressed indifferently either as the descent to earth of the Heavenly Presence of our Lord or as the lifting up to Heaven of our gifts, there on the heavenly altar to be united with Him. The truth that they strive to express is that heaven and earth are made one.[1] So in the Holy Eucharist our Lord is present in His Heavenly glory, to be the food of our souls, and since He is present, His sacrifice is present too. Our Lord presides at the Board not only as Host but as Priest. 'He pleads by what He is.' His presence in Heaven eternally intercedes for us, and His presence in the Eucharist is no less a presence of intercession. We, as His members, join with Him in presenting His sacrifice before the Father.

> 'Having with us Him that pleads above,
> We here present, we here spread forth to Thee,
> That only offering perfect in Thine eyes,
> The one true pure immortal sacrifice.'

Thus, what the Church does in the Eucharist is on a level, not with what our Lord did once for all on Calvary, but with what He is now

---

[1] Cp. the language of the Leonine Sacramentary:

'On Thy altars, O Lord, we thankfully offer earthly gifts that we may win heavenly: we give earthly things that we may receive eternal.'

doing in Heaven. That death can never be repeated. Through it He has become all that He now is. Our Lord's historical acts 'had value only as expressing and perfecting His will, and they live eternally in the will expressed and "perfected" through them: so that He offers Himself for ever. Through the commemorative thanksgiving the Church co-operates with the eternal act of His will and offers Him to the Father.'[1] Our Lord, as the 'Lamb that hath been slain', is an eternal and abiding sacrifice, interceding for us by His presence in Heaven. In the Eucharist we on earth join with Him in pleading His sacrifice, even as He pleads it above.[2]

> 'His manhood pleads where now it lives
>   On Heaven's eternal throne,
> And where in mystic rite (*i.e.* the Eucharist) He gives
>   Its presence (*i.e.* the presence of His manhood) to His own.'

As His members we identify ourselves with our Head. As 'in Christ', we hold up before the Father His Cross and Passion, as

---

[1] Article 'Sacrifice in N.T.' by F. E. Brightman, p. 768*b*, Murray's *Bible Dictionary*. The whole article should be studied.

[2] It is important to notice two ambiguities that lurk under the expression 'the finished sacrifice of Christ'. The word 'sacrifice' may mean either 'the act of sacrificing' or 'the victim sacrificed'. If it is used in the first sense our Lord's sacrifice is an act that lies in the past. If it is used in the second sense, 'our Lord is our sacrifice', He is the 'Lamb as it had been slain'. Again, the word 'finished' may mean no more than 'past', 'no longer going on,' as, *e.g.* a day is 'finished' when it comes to an end. But it may also mean 'completed', 'able to do its work,' as, *e.g.* a house is finished when we can live in it. More than half the controversies about the Eucharistic sacrifice have turned on a confusion in the use of these two words. In one sense we rightly speak of the finished sacrifice of Christ, meaning that He has died and risen and ascended and will never die again. In another sense, no less rightly, we regard our Lord Himself as an abiding sacrifice. Through all that He has accomplished, He has become the perfect instrument of our redemption. He is for all eternity 'the Lamb that hath been slain' (ὡς ἐσφαγμένον, Rev 5⁶), *i.e.* alive through death. 'He is' (not was) 'the propitiation for our sins' (1 Jn 2²). It is through the living and glorified Christ, not simply through what He once did, but through what He now is, that we have access unto the Father (Eph 2¹⁶⁻¹⁸). In other words, His sacrifice is finished in that we can now enjoy all its benefits. The one view that contradicts all Scripture teaching is to maintain that our Lord's death is in any sense repeated.

Certain teachers of very different schools of thought have used language that implies that in the Eucharist we feed on the Body and Blood of the dead Christ: that we go, in the words of Bishop Andrewes, 'ad cadaver,' or in the words of a leading Evangelical teacher, that 'The *res sacramenti* is not Christ as He now is, but Christ's Body and Blood as separated in Sacrificial Death for our sins.' In other words, at each communion 'by the omnipotency of Christ's word the actual moment of His redemptive death upon the Cross is made to be present again to faith'. Such a view would seem to demand a new miracle at each Eucharist no less than the doctrine of Transubstantiation demands it. Further, it rests on an unreal distinction between the sacrificed and the glorified Body. There is but one Body of Christ, that which has passed through death to glory. His Body is not νεκρόν but ἐσφαγμένον. The view in question is anxious to safeguard the immediate connexion between the Eucharist and Calvary. But it rests on a false antithesis. The Crucifixion and the Ascended Life of our Lord are in the most intimate connexion. The latter derives its saving potency solely from the former. It is as He that 'became dead and liveth' (Rev 1¹⁸) that Christ is our Saviour. Just as the saving efficacy of the Cross lives on in the living Christ, so in the Eucharist our faith rests not on a single act of past time but on an eternal present. (For a full discussion see Moberly, *Problems and Principles*, No. 5.)

being the realization of that antagonism to sin and filial obedience to the Father's will, which we would fain attain, but from which we know ourselves to fall short. We claim the forgiveness won for us. We thank God for the great act of redemption. We ask God, as it were, to look upon Christ as being that which by His grace we hope one day to become. Thus, through Christ we dare to enter into communion with the Father. He is our at-one-ment. Through Him we can enjoy that fellowship with God which ancient sacrifices aspired to achieve. And through Christ we offer our prayers and thanksgivings for our fellow-members in His Body and plead His death for all the faithful living and departed.

(iii) Not only do we commemorate all that our Lord has done for us, but in and through Him we offer ourselves to the Father. Our Lord in Heaven presents to the Father not only Himself but His Body, the Church. We, as parts or 'members' of Christ, filled anew by the act of communion with His life, join with Him in offering ourselves, 'our souls and bodies.' We in and with Him intercede for the whole Church, and offer to God the whole body of the faithful living and departed and ourselves as part of it. This is the culmination of the Eucharistic sacrifice. Not the mere presentation of Christ's sacrifice as something done for us or outside us, but rather our own self-identification with that sacrifice. In the language of S. Augustine, 'The whole redeemed city . . . is offered as a universal sacrifice to God by the high priest, who offered nothing less than Himself in suffering for us, that we might become the body of so glorious a head.' The priest who celebrates the Eucharist does not act simply as an individual, but as the minister and representative of the whole Body of Christ—not only the particular congregation gathered within the walls of a building, but the whole body of the faithful living and departed. Without our own self-oblation the Eucharistic sacrifice is incomplete. 'This is the Christian sacrifice, the many become one body in Christ. And it is this that the Church celebrates by means of the Sacrament of the Altar . . . when it is shown to her that in what she offers she herself is offered.'

(c) In such thoughts as these we find the Church making explicit to herself the wealth of meaning contained in her chief act of worship. It was her supreme act of homage, the commemoration of the atoning sacrifice of Calvary, the means of Communion. All that the old sacrifices prefigured found its fulfilment here. There is little or no attempt to construct any formal theological statement of the Eucharistic sacrifice till quite a late date. Even the earlier Schoolmen refrained from precise definitions on the subject. The corruption of doctrine attacked in our Article may be said to start from certain informal statements of Thomas Aquinas. These combined with current tendencies of popular religion to produce a debased and disproportionate teaching of the Eucharistic sacrifice. Not only did he define sacrifice as 'something done for the honour properly due to God in order to appease Him',[1] but he asserted that it involved a change of some kind in the object offered, as 'that animals were killed, that bread is broken and eaten and blessed.'[2] This a priori view is quite out of touch with history. It isolates the act of sacrifice and attempts to treat it independently of the results attained by sacrifice. We can hardly wonder if the fruit of such treatment is an abstract and one-sided theology. The study of the Eucharistic sacrifice got, as it were, shunted on to a very barren side-track. The absorbing question came to be, if Christ is the victim in every Eucharist, what change does He undergo in each offering, so that it may rightly be termed a sacrifice? Thomas Aquinas was far too good a theologian to suppose that the sacrifice of Calvary was in any sense repeated or added to in the Eucharist, but his definition of sacrifice was the parent of theories that came dangerously near such teaching.

Again, current practice lent itself to a distorted theology. By every analogy communion is an essential part of sharing fully in the Eucharistic sacrifice. In the first days of the Church every Christian attended the Eucharist as a matter of duty at least every Sunday and communicated. We hear first of non-communicating attendance at the close of the second century. Tertullian mentions those who on days other than Sunday did not wish to break their fast, and so were present at the service and took away the Lord's Body for private communion at home. Again, Clement of Alexandria contemplates its being left to the conscience of persons present to receive or not: but he states that such permission was only the practice of some. The habit of non-communicating attendance only became general when Christianity had become popular and the world had invaded the Church. Many Christians no longer desired to make the effort of frequent communion, nor indeed were spiritually capable of it. S. Chrysostom found it necessary to condemn the habit of substituting mere attendance at the Eucharist for communion, and allowed it only to those in the final stage of ecclesiastical penance. Otherwise he insisted that those who felt themselves unworthy to communicate ought to go out with the penitents. The same condemnation is found elsewhere, as, for instance, in the 'Apostolical Canons'. It is clear that the Church was being faced with a real problem, how to deal with the lowered standard of personal holiness in ordinary Christians, The problem was solved by allowing non-communicating attendance. This, at least, preserved the Lord's service as the chief service on the Lord's Day. Even so, those present were said to 'assist at the prayers' rather than 'assist at the Sacrifice'. As time went on infrequency of communion on the part of the lay-folk tended to increase. The well-meant attempt of the Lateran Council to enforce a minimum of once a year was perverted into a restriction of communion to once a year.

[1] *Summa*, III. 48. 3.   [2] *Summa*, IIa, IIae, 85. 3. *ad.* 3.

This inevitably tended to thrust into the background the great truth that the Eucharistic sacrifice culminates in the self-oblation of the whole Church. Stress was laid rather on the priest's part, and the priest was no longer regarded as the representative of the whole priestly body, but only as the representative of Christ. This tendency was furthered by the withdrawal of the cup from the laity.

Again, the Eucharist was at the first the common sacrificial meal of the united Christian brotherhood. Not till the fifth century do we hear of the possibility of more than one Eucharist in the same Church on the same day with rare exceptions. About 445 Pope Leo wrote to Bishop Dioscorus of Alexandria, pointing out that this rule might prevent some from offering the sacrifice, and urging him to bring Alexandria into line with Rome, where there was more than one celebration in a day in the same Church—'as often as there was a congregation to fill the Church.' The condition is worth notice. Gradually in the West there developed the ordinary method of the Middle Ages. Many priests celebrated daily. In many churches Masses were multiplied.[1] This development was partly due to a desire to suit the convenience of the congregation, more largely to the growing custom of saying Masses for special purposes. It received a great impetus by the growth of the doctrine of Purgatory. The whole system of chantries and the traffic in 'solitary Masses' were the result of this doctrine. The Mass came to be viewed chiefly as a means of delivering souls from Purgatory. Once again this increase in the number of Masses led to a diminution in the number of persons required to take part, until in 'Low Mass' all that remained was concentrated in the hands of the priest.[2]

So the idea of the Eucharist was externalized. The neglect of communion fixed attention on the moment of Consecration. Excessive attention was paid to the question of the relation of the elements to the presence of Christ. The consecration itself became regarded as the sacrificial act performed by Christ through the priest. The words of consecration were in danger of being viewed as a magical charm in obedience to which the miracle of transubstantiation took place. The priest came to be regarded, not as the organ of the whole priestly body, but as an individual possessed of certain wonderful powers. So the corporate aspect of the Eucharist was obscured. Again, as a result of the mechanical view of sacrifice, each Eucharist was regarded as having, so to say, a special value of its own and as purchasing an instalment of salvation. The more Masses that were offered, the greater amount of benefit was secured. Here again the influence of Thomas Aquinas was unfortunate. He asserted that the Sacrifice of

[1] In the East every church has still only one altar. The Eucharist is celebrated on Sunday and festivals.

[2] Here again the East shows its conservatism. Low Mass is unknown. The East preferred to maintain the full dignity of the Eucharist and to be content with fewer celebrations.

the Mass was efficacious in winning blessings for all who had a right disposition. This is capable of a perfectly right interpretation, but it was perverted into the teaching that the sacrifice of the Mass apart from Communion could automatically obtain blessings for those on whose behalf the priest intended to offer it, whatever their moral state. So attainment of salvation became little more than a question of getting sufficient Masses offered for oneself either in one's lifetime or after death. To meet the demand a worthless class of priests sprang up who earned their living simply by saying Masses.

Again, in later mediaeval teaching we find an idea that, while the sacrifice of the Cross availed only for the forgiveness of original sin, that of the Mass was instituted to make satisfaction for actual sins. This opinion was condemned in the Confession of Augsburg, which had influence on our Article XXXI. The Roman party repudiated any such teaching, and certainly after attention had been drawn to it the doctrine was not repeated. But the idea in question is found in sermons ascribed wrongly to Thomas Aquinas and was probably held by Catharinus, a bishop who was present at Trent. The existence of the sermons, whoever composed them, is proof that such a doctrine was taught.

The Church of England at the Reformation endeavoured to get back to a truer view of the Eucharist, one that preserved the due proportion of things, and was in complete accord with Scripture and primitive teaching. Hence the emphasis on communion as an integral part of Eucharistic worship, and the attempt, not altogether successful, to restore frequent communion. So this Article has its eye throughout on mediaeval abuses and on the attempt of the Council of Trent to shelter them as far as possible.

The offering of Christ, once made, is the perfect redemption, propitiation and satisfaction for all the sins of the whole world, both original and actual: and there is none other satisfaction for sin but that alone. This assertion of the atonement, similar in language to the opening words of the Prayer of Consecration, is only made here, as the structure of the Article shows, to be ground of the subsequent condemnation. It is based on Heb 7^{27}, $9^{14, \ 26-28}$, 10^{10}, where the death of Christ once for all ($\dot{\epsilon}\phi\acute{a}\pi a\xi$) is contrasted with the repeated sacrifices of the Jewish system (cp. Rom 6^{9-10}). *Wherefore the sacrifices of Masses in the which it was commonly (vulgo) said that the priests did offer Christ for the quick and the dead, to have remission of pain or guilt, were blasphemous fables and dangerous deceits.* The language is most carefully chosen. There is no denial of the Eucharistic sacrifice, but of current popular perversions of it, as embodied in the practical system of worship during the Middle Ages. The plural 'sacrifices' condemns any idea that each Eucharist is in any sense a repetition of the sacrifice once offered on Calvary or an addition to it, or that by multiplying Eucharists blessings could automatically be multiplied.

So, too, the plural '*Masses*' makes plain that the idea condemned is that each Mass possesses a supplementary value of its own. Again, the plural '*priests*' emphasizes the condemnation of this idea. So it is not 'the sacrifice of the Mass' but the '*sacrifices of masses*' that is condemned : not any formal theological statement of doctrine,—for such did not exist,—but popular errors (*quod vulgo dicebatur*).

The decrees of the Council of Trent bear evidence of a double purpose. As theologians they wished to preserve themselves from making the sacrifice of the Mass a repetition of that of Calvary. As ecclesiastical statesmen they did not wish to upset established ideas and practice. Hence on the one hand they distinguished between the bloody oblation of Calvary and the unbloody oblation of the Eucharist. The latter was instituted to be the representation of the sacrifice on the Cross, till Christ should come. Through this unbloody offering the fruits of the bloody offering are received. On the other hand, they spoke of the sacrifice of the Mass as 'truly propitiatory', a phrase capable of an innocent but also of a perverted meaning,[1] especially as it is elsewhere called 'a true and proper sacrifice' (*verum et proprium sacrificium*). From this dubious teaching of the Council of Trent have arisen two types of Roman teaching, the one minimizing, the other exalting, the Sacrifice of the Mass. Both, however, are hampered by the unsound tradition based on the teaching of Aquinas, which regards the destruction or physical modification of the victim as the essential part of sacrifice and connects the Eucharistic sacrifice, not with our Lord's Heavenly priesthood, but with His death on the Cross placed in an unreal isolation. The dominant school in the Church of Rome hold that in some sense Christ suffers change or destruction in each Mass and that the Eucharist is in virtue of this act a distinct sacrifice in itself. Christ is regarded as in each Mass undergoing a new humiliation, a new self-emptying.[2] As we saw, the latest Roman denial of our orders is based on our rejection of any such view which makes the sacrifice of the

---

[1] 'Now undoubtedly there are two senses in which an act may be said to be propitiatory. The act of Christ's sacrifice on the Cross had an original propitiatory power . . . all the power that any action of man can have for this end is a derived power, derived from Christ's sacrifice, from which any other sacrifice, the Eucharistic one included, borrows its virtue and without which it would be wholly null and void. There is then an original propitiation and a borrowed propitiation, a first propitiation and a secondary one. Why did the Fathers of Trent, when they had all human language at their command, deliberately choose to call the sacrifice of the Mass *vere propitiatorium*? They may have said that it was *vere propitiatorium* in the secondary sense; but no man can fail to see the misleading effect of such language and that nothing could have been easier to the divines of Trent, had they chosen, than to draw a far more clear distinction than they did between the sacrifice of the Mass and the sacrifice on the Cross' (Mozley, *Lectures and Theological Papers*, p. 216).

[2] Cp. Gore, *R.C. Claims*, p. 175, and Dom Chapman's reply. The statements of the Council of Trent appear to be the only definitions of the eucharistic sacrifice officially binding on Roman Catholics. Some modern Roman writers (*e.g.* de la Taille, Masure, Vonier) expressly reject the view that the eucharistic sacrifice involves any kind of 'immolation' of Christ other than that once made on the Cross.

Eucharist additional to that of Calvary. As long as it is taught, in however refined a form, the protest of our Article will not be out of date.

We need to get back to broader and truer notions of sacrifice. As we have seen, the culminating point of animal sacrifice was not the death of the victim but the presentation of the 'blood which is the life' before God. The death was not the climax, but rather the means through which the life was set free. So, too, a sacrifice does not necessarily involve a change or destruction of anything. The 'meal offering' and the shewbread were both sacrifices, and they are typical of a multitude of similar sacrifices found all over the world. The root idea of sacrifice is found to be communion rather than propitiation. The Roman interpretation of the sacrifice of the Eucharist rests on the later and debased mediaeval theology. Against it we appeal to a nobler and wider conception of sacrifice, more faithful alike to history and to Scripture.†

ARTICLES XXXVII–XXXIX

CHURCH AND STATE

ARTICLE XXXVII

Of the Civil Magistrates

The Queen's Majesty hath the chief power in this Realm of *England*, and over her dominions, unto whom the chief government of all estates of this Realm, whether they be Ecclesiastical or Civil, in all causes doth appertain, and is not, nor ought to be, subject to any foreign jurisdiction.

Where we attribute to the Queen's Majesty the chief government, by which titles we understand the minds of some slanderous folk to be offended; we give not to our princes the ministering either of God's Word, or of Sacraments, the which thing the Injunctions also lately set forth by *Elizabeth* our Queen doth most plainly testify: But that only prerogative, which we see to have been given always to all godly princes in holy Scriptures by God himself; that is, that they should rule all estates and degrees committed to their charge by God, whether they be Ecclesiastical or Temporal, and restrain with the civil sword the stubborn and evil-doers.

The Bishop of *Rome* hath no jurisdiction in this Realm of *England*.

De civilibus Magistratibus

Regia Majestas in hoc Angliae regno, ac caeteris ejus dominiis, summam habet potestatem, ad quam omnium statuum hujus regni, sive illi ecclesiastici sint, sive civiles, in omnibus causis, suprema gubernatio pertinet, et nulli externae jurisdictioni est subjecta, nec esse debet.

Cum Regiae Majestati summam gubernationem tribuimus, quibus titulis intelligimus animos quorundam calumniatorum offendi, non damus Regibus nostris, aut verbi Dei, aut Sacramentorum administrationem, quod etiam Injunctiones ab Elizabetha Regina nostra, nuper editae, apertissime testantur: sed eam tantum praerogativam, quam in sacris Scripturis a Deo ipso, omnibus piis Principibus, videmus semper fuisse attributam: hoc est, ut omnes status atque ordines fidei suae a Deo commissos, sive illi ecclesiastici sint, sive civiles, in officio contineant et contumaces ac delinquentes gladio civili coerceant.

Romanus pontifex nullam habet jurisdictionem in hoc regno Angliae.

420

The laws of the Realm may punish Christian men with death, for heinous and grievous offences.	Leges regni possunt Christianos propter capitalia, et gravia crimina, morte punire.
It is lawful for Christian men, at the commandment of the Magistrate, to wear weapons, and serve in the wars.	Christianis licet, ex mandato magistratus, arma portare, et justa bella administrare.

The history is important. In 1563 the whole of the opening paragraph was rewritten and the second paragraph added for the first time. Its objects were:

   (i) To explain and defend 'The Royal supremacy';
   (ii) To repudiate all papal jurisdiction;
   (iii) To condemn Anabaptist attacks on the authority of the State.

§ 1. The relations between Church and State

(a) We find in Scripture no formal discussion of the relations between Church and State. As we have seen, the Church is there pictured as a society with a life of its own, drawing a sharp distinction between those within and those without, exercising over its own members judicial authority in its own courts according to its own laws. Nothing is clearer than that the rules of the Church in no way depended upon the authority of the State. For instance, the Roman Empire had its own laws of marriage binding upon all its subjects alike. But the Church had her own far stricter laws of marriage based upon the teaching of Christ. These S. Paul claimed to enforce upon Christians. At the Council of Jerusalem definite rules were made on subjects about which the laws of the Empire had no concern, e.g. fornication and eating certain kinds of meat. On all questions of discipline and order the Church claimed to interpret the will of Christ under the guidance of the Spirit and demanded from her members obedience to her interpretation. She acted upon her own authority.

But since the Church existed within the Roman Empire she could not escape all relationship with it. In the very early days Christians would be regarded simply as a new Jewish sect. They shared the toleration accorded to Judaism. But it soon became apparent that Christianity was more than a reformed Judaism. As the Church developed an independent existence and a vigorous life of her own, conflict with the State became inevitable. The Roman Empire had a great suspicion of all smaller societies within itself. Christianity was a religion not sanctioned by law. The Church's very existence might at any time lay her open to the hostility of the State. Further, the State required of all who were not Jews a willingness to participate in idolatrous worship, especially the worship of the Emperor. Such commands Christians, out of loyalty to Christ, could not obey. Their refusal appeared an act of disloyalty to the Emperor. Again, civil and social life were so bound up with idolatry that it was almost impossible for Christians to take part in it. They were made to appear

unsocial and unpatriotic. Hence arose persecution and the attempts
to compel Christians to do sacrifice. Even the most reluctant witness
must confess that under such circumstances obedience to Christ was
inconsistent with obedience to the State.[1]

At the same time, the Church had no hostility to the State as such.
By His example and teaching Christ Himself had inculcated loyalty
to the civil power in its own sphere. He showed that Caesar's head on
the coinage implied the duty of paying taxes to Caesar. There was no
necessary conflict between the claims of Caesar and the claims of
God (Mk 12[13] ff.). He submitted Himself to the authority of Pilate as
being given to him from above (Jn 19[11]), so long as he acted within the
limits of his office (Jn 18[33] ff.). S. Paul commands whole-hearted
obedience to the civil authority. 'The powers that be are ordained
of God' (Rom 13[1-7]). S. Peter ends a long exhortation on the respect due to the State with the injunction (1 Pet 2[13-17]), 'Honour the
king'—a hard duty when Nero was on the throne. It is true that in
the Apocalypse we find denunciation of Rome as the persecutor of
Christians (Rev 13 and 17). Pergamum, the centre of the cult of the
Emperor in Asia Minor, is 'where Satan's throne is' (2[13]). But this
was hostility not towards the Empire as such, but towards the Empire
as persecuting Christians. In early Christian writers we find side by
side professions of loyalty to Emperor and bitter denunciation of
persecutors.[2]

(b) The accession of Constantine ushered in a new era. The State
had failed to suppress the Church. Constantine saw that the only
course was to make an alliance with the Church. Relations became
openly friendly. By the Edict of Milan universal toleration of all
religions was proclaimed. The laws of Constantine were tinged by
Christian morality, but they were not specifically Christian. The
clergy were given equal privileges with pagan priests. The Church was
allowed to receive gifts. During the lifetime of Constantine paganism
was discouraged and immoral worship put down, but it was left for
his successor to issue definite edicts against heathenism as heathenism. But very soon we find evidence of a tendency to be content no
longer with a mere alliance of Church and State, but to aim at something like identification. The State was ready to purchase the support
of the Church by lending the support of the secular arm for the sup-
pression of heretics or heathen. Before the close of the fourth century
heresy and paganism had become offences against the civil law.
Further, the State began to find in bishops valuable civil servants and
to assign to them a share in the civil administration. The Church had
in time to pay the price. If the Church's laws were enforced by the
power of the State upon those who defied them, the State might not

[1] Cp. Hobhouse, *The Church and the World*, p. 41, 'Christians were . . . persecuted
not so much for individual beliefs, as for being members of a Church and of a Church
which acknowledged no divided allegiance.'
[2] *E.g.* Tertullian, *ad Scap.* 2.

unreasonably claim a voice in the making and amending of such laws. If a bishop was an important government official, the State might not unreasonably expect to be consulted in his selection and appointment. Above all the Emperor assumed a position of supreme importance in the Church. If a heathen Emperor was a minister of God, a Christian Emperor was 'the Lord's anointed', endowed with an almost priestly office. Even Constantine could say 'You are bishops of matters within the Church: I also am the bishop ordained by God of matters without the Church.' The line of distinction between the Church and the State became more and more obliterated. A new ideal grew up of a great Christian commonwealth, at once State and Church, like Israel of old. Heresy was regarded not only as disloyalty to the Church but as treason to the State. Old Testament notions were freely applied. The State and the Church were regarded as two aspects of one visible Christian society, 'the City of God.' So far as the old conflict between State and Church survived, it passed into a conflict between the civil authorities and the spiritual authorities, regarded as different classes of officials in one and the same society. Since we are still suffering from the effects of this fusion of Church and State, it may be well to pause and consider some of the features of the change.

(i) The first result was a confusion between the principles of civil and the principles of ecclesiastical authority. The State has not only the right but the duty of compelling obedience to its laws, if need be, by methods of force. Such laws are binding upon all its subjects alike. On the other hand the Church, if she is loyal to the teaching of Christ, can only enforce obedience to her laws by spiritual penalties, in the last resort by expulsion from her fellowship. Further, she can only claim such obedience from her own children. Persecution and the employment of force to compel men to come into the Church or to submit to her laws is wrong and contrary to the spirit of the Gospel.[1] The source of all the Church's life and order is loyalty to Christ, and personal adhesion to Christ cannot be brought about by compulsion. If by persecution the Church could make men Christians, the Church would be right to persecute. But methods of force can only make nominal Christians: they cannot create a lively faith. The immediate result of the identification of Church and State was to flood the Church with nominal Christians. It cost less to profess to be a Christian than to make no profession.

(ii) Further, the authority of the Church should go deeper than that of the State. Civil legislation can never go very far in advance of public opinion. The State should indeed enforce the principles of universal morality. It has been well called 'the armed conscience of the community': but just because the community contains many who are not prepared to accept the full Christian standard of living, the

[1] For certain qualifications, see W. Temple, *Church and Nation*, pp. 16–19.

State cannot go beyond the public conscience of the day. The Church, on the other hand, is bound to enforce upon her members the full moral teaching of Christ: she asserts not only those laws of morality that the State asserts, but others which it would not be reasonable to expect any who are not Christians to accept. The confusion between the laws of the Church and the laws of the State inevitably resulted in a lowering of the Christian standard. The attempt to enforce full Christian morality could only end in failure. In popular practice the moral demands of Christ were identified with the average morality of the day—the morality of a world that had become Christian only in name. A double standard of Christian practice was set up. Full Christian morality was expected at most from the clergy. The laity were to be content with something less exacting.

(c) In mediaeval times the relations between Church and State were dominated by ideas that were inherited from earlier days. In theory the Emperor and the Pope were the two heads of one 'Holy Roman Empire'. In England the same ideal was reproduced in miniature. In Saxon times there was very considerable confusion between Church and State. There were no separate Church courts and no clear distinction between national and ecclesiastical assemblies. The fellowship between Church and State was so intimate and their mutual understanding so complete that there arose no necessity for any exact definition of their relationship. With the coming of the Normans England was brought into closer connexion with the Continent and the papacy. A separation was effected between civil and ecclesiastical courts. A distinction was recognized between the canon law which was administered in the Church courts and the common law which was administered in the civil courts. But Church and State were none the less identified. Every Englishman was regarded as *ipso facto* a member of the national Church. Whatever laws existed were enforced upon all Englishmen alike. Breaches of the Church's law were punished by civil penalties and breaches of civil law by ecclesiastical penalties. Excommunication involved not only loss of Church privileges but loss of civil rights.[1] When the Church claimed to withdraw her officers from the jurisdiction of the civil courts and to try them in her own courts, there was no idea of any rebellion against the State. The claim is rather to be viewed as a dispute between two sets of officials of one single Church-State as to the limits of their respective jurisdiction. Church and State were not even regarded as two distinct societies composed of the same people, but as one great all-

---

[1] It is from this point of view that we must consider persecution, namely, as the lending to the Church by the State of the force of secular authority in order to compel obedience to the Church's authority on questions of doctrine or practice. So in 1400 Parliament supported the Church by passing a statute for the burning of heretics, and fourteen years later by a supplementary Act put at the disposal of the Church the organization of the State for hunting out the Lollards. Heresy was regarded not only as disloyalty to the Church but as disloyalty to the State.

embracing divine society. The quarrels between kings and bishops were quarrels between heads of two departments in one community.[1]

This mediaeval point of view was destined to be shattered by the Reformation, but it explains many of the features of that troubled time. All parties persecuted because all parties could have no conception of a state of society in which more than one religion was tolerated. Catholics and Protestants agreed that Church and State must remain co-extensive. They differed as to the nature of the Church that they desired. Even the Puritans for a long time did not wish to separate from the Church of England: they wished to change the Church of England into the kind of Church that they preferred and to make all Englishmen submit to it. Hooker can still write: 'There is not any man of the Church of England but the same man is also a member of the commonwealth; nor any man a member of the commonwealth, who is not also of the Church of England.'[2] Hooker did not suppose that the Church's spiritual authority was derived from the State or that the Church was simply a Government department for dealing with religion. But his eyes were blinded by the traditional thought and customs of centuries. He could not conceive of a day when Church and State should no longer be coextensive. Moreover, in Elizabeth's day it was easy to confuse the desire for national unity against external foes with the desire for the religious unity of the English nation. But even while Hooker wrote, his theory was breaking down. Elizabeth was, in practice, compelled to tolerate nonconformists even though they had to endure severe restrictions. Since her day the idea that the Church of England is simply the 'nation on its religious side' has become more and more contrary to the facts. The spread of toleration has wrecked any identification of Church and State. Quite rightly we enjoy the fullest toleration of all religious beliefs. With a very few exceptions the fullest rights of citizenship are granted to men of every creed or none. Accordingly a new situation has arisen, demanding a fresh consideration of the relations between Church and State.

§ 2. We may now turn to the changes in the relations between Church and State made at the Reformation.

(a) As we saw, the Church assigned to the Christian Emperor a

---

[1] 'The word Churchman means to-day one who belongs to the Church as against others. In the Middle Ages there were no others, or if there were they were occupied in being burnt. A Churchman meant one who belonged to the Church in the narrower sense of its governing body—an ecclesiastic, as the word implies; just as statesman to-day means not a member but an officer actual or potential of the State' (Figgis, *Churches in the Modern State*, p. 189). There were, of course, the Jews, who carried on a precarious existence without any assured rights, dependent upon the caprice or the poverty of the ruling classes. But no mediaeval Christian would have taken much account of the Jews.

[2] *Eccl. Pol.* viii.

unique position. He was regarded as the Lord's anointed, the successor of the sacred kings of Judah. In mediaeval theory the Emperor was the coequal head with the Pope of the City of God. So, too, in England there has been from the first a very real Royal Supremacy. It was in no sense created at the Reformation. Our Article asserts no new doctrine when it claims for Elizabeth '*that . . . prerogative which we see to have been given to all godly princes in Holy Scriptures by God Himself, that they should rule all estates and degrees committed to their charge by God, whether they be Ecclesiastical or Temporal, and restrain with the civil sword the stubborn and evildoers.*' In practice the Royal supremacy was exercised in the following directions:

(i) The King regarded himself as the guardian of justice within his realm. It was his duty to see to the safety of the bodies and property of his subjects. Their souls were in the care of the Church. As such he claimed to prevent any external power, such as the Pope, from exercising authority over persons or property within his kingdom, except by permission.[1] Further, he saw that the Church obeyed her own laws and did not encroach upon the authority of the State. New canons could only be made subject to the King's approval. The Supremacy 'was essentially, therefore, a regulating force, the function of which was to decide in what spheres and under what conditions the spiritual power which it recognized as independent in origin and authority should act.'[2] The King did not claim any spiritual authority. Rather he supervised the administration of the Church from outside.

(ii) But the King was no less the first layman of the Church and her champion. As such it was his duty to protect the Church and see that she had free scope for her work.

(*b*) We must consider the changes made by Henry VIII in the light of such ideas as these. What changes were actually made?

(i) The authority of the Pope was disallowed. In theory the jurisdiction claimed by the Pope was purely spiritual. The term 'papal supremacy' came to be used only after his power in England had come to an end. 'From the point of view of the King it was simply a part of the Church system which he allowed or disallowed so far as it seemed harmless or harmful to the realm at large.'[3] No doubt there were times, especially between the eleventh and fourteenth centuries, when the Pope claimed temporal authority in England. A weak King was not above purchasing the support of the Pope by allowing his claim to bestow the crown of England on whom he would. But any such recognition of papal authority was vigorously repudiated, *e.g.* in the statute of Praemunire, and was never generally allowed. So the relation of the Pope towards the English Church was a spiritual rela-

---

[1] In theory, at least, no appeal might be made from the Church courts to Rome without the royal permission. Papal legates needed the King's consent before landing in England. English bishops could only act as papal legates with the King's sanction.
[2] Wakeman, *History of the Church of England*, note D.
[3] Collins, *C.H.S. Lectures*, III .p. 34.

tion. There is no denying that, especially at certain times, he exercised very considerable authority over the English Church. It became customary for archbishops to receive from him the gift of the Pallium and to take an oath of obedience to him on receiving it. He often filled vacant sees. Appeals of all kinds were made to him. The theory came to be held that canon law derived its authority from the Pope, and hence the Pope and the Pope alone could dispense from it. Accordingly, we find an exceedingly strict and logical system of Church law which was in practice never observed, because it could be evaded by dispensations. Its strictness was only a source of profit to the papal officials. When we consider the very wide field that this system covered, we can see that the power of dispensation gave to the Pope immense political importance, *e.g.* in the matter of marriages. The immediate cause of Henry's breach with Rome was the refusal of the Pope to declare his marriage with Catherine null and void, and that refusal was based on purely political calculations. But England was tired of papal exactions. The loyalty of the Church to the Holy Father had expired under the burdens that he had laid upon her. In 1534 Convocation declared that 'The Pope of Rome hath no greater jurisdiction conferred on him by God in Holy Scripture, in this kingdom of England, than any other foreign Bishop.' The Church of England claimed that such jurisdiction over her as he had enjoyed had only been by her free consent. He had proved himself unworthy to exercise it, and therefore, since she was in no way bound to bestow it, it was taken away. This repudiation of papal authority was accepted by the whole Church under pressure from the Crown. 'The civil power forbade, under penalties, any recourse to the authority which, as a matter of fact, the Church of England had just repudiated.'

(ii) In 1531 Henry, in order to ensure the submission of the clergy, demanded the consent of Convocation to a new form of title. He claimed to be 'Supreme Head of the English Church and Clergy'. The title was accepted by Convocation, with the important qualification, 'so far as the law of Christ allows.' In a letter addressed to the Northern Convocation, Henry expressly disclaimed any new authority in spiritual matters. In 1534 he was recognized by Parliament as 'only supreme head on earth of the Church of England'. Further, in the same year the act for the submission of the clergy gave the authority of Parliament to arrangements already agreed to by Convocation in 1532. Convocation had consented that it should only meet by the King's writ and that new canons might only be promulgated by the King's license. On the other hand, the King's assent to the meeting and the promulgation of canons was not to be withheld arbitrarily. So far nothing revolutionary had been done. The novel title 'Supreme head' was capable of a good interpretation.[1] The control claimed by

---

[1] Cranmer, indeed, in his examination shortly before his death gave a very mild interpretation of the title: 'Every king in his own realm is supreme head.... Nero was

the Crown over ecclesiastical legislation was no greater than had been claimed by earlier kings: it was only made more positive and definite. On the other hand, 'Although it is true that nothing had been done except to define and formulate rights of the Crown in relation to the Church which had been frequently insisted upon and exercised in past ages, still it was equally true that their revival and exercise by a King of the character of Henry VIII at a time in the history of England when kingly authority was exceptionally strong, practically introduced a new state of things. There was no new principle involved in the relations of Church and State, but the mutual influence of the two bodies upon each other was altered.'[1]

(iii) But the use by Henry VIII of his supremacy did not stay here. The Supremacy Act in 1534 included among his powers 'full power and authority . . . to visit, repress, redress, reform, order, correct, restrain and amend all such errors, heresies, abuses, offences, contempts and enormities, whatsoever they be, which by any manner spiritual authority or jurisdiction ought or may lawfully be reformed . . . or amended.' This implied a claim not only to supervise the fulfilment of their proper duties by spiritual authorities but also himself to exercise spiritual jurisdiction. This new claim was exercised without any hesitation or scruple. After being dropped by Mary, it was revived by Elizabeth in the form of the Court of High Commission, which was only finally abolished in 1641. Further, in 1535 Henry delegated his powers to Cromwell, who carried out a visitation in the King's name. This was only one act that showed that the Crown claimed to govern the Church just in the same manner as it governed the State. There is no need to enter into details. It was a period of constitutional anarchy in Church and State alike. The Church was powerless in Henry's hands. He was restrained by no scruples from carrying out his will. No precedents for the use of the Royal Supremacy can fairly be quoted from such a time.

(c) The use of the title 'Supreme Head' was continued by Edward VI and by Mary up to the time of her marriage with Philip in 1554. It was then dropped and has never since been revived. When Elizabeth came to the throne in 1558 she only claimed the title 'Supreme Governor'. The 'Supreme Head' statute was never re-enacted. She was unwilling to be addressed as the head of the Church of England, maintaining 'that this honour is due to Christ alone, and cannot belong to any human being soever.' Accordingly the old Article was very largely rewritten, and our present Article simply explains the title 'Supreme Governor'—'*We attribute to the Queen's Majesty the chief*

head of the Church, that is in worldly respect of the temporal bodies of men, of whom the Church consisteth: for so he beheaded Peter and the Apostles. And the Turk, too, is head of the Church of Turkey. . . . The king is head and governor of his people which are the visible Church . . . wherein he was named supreme head of the Church, there was never other thing meant.'

[1] Wakeman, *History of the Church of England*, p. 215.

government.' Elizabeth took the greatest pains to define and limit the constitutional meaning of her supremacy. In 1559 she appended the Injunctions, 'An admonition to simple men deceived by the malicious,' referred to in our Article. This, in very similar language to the Article, insisted that she only claimed the authority 'of ancient time due to the Imperial Crown of this realm, that is, under God to have the sovereignty and rule over all manner of persons born within these, her realms, dominions and countries, of what estate, either ecclesiastical or temporal they be, so as no other foreign power shall, or ought to have, any superiority over them.' Further, the Queen wrote with her own hand the addition to Article XX stating that '*The Church*' (not the Crown) '*hath power to decree rites and ceremonies and authority in controversies of faith.*' In the Royal Supremacy, as defined in our present Article, there is nothing to which the Church can reasonably object. In practice it includes the following claims:

(i) No Englishman can claim to be withdrawn from the jurisdiction of the Crown in virtue of any office that he may hold in the Church. The Crown is to rule '*all estates and degrees committed to their charge by God, whether they be Ecclesiastical or Temporal.*'

(ii) The King is to be the guardian of all forms of justice. In the civil courts judges act in the King's name. They receive authority not to make but to interpret and administer laws. So in the enforcement of the Church's laws, the King, in virtue of his sacred office as first layman, is to dispense justice. That does not mean that he makes the laws of the Church or can alter them, but that he undertakes to see that the Church observes her own laws and that justice is meted out in accordance with them.

(iii) It is his duty to keep the balance between Church and State and to see that each side faithfully observes its side of the compact. Thus Queen Elizabeth in 1572 forbade Parliament to discuss bills concerning religion 'unless the same should be first considered and liked by the clergy'. Again, in 1593 she wrote to the Speaker: 'If you perceive any idle heads . . . which will meddle with reforming the Church or transforming the commonwealth and do exhibit any Bills to such purpose, that you receive them not, until they be viewed and considered of those who it is fitter should consider of such things and can better judge of them.'

§ 3. The relation of the Church of England to the State to-day can only be understood in the light of previous history. It is not the result of the consistent working out of any theory, but of gradual growth and development. Much that appears at first sight illogical and absurd is a survival from past days when conditions were very different from the present.

(*a*) We find the Crown in possession of considerable authority in Church matters. We saw how from the time of Constantine such a position was given to the Christian King. This position was a personal

2 F   B.T.A.

one. It was given to him as a loyal son of the Church, 'a godly prince,'
at a time when princes governed in person. Further, it was no
arbitrary or unlimited power that was bestowed, but it was assumed
that the King would exercise it subject to certain limitations and with
due respect to the Church's own rights and laws, according to precedent and custom.[1] To-day the personal position of the King has
completely changed. The real power has been transferred to the Prime
Minister, the Cabinet and Parliament. The King no longer governs
in person. As Churchmen we maintain that this has made all the
difference. The King has no moral right to delegate the authority
given by the Church to him personally, as the 'eldest son of the
Church', to some secular official or body, whose relation to the
Church in no way resembles his own. The Prime Minister is not
bound to be a Christian. The Cabinet or Parliament may contain at
any time a majority of Jews or agnostics. Further, there is a tendency
to regard the authority of Parliament as absolutely unlimited, even
in dealing with the Church. The respect for the Church's independence which was tacitly implied and acted on in the original relationship to the Crown is in danger of being ignored.[2]

(b) A clear instance of the fruits of this change is seen in the appointment of bishops and the exercise of Crown patronage. It was one
thing for the King as first layman of the Church to nominate bishops.
It is quite another thing for a Prime Minister who may not be a
churchman to do so. No doubt this implies no claim on the part of
the Crown to bestow spiritual authority. The man nominated receives his spiritual authority solely through consecration.[3] But logically the system is quite indefensible. It can only be urged that on the
whole it works very well. Prime Ministers of all parties have of late
years conscientiously tried to find the best men. It avoids the creation
of anything like parties in a diocese supporting rival candidates. But
we must remember it may cause trouble at any time. An unscrupulous

---

[1] 'No one would probably deny that, as a matter of fact, when the Church admitted
the Crown to a share in her concerns, whether it was in Constantine's day or Charle-
magne's, or at the Reformation or under Louis XIV, it was to a real King understood
to be both a Christian and a Churchman that she consented to yield this power' (Dean
Church, *On the Relations between Church and State*, p. 17).

[2] 'Legally the position of the Crown in the civil government is not much changed
from the days of Edward the Confessor: politically and constitutionally it is altogether
changed. As a power it is a ministry or a Parliament: as a person, the Crown stands at
the head of a nation, like all other nations broken up into recognized and tolerated
parties, and is bound to neutrality. . . . Statesmen cling with inconsistent tenacity to a
notion of ecclesiastical supremacy entirely different from that which they entertain of
temporal: and are taken aback at the idea of limitations in the one, which they have
all their lives assumed as first principles in the other' (*op. cit.* p. 51).

[3] The actual process is this. The Crown nominates a man and issues a writ command-
ing the chapter of the diocese to elect him and the archbishop to confirm the election.
Disobedience would legally incur severe penalties. But resistance has more than once
been threatened, and the possibility of it is a certain safeguard. In 1733 the appointment of Rundle to the bishopric of Gloucester was successfully opposed on the ground
of Deism. He was consoled with a bishopric in Ireland!

Prime Minister might force a conflict upon the Church by a series of political choices or the deliberate selection of an unorthodox candidate.

(c) A more serious grievance increasingly felt in the early years of this century is the inability of the Church to legislate for herself. All new legislation requires the consent of the Crown, of Convocation representing the clergy, and of Parliament. In old days Parliament was in a real sense a 'House of Laymen'. All members were churchmen and were elected by churchmen. As representing the laity they could rightly claim a voice in Church legislation. To-day, as the result of toleration, there are quite rightly no religious tests either for members of Parliament or for electors. Under present conditions there is nothing to prevent the majority of members from being Roman Catholics, Nonconformists, Jews or atheists. Yet all fresh Church legislation, on however sacred or domestic a subject, requires their consent before it can be enforced.[1] We may fairly claim that men who do not profess the Christian religion or who belong to bodies that have deliberately separated themselves from the Church and organized themselves in opposition to her, have no moral right to interfere in matters that belong to her own internal life and organization. The whole situation is a relic of the days when every citizen was a member of the Church.

This grievance has been alleviated by the passing of the Enabling Act in 1919. By this Act a National Assembly of the Church of England has been set up with the power of initiating legislation under conditions that give it a reasonable chance of receiving the sanction of Parliament. The Assembly consists of three Houses. The House of Bishops is composed of the members of the Upper Houses of Convocation, the House of Clergy of the members of the Lower Houses of Convocation, and the House of Laity of representatives elected by the representative electors in the several Diocesan Conferences. The method of procedure is as follows. The Assembly resolves that legislation on some matter relating to the Church is desirable. In order to give practical effect to the resolution, it is embodied in a 'measure'. The measure in the form that it is passed after discussion by the Assembly is passed on to a Legislative Committee of the Assembly, which forwards the measure to a special Ecclesiastical Committee of both Houses of Parliament, with any comments or explanations that it thinks desirable. The Ecclesiastical Committee then drafts a report on the measure containing its views on its expediency and its relation to the constitutional rights of all His Majesty's subjects. This report before being presented to Parliament must be shown to the Legisla-

---

[1] 'The understanding never was that the ecclesiastical power should be transferred to a body of men, neither representing the Church nor identified with her in feeling, in purpose, in belief, into whose hands by the effect of political changes, had passed in reality the old civil and temporal functions of the Crown' (op. cit. p. 52).

tive Committee of the Assembly and the two committees may if they desire confer together. The next step lies with the Legislative Committee. If it so desires, the measure and report together are presented to Parliament, but it has the power of withdrawing the measure at this stage, so as to avoid a direct conflict between the Assembly and Parliament in the case of an unfavourable report. After the report has once been presented, any member of either House of Parliament may propose a resolution that the measure be submitted to the King for his assent. A resolution of both Houses is necessary, and, after receiving the Royal Assent, the measure has all the force of an Act of Parliament. It is to be noticed that Parliament may approve or reject but cannot alter the measure.

By this Act the possibility of new legislation receiving the consent of Parliament has been considerably increased. Under the old conditions time was grudged for Church measures and as they were in no way a source of party profit, the Government was unwilling to grant special facilities. This gave opportunity for an individual member who was hostile to the Church to block the motion. The enemies of the Church deliberately opposed all proposals which would increase her efficiency. Since the Enabling Act came into operation, many useful measures of the Assembly have passed through Parliament and received the Royal Assent. With the pressure on the time of Parliament arising from the troubled events of the period since 1919 the legislation demanded by the changing circumstances of the Church could hardly have received proper attention in any other way. The rejection of the proposed Revised Prayer-Book by Parliament in 1927 and again in 1928 brought disappointment and dismay to many church people. A serious point of principle was no doubt involved in Parliament's decision to reject a Book officially proposed by the Convocations and the Assembly, but since 1928 general opinion in the Church has become much less disposed to regard the decision as a disaster.[1] A fresh and more promising approach to the revision of the ordering of the Church's life and worship is now being made by the discussion of a new body of Canons. If in this way the ecclesiastical law is clarified and adapted to present conditions and the system of Church Courts is revised so as to command general confidence, the Church will be in a better position to undertake the work of liturgical revision with an orderly and united purpose.†

Until new Canons are made it remains by no means easy to determine what the law of the Church is on many points. During the Middle Ages the Church of England accepted the canon law of the Western Church with a certain amount of local canon law. In origin this canon law was partly the customary law of the Church, partly

---

[1] There was a strong minority opinion in the Church against some features of the new Book; Parliament probably rightly judged that if sanctioned it would not have brought about a real settlement.

the decisions of councils, partly the decrees of Popes either genuine or forged. At first it simply represented the mind of the Church as declared in her decisions on particular cases with references to particular circumstances and was observed only in so far as it was enforced by the bishops, and thus continued to represent the mind of the Church. In time this was systematized and came to be viewed as resting not on the mind of the Church but on the authority of the Pope and was administered as a legal system. When the authority of the Pope was repudiated, the system was shattered. A return was made to earlier principles. Much of the old canon law no longer represented the mind of the Church and was therefore rightly abolished. A revision was needed, and a committee was appointed to make such a revision with a view to giving it the authority of statute law. Till then the old canon law was declared still binding on the clergy 'so far as it be not contrary to the statutes of the realm'. An attempt at revision was made, the 'Reformatio Legum Ecclesiasticarum', but it never received authority, so that we are theoretically bound to what was left of the old canon law. This position is, however, modified by three considerations: (i) Much of the old law was deliberately abrogated by the Church's own acts during the Reformation and the laying down of new rules of worship, *e.g.* the restoration of communion in both kinds and the abolition of compulsory confession. (ii) It is a principle of canon law that it is abrogated by 'desuetude', *i.e.* by the deliberate giving up of a practice or by the adoption of a definite practice to the contrary. This is evidence that the law abrogated no longer represents the mind of the Church. Much of the old law has in this way ceased to be authoritative. In other words, the present canon law of the English Church is that which the English Church to-day as a matter of fact uses. (iii) From time to time the Church of England has made new canons, *e.g.* those of 1603, and changes have been made in the Prayer-Book.

The Report of the Archbishop's Commission on Canon Law, issued in 1947, under the title 'The Canon Law of the Church of England', contains a draft of a complete body of new Canons to take the place of the Canons of 1603. Such a new body of Canons, together with the Book of Common Prayer and Statutory Provisions, will, it is hoped, 'give the Church a body of law, simple, up-to-date, and sufficient for its needs, without either being too detailed or revolutionizing the characteristics of our law, and will, at the same time, leave the ancient Canon Law as the source of the principles of our ecclesiastical jurisprudence'.[1]†

(*d*) Yet another disturbing result of the transference of authority from the King to a secular body is seen when we turn to the disciplinary system of the Church. In the Middle Ages the Church had her own system of courts, the archdeacon's, the bishop's, the arch-

[1] See Report, p. 86.

bishop's.[1] Appeals could be made from a lower to a higher court. In practice appeals were carried from the archbishop's court to the Pope, in spite of many efforts to check this by legislation. In fact, in order to save time and trouble appeals were often made to the Pope in the first instance. The result of this custom and of the centralization of authority in the Pope was to weaken the Church courts. They naturally tended to fall into disuse, being superseded by papal jurisdiction. At the Reformation appeals to Rome were forbidden. It was laid down in the statute of the Submission of the Clergy that they should be made to the Crown instead, and that the King should on each occasion appoint a court of commissioners to try the particular case. This was only intended as a temporary measure, until the reformation of canon law was completed and the system of Church courts reconstituted. As we have seen, this reform was never carried through, and the Crown by repeated use of its powers acquired the right of appointing the members of a final court of appeal for ecclesiastical cases known as the Court of Delegates. The position of such a court, so long as ecclesiastics were appointed, might be perfectly satisfactory, though there was no guarantee that it would be so. But in 1833 by Act of Parliament, without the consent of the Church, as the result not of any deliberate policy, but of a series of accidents, muddles and misadventures, the jurisdiction of the Court of Delegates was transferred to the Judicial Committee of the Privy Council. This committee is a purely civil body, originally called into being for purely civil purposes. It may consist entirely of lawyers who are not even Christians and may possess no sympathy with the life of the Church and no qualifications for deciding on questions of doctrine, which call for more than a merely legal knowledge. So by an Act of very doubtful authority the judicial supremacy granted to the King personally as a churchman has been transferred to a purely secular court. Its unspiritual nature is sufficiently shown by the fact that it cannot inflict those spiritual punishments which are the only fitting penalty for grave cases of spiritual disobedience, such as excommunication or deprivation of orders. The appointment of two bishops to act as assessors since 1876 cannot turn a civil court into a spiritual court. Hence churchmen have as a matter of conscience widely refused to recognize the authority of this court. They hold that, 'The Crown being supreme over all causes has the right to appoint such a court' (*i.e.* a court of final appeal). 'But this right must be exercised in accordance with the Church constitution, otherwise the court will lack spiritual authority, which can only be derived from the Church, and therefore its decision cannot be accepted as valid.'[2] The Church

---

[1] We must remember that Church courts dealt with a very wide range of cases. They included not only questions of Church discipline and property, but *e.g.* marriages and wills.

[2] Crosse, *Church and State*, p. 100.

of England is placed in the unhappy position of having no final court of appeal for questions of Church order and discipline whose decisions are binding on the conscience of all her members. The result is disciplinary chaos tempered by episcopal good advice and a practical disuse of ecclesiastical courts. Much is said about 'clerical lawlessness'. Such lawlessness can only be remedied by a revival of a proper system of Church courts.[1] It is well also to remember that lay members should equally be subject to Church discipline. Our present unhappy condition is partly a legacy from days when civil and ecclesiastical courts were looked on as parts of the judicial system of one single Church-State, partly the result of the transference to the Crown of powers that had been seized by the Pope, partly the result of sheer dullness of imagination. But the Church of England can never do her work satisfactorily until it is remedied.[2]†

(e) It may be perhaps urged that these conditions are the inevitable result of Establishment. The reply is that they are not the result of Establishment as such, but of the unfortunate terms on which the Church of England is established. We have only to turn to Scotland to see a Church there established on very different terms. The Established Church of Scotland appoints its own chief ministers: it is free to legislate for itself, and such legislation is recognized as valid by the civil courts: it possesses a complete system of Church courts, with a final court of appeal possessed of due spiritual authority. It combines establishment with spiritual autonomy. Further, there has been much confusion about the meaning of 'established'. The Church of England 'as by law established' in the original use of the phrase, e.g. in the canons of 1604, means 'not as by law founded, but as by law settled: it refers not to the origin of the Church but to its control.'[3] There was no idea of drawing any contrast between Churches that are established and Churches that are not; the reference rather was to the actual terms of the relationship to the State. Nor does the word imply that the State claims to have founded the Church. In itself there need be nothing in State recognition to limit the liberty of the Church.

The State might bestow privileges upon the ministers of the Church, give special facilities for Church worship and teaching and even make grants of land or money because it considered Christianity a

---

[1] Cp. *The Report of the Royal Commission on Ecclesiastical Discipline*, c. x., esp. the following sentences: 'A court dealing with matters of conscience and religion must, above all others, rest on moral authority if its judgments are to be effective. As thousands of clergy, with strong lay support, refuse to recognize the jurisdiction of the Judicial Committee, its judgments cannot practically be enforced. Those who most desire to repress irregularities are those who have most to gain by the substitution of an effective tribunal for a court which, because it is powerless, encourages rather than represses disorder. The establishment of a court, the authority of which could not be disputed, would destroy any foundation for the claim now in fact made by a section of the clergy to decide for themselves the limits of canonical obedience' (p. 67).

[2] The proposed new Canons include a revised system of Church Courts.

[3] Figgis, *Churches in the Modern State*, p. 9.

desirable religion for its subjects, without affecting the discipline of the Church at all. Whether the State decides to give to the Church any such privileged position, the State alone can determine. 'Establishment is in its nature a political fact: the adoption or maintenance of a national relation towards the Church.'[1] The Church cannot either establish or disestablish herself.

Further, from the nature of things the Church cannot at any time be entirely free from all relation to the State. The Church is called to work in the world. She avails herself of all the resources of civilized society. The safety of her gatherings depends upon the strong arm of the civil law. Again, the tenure of all property depends upon the State for its security. If it is given for a certain purpose it is the duty of the State to see that it is used for that purpose. As early as A.D. 269 we find the Church appealing to the heathen Emperor Aurelian in order to recover Church property which Paul of Samosata refused to give up after his deposition by the Council of Antioch. So the Free Churches are in varying degrees bound down by the possession of property. If, say, a minister preached doctrine not in accordance with the trust-deed of his chapel and an action were brought to eject him, that action, involving questions of doctrine, would be tried by a civil court. Some years ago the majority of the Wesleyan Methodist body desired to extend the number of years during which a minister could remain at one chapel. To effect this they were compelled to apply to Parliament for leave to alter the terms of the trust on which their property was held. A minority within the body threatened opposition, so that there was no chance of Parliamentary support. Accordingly the reform was dropped. Again, the same principle can be seen in the famous case of the Free Church of Scotland. This body by a very large majority decided to amalgamate with a smaller Presbyterian body, the United Presbyterians. The union was effected in face of the resistance of a small minority. But this minority brought an action in the civil courts claiming the whole of the property on the ground that this union involved a change of doctrine, since the formularies of the United Presbyterians were looser than those of the Free Church. Before the House of Lords the action was finally decided in favour of the minority, and it needed a special Act of Parliament to make possible an equitable apportionment of the property. These examples are enough to show that the present limitations of self-government in the Church of England are not due simply to the Royal Supremacy or to Establishment. If the Church were disestablished to-morrow the amount of liberty she possessed would depend upon the terms of disestablishment, that is, on the conditions on which she held whatever property she retained.

Accordingly, behind any question of establishment, and in reality distinct from it, there lies the further and greater question: how far

[1] Moberly, *Problems and Principles*, p. 160.

is the State ready to recognize the independent life of smaller societies within itself, to regard them as containing within themselves powers of development and growth, and to allow them to adapt their rules and constitutions to fresh circumstances? That is one of the big problems of the future. It affects not only the Church, but many other societies, such as trade-unions. We can only consider it here so far as it affects the Church. Let us take one divergence which has already arisen between Church and State. The State has by Act of Parliament seriously relaxed its laws of marriage. It allows, for instance, the re-marriage of divorced persons, innocent and guilty alike. The man in the street cannot understand that the Church has not changed her law too. Hence he cannot see why, when two persons are married according to the law of the land, they may be repelled from communion in church, on the ground that they are not married according to the Church's law. In other words, he cannot imagine that the Church can have a law of her own resting on other authority than that of the State. The question may be obscured by establishment, but is at bottom independent of it. Again, the case of the Free Church of Scotland suggests that the State is unwilling to allow a religious body the right to make new rules for itself. It is quite possible that if we were disestablished we might be bound down, with very little power, say, to alter our Prayer-Book or make new canons.

(f) In the face of present difficulties we are being thrown back upon first principles. There exists to-day in Europe a greater variety of belief and practice than can be found at any time probably since the Empire became Christian. We must face facts. It is both useless and impertinent to pretend that a Theosophist or a Buddhist, or a votary of the 'New Thought' or an agnostic is a Christian or a churchman because he is an English citizen. It is not that such men interpret the will of Christ in one way and the Church in another way. They do not recognize the authority of Christ at all, and do not even wish to discover what His will is, still less to submit to it. More and more men are rejecting not simply Christian doctrine, but the whole Christian standard of morality. It is becoming clear that the two in the long run stand or fall together. The present age is impatient of mere convention. Open disbelief is taking the place of secret indifference. A bored acquiescence in Christianity, as the correct thing, is changing into a calculated rejection of Christ. It is doubtful how long the current relations between Church and State will bear the strain. Pressure of fact compels us to look for guidance to Scripture and the early Church. We may find help, too, in a study of the mission field, where the essential principles of Church life stand out more clearly than at home. The following lines of thought may be suggested as an outline of practical policy.

(i) Perhaps the greatest danger that besets the English Church in its relation to the State is Erastianism. On this view the supreme authority over religion rests with the State. The Church is simply the Government department for dealing with religion and the clergy are a class of civil servants. Hence it rests with the State to decide questions of doctrine, worship and discipline. There is a good deal of Erastian thought current, all the more dangerous because it has not been put into words. It is shown in the idea that all Englishmen have a right to be admitted to communion or that the law of the State concerning marriage binds the Church. Against this we must insist that the authority of the Church, her rule of life and her ministry, depend not on the State but on Christ.[1] Were the Church disestablished tomorrow she would still be the Body of Christ: she would still preach God's word and minister His sacraments. Christ Himself gave authority to His Church to 'bind and loose': to submit to the commands of the State when they conflict with the law of Christ would be disloyalty to Him. It would be to give to Caesar what belongs to God. It is always possible that the Church may be faced with the alternative of consenting to the usurpation of authority by the State in deciding matters of doctrine and ordaining rites and ceremonies or else of going out into the wilderness naked and bleeding and stripped of all her possessions.

(ii) Positively, we must work for Church reform, not necessarily disestablishment at all. We believe as English citizens that we have a duty to the nation and that every opportunity should be given to the Church to influence the national life. We must be prepared to sacrifice our own preferences on matters that are not vital in order to meet the needs and desires and even the prejudices of the nation (cp. 1 Cor 9[22]). On the other hand, in order that the Church may be her best self she needs greater power of action. What is required is some means by which the Church may express her mind and alter or amend her rules. It may be claimed that some improvement in this respect has taken place since the end of the first great war. Certain reforms in the representation of the clergy in the Convocations were carried through by new Canons which received the Royal Assent in 1921. The preponderance of the official element is now diminished, and more adequate representation is given to the parochial clergy, including the unbeneficed. The setting up of the Church Assembly with a House of Laity has provided a statutory central organ for the expression of lay opinion, and, more locally, Diocesan Conferences and Parochial Church Councils have helped to bring the laity into active participation in the affairs of the Church. But it cannot be said that the problem of forming, expressing, and giving effect to a corporate mind in the Church on important matters concerning her life and witness has

[1] The taunt that we wish to reduce the Church to the level of a sect loses its force when we remember that the word 'sect' comes from *sequor*, not *seco*. The Church as a whole must be in the strict sense of the term a 'sect' since it consists of those who follow Christ and are thereby distinguished from all others. It is more important that the Church should consist of true Christians than that it should include all Englishmen.

yet been completely solved. Again, we must strive for the restoration of an efficient system of Church courts leading up to a final court of appeal, such as will bind the consciences of all Church people. Only when this has been attained can we hope for any efficient exercise of Church discipline over all who claim to be her members.[1] In short, the Church of England must demand from the State a fuller recognition of the independence of her own life, even if a price has to be paid for such recognition.

(iii) On the other hand, the Church must fairly recognize the independence of the State. Just as she no longer expects the State to compel all citizens to attend her services, so she must not expect the State to enforce on all its citizens the full Christian standard of morality. Probably there never was a time when all the members of any State were at heart Christian. To-day it is unreasonable to expect men who reject the authority of Christ to accept, say, a strict law of marriage that is based on His authority. The Church must be content to be able to enforce the Christian standard of life upon those who voluntarily are her members. Those without we must leave to God's judgment. To attempt to enforce upon the world at large the full Christian standard can only end in degrading that standard. What will in practice be enforced will be something lower than Christian which will at the same time be supposed to be Christian.

Let us in conclusion recall the true work of the Church. The Church exists to forward the Kingdom of God on earth, to lead all men to Christ, that in Him they may find their truest life. She is to be 'in the world but not of the world'. She recognizes to the full the authority of the State as coming from God. If she desires to preserve her own life from worldliness and from the intrusion of secular authority, it is not from any selfish motive, but because only so can she preserve within herself that salt of Christian living which is to be her gift to the world. What is best for the Church will be best for the State in the long run.

§ 4. As we saw, the discipline of the State differs from that of the Church, in that the State has the right of employing force to compel obedience. The Church has always recognized the divinely given authority of the State (cp. Rom 13, 1 Pet 2^{13-17}). The State exists because men as social beings can only realize themselves through a common life. The existence of the State may be threatened in either of two ways, by lawlessness within or by enemies without. In either case the State is bound to use force to maintain its own existence. Public order is something that a right and wise use of force can ensure. The State is concerned primarily with acts and not motives, and hence its discipline can differ from that of the Church. The strong arm of the law is able to effect that outward obedience in those matters that are the concern of the State.

[1] See note on p. 435.

(*a*) This is justification of that police action which is defended in the Article against the anarchial theories of Anabaptism. The rulers have authority '*to restrain with the sword the stubborn and evildoers*'. Our whole social order is backed in the last resort by force. Under normal circumstances this is disguised. Even so, unpleasant duties, such as paying taxes, are enforced by the aid of the policeman. Men do them because they are obliged to. So, too, in primitive communities disputes are settled by open violence. The stronger party carries the day. Among ourselves we have political conflicts. At bottom the effective principle is the same. 'We count heads instead of breaking them.' Modern events have shown that a powerful minority, smarting under a sense of injustice, may even now tear down the disguise and appeal to the sword. Thus from its very constitution the State has the inherent right of using force for self-preservation. This is not to say that the authority of the State is simply the will of the stronger or that the only motive to obedience is fear of punishment. As civilization advances the use of force is abated. Conduct becomes moralized. Higher motives for obedience tend to supplant the lower. But at bottom there must always be the appeal to force to put down disorder.

(*b*) So, too, when the State's existence is threatened by an external enemy, force may rightly be used to repel him. That is, the State can call upon its citizens to take up arms in its defence. Hence '*It is lawful for Christian men, at the command of the Magistrate, to wear weapons and serve in the wars*' (Latin, *iusta bella*). This position was contested by the Anabaptists. So to-day the Quakers and many other individual Christians argue that all war is evil, and the Christian, as such, is bound not to take part in it and even to endure suffering or death rather than fight. The ordinary man finds it difficult to understand how the same persons can avail themselves of the protection of the State for their lives and property, which protection against internal disorder, as we have seen, depends in the last resort on force, and yet refuse to support the State in defending itself by war against destruction and pillage by external foes. But their position raises in an acute form the problem of the Christian's attitude to war.

When we turn to the New Testament we find that our Lord accepted social conditions as He found them. He did not directly attack abuses, such as war or slavery, rather He laid down principles through the acceptance of which such abuses would be abolished. In the case of slavery there is no explicit condemnation in the New Testament. S. Paul does not even bid Philemon set free Onesimus (Philemon v. [16]). Rather he exhorts slaves to do their work faithfully. Yet in due time the conscience of Christendom came to see with increasing clearness that slavery was inconsistent with the principles of the Gospel, such as the unique value of the individual and the brotherhood of humanity. Accordingly, slavery was mitigated and in time abolished. So in the case of war, soldiers are not bidden to abandon their profession (*e.g.* Lk 3¹⁴, Acts 10⁴⁸) and metaphors from the soldier's life are freely employed. War is recognized as a training ground of manly virtues. Our Lord seems to approve of the use of armed force by the 'kingdoms of this world' (ἐκ τοῦ κόσμου τούτου, *i.e.* having their origin from this world, Jn 18³⁶).¹ On the other hand, we are coming increasingly to see that if men and nations were really Christian, war would be impossible. War is simply the result of human sin and self-seeking. It is a symptom of the depravity of the human heart. Christianity sets itself not to abolish the symptom only but to root out the cause of the evil. After all, war is simply the exhibition on the largest and most destructive scale of those fierce and anti-social passions which lie equally behind all acts of cruelty and injustice and are in utter antagonism to the Christian spirit of love. The more Christian we become the more we are shocked at the horrors of war. Only when the whole world is Christian can we hope for war to cease. It cannot be put down by any external legislation.

It may be asked, however, ought not the Christian to carry out literally the precepts of the Sermon on the Mount and refuse to offer resistance to any enemy? One line of answer would be to point out that we have obligations not only to self but to society. What our Lord forbids is the spirit of personal revenge. If we ourselves alone are injured, we may be called on not to resist our enemy and even to suffer death. Such non-resistance may be truly Christian. But when the injury affects others, then we may be called on to resist. The evil-doer is to be resisted not that we may gratify our own spite, but that he may himself learn from his punishment and be reformed, and that society may be protected. All war is sinful, and arises from unchristian ambitions and jealousies. Yet the Christian fights not from personal animosity but to save his country.

Further, as we have seen, the State is not as yet fully Christian. It contains many citizens who are not even Christian in name. It is arguable that a perfectly Christian State might be called on to render a literal obedience to the Sermon on the Mount by a policy of non-resistance, and to witness for Christ by suffering wrong patiently as our Lord did. But a semi-Christian State cannot be under any such obligation. The difficulty for the individual Christian is that he is compelled to live, as it were, on two levels. As a member of the State he must assist the State to live up to its highest standard, and that standard includes resistance to evil by force. As a Christian he believes that evil can never be conquered by force. If he accepts State protection for his own personal safety, he can hardly refuse to help the State to defend itself against external enemies. In a sinful world

¹ So, too, our Lord seems to teach that force is not intrinsically evil, but can be consecrated to the service of God, when He pictures the Good Shepherd as employing it to defend the sheep. Jn 10¹¹⁻¹³.

this dual standard is unavoidable. Human sin has made the best impossible. We must choose the second best.

Political and scientific developments in the first half of the twentieth century have, however, made the problem of war both more urgent and more difficult. The total character of modern warfare, involving the mobilization of whole populations and their exposure to mass destruction by weapons of ever-increasing power, has made the idea of engaging in war repugnant to the conscience of the majority of mankind. But this fact does not in itself preclude the possibility of a new war. On the other hand the rise of totalitarian forms of government has increased the seriousness of the issues at stake in any conflict. A desire to extend the range of their power and the domination of their ideas is characteristic of these governments, and their claim to control men's minds as well as their actions makes the threat of their ultimate victory much more serious than a threat of conquest would have been in earlier ages. A nation and society united in Christian conviction might renounce war and face the probable consequences, spiritual and material, with confidence. But such a society does not anywhere yet exist. Meanwhile the Church has a clear duty to work for the promotion of international justice and co-operation and for the elimination of poverty and discontent which in different parts of the world invite a resort to tyrannical forms of government.†

(c) Again, the supreme penalty that the State can inflict is death. Without doubt in earlier stages of society the death penalty was absolutely necessary as a deterrent. It is approved by the conscience of the writers of the Old Testament and of the New (Gen 9⁶, Exod 21¹², Acts 25¹¹, etc.). Hence the cautious wording of the Article can hardly be criticized. '*The laws of the realm may punish Christian men with death, for heinous and grievous offences.*' Whether at any given time it is desirable to inflict the death penalty is left open. That is a question that can only be decided by the reason and conscience of the particular community.†

ARTICLE XXXVIII

Of Christian men's Goods, which are not common	*De illicita bonorum communicatione*
The riches and goods of Christians are not common as touching the right, title, and possession of the same, as certain Anabaptists do falsely boast. Notwithstanding, every man	Facultates et bona Christianorum non sunt communia, quoad jus et possessionem (ut quidam Anabaptistae falso jactant); debet tamen quisque de his quae possidet, pro facultatum ratione,

ought, of such things as he possesseth, liberally to give alms to the poor, according to his ability.

pauperibus eleemosynas benigne distribuere.

Composed in 1553.

§ 5. At the time of the Reformation certain Anabaptists advocated communism as an essential part of Christianity. They based their claim on a literal imitation of the life of the earliest Christian community as described in the opening chapters of Acts. There Christians are described as having 'all things in common' (see esp. 2^{44-45} and 4^{32}). Such a claim, however, fails to take account of all the facts. It is quite clear that such communism was the spontaneous product of the new spirit of brotherhood. It was based not on any formal legislation but the sharing of a common temper and outlook. It was neither compulsory nor universal. S. Peter clearly asserts that Ananias had the right, if he so wished, to retain either his property or the money for which he sold it (5^4). Mary the mother of S. Mark clearly possessed her own house, though she put it at the disposal of the community (Acts 12^{12}). It is a certain inference from the facts of S. Paul's life that he was able at times of crisis to draw upon considerable resources. Both our Lord and the teaching of the New Testament generally inculcate the duty of almsgiving, which presupposes the retention of at least some private property (Mt 6^1 ff., etc., Rom 12^{13}, 1 Cor 16^2, 2 Cor 9^7, Heb 13^{16}, 1 Jn 3^{17}, etc.). Outside Jerusalem no trace of communism is found. Before many years had passed the Church of Jerusalem was in urgent need of financial assistance (Rom 15^{25-28}, etc.). How far this was due to the conduct described above is an interesting question.

To-day a very similar demand is often made that the Church should definitely commit herself to that economic theory known as 'socialism'.[1] Our Lord is claimed as a socialist. This demand rests upon unsound arguments. Our Lord laid down general principles. He did not formulate any system. He left it to His disciples to work out those principles to meet the needs of successive ages. If we believe that socialism is economically sound and will minister to the highest welfare of mankind, then we are bound to propagate it. But we must allow that our views are not an essential part of the Christian faith. Socialism has no place in the revelation of God. Christians must be prepared to differ on such a subject. All that loyalty to Christ demands is that whatever views they hold, they adopt them from Christian motives as the result of prayer, thought and study, not

[1] It is much to be wished that the term 'socialism' would only be employed in its proper sense. As so used it signifies the view that the community as a whole should own all the means of production. It is too often employed in a vague sense as meaning little more than 'social reform'. Socialism is not the same as communism, since it leaves room for a limited possession of private property.

simply because they will fill their own pockets and keep them full. Our Lord's teaching about wealth may be summed up in two leading thoughts. First, it is a great responsibility, to be used for the good not only of its owner but of others. Secondly, it is a great temptation, leading its possessor to rely on self rather than God. This teaching, we must note, applies not only to money but to all conspicuous gifts whether of mind or body.

The Church is not tied down to any one economic theory, but it is bound to assert Christian principles. That is where the Church has often failed. It has made little or no protest against the exploitation of the poor and weak.[1] Men have been allowed to suppose that Christian morality applies only to private life and not to business relationships. Prominent members of the Church have been known to be getting money by means that involved the suffering and loss of their fellow men and women and the Church has never rebuked them. Men have salved their conscience by gifts to the Church taken from money gained at the cost of the lives of their employees. The Christian conscience has acquiesced in the existence of slums and the employment of sweated labour. In all attempts at reform the Church has too often taken the side of wealth rather than righteousness. These ugly facts underlie the demand that the Church should adopt socialism. The Church is bound to face, in the light of the Gospel, the evils for which socialism claims to supply a remedy. But she is not bound to accept any particular political or economic remedy without investigation. She must always insist that external conditions by themselves cannot secure righteousness, though they may do much to hinder it. The real root of all social problems lies in the perverted will and heart of man, in other words, in human sin. No economic reconstruction apart from love can bring true and lasting satisfaction.

The social measures which since the second world war have set up in this country, with the general support of public opinion, what is called 'the Welfare State' must be welcomed by the Christian conscience as supplying remedies for many social evils. Some credit for these measures must go to the diffusion of Christian ideals among our people, but circumstances arising from the war probably hastened what might otherwise have taken a long time to accomplish. In this new situation the emphasis and direction of the duty of the Church to society will need some re-thinking. The Welfare State may go far towards giving 'social security' at the cost of the sense of personal responsibility for self and others, a danger which can be counteracted only by an intelligent propagation of Christian teaching on family and social relations. If the opportunities are wisely discerned and used, a wide sphere of voluntary service and influence remains open to effective Christian effort, and the official services themselves will not fulfil their possibilities unless individual Christians are ready to

[1] See the excellent statement, W. Temple, *Church and Nation*, p. 80 ff.

find a vocation in them. The problem of the relation of the Church to contemporary society has thus changed in character. The relief of economic need is no longer a primary concern. The Church now has to discover how to make Christian standards effective in a society in which education is mainly under the direct control of the State, and the large-scale influence of rapid transport, the cinema, radio and television is a constant factor.†

ARTICLE XXXIX

Of a Christian man's oath

As we confess that vain and rash Swearing is forbidden Christian men by our Lord Jesus Christ, and *James* his Apostle: So we judge, that Christian Religion doth not prohibit, but that a man may swear when the Magistrate requireth, in a cause of faith and charity, so it be done according to the Prophet's teaching, in justice, judgment, and truth.

De jurejurando

Quemadmodum juramentum vanum et temerarium a Domino nostro Jesu Christo, et Apostolo ejus Jacobo, Christianis hominibus interdictum esse fatemur; ita Christianorum Religionem minime prohibere censemus, quin jubente magistratu in causa fidei et charitatis jurare liceat, modo id fiat juxta Prophetae doctrinam, in justitia, in judicio, et veritate.

Composed in 1553.

§ 6. The objection of the Anabaptists, like that of the Quakers in later days, to the use of oaths rests upon a misunderstanding of Scripture of the same kind as those that we have already considered. In Mt 5³³ ff. our Lord says, 'Ye have heard that it was said to them of old time, Thou shalt not forswear thyself but shalt perform unto the Lord thine oaths: but I say unto you, Swear not at all. . . . But let your speech be, Yea, yea; Nay, nay; and whatsoever is more than these is of the evil one.' His words are re-echoed by S. James 5¹², 'Above all things, my brethren, swear not, neither by the heaven, nor by the earth, nor by any other oath; but let your yea be yea, and your nay, nay (let yours be the yea, yea and the nay, nay, R.V. mg.), that ye fall not under judgment.' These are the passages alluded to in the Article.

To grasp the spirit of our Lord's command, we must consider the meaning of an oath. The idea of any obligation to speak the truth at all times and to all men is quite a late idea. Primitive man only felt himself bound to speak the truth to particular men, *e.g.* his own kinsfolk, or under particular circumstances. As the narratives of the Old Testament show, no moral blame whatever was felt to attach to untruthfulness to a stranger or an enemy. Gradually the circle of men to whom truthfulness was felt to be a duty widened. Christian morality proclaims that all men have a right to expect the truth (Eph 4²⁵). Lying is anti-social. The Christian, if he is faithful to Christ, is bound to speak the truth. This is the real thought that underlies the exhortations of our Lord and S. James. The oath is in origin a device to obtain truthfulness on a particular occasion, when truthfulness was not necessarily to be expected. It is the solemn calling upon God to bear witness that a statement is true. The use of oaths has always tended to produce a double standard of truthfulness. Men come to feel that they are bound to speak the truth when they are on oath, but not otherwise. Further, men try to evade the sanctity of oaths by quibbles and subterfuges. Some oaths are held to be binding and others not (cp. Mt 23¹⁶⁻²²). In short, the whole system of oaths, though necessary, is at best a makeshift. What is wanted is not a code of oaths but a spirit of truthfulness. Human selfishness and ingenuity will always endeavour to evade an oath, unless there is the right inward disposition. Our Lord commands His disciples to speak the truth always, as being always in the presence of God. Hence the need of oaths is removed. The Christian will not have two standards of truth, one when he is on oath and one when he is not. His simple 'yea' or 'nay' will be sufficient. His whole speech will be on that high moral level to which the speech of the non-Christian is raised only temporarily and partially by the taking of an oath.

If, then, the world was a Christian world and all men were disciples, our Lord's command would be obeyed literally. Oaths would rightly be abolished as contrary to the spirit of Christ. But, as we saw, the State is not as yet a Christian society. Its members are not all Christians. Its action, therefore, cannot be guided by the full principles of Christian morality. Hence it is compelled to retain and enforce oaths. And the Christian, as a member of the State, will conform to the State's rule in matters that concern the State. To him, indeed, the oath will be superfluous, as he is equally bound to speak the truth at all times. He will, however, be content to follow the example of His Master, who, though He gave the command 'swear not at all', yet was willing to be put on oath by Caiaphas and recognized the authority of the State (Mt 26⁶³).[1]

---

[1] The solemn asseverations used from time to time by S. Paul (e.g. 2 Cor 1²³, Gal 1²⁰, etc.) may be considered a form of oath. They were needed because his converts had hardly yet reached the full Christian standard of morality. They do not violate any Christian principle, since they in no way imply a double standard of truthfulness.

LIST OF BOOKS FOR FURTHER STUDY

INTRODUCTION

Page
2 See N. Micklem, *Religion* (Home University Library); E. O. James in *The Study of Theology*, c. ii (with bibliography).

4 On faith and conduct, see L. S. Thornton, *Conduct and the Supernatural*; V. A. Demant, *The Religious Prospect* (for Christian dogma in relation to social and political theories).

6 On the nature of Theology, see *Lux Mundi*, Essay ii, § 6, and Essay vi, § 1; Webb, *A Century of Anglican Theology*, Lect. iii; W. R. Matthews (editor), *Dogma in History and Thought*; essays by N. P. Williams and N. Micklem in *The Study of Theology*; Taylor, *The Faith of a Moralist*, esp. Vol. ii, c. ii; K. Barth, *The Doctrine of the Word of God*; E. Brunner, *The Christian Doctrine of God, Dogmatics*, Vol. i; E. L. Mascall, *Christ, the Christian and the Church*, c. xiii.

THE THIRTY-NINE ARTICLES. THEIR HISTORY AND PLACE IN THEOLOGY

21 For the background of English Church History, see J. R. H. Moorman, *A History of the Church in England* and the volumes in Stephens and Hunt's *History of the English Church*, and for an excellent brief account, T. M. Parker, *The English Reformation to 1558* (Home University Library). For the Continental Reformation, see Kidd, *The Continental Reformation*, and *Documents of the Continental Reformation*, and for the Council of Trent his *The Counter-Reformation*. See also Pullan, *Religion Since the Reformation*, Lects. i–iii. The Protestant standpoint can be studied in Lindsay, *History of the Reformation* (two Vols.). For a full history of the Articles, see Hardwick, *A History of the Articles of Religion*.

THE BEING OF GOD

23 For a defence of theism see Taylor's essay in *Essays Catholic and Critical* and his article, 'Theism,' in *E.R.E.* For a clear statement of the Scholastic proofs of the existence of God, Joyce, *Principles of Natural Theology*. Among larger works are A. M. Farrer, *Finite and Infinite* (a brilliant critical and constructive discussion of rational theology); E. L. Mascall, *He Who Is* (a discussion along modern Thomistic lines); Temple, *Nature, Man and God*; H. H. Farmer, *The World and God* and *Towards Belief in God* (the last three works containing a more idealistic and experiential approach).

Page
23   On Israel's faith in God see Hamilton, *The People of God*, Vol. i;
      Wheeler Robinson, *Religious Ideas of the Old Testament*; G. E.
      Wright, *The Old Testament against its Environment* (S.C.M. Press).

27   On divine personality, see Webb, *God and Personality*; Illingworth,
      Personality, Human and Divine, Lects. i–v. Among more recent dis-
      cussions, Quick, *Doctrines of the Creed*, c. iv; and on the use of the
      principle of analogy, A. M. Farrer, *Finite and Infinite*, esp. Part I;
      E. L. Mascall, *Existence and Analogy* (Longmans).

29   See for a discussion of reserve in ascribing 'passibility' to God,
      Mozley, *The Impassibility of God*; von Hügel, *Essays*, Vol. ii, pp.
      165 ff.; Taylor, *The Faith of a Moralist*, Vol. ii, Lect. viii.

31   On divine providence, see H. H. Farmer, *The World and God*, cc.
      vi, xiii and xvi.

33   On the being and attributes of God see the books referred to above
      (pages 23 and 27) and Headlam, *Christian Theology, The Doctrine
      of God*; W. R. Matthews, *God in Christian Thought and Experience*;
      E. Brunner, *The Christian Doctrine of God, Dogmatics*, Vol. i. For a
      discussion of divine transcendence and immanence see Temple,
      Nature, Man and God, esp. Lectures x and xi.

THE HOLY TRINITY

34   For a discussion of our Lord's miracles, see A. Richardson, *The
      Miracle Stories of the Gospels* (S.C.M. Press).

37   For a study of the New Testament evidence, see A. E. J. Rawlinson,
      The New Testament Doctrine of the Christ.

39   See Glover, *Conflict of Religions in the Early Roman Empire*; Bevan,
      Stoics and Sceptics and *Hellenism and Christianity*; Halliday, *The
      Pagan Background of Early Christianity*; A. D. Nock's essay in
      Essays on the Trinity and the Incarnation, ed. Rawlinson, on 'Early
      Gentile Christianity and its Hellenistic Background'.

41   On the preparation for the doctrine of the Trinity in Judaism, see
      K. E. Kirk, 'The Evolution of the Doctrine of the Trinity' in *Essays on
      the Trinity and the Incarnation*; J. Lebreton, *Les Origines du Dogme
      de la Trinité*.

44   For ebionism, see Bethune Baker, *Christian Doctrine*, pp. 62–68;
      Du Bose, *Ecumenical Councils*, c. iii; Tixeront, *History of Dogmas*,
      Vol. i, c. iv.

45   For docetism, see art. 'Docetism' in *E.R.E.*; Du Bose, *Ecumenical
      Councils*, c. iii.

46   On dynamic and modalist monarchianism, see Mackintosh, *Person
      of Christ*, pp. 147 ff.; Tixeront, *History of Dogmas*, Vol. i, c. viii.

47   For Arianism, besides the histories of dogma, see Mackintosh,
      Person of Christ, c iv; Du Bose, *Ecumenical Councils*, cc. v and vi;
      Gwatkin, *Studies of Arianism*.

Page

50   On the meaning of *ousia, hypostasis* and *homoousios*, see G. L. Prestige, *God in Patristic Thought*.

52   The early history of the doctrine of the Trinity may be studied in the standard histories of doctrine, of which Tixeront is the best for general use. For more detailed treatment of the history see G. L. Prestige, *God in Patristic Thought*; *Essays on the Trinity and the Incarnation*, esp. iv, v, and vi; and for more systematic treatment, L. Hodgson, *The Doctrine of the Trinity*; K. Barth, *The Doctrine of the Word of God*; R. S. Franks, *The Doctrine of the Trinity* (Duckworth).

53   On the subject of this note see Temple, *Nature, Man and God*, esp. Lects. i, xii and xx, and Quick, *Doctrines of the Creed*, c. ii (for criticism of the traditional distinction between natural and revealed theology); for the neo-Reformed view, see E. Brunner, *Revelation and Reason*; K. Barth, *The Doctrine of the Word of God*; differences between Barth and Brunner on natural theology are set out in their discussion in E. Brunner and K. Barth, *Natural Theology* (Centenary Press); for a defence and exposition of the distinction between natural reason and supernatural revelation, see A. M. Farrer, *The Glass of Vision*, cc. i and ii. Cp. E. Gilson, *Reason and Revelation in the Middle Ages*.

THE INCARNATION

55   On the figure of Christ in the Gospels and on questions concerning faith and history in relation to the Gospels, see Hoskyns in *Essays Catholic and Critical*; *Mysterium Christi* (ed. Bell), Essays ii, iii and iv; A. E. J. Rawlinson, *Christ in the Gospels*; T. W. Manson, *The Servant-Messiah*; E. Brunner, *The Mediator*, cc. vi, xiii and xiv; D. M. Baillie, *God Was in Christ*, Sections i and ii. On the moral perfection of Jesus, Quick, *Doctrines of the Creed*, c. xvii.

56   The best brief account of Apollinarius and his teaching is G. L. Prestige, *Fathers and Heretics*, c. v. C. E. Raven, *Apollinarianism*, gives a fuller historical discussion. See also Mackintosh, *Person of Christ*, pp. 196 ff.; R. V. Sellers, *Two Ancient Christologies* (for the place of Apollinarius in 'Alexandrine' Christology).

58   For recent brief and sympathetic accounts, see G. L. Prestige, *Fathers and Heretics*, c. vi, and R. V. Sellers, *Two Ancient Christologies*, c. ii (on Antiochene Christology). L. Hodgson in Appendix iv to *Nestorius, The Bazaar of Heracleides* (ed. Driver and Hodgson) raises some valuable points about the metaphysics of Nestorius. Bethune Baker, *Nestorius and his Teaching*, defends Nestorius' orthodoxy.

59   On the Council of Chalcedon and the merits of its Definition, see Mackintosh, *Person of Christ*, cc. x and xi; Temple, *Christus Veritas*, c. viii; Mozley's essay in *Essays Catholic and Critical*; L. Hodgson's essay in *Essays on the Trinity and the Incarnation*, esp. pp. 387 ff.; R. V. Sellers, *The Council of Chalcedon* (S.P.C.K.). See also Bindley, *The Oecumenical Documents of the Faith* (ed. Green, 1950).

Page

68   On the theology of the Incarnation, see, among older works, Gore, *The Incarnation of the Son of God* (Bampton Lectures) and *Dissertations*; Mackintosh, *The Person of Christ*; among more recent works, H. M. Relton, *A Study in Christology*; L. Hodgson, *And Was Made Man* and his essay in *Essays on the Trinity and the Incarnation*; L. S. Thornton, *The Incarnate Lord*; E. Brunner, *The Mediator*; D. M. Baillie, *God Was in Christ*. On the relation between Christology and soteriology, Mozley's essay in *Mysterium Christi* is most valuable. For discussion of the kenotic theory see Temple, *Christus Veritas*, c. viii; Quick, *Doctrines of the Creed*, c. xiii; Baillie, *op. cit.*, c. iv. For a survey of the history of the doctrine, see Ottley, *The Doctrine of the Incarnation* (two Vols.).

71   On our Lord's human knowledge, see Gore, *Dissertations*; Quick, *Doctrines of the Creed*, c. xvi; E. L. Mascall, *Christ, the Christian and the Church*, c. iii.

74   On our Lord's temptations and moral perfection, see L. Hodgson, *And Was Made Man*, c. iii; Quick, *Doctrines of the Creed*, c. xvii.

81   On the Virgin-birth, see Box, *The Virgin Birth of Jesus*; Gore, *Dissertations*; Headlam, *Miracles of the New Testament*, Lect. vii; Quick, *Doctrines of the Creed*, c. xv.

THE ATONEMENT

93   Only a few of the numerous books on the Atonement are here mentioned. Among older works, see Dale, *The Atonement*; Denney, *The Death of Christ*; Forsyth, *The Work of Christ*; Moberly, *Atonement and Personality*. Among more recent works, Mozley, *The Doctrine of the Atonement* (an excellent historical and systematic survey); E. Brunner, *The Mediator*; Quick, *The Gospel of the New World* and *Doctrines of the Creed*, cc.xix–xxi; G. Aulen, *Christus Victor*; Mackintosh, *The Christian Experience of Forgiveness*; L. Hodgson, *The Doctrine of the Atonement*; and for a valuable brief discussion, K. E. Kirk's essay in *Essays Catholic and Critical*. See also, esp. for New Testament teaching, the three works by Vincent Taylor, *Jesus and His Sacrifice*, *The Atonement in New Testament Teaching*, and *Forgiveness and Reconciliation*. For a sustained and learned exposition of the 'subjective' theory, see Rashdall, *The Idea of Atonement in Christian Theology*, and more briefly R. S. Franks, *The Atonement* (Oxford University Press).

THE RESURRECTION AND ASCENSION

104   Among older books, Swete, *The Appearances of our Lord after the Passion*; Westcott, *The Revelation of the Risen Lord* and *The Gospel of the Resurrection* are very valuable. The best recent survey of the evidence and the theology is A. M. Ramsey, *The Resurrection of Christ*. See also the essays by E. G. Selwyn in *Essays Catholic and Critical* and H. Sasse in *Mysterium Christi*.

Page

118   On the eschatological elements in our Lord's teaching, see Schweitzer, *The Quest of the Historical Jesus* (the last two chapters); von Hügel, *Essays and Addresses* (First Series) v and vii; and more recently, C. H. Dodd, *The Parables of the Kingdom* ('realized eschatology'); Hoskyns' essay in *Essays Catholic and Critical* (on the 'Liberal' view of the Gospels); H. E. W. Turner, *Jesus, Master and Lord*, esp. c. ix. On the doctrine of the Last Things (Judgment, Resurrection) see Darragh, *The Resurrection of the Flesh*; Quick, *Doctrines of the Creed*, cc. xxii–xxiv and *The Gospel of the New World*, c. viii.

THE HOLY SPIRIT

122   On the development of the doctrine of the Holy Spirit, see Swete, art. 'Holy Spirit' in *H.D.B.* and *The Holy Spirit in the New Testament* and *The Holy Spirit in the Ancient Church*. See also Wheeler Robinson, *The Christian Experience of the Holy Spirit*. For the relation of the Holy Spirit to the Person and Work of Christ, see L. S. Thornton, *The Incarnate Lord*, c. xii.

124   On the question of the 'double procession', see Swete, *The Holy Spirit in the Ancient Church*, c. ix. On *Filioque* in the Creed, see J. N. D. Kelly, *Early Christian Creeds*, pp. 358 ff.

THE SCRIPTURES

138   On the inspiration and interpretation of the Bible, see Gore, *Lux Mundi*, Essay viii; Sanday, *Inspiration*, Lect. viii; and, among more recent books, A. Richardson, *A Preface to Bible Study*; C. W. Dugmore (editor), *The Interpretation of the Bible* (S.P.C.K.); McNeile (ed. C. S. C. Williams, 1953), *Introduction to the New Testament*; Wheeler Robinson, *Ancient and Modern Versions of the Bible*, Essay ix; Mozley's essay in *The Christian Faith* (ed. Matthews); A. M. Farrer, *The Glass of Vision*.

143   For the history of the Canon, see Westcott, *The Bible in the Church* and *The Canon of the New Testament*; Sanday, *Inspiration*; McNeile (1953 edn.), *Introduction to the New Testament*.

146   On the importance of the Old Testament, see G. E. Phillips, *The Old Testament in the World Church*; Wheeler Robinson (editor), *Record and Revelation*, Essay x; A. Richardson, *A Preface to Bible Study*, esp. cc. vi and vii; C. H. Dodd, *According to the Scriptures*.

THE CREEDS

161   Earlier works on the Creeds have been largely superseded on of the Kelly, *Early Christian Creeds*, which contains a full die Creeds. history and interpretation of the Apostles' and *and Use of* Swete, *The Apostles' Creed* and Turner, *The H\` Creeds and Anathemas* are still valuable.

Page

170   For a convenient exposition of Brewer's theory of the origin of the *Quicunque*, see Badcock, *The History of the Creeds*. Cp. Burn's article in *J.Th.S.*, Vol. xxvii (1926), pp. 19 ff., and for a criticism of Brewer, see F. Homes Dudden, *The Life and Times of S. Ambrose*, pp. 676 ff. For Burn's earlier views, see his books *An Introduction to the Creeds* (1899) and *The Athanasian Creed* (1912).

THE NATURE OF MAN, AND GRACE

175   For an account of primitive man, see E. O. James, *The Origin of Man*.

190   On the Christian doctrine of man, see R. Niebuhr, *The Nature and Destiny of Man*; E. Brunner, *Man in Revolt*; Quick, *The Gospel of the New World*; E. L. Mascall, *Christ, the Christian, and the Church*; D. Cairns, *The Image of God in Man*.

On sin, see Strong, *Christian Ethics*, Lect. v; Taylor, *The Faith of a Moralist*, Vol. i, Lect. v; Mackintosh, *The Christian Experience of Forgiveness*; K. E. Kirk, *Some Principles of Moral Theology*, c. x.

On original sin, see Williams, *The Doctrines of the Fall and of Original Sin* (for the history); Bicknell, *The Christian Idea of Sin and of Original Sin*, and his essay in *Essays Catholic and Critical*; C. E. Barbour, *Sin and the New Psychology*; Tennant's works referred to in the text; Quick, *op. cit.*, esp. c. ii. *Doctrine in the Church of England* (S.P.C.K.) gives a concise review of questions relating to sin and original sin.

198   On mortal and venial sins, see K. E. Kirk, *Some Principles of Moral Theology*, cc. x and xi, and on questions of penance, discipline and their relation to the Christian *summum bonum*, see his book *The Vision of God*.

On grace, see Taylor, *The Faith of a Moralist*, Vol. i, Lect. vi; Williams, *The Grace of God*; L. Hodgson, *The Grace of God in Faith and Philosophy*; *The Doctrine of Grace* (S.C.M. Press, 1932), a symposium expounding the doctrine and its history in different parts of the Church. On grace and freedom see esp. Mozley's essay in *Essays Catholic and Critical*. On the Pelagian controversy and S. Augustine, see Tixeront, *History of Dogmas*, Vol. ii, c. xi.

SALVATION

207   On justification, see the commentaries on Romans by Sanday and Headlam, C. H. Dodd (Moffatt) and K. E. Kirk (Clarendon Bible); Vincent Taylor, *Forgiveness and Reconciliation*; E. L. Mascall, *Christ, the Christian and the Church*, esp. c. v (on imputation and imputation). See also C. H. Dodd, *Gospel and Law*.

228   On Predestination, see Mozley, *The Augustinian Doctrine of Predestination* (a classical exposition); F. H. Brabant, *Time and Eternity in Christian Thought*, Lect. vii; and for a modern Thomist treatment, R. Garrigou-Lagrange (trans. Rose), *Predestination* (E.

THE CHURCH

On the doctrine of the Church, see for particular aspects the books mentioned lower down on the Authority and Ministry of the Church. On the doctrine of the Church in general, see among older books, F. D. Maurice, *The Kingdom of Christ*; Swete, *The Holy Catholic Church*; Stone, *The Christian Church*; Gore, *The Reconstruction of Belief*, Part iii; among more recent books, A. M. Ramsey, *The Gospel and the Catholic Church*; A. G. Hebert, *The Form of the Church*; K. E. Kirk (editor), *The Apostolic Ministry*; E. L. Mascall, *Christ, the Christian and the Church*; S. Neill, *The Christian Society*. See also *The Parish Communion* (S.P.C.K.), esp. Essays iv, v and vi; *The Church of God* (S.P.C.K.), an Anglo-Russian symposium; W. A. Visser't Hooft and J. H. Oldham, *The Church and its Function in Society* (Allen and Unwin, 1937); E. Mersch, *The Whole Christ* (an English translation of *Le Corps Mystique du Christ*, on the historical development of the doctrine of the mystical body).

On the New Testament doctrine (in addition to most of the above), see R. Newton Flew, *Jesus and His Church*; L. S. Thornton, *The Common Life in the Body of Christ*; K. L. Schmidt, *The Church* (Bible Key Words—A. & C. Black).

On the nature of 'catholicity', see *Catholicity* (Dacre Press, 1947), *The Fulness of Christ* (S.P.C.K. 1950), and *The Catholicity of Protestantism* (Lutterworth Press, 1950), three reports presented to the Archbishop of Canterbury. See also D. T. Jenkins, *The Nature of Catholicity* (Faber), for a modern Congregationalist point of view. A more radical Protestant view is given in E. Brunner, *The Misunderstanding of the Church* (Lutterworth Press, 1952).

Questions concerning re-union may be studied in G. K. A. Bell, *Documents on Christian Unity* (Oxford University Press), three volumes; *Reports of the Lambeth Conferences* of 1920, 1930 and 1948; *The Church* (S.C.M. Press, 1951), a report of the Faith and Order Commission of the World Council of Churches; A. M. Ramsey, K. E. Kirk, *op. cit.*; A. E. J. Rawlinson, *The Church of England and the Church of Christ* and *Problems of Re-union*; W. Nicholls, *Ecumenism and Catholicity*; M. J. Congar, O.P., *Divided Christendom* (throws light on some currents of thought in the Roman Church, the French original *Chrétiens Désunis* should be used if possible). For a full bibliography of books and periodicals on the subject, see H. R. T. Brandreth, *Unity and Reunion* (second edition, 1948).

On the question of the papacy, see list of books for page 350.

THE CHURCH'S AUTHORITY IN DOCTRINE

On the authority of the Church, see Salmon, *Infallibility of the Church* (1952 edn.); Gore, *Reconstruction of Belief*, Book III, cc. v–x; essays in *Essays Catholic and Critical* by A. E. J. Rawlinson and Knox; essay by N. P. Williams in *Northern Catholicism* esp. pp. 154 ff.

Page

260   On development in doctrine, see Mozley, *Theory of Development*; Darwell Stone, *The Christian Church*, c. xiv; Turner, *Catholic and Apostolic*, cc. ii and iii; R. Hanson and R. Fuller, *The Church of Rome* (S.C.M. Press), c. iv.

267   On modernism, see A. R. Vidler, *The Modernist Movement in the Roman Church*. English Modernism may be studied in H. D. A. Major, *English Modernism*, and E. W. Barnes, *The Rise of Christianity*. Harnack, *What is Christianity?* remains a classical exposition of the older type of Liberal Protestantism. For a review of the whole subject, see Quick, *Liberalism, Modernism and Tradition* and the Report entitled *Catholicity* (Dacre Press, 1947).

272   On general councils, see Darwell Stone, *The Christian Church*, c. xiii.

287   On purgatory, see Mason, *Purgatory*, and the brief treatment in *Doctrine in the Church of England*.
         Modern Roman teaching on indulgences is set out conveniently in H. Davis, S.J., *Moral and Pastoral Theology*, Vol. iii.

298   On the invocation of saints, see *Doctrine in the Church of England*, pp. 213–216; Darwell Stone, *The Invocation of Saints*; Williams' essay in *Northern Catholicism*, pp. 221 ff.

THE CHURCH'S AUTHORITY IN DISCIPLINE

307   The Report on *The Canon Law of the Church of England* (S.P.C.K., 1947) should be consulted. See also Hooker, *Eccl. Pol.*, V, cc. v–x, for the classical defence of Prayer-Book ceremonies and customs.

314   On celibacy and the monastic ideal, see K. E. Kirk, *The Vision of God*. On clerical celibacy, see Wordsworth, *Ministry of Grace*, iv; Lea, *History of Sacerdotal Celibacy*; the article 'Célibat Ecclésiastique' in *Dictionnaire de Théol. Catholique*.

319   On the early history of excommunication, see K. E. Kirk, *op. cit.*

THE MINISTRY OF THE CHURCH

329   On the early history of the ministry, see Lightfoot's Excursus in his *Commentary* on Philippians, with Moberly's criticism in his *Ministerial Priesthood*; Gore and Turner, *The Church and the Ministry*; Swete (editor), *The Early History of the Church and the Ministry*; C. Jenkins and K. D. Mackenzie (editors), *Episcopacy, Ancient and Modern*; K. E. Kirk (editor), *The Apostolic Ministry*, with the criticism in *The Ministry of the Church*, by S. Neill and others (Canterbury Press).

337   For the doctrine of the apostolic succession, see the books cited above, esp. essay iii (Turner) in *The Early History of the Church and the Ministry*; A. M. Ramsey, *The Gospel and the Catholic Church*. For another view, see Headlam, *The Doctrine of the Church and Christian Reunion*; A. Ehrhardt, *The Apostolic Succession*. For Free

Page

Church expositions, see Lindsay, *The Church and the Ministry in the Early Centuries*; and more recently D. Jenkins, *The Nature of Catholicity* and *The Gift of Ministry;* T. W. Manson, *The Church's Ministry.*

341 On the validity of Anglican orders, see Puller, *The Bull 'Apostolicae Curae' and the Edwardine Ordinal*; Moberly, *op. cit.*, c. vii and Appendix; the essay on the Ordinal in *Liturgy and Worship*; Dix, *The Question of Anglican Orders* (Dacre Press). For a formal statement on priesthood and sacrifice in the Church of England, see *Responsio Archiepiscoporum Angliae ad Litteras Apostolicas Leonis Papae XIII*, issued by the Archbishops of Canterbury and York (Temple and Maclagan) in 1897 (now published by the Church Historical Society, S.P.C.K., under the title 'Anglican Orders').

350 On the question of the papacy, see Puller, *The Primitive Saints and the See of Rome*; Salmon, *Infallibility of the Church*, 1952 edition, cc. xi–xv; Stone, *The Christian Church*, cc. vi, viii, ix; Kidd, *The Roman Primacy to 461*; T. E. Jalland, *The Church and the Papacy.*

THE SACRAMENTS

357 On the general theology of the sacraments, see *Lux Mundi*, essay x; Quick, *The Christian Sacraments* and *The Gospel of Divine Action*; A. E. Taylor, *The Faith of a Moralist*, Vol. ii, Lect. vii; H. J. Wotherspoon, *Religious Values in the Sacraments*; the section in *Doctrine in the Church of England*. On the origin of the Christian sacraments, see Williams' essay in *Essays Catholic and Critical*; A. D. Nock's essay in *Essays on the Trinity and the Incarnation* (the 'mystery-religions' question); Dix, *The Shape of the Liturgy.*

364 On the history of penance, see O. D. Watkins, *A History of Penance* (fully documented); K. E. Kirk, *The Vision of God*; R. C. Mortimer, *The Origins of Private Penance*. On the practice of sacramental confession, see O. Hardman (editor), *The Christian Life*, Vol. ii. Roman Catholic theory and practice may be studied in H. Davis, *Moral and Pastoral Theology*, Vol. iii, cc. v–ix.

265 On the anointing of the sick, see *Liturgy and Worship*, pp. 472 ff.; *The Report on the Ministry of Healing*, (S.P.C.K., 1924); and the forms of service approved by the Convocation of Canterbury, June 1935.

HOLY BAPTISM

375 On baptism, see Darwell Stone, *Holy Baptism*; G. W. H. Lampe, *The Seal of the Spirit*; W. F. Flemington, *The New Testament Doctrine of Baptism*; O. Cullman, *Baptism in the New Testament* (S.C.M. Press).

381 For the view that confirmation for the first time bestows the Holy Spirit, see Mason, *Relation of Baptism to Confirmation*; Hall, *Confirmation*; and the lecture by Dix, *The Theology of Confirmation in Relation to Baptism* (Dacre Press). For a different view, see Stone,

Holy Baptism; Quick, *The Christian Sacraments*, p. 181; and the extensive review of New Testament and patristic evidence in G. W. H. Lampe, *The Seal of the Spirit*. Recent discussions of theory and practice may be studied in the following Reports: *Confirmation Today* (1944) and *Baptism Today* (1949, Press and Publications Board); *The Theology of Christian Initiation* (1948, S.P.C.K., the report of a Theological Commission). See also the two volumes *Confirmation* (S.P.C.K.) and the essays by evangelical authors in *Baptism and Confirmation* (Church Book Room Press).

THE HOLY COMMUNION

392   For a review of the history of teaching on the Holy Communion in the Church of England, see Waterland, *A Review of the Doctrine of the Eucharist* (1736); A. J. Macdonald (editor), *The Evangelical Doctrine of the Holy Communion*; C. W. Dugmore, *Eucharistic Doctrine in England from Hooker to Waterland*; Darwell Stone, *A History of the Doctrine of the Holy Eucharist*, Vol. ii (with full quotations). Cp. Y. Brilioth, *Eucharistic Faith and Practice* (a review of the various traditions by a Swedish scholar).

395   On the doctrine of the real presence, see Strong, *The Real Presence*; Gore, *The Body of Christ*; Quick, *The Christian Sacraments*, c. ix; E. L. Mascall, *Christ, the Christian and the Church*, cc. ix–xi, and *Corpus Christi*; Stone, *The Holy Communion*.

399   For the history of the doctrine of transubstantiation see Gore, *Dissertations*, iii; Stone, *op. cit.* (both volumes).

407   For a history of reservation, see Freestone, *The Sacrament Reserved* (Alcuin Club). The Article by Harris on 'The Communion of the Sick' in *Liturgy and Worship* contains much important material. *Reservation* (S.P.C.K., 1926), the Report of a representative conference, provides a full discussion of the questions at issue, and the paper by E. G. Selwyn and the Chairman's summary at the end ably state the case respectively for and against extra-liturgical devotions.

419   On the sacrificial aspect of the eucharist, see the works by Stone, Gore, Quick and E. L. Mascall already cited; Kidd, *The Later Medieval Doctrine of the Eucharistic Sacrifice*; Hicks, *The Fulness of Sacrifice*. Essays iii, iv and v in *The Parish Communion* (S.P.C.K.) contain valuable discussions of the corporate character and significance of the eucharistic action. See also A. G. Hebert, *Liturgy and Society*. On the history of the liturgy, see J. H. Srawley, *The Early History of the Liturgy*; Dix, *The Shape of the Liturgy*.

CHURCH AND STATE

432   Recent discussions will be found in *Report of the Archbishops' Committee on Church and State*, 1916; *Report of the Archbishops' Commission on the Relations between Church and State*, 1935; *Church and State, being the Report of a Commission appointed by the Church*

Page

Assembly, 1952. See also Dibdin, *Establishment in England* (essays by a distinguished authority on ecclesiastical law, 1932); C. Garbett, *Church and State in England* (1950).

For a more general treatment of the subject, see Hobhouse, *The Church and the World*; Figgis, *Churches in the Modern State*.

For an account of the Enabling Act, the Constitution of the Church Assembly and a list of the Measures passed since its inception, see the annual *Official Year-Book of the Church of England*.

433   See *The Canon Law of the Church of England*, being the Report of the Archbishops' Commission on Canon Law (S.P.C.K., 1947), which contains essays on the history of Canon Law, proposals for a Revised Body of Canons, and a Memorandum '*Lawful Authority*' by Mr Justice Vaisey. See also R. C. Mortimer, *Western Canon Law*.

435   See the *Report of the Ecclesiastical Courts Commission*, 1926, which is reprinted as Appendix IV in the 1935 Report on Church and State, Vol. i, mentioned above. See also the Report on Canon Law mentioned above.

442   (i) For a brief review of the problems connected with war, see the Report of the Lambeth Conference 1948 (Report of Committee No. ii on The Church and the Modern World). For a fuller discussion, see 'The Church and the Atom', a study of the moral and theological aspects of peace and war being the Report of a Commission appointed by the Archbishops at the request of the Church Assembly to consider the Report of the British Council of Churches' Commission entitled 'The Era of Atomic Power'.
(ii) See W. Temple, *The Ethics of Penal Action* (Clarke Hall Fellowship Lecture, 1934).

445   For a general review of the relation of the Church to modern society, see the Report of the Lambeth Conference 1948 (Report of Committee No. ii on The Church and the Modern World).

The following books deal with various aspects of this problem more fully: E. Brunner, *Christianity and Civilization* and *Justice and the Social Order*; H. Butterfield, *Christianity, Diplomacy and War*; V. A. Demant, *Theology of Society* and *Religion and the Decline of Capitalism*; T. S. Eliot, *The Idea of a Christian Society*; D. M. Mackinnon (editor), *Christian Faith and Communist Faith*; J. Maritain, *Man and the State*; Richard Niebuhr, *Christ and Culture*; M. B. Reckitt, *Maurice to Temple*; W. Temple, *Christianity and Social Order*.

INDEX

Where several references are given, the most important are italicised